THE
MACRO ECONOMY
TODAY

TWELFTH EDITION

The McGraw-Hill Series Economics

ESSENTIALS OF ECONOMICS

Brue, McConnell, and Flynn
Essentials of Economics
Second Edition

Mandel
Economics: The Basics
First Edition

Schiller
Essentials of Economics
Seventh Edition

PRINCIPLES OF ECONOMICS

Colander
Economics, Microeconomics, and Macroeconomics
Eighth Edition

Frank and Bernanke
Principles of Economics, Principles of Microeconomics, Principles of Macroeconomics
Fourth Edition

Frank and Bernanke
Brief Editions: Principles of Economics, Principles of Microeconomics, Principles of Macroeconomics
First Edition

McConnell, Brue, and Flynn
Economics, Microeconomics, and Macroeconomics
Eighteenth Edition

McConnell, Brue, and Flynn
Brief Editions: Microeconomics and Macroeconomics
First Edition

Miller
Principles of Microeconomics
First Edition

Samuelson and Nordhaus
Economics, Microeconomics, and Macroeconomics
Nineteenth Edition

Schiller
The Economy Today, The Micro Economy Today, and The Macro Economy Today
Twelfth Edition

Slavin
Economics, Microeconomics, and Macroeconomics
Ninth Edition

ECONOMICS OF SOCIAL ISSUES

Guell
Issues in Economics Today
Fifth Edition

Sharp, Register, and Grimes
Economics of Social Issues
Nineteenth Edition

ECONOMETRICS

Gujarati and Porter
Basic Econometrics
Fifth Edition

Gujarati and Porter
Essentials of Econometrics
Fourth Edition

MANAGERIAL ECONOMICS

Baye
Managerial Economics and Business Strategy
Seventh Edition

Brickley, Smith, and Zimmerman
Managerial Economics and Organizational Architecture
Fifth Edition

Thomas and Maurice
Managerial Economics
Tenth Edition

INTERMEDIATE ECONOMICS

Bernheim and Whinston
Microeconomics
First Edition

Dornbusch, Fischer, and Startz
Macroeconomics
Tenth Edition

Frank
Microeconomics and Behavior
Eighth Edition

ADVANCED ECONOMICS

Romer
Advanced Macroeconomics
Third Edition

MONEY AND BANKING

Cecchetti
Money, Banking, and Financial Markets
Second Edition

URBAN ECONOMICS

O'Sullivan
Urban Economics
Seventh Edition

LABOR ECONOMICS

Borjas
Labor Economics
Fifth Edition

McConnell, Brue, and Macpherson
Contemporary Labor Economics
Ninth Edition

PUBLIC FINANCE

Rosen and Gayer
Public Finance
Ninth Edition

Seidman
Public Finance
First Edition

ENVIRONMENTAL ECONOMICS

Field and Field
Environmental Economics: An Introduction
Fifth Edition

INTERNATIONAL ECONOMICS

Appleyard, Field, and Cobb
International Economics
Seventh Edition

King and King
International Economics, Globalization, and Policy: A Reader
Fifth Edition

Pugel
International Economics
Fourteenth Edition

THE
MACRO ECONOMY TODAY

TWELFTH EDITION

BRADLEY R. SCHILLER
The University of Nevada–Reno

McGraw-Hill Irwin

THE MACRO ECONOMY TODAY
Published by McGraw-Hill/Irwin, a business unit of The McGraw-Hill Companies, Inc., 1221 Avenue of the Americas, New York, NY, 10020.
Copyright © 2010, 2008, 2006, 2003, 2000, 1997, 1994, 1991, 1989, 1986, 1983, 1980 by The McGraw-Hill Companies, Inc. All rights reserved.
No part of this publication may be reproduced or distributed in any form or by any means, or stored in a database or retrieval system, without
the prior written consent of The McGraw-Hill Companies, Inc., including, but not limited to, in any network or other electronic storage or
transmission, or broadcast for distance learning.

Some ancillaries, including electronic and print components, may not be available to customers outside the United States.

This book is printed on acid-free paper.

2 3 4 5 6 7 8 9 0 DOW/DOW 0

ISBN 978-0-07-724740-9
MHID 0-07-724740-X

Vice president and editor-in-chief: *Brent Gordon*
Publisher: *Douglas Reiner*
Director of development: *Ann Torbert*
Development editor: *Anne E. Hilbert*
Editorial coordinator: *Marianne L. Magday*
Vice president and director of marketing: *Robin J. Zwettler*
Senior marketing manager: *Melissa Larmon*
Vice president of editing, design and production: *Sesha Bolisetty*
Senior project manager: *Harvey Yep*
Production supervisor: *Gina Hangos/Michael McCormick*
Lead designer: *Matthew Baldwin*
Senior photo research coordinator: *Lori Kramer*
Photo researcher: *Mary Reeg*
Senior media project manager: *Susan Lombardi*
Cover design: *Evan Modesto*
Cover image: *© Getty Images*
Interior design: *Matthew Baldwin*
Typeface: *10/12 Times New Roman*
Compositor: *Aptara®, Inc.*
Printer: *R. R. Donnelley*

Library of Congress Cataloging-in-Publication Data

Schiller, Bradley R., 1943–
    The macro economy today / Bradley R. Schiller.—12th ed.
      p. cm.
    Includes index.
    ISBN-13: 978-0-07-724740-9 (alk. paper)
    ISBN-10: 0-07-724740-X (alk. paper)
    1. Macroeconomics. I. Title.
HB172.5.S3425 2010
339—dc22

2009032687

Bradley R. Schiller has over four decades of experience teaching introductory economics at the University of Nevada, American University, the University of California (Berkeley and Santa Cruz), and the University of Maryland. He has given guest lectures at more than 300 colleges ranging from Fresno, California, to Istanbul, Turkey. Dr. Schiller's unique contribution to teaching is his ability to relate basic principles to current socioeconomic problems, institutions, and public policy decisions. This perspective is evident throughout *The Economy Today.*

Dr. Schiller derives this policy focus from his extensive experience as a Washington consultant. He has been a consultant to most major federal agencies, many congressional committees, and political candidates. In addition, he has evaluated scores of government programs and helped design others. His studies of poverty, discrimination, training programs, tax reform, pensions, welfare, Social Security, and lifetime wage patterns have appeared in both professional journals and popular media. Dr. Schiller is also a frequent commentator on economic policy for television and radio, and his commentary has appeared in *The Wall Street Journal, The Washington Post, The New York Times,* and *Los Angeles Times,* among other major newspapers.

Dr. Schiller received his PhD from Harvard in 1969. He earned a B.A. degree, with great distinction, from the University of California (Berkeley) in 1965. He is now a professor of economics at the University of Nevada in Reno, where he hosts McGraw-Hill's annual West Coast Teaching Economics Conference. On his days off, Brad is on the tennis courts, the ski slopes, or the crystal-blue waters of Lake Tahoe.

LEARNING FROM CRISES

The Great Recession of 2008–9 caused a lot of pain. Millions of workers lost their jobs. Homeowners experienced huge declines in their wealth. Stockholders saw the value of their portfolios shrink. Economic insecurity spread across the population. No one wanted the recession and few people anticipated it.

The Great Recession did have a sliver of silver lining, however, especially for the economics profession. That setback woke people up to potential economic problems. The long economic expansions of the 1980s, 1990s, and 2002–7 raised American living standards, wealth, and confidence. Consumers felt comfortable running up debts and driving the marginal propensity to save into negative territory. Even the economics profession got caught up in the euphoria. In the mid-1990s some of the most prominent economists asserted that the business cycle had been forever tamed.

We know better now. The recession of 2008–9 shocked us back into reality. We certainly do a better job now of managing the macro economy than we did in the 1930s, but business cycles are far from extinct. The Great Recession of 2008–9 was in fact the twelfth recession since World War II. It wasn't even that "great" in terms of GDP losses. Nine of the 12 post–World War II recessions entailed much deeper GDP contractions; in two of those recessions, the unemployment rate peaked higher. Although President Obama repeatedly compared the Great Recession of 2008–9 to the Great Depression of the 1930s, the two experiences were never remotely similar. The speed and suddenness of the 2008–9 downturn were severe enough, however, to scare market participants and energize policy makers. It even got our students interested in discovering what makes markets "tick."

Markets vs. Government

Of special relevance to economics courses is the resurgence of the basic choice between market reliance and government intervention. Liberals blamed the Great Recession on market failures and championed more government regulation. Conservatives, on the other hand, blamed excessive and inefficient government regulation for many of our macro problems. As they saw it, *less* government regulation was needed, not more. The public wasn't sure which position was right. According to an April 2009 poll, Americans were equally divided over the question of whether more or less government intervention in markets is desirable (see News).

IN THE NEWS

Markets vs. Government

Q: Which statement about the role of government comes closest to your point of view?

A1:   Government should do more to solve problems and help meet the needs of people. — 47%

A2:   Government is doing too many things better left to businesses and individuals. — 46%

A3:   Other; not sure — 7%

Source: NBC News/Wall Street Journal Survey, April 2009. Hart/McInturff.

Analysis: American opinion is equally divided over the core question of whether *more* or *less* government intervention in the marketplace is desired.

This debate takes us to the very core of macro theory and policy: deciding when (and how) government should intervene in the economy, at either the macro level (fiscal, monetary, and supply-side policies) or the micro level (regulation of product and resource markets).

The debate about markets versus government has always been a central theme of *The Macro Economy Today*. In the very first chapter students are introduced to the goals of the economy—optimal resolutions of the core WHAT, HOW, and FOR WHOM questions—and alternative strategies for attaining them. In that very first chapter, the concepts of *both* market failure and government failure are introduced and discussed. In every subsequent macro and international chapter the debate continues. The "Economy Tomorrow" feature at the end of every chapter challenges students to apply the markets versus government options to specific policy issues. There are no pat answers, as this is not a "point of view" text. The goal of *The Macro Economy Today* is instead to introduce students to the central debates in economic theory and policy—and challenge them to think about these debates analytically.

Unique Macro Approach

In *The Macro Economy Today* I have always emphasized the problems associated with short-run instability. This emphasis reflects not only the historical record of recurrent recessions, but also my long experience in Washington, DC. In the nation's capitol the *long run* is the next election. As experience has shown (sadly), very little attention is paid to long-run strategies or even the long-run consequences of short-run policies. Although President Obama has tried to lengthen the policy horizon, the reality remains that the policy cycle is rarely longer than the two-year Congressional election cycle. Under these circumstances, the challenge is to implement policies that help the economy in the short run without inflicting too much damage in the long run. The debates over the 2009 stimulus program and its longer-run deficit implications epitomize this dilemma.

The Macro Economy Today maintains an objective, *balanced* assessment of contrasting views and theories. No other text offers such a fair and complete discussion of Keynesian, monetarist, and supply-side perspectives, each presented in its own best light. My goal is to assure that students understand these contrasting macro perspectives well enough to see when and how they might be helpful.

Unique Theme

These central themes of markets versus government, balanced perspectives, and a policy focus permeate *The Macro Economy Today*. ***By infusing the presentation of core concepts with a unifying theme and pervasive real-world applications,* The Macro Economy Today *offers a unique and exciting introduction to economics.***

Unique Chapters

As you compare this text to others, take special note of the unique combination of topics covered. For example, in the Introduction, Chapter 2: The U.S. Economy: A Global View, offers a descriptive profile of the U.S. economy in a comparative framework, organized around the core WHAT, HOW, FOR WHOM questions.

Chapter 6: Unemployment and Chapter 7: Inflation provide chapter-long descriptions of these core macro problems, their socioeconomic consequences and their measurement. Chapter 16: Supply-Side Policy: Short-Run Options is solely devoted to policy options for shifting the aggregate supply curve, as an alternative to fiscal and monetary policies. Finally, Chapter 18: Theory versus Reality is the capstone to Macro, offering a theory synthesis and a nuts-and-bolts discussion of the problems in attaining policy perfection.

In International, Chapter 21: Global Poverty wraps everything up with a penetrating look at the magnitude and causes of global deprivation that reinforces the importance of policy choices.

Every one of these chapters is designed to lay a solid empirical foundation that will spark students' interest and motivate them to learn more about what makes real-world economies "tick." Does the text you are now using offer a comparable set of attractions?

Unique One-Model Macro

Last, but far from least on the list of unique features for *The Macro Economy Today,* is its consistent use of a single macro framework to illustrate the entire spectrum of macro theories and policy options. All other textbooks and too many instructors still use the Keynesian cross to teach Keynesian theory. As you know, this always ends up in an inflationary dead end, because inflation can't be illustrated in that framework. So a *second* framework—the AS/AD model—is introduced. Introducing two separate frameworks into the principles courses not only unduly confuses students but also wastes precious course time. As I demonstrated long ago, the entire gamut of Keynesian theory—including the critical multiplier—can be accurately and more efficiently illustrated in the AS/AD framework. The building blocks for the AD curve—consumption and investment functions—are identical to those used to build a Keynesian cross. But the addition proceeds horizontally rather than vertically (see p. 190). This simplification eliminates the intermediate step—the Keynesian cross itself—completely. Peruse Chapters 9 and 10 (especially the multiplier illustrations on pp. 210–215) to see how this works.

Texts that apologetically offer to let students "skip" the Keynesian cross chapter and proceed to the AS/AD model are not a substitute for this one-model approach. In every such case, students are skipping over core concepts (e.g., the consumption function) that are critical to understanding macro dynamics. If you haven't yet tried the one-model approach, you should. Both you and your students will benefit from the greater efficiency and efficacy that result.

EFFECTIVE PEDAGOGY

Clean, Clear Theory

Despite the abundance of real-world applications, this is at heart a *principles* text, not a compendium of issues. Good theory and interesting applications are not mutually exclusive. This is a text that wants to *teach economics,* not just increase awareness of policy issues. To that end, *The Macro Economy Today* provides a logically organized and uncluttered theoretical structure for macro and international theory. What distinguishes this text from others on the market is that it conveys theory in a lively, student-friendly manner.

Concept Reinforcement

Student comprehension of core theory is facilitated with careful, consistent, and effective pedagogy. This distinctive pedagogy includes the following features:

Chapter Learning Objectives. Each chapter contains a set of chapter-level Learning Objectives. Students and professors can be confident that the organization of each chapter surrounds common themes outlined by three to five learning objectives listed on the first page of each chapter. End-of-chapter material including the chapter summary, Discussion Questions, and *Student Problem Sets* is tagged to these Learning Objectives as is the supplementary material, which includes the *Test Bank, Instructor's Resource Manual,* and *Study Guide.*

Self-Explanatory Graphs and Tables. Graphs are *completely* labeled, colorful, and positioned on background grids as the following graph illustrates. Because students often enter the principles course as graph-phobics, graphs are frequently accompanied by synchronized tabular data. Every table is also annotated. This shouldn't be a product-differentiating feature but, sadly, it is. Putting a table in a textbook without an annotation is akin to writing a cluster of numbers on the board, then leaving the classroom without any explanation.

Reinforced Key Concepts. Key terms are defined in the margin when they first appear and, unlike in other texts, redefined in the margin as necessary in subsequent chapters. Web site references are directly tied to the book's content, not hung on like ornaments. End-of-chapter Discussion Questions use tables, graphs, and boxed news stories from the text, reinforcing key concepts, and are linked to the chapter's Learning Objectives.

Boxed and Annotated Applications. In addition to the real-world applications that run through the body of the text, the new design of *The Macro Economy Today* intersperses boxed domestic (In the News) and global (World View) case studies intertextually for further understanding and reference. Although nearly every text on the market now offers boxed applications, *The Economy Today*'s presentation is distinctive. First, the sheer number of In the News and World View boxes is unique. Second, and more important, *every*

FIGURE 3.3
Shifts vs. Movements

A demand curve shows how a consumer responds to price changes. If the determinants of demand stay constant, the response is a *movement* along the curve to a new quantity demanded. In this case, the quantity demanded increases from 5 (point d_1), to 12 (point g_1), when price falls from $35 to $20 per hour.

If the determinants of demand change, the entire demand curve *shifts*. In this case, an increase in income increases demand. With more income, Tom is willing to buy 12 hours at the initial price of $35 (point d_2), not just the 5 hours he demanded before the lottery win.

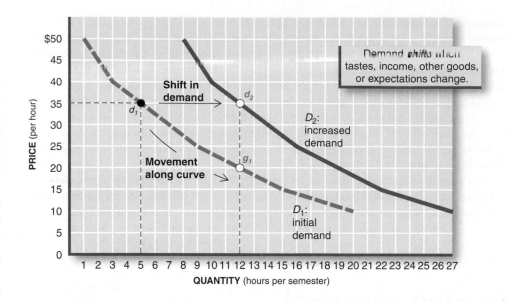

Demand shifts when tastes, income, other goods, or expectations change.

		Quantity Demanded (hours per semester)	
	Price (per hour)	Initial Demand	After Increase in Income
A	$50	1	8
B	45	2	9
C	40	3	10
D	35	5	12
E	30	7	14
F	25	9	16
G	20	12	19
H	15	15	22
I	10	20	27

WORLD VIEW

U.S. Downturn Dragging World Into Recession

The world is falling into the first global recession since World War II as the crisis that started in the United States engulfs once-booming developing nations, confronting them with massive financial shortfalls that could turn back the clock on poverty reduction by years, the World Bank warned yesterday. . . .

The report predicted that the global economy will shrink this year for the first time since the 1940s, reducing earlier estimates that emerging markets would propel the world to positive growth even as the United States, Europe and Japan tanked. The dire prediction underscored what many are calling a mounting crisis within a crisis, as the downturn that started in the wealthy nations of the West washes over developing countries through a pullback in investment, trade and credit.

—Anthony Faiola

Source: *The Washington Post*, March 9, 2009, p. A01. © 2009 The Washington Post. Used with permission by PARS International Corp.

Analysis: In an increasingly global economy a recession in one nation—particularly the world's richest—causes output contractions in other nations.

boxed application is referenced in the body of the text. Third, *every* News and World View comes with a brief, self-contained explanation as the previous example illustrates. Fourth, the News and World View boxes are the explicit subject of the end-of-chapter Discussion Questions and *Student Problem Set* exercises. In combination, these distinctive features assure that students will actually *read* the boxed applications and discern their economic content. The *Test Bank* provides subsets of questions tied to the News and World View boxes so that instructors can confirm student use of this feature.

Photos and Cartoons. The text presentation is also enlivened with occasional photos and cartoons that reflect basic concepts. The photos on page 36 are much more vivid testimony to the extremes of inequality than the data in Figure 2.3 (p. 35). Every photo and cartoon is annotated and referenced in the body of the text. These visual features are an integral part of the presentation, not diversions.

Readability

The one adjective invariably used to describe *The Macro Economy Today* is "readable." Professors often express a bit of shock when they realize that students actually enjoy reading the book. (Well, not as much as a Stephen King novel, but a whole lot better than most textbooks they've had to plow through.) The writing style is lively and issue-focused. Unlike any other textbook on the market, every boxed feature, every graph, every table, and every cartoon is explained and analyzed. Every feature is also referenced in the text, so students actually learn the material rather than skipping over it. Because readability is ultimately in the eye of the beholder, you might ask a couple of students to read and compare a parallel chapter in *The Macro Economy Today* and in another text. This is a test *The Macro Economy Today* usually wins.

Student Problem Set

I firmly believe that students must *work* with key concepts in order to really learn them. Weekly homework assignments are *de rigueur* in my own classes. To facilitate homework assignments, I have prepared the *Student Problem Set,* which includes built-in numerical and graphing problems that build on the tables, graphs, and boxed material that aligns with each chapter's Learning Objectives. Grids for drawing graphs are also provided. Students cannot complete all the problems without referring to material in the chapter. This increases the odds of students actually *reading* the chapter, the tables, and the boxed applications.

The *Student Problem Set* at the end of each chapter is reproduced in the online student tutorial software (*Connect Economics,* discussed on the following page). This really helps students transition between the written material and online supplements. It also means that the online assignments are totally book specific.

© Santokh Kochar/Getty Images/DAL

Gene Alexander, USDA Natural Resources Conservation Service/DAL

Analysis: An abundance of capital equipment and advanced technology make American farmers and workers far more productive than workers in poor nations.

DISTINCTIVE WEB SUPPORT

The Twelfth edition of *The Macro Economy Today* continues to set the pace for Web applications and support of the principles course.

Web Analysis Boxes

A mini Web site directory is provided in each chapter's marginal Web Analysis boxes, created and updated by Shane Sanders of Nicholls State University. These URLs aren't random picks; they were selected because they let students extend and update adjacent in-text discussions.

www.mhhe.com/ schiller12e

The Macro Economy Today's Web site now includes even more features that both instructors and students will find engaging and instructive. The Online Learning Center is user-friendly. Upon entering the site at **www.mhhe.com/schiller12e,** students and instructors will find three separate book covers: one for *The Economy Today,* one for *The Macro Economy Today,* and one for *The Micro Economy Today.* By clicking on the appropriate cover, users will link to a specific site for the version of the book they are using.

Proceeding into the Student Center, students will find lots of brand-new interactive study material. Brian Lynch of Lake Land College has revised 10 self-grading multiple-choice questions per chapter, which are ideal for self-quizzing before a test. In addition, Shane Sanders has enhanced the Auxiliary Problem Sets for the site by updating the problems for added practice. Professors can assign the additional problems as homework or students can access them for additional skills practice. Answers can be found on the password-protected Instructor's Edition of the Web site. Professor Sanders also revised and created new Web Activities for each chapter. On top of all that, students have access to my periodic News Flashes along with my e-mail address to ask me any questions directly, under "ask Brad."

The password-protected Instructor Center includes some wonderful resources for instructors who want to include more interactive student activities in their courses. The downloadable *Instructor's Resource Manual* and PowerPoints, Auxiliary Problem Sets and answers, and Instructor's Notes for the Web Activities are available to provide guidance for instructors who collect these assignments and grade them.

Premium Content. The Online Learning Center now offers students the opportunity to purchase Premium Content. Like an electronic study guide, the OLC Premium Content enables students to take pre- and post-tests (revised by Brian Lynch) for each chapter as well as to download Schiller-exclusive iPod content including podcasts by Brad Schiller, practice quizzes, Paul Solman videos, and chapter summaries—all accessible through the student's MP3 device.

McGraw-Hill *Connect* Economics

Less Managing. More Teaching. Greater Learning. McGraw-Hill *Connect Economics* is an online assignment and assessment solution that connects students with the tools and resources they'll need to achieve success.

McGraw-Hill *Connect Economics* helps prepare students for their future by enabling faster learning, more efficient studying, and higher retention of knowledge.

Features. *Connect Economics* offers a number of powerful tools and features to make managing assignments easier, so faculty can spend more time teaching. With *Connect Economics,* students can engage with their coursework anytime and anywhere, making the learning process more accessible and efficient. *Connect Economics* offers you the features described below.

Simple Assignment Management With *Connect Economics,* creating assignments is easier than ever, so you can spend more time teaching and less time managing. The assignment management function enables you to:

- Create and deliver assignments easily with selectable end-of-chapter questions and test bank items.

- Streamline lesson planning, student progress reporting, and assignment grading to make classroom management more efficient than ever.
- Go paperless with the eBook and online submission and grading of student assignments.

Smart Grading   When it comes to studying, time is precious. *Connect Economics* helps students learn more efficiently by providing feedback and practice material when they need it, where they need it. When it comes to teaching, your time also is precious. The grading function enables you to:

- Have assignments scored automatically, giving students immediate feedback on their work and side-by-side comparisons with correct answers.
- Access and review each response; manually change grades or leave comments for students to review.
- Reinforce classroom concepts with practice tests and instant quizzes.

Instructor Library   The *Connect Economics* Instructor Library is your repository for additional resources to improve student engagement in and out of class. You can select and use any asset that enhances your lecture. The *Connect Economics* Instructor Library includes:

- eBook
- PowerPoint presentations
- Test Bank
- Solutions Manual
- Instructor's Manual
- Auxiliary Problem Sets and Answers
- Web Activities and Answers
- Digital Image Library

Student Study Center   The *Connect Economics* Student Study Center is the place for students to access additional resources. The Student Study Center:

- Offers students quick access to lectures, practice materials, eBooks, and more.
- Provides instant practice material and study questions, easily accessible on-the-go.
- Gives students access to the Personal Learning Plan described below.

Personal Learning Plan   The Personal Learning Plan (PLP) connects each student to the learning resources needed for success in the course. For each chapter, students:

- Take a practice test to initiate the Personal Learning Plan.
- Immediately upon completing the practice test, see how their performance compares to content by sections within chapters.
- Receive a Personal Learning Plan that recommends specific readings from the text, supplemental study material, and practice work that will improve their understanding and mastery of each learning objective.

Diagnostic and Adaptive Learning of Concepts: LearnSmart   Students want to make the best use of their study time. The LearnSmart adaptive self-study technology within *Connect Economics* provides students with a seamless combination of practice, assessment, and remediation for every concept in the textbook. LearnSmart's intelligent software adapts to every student response and automatically delivers concepts that advance the student's understanding while reducing time devoted to the concepts already mastered. The result for every student is the fastest path to mastery of the chapter concepts. LearnSmart:

- Applies an intelligent concept engine to identify the relationships between concepts and to serve new concepts to each student only when he or she is ready.

- Adapts automatically to each student, so students spend less time on the topics they understand and practice more those they have yet to master.
- Provides continual reinforcement and remediation, but gives only as much guidance as students need.
- Integrates diagnostics as part of the learning experience.
- Enables you to assess which concepts students have efficiently learned on their own, thus freeing class time for more applications and discussion.

Student Progress Tracking   *Connect Economics* keeps instructors informed about how each student, section, and class is performing, allowing for more productive use of lecture and office hours. The progress-tracking function enables you to:

- View scored work immediately and track individual or group performance with assignment and grade reports.
- Access an instant view of student or class performance relative to learning objectives.
- Collect data and generate reports required by many accreditation organizations, such as AACSB.

McGraw-Hill Connect Plus Economics   McGraw-Hill reinvents the textbook learning experience for the modern student with *Connect Plus Economics*. A seamless integration of an eBook and *Connect Economics, Connect Plus Economics* provides all of the *Connect Economics* features plus the following:

- An integrated eBook, allowing for anytime, anywhere access to the textbook.
- Dynamic links between the problems or questions you assign to your students and the location in the eBook where that problem or question is covered.
- A powerful search function to pinpoint and connect key concepts in a snap.

In short, *Connect Economics* offers you and your students powerful tools and features that optimize your time and energies, enabling you to focus on course content, teaching, and student learning. *Connect Economics* also offers a wealth of content resources for both instructors and students. This state-of-the-art, thoroughly tested system supports you in preparing students for the world that awaits.

For more information about Connect, go to **www.mcgrawhillconnect.com,** or contact your local McGraw-Hill sales representative.

Tegrity Campus: Lectures 24/7

Tegrity Campus is a service that makes class time available 24/7 by automatically capturing every lecture in a searchable format for students to review when they study and complete assignments. With a simple one-click start-and-stop process, you capture all computer screens and corresponding audio. Students can replay any part of any class with easy-to-use browser-based viewing on a PC or Mac.

Educators know that the more students can see, hear, and experience class resources, the better they learn. In fact, studies prove it. With Tegrity Campus, students quickly recall key moments by using Tegrity Campus's unique search feature. This search helps students efficiently find what they need, when they need it, across an entire semester of class recordings. Help turn all your students' study time into learning moments immediately supported by your lecture.

To learn more about Tegrity, watch a 2-minute Flash demo at **http://tegritycampus. mhhe.com.**

Assurance-of-Learning Ready

Many educational institutions today are focused on the notion of *assurance of learning*, an important element of some accreditation standards. *The Macro Economy Today* is designed specifically to support your assurance-of-learning initiatives with a simple, yet powerful solution.

Each test bank question for *The Macro Economy Today* maps to a specific chapter learning outcome/objective listed in the text. You can use our test bank software, EZ Test and EZ Test Online, or *Connect Economics* to easily query for learning outcomes/objectives that directly relate to the learning objectives for your course. You can then use the reporting features of EZ Test to aggregate student results in similar fashion, making the collection and presentation of assurance of learning data simple and easy.

The McGraw-Hill Companies is a proud corporate member of AACSB International. Understanding the importance and value of AACSB accreditation, *The Macro Economy Today* recognizes the curricula guidelines detailed in the AACSB standards for business accreditation by connecting selected questions in the text and the test bank to the six general knowledge and skill guidelines in the AACSB standards.

The statements contained in *The Macro Economy Today* are provided only as a guide for the users of this textbook. The AACSB leaves content coverage and assessment within the purview of individual schools, the mission of the school, and the faculty. While *The Macro Economy Today* and the teaching package make no claim of any specific AACSB qualification or evaluation, we have labeled within *The Macro Economy Today* selected questions according to the six general knowledge and skills areas.

McGraw-Hill Customer Care Contact Information

At McGraw-Hill, we understand that getting the most from new technology can be challenging. That's why our services don't stop after you purchase our products. You can e-mail our Product Specialists 24 hours a day to get product-training online. Or you can search our knowledge bank of Frequently Asked Questions on our support Web site. For Customer Support, call **800-331-5094,** e-mail **hmsupport@mcgraw-hill.com,** or visit **www.mhhe.com/support.** One of our Technical Support Analysts will be able to assist you in a timely fashion.

CourseSmart is a new way for faculty to find and review eTextbooks. It's also a great option for students who are interested in accessing their course materials digitally. CourseSmart offers thousands of the most commonly adopted textbooks across hundreds of courses from a wide variety of higher education publishers. It is the only place for faculty to review and compare the full text of a textbook online. At CourseSmart, students can save up to 50% off the cost of a print book, reduce their impact on the environment, and gain access to powerful web tools for learning including full text search, notes and highlighting, and email tools for sharing notes between classmates. Complete tech support is also included in each title.

Finding your eBook is easy. Visit **www.CourseSmart.com** and search by title, author, or ISBN.

WHAT'S NEW IN THE TWELFTH

To previous users of *The Macro Economy Today,* all of its distinctive features have become familiar—and, hopefully, welcome. For those instructors already familiar with *The Macro Economy Today,* the more urgent question is, What's new? The answer is *a lot.* By way of brief summary, you may want to note the following:

The Great Recession of 2008-9

For a text that emphasizes short-run instability, the Great Recession of 2008–9 was a kind of windfall. That GDP contraction not only reinvigorated both student and faculty interest in business cycles, but provided scores of fresh illustrations of cyclical forces and policy responses.

There are many aspects of the recession that are tied in to each chapter. For example, Chapter 3's introduction is based around the 2008–9 gyration in gasoline prices. Chapter 6 emphasizes labor-force growth and discusses 2008–9 job losses and the jobless surge. Chapter 8 centers on the 2008–9 recession and includes a new debate on policy options for ending the recession. Chapter 9's introduction ties to the 2008–9 recession and contains articles representing the plunge in consumer confidence in 2008–9 and disposable income and spending overall in 2009. The multiplier is traced through the recession from 2007 to 2009 in Chapter 10 with references to the 2008–9 multiplier effects, the risk of deflation in 2008–9, and the 2008 decline in consumption. The monetary policy option chapters (Chapters 13–15) discuss the 2008–9 credit crisis, the Fed funds rate cut, and bank credit tightening, respectively.

The Obama Presidency

The new "Economist in Chief" has certainly changed the tone and substance of economic policy. Almost every chapter refers to the goals, the options, and choices associated with the Obama administration. Chapter 10's introduction is tied to Obama's Keynesian approach, while Chapter 11 examines the debates of Obama's 2009 stimulus plan and the CBO's analyses of the package. Deficit implications of Obama's stimulus program are a new focus in Chapter 12. The supply-side option chapters (Chapters 16 and 17) cite Obama's infrastructure spending and incorporate Obama's 2009 growth-enhancing stimulus components accordingly. Chapter 18 centers on the 2009 battle over Obama's stimulus package with mentions of the 2009 tax cuts versus spending debate and the CBO's forecasts.

New "Economy Tomorrow"s

Chapter 1 has a new "Economy Tomorrow" focused on the benefits and opportunity costs of the 2008 discovery of water on Mars. Chapter 3 incorporates the market for human organs with a detailed illustration of the shortage of organs, market incentives, and zero price ceiling. The expanded government's share of total output of the global recession of 2008–9 is mentioned in Chapter 4's "Economy Tomorrow." A new "Economy Tomorrow" at the end of Chapter 8 surveys the broad policy options for ending the Great Recession of 2008–9. Chapter 10 showcases consumer confidence, explaining the slip in 2007 and the deep plunge in 2008 and recognizing the "paradox of thrift" directly affecting aggregate demand. Chapter 12 focuses on bank failures and integrates the 2008 credit crisis and the intent of the 2008–9 bank bailout with an example of Washington Mutual's failure. Obama's view is noted within the overall explanation in Chapter 18.

New "In the News" Boxes

The "In the News" boxes are all annotated with analytical captions and referred to in the body of the text. They cover everything from tuition hikes (p. 132) to Treasury auction prices and yields (p. 298). Some of my favorites are:

- The scalping of Obama inaugural tickets (p. 57)
- The 2008–9 surge in joblessness (p. 123)
- Domestic (p. 211) and global (p. 212) multiplier effects of the Great Recession
- The lobbyists' scramble for stimulus funds (p. 395)

New "World View" Boxes

The "World Views" are also festooned with analytical captions and referred to explicitly in the body of the text. These include new "World Views" on China's fiscal stimulus (p. 230), monetary policy restraint (p. 303), and U.S. competitiveness (p. 366). The dual World View (p. 91) is a great illustration of the North Korean guns versus butter trade-off. Another favorite of mine is the Zimbabwean hyperinflation of 200 million-plus percent (p. 136).

New Problems

The problems in *The Macro Economy Today* are more numerous, more challenging, and more explicitly tied to the content of each chapter than is the case with other texts. The same problems, in exactly the same format, appear in the *Connect Economics* tutorial software. My own teaching assistant, Karl Geisler, and I checked every question and answer.

New Discussion Questions

Like the *Student Problem Sets,* the Questions for Discussion at the end of each chapter are tied to the content of the text, including News and World View boxes.

Thorough Updating

Besides all these salient updates, the entire text has been rendered up-to-date with the latest statistics and case studies. ***This unparalleled currency is a distinctive feature of* The Macro Economy Today.**

NEW AND IMPROVED SUPPLEMENTS

Instructor Aids

Test Bank. Robert Shoffner of Central Piedmont Community College and Roberta Biby of Grand Valley State University have thoroughly revised the *Test Bank* for the Twelfth edition. This team assures a high level of quality and consistency of the test questions and the greatest possible correlation with the content of the text as well as the *Study Guide,* which was prepared by Linda Wilson of the University of Texas, Arlington, with Mark Maier of Glendale Community College. All questions are coded according to chapter Learning Objectives, AACSB Assurance of Learning, and Bloom's Taxonomy guidelines. The computerized *Test Bank* is available in EZ Test, a flexible and easy-to-use electronic testing program that accommodates a wide range of question types including user-created questions. Tests created in EZ Test can be exported for use with course management systems such as WebCT, BlackBoard, or PageOut. The program is available for Windows, Macintosh, and Linux environments. *Test Banks* are offered in micro and econ versions, each of which contains thousands of questions including essay questions.

PowerPoint Presentations. David Doorn of the University of Minnesota, Duluth, created new presentation slides for the Twelfth edition. Developed using Microsoft Power-Point software, these slides are a step-by-step review of the key points in the book's 21 chapters. They are equally useful to the student in the classroom as lecture aids or for personal review at home or the computer lab. The slides use animation to show students how graphs build and shift.

Digital Image Library. All of the text's tables and graphs have been reproduced as full-color images on the Web site for instructor access.

Instructor's Resource Manual. Ronald Nate of Brigham Young University, Idaho, has prepared the *Instructor's Resource Manual*. The *Instructor's Resource Manual* is available online, and it includes chapter summaries and outlines, "lecture launchers" to stimulate class discussion, and media exercises to extend the analysis. New features include the complete integration of chapter Learning Objectives, AACSB, and Bloom's Taxonomy guidelines.

News Flashes. As up-to-date as *The Macro Economy Today* is, it can't foretell the future. As the future becomes the present, however, I write two-page News Flashes describing major economic events and relating them to specific text references. These News Flashes provide good lecture material and can be copied for student use. Adopters of *The Macro Economy Today* have the option of receiving News Flashes via fax or mail. They're also available on the Schiller Web site. Four to six News Flashes are sent to adopters each year. (Contact your local McGraw-Hill/Irwin sales representative to get on the mailing list.)

Student Aids

At the instructor's discretion, students have access to the News Flashes described above. In addition, the following supplements can facilitate learning.

Built-in Student Problem Set. The built-in *Student Problem Set* is found at the end of every chapter of *The Macro Economy Today*. Each chapter has 8 to 10 numerical and graphing problems tied to the content of the text. Graphing grids are provided. The answer blanks are formatted to facilitate grading and all answers are contained in the *Instructor's Resource Manual*. For convenience, the *Student Problem Set* pages can also be found on the textbook's Web site, in exactly the same order and format. This facilitates either manual or electronic retrieval of homework assignments.

Study Guide. The new *Study Guide* has been completely updated by Linda Wilson of the University of Texas, Arlington, and Mark Maier of Glendale Community College. The *Study Guide* develops quantitative skills and the use of economic terminology, and enhances critical thinking capabilities. Each chapter includes a Quick Review that lists the key points in an easy-to-read bulleted format, Learning Objectives for the chapter, a crossword puzzle using key terms, 10 true-false questions with explanations, 20 multiple-choice questions, problems and applications that relate directly back to the text, and common student errors. Answers to all problems, exercises, and questions are provided at the end of each chapter.

ACKNOWLEDGMENTS

This Twelfth edition is unquestionably the finest edition of *The Macro Economy Today,* and I am deeply grateful to all those people who helped develop it. Marianne Magday was my faithful, fastidious, and cheerful Editorial Coordinator under the watchful eye of Anne

Hilbert, the Development Editor. Harvey Yep, the Project Manager, once again did an exceptional job in assuring that every page of the text was visually pleasing, properly formatted, error-free, and timely produced. Douglas Reiner continued to serve as the Publisher, offering sage advice and savvy leadership. The design team, led by Matt Baldwin, created a cool pallette of colors and features that enhanced *The Macro Economy Today*'s readability. My thanks to all of them and their supporting staff. My UNR teaching assistant, Karl Geisler, also deserves thanks for his valuable research assistance and careful integration of the Student Problem Set into *Connect Economics*.

I also want to express my heartfelt thanks to the professors who have shared their reactions (both good and bad) with me. Direct feedback from these users and reviewers has been a great source of continuing improvements in *The Macro Economy Today:*

Reviewers

Richard Agesa
Marshall University

Ben Artz
University of Wisconsin, Whitewater

Christopher Azevedo
University of Central Missouri

Rebecca Tuttle Baldwin
Bellevue College

Hamid Bastin
Shippensburg University

Doris S. Bennett
Jacksonville State University

John Bishop
East Carolina University

Ralph Bradburd
Williams College

Bruce C. Brown
California State Polytechnic University,
    Pomona

Tony Caporale
University of Dayton

J. Lon Carlson
Illinois State University

Adhip Chaudhuri
Georgetown University

Dennis Debrecht
Carroll University

David J. Doorn
University of Minnesota, Duluth

Tran Dung
Wright State University

Harold Elder
The University of Alabama

Fred Foldvary
Santa Clara University

James Fort
SUNY Cobleskill

Ralph Gamble
Fort Hays State University

Frank Garland
TriCounty Technical College

Fusun Gonul
Slippery Rock University of
    Pennsylvania

Homer Guevara
Northwest Vista College

Darrin Gulla
University of Kentucky

Becky Haney
Oklahoma City University

Christine Harrington
SUNY Oneonta

Glenn S. Haynes
Western Illinois University

Susan He
Washington State University

Daniel J. Horton
Cleveland State University

Robert G. James
California State University,
    Chico

Elizabeth Sawyer Kelley
University of Wisconsin, Madison

Frederic Kolb
University of Wisconsin, Eau Claire

Carsten Lange
California State Polytechnic University,
    Pomona

Daniel Marburger
Arkansas State University,
    Jonesboro

Christopher McIntosh
University of Minnesota, Duluth

Evelina Mengova
California State University, Fullerton

Douglas Miller
University of Missouri, Columbia

Daniel Nguyen
Purdue University

Lolita Paff
Pennsylvania State University,
    Berks

Stephen Paulone
Post University
Gregory Pratt
Mesa Community College
Ratha Ramoo
Diablo Valley College
Bill Robinson
University of Nevada, Las Vegas
Brian Rosario
University of California, Davis
Djavad Salehi-Isfahani
Virginia Polytechnic Institute and State
   University

Evgenia Shumilkina
Northeastern University
Richard Stratton
The University of
   Akron
Zhi Su
Northeastern
   University
Manjuri Talukdar
Northern Illinois
   University

Finally, I'd like to thank all the professors and students who are going to use *The Macro Economy Today* as an introduction to economics principles. I welcome any responses (even the bad ones) you'd like to pass on for future editions.

—Bradley R. Schiller

CONTENTS

THE
MACRO ECONOMY
TODAY

TWELFTH EDITION

PART 1 The Economic Challenge

People around the world want a better life. Whether rich or poor, everyone strives for a higher standard of living. Ultimately, the performance of the economy will determine who attains that goal.

These first few chapters examine how the *limits* to output are determined and how the interplay of market forces and government intervention utilize and expand those limits.

  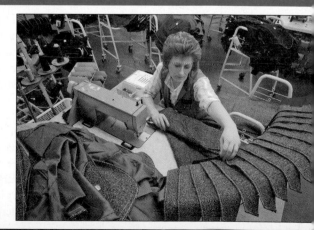

Economics:
The Core Issues

◀ "The Economist in Chief"

Barack Obama was elated when he won the presidential election on November 4, 2008. Like his predecessors, however, he was also anxious about his new responsibilities. As president, Obama would not only be the Commander in Chief, but also the Economist in Chief. He would be the one held responsible for the success or failure of the U.S. economy for the next 4 years. And his *re-election* prospects would depend heavily on how well the economy did. The economic showdown of 2007–8 had helped him defeat his Republican opponent; Obama wanted to avoid a similar fate. What should he do? What *could* he do?

The recession he inherited added a sense of urgency to these policy questions. In the weeks following the election, all the economic alarms were ringing: unemployment was rising, output was falling, the U.S. dollar was weakening, consumer confidence was deteriorating, and the stock market was plummeting. He had to formulate an economic-action plan even *before* his inauguration. As president-elect Obama himself observed, "With our economy in distress, we cannot hesitate, and we cannot delay." Weeks before his inauguration, he assembled a team of economic advisers to help him develop an action plan. Obama asked them whether the economy would recover from recession without further government intervention. If further government intervention was needed, how large should the additional tax cuts, spending hikes, or interest-rate reductions be? Should an Obama administration extend government regulation deeper into the economy—for example, more regulation of banks, labor markets, international trade,

health care, the housing market—or instead rely more on the private sector (markets) to keep the economy going?

To make the right policy decisions, President Obama needed the help of economic theory. He and his advisers needed to know what makes an economy "tick"—what forces drive an economy to keep producing goods and services. And what causes the economic engine to sometimes sputter and stall, as it did in 2008. They needed to know when government intervention can help fix our economic problems and also when, regrettably, government intervention can actually make things worse.

This chapter starts down the path of economic understanding with an overview of the big questions every economy (and its Economist in Chief) must answer. What do we want the economy to produce? How can we assure that outcome? Will the output of the economy be distributed fairly? Will the environment be protected? What role should the government play in answering these questions? How much should we rely on the private sector—on *markets*—to produce the goods we desire, the jobs we want, and to protect the environment?

We also begin in this chapter to examine some of the little questions we confront as individuals. How much time should you spend reading this book? Why, for that matter, are you reading this book at all? Are you expecting a better grade if you complete your assignments? Will better grades lead to better jobs after graduating? How much money do you plan to spend this weekend? What products will you buy?

Although the Big Questions an economy confronts and the little questions individuals confront are very different, they do have a common thread—an *economic* thread. In a world of unlimited resources, we could have all the goods we desired. We'd have time to do everything we wanted, enough money to buy everything we desired. We could produce enough to make everyone rich, while protecting the environment and exploring the universe. The Economist in Chief could deliver everything voters asked for. Unfortunately, we don't live in that utopia: we live in a world of *limited* resources. So we have to make difficult decisions about how *best* to use our time, our money, and our resources. President Obama has to decide how *best* to use the nation's limited resources. These are *economic* decisions.

In this first chapter we'll examine how the problem of limited resources arises and the kinds of choices it forces us to make. As we'll see, **three core choices confront every nation:**

- **WHAT to produce with our limited resources.**
- **HOW to produce the goods and services we select.**
- **FOR WHOM goods and services are produced; that is, who should get them.**

We also have to decide who should answer these questions. Should people take care of their own health and retirement, or should the government provide a safety net of health care and pensions? Should the government regulate airfares or let the airlines set prices? Should Microsoft decide what features get included in a computer's operating system or should the government make that decision? Should interest rates be set by private banks alone, or should the government try to control interest rates? The battle over *who* should answer the core questions is often as contentious as the questions themselves.

THE ECONOMY IS US

To learn how the economy works, let's start with a simple truth: *The economy is us*. "The economy" is simply an abstraction referring to the grand sum of all our production and consumption activities. What we collectively produce is what the economy produces; what we collectively consume is what the economy consumes. In this sense, the concept of "the economy" is no more difficult than the concept of "the family." If someone tells you that the Jones family has an annual income of $42,000, you know that the reference is to the collective earnings of all the Joneses. Likewise, when someone reports that the nation's income is $15 trillion per year—as it now is—we should recognize that the reference is to the grand total of everyone's income. If we work fewer hours or get paid less, both family income *and* national income decline. The "meaningless statistics" (see cartoon below) often cited in the news are just a summary of our collective market behavior.

"Meaningless statistics were up one-point-five per cent this month over last month."

Analysis: Many people think of economics as dull statistics. But economics is really about human behavior—how people decide to use scarce resources and how those decisions affect market outcomes.

The same relationship between individual behavior and aggregate behavior applies to specific outputs. If we as individuals insist on driving cars rather than taking public transportation, the economy will produce millions of cars each year and consume vast quantities of oil. In a slightly different way, the economy produces billions of dollars of military hardware to satisfy our desire for national defense. In each case, the output of the economy reflects the collective behavior of the 310 million individuals who participate in the U.S. economy.

We may not always be happy with the output of the economy. But we can't ignore the link between individual action and collective outcomes. If the highways are clogged and the air is polluted, we can't blame someone else for the transportation choices we made. If we're disturbed by the size of our military arsenal, we must still accept responsibility for our choices (or nonchoices, if we failed to vote). In either case, we continue to have the option of reallocating our resources. We can create a different outcome the next day, month, or year.

SCARCITY: THE CORE PROBLEM

Although we can change economic outcomes, we can't have everything we want. If you go to the mall with $20 in your pocket, you can buy only so much. The money in your pocket sets a *limit* to your spending.

The output of the entire economy is also limited. The limits in this case are set not by the amount of money in people's pockets, but by the resources available for producing goods and services. Everyone wants more housing, new schools, better transit systems, and a new car. We also want to explore space and bring safe water to the world's poor. But even a country as rich as the United States can't produce everything people want. So, like every other nation, we have to grapple with the core problem of **scarcity**—the fact that there aren't enough resources available to satisfy all our desires.

scarcity: Lack of enough resources to satisfy all desired uses of those resources.

Factors of Production

factors of production: Resource inputs used to produce goods and services, such as land, labor, capital, and entrepreneurship.

The resources used to produce goods and services are called **factors of production.** *The four basic factors of production are*

- *Land*
- *Labor*
- *Capital*
- *Entrepreneurship*

These are the *inputs* needed to produce desired *outputs*. To produce this textbook, for example, we needed paper, printing presses, a building, and lots of labor. We also needed people with good ideas who could put it together. To produce the education you're getting in this class, we need not only a textbook but a classroom, a teacher, a blackboard, and maybe a computer as well. Without factors of production, we simply can't produce anything.

Land. The first factor of production, land, refers not just to the ground but to all natural resources. Crude oil, water, air, and minerals are all included in our concept of "land."

Labor. Labor too has several dimensions. It's not simply a question of how many bodies there are. When we speak of labor as a factor of production, we refer to the skills and abilities to produce goods and services. Hence, both the quantity and the quality of human resources are included in the "labor" factor.

capital: Final goods produced for use in the production of other goods, e.g., equipment, structures.

Capital. The third factor of production is capital. In economics the term **capital** refers to final goods produced for use in further production. The residents of fishing villages in southern Thailand, for example, braid huge fishing nets. The sole purpose of these nets is to catch more fish. The nets themselves become a factor of production in obtaining the final goods (fish) that people desire. Thus, they're regarded as *capital.* Blast furnaces used to make steel and desks used to equip offices are also capital inputs.

Entrepreneurship. The more land, labor, and capital available, the greater the amount of potential output. A farmer with 10,000 acres, 12 employees, and six tractors can grow more crops than a farmer with half those resources. But there's no guarantee that he will. The farmer with fewer resources may have better ideas about what to plant, when to irrigate, or how to harvest the crops. ***It's not just a matter of what resources you have but also of how well you use them.*** This is where the fourth factor of production—**entrepreneurship**—comes in. The entrepreneur is the person who sees the opportunity for new or better products and brings together the resources needed for producing them. If it weren't for entrepreneurs, Thai fishermen would still be using sticks to catch fish. Without entrepreneurship, farmers would still be milking their cows by hand. If someone hadn't thought of a way to miniaturize electronic circuits, you wouldn't have a cell phone.

> **entrepreneurship:** The assembling of resources to produce new or improved products and technologies.

The role of entrepreneurs in economic progress is a key issue in the market versus government debate. The Austrian economist Joseph Schumpeter argued that free markets unleash the "animal spirits" of entrepreneurs, propelling innovation, technology, and growth. Critics of government regulation argue that government interference in the marketplace, however well intentioned, tends to stifle those very same animal spirits.

Limits to Output

No matter how an economy is organized, there's a limit to how much it can produce. The most evident limit is the amount of resources available for producing goods and services. One reason the United States can produce so much is that it has over 3 *million* acres of land. Tonga, with less than 500 acres of land, will never produce as much. The U.S. also has a population of over 300 million people. That's a lot less than China (1.4 *billion*), but far larger than 200 other nations (Tonga has a population of less than 125,000). So an abundance of "raw" resources gives us the potential to produce a lot of output. But that greater production capacity isn't enough to satisfy all our desires. We're constantly scrambling for additional resources to build more houses, make better movies, provide more health care, and colonize the moon. That imbalance between available resources and our wish list is one of the things that makes the job of Economist in Chief so difficult.

The science of **economics** helps us frame these choices. In a nutshell, economics is the study of how people use scarce resources. How do you decide how much time to spend studying? How does Google decide how many workers to hire? How does Ford decide whether to use its factories to produce sports utility vehicles or sedans? What share of a nation's resources should be devoted to space exploration, the delivery of health care services, or pollution control? In every instance, alternative ways of using scarce labor, land, and capital resources are available, and we have to choose one use over another.

> **economics:** The study of how best to allocate scarce resources among competing uses.

Opportunity Costs

President Obama vowed to continue the journey to Mars initiated by President Bush. Scientists believe that the biological, geophysical, and technical knowledge gained from the exploration of Mars will improve life here on Earth. But that expedition won't be costless. ***Every time we use scarce resources in one way, we give up the opportunity to use them in other ways.*** If we use more resources to explore space, we have fewer resources available for producing earthly goods. The forgone earthly goods represent the **opportunity costs** of a Mars expedition. ***Opportunity cost is what is given up to get something else.*** Even a so-called free lunch has an opportunity cost (see following cartoon). The resources used to produce the lunch could have been used to produce something else. A trip to Mars has a much higher opportunity cost.

> **opportunity cost:** The most desired goods or services that are forgone to obtain something else.

Your economics class also has an opportunity cost. The building space used for your economics class can't be used to show movies at the same time. Your professor can't lecture (produce education) and repair motorcycles simultaneously. The decision to use these scarce resources (capital, labor) for an economics class implies producing less of other goods.

Even reading this book is costly. That cost is not measured in dollars and cents. The true (economic) cost is, instead, measured in terms of some alternative activity. What would you

"There's no such thing as a free lunch."

Analysis: All goods and services have an opportunity cost. Even the resources used to produce a "free lunch" could have been used to produce something else.

---

like to be doing right now? The more time you spend reading this book, the less time you have available for other uses of your time. The opportunity cost of reading this text is the best alternative use of your scarce time. If you are missing your favorite TV show, we'd say that show is the opportunity cost of reading this book. It is what you gave up to do this assignment. Hopefully, the benefits you get from studying will outweigh that cost. Otherwise this wouldn't be the best way to use your scarce time.

Guns vs. Butter

One of the persistent national choices about resource use entails defense spending. After the September 11, 2001, terrorist attacks on the World Trade Center and Pentagon, American citizens overwhelmingly favored an increase in military spending. Even the unpopularity of the war in Iraq didn't quell the desire for more national defense. But national defense, like Mars exploration, requires the use of scarce resources. The 1.4 million men and women who serve in the armed forces aren't available to build schools, program computers, or teach economics. Similarly, the land, labor, capital, and entrepreneurship devoted to producing military hardware aren't available for producing civilian goods. An *increase* in national defense implies still more sacrifices of civilian goods and services. How many schools, hospitals, or cars are we willing to sacrifice in order to "produce" more national security? This is the "guns versus butter" dilemma that all nations confront.

PRODUCTION POSSIBILITIES

The opportunity costs implied by our every choice can be illustrated easily. Suppose a nation can produce only two goods, trucks and tanks. To keep things simple, assume that labor (workers) is the only factor of production needed to produce either good. Although other factors of production (land, machinery) are also needed in actual production, ignoring them for the moment does no harm. Let us assume further that we have a total of only 10 workers available per day to produce either trucks or tanks. Our initial problem is to determine the *limits* of output. How many trucks or tanks *can* be produced in a day with available resources?

Before going any further, notice how opportunity costs will affect the answer. If we use all 10 workers to produce trucks, no labor will be available to assemble tanks. In this case, forgone tanks would become the *opportunity cost* of a decision to employ all our resources in truck production.

We still don't know how many trucks could be produced with 10 workers or exactly how many tanks would be forgone by such a decision. To get these answers, we need more details about the production processes involved—specifically, how many workers are required to manufacture either good.

TABLE 1.1
A Production Possibilities Schedule

As long as resources are limited, their use entails an opportunity cost. In this case, resources (labor) used to produce trucks can't be used for tank assembly at the same time. Hence, the forgone tanks are the opportunity cost of additional trucks. If all our resources were used to produce trucks (row *A*), no tanks could be assembled.

Resources can't transfer equally.

	Total Available Labor	Output of Trucks per Day	×	Labor Needed per Truck	=	Total Labor Required for Trucks	Labor Not Used for Trucks	Potential Output of Tanks per Day		Increase in Tank Output
		Truck Production						**Tank Production**		
A	10	5		2		10	0	0		
B	10	4		2		8	2	2.0	>	2.0
C	10	3		2		6	4	3.0	>	1.0
D	10	2		2		4	6	3.8	>	0.8
E	10	1		2		2	8	4.5	>	0.7
F	10	0		2		0	10	5.0	>	0.5

Table 1.1 summarizes the hypothetical choices, or **production possibilities,** that we confront in this case. Suppose we wanted to produce only trucks (i.e., no tanks). Row *A* of the table shows the *maximum* number of trucks we could produce. With 10 workers available and a labor requirement of 2 workers per truck, we can manufacture a maximum of five trucks per day.

Producing five trucks per day leaves no workers available to produce tanks. On row *A* of Table 1.1 we've got "butter" but no "guns." If we want tanks, we'll have to cut back on truck production. The remainder of Table 1.1 illustrates the trade-offs we confront in this simple case. By cutting back truck production from five to four trucks per day (row *B*), we reduce labor use in truck production from 10 workers to 8. That leaves 2 workers available for other uses, including the production of tanks.

If we employ these remaining 2 workers to assemble tanks, we can build two tanks a day. We would then end up with four trucks and two tanks per day. What's the opportunity cost of these two tanks? It's the one additional truck (the fifth truck) that we could have produced but didn't.

As we proceed down the rows of Table 1.1, the nature of opportunity costs becomes apparent. Each additional tank built implies the loss (opportunity cost) of truck output. Likewise, every truck produced implies the loss of some tank output.

These trade-offs between truck and tank production are illustrated in the production possibilities curve of Figure 1.1. *Each point on the production possibilities curve depicts an alternative mix of output* **that could be produced.** In this case, each point represents a different combination of trucks and tanks that we could produce in a single day using all available resources (labor in this case).

Notice in particular how points *A* through *F* in Figure 1.1 represent the choices described in each row of Table 1.1. At point *A*, we're producing five trucks per day and no tanks. As we move down the curve from point *A* we're producing fewer trucks and more tanks. At point *B*, truck production has dropped from five to four vehicles per day while tank assembly has increased from zero to two. In other words, we've given up one truck to get two tanks assembled. The opportunity cost of those tanks is the one truck that is given up. A production possibilities curve, then, is simply a graphic summary of production possibilities, as described in Table 1.1. As such, *the production possibilities curve illustrates two essential principles:*

- *Scarce resources.* There's a limit to the amount of output we can produce in a given time period with available resources and technology.
- *Opportunity costs.* We can obtain additional quantities of any particular good only by reducing the potential production of another good.

The Production Possibilities Curve

production possibilities: The alternative combinations of final goods and services that could be produced in a given time period with all available resources and technology.

FIGURE 1.1

A Production Possibilities Curve

A production possibilities curve (PPC) describes the various output combinations that could be produced in a given time period with available resources and technology. It represents a menu of output choices an economy confronts.

Point *B* indicates that we could produce a *combination* of four trucks and two tanks per day. By producing one less truck, we could assemble a third tank, and thus move to point *C*.

Points *A, D, E,* and *F* illustrate still other output combinations that could be produced. This curve is a graphic illustration of the production possibilities schedule in Table 1.1.

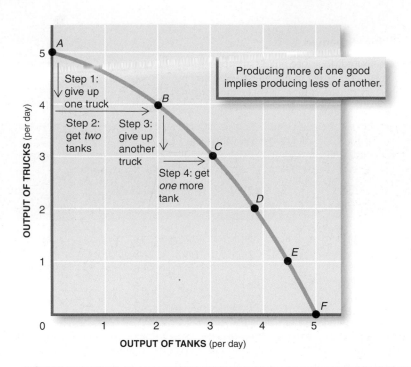

Increasing Opportunity Costs

The shape of the production possibilities curve reflects another limitation on our choices. Notice how opportunity costs increase as we move along the production possibilities curve. When we cut truck output from five to four (step 1, Figure 1.1), we get two tanks (step 2). When we cut truck production further, however (step 3), we get only one tank per truck given up (step 4). The opportunity cost of tank production is increasing. This process of increasing opportunity cost continues. By the time we give up the last truck (row *F*), tank output increases by only 0.5: We get only half a tank for the last truck given up. These increases in opportunity cost are reflected in the outward bend of the production possibilities curve.

Why do opportunity costs increase? Mostly because it's difficult to move resources from one industry to another. It's easy to transform trucks to tanks on a blackboard. In the real world, however, resources don't adapt so easily. Workers who assemble trucks may not have the same skills for tank assembly. As we continue to transfer labor from one industry to the other, we start getting fewer tanks for every truck we give up.

The difficulties entailed in transferring labor skills, capital, and entrepreneurship from one industry to another are so universal that we often speak of the *law* of *increasing opportunity cost*. This law says that we must give up ever-increasing quantities of other goods and services in order to get more of a particular good. The law isn't based solely on the limited versatility of individual workers. The *mix* of factor inputs makes a difference as well. Truck assembly requires less capital than tank assembly. In a pinch, wheels can be mounted on a truck almost completely by hand, whereas tank treads require more sophisticated machinery. As we move labor from truck assembly to tank assembly, available capital may restrict our output capabilities.

The Cost of North Korea's Military

The production possibilities curve illustrates why the core economic decision about WHAT to produce is so difficult. Consider, for example, North Korea's decision to maintain a large military. North Korea is a relatively small country: Its population of 24 million ranks fortieth in the world. Yet North Korea maintains the fourth-largest army in the world and continues to develop a nuclear weapons capability. To do so, it must allocate 16 percent of all its resources to feeding, clothing, and equipping its military forces. As a consequence, there aren't enough resources available to produce food. Without adequate machinery, seeds,

WORLD VIEW

Chronic Food Shortage Shows Despite Efforts by N. Korea to Hide It

NAMPO, North Korea—Along the sides of the road, people comb through the grass looking for edible weeds. In the center of town, a boy about 9 years old wears a tattered army jacket hanging below his knees. He has no shoes.

Sprawled on the lawn outside a bath house, poorly dressed people lie on the grass, either with no place better to go or no energy to do so at 10 A.M. on a weekday.

Despite efforts to keep North Korea's extreme poverty out of view, a glance around the countryside shows a population in distress. At the heart of the problem is a chronic food shortage. . . .

The UN World Food Program reached similar conclusions. In a recent survey of 375 North Korean households, more than 70 percent of North Koreans were found to be supplementing their diet with weeds and grasses foraged from the countryside. Such wild foods are difficult to digest, especially for children and the elderly.

The survey also determined that most adults had started skipping lunch, reducing their diet to two meals a day to cope with the food shortage.

These are some of the same signs that augured the mid-1990s famine that killed as many as 2 million people, 10 percent of the population.

—Barbara Demick

Source: *Los Angeles Times,* November 9, 2008. Used with permission.

Rocket Launch Cost Enough to End Famine in North Korea for a Year

SEOUL—The rocket launched by North Korea on Sunday is believed to be an upgraded version of the country's Taepodong-2 missile, which was used in a failed missile test in 2006, according to a report by the South Korean military . . .

A researcher at the National Intelligence Service estimated the cost of developing the missile at 300–500 million dollars, based on a previous statement by North Korean leader Kim Jong Il that the Taepodong-1 missile launched in 1998 cost between 200–300 million dollars.

Insiders close to South Korean President Lee Myung-bak say the launch itself cost around 300 million dollars, enough to break the famine sweeping much of the nation for a year.

Source: *The Mainichi Newspapers.* Copyright © April 6, 2009. Used with permission.

AP Wide World Photo

Analysis: North Korea's inability to feed itself is partly due to maintaining its large army: Resources used for the military aren't available for producing food.

fertilizer, or irrigation, Korea's farmers can't produce enough food to feed the population (see World View above). As Figure 1.2 illustrates, the opportunity cost of "guns" in Korea is a lot of needed "butter."

During World War II, the United States confronted a similar trade-off. In 1944, nearly 40 percent of all U.S. output was devoted to the military. Civilian goods were so scarce that

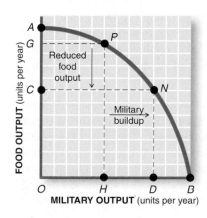

FIGURE 1.2
The Cost of War

North Korea devotes 16 percent of its output to the military. The opportunity cost of this decision is reduced output of food. As the military expands from *OH* to *OD,* food output drops from *OG* to *OC.*

web analysis

To see how the share of United States output allocated to national defense has changed in recent decades, visit the Government Printing Office Web site **www.gpoaccess.gov/usbudget** and click on "About the Budget."

FIGURE 1.3
The Military Share of Output

The share of total output allocated to the military indicates the opportunity cost of maintaining an army. North Korea has the highest cost, using 16 percent of its resources for military purposes. Although China and the United States have much larger armies, their military *share* of output is much smaller.

Source: U.S. Central Intelligence Agency (2006–2007 data).

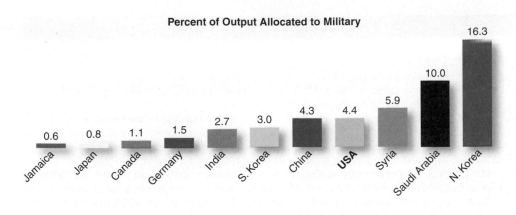

Percent of Output Allocated to Military

they had to be rationed. Staples like butter, sugar, and gasoline were doled out in small quantities. Even golf balls were rationed. In North Korea, golf balls would be a luxury even without a military buildup. As the share of North Korea's output devoted to the military increased, even basic food production became more difficult.

Figure 1.3 illustrates how other nations divide up available resources between military and civilian production. The $640 billion the United States now spends on national defense absorbs only 4.4 percent of total output. This made the opportunity costs of the post-9/11 military buildup, and the wars in Iraq and Afghanistan less painful.

Efficiency

> **efficiency:** Maximum output of a good from the resources used in production.

Not all of the choices on the production possibilities curve are equally desirable. They are, however, all *efficient*. Efficiency means squeezing *maximum* output out of available resources. Every point of the PPC satisfies this condition. Although the *mix* of output changes as we move around the production possibilities curve (Figures 1.1 and 1.2), at every point we are getting as much *total* output as physically possible. Since **efficiency** in production means simply "getting the most from what you've got," **every point on the production possibilities curve is efficient.** At every point on the curve we are using all available resources in the best way we know how.

Inefficiency

There's no guarantee, of course, that we'll always use resources so efficiently. *A production possibilities curve shows* potential *output, not necessarily* actual *output.* If we're inefficient, actual output will be less than that potential. This happens. In the real world, workers sometimes loaf on the job. Or they call in sick and go to a baseball game instead of working. Managers don't always give the clearest directions or stay in touch with advancing technology. Even students sometimes fail to put forth their best effort on homework assignments. This kind of slippage can prevent us from achieving maximum production. When that happens, we end up *inside* the PPC rather than *on* it.

Point *Y* in Figure 1.4 illustrates the consequences of inefficient production. At point *Y*, we're producing only three trucks and two tanks. This is less than our potential. We could assemble a third tank without cutting back truck production (point *C*). Or we could get an extra truck without sacrificing any tank output (point *B*). Instead, we're producing *inside* the production possibilities curve at point *Y*. Whenever we're producing inside the production possibilities curve we are forgoing the opportunity of producing (and consuming) additional output.

[Handwritten note: All points on PPC represent efficiency. It also shows predicted / potential output. Not Real.]

Unemployment

We can end up inside the production possibilities curve by utilizing resources inefficiently or simply by not using all available resources. This happened in 2008–9. In early 2009 more than 11 *million* Americans were *unemployed* (see following News). These men and women were ready, willing, and available to work, but no one hired them. As a result, we were stuck *inside* the PPC, producing less output than we could have. One of President Obama's first challenges was to develop economic policies that would create more jobs and get the U.S. back on its production possibilities curve.

FIGURE 1.4

Points Inside and Outside the PPC Curve

Points outside the production possibilities curve (point *X*) are unattainable with available resources and technology. Points inside the PPC (point *Y*) represent the incomplete use of available resources. Only points on the PPC (*A, B, C*) represent maximum use of our production capabilities.

U.S. Jobless Rate at Highest Level Since '93

At 7.2%, 11.1 Million Americans Are Out of Work—a Total of 2.6 Million Jobs Were Lost in 2008

The nation's unemployment rate jumped to 7.2 percent in December, the highest level since 1993, with 11.1 million Americans forced to pound the streets amid a job-destroying recession.

In a report issued Friday, the Labor Department said employers cut payrolls by 524,000 in December, bringing to 2.6 million the total number of jobs lost last year.

Wells Fargo economist Eugenio Aleman said 1.9 million of those jobs were lost since September, when the global financial system nearly collapsed.

"The worst news about this release is that we expect the employment situation to continue to deteriorate for some time to come," Aleman said.

The grim figures arrived a day after President-elect Barack Obama called for quick congressional action on a combination of public spending and tax cuts to stimulate the sagging economy and create or save 3 million jobs . . .

—Tom Abate

Source: *San Francisco Chronicle,* January 10, 2009. Copyright 2006 by San Francisco Chronicle. Reproduced with permission of San Francisco Chronicle in the format Textbook via Copyright Clearance Center.

Analysis: In 2009 the U.S. economy failed to reach its production possibilities curve, leaving millions of workers jobless.

ECONOMIC GROWTH

The challenge of getting to the production possibilities curve increases with each passing day. People are born every day. As they age, they enter the labor force as new workers. Technology, too, keeps advancing each year. These increases in available labor and technology keep pushing the producing possibilities curve outward. This **economic growth** is a good thing in the sense that it allows us to produce more goods and raise living standards. But it also means that we have to keep creating *more* jobs every year just to stay on the PPC.

Figures 1.4 and 1.5 illustrate how economic growth raises our living standards. Point *X* in Figure 1.4 lies *outside* the PPC. It is an enticing point because it suggests we could get more trucks (five) without sacrificing any tanks (two). Unfortunately, point *X* is only a mirage. ***All output combinations that lie outside the PPC are unattainable in the short run.***

In the long run, however, resources and technology increase, shifting the PPC outward, as in Figure 1.5. Before the appearance of new resources or better technology, our production

economic growth: An increase in output (real GDP); an expansion of production possibilities.

More resources or better technology expand output limits.

FIGURE 1.5

Growth: Increasing Production Possibilities

A production possibilities curve is based on *available* resources and technology. If more resources or better technology becomes available, production possibilities will increase. This economic growth is illustrated by the *shift* from PP_1 to PP_2.

possibilities were limited by the curve PP_1. *With more resources or better technology, our production possibilities increase.* This greater capacity to produce is represented by curve PP_2. This outward shift of the production possibilities curve is the essence of economic growth. With economic growth, countries can have more guns *and* more butter. Without economic growth, living standards decline as the population grows. This is the problem that plagues some of the world's poorest nations, where population increases every year but output often doesn't (see Table 2.1).

BASIC DECISIONS

Production possibilities define the output choices that a nation confronts. From these choices every nation must make some basic decisions. As we noted at the beginning of this chapter, the three core economic questions are

- *WHAT to produce.*
- *HOW to produce.*
- *FOR WHOM to produce.*

WHAT

There are millions of points along a production possibilities curve, and each one represents a different mix of output. We can choose only *one* of these points at any time. The point we choose determines what mix of output gets produced. That choice determines how many guns are produced, and how much butter. Or how many space expeditions and how many water-treatment facilities.

The production possibilities curve doesn't tell us which mix of output is best; it just lays out a menu of available choices. It's up to us to pick out the one and only mix of output that will be produced at a given time. This WHAT decision is a basic decision every nation must make.

HOW

Decisions must also be made about HOW to produce. Should we generate electricity by burning coal, smashing atoms, or transforming solar power? Should we harvest ancient forests even if that destroys endangered owls or other animal species? Should we dump municipal and industrial waste into nearby rivers, or should we dispose of it in some other way? Should we use children to harvest crops and stitch clothes or should we use only adult labor? There are lots of different ways of producing goods and services, and someone has to make a decision about which production methods to use. The HOW decision is a question not just of efficiency but of social values as well.

FOR WHOM

After we've decided what to produce and how, we must address a third basic question: FOR WHOM? Who is going to get the output produced? Should everyone get an equal share? Should everyone wear the same clothes and drive identical cars? Should some people get to enjoy seven-course banquets while others forage in garbage cans for food scraps? How should the goods and services an economy produces be distributed? Are we satisfied with the way output is now distributed?

THE MECHANISMS OF CHOICE

Answers to the questions of WHAT, HOW, and FOR WHOM largely define an economy. But who formulates the answers? Who actually decides which goods are produced, what technologies are used, or how incomes are distributed?

The Invisible Hand of a Market Economy

Adam Smith had an answer back in 1776. In his classic work *The Wealth of Nations,* the Scottish economist Smith said the "invisible hand" determines what gets produced, how, and for whom. The invisible hand he referred to wasn't a creature from a science fiction movie but, instead, a characterization of the way markets work.

Consider the decision about how many cars to produce in the United States. Who decides to produce over 15 million cars and trucks a year? There's no "auto czar" who dictates production. Not even General Motors can make such a decision. Instead, the *market* decides how many cars to produce. Millions of consumers signal their desire to have a car by browsing the Internet, visiting showrooms, and buying cars. Their purchases flash a green light to producers, who see the potential to earn more profits. To do so, they'll increase auto output. If consumers stop buying cars, profits will disappear. Producers will respond by reducing output, laying off workers, and even closing factories as they did in 2008–9.

Notice how the invisible hand moves us along the production possibilities curve. If consumers demand more cars, the mix of output will include more cars and less of other goods. If auto production is scaled back, the displaced autoworkers will end up producing other goods and services, changing the mix of output in the opposite direction.

Adam Smith's invisible hand is now called the **market mechanism.** Notice that it doesn't require any direct contact between consumers and producers. Communication is indirect, transmitted by market prices and sales. Indeed, *the essential feature of the market mechanism is the price signal.* If you want something and have sufficient income, you can buy it. If enough people do the same thing, the total sales of that product will rise, and perhaps its price will as well. Producers, seeing sales and prices rise, will want to exploit this profit potential. To do so, they'll attempt to acquire a larger share of available resources and use it to produce the goods we desire. That's how the "invisible hand" works.

The market mechanism can also answer the HOW question. To maximize their profits, producers seek the lowest-cost method of producing a good. By observing prices in the marketplace, they can identify the cheapest method and adopt it.

The market mechanism can also resolve the FOR WHOM question. A market distributes goods to the highest bidder. Individuals who are willing and able to pay the most for a product tend to get it in a pure market economy.

Adam Smith was so impressed with the ability of the market mechanism to answer the basic WHAT, HOW, and FOR WHOM questions that he urged government to "leave it alone" **(laissez faire).** In his view, the price signals and responses of the marketplace were likely to do a better job of allocating resources than any government could.

> **market mechanism:** The use of market prices and sales to signal desired outputs (or resource allocations).

> **laissez faire:** The doctrine of "leave it alone," of nonintervention by government in the market mechanism.

Government Intervention and Command Economies

The laissez-faire policy Adam Smith favored has always had its share of critics. The German economist Karl Marx emphasized how free markets tend to concentrate wealth and power in the hands of the few, at the expense of the many. As he saw it, unfettered markets permit the capitalists (those who own the machinery and factories) to enrich themselves while the proletariat (the workers) toil long hours for subsistence wages. Marx argued that the government not only had to intervene but had to *own* all the means of production—the factories, the machinery, the land—in order to avoid savage inequalities. In *Das Kapital* (1867) and the revolutionary *Communist Manifesto* (1848), he laid the foundation for a communist state in which the government would be the master of economic outcomes.

The British economist John Maynard Keynes offered a less drastic solution. The market, he conceded, was pretty efficient in organizing production and building better mousetraps. However, individual producers and workers had no control over the broader economy. The cumulative actions of so many economic agents could easily tip the economy in the wrong direction. A completely unregulated market might veer off in one direction and then another as producers all rushed to increase output at the same time or throttled back production in a herdlike manner. The government, Keynes reasoned, could act like a pressure gauge, letting off excess steam or building it up as the economy needed. With the government maintaining overall balance in the economy, the market could live up to its performance expectations. While assuring a stable, full-employment environment, the government might also be able to redress excessive inequalities. In Keynes's view, government should play an active but not all-inclusive role in managing the economy.

Continuing Debates

These historical views shed perspective on today's political debates. The core of most debates is some variation of the WHAT, HOW, or FOR WHOM questions. Much of the debate is how these questions should be answered. Conservatives favor Adam Smith's laissez-faire approach, with minimal government interference in the markets. Liberals, by contrast, think government intervention is needed to improve market outcomes. Conservatives resist workplace regulation, price controls, and minimum wages because such interventions might impair market efficiency. Liberals argue that such interventions temper the excesses of the market and promote both equity and efficiency.

WORLD VIEW

Market Reliance vs. Government Reliance?

A public opinion poll conducted in countries from around the world found a striking global consensus that the free market economic system is best. In all but one country polled, a majority or plurality agreed with the statement that "the free enterprise system and free market economy is the best system on which to base the future of the world."

Source: GlobeScan 2005 poll for Program on International Policy Attitudes, University of Maryland.

The free enterprise system and free market economy is the best system on which to base the future of the world.

Country	Agree	Disagree
United States	71	24
Canada	65	29
Mexico	61	38
Brazil	57	30
Argentina	42	29
Great Britain	66	27
Germany	65	32
Spain	63	28
Turkey	47	36
Russia	43	34
France	36	50
China	74	20
South Korea	70	19
India	70	17
Nigeria	66	29
Kenya	59	25
World Average	61	28

Analysis: People around the world believe that markets can do a good job of fostering economic growth.

web analysis

Comparative data on the percentage of goods and services the various national governments provide are available from the Penn World Tables at **www.pwt.econ.upenn.edu**.

The debate over how best to manage the economy is not unique to the United States. Countries around the world confront the same choice, between reliance on the market and reliance on the government. Public opinion clearly favors the market system, as the above World View documents. Yet, few countries have ever relied exclusively on either the markets or the government to manage their economy. Even the former Soviet Union, where the government owned all the means of production and central planners dictated how they were to be used, made limited use of free markets. In Cuba, the government still manages the economy's resources but encourages farmers' markets and some private trade and investment.

The World View on page 15 categorizes nations by the extent of their market reliance. Hong Kong scores high on this "Index of Economic Freedom" because its tax rates are relatively low, the public sector is comparatively small, and there are few restrictions on private investment or trade. By contrast, North Korea scores extremely low because the government owns

WORLD VIEW

Index of Economic Freedom

Hong Kong ranks number one among the world's nations in economic freedom. It achieves that status with low tax rates, free-trade policies, minimal government regulation, and secure property rights. These and other economic indicators place Hong Kong at the top of the Heritage Foundation's 2009 country rankings by the degree of "economic freedom." The "most free" and the "least free" (repressed) economies on the list of 179 countries are

Greatest Economic Freedom	Least Economic Freedom
Hong Kong	North Korea
Singapore	Zimbabwe
Australia	Cuba
Ireland	Myanmar (Burma)
New Zealand	Eritrea
United States	Venezuela
Canada	Congo
Denmark	Libya
Switzerland	Comoros
United Kingdom	Turkmenistan

Source: Heritage Foundation, *2009 Index of Economic Freedom,* Washington, DC, 2009. Used with permission. **www.heritage.org.**

Analysis: All nations must decide whether to rely on market signals or government directives to determine economic outcomes. Nations that rely the least on government intervention score highest ("most free") on this Index of Economic Freedom.

web analysis

To learn how the Heritage Foundation defines economic freedom, visit its Web site at **www.heritage.org.**

all property, directly allocates resources, sets wages, and limits trade. In other words, Hong Kong is the most market reliant; North Korea is the most government reliant.

The rankings shown are neither definitive nor stable. In 1989, Russia began a massive transformation from a state-controlled economy to a more market-oriented economy. Some of the former republics (e.g., Estonia) became relatively free, while others (e.g., Turkmenistan) still rely on extensive government control of the economy. China has greatly expanded the role of private markets and Cuba is moving in the same direction in fits and starts. Even Libya—the ninth "least-free" nation on the Heritage list—is just now experimenting with some market reforms.

In the United States, the changes have been less dramatic. The most notable shift was President Franklin Roosevelt's New Deal, which greatly expanded the government's role in the economy. In more recent times, the tug-of-war between laissez faire and government intervention has been much less decisive. Although President Reagan often said that "government *is* the problem," he hardly made a dent in government growth during the eight years of his presidency. Likewise, President Clinton's very different conviction that the government can *fix* problems, not cause them, had only minor effects on the size and scope of government activity. President George W. Bush not only lowered taxes but also lessened government regulation of HOW goods are produced. By the time President Obama took office, the economy was in such a mess that people demanded *more* government intervention to help fix the market's problems.

No one advocates *complete* dependence on markets, nor *total* government control of economic resources. Neither Adam Smith's invisible hand nor the governments' very visible hand always works perfectly. As a result, *the United States, like most nations, uses a combination of market signals and government directives to direct economic outcomes.* The resulting compromises are called **mixed economies.**

The reluctance of countries around the world to rely exclusively on either market signals or government directives is due to the recognition that both mechanisms can and do fail on

A Mixed Economy

mixed economy: An economy that uses both market signals and government directives to allocate goods and resources.

occasion. As we've seen, market signals are capable of answering the three core questions of WHAT, HOW, and FOR WHOM. But the answers may not be the best possible ones.

Market Failure

> market failure: An imperfection in the market mechanism that prevents optimal outcomes.

When market signals don't give the best possible answers to the WHAT, HOW, and FOR WHOM questions, we say that the market mechanism has *failed*. Specifically, **market failure** means that the invisible hand has failed to achieve the best possible outcomes. If the market fails, we end up with the wrong (*sub*optimal) mix of output, too much unemployment, polluted air, or an inequitable distribution of income.

In a market-driven economy, for example, producers will select production methods based on cost. Cost-driven production decisions, however, may encourage a factory to spew pollution into the environment rather than to use cleaner but more expensive methods of production. The resulting pollution may be so bad that society ends up worse off as a result of the extra production. In such a case we may need government intervention to force better answers to the WHAT and HOW questions.

We could also let the market decide who gets to consume cigarettes. Anyone who had enough money to buy a pack of cigarettes would then be entitled to smoke. What if, however, children aren't experienced enough to balance the risks of smoking against the pleasures? What if nonsmokers are harmed by secondhand smoke? In this case as well, the market's answer to the FOR WHOM question might not be optimal.

Government Failure

> government failure: Government intervention that fails to improve economic outcomes.

Government intervention may move us closer to our economic goals. If so, the resulting mix of market signals and government directives would be an improvement over a purely market-driven economy. But government intervention may fail as well. **Government failure** occurs when government intervention fails to improve market outcomes or actually makes them worse.

Government failure often occurs in unintended ways. For example, the government may intervene to force an industry to clean up its pollution. The government's directives may impose such high costs that the industry closes factories and lays off workers. Some cutbacks in output might be appropriate, but they could also prove excessive. The government might also mandate pollution control technologies that are too expensive or even obsolete. None of this has to happen, but it might. If it does, government failure will have worsened economic outcomes.

[handwritten annotation: B/c of regulation increased cost for a company therefore cut backs may be necessary]

The government might also fail if it interferes with the market's answer to the FOR WHOM question. For 50 years, communist China distributed goods by government directive, not market performance. Incomes were more equal, but uniformly low. To increase output and living standards, China turned to market incentives. As entrepreneurs responded to these incentives, living standards rose dramatically—even while inequality increased. That surge in living standards made the vast majority of Chinese "true believers" in the power of free markets (see World View on p. 14).

[handwritten annotation: gov't →] Excessive taxes and transfer payments can also worsen economic outcomes. If the government raises taxes on the rich to pay welfare benefits for the poor, neither the rich nor the poor may see much purpose in working. In that case, the attempt to give everybody a "fair" share of the pie might end up shrinking the size of the pie. If that happened, society could end up worse off.

Seeking Balance

None of these failures has to occur. But they might. The challenge for society is to minimize failures by selecting the appropriate balance of market signals and government directives. This isn't an easy task. It requires that we know how markets work and why they sometimes fail. We also need to know what policy options the government has and how and when they might work.

WHAT ECONOMICS IS ALL ABOUT

Understanding how economies function is the basic purpose of studying economics. We seek to know how an economy is organized, how it behaves, and how successfully it achieves its basic objectives. Then, if we're lucky, we can discover better ways of attaining those same objectives.

Economists don't formulate an economy's objectives. Instead, they focus on the *means* available for achieving given *goals.* In 1978, for example, the U.S. Congress identified "full employment" as a major economic goal. Congress then directed future presidents (and their economic advisers) to formulate policies that would enable us to achieve full employment. The economist's job is to help design policies that will best achieve this and other economic goals.

End vs. Means

The study of economics is typically divided into two parts: macroeconomics and microeconomics. Macroeconomics focuses on the behavior of an entire economy—the "big picture." In macroeconomics we worry about such national goals as full employment, control of inflation, and economic growth, without worrying about the well-being or behavior of specific individuals or groups. The essential concern of **macroeconomics** is to understand and improve the performance of the economy as a whole.

Macro vs. Micro

macroeconomics: The study of aggregate economic behavior, of the economy as a whole.

Microeconomics is concerned with the details of this big picture. In microeconomics we focus on the individuals, firms, and government agencies that actually compose the larger economy. Our interest here is in the behavior of individual economic actors. What are their goals? How can they best achieve these goals with their limited resources? How will they respond to various incentives and opportunities?

microeconomics: The study of individual behavior in the economy, of the components of the larger economy.

A primary concern of *macro*economics, for example, is to determine how much money, *in total,* consumers will spend on goods and services. In *micro*economics, the focus is much narrower. In micro, attention is paid to purchases of *specific* goods and services rather than just aggregated totals. Macro likewise concerns itself with the level of *total* business investment, while micro examines how *individual* businesses make their investment decisions.

Although they operate at different levels of abstraction, macro and micro are intrinsically related. Macro (aggregate) outcomes depend on micro behavior, and micro (individual) behavior is affected by macro outcomes. One can't fully understand how an economy works until one understands how all the individual participants behave. But just as you can drive a car without knowing how its engine is constructed, you can observe how an economy runs without completely disassembling it. In macroeconomics we observe that the car goes faster when the accelerator is depressed and that it slows when the brake is applied. That's all we need to know in most situations. At times, however, the car breaks down. When it does, we have to know something more about how the pedals work. This leads us into micro studies. How does each part work? Which ones can or should be fixed?

Our interest in microeconomics is motivated by more than our need to understand how the larger economy works. The "parts" of the economic engine are people. To the extent that we care about the well-being of individuals, we have a fundamental interest in microeconomic behavior and outcomes. In this regard, we examine how individual consumers and business firms seek to achieve specific goals in the marketplace. The goals aren't always related to output. Gary Becker won the 1992 Nobel Prize in Economics for demonstrating how economic principles also affect decisions to marry, to have children, to engage in criminal activities—or even to complete homework assignments in an economics class.

The distinction between macroeconomics and microeconomics is one of many simplifications we make in studying economic behavior. The economy is much too vast and complex to describe and explain in one course (or one lifetime). Accordingly, we focus on basic relationships, ignoring annoying detail. In so doing, we isolate basic principles of economic behavior and then use those principles to predict economic events and develop economic policies. This means that we formulate theories, or *models,* of economic behavior and then use those theories to evaluate and design economic policy.

Theory vs. Reality

Our model of consumer behavior assumes, for example, that people buy less of a good when its price rises. In reality, however, people *may* buy *more* of a good at increased prices, especially if those high prices create a certain snob appeal or if prices are expected to increase still further. In predicting consumer responses to price increases, we typically ignore such possibilities by *assuming* that the price of the good in question is the *only* thing that changes. This assumption of "other things remaining equal" (unchanged) (in Latin, **ceteris paribus**) allows us to make straightforward predictions. If instead we described consumer responses to increased prices in any and all circumstances (allowing everything

ceteris paribus: The assumption of nothing else changing.

to change at once), every prediction would be accompanied by a book full of exceptions and qualifications. We'd look more like lawyers than economists.

Although the assumption of *ceteris paribus* makes it easier to formulate economic theory and policy, it also increases the risk of error. If other things do change in significant ways, our predictions (and policies) may fail. But, like weather forecasters, we continue to make predictions, knowing that occasional failure is inevitable. In so doing, we're motivated by the conviction that it's better to be approximately right than to be dead wrong.

Politics. Politicians can't afford to be quite so complacent about economic predictions. Policy decisions must be made every day. And a politician's continued survival may depend on being more than approximately right. Barack Obama won votes by tying his opponent's economic views to those of President George W. Bush. He argued that Senator John McCain, like President Bush, was too optimistic about the ability of markets to self-correct. He insisted that more government intervention was needed to get the economy back on track.

After he took office, President Obama introduced a massive stimulus program of tax cuts and increased government spending, especially on infrastructure (roads, rails, bridges, etc.). Were these the right choices? Economic theory can't completely answer that question. Choices about the mix of output are ultimately political—decisions that must take into account not only economic trade-offs (opportunity costs) but also social values. "Politics"—the balancing of competing interests—is an inevitable ingredient of economic policy.

Imperfect Knowledge. One last word of warning before you read further. Economics claims to be a science, in pursuit of basic truths. We want to understand and explain how the economy works without getting tangled up in subjective value judgments. This may be an impossible task. First, it's not clear where the truth lies. For more than 200 years economists have been arguing about what makes the economy tick. None of the competing theories has performed spectacularly well. Indeed, few economists have successfully predicted major economic events with any consistency. Even annual forecasts of inflation, unemployment, and output are regularly in error. Worse still, never-ending arguments about what caused a major economic event continue long after it occurs. In fact, economists are still arguing over the primary causes of the Great Depression of the 1930s!

In view of all these debates and uncertainties, don't expect to learn everything there is to know about the economy today in this text or course. Our goals are more modest. We want to develop a reasonable perspective on economic behavior, an understanding of basic principles. With this foundation, you should acquire a better view of how the economy works. Daily news reports on economic events should make more sense. Congressional debates on tax and budget policies should take on more meaning. You may even develop some insights that you can apply toward running a business, planning a career, or simply managing your scarce time and money more efficiently.

THE ECONOMY TOMORROW

THE JOURNEY TO MARS

Stocktrek/Getty Images/RF

May 25, 2008, was a milestone in space exploration. That was the day the spacecraft *Phoenix* completed its 171-million-mile journey and successfully landed on Mars. That was not the first landing on Mars (five other spacecraft preceded it), but it was one of the most important. Earlier missions had found evidence of water on Mars's surface. The goal of *Phoenix* was to use its robotic arms to dig into Mars's surface and confirm that water once flowed there. If water did exist as recently as 100,000 years ago, life could have existed as well. Scientists from around the world viewed the *Phoenix* landing as a new frontier in our understanding of space, biology, and other spheres of knowledge. Both President Bush and President Obama supported NASA's goal of sending human missions to Mars (via intermediate settlements on the Moon) within a decade's time.

Opportunity Costs. The journey to Mars is not only a technological commitment but an economic commitment as well. The cost of the *Phoenix* mission alone was $457 million. The cost of continuing the human journey to Mars will approach $1 trillion. All of the resources used for this journey have alternative uses here on Earth. Some of the same scientists could be developing high-speed *rail* systems, safer domestic flights, or more eco-friendly technologies. The technological resources being poured into space exploration could be perfecting cell phone quality or simply accelerating online data transmissions. If we devoted as many resources to medical research as space research, we might find more ways to extend and improve life here on Earth. Or we could use all those resources to develop safe water and sanitation systems for the globally poor. In other words, the journey to Mars will entail opportunity costs, that is, the sacrifice of earthly goods and services that could be produced with those same resources.

Earthly Benefits. NASA says the benefits of the Mars journey will outweigh those opportunity costs. Space exploration has already generated tangible benefits for us earthlings. NASA cites advances in weather forecasting, in communications technology, in robotics, in computing and electronics, and in search and rescue technology. The research behind the space program has also helped create the satellite telecommunications network and the Global Positioning System (GPS). Medical technologies such as the image processing used in CAT scanners and MRI machines also trace their origins to engineering work for space exploration. Scientists say we should expect still further benefits from the journey to Mars: not only tangible benefits like new resources and technological advance but also intangibles like the spiritual uplifting and heightened quest for knowledge that exploration promotes.

Resource Allocations. As a society, we're going to have to make important choices about the economy tomorrow. Do we want to take the journey to Mars? If so, how fast do we want to get there? How many earthly goods and services do we want to give up to pay for the journey? Every year, the President and the U.S. Congress have to answer these questions. Their answers are reflected in the funds allocated to NASA (rather than other programs) in each year's federal budget. If you were in charge of the budget, how would you allocate scarce resources between space exploration and earthly activities?

web analysis

For a review of NASA's budget, visit **www.nasa.gov** and search "budget."

SUMMARY

- Scarcity is a basic fact of economic life. Factors of production (land, labor, capital, entrepreneurship) are scarce in relation to our desires for goods and services. LO1

- All economic activity entails opportunity costs. Factors of production (resources) used to produce one output cannot simultaneously be used to produce something else. When we choose to produce one thing, we forsake the opportunity to produce some other good or service. LO1

- A production possibilities curve (PPC) illustrates the limits to production—the various combinations of goods and services that could be produced in a given period if all available resources and technology are used efficiently. The PPC also illustrates opportunity costs—what is given up to get more of something else. LO1

- The bent shape of the PPC reflects the law of increasing opportunity costs: Increasing quantities of any good can be obtained only by sacrificing ever-increasing quantities of other goods. LO1

- Inefficient or incomplete use of resources will fail to attain production possibilities. Additional resources or better technologies will expand them. This is the essence of economic growth. LO1

- Every country must decide WHAT to produce, HOW to produce, and FOR WHOM to produce with its limited resources. LO2

- The WHAT, HOW, and FOR WHOM choices can be made by the market mechanism or by government directives. Most nations are mixed economies, using a combination of these two choice mechanisms. LO3

- Market failure exists when market signals generate sub-optimal outcomes. Government failure occurs when government intervention worsens economic outcomes. The challenge for economic theory and policy is to find the mix of market signals and government directives that best fulfills our social and economic goals. LO3

- The study of economics focuses on the broad question of resource allocation. Macroeconomics is concerned with allocating the resources of an entire economy to achieve aggregate economic goals (e.g., full employment). Microeconomics focuses on the behavior and goals of individual market participants, LO3

Key Terms

scarcity
factors of production
capital
entrepreneurship
economics
opportunity cost

production possibilities
efficiency
economic growth
market mechanism
laissez faire
mixed economy

market failure
government failure
macroeconomics
microeconomics
ceteris paribus

Questions for Discussion

1. What opportunity costs did you incur in reading this chapter? If you read another chapter today, would your opportunity cost (per chapter) increase? Explain. LO1
2. How much time could you spend on homework in a day? How much do you spend? How do you decide? LO1
3. What's the real cost of the food in the "free lunch" cartoon on page 6? LO1
4. How might a nation's production possibilities be affected by the following? LO2
   a. A decrease in taxes.
   b. An increase in government regulation.
   c. An increase in military spending.
   d. An increase in college tuition.
   e. Faster, more powerful electronic chips.
5. Markets reward individuals according to their output; communism rewards people according to their needs. How might these different systems affect work effort? LO3
6. Who would go to college in a completely private (market) college system? How does government intervention change this FOR WHOM outcome? LO3
7. Why do people around the world have so much faith in free markets (World View, p. 14)? LO2
8. How many resources should we allocate to space exploration? How will we make this decision? LO2
9. What is the connection between North Korea's missile program and its hunger problem? (World View, p. 9) LO3
10. What is the opportunity cost of President Obama's increased infrastructure spending? LO1

 web activities to accompany this chapter can be found on the Online Learning Center:
http://www.mhhe.com/schiller12e

APPENDIX

USING GRAPHS

Economists like to draw graphs. In fact, we didn't even make it through the first chapter without a few graphs. This appendix looks more closely at the way graphs are drawn and used. The basic purpose of a graph is to illustrate a relationship between two *variables*. Consider, for example, the relationship between grades and studying. In general, we expect that additional hours of study time will lead to higher grades. Hence, we should be able to see a distinct relationship between hours of study time and grade-point average.

Suppose that we actually surveyed all the students taking this course with regard to their study time and grade-point averages. The resulting information can be compiled in a table such as Table A.1.

According to the table, students who don't study at all can expect an F in this course. To get a C, the average student apparently spends 8 hours a week studying. All those who study 16 hours a week end up with an A in the course.

These relationships between grades and studying can also be illustrated on a graph. Indeed, the whole purpose of a graph is to summarize numerical relationships.

We begin to construct a graph by drawing horizontal and vertical boundaries, as in Figure A.1. These boundaries are called the *axes* of the graph. On the vertical axis (often called the *y*-axis) we measure one of the variables; the other variable is measured on the horizontal axis (the *x*-axis).

In this case, we shall measure the grade-point average on the vertical axis. We start at the *origin* (the intersection of the two axes) and count upward, letting the distance between horizontal lines represent half (0.5) a grade point. Each horizontal line is numbered, up to the maximum grade-point average of 4.0.

The number of hours each week spent doing homework is measured on the horizontal axis. We begin at the origin again, and count to the right. The *scale* (numbering) proceeds in increments of 1 hour, up to 20 hours per week.

When both axes have been labeled and measured, we can begin illustrating the relationship between study time and grades. Consider the typical student who does 8 hours of homework per week and has a 2.0 (C) grade-point average. We illustrate this relationship by first locating 8 hours on the horizontal axis. We then move up from that point a distance of 2.0 grade points, to point *M*. Point *M* tells us that 8 hours of study time per week is typically associated with a 2.0 grade-point average.

The rest of the information in Table A.1 is drawn (or *plotted*) on the graph the same way. To illustrate the average grade for people who study 12 hours per week, we move upward from the number 12 on the horizontal axis until we reach the height of 3.0 on the vertical axis. At that intersection, we draw another point (point *N*).

Once we've plotted the various points describing the relationship of study time to grades, we may connect them with a line or curve. This line (curve) is our summary. In this case, the line slopes upward to the right—that is, it has a *positive* slope. This slope indicates that

TABLE A.1

Hypothetical Relationship of Grades to Study Time

Study Time (hours per week)	Grade-Point Average
16	4.0 (A)
14	3.5 (B+)
12	3.0 (B)
10	2.5 (C+)
8	2.0 (C)
6	1.5 (D+)
4	1.0 (D)
2	0.5 (F+)
0	0.0 (F)

web analysis

For online practice with graphs, visit **www.econweb.com** and use the "Intro Micro" and "Intro Macro" links.

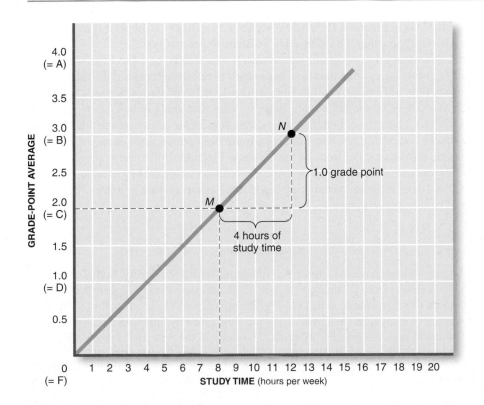

FIGURE A.1

The Relationship of Grades to Study Time

The upward (positive) slope of the curve indicates that additional studying is associated with higher grades. The average student (2.0, or C grade) studies 8 hours per week. This is indicated by point *M* on the graph.

more hours of study time are associated with *higher* grades. Were higher grades associated with *less* study time, the curve in Figure A.1 would have a *negative* slope (downward from left to right).

Slopes

The upward slope of Figure A.1 tells us that higher grades are associated with increased amounts of study time. That same curve also tells us *by how much* grades tend to rise with study time. According to point *M* in Figure A.1, the average student studies 8 hours per week and earns a C (2.0 grade-point average). To earn a B (3.0 average), students apparently need to study an average of 12 hours per week (point *N*). Hence an increase of 4 hours of study time per week is associated with a 1-point increase in grade-point average. This relationship between *changes* in study time and *changes* in grade-point average is expressed by the steepness, or *slope,* of the graph.

The slope of any graph is calculated as

$$\text{Slope} = \frac{\text{vertical distance between two points}}{\text{horizontal distance between two points}}$$

In our example, the vertical distance between *M* and *N* represents a change in grade-point average. The horizontal distance between these two points represents the change in study time. Hence the slope of the graph between points *M* and *N* is equal to

$$\text{Slope} = \frac{3.0 \text{ grade} - 2.0 \text{ grade}}{12 \text{ hours} - 8 \text{ hours}} = \frac{1 \text{ grade point}}{4 \text{ hours}}$$

In other words, a 4-hour increase in study time (from 8 to 12 hours) is associated with a 1-point increase in grade-point average (see Figure A.1).

Shifts

The relationship between grades and studying illustrated in Figure A.1 isn't inevitable. It's simply a graphical illustration of student experiences, as revealed in our hypothetical survey. The relationship between study time and grades could be quite different.

Suppose that the university decided to raise grading standards, making it more difficult to achieve higher grades. To achieve a C, a student now would need to study 12 hours per week, not just 8 (as in Figure A.1). Whereas students could previously get a B by studying 12 hours per week, now they'd have to study 16 hours to get that grade.

Figure A.2 illustrates the new grading standards. Notice that the new curve lies to the right of the earlier curve. We say that the curve has *shifted* to reflect a change in the relationship between study time and grades. Point *R* indicates that 12 hours of study time now "produce" a C, not a B (point *N* on the old curve). Students who now study only 4 hours per week (point *S*) will fail. Under the old grading policy, they could have at least gotten a D. ***When a curve shifts, the underlying relationship between the two variables has changed.***

A shift may also change the slope of the curve. In Figure A.2, the new grading curve is parallel to the old one; it therefore has the same slope. Under either the new grading policy or the old one, a 4-hour increase in study time leads to a 1-point increase in grades. Therefore, the slope of both curves in Figure A.2 is

$$\text{Slope} = \frac{\text{vertical change}}{\text{horizontal change}} = \frac{1}{4}$$

This too may change, however. Figure A.3 illustrates such a possibility. In this case, zero study time still results in an F. But now the payoff for additional studying is reduced. Now it takes 6 hours of study time to get a D (1.0 grade point), not 4 hours as before. Likewise, another 4 hours of study time (to a total of 10) raise the grade by only two-thirds of a point. It takes 6 hours to raise the grade a full point. The slope of the new line is therefore

$$\text{Slope} = \frac{\text{vertical change}}{\text{horizontal change}} = \frac{1}{6}$$

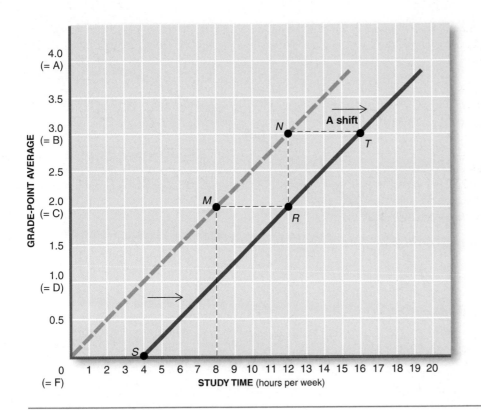

FIGURE A.2
A Shift

When a relationship between two variables changes, the entire curve *shifts*. In this case a tougher grading policy alters the relationship between study time and grades. To get a C, one must now study 12 hours per week (point *R*), not just 8 hours (point *M*).

The new curve in Figure A.3 has a smaller slope than the original curve and so lies below it. What all this means is that it now takes a greater effort to *improve* your grade.

In Figures A.1–A.3 the relationship between grades and studying is represented by a straight line—that is, a *linear curve*. A distinguishing feature of linear curves is that they

Linear vs. Nonlinear Curves

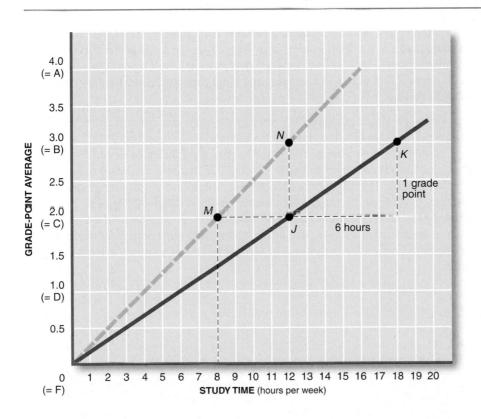

FIGURE A.3
A Change in Slope

When a curve shifts, it may change its slope as well. In this case, a new grading policy makes each higher grade more difficult to reach. To raise a C to a B, for example, one must study 6 additional hours (compare points *J* and *K*). Earlier it took only 4 hours to move the grade scale up a full point. The slope of the line has declined from 0.25(= 1 ÷ 4) to 0.17(= 1 ÷ 6).

FIGURE A.4
A Nonlinear Relationship

Straight lines have a constant slope, implying a constant relationship between the two variables. But the relationship (and slope) may vary. In this case, it takes 6 extra hours of study to raise a C (point *W*) to a B (point *X*) but 8 extra hours to raise a B to an A (point *Y*). The slope decreases as we move up the curve.

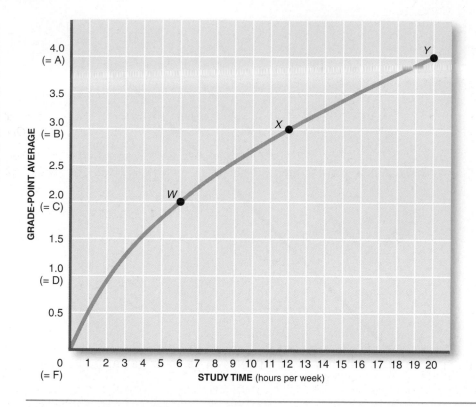

have the same (constant) slope throughout. In Figure A.1, it appears that *every* 4-hour increase in study time is associated with a 1-point increase in average grades. In Figure A.3, it appears that every 6-hour increase in study time leads to a 1-point increase in grades. But the relationship between studying and grades may not be linear. Higher grades may be more difficult to attain. You may be able to raise a C to a B by studying 4 hours more per week. But it may be harder to raise a B to an A. According to Figure A.4, it takes an additional 8 hours of studying to raise a B to an A. Thus the relationship between study time and grades is *nonlinear* in Figure A.4; the slope of the curve changes as study time increases. In this case, the slope decreases as study time increases. Grades continue to improve, but not so fast, as more and more time is devoted to homework. You may know the feeling.

Causation

Figure A.4 doesn't by itself guarantee that your grade-point average will rise if you study 4 more hours per week. In fact, the graph drawn in Figure A.4 doesn't prove that additional study ever results in higher grades. The graph is only a summary of empirical observations. It says nothing about cause and effect. It could be that students who study a lot are smarter to begin with. If so, then less-able students might not get higher grades if they studied harder. In other words, the *cause* of higher grades is debatable. At best, the empirical relationship summarized in the graph may be used to support a particular theory (e.g., that it pays to study more). Graphs, like tables, charts, and other statistical media, rarely tell their own story; rather, they must be *interpreted* in terms of some underlying theory or expectation.

PROBLEMS FOR CHAPTER 1   Name: _____

LO1 1. According to Table 1.1 (or Figure 1.1), what is the opportunity cost of the

    (a) Fourth truck? _____

    (b) Fifth truck? _____

LO2 2. (a) According to Figure 1.2, what is the opportunity cost of North Korea's military force at point *N*? _____

    (b) How much more food could North Korea produce if it cut military output from *OD* to *OH*? _____

LO2 3. (a) What was the dollar cost of the North Korean 2009 missile launch, according to South Korea? _____

    (b) How many people could have been fed for a year at the World Bank Standard of $2 per day with that money? _____

LO2 4. What is the opportunity cost (in civilian output) of a defense buildup that raises military spending from 4.0 to 4.4 percent of a $15 trillion economy? $_____

LO1 5. What is the opportunity cost (in dollars) to attend an hour-long econ lecture for

    (a) A minimum-wage teenager in fall 2009? $_____

    (b) A $100,000 per year corporate executive who works 2,000 hours per year? $_____

LO1 6. Suppose either computers or televisions can be assembled with the following labor inputs:

Units produced	1	2	3	4	5	6	7	8	9	10
Total labor used	3	7	12	18	25	33	42	54	70	90

    (a) Draw the production possibilities curve for an economy with 54 units of labor. Label it P54.

    (b) What is the opportunity cost of the eighth computer? _____

    (c) Suppose immigration brings in 36 more workers. Redraw the production possibilities curve to reflect this added labor. Label the new curve P90.

    (d) Suppose advancing technology (e.g., the miniaturization of electronic circuits) increases the productivity of the 90-laborer workforce by 20 percent. Draw a third production possibilities curve (PT) to illustrate this change.

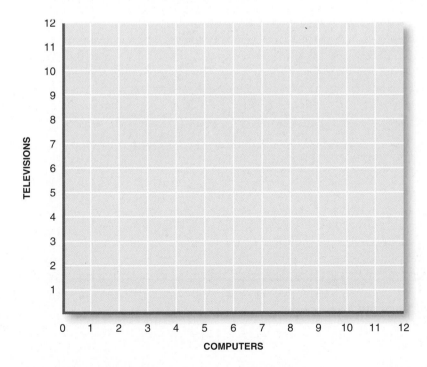

LO3 7. According to the World View on page 14, which nation has

    (a) The most faith in the market system? _____

    (b) The least faith in the market system? _____

LO1 8. Suppose there's a relationship of the following sort between study time and grades:

	(a)	(b)	(c)	(d)	(e)
Study time (hours per week)	0	2	6	12	20
Grade-point average	0	1.0	2.0	3.0	4.0

If you have only 20 hours per week to use for either study time or fun time,
(a) Draw the (linear) production possibilities curve on the graph below that represents the alternative uses of your time.
(b) Indicate on the graph the point C that would get you a 2.0 grade average.
(c) What is the cost, in lost fun time, of raising your grade-point average from 2.0 to 3.0? Illustrate this effort on the graph (point C to point D).   _____
(d) What is the opportunity cost of increasing your grades from 3.0 to 4.0? Illustrate as point D to point E.   _____

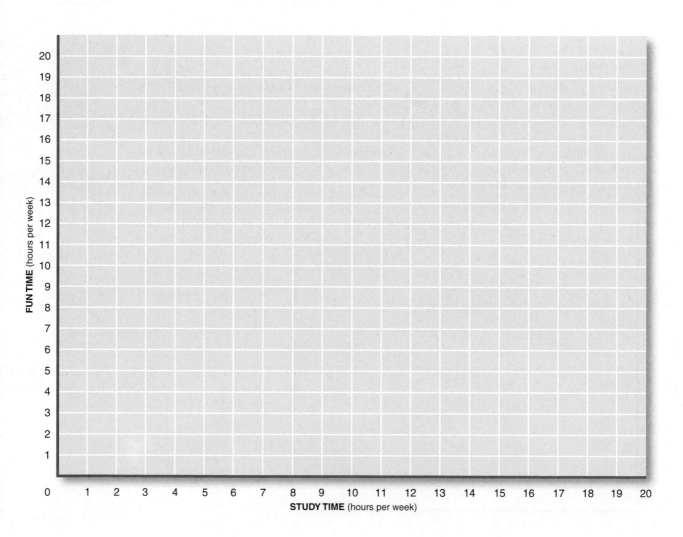

2

The U.S. Economy: A Global View

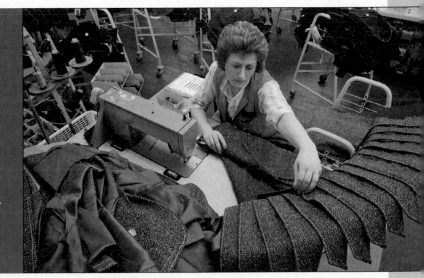

LEARNING OBJECTIVES

After reading this chapter, you should be able to:

LO1. Describe the relative size and content of U.S. output (GDP).

LO2. Explain how America is able to produce so much output.

LO3. Discuss how incomes are distributed in the U.S. and elsewhere.

All nations must confront the central economic questions of WHAT to produce, HOW to produce, and FOR WHOM to produce it. However, the nations of the world approach these issues with vastly different production possibilities. China, Canada, the United States, and Brazil have more than *3 million* acres of land each. All that land gives them far greater production possibilities than Dominica, Tonga, Malta, or Lichtenstein, each of which has less than 500 acres of land. The population of China totals more than 1.4 billion people, nearly five times that of the United States, and 25,000 times the population of Greenland. Obviously, these nations confront very different output choices.

In addition to vastly uneven production possibilities, the nations of the world use different mechanisms for deciding WHAT, HOW, and FOR WHOM to produce. Belarus, Romania, North Korea, and Cuba still rely heavily on central planning.

By contrast, Singapore, New Zealand, Ireland, and the United States permit the market mechanism to play a dominant role in shaping economic outcomes.

With different production possibilities and mechanisms of choice, you'd expect economic outcomes to vary greatly across nations. And they do. This chapter assesses how the U.S. economy stacks up. Specifically,

- **WHAT goods and services does the United States produce?**
- **HOW is that output produced?**
- **FOR WHOM is the output produced?**

In each case, we want to see not only how the United States has answered these questions but also how America's answers compare with those of other nations.

WHAT AMERICA PRODUCES

The United States has less than 5 percent of the world's population and only 12 percent of the world's arable land, yet it produces more than 20 percent of the world's output.

GDP Comparisons

> **gross domestic product (GDP):** The total market value of all final goods and services produced within a nation's borders in a given time period.

$$GDP = C + I + G + (N_E)$$

The World View below shows how total U.S. production compares with that of other nations. These comparisons are based on the total market value of all the goods and services a nation produces in a year—what we call **gross domestic product (GDP).** In effect, GDP is the "pie" of output we bake each year.

In 2007, the U.S. economy baked a huge pie—one containing nearly $14 trillion worth of output. That was far more output than any other nation produced. The second-largest economy, China, produced only two-thirds that much. Japan came in third, with about a third of U.S. output. Cuba, by contrast, produced only $1.6 *billion* of output, less than the state of South Dakota. Russia, which was once regarded as a superpower, produced only $1.3 trillion, about as much as New York State. The entire 27-member European Union produces less output than the United States.

WORLD VIEW

Comparative Output (GDP)

The United States is by far the world's largest economy. Its annual output of goods and services is one and a half times that of China's, three times Japan's, and equal to all of the European Union's. The output of Third World countries is only a tiny fraction of U.S. output.

Source: From *World Development Report 2009.* **www.worldbank.org.**

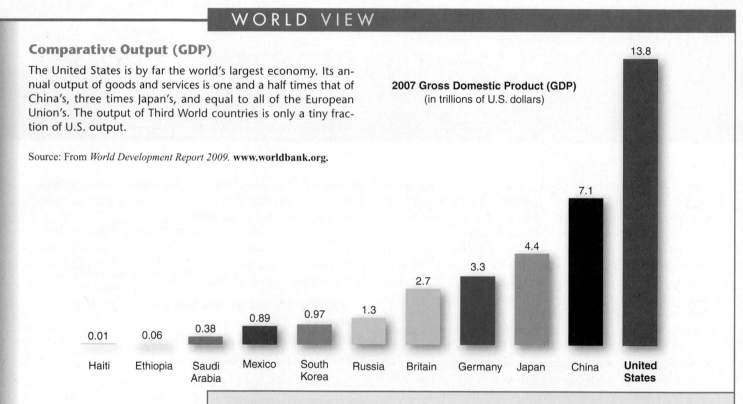

2007 Gross Domestic Product (GDP)
(in trillions of U.S. dollars)

Haiti	Ethiopia	Saudi Arabia	Mexico	South Korea	Russia	Britain	Germany	Japan	China	United States
0.01	0.06	0.38	0.89	0.97	1.3	2.7	3.3	4.4	7.1	13.8

Analysis: The market value of output (GDP) is a basic measure of an economy's size. The U.S. economy is far larger than any other and accounts for over one-fifth of the entire world's output of goods and services.

$$\frac{GDP}{population} = per\ capita$$

> **per capita GDP:** The dollar value of GDP divided by total population; average GDP.

Per Capita GDP. What makes the U.S. share of world output so remarkable is that we do it with so few people. The U.S. population of 310 million amounts to less than 5 percent of the world's total (6.7 billion). Yet we produce over 20 percent of the world's output. That means we're producing a lot of output *per person.* China, by contrast, has the opposite ratios: 20 percent of the world's population producing less than 14 percent of the world's output. So China is producing a lot of output but relatively less *per person.*

This people-based measure of economic performance is called **per capita GDP.** Per capita GDP is simply a nation's total output divided by its total population. Per capita GDP doesn't tell us how much any specific person gets. ***Per capita GDP is an indicator of how much output*** *the average person would get if all output were divided up evenly among the population.* In effect, GDP per capita tells us how large a slice of the GDP pie the average citizen gets.

In 2007, per capita GDP in the United States was roughly $46,000. That means that the average U.S. citizen could have consumed as much as $46,000 worth of goods and services. That's a staggering amount by global standards—nearly five times the world average. The following World View provides a global perspective on just how "rich" America is. Some of the country-specific comparisons are startling. China, which produces the world's second-largest GDP, has such a low *per capita* income that most of its citizens would be considered "poor" by official American standards. Yet people in other nations (e.g., Haiti, Ethiopia) don't even come close to that low standard. According to the World Bank, nearly half of the people on Earth subsist on incomes of less than $2 a day—a level completely unimaginable to the average American. *Homeless* people in the U.S. enjoy a higher living standard than billions of poor people in other nations (see Chapter 36). In this context, it's easy to understand why the rest of the world envies (and sometimes resents) America's prosperity.

WORLD VIEW

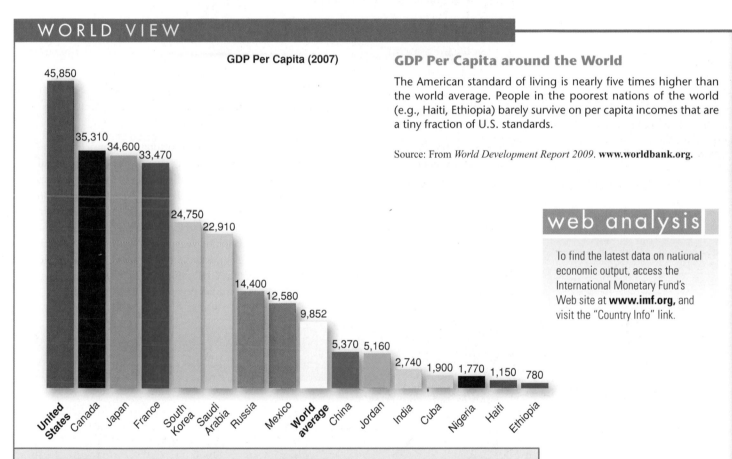

GDP Per Capita (2007)

GDP Per Capita around the World

The American standard of living is nearly five times higher than the world average. People in the poorest nations of the world (e.g., Haiti, Ethiopia) barely survive on per capita incomes that are a tiny fraction of U.S. standards.

Source: From *World Development Report 2009*. **www.worldbank.org**.

web analysis

To find the latest data on national economic output, access the International Monetary Fund's Web site at **www.imf.org,** and visit the "Country Info" link.

Analysis: Per capita GDP is a measure of output that reflects average living standards. America's exceptionally high GDP per capita implies access to far more goods and services than people in other nations have.

GDP Growth. What's even more startling about global comparisons is that the GDP gap between the United States and the world's poor nations keeps growing. The reason for that is **economic growth.** With few exceptions, U.S. output increases nearly every year: the pie keeps getting larger. *On average, U.S. output has grown by roughly 3 percent a year, nearly three times faster than population growth (1 percent).* So the U.S. pie is growing faster than the number of people coming to the table. Hence, not only does *total* output keep rising, but *per capita* output keeps rising as well (see Figure 2.1).

economic growth: An increase in output (real GDP); an expansion of production possibilities.

FIGURE 2.1

U.S. Output and Population Growth since 1900

Over time, the growth of output in the United States has greatly exceeded population growth. As a consequence, GDP per capita has grown tremendously. GDP per capita was five times higher in 2000 than in 1900.

Source: U.S. Department of Labor.

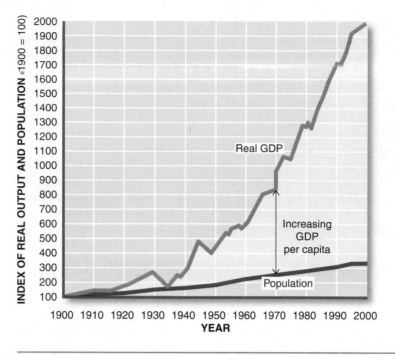

Poor Nations. People in the world's poorest countries aren't so fortunate. China's economy has grown exceptionally fast in the last 20 years, propelling it to second place in the global GDP rankings. But in many other nations total output has actually *declined* year after year, further depressing living standards. Notice in Table 2.1, for example, what's been happening in Zambia. From 2000 to 2007, Zambia's output of goods and services (GDP) *declined* by an average of 5.7 percent a year. As a result, total Zambian output in 2007 was 50 percent *smaller* than in 2000. During those same years, the Zambian population kept growing—by 1.9 percent a year. So the Zambian pie was shrinking every year even as the number of people coming to the table was increasing. As a result, Zambia's per capita GDP fell below $1,300 a year. That low level of per capita GDP left nearly two-thirds of Zambia's population undernourished.

TABLE 2.1

GDP Growth vs. Population Growth

The relationship between GDP growth and population growth is very different in rich and poor countries. The populations of rich countries are growing very slowly, and gains in per capita GDP are easily achieved. In the poorest countries, population is still increasing rapidly, making it difficult to raise living standards. Notice how per capita incomes are *declining* in many poor countries (such as Zimbabwe, Haiti, and Zambia).

	Average Growth Rate (2000–2007) of		
	GDP	**Population**	**Per Capita GDP**
High-income countries			
United States	2.7	0.9	1.8
Canada	2.7	1.0	1.7
Japan	1.7	0.1	1.6
France	1.7	0.7	1.0
Low-income countries			
China	10.2	0.6	9.6
India	7.8	1.4	6.4
Madagascar	3.3	2.8	0.5
Niger	3.9	3.5	0.4
Haiti	0.2	1.6	−1.4
Ivory Coast	0.2	1.7	−1.5
Zimbabwe	−4.4	0.8	−5.2
Zambia	−5.7	1.9	−7.6

Source: From *World Development Report, 2009.* **www.worldbank.org.**

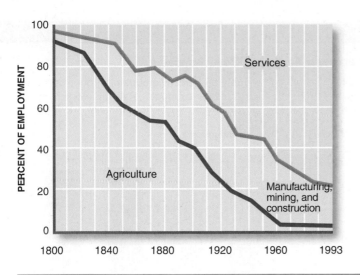

FIGURE 2.2
The Changing Mix of Output

Two hundred years ago, almost all U.S. output came from farms. Today, 75 percent of output consists of services, not farm or manufactured goods.

Source: U.S. Department of Commerce.

web analysis

Data on the mix of output in different nations are compiled in the World Bank's annual World Development Report, available at **www.worldbank.org.**

As Table 2.1 shows, the economic situation deteriorated nearly as fast in Zimbabwe. Even some poor nations that had *positive* GDP growth in recent years (e.g., Haiti, Ivory Coast) didn't grow fast enough to raise living standards. As a result, they fell even further behind America's (rising) level of prosperity.

The Mix of Output

Regardless of how much output a nation produces, the *mix* of output always includes both *goods* (such as cars, plasma TVs, potatoes) and *services* (like this economics course, visits to a doctor, or a professional baseball game). A century ago, about two-thirds of U.S. output consisted of farm goods (37 percent), manufactured goods (22 percent), and mining (9 percent). Since then, over 25 *million* people have left the farms and taken jobs in other sectors. As a result, today's mix of output is completely reversed: *Nearly 75 percent of U.S. output now consists of services, not goods* (see Figure 2.2).

The *relative* decline in goods production (manufacturing, farming) doesn't mean that we're producing *fewer* goods today than in earlier decades. Quite the contrary. While some industries such as iron and steel have shrunk, others, such as chemicals, publishing, and telecommunications equipment, have grown tremendously. The result is that manufacturing output has increased fourfold since 1950. The same kind of thing has happened in the farm sector, where output keeps rising even though agriculture's *share* of total output has declined. It's just that our output of *services* has increased so much faster.

Development Patterns. The transformation of the United States into a service economy is a reflection of our high incomes. In Ethiopia, where the most urgent concern is to keep people from starving, over 50 percent of output still comes from the farm sector. Poor people don't have enough income to buy dental services, vacations, or even an education, so the mix of output in poor countries is weighted toward goods, not services.

HOW AMERICA PRODUCES

Regardless of how much output a nation produces, every nation ultimately depends on its resources—its **factors of production**—to produce goods and services. So *differences* in GDP must be explained by HOW those resources are used.

factors of production: Resource inputs used to produce goods and services, such as land, labor, capital, entrepreneurship.

We've already observed that America's premier position in global GDP rankings isn't due to the number of humans within our borders. We have far fewer bodies than China, India, Indonesia, and Brazil, yet produce far more output than any of those nations. What counts for production purposes is not just the *number* of workers a nation has, but the *skills* of those workers—what we call **human capital.**

Human Capital

Over time, the United States has invested heavily in human capital. In 1940, only 1 out of 20 young Americans graduated from college; today, over 30 percent of young people are

human capital: The knowledge and skills possessed by the workforce.

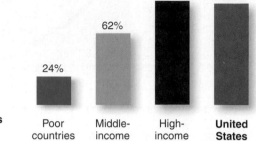

The Education Gap between Rich and Poor Nations

Virtually all Americans attend high school and roughly 85 percent graduate. In poor countries, relatively few workers attend high school and even fewer graduate. Half the workers in the world's poorest nations are illiterate.

Source: From *World Development Indicators, 2009.* **www.worldbank.org.**

web analysis

The Central Intelligence Agency provides cross-country data on educational attainment. Visit **www.cia.gov** and click on "World Factbook" to view this information.

Enrollment in Secondary Schools (percent of school-age youth attending secondary schools)

- Poor countries: 24%
- Middle-income countries: 62%
- High-income countries: 90%
- **United States**: 88%

Analysis: The high productivity of the American economy is explained in part by the quality of its labor resources. Workers in poorer, less developed countries get much less education and training.

college graduates. High school graduation rates have jumped from 38 percent to over 85 percent in the same time period. In the less developed countries, only 1 out of 2 youth ever *attend* high school, much less graduate (see above World View). As a consequence, the United Nations estimates that 1.2 billion people—a fifth of humanity—are unable to read a book or even write their own names. Without even functional literacy, such workers are doomed to low-productivity jobs. Despite low wages, they are not likely to "steal" many jobs from America's highly educated and trained workforce.

Capital Stock

capital-intensive: Production processes that use a high ratio of capital to labor inputs.

America has also accumulated a massive stock of capital—over $50 *trillion* worth of machinery, factories, and buildings. As a result of all this prior investment, U.S. production tends to be very **capital-intensive.** The contrast with *labor-intensive* production in poorer countries is striking. A farmer in India still works mostly with his hands and crude implements, whereas a U.S. farmer works with computers, automated irrigation systems, and mechanized equipment (see photos on p. 33). Russian business managers don't have the computer networks or telecommunications systems that make U.S. business so efficient. In Haiti and Ethiopia, even telephones, indoor plumbing, and dependable sources of power are scarce.

High Productivity

productivity: Output per unit of input, such as output per labor-hour.

When you put educated workers together with sophisticated capital equipment, you tend to get more output. This relationship largely explains why the United States has such a lead in worker **productivity**—the amount of output produced by the average worker. *American households are able to consume so much because American workers produce so much.* It's really that simple.

The huge output of the United States is thus explained not only by a wealth of resources but by their quality as well. *The high productivity of the U.S. economy results from using highly educated workers in capital-intensive production processes.*

Factor Mobility. Our continuing ability to produce the goods and services that consumers demand also depends on our agility in *reallocating* resources from one industry to another. Every year, some industries expand and others contract. Thousands of new firms start up

Analysis: An abundance of capital equipment and advanced technology make American farmers and workers far more productive than workers in poor nations.

each year and almost as many others disappear. In the process, land, labor, capital, and entrepreneurship move from one industry to another in response to changing demands and technology. In 1975, Federal Express, Dell Computer, Staples, Oracle, and Amgen didn't even exist. Wal-Mart was still a small retailer. Starbucks was selling coffee on Seattle street corners, and the founders of Google and YouTube weren't even born. Today, these companies employ over a million people. These workers came from other firms and industries that weren't growing as fast.

Technological Advance. One of the forces that keeps shifting resources from one industry to another is continuing advances in technology. Advances in technology can be as sophisticated as microscopic miniaturization of electronic circuits or as simple as the reorganization of production processes. Either phenomenon increases the productivity of the workforce and potential output. *Whenever technology advances, an economy can produce more output with existing resources.*

Outsourcing and Trade. The same technological advances that fuel economic growth also facilitate *global* resource use. Telecommunications has become so sophisticated and inexpensive that phone workers in India or Grenada can answer calls directed to U.S. companies. Likewise, programmers in India can work online to write computer code, develop software, or perform accounting chores for U.S. corporations. Although such "outsourcing" is often viewed as a threat to U.S. jobs, it is really another source of increased U.S. output. By outsourcing routine tasks to foreign workers, U.S. workers are able to focus on higher-value jobs. U.S. computer engineers do less routine programming and more systems design. U.S. accountants do less cost tabulation and more cost analysis. By utilizing foreign resources in the production process, U.S. workers are able to pursue their *comparative advantage* in high-skill, capital-intensive jobs. In this way, both productivity and total output increase. Although some U.S. workers suffer temporary job losses in this process, the economy overall gains.

Role of Government

In assessing HOW goods are produced and economies grow, we must also take heed of the role the government plays. As we noted in Chapter 1, the amount of economic freedom varies greatly among the 200-plus nations of the world. Moreover, the Heritage Foundation has documented a positive relationship between the degree of economic freedom and economic growth. Quite simply, when entrepreneurs are unfettered by regulation or high taxes, they are more likely to design and produce better mousetraps. When the government owns the factors of production, imposes high taxes, or tightly regulates output, there is little opportunity or incentive to design better products or pursue new technology.

Recognizing the productive value of economic freedom isn't tantamount to rejecting all government intervention. No one really advocates the complete abolition of government.

On the contrary, the government plays a critical role in establishing a framework in which private businesses can operate.

- *Providing a legal framework.* One of the most basic functions of government is to establish and enforce the rules of the game. In some bygone era maybe a person's word was sufficient to guarantee delivery or payment. Businesses today, however, rely more on written contracts. The government gives legitimacy to contracts by establishing the rules for such pacts and by enforcing their provisions. In the absence of contractual rights, few companies would be willing to ship goods without prepayment (in cash). Even the incentive to write textbooks would disappear if government copyright laws didn't forbid unauthorized photocopying. By establishing ownership rights, contract rights, and other rules of the game, the government lays the foundation for market transactions.

- *Protecting the environment.* The government also intervenes in the market to protect the environment. The legal contract system is designed to protect the interests of a buyer and a seller who wish to do business. What if, however, the business they contract for harms third parties? How are the interests of persons who *aren't* party to the contract to be protected?

Numerous examples abound of how unregulated production may harm third parties. Earlier in the century, the steel mills around Pittsburgh blocked out the sun with clouds of sulfurous gases that spewed out of their furnaces. Local residents were harmed every time they inhaled. In the absence of government intervention, such side effects would be common. Decisions on how to produce would be based on costs alone, not on how the environment is affected. However, such **externalities**—spillover costs imposed on the broader community—affect our collective well-being. To reduce the external costs of production, the government limits air, water, and noise pollution and regulates environmental use.

- *Protecting consumers.* The government also uses its power to protect the interests of consumers. One way to do this is to prevent individual business firms from becoming too powerful. In the extreme case, a single firm might have a **monopoly** on the production of a specific good. As the sole producer of that good, a monopolist could dictate the price, the quality, and the quantity of the product. In such a situation, consumers would likely end up with the short end of the stick—paying too much for too little.

To protect consumers from monopoly exploitation, the government tries to prevent individual firms from dominating specific markets. Antitrust laws prohibit mergers or acquisitions that would threaten competition. The U.S. Department of Justice and the Federal Trade Commission also regulate pricing practices, advertising claims, and other behavior that might put consumers at an unfair disadvantage in product markets.

Government also regulates the safety of many products. Consumers don't have enough expertise to assess the safety of various medicines, for example. If they rely on trial and error to determine drug safety, they might not get a second chance. To avoid this calamity, the government requires rigorous testing of new drugs, food additives, and other products.

- *Protecting labor.* The government also regulates how labor resources are used in the production process. In most poor nations, children are forced to start working at very early ages, often for minuscule wages. They often don't get the chance to go to school or to stay healthy. In Africa, 40 percent of children under age 14 work to survive or to help support their families. In the United States, child labor laws and compulsory schooling prevent minor children from being exploited. Government regulations also set standards for workplace safety, minimum wages, fringe benefits, and overtime provisions.

externalities: Costs (or benefits) of a market activity borne by a third party.

monopoly: A firm that produces the entire market supply of a particular good or service.

Striking a Balance

All these government interventions are designed to change the way resources are used. Such interventions reflect the conviction that the market alone might not select the best possible way of producing goods and services. There's no guarantee, however, that government regulation of HOW goods are produced always makes us better off. Excessive regulation may inhibit production, raise product prices, and limit consumer choices. As noted in Chapter 1, *government* failure might replace *market* failure, leaving us no better off—possibly even worse off. This possibility underscores the importance of striking the right balance between market reliance and government regulation.

FOR WHOM AMERICA PRODUCES

As we've seen, America produces a huge quantity of output, using high-quality labor and capital resources. That leaves one basic question unanswered: FOR WHOM is all this output produced?

How many goods and services one gets largely depends on how much income one has to spend. The U.S. economy uses the market mechanism to distribute most goods and services. Those who receive the most income get the most goods. This goes a long way toward explaining why millionaires live in mansions and homeless people seek shelter in abandoned cars. This is the kind of stark inequality that fueled Karl Marx's denunciation of capitalism. Even today, people wonder how some Americans can be so rich while others are so poor.

Figure 2.3 illustrates the actual distribution of income in the United States. For this illustration the entire population is sorted into five groups of equal size, ranked by income. In this depiction, all the rich people are in the top **income quintile;** the poor are in the lowest quintile. To be in the top quintile in 2007, a household needed at least $100,000 of income. All the households in the lowest quintile had incomes under $20,000.

The most striking feature of Figure 2.3 is how large a slice of the income pie rich people get: ***The top 20 percent (quintile) of U.S. households get half of all U.S. income.*** By contrast, the poorest 20 percent (quintile) of U.S. households get only a sliver of the income pie—less than 4 percent. Those grossly unequal slices explain why nearly half of all Americans believe the nation is divided into "haves" and "have nots."

As unequal as U.S. incomes are, income disparities are actually greater in many other countries. Ironically, income inequalities are often greatest in the poorest countries. The richest *tenth* of U.S. families gets 30 percent of America's income pie. The richest tenth of South Africa's families gets 45 percent of that nation's income (see World View on p. 36). Given the small size of South Africa's pie, the *bottom* tenth of South African families is left with

U.S. Income Distribution

income quintile: One-fifth of the population, rank-ordered by income (e.g., top fifth).

Global Inequality

Motive of Occupy Wallstreet.

US incomes are distributed Very unequally

Poorest fifth

Income Quintile	2007 Income	Average Income	Share of Total Income (%)
Highest fifth	above $100,000	$168,000	49.7
Second fifth	$62,000–100,000	$ 79,000	23.4
Third fifth	$39,000–62,000	$ 50,000	14.8
Fourth fifth	$20,000–39,000	$ 29,000	8.7
Lowest fifth	$0–20,000	$ 12,000	3.4

Source: U.S. Department of Commerce, Bureau of the Census (averages rounded to thousands of dollars; 2007 data).

web analysis

Past and present data on the United States income distribution are available at **www.census.gov.** Click on the "Income" link.

FIGURE 2.3
The U.S. Distribution of Income

The richest fifth of U.S. households gets half of all the income—a huge slice of the income pie. By contrast, the poorest fifth gets only a sliver.

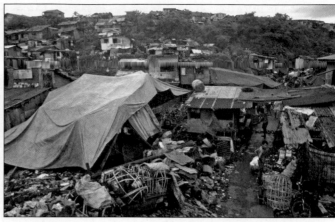

Analysis: The market distributes income (and, in turn, goods and services) according to the resources an individual owns and how well they are used. If the resulting inequalities are too great, some redistribution via government intervention may be desired.

mere crumbs. As we'll see in Chapter 36, 40 percent of South Africa's population live in "severe poverty," defined by the World Bank as an income of less than $2 a day.

Comparisons across countries would manifest even greater inequality. As we saw earlier, Third World GDP per capita is far below U.S. levels. As a consequence, even **poor** *people in the United States receive far more goods and services than the* **average** *household in most low-income countries.*

WORLD VIEW

Income Share of the Rich

Inequality tends to diminish as a country develops. In poor, developing nations, the richest tenth of the population typically gets 40 to 50 percent of all income. In developed countries, the richest tenth gets 20 to 30 percent of total income.

Source: From *World Development Indicators, 2009.* **www.worldbank.org.**

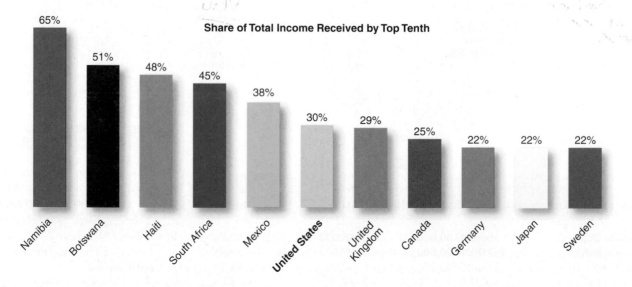

Share of Total Income Received by Top Tenth

Namibia	Botswana	Haiti	South Africa	Mexico	United States	United Kingdom	Canada	Germany	Japan	Sweden
65%	51%	48%	45%	38%	30%	29%	25%	22%	22%	22%

Analysis: The FOR WHOM question is reflected in the distribution of income. Although the U.S. distribution of income is very unequal, inequalities are even more severe in most poor nations.

THE ECONOMY TOMORROW

ENDING GLOBAL POVERTY

Global answers to the basic questions of WHAT, HOW, and FOR WHOM have been shaped by market forces and government intervention. Obviously, the answers aren't yet fully satisfactory.

Millions of Americans still struggle to make ends meet. Worse yet, nearly 3 *billion* people around the world live in abject poverty—with incomes of less than $2 a day. Over a fourth of the world's population is illiterate, nearly half has no access to sanitation facilities, and a fifth is chronically malnourished.

The World Bank thinks we can do a lot better. In fact, it has set ambitious goals for the economy tomorrow. In the Millennium Declaration of October 2000, the 180 nation-members of the World Bank set specific goals for world development. By 2015, they agreed to

- Reduce extreme poverty and hunger by at least half.
- Achieve universal primary education.
- Reduce child and maternal mortality by two-thirds.
- Reduce by half the number of people without access to potable water.

Achieving these goals would obviously help billions of people. But how will we fulfill them?

People in rich nations also aspire to higher living standards in the economy tomorrow. They already enjoy more comforts than people in poor nations even dream of. But that doesn't stop us from wanting more consumer goods, better schools, improved health care, a cleaner environment, and greater economic security. How will we get them?

A magic wand could transform the economy tomorrow into utopia. But short of that, we're saddled with economic reality. All nations have limited resources and technology. To get to a better place tomorrow, we've got to put those resources to even better uses. Will the market alone head us down the right path? As we've observed, economies that have relied more on market mechanisms than on government directives have prospered the most. But that doesn't mean we must fully embrace laissez faire. Government intervention still has potential to accelerate economic growth, reduce poverty, raise health and education standards, and protect the environment. The challenge for the economy both today and tomorrow is to find the right balance of market and government forces. We'll explore this quest in more detail as the text proceeds and revisit the challenge of global poverty in Chapter 36.

SUMMARY

- Answers to the core WHAT, HOW, and FOR WHOM questions vary greatly across nations. These differences reflect varying production possibilities, choice mechanisms, and values. LO1
- Gross domestic product (GDP) is the basic measure of how much an economy produces. The United States produces roughly $15 trillion of output per year, more than one-fifth of the world's total. LO1
- Per capita GDP is a nation's total output divided by its population. It indicates the average standard of living. The U.S. GDP per capita is five times the world average. LO1

- The high level of U.S. per capita GDP reflects the high productivity of U.S. workers. Abundant capital, education, technology, training, and management all contribute to high productivity. The relatively high degree of U.S. economic freedom (market reliance) is also an important cause of superior economic growth. LO2
- Over 75 percent of U.S. output consists of services, including government services. This is a reversal of historical ratios and reflects the relatively high incomes in the United States. Poor nations produce much higher proportions of food and manufactured goods. LO2

- U.S. incomes are distributed very unequally, with households in the highest income class (quintile) receiving over 10 times more income than low-income households. Incomes are even less equally distributed in most poor nations.   LO3

- The mix of output, production methods, and the income distribution continues to change. The WHAT, HOW, and FOR WHOM answers in tomorrow's economy will depend on the continuing interplay of (changing) market signals and (changing) government policy.   LO3

Key Terms

gross domestic product (GDP)
per capita GDP
economic growth
factors of production

human capital
capital-intensive
productivity
externalities

monopoly
income quintile

Questions for Discussion

1. Americans already enjoy living standards that far exceed world averages. Do we have enough? Should we even try to produce more?   LO1

2. Why is per capita GDP so much higher in the United States than in Mexico?   LO2

3. Can we continue to produce more output every year? Is there a limit?   LO2

4. The U.S. farm population has shrunk by over 25 million people since 1900. Where did all the people go? Why did they move?   LO2

5. How might the following government interventions affect a nation's economic growth?   LO2
    a. Mandatory school attendance.
    b. High income taxes.
    c. Copyright and patent protection.
    d. Political corruption.

6. How many people are employed by your local or state government? What do they produce? What is the opportunity cost of that output?   LO1

7. Why should the government regulate how goods are produced? Can regulation ever be excessive?   LO1

8. Should the government try to equalize incomes more by raising taxes on the rich and giving more money to the poor? How might such redistribution affect total output and growth?   LO3

9. Why are incomes so much more unequal in poor nations than in rich ones?   LO3

10. How might free markets help reduce global poverty? How might they impede that goal?   LO3

! **web activities** to accompany this chapter can be found on the Online Learning Center:
http://www.mhhe.com/schiller12e

LO1   1. In 2007, the world's total output (real GDP) was roughly $65 trillion. What percent of this total
was produced by the three largest economies (World View, p. 28)?   _____%

LO3   2. According to the World View on page 29, what percentage of America's GDP per capita is
available to the average citizen of

(a) Mexico?	_____%
(b) China?	_____%
(c) Ethiopia?	_____%

LO3   3. According to Table 2.1, how fast does total output have to grow in order to raise
per capita GDP in

(a) Japan?	_____
(b) Niger?	_____

LO3   4. If Haiti's per capita GDP of roughly $1,150 were to increase as fast as China's (see Table 2.1),
what would its per capita GDP be in

(a) 10 years?	$_____
(b) 20 years?	$_____

LO1   5. U.S. real gross domestic product increased from $10 trillion in 1998 to $14 trillion in 2008.
During that same decade the share of manufactured goods (e.g., cars, appliances) fell from
16 percent to 12 percent. What was the dollar value of manufactured output
  (a) In 1998? $_____
  (b) In 2008? $_____
  (c) By how much did durable output change?   _____%

LO3   6. Using the data in Figure 2.3,
  (a) Compute the average income of U.S. households. $_____
  (b) If all incomes were equalized by government taxes and transfer payments, how much would
      the average household in each income quintile gain (via transfers) or lose (via taxes)?

(i) Highest fifth	$_____
(ii) Second fifth	$_____
(iii) Third fifth	$_____
(iv) Fourth fifth	$_____
(v) Lowest fifth	$_____

  (c) What is the implied tax rate (i.e., tax ÷ average income) on the highest quintile?   _____%

LO2   7. If 150 million workers produced America's GDP in 2007 (World View, p. 28), how much output
did the average worker produce? $_____

LO3   8. How much more output (income) per year will have to be produced in the world
  (a) Just to provide the 2.7 billion "severely" poor population with $1 more output per day? $_____
  (b) To raise the incomes of the world's "severely poor" population (income less than $2 per day)
      to the official threshold of U.S. poverty (roughly $5,000 per year per person)? $_____

LO1 9. Using data from Table 2.1, illustrate on the following graphs real GDP and population growth since 2000 (in the manner of Figure 2.1) for the nations indicated.

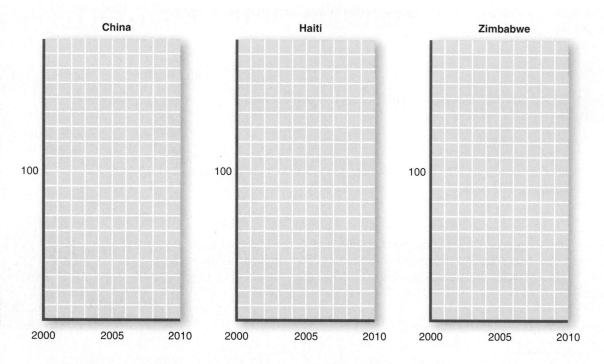

LO1 10. Using data from the endpapers, illustrate on the graph below
   (*a*) The federal government's share of the total output.
   (*b*) The state/local government's share of total output.

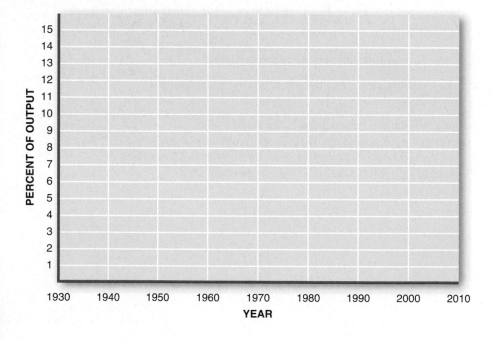

3

Supply and Demand

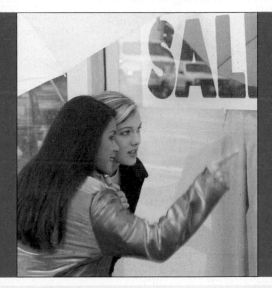

After reading this chapter, you should be able to:

LO1. Define the meaning of market demand and supply.

LO2. Show how market prices are established.

LO3. Explain what causes market prices to change.

LO4. Describe how government price controls affect market outcomes.

Gasoline prices surged in early 2008, rising from $2.99 a gallon in January to $4.05 in July. Consumers were angry every time they filled up their tanks. Popular opinion blamed the "Big Oil" companies and "speculators" for the sky-high prices. They demanded that the government intervene and force prices back down. Congressional hearings were conducted, government investigations were initiated, and "excess profits" taxes on oil companies were proposed.

By the end of 2008, gasoline prices had receded. In early 2009, pump prices were back to less than $2 a gallon. No oil executives or speculators had been arrested. No congressional reports had been completed. No government indictments had been issued. Economists explained this turn of events with "supply and demand." Surging demand and limited supply had caused the price spike; slowing demand and increased supply had pushed pump prices back down. Motorists weren't entirely convinced, but were happy. They filled their tanks and drove off to other economic concerns.

The goal of this chapter is to explain how supply and demand really works. How do *markets* establish the price of gasoline and other products? Why do prices change so often? More broadly, how does the market mechanism decide WHAT to produce, HOW to produce, and FOR WHOM to produce? Specifically,

- **What determines the price of a good or service?**
- **How does the price of a product affect its production and consumption?**
- **Why do prices and production levels often change?**

Once we've seen how unregulated markets work, we'll observe how government intervention may alter market outcomes—for better or worse.

MARKET PARTICIPANTS

A good way to start figuring out how markets work is to see who participates in them. The answer is simple: just about every person and institution on the planet. Domestically, over 310 million consumers, about 25 million business firms, and tens of thousands of government agencies participate directly in the U.S. economy. Millions of international buyers and sellers also participate in U.S. markets.

Maximizing Behavior

All these market participants enter the marketplace to pursue specific goals. Consumers, for example, come with a limited amount of income to spend. Their objective is to buy the most desirable goods and services that their limited budgets will permit. We can't afford *everything* we want, so we must make *choices* about how to spend our scarce dollars. Our goal is to *maximize* the utility (satisfaction) we get from our available incomes.

Businesses also try to maximize in the marketplace. In their case, the quest is for maximum *profits.* Business profits are the difference between sales receipts and total costs. To maximize profits, business firms try to use resources efficiently in producing products that consumers desire.

The public sector also has maximizing goals. The economic purpose of government is to use available resources to serve public needs. The resources available for this purpose are limited too. Hence, local, state, and federal governments must use scarce resources carefully, striving to maximize the general welfare of society. International consumers and producers pursue these same goals when participating in our markets.

Market participants sometimes lose sight of their respective goals. Consumers sometimes buy impulsively and later wish they'd used their income more wisely. Likewise, a producer may take a 2-hour lunch, even at the sacrifice of maximum profits. And elected officials sometimes put their personal interests ahead of the public's interest. In all sectors of the economy, however, ***the basic goals of utility maximization, profit maximization, and welfare maximization explain most market activity.***

Specialization and Exchange

We are driven to buy and sell goods and services in the market by two simple facts. First, most of us are incapable of producing everything we want to consume. Second, even if we *could* produce all our own goods and services, it would still make sense to *specialize,* producing only one product and *trading* it for other desired goods and services.

Suppose you were capable of growing your own food, stitching your own clothes, building your own shelter, and even writing your own economics text. Even in this little utopia, it would still make sense to decide how *best* to expend your limited time and energy, relying on others to fill in the gaps. If you were *most* proficient at growing food, you would be best off spending your time farming. You could then *exchange* some of your food output for the clothes, shelter, and books you wanted. In the end, you'd be able to consume *more* goods than if you'd tried to make everything yourself.

Our economic interactions with others are thus necessitated by two constraints:

1. Our absolute inability as individuals to produce all the things we need or desire.
2. The limited amount of time, energy, and resources we have for producing those things we could make for ourselves.

Together, these constraints lead us to specialize and interact. Most of the interactions that result take place in the market.

THE CIRCULAR FLOW

Figure 3.1 summarizes the kinds of interactions that occur among market participants. Note first that the figure identifies four separate groups of participants. Domestically, the rectangle labeled "Consumers" includes all 310 million consumers in the United States. In the "Business firms" box are grouped all the domestic business enterprises that buy and sell goods and services. The third participant, "Governments," includes the many separate agencies of the federal government, as well as state and local governments. Figure 3.1 also illustrates the role of global actors.

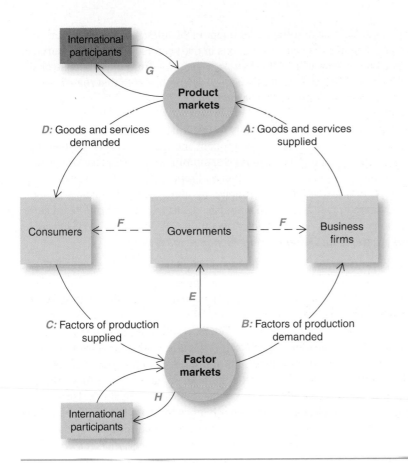

FIGURE 3.1
The Circular Flow

Business firms supply goods and ser-vices to product markets (point *A*) and purchase factors of production in factor markets (*B*). Individual consumers supply factors of pro-duction such as their own labor (*C*) and purchase final goods and ser-vices (*D*). Federal, state, and local governments acquire resources in factor markets (*E*) and provide ser-vices to both consumers and busi-ness (*F*). International participants also take part by supplying imports, purchasing exports (*G*), and buying and selling factors of production (*H*).

The easiest way to keep track of all this activity is to distinguish two basic markets. Figure 3.1 makes this distinction by portraying separate circles for product markets and factor mar-kets. In **factor markets,** factors of production are exchanged. Market participants buy or sell land, labor, or capital that can be used in the production process. When you go looking for work, for example, you're making a factor of production—your labor—available to producers. The producers will hire you—purchase your services in the factor market—if you're offering the skills they need at a price they're willing to pay. The same kind of inter-action occurs in factor markets when the government enlists workers into the armed services or when the Japanese buy farmland in Montana.

Interactions within factor markets are only half the story. At the end of a hard day's work, consumers go to the grocery store (or to a virtual store online) to buy desired goods and services—that is, to buy *products.* In this context, consumers again interact with busi-ness firms, this time purchasing goods and services those firms have produced. These interactions occur in **product markets.** Foreigners also participate in the product market by supplying goods and services (imports) to the United States and buying some of our output (exports).

The government sector also supplies services (e.g., education, national defense, high-ways). Most government services aren't explicitly sold in product markets, however. Typically, they're delivered "free," without an explicit price (e.g., public elementary schools, highways). This doesn't mean government services are truly free, though. There's still an **opportunity cost** associated with every service the government provides. Con-sumers and businesses pay that cost indirectly through taxes rather than directly through market prices.

In Figure 3.1, the arrow connecting product markets to consumers (point *D*) emphasizes the fact that consumers, by definition, don't supply products. When individuals produce

The Two Markets

factor market: Any place where factors of production (e.g., land, labor, capital) are bought and sold.

product market: Any place where finished goods and services (products) are bought and sold.

opportunity cost: The most desired goods or services that are forgone in order to obtain something else.

goods and services, they do so within the government or business sector. For instance, a doctor, a dentist, or an economic consultant functions in two sectors. When selling services in the market, this person is regarded as a "business"; when away from the office, he or she is regarded as a "consumer." This distinction is helpful in emphasizing that *the consumer is the final recipient of all goods and services produced.*

Locating Markets. Although we refer repeatedly to two kinds of markets in this book, it would be a little foolish to go off in search of the product and factor markets. Neither market is a single, identifiable structure. The term *market* simply refers to a place or situation where an economic exchange occurs—where a buyer and seller interact. The exchange may take place on the street, in a taxicab, over the phone, by mail, or in cyberspace. In some cases, the market used may in fact be quite distinguishable, as in the case of a retail store, the Chicago Commodity Exchange, or a state employment office. But whatever it looks like, *a market exists wherever and whenever an exchange takes place.*

Dollars and Exchange

Figure 3.1 provides a useful summary of market activities, but it neglects one critical element of market interactions: dollars. Each arrow in the figure actually has two dimensions. Consider again the arrow linking consumers to product markets: It's drawn in only one direction because consumers, by definition, don't provide goods and services directly to product markets. But they do provide something: dollars. If you want to obtain something from a product market, you must offer to pay for it (typically, with cash, check, debit or credit card). Consumers exchange dollars for goods and services in product markets.

The same kinds of exchange occur in factor markets. When you go to work, you exchange a factor of production (your labor) for income, typically a paycheck. Here again, the path connecting consumers to factor markets really goes in two directions: one of real resources, the other of dollars. Consumers receive wages, rent, and interest for the labor, land, and capital they bring to the factor markets. Indeed, nearly *every market transaction involves an exchange of dollars for goods (in product markets) or resources (in factor markets).* Money is thus critical in facilitating market exchanges and the specialization the exchanges permit.

Supply and Demand

supply: The ability and willingness to sell (produce) specific quantities of a good at alternative prices in a given time period, *ceteris paribus.*

demand: The ability and willingness to buy specific quantities of a good at alternative prices in a given time period, *ceteris paribus.*

In every market transaction there must be a buyer and a seller. The seller is on the **supply** side of the market; the buyer is on the **demand** side. As noted earlier, we *supply* resources to the market when we look for a job—that is, when we offer our labor in exchange for income. We *demand* goods when we shop in a supermarket—that is, when we're prepared to offer dollars in exchange for something to eat. Business firms may *supply* goods and services in product markets at the same time they're *demanding* factors of production in factor markets. Whether one is on the supply side or the demand side of any particular market transaction depends on the nature of the exchange, not on the people or institutions involved.

DEMAND

To get a sense of how the demand side of market transactions works, we'll focus first on a single consumer. Then we'll aggregate to illustrate *market* demand.

Individual Demand

We can begin to understand how market forces work by looking more closely at the behavior of a single market participant. Let us start with Tom, a senior at Clearview College. Tom has majored in everything from art history to government in his 3 years at Clearview. He didn't connect to any of those fields and is on the brink of academic dismissal. To make matters worse, his parents have threatened to cut him off financially unless he gets serious about his course work. By that, they mean he should enroll in courses that will lead to a job after graduation. Tom thinks he has found the perfect solution: Web design. Everything associated with the Internet pays big bucks. Plus, the girls seem to think Webbies are "cool." Or at least so Tom thinks. And his parents would definitely approve. So Tom has enrolled in Web-design courses.

Unfortunately for Tom, he never developed computer skills. Until he got to Clearview College, he thought mastering Sony's latest alien-attack video game was the pinnacle of electronic wizardry. Tom didn't have a clue about "streaming," "interfacing," "animation," or the other concepts the Web-design instructor outlined in the first lecture.

Given his circumstances, Tom was desperate to find someone who could tutor him in Web design. But desperation is not enough to secure the services of a Web architect. In a market-based economy, you must also be willing to *pay* for the things you want. Specifically, *a demand exists only if someone is willing and able to pay for the good*—that is, exchange dollars for a good or service in the marketplace. Is Tom willing and able to *pay* for the Web-design tutoring he so obviously needs?

Let us assume that Tom has some income and is willing to spend some of it to get a tutor. Under these assumptions, we can claim that Tom is a participant in the *market* for Web-design services.

But how much is Tom willing to pay? Surely, Tom is not prepared to exchange *all* his income for help in mastering Web design. After all, Tom could use his income to buy more desirable goods and services. If he spent all his income on a Web tutor, that help would have an extremely high *opportunity cost.* He would be giving up the opportunity to spend that income on other goods and services. He'd pass his Web-design class but have little else. It doesn't sound like a good idea.

It seems more likely that there are *limits* to the amount Tom is willing to pay for any given quantity of Web-design tutoring. These limits will be determined by how much income Tom has to spend and how many other goods and services he must forsake in order to pay for a tutor.

Tom also knows that his grade in Web design will depend in part on how much tutoring service he buys. He can pass the course with only a few hours of design help. If he wants a better grade, however, the cost is going to escalate quickly.

Naturally, Tom wants it all: an A in Web design and a ticket to higher-paying jobs. But here again the distinction between *desire* and *demand* is relevant. He may *desire* to master Web design, but his actual proficiency will depend on how many hours of tutoring he is willing to *pay* for.

We assume, then, that when Tom starts looking for a Web-design tutor he has in mind some sort of **demand schedule,** like that described in Figure 3.2. According to row *A* of this schedule, Tom is willing and able to buy only 1 hour of tutoring service per semester if he must pay $50 an hour. At such an outrageous price he will learn minimal skills and just pass the course.

At lower prices, Tom would behave differently. According to Figure 3.2, Tom would purchase more tutoring services if the price per hour were less. At lower prices, he would not have to give up so many other goods and services for each hour of technical help. Indeed, we see from row *I* of the demand schedule that Tom is willing to purchase 20 hours per semester—the whole bag of design tricks—if the price of tutoring is as low as $10 per hour.

Notice that the demand schedule doesn't tell us anything about *why* this consumer is willing to pay specific prices for various amounts of tutoring. Tom's expressed willingness to pay for Web-design tutoring may reflect a desperate need to finish a Web-design course, a lot of income to spend, or a relatively small desire for other goods and services. All the demand schedule tells us is what the consumer is *willing and able* to buy, for whatever reasons.

Also observe that the demand schedule doesn't tell us how many hours of design help the consumer will *actually* buy. Figure 3.2 simply states that Tom is *willing and able* to pay for 1 hour of tutoring per semester at $50 per hour, for 2 hours at $45 each, and so on. How much tutoring he purchases will depend on the actual price of such services in the market. Until we know that price, we cannot tell how much service will be purchased. Hence *"demand" is an expression of consumer buying intentions, of a willingness to buy, not a statement of actual purchases.*

The Demand Schedule

demand schedule: A table showing the quantities of a good a consumer is willing and able to buy at alternative prices in a given time period, *ceteris paribus.*

FIGURE 3.2

A Demand Schedule and Curve

A demand schedule indicates the quantities of a good a consumer is able and willing to buy at alternative prices (*ceteris paribus*). The demand schedule below indicates that Tom would buy 5 hours of Web tutoring per semester if the price were $35 per hour (row *D*). If Web tutoring were less expensive (rows *E–I*), Tom would purchase a larger quantity.

A demand curve is a graphical illustration of a demand schedule. Each point on the curve refers to a specific quantity that will be demanded at a given price. If, for example, the price of Web tutoring were $35 per hour, this curve tells us the consumer would purchase 5 hours per semester (point *D*). If Web tutoring cost $30 per hour, 7 hours per semester would be demanded (point *E*). Each point on the curve corresponds to a row in the schedule.

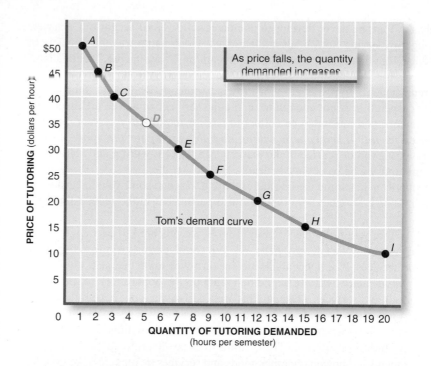

As price falls, the quantity demanded increases

Tom's demand curve

	Tom's Demand Schedule	
	Price of Tutoring (per hour)	**Quantity of Tutoring Demanded (hours per semester)**
A	$50	1
B	45	2
C	40	3
D	35	5
E	30	7
F	25	9
G	20	12
H	15	15
I	10	20

web analysis

The Demand Curve

demand curve: A curve describing the quantities of a good a consumer is willing and able to buy at alternative prices, *ceteris paribus.*

A convenient summary of buying intentions is the **demand curve,** a graphical illustration of the demand schedule. The demand curve in Figure 3.2 tells us again that this consumer is willing to pay for only 1 hour of tutoring per semester if the price is $50 per hour (point *A*), for 2 if the price is $45 (point *B*), for 3 at $40 an hour (point *C*), and so on. Once we know what the market price of tutoring actually is, a glance at the demand curve tells us how much service this consumer will buy.

What the notion of *demand* emphasizes is that *the amount we buy of a good depends on its price.* We seldom if ever decide to buy only a certain quantity of a good at whatever price is charged. Instead, we enter markets with a set of desires and a limited amount of money to spend. How much we actually buy of any particular good will depend on its price.

A common feature of demand curves is their downward slope. *As the price of a good falls, people purchase more of it.* In Figure 3.2 the quantity of Web-tutorial services demanded increases (moves rightward along the horizontal axis) as the price per hour decreases (moves down the vertical axis). This inverse relationship between price and

IN THE NEWS

Auto Makers Return to Deep Discounts

GM's Problems Prompt Price Cuts of up to $10,000; Ford, Chrysler Likely to Follow

General Motors reintroduced heavy incentives on many of its 2005 and 2006 models yesterday, slashing sticker prices by as much as $10,000 on some cars and trucks.

The huge price cuts come after General Motors Corp.'s sales plunged in October and are an acknowledgment that the world's largest auto maker needs to boost sales as it grapples with a $1.6 billion loss in the third quarter and decreasing market share. Some of the new discounts are even better deals for car buyers than this summer's popular employee-discount program.

All three U.S. car makers enjoyed a surge in sales this summer when they offered customers the same prices they had previously given their own employees. That boosted sales but cut deeply into profit margins, especially for GM and Ford. Each reported massive losses in North America in the third quarter.

More than a month ago, the Big Three cut off the employee-pricing discounts in a bid to set new prices that are above employee levels.

—Gina Chon

Source: *The Wall Street Journal,* November 15, 2005, p. D1. Copyright 2005 by Dow Jones & Company, Inc. Reproduced with permission of Dow Jones & Company, Inc. in the format Textbook via Copyright Clearance Center.

Analysis: The law of demand predicted that General Motors would sell fewer cars if it raised its price and more cars if it reduced their price. That is exactly what happened.

quantity is so common we refer to it as the **law of demand.** General Motors used this law to increase auto sales in 2005–2006 (see News above).

The demand curve in Figure 3.2 has only two dimensions—quantity demanded (on the horizontal axis) and price (on the vertical axis). This seems to imply that the amount of tutoring demanded depends only on the price of that service. This is surely not the case. A consumer's willingness and ability to buy a product at various prices depend on a variety of forces. *The determinants of market demand include*

- *Tastes* (desire for this and other goods).
- *Income* (of the consumer).
- *Other goods* (their availability and price).
- *Expectations* (for income, prices, tastes).
- *Number of buyers.*

Tom's "taste" for tutoring has nothing to do with taste buds. *Taste* is just another word for desire. In this case Tom's taste for Web-design services is clearly acquired. If he didn't have to pass a Web-design course, he would have no desire for related services, and thus no demand. If he had no income, he couldn't *demand* any Web-design tutoring either, no matter how much he might *desire* it.

Other goods also affect the demand for tutoring services. Their effect depends on whether they're *substitute* goods or *complementary* goods. A **substitute good** is one that might be purchased instead of tutoring services. In Tom's simple world, pizza is a substitute for tutoring. If the price of pizza fell, Tom would use his limited income to buy more pizzas and cut back on his purchases of Web tutoring. When the price of a substitute good falls, the demand for tutoring services declines.

A **complementary good** is one that's typically consumed with, rather than instead of, tutoring. If textbook prices or tuition increases, Tom might take fewer classes and demand

Demand ↗ (inverse)
Price ↓

law of demand: The quantity of a good demanded in a given time period increases as its price falls, *ceteris paribus.*

Determinants of Demand

Butter/margarine

substitute goods: Goods that substitute for each other; when the price of good *x* rises, the demand for good *y* increases, *ceteris paribus.*

complementary goods: Goods frequently consumed in combination; when the price of good *x* rises, the demand for good *y* falls, *ceteris paribus.*

hot dogs & buns

less Web-design assistance. In this case, a price increase for a complementary good causes the demand for tutoring to decline.

Expectations also play a role in consumer decisions. If Tom expected to flunk his Web-design course anyway, he probably wouldn't waste any money getting tutorial help; his demand for such services would disappear. On the other hand, if he expects a Web tutor to determine his college fate, he might be more willing to buy such services.

Ceteris Paribus

ceteris paribus: The assumption of nothing else changing.

If demand is in fact such a multidimensional decision, how can we reduce it to only the two dimensions of price and quantity? In Chapter 1 we first encountered this *ceteris paribus* trick. To simplify their models of the world, economists focus on only one or two forces at a time and *assume* nothing else changes. We know a consumer's tastes, income, other goods, and expectations all affect the decision to hire a tutor. But we want to focus on the relationship between quantity demanded and price. That is, we want to know what *independent* influence price has on consumption decisions. To find out, we must isolate that one influence, price, and assume that the determinants of demand remain unchanged.

The *ceteris paribus* assumption is not as farfetched as it may seem. People's tastes, income, and expectations do not change quickly. Also, the prices and availability of other goods don't change all that fast. Hence, a change in the *price* of a product may be the only factor that prompts an immediate change in quantity demanded.

The ability to predict consumer responses to a price change is important. What would happen, for example, to enrollment at your school if tuition doubled? Must we guess? Or can we use demand curves to predict how the quantity of applications will change as the price of college goes up? ***Demand curves show us how changes in market prices alter consumer behavior.*** We used the demand curve in Figure 3.2 to predict how Tom's Web-design ability would change at different tutorial prices.

Shifts in Demand

Although demand curves are useful in predicting consumer responses to market signals, they aren't infallible. The problem is that ***the determinants of demand can and do change.*** When they do, a specific demand curve may become obsolete. A ***demand curve (schedule) is valid only so long as the underlying determinants of demand remain constant.*** If the *ceteris paribus* assumption is violated—if tastes, income, other goods, or expectations change—the ability or willingness to buy will change. When this happens, the demand curve will **shift** to a new position.

shift in demand: A change in the quantity demanded at any (every) given price.

Suppose, for example, that Tom won $1,000 in the state lottery. This increase in his income would greatly increase his ability to pay for tutoring services. Figure 3.3 shows the effect of this windfall on Tom's demand. The old demand curve, D_1, is no longer relevant. Tom's lottery winnings enable him to buy *more* tutoring at any price, as illustrated by the new demand curve, D_2. According to this new curve, lucky Tom is now willing and able to buy 12 hours per semester at the price of $35 per hour (point d_2). This is a large increase in demand; previously (before winning the lottery) he demanded only 5 hours at that price (point d_1).

With his higher income, Tom can buy more tutoring services at every price. Thus, ***the entire demand curve shifts to the right when income goes up.*** Figure 3.3 illustrates both the old (prelottery) and the new (postlottery) demand curves.

Income is only one of the basic determinants of demand. Changes in any of the other determinants of demand would also cause the demand curve to shift. Tom's taste for Web tutoring might increase dramatically, for example, if his parents promised to buy him a new car for passing Web design. In that case, he might be willing to forgo other goods and spend more of his income on tutors. ***An increase in taste (desire) also shifts the demand curve to the right.***

Pizza and Politics. A similar demand shift occurs at the White House when a political crisis erupts. On an average day, White House staffers order about $180 worth of pizza from the nearby Domino's. When a crisis hits, however, staffers work well into the night and their demand for pizza soars. On the days preceding the March 2003 invasion of Iraq,

Shift (n/e) depend on consumer tastes, income, expectations, other goods.

FIGURE 3.3
Shifts vs. Movements

A demand curve shows how a consumer responds to price changes. If the determinants of demand stay constant, the response is a *movement* along the curve to a new quantity demanded. In this case, the quantity demanded increases from 5 (point d_1), to 12 (point g_1), when price falls from $35 to $20 per hour.

If the determinants of demand change, the entire demand curve *shifts*. In this case, an increase in income increases demand. With more income, Tom is willing to buy 12 hours at the initial price of $35 (point d_2), not just the 5 hours he demanded before the lottery win.

$Q \uparrow$ as $P \downarrow$ (Demand)

		Quantity Demanded (hours per semester)	
	Price (per hour)	Initial Demand	After Increase in Income
A	$50	1	8
B	45	2	9
C	40	3	10
D	35	5	12
F	30	7	14
F	25	9	16
G	20	12	19
H	15	15	22
I	10	20	27

White House staffers ordered more than $1,000 worth of pizza per day! Political analysts now use pizza deliveries to predict major White House announcements.

It's important to distinguish shifts of the demand curve from movements along the demand curve. *Movements along a demand curve are a response to price changes for that good.* Such movements assume that determinants of demand are unchanged. By contrast, *shifts of the demand curve occur when the determinants of demand change.* When tastes, income, other goods, or expectations are altered, the basic relationship between price and quantity demanded is changed (shifts).

For convenience, movements along a demand curve and shifts of the demand curve have their own labels. Specifically, take care to distinguish

- *Changes in quantity demanded:* movements along a given demand curve, in response to price changes of that good.
- *Changes in demand:* shifts of the demand curve due to changes in tastes, income, other goods, or expectations.

Tom's behavior in the Web-tutoring market will change if either the price of tutoring changes (a movement) or the underlying determinants of his demand are altered (a shift).

Movements vs. Shifts

Mvmt - $P \downarrow$ $Q \uparrow$

Shift ⟨ expects. change
taste changes
income changes

Notice in Figure 3.3 that he ends up buying 12 hours of Web tutoring if either the price of tutoring falls (to $20 per hour) or his income increases. Demand curves help us predict those market responses.

Market Demand

Whatever we say about demand for Web-design tutoring on the part of one wannabe Webmaster, we can also say about every student at Clearview College (or, for that matter, about all consumers). Some students have no interest in Web design and aren't willing to pay for related services: They don't participate in the Web-tutoring market. Other students want such services but don't have enough income to pay for them: They too are excluded from the Web-tutoring market. A large number of students, however, not only have a need (or desire) for Web tutoring but also are willing and able to purchase such services.

What we start with in product markets, then, is many individual demand curves. Fortunately, it's possible to combine all the individual demand curves into a single **market demand.** The aggregation process is no more difficult than simple arithmetic. Suppose you would be willing to buy 1 hour of tutoring per semester at a price of $80 per hour. George, who is also desperate to learn Web design, would buy 2 at that price; and I would buy none, since my publisher (McGraw-Hill) creates a Web page for me (try **mhhe.com/ schiller12e**). What would our combined (market) demand for hours of tutoring be at that price? Clearly, our individual inclinations indicate that we would be willing to buy a total of 3 hours of tutoring per semester if the price were $80 per hour. Our combined willingness to buy—our collective market demand—is nothing more than the sum of our individual demands. The same kind of aggregation can be performed for all consumers, leading to a summary of the total market demand for a specific good or service. Thus *market demand is determined by the number of potential buyers and their respective tastes, incomes, other goods, and expectations.*

> **market demand:** The total quantities of a good or service people are willing and able to buy at alternative prices in a given time period; the sum of individual demands.

The Market Demand Curve

Figure 3.4 provides the basic market demand schedule for a situation in which only three consumers participate in the market. It illustrates the same market situation with demand curves. The three individuals who participate in the market demand for Web tutoring at Clearview College obviously differ greatly, as suggested by their respective demand schedules. Tom's demand schedule is portrayed in the first column of the table (and is identical to the one we examined in Figure 3.2). George is also desperate to acquire some job skills and is willing to pay relatively high prices for Web-design tutoring. His demand is summarized in the second column under Quantity Demanded in the table.

The third consumer in this market is Lisa. Lisa already knows the nuts and bolts of Web design, so she isn't so desperate for tutorial services. She would like to upgrade her skills, however, especially in animation and e-commerce applications. But her limited budget precludes paying a lot for help. She will buy some technical support only if the price falls to $30 per hour. Should tutors cost less, she'd even buy quite a few hours of design services. Finally, there is my demand schedule (column 4 under Quantity Demanded), which confirms that I really don't participate in the Web-tutoring market.

The differing personalities and consumption habits of Tom, George, Lisa, and me are expressed in our individual demand schedules and associated curves in Figure 3.4. To determine the *market* demand for tutoring from this information, we simply add these four separate demands. The end result of this aggregation is, first, a *market* demand schedule and, second, the resultant *market* demand curve. These market summaries describe the various quantities of tutoring that Clearview College students are *willing and able* to purchase each semester at various prices.

How much Web tutoring will be purchased each semester? Knowing how much help Tom, George, Lisa, and I are willing to buy at various prices doesn't tell you how much we're actually going to purchase. To determine the actual consumption of Web tutoring, we have to know something about prices and supplies. Which of the many different prices illustrated in Figures 3.3 and 3.4 will actually prevail? How will that price be determined?

(e) The market demand curve

FIGURE 3.4
Construction of the Market Demand Curve

Market demand represents the combined demands of all market participants. To determine the total quantity of Web tutoring demanded at any given price, we add the separate demands of the individual consumers. Row G of this schedule indicates that a *total* quantity of 39 hours per semester will be demanded at a price of $20 per hour. This same conclusion is reached by adding the individual demand curves, leading to point G on the market demand curve (see above).

	Price (per hour)	Tom	+	George	+	Lisa	+	Me	=	Market Demand
A	$50	1		4		0		0		5
B	45	2		6		0		0		8
C	40	3		8		0		0		11
D	35	5		11		0		0		16
E	30	7		14		1		0		22
F	25	9		18		3		0		30
G	20	12		22		5		0		39
H	15	15		26		6		0		47
I	10	20		30		7		0		57

Quantity of Tutoring Demanded (hours per semester)

market supply: The total quantities of a good that sellers are willing and able to sell at alternative prices in a given time period, *ceteris paribus.*

SUPPLY

To understand how the price of Web tutoring is established, we must also look at the other side of the market: the supply side. We need to know how many hours of tutoring services people are willing and able to *sell* at various prices, that is, the **market supply.** As on the demand side, the *market supply* depends on the behavior of all the individuals willing and able to supply Web tutoring at some price.

Determinants of Supply

Let's return to the Clearview campus for a moment. What we need to know now is how much tutorial help people are willing and able to provide. Generally speaking, Web-page design can be fun, but it can also be drudge work, especially when you're doing it for someone else. Software programs like PhotoShop, Flash, and Fireworks have made Web-page design easier and more creative. And Wi-Fi access has made the job more convenient. But teaching someone else to design Web pages is still work. So why does anyone do it? Easy answer: for the money. People offer (supply) tutoring services to earn income that they, in turn, can spend on the goods and services *they* desire.

How much income must be offered to induce Web designers to do a job depends on a variety of things. The *determinants of market supply include*

- *Technology*
- *Factor cost*
- *Other goods*
- *Taxes and subsidies*
- *Expectations*
- *Number of sellers*

The technology of Web design, for example, is always getting easier and more creative. With a program like PageOut, for example, it's very easy to create a bread-and-butter Web page. A continuous stream of new software programs (e.g., Fireworks, DreamWeaver) keeps stretching the possibilities for graphics, animation, interactivity, and content. These technological advances mean that Web-design services can be supplied more quickly and cheaply. They also make *teaching* Web design easier. As a result, they induce people to supply more tutoring services at every price.

How much Web-design service is offered at any given price also depends on the cost of factors of production. If the software programs needed to create Web pages are cheap (or, better yet, free), Web designers can afford to charge lower prices. If the required software inputs are expensive, however, they will have to charge more money per hour for their services.

Other goods can also affect the willingness to supply Web-design services. If you can make more income waiting tables than you can tutoring lazy students, why would you even boot up the computer? As the prices paid for other goods and services change, they will influence people's decision about whether to offer Web services.

In the real world, the decision to supply goods and services is also influenced by the long arm of Uncle Sam. Federal, state, and local governments impose taxes on income earned in the marketplace. When tax rates are high, people get to keep less of the income they earn. Once taxes start biting into paychecks, some people may conclude that tutoring is no longer worth the hassle and withdraw from the market.

Expectations are also important on the supply side of the market. If Web designers expect higher prices, lower costs, or reduced taxes, they may be more willing to learn new software programs. On the other hand, if they have poor expectations about the future, they may just sell their computers and find something else to do.

Finally, we note that the number of potential tutors will affect the quantity of service offered for sale at various prices. If there are lots of willing tutors on campus, a lot of tutorial service will be available at reasonable prices.

All these considerations—factor costs, technology, expectations—affect the decision to offer Web services and at what price. In general, we assume that Web architects will be willing to provide more tutoring if the per-hour price is high and less if the price is low. In other words, there is a **law of supply** that parallels the law of demand. *The law of supply says that larger quantities will be offered for sale at higher prices.* Here again, the laws rest on the *ceteris paribus* assumption: The quantity supplied increases at higher prices *if* the determinants of supply are constant. *Supply curves are upward-sloping to the right,* as

law of supply: The quantity of a good supplied in a given time period increases as its price increases, *ceteris paribus.*

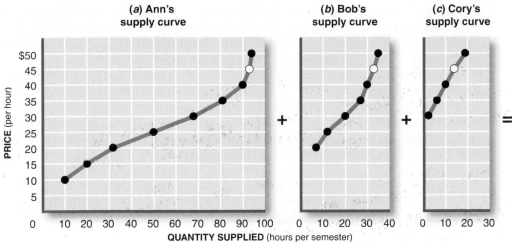

(a) Ann's supply curve   **(b) Bob's supply curve**   **(c) Cory's supply curve**

QUANTITY SUPPLIED (hours per semester)

Quantity supplied increases as price rises.

QUANTITY SUPPLIED (hours per semester)

FIGURE 3.5
Market Supply

The market supply curve indicates the *combined* sales intentions of all market participants; i.e., the total quantities they are willing and able to sell at various prices. If the price of tutoring were $45 per hour (point *i*), the *total* quantity of services supplied would be 140 hours per semester. This quantity is determined by adding the supply decisions of all individual producers. In this case, Ann supplies 93 hours, Bob supplies 33, and Cory supplies the rest.

| | Price per hour | **Quantity of Tutoring Supplied by** | | | | | | |
		Ann	+	Bob	+	Cory	=	Market
j	$50	94		35		19		148
i	45	93		33		14		140
h	40	90		30		10		130
g	35	81		27		6		114
f	30	68		20		2		90
e	25	50		12		0		62
d	20	32		7		0		39
c	15	20		0		0		20
b	10	10		0		0		10

in Figure 3.5. Note how the *quantity supplied* jumps from 39 hours (point *d*) to 130 hours (point *h*) when the price of Web service doubles (from $20 to $40 per hour).

Figure 3.5 also illustrates how *market* supply is constructed from the supply decisions of individual sellers. In this case, only three Web masters are available. Ann is willing to provide a lot of tutoring at low prices, whereas Bob requires at least $20 an hour. Cory won't talk to students for less than $30 an hour.

Market Supply

By adding the quantity each Webhead is willing to offer at every price, we can construct the market supply curve. Notice in Figure 3.5, how the quantity supplied to the market at $45 (point *i*) comes from the individual efforts of Ann (93 hours), Bob (33 hours), and Cory (14 hours). *The market supply curve is just a summary of the supply intentions of all producers.*

None of the points on the market supply curve (Figure 3.5) tells us how much Web tutoring is actually being sold on the Clearview campus. *Market supply is an expression of sellers' intentions—an offer to sell—not a statement of actual sales.* My next-door neighbor may be willing to sell his 1994 Honda Civic for $8,000, but most likely he'll never find a buyer at that price. Nevertheless, his *willingness* to sell his car at that price is part of the *market supply* of used cars. (See Web analysis for more detail on the market supply of used cars.)

Shifts of Supply

As with demand, there's nothing sacred about any given set of supply intentions. Supply curves *shift* when the underlying determinants of supply change. Thus, *it is important to distinguish*

- *Changes in quantity supplied:* movements along a given supply curve.
- *Changes in supply:* shifts of the supply curve.

Our Latin friend *ceteris paribus* is once again the decisive factor. If the price of a product is the only variable changing, then we can **track changes in quantity supplied along the supply curve.** But if *ceteris paribus* is violated—if technology, factor costs, the profitability of producing other goods, tax rates, expectations, or the number of sellers change—then **changes in supply are illustrated by shifts of the supply curve.**

The accompanying News illustrates how a supply shift sent gasoline prices soaring in 2005. When Hurricane Katrina shut down oil-producing facilities in the Gulf of Mexico, the gasoline supply curve shifted leftward and price jumped.

IN THE NEWS

Another Storm Casualty: Oil Prices

The region that produces and refines a major portion of the nation's oil and natural gas was largely shut down by Hurricane Katrina yesterday, further tightening strained energy markets and sending prices to new highs.

As oil companies evacuated offshore operations throughout the Gulf of Mexico, oil production in that region was reduced by 92 percent and gas output was cut by 83 percent.

The latest interruptions in oil supplies are likely to send retail gasoline prices even higher than the current average of $2.60 a gallon. . . .

The Gulf of Mexico, which produces 27 percent of the nation's oil and a fifth of its natural gas, is dotted with nearly 4,000 platforms linked by 33,000 miles of underwater pipelines. Over the weekend, oil companies withdrew their workers from 615 platforms and 96 drilling rigs in the gulf.

—Jad Mouawad and Simon Romero

Source: From "Another Storm Casualty: Oil Prices" by Jad Mouawad and Simon Romero, *The New York Times*, August 30, 2005, p. 1. Copyright © 2005 by The New York Times. Used with permission by PARS International.

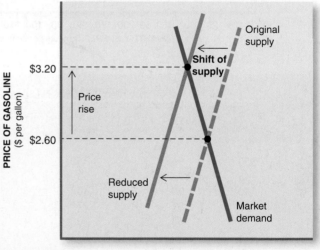

Analysis: When factor costs or availability worsen, the supply curve *shifts* to the left. Such leftward supply-curve shifts push prices up the market demand curve.

EQUILIBRIUM

That post-Katrina spike in oil prices offers some clues as to how the forces of supply and demand set—and change—market prices. For a closer look at how those forces work, we'll return to Clearview College for a moment. How did supply and demand resolve the WHAT, HOW, and FOR WHOM questions in that Web-tutoring market?

Figure 3.6 helps answer that question by bringing together the market supply and demand curves we've already examined (Figures 3.4 and 3.5). When we put the two curves together, we see that *only one price and quantity combination is compatible with the existing intentions of both buyers and sellers. This equilibrium occurs at the intersection of the supply and demand curves.* Notice in Figure 3.6 where that intersection occurs—at the price of $20 and the quantity of 39 hours. So, $20 is the **equilibrium price:** Campus Webheads will sell a total of 39 hours of tutoring per semester—the same amount that students wish to buy at that price. Those 39 hours of tutoring service will be part of WHAT is produced.

An equilibrium doesn't imply that everyone is happy with the prevailing price or quantity. Notice in Figure 3.6, for example, that some students who want to buy Web-design assistance services don't get any. These would-be buyers are arrayed along the demand curve *below* the equilibrium. Because the price they're *willing* to pay is less than the equilibrium

equilibrium price: The price at which the quantity of a good demanded in a given time period equals the quantity supplied.

Market Clearing

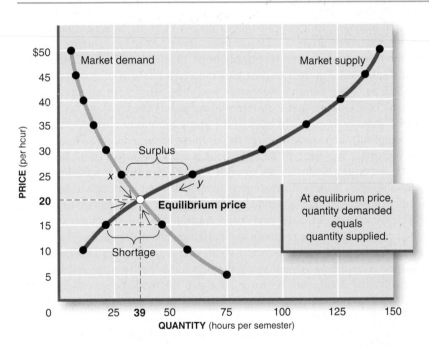

FIGURE 3.6
Equilibrium Price

The intersection of the demand and supply curves establishes the *equilibrium* price and output. Only at equilibrium is the quantity demanded equal to the quantity supplied. In this case, the equilibrium price is $20 per hour, and 39 hours is the equilibrium quantity.

At above-equilibrium prices, a market surplus exists—the quantity supplied exceeds the quantity demanded. At prices below equilibrium, a market shortage exists.

Price (per hour)	Quantity Supplied (hours per semester)		Quantity Demanded (hours per semester)
$50	148		5
45	140		8
40	130	market surplus	11
35	114		16
30	90		22
25	62		30
20	39	equilibrium	39
15	20	market shortage	47
10	10		57

*Non*equilibrium prices create surpluses or shortages

price, they don't get any Web-design help. The market's FOR WHOM answer includes only those students willing and able to pay the equilibrium price.

Likewise, some would-be sellers are frustrated by this market outcome. These people are arrayed along the supply curve *above* the equilibrium. Because they insist on being paid *more* than the equilibrium price, they don't actually sell anything.

Although not everyone gets full satisfaction from the market equilibrium, that unique outcome is efficient. ***The equilibrium price and quantity reflect a compromise between buyers and sellers. No other compromise yields a quantity demanded that's exactly equal to the quantity supplied.***

The Invisible Hand. The equilibrium price isn't determined by any single individual. Rather, it's determined by the collective behavior of many buyers and sellers, each acting out his or her own demand or supply schedule. It's this kind of impersonal price determination that gave rise to Adam Smith's characterization of the market mechanism as "the invisible hand." In attempting to explain how the **market mechanism** works, the famed eighteenth-century economist noted a remarkable feature of market prices. The market behaves as if some unseen force (the invisible hand) were examining each individual's supply or demand schedule and then selecting a price that assured an equilibrium. In practice, the process of price determination isn't so mysterious: It's a simple process of trial and error.

market mechanism: The use of market prices and sales to signal desired outputs (or resource allocations).

Surplus and Shortage

price floor: Lower limit set for the price of a good.

market surplus: The amount by which the quantity supplied exceeds the quantity demanded at a given price; excess supply.

Market Surplus. To appreciate the power of the market mechanism, consider interference in its operation. Suppose, for example, that campus Webheads banded together and agreed to charge a minimum price of $25 per hour. By establishing a **price floor,** a minimum price for their services, the Webheads hope to increase their incomes. But they won't be fully satisfied. Figure 3.6 illustrates the consequences of this *dis*equilibrium pricing. At $25 per hour, campus Webheads would be offering more tutoring services (point *y*) than Tom, George, and Lisawere willing to buy (point *x*) at that price. A **market surplus** of Web services would exist in the sense that more tutoring was being offered for sale (supplied) than students cared to purchase at the available price.

As Figure 3.6 indicates, at a price of $25 per hour, a market surplus of 32 hours per semester exists. Under these circumstances, campus Webheads would be spending many idle hours at their keyboards waiting for customers to appear. Their waiting will be in vain because the quantity of Web tutoring demanded will not increase until the price of tutoring falls. That is the clear message of the demand curve. As would-be tutors get this message, they'll reduce their prices. This is the response the market mechanism signals.

As sellers' asking prices decline, the quantity demanded will increase. This concept is illustrated in Figure 3.6 by the movement along the demand curve from point *x* to lower prices and greater quantity demanded. As we move down the market demand curve, the *desire* for Web-design help doesn't change, but the quantity people are *able and willing to buy* increases. When the price falls to $20 per hour, the quantity demanded will finally equal the quantity supplied. This is the *equilibrium* illustrated in Figure 3.6.

Market Shortage. A very different sequence of events would occur if a market shortage existed. Suppose someone were to spread the word that Web-tutoring services were available at only $15 per hour. Tom, George, and Lisa would be standing in line to get tutorial help, but campus Web designers wouldn't be willing to supply the quantity demanded at that price. As Figure 3.6 confirms, at $15 per hour, the quantity demanded (47 hours per semester) greatly exceeds the quantity supplied (20 hours per semester). In this situation, we speak of a **market shortage,** that is, an excess of quantity demanded over quantity supplied. At a price of $15 an hour, the shortage amounts to 27 hours of tutoring services.

market shortage: The amount by which the quantity demanded exceeds the quantity supplied at a given price; excess demand.

When a market shortage exists, not all consumer demands can be satisfied. Some people who are *willing* to buy Web help at the going price ($15) won't be able to do so. To assure themselves of sufficient help, Tom, George, Lisa, or some other consumer may offer to pay a *higher* price, thus initiating a move up the demand curve in Figure 3.6. The higher prices offered will in turn induce other enterprising Webheads to tutor more, thus ensuring an upward movement along the market supply curve. Notice, again, that the *desire* to tutor Web design hasn't changed; only the quantity supplied has responded to a change in price. As this process continues, the quantity supplied will eventually equal the quantity demanded (39 hours in Figure 3.6).

Self-Adjusting Prices. What we observe, then, is that *whenever the market price is set above or below the equilibrium price, either a market surplus or a market shortage will emerge.* To overcome a surplus or shortage, buyers and sellers will change their behavior. Sellers will have to compete for customers by reducing prices when a market surplus exists. If a shortage exists, buyers will compete for service by offering to pay higher prices. Only at the *equilibrium* price will no further adjustments be required.

Sometimes the market price is slow to adjust, and a disequilibrium persists. This is often the case with tickets to rock concerts, football games, and other one-time events. People initially adjust their behavior by standing in ticket lines for hours, or hopping on the Internet, hoping to buy a ticket at the below-equilibrium price. The tickets are typically resold ("scalped"), however, at prices closer to equilibrium. This kind of market adjustment was evident even at President Obama's inauguration (see News below).

IN THE NEWS

Historic Inauguration Could Lead to Ticket Scalping

November 11, 2008. Sen. Dianne Feinstein (D-CA) says she's disturbed by reports that tickets to President-elect Barack Obama's inauguration are being sold online for as much as $40,000. She says she's writing to eBay and other sites to make sure they're not involved in ticket scalping. The 240,000 available tickets are supposed to be free to the public and are given out through congressional offices. Feinstein is also working on a bill that would make it a federal crime to sell tickets to the inauguration.

National Public Radio, November 11, 2008, morning edition.

Analysis: When tickets are sold initially at below-equilibrium prices, a market shortage is created. Scalpers resell tickets at prices closer to equilibrium, reaping a profit in the process.

Business firms can discover equilibrium prices by trial and error. If consumer purchases aren't keeping up with production, a firm may conclude that price is above the equilibrium price. To get rid of accumulated inventory, the firm will have to lower its price (a Grand End-of-Year Sale, perhaps). In the happier situation where consumer purchases are outpacing production, a firm might conclude that its price was a trifle too low and give it a nudge upward. In either case, the equilibrium price can be established after a few trials in the marketplace.

No equilibrium price is permanent. The equilibrium price established in the Clearview College tutoring market, for example, was the unique outcome of specific demand and supply schedules. Those schedules themselves were based on our assumption of *ceteris paribus.* We assumed that the "taste" (desire) for Web-design assistance was given, as were consumers' incomes, the price and availability of other goods, and expectations. Any of these determinants of demand could change. When one does, the demand curve has to be redrawn. Such a shift of the demand curve will lead to a new equilibrium price and quantity. Indeed, *the equilibrium price will change whenever the supply or demand curve shifts.*

Changes in Equilibrium

A Demand Shift. We can illustrate how equilibrium prices change by taking one last look at the Clearview College tutoring market. Our original supply and demand curves, together with the resulting equilibrium (point E_1), are depicted in Figure 3.7. Now suppose that all the professors at Clearview begin requiring class-specific Web pages from each student.

The increased need (desire) for Web-design ability will affect market demand. Tom, George, and Lisa will be willing to buy more Web tutoring at every price than they were before. That is, the *demand* for Web services has increased. We can represent this increased demand by a rightward *shift* of the market demand curve, as illustrated in Figure 3.7a.

Note that the new demand curve intersects the (unchanged) market supply curve at a new price (point E_2); the equilibrium price is now $30 per hour. This new equilibrium price will persist until either the demand curve or the supply curve shifts again.

A Supply Shift. Figure 3.7b illustrates a *supply* shift. The decrease (leftward shift) in supply might occur if some on-campus Webheads got sick. Or approaching exams might

FIGURE 3.7
Changes in Equilibrium

If demand or supply changes (shifts), market equilibrium will change as well.

Demand shift. In (*a*), the rightward shift of the demand curve illustrates an increase in demand. When demand increases, the equilibrium price rises (from E_1 to E_2).

Supply shift. In (*b*), the leftward shift of the supply curve illustrates a decrease in supply. This raises the equilibrium price to E_3.

Demand and supply curves shift only when their underlying determinants change, that is, when *ceteris paribus* is violated.

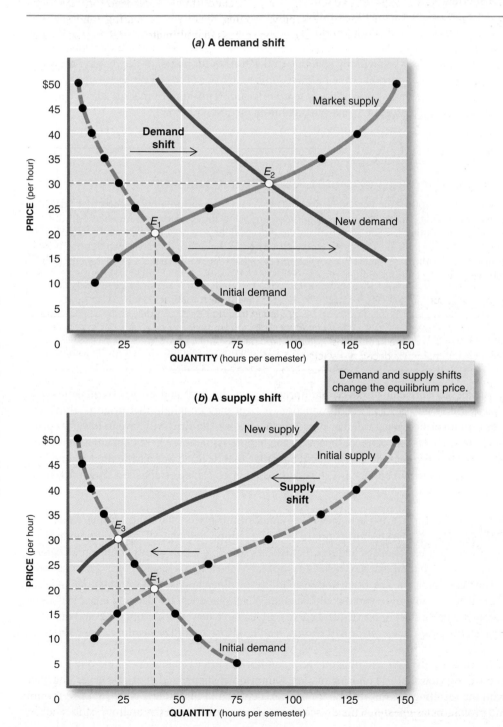

(*a*) A demand shift

(*b*) A supply shift

Demand and supply shifts change the equilibrium price.

convince would-be tutors that they have no time to spare. ***Whenever supply decreases (shifts left), price tends to rise,*** as in Figure 3.7*b*.

The rock band U2 learned about changing equilibriums the hard way. Ticket prices for the band's 1992 tour were below equilibrium, creating a *market shortage.* So U2 raised prices to as much as $52.50 a ticket for their 1997 tour—nearly double the 1992 price. By then, however, demand had shifted to the left, due to a lack of U2 hits and an increased number of competing concerts. By the time they got to their second city they were playing in stadiums with lots of empty seats. The apparent *market surplus* led critics to label the 1997 "Pop Mart" tour a disaster. For their 2001 "Elevation Tour," U2 offered "festival seating" for only $35 in order to fill stadiums and concert halls. Demand shifted again in 2005. Buoyed by a spike of new hit songs (e.g., "Beautiful Day"), demand for U2's "Vertigo Tour" far outstripped available supply, sending ticket prices soaring (and scalpers celebrating). This is the kind of trial and error process that ultimately establishes an equilibrium price.

The accompanying World View shows how rapid price adjustments can alleviate market shortages and surpluses. In this unusual case, a restaurant continuously adjusts its prices to ensure that everything on the menu is ordered and no food is wasted. It's an ingenious use of the market mechanism.

WORLD VIEW

Dining on the Downtick

Americans aren't the only consumers who fall for packaging. Since late January, Parisians (not to mention TV crews from around the world) have been drawn to 6 rue Feydeau to try La Connivence, a restaurant with a new gimmick. The name means "collusion," and yes, of course, La Connivence is a block away from the Bourse, the French stock exchange.

What's the gimmick? Just that the restaurant's prices fluctuate according to supply and demand. The more a dish is ordered, the higher its price. A dish that's ignored gets cheaper.

Customers tune in to the day's menu (couched in trading terms) on computer screens. Among a typical day's options: *forte baisse du haddock* ("precipitous drop in haddock"), *vif recul de la côte de boeuf* ("rapid decline in beef ribs"), *la brochette de lotte au plus bas* ("fish kabob hits bottom"). Then comes the major decision—whether to opt for the price that's listed when you order or to gamble that the price will have gone down by the time you finish your meal.

So far, only main dishes are open to speculation, but co-owners Pierre Guette, an ex-professor at a top French business school, and Jean-Paul Trastour, an ex-journalist at *Le Nouvel Observateur*, are adding wine to the risk list.

La Connivence is open for dinner, but the midday "session" (as the owners call it) is the one to catch. That's when the traders of Paris leave the floor to push their luck *à table*. But here, at least, the return on their $15 investment (the average price of a meal) is immediate—and usually good.

—Christina de Liagre

Source: *New York,* April 7, 1986.

Analysis: A market surplus signals that price is too high; a market shortage suggests that price is too low. This restaurant adjusts price until the quantity supplied equals the quantity demanded.

MARKET OUTCOMES

Notice how the market mechanism resolves the basic economic questions of WHAT, HOW, and FOR WHOM.

WHAT

The WHAT question refers to the mix of output society produces. How much Web tutorial services will be included in that mix? The answer at Clearview College was 39 hours of tutoring per semester. This decision wasn't reached in a referendum, but instead in the market equilibrium (Figure 3.6). In the same way but on a larger scale, millions of consumers and a handful of auto producers decide to include 15 million or so cars and trucks in each year's mix of output. Auto manufacturers use rebates, discounts, and variable interest rates to induce consumers to buy the same quantity that auto manufacturers are producing.

HOW

The market mechanism also determines HOW goods are produced. Profit-seeking producers will strive to produce Web designs and automobiles in the most efficient way. They'll use market prices to decide not only WHAT to produce but also what resources to use in the production process. If new software simplifies Web design—and is priced low enough—Webheads will use it. Likewise, auto manufacturers will use robots rather than humans on the assembly line if robots reduce costs and increase profits.

FOR WHOM

Finally, the invisible hand of the market will determine who gets the goods produced. At Clearview College, who got Web tutoring? Only those students who were willing and able to pay $20 per hour for that service. FOR WHOM are all those automobiles produced each year? The answer is the same: those consumers who are willing and able to pay the market price for a new car.

Optimal, Not Perfect

Not everyone is happy with these answers, of course. Tom would like to pay only $10 an hour for a tutor. And some of the Clearview students don't have enough income to buy any tutoring. They think it's unfair that they have to design their own Web pages while rich students can have someone else do their design work for them. Students who can't afford cars are even less happy with the market's answer to the FOR WHOM question.

Although the outcomes of the marketplace aren't perfect, they're often optimal. Optimal outcomes are the best possible *given* our incomes and scarce resources. Sure, we'd like everyone to have access to tutoring and to drive a new car. But there aren't enough resources available to create such a utopia. So we have to ration available tutors and cars. The market mechanism performs this rationing function. People who want to supply tutoring or build cars are free to make that choice. And consumers are free to decide how they want to spend their income. In the process, we expect market participants to make decisions that maximize their own welfare. If they do, then we conclude that everyone is doing as well as possible, given their available resources.

THE ECONOMY TOMORROW

DEADLY SHORTAGES: THE ORGAN-TRANSPLANT MARKET

As you were reading this chapter, dozens of Americans were dying from failed organs. More than 100,000 Americans are waiting for life-saving kidneys, livers, lungs, and other vital organs. They can't wait long, however. Every day at least 20 of these organ-diseased patients die. The clock is always ticking.

Modern technology can save most of these patients. Vital organs can be transplanted, extending the life of diseased patients. How many people are saved, however, depends on how well the organ "market" works.

The Supply of Organs. The only cure for liver disease and some other organ failures is a replacement organ. Over 50 years ago, doctors discovered that they could transplant an organ from one individual to another. Since then, medical technology has advanced to the point where organ transplants are exceptionally safe and successful. The constraint on this life-saving technique is the *supply* of transplantable organs.

Although over 2 million Americans die each year, most deaths do not create transplantable organs. Only 20,000 or so people die in circumstances—such as brain death after a car crash—that make them suitable donors for life-saving transplants. Additional kidneys can be "harvested" from live donors (we have two kidneys, but can function with only one; not true for liver, heart, or pancreas).

You don't have to die to supply an organ. Instead, you become a donor by agreeing to release your organs after death. The agreement is typically certified on a driver's license and sometimes on a bracelet or "dog tag." This allows emergency doctors to identify potential organ supplies.

People become donors for many reasons. Moral principles, religious convictions, and humanitarianism all play a role in the donation decision. It's the same with blood donations: People give blood (while alive!) because they want to help save other individuals.

Market Incentives. Monetary incentives could also play a role. When blood donations are inadequate, hospitals and medical schools *buy* blood in the marketplace. People who might not donate blood come forth to *sell* blood when a price is offered. In principle, the same incentive might increase the number of *organ* donors. If offered cash now for a postmortem organ, would the willingness to donate increase? The law of supply suggests it would. Offer $1,000 in cash for signing up, and potential donors will start lining up. Offer more, and the quantity supplied will increase further.

Zero Price Ceiling. The government doesn't permit this to happen. In 1984 Congress forbade the purchase or sale of human organs in the United States (the National Organ Transplantation Act). In part, the prohibition was rooted in moral and religious convictions. It was also motivated by equity concerns—the For Whom question. If organs could be bought and sold, then the rich would have a distinct advantage in living.

The prohibition on market sales is effectively a **price ceiling** set at zero. As a consequence, the only available organs are those supplied by altruistic donors. The quantity supplied can't be increased with price incentives. In general, *price ceilings have three predictable effects; they*

price ceiling: Upper limit imposed on the price of a good.

- *Increase the quantity demanded.*
- *Decrease the quantity supplied.*
- *Create a market shortage.*

The Deadly Shortage. Figure 3.8 illustrates the consequences of this price ceiling. At a price of zero, only the quantity q_a of "altruistic" organs is available (roughly one-third of the potential supply). But the quantity q_d is demanded by all the organ-diseased individuals. The market shortage $q_d - q_a$ tells us how many patients will die.

The News on page 62 argues that many of these deaths are unnecessary. Without the government-set price ceiling, more organ-diseased patients would live. Figure 3.8 shows that q_E people would get transplants in a market-driven system rather than only q_a in the government-regulated system. But they'd have to pay the price p_E—a feature regulators say is unfair. In the absence of the market mechanism, however, the government must set rules for who gets the even smaller quantity of organs supplied. That rationing system may be unfair as well.

QUANTITY (organs per year)

web analysis

The United Network for Organ Sharing (**www.UNOS.org**) maintains data on organ waiting lists and transplants.

FIGURE 3.8
Organ-Transplant Market

A market in human organs would deliver the quantity q_E at a price of p_E. The government-set price ceiling ($p = 0$) reduces the quantity supplied to q_a.

IN THE NEWS

Are Kidneys a Commodity?

As of last Wednesday at 5:44 P.M., according to the minute-by-minute count on the Web site of the United Network for Organ Sharing, there were 75,629 people awaiting kidney transplants in the United States. Here's roughly what we can expect to happen over the next 12 months, based on the experience of recent years. About 10,000 of them will receive transplants from deceased strangers, awarded by UNOS roughly in order of waiting time. An additional 6,000 or so on the waiting list will get a transplant from a living donor, almost invariably a close friend or relative. About 5,000 will either die or become too sick to qualify for a transplant. Most of the rest will still be waiting a year from now. They might want to consider talking to Lloyd Cohen.

© Owen Franken/Corbis

Cohen thinks people should have the right to buy or sell major organs, an idea reviled by docs.

Cohen is a professor of law at George Mason University who for two decades has been fighting for the right to sell off his major organs—or to buy one from someone else, should he need it. These are practices currently prohibited by U.S. law, and widely reviled by doctors, who like to believe they occupy one of the last bastions of selfless altruism in the American economy. . . . Cohen has made his case at length in articles and books, but he can summarize it in a dozen words: "If you pay people for something, they will provide more of it." This, he says, is as true of body parts as anything else.

—Jerry Adler

Source: *Newsweek*, May 26, 2008. Copyright 2008 Newsweek. Reprinted with permission by PARS International.

Analysis: A prohibition against selling organs is effectively a price ceiling at zero. A positive price would increase the quantity supplied.

SUMMARY

- People participate in the marketplace by offering to buy or sell goods and services, or factors of production. Participation is motivated by the desire to maximize utility (consumers), profits (business firms), or the general welfare (government agencies) from the limited resources each participant has. LO1
- All market transactions involve the exchange of either factors of production or finished products. Although the actual exchanges can occur anywhere, they take place in product markets or factor markets, depending on what is being exchanged. LO1
- People willing and able to buy a particular good at some price are part of the market demand for that product. All those willing and able to sell that good at some price are part of the market supply. Total market demand or supply is the sum of individual demands or supplies. LO1

- Supply and demand curves illustrate how the quantity demanded or supplied changes in response to a change in the price of that good, if nothing else changes *(ceteris paribus)*. Demand curves slope downward; supply curves slope upward. LO2
- Determinants of market demand include the number of potential buyers and their respective tastes (desires), incomes, other goods, and expectations. If any of these determinants changes, the demand curve shifts. Movements along a demand curve are induced only by a change in the price of that good. LO3
- Determinants of market supply include factor costs, technology, profitability of other goods, expectations, tax rates, and number of sellers. Supply shifts when these underlying determinants change. LO3

- The quantity of goods or resources actually exchanged in each market depends on the behavior of all buyers and sellers, as summarized in market supply and demand curves. At the point where the two curves intersect, an equilibrium price—the price at which the quantity demanded equals the quantity supplied—is established.   LO3
- A distinctive feature of the market equilibrium is that it's the only price-quantity combination acceptable to buyers and sellers alike. At higher prices, sellers supply more than buyers are willing to purchase (a market surplus); at lower prices, the amount demanded exceeds the quantity supplied (a market shortage). Only the equilibrium price clears the market.   LO3
- Price ceilings are disequilibrium prices imposed on the marketplace. Such price controls create an imbalance between quantities demanded and supplied, resulting in market shortages.   LO4

Key Terms

factor market	law of demand	law of supply
product market	substitute goods	equilibrium price
opportunity cost	complementary goods	market mechanism
supply	*ceteris paribus*	price floor
demand	shift in demand	market surplus
demand schedule	market demand	market shortage
demand curve	market supply	price ceiling

Questions for Discussion

1. In our story of Tom, the student confronted with a Web-design assignment, we emphasized the great urgency of his desire for Web tutoring. Many people would say that Tom had an "absolute need" for Web help and therefore was ready to "pay anything" to get it. If this were true, what shape would his demand curve have? Why isn't this realistic?   LO1

2. With respect to the demand for college enrollment, which of the following would cause (1) a movement along the demand curve or (2) a shift of the demand curve?   LO3
   a. An increase in incomes.
   b. Lower tuition.
   c. More student loans.
   d. An increase in textbook prices.

3. What would have happened to gasoline production and consumption if the government had prohibited post-Katrina price increases (see News, p. 54)?   LO4

4. Which determinants of pizza demand change when the White House is in crisis (pp. 48–49)?   LO3

5. What do the demand and supply of Inaugural tickets look like? Who attends if tickets are openly sold? Who attends if "scalping" is outlawed? (News, p. 57)   LO2

6. In Figure 3.8, why is the organ demand curve downward-sloping rather than vertical?   LO1

7. The shortage in the organ market (Figure 3.8) requires a nonmarket rationing scheme. Who should get the available (q_a) organs? Is this fairer than the market-driven distribution?   LO4

8. What would happen in the apple market if the government set a *minimum* price of $2.00 per apple? What might motivate such a policy?   LO4

9. The World View on page 59 describes the use of prices to achieve an equilibrium in the kitchen. What happens to the food at more traditional restaurants?   LO2

10. Is there a shortage of on-campus parking at your school? How might the shortage be resolved?   LO2

 web activities to accompany this chapter can be found on the Online Learning Center:
http://www.mhhe.com/schiller12e

connect
|ECONOMICS

LO1 1. According to Figure 3.3, at what price would Tom buy 9 hours of Web tutoring?

(a) Without a lottery win.   _____

(b) With a lottery win.   _____

LO2 2. According to Figures 3.5 and 3.6, what would the new equilibrium price of tutoring services be if Ann decided to stop tutoring?   _____

LO2 3. Given the following data on gasoline supply and demand,

(a) What is the equilibrium price?   _____

(b) How large a market shortage would exist if government set a price ceiling of $1 per gallon?   _____

A. Price per gallon	$5.00	$4.00	$3.00	$2.00	$1.00			$5.00	$4.00	$3.00	$2.00	$1.00
B. Quantity demanded (gallons per day)						C. Quantity supplied (gallons per day)						
Al	1	2	3	4	5	Alice	3	3	3	3	3
Betsy	0	1	1	1	2	Butch	7	5	4	4	2
Casey	2	2	3	3	4	Connie	6	4	3	3	1
Daisy	1	3	4	4	6	Dutch	6	5	4	3	0
Eddie	1	2	2	3	5	Ellen	4	2	2	2	1
Market total	__	__	__	__	__	Market total	__	__	__	__	__

LO3 4. As a result of Katrina damage (News, p. 54), which of the following changed (answer yes or no):

(a) Demand   _____

(b) Quantity demanded   _____

(c) Price   _____

LO2 5. In the World View on page 59, menu prices are continuously adjusted. Graph the initial and final (adjusted) prices for the following situation. Be sure to label axes and graph completely.

(a) **Customers are ordering too little haddock.**

(b) **The kitchen is running out of beef ribs.**

LO4 6. According to Figure 3.8,

(a) How many people die in the market-driven economy?   _____

(b) How many people die in the government-regulated economy?   _____

LO1 7. The goal of the price incentives described in the News on page 47, is to (select one):

(a) Increase supply.   _____

(b) Increase quantity supplied.   _____

(c) Increase demand.   _____

(d) Increase quantity demanded.   _____

LO4 8. In Figure 3.8, when a price ceiling of zero is imposed on the organ market by how much does
   (a) The quantity of organs demanded increase? _____
   (b) The demand increase? _____
   (c) The quantity of organs supplied decrease? _____
   (d) The supply decrease? _____

LO2 9. Use the following data to draw supply and demand curve on the accompanying graph.

Price	$ 8	7	6	5	4	3	2	1
Quantity demanded	2	3	4	5	6	7	8	9
Quantity supplied	10	9	8	7	6	5	4	3

   (a) What is the equilibrium price? _____
   (b) If a *minimum* price (price floor) of $6 is set,
       (i) What kind of disequilibrium results? _____
       (ii) How large is it? _____
   (c) If a *maximum* price (price ceiling) of $3 is set,
       (i) What disequilibrium results? _____
       (ii) How large is it ? _____

Illustrate these answers.

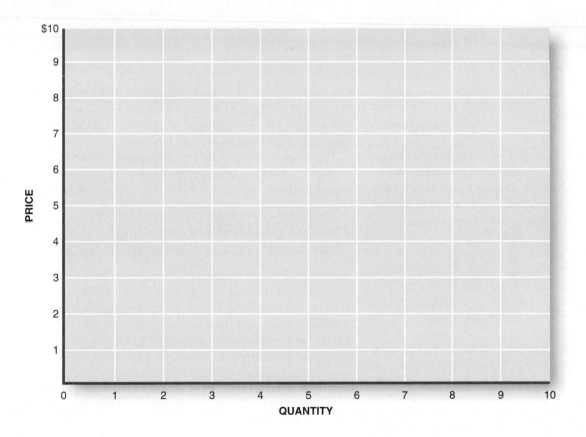

The Role of Government

4

After reading this chapter, you should be able to:

LO1. Analyze the nature and causes of market failure.

LO2. Demonstrate how government budgets are financed and spent.

LO3. Discuss the meaning of government failure.

The market has a keen ear for private wants, but a deaf ear for public needs.

—Robert Heilbroner

Markets do work: The interaction of supply and demand in product markets *does* generate goods and services. Likewise, the interaction of supply and demand in labor markets *does* yield jobs, wages, and a distribution of income. As we've observed, the market is capable of determining WHAT goods to produce, HOW, and FOR WHOM.

But are the market's answers good enough? Is the mix of output produced by unregulated markets the best possible mix? Will producers choose the production process that protects the environment? Will the market-generated distribution of income be fair enough? Will there be enough jobs for everyone who wants one?

In reality, markets don't always give us the best-possible outcomes. Markets dominated by a few powerful corporations may charge excessive prices, limit output, provide poor service, or even retard technological advance. In the quest for profits, producers may sacrifice the environment for cost savings. In unfettered markets, some people may not get

life-saving health care, basic education, or even adequate nutrition. When markets generate such outcomes, government intervention may be needed to ensure better answers to the WHAT, HOW, and FOR WHOM questions.

This chapter identifies the circumstances under which government intervention is desirable. To this end, we answer the following questions:

- **Under what circumstances do markets fail?**
- **How can government intervention help?**
- **How much government intervention is desirable?**

As we'll see, there's substantial agreement about how and when markets fail to give us the best WHAT, HOW, and FOR WHOM answers. But there's much less agreement about whether government intervention improves the situation. Indeed, an overwhelming majority of Americans are ambivalent about government intervention. They want the government to "fix" the mix of output, protect the environment, and ensure an adequate level of income for everyone. But voters are equally quick to blame government meddling for many of our economic woes.

COMPUTERS (units per time period)

Production possibilities

The market fails when it produces the wrong (suboptimal) mix of output

X (Optimal mix)

M (Market mix)

ALL OTHER GOODS (units per time period)

FIGURE 4.1
Market Failure

We can produce any mix of output on the production possibilities curve. Our goal is to produce the optimal (best-possible) mix of output, as represented by point X. Market forces, however, might produce another combination, like point M. In that case, the market fails—it produces a *sub*optimal mix of output.

MARKET FAILURE

We can visualize the potential for government intervention by focusing on the WHAT question. Our goal here is to produce the best-possible mix of output with existing resources. We illustrated this goal earlier with production possibilities curves. Figure 4.1 assumes that of all the possible combinations of output we could produce, the unique combination at point X represents the most desirable one. In other words, it's the **optimal mix of output,** the one that maximizes our collective social utility. We haven't yet figured out how to pinpoint that optimal mix; we're simply using the arbitrary point X in Figure 4.1 to represent that best-possible outcome.

Ideally, the **market mechanism** would lead us to point X. Price signals in the marketplace are supposed to move factors of production from one industry to another in response to consumer demands. If we demand more computers—offer to buy more at a given price— more resources (labor) will be allocated to computer manufacturing. Similarly, a fall in demand will encourage producers to stop making computers and offer their services in another industry. *Changes in market prices direct resources from one industry to another, moving us along the perimeter of the production possibilities curve.*

Where will the market mechanism take us? Will it move resources around until we end up at the optimal point X? Or will it leave us at another point on the production possibilities curve, with a *sub*optimal mix of output? (If point X is the *optimal,* or best-possible, mix, all other output mixes must be *sub*optimal.)

We use the term **market failure** to refer to situations where the market generates less-than-perfect (suboptimal) outcomes. If the invisible hand of the marketplace produces a mix of output that's different from the one society most desires, then it has failed. *Market failure implies that the forces of supply and demand haven't led us to the best point on the production possibilities curve.* Such a failure is illustrated by point M in Figure 4.1. Point M is assumed to be the mix of output generated by market forces. Notice that the market mix (M) doesn't represent the optimal mix, which is assumed to be at point X. The market in this case *fails;* we get the wrong answer to the WHAT question.

Market failure opens the door for government intervention. If the market can't do the job, we need some form of *nonmarket* force to get the right answers. In terms of Figure 4.1, we need something to change the mix of output—to move us from point M (the market mix of output) to point X (the optimal mix of output). Accordingly, *market failure establishes a basis for government intervention.* We look to the government to push market outcomes closer to the ideal.

Causes of Market Failure. Because market failure is the justification for government intervention, we need to know how and when market failure occurs. *The four specific sources of market failure are*

- *Public goods*
- *Externalities*
- *Market power*
- *Equity*

optimal mix of output: The most desirable combination of output attainable with existing resources, technology, and social values.

market mechanism: The use of market prices and sales to signal desired outputs (or resource allocations).

market failure: An imperfection in the market mechanism that prevents optimal outcomes.

We will first examine the nature of these problems, then see why government intervention is called for in each case.

Public Goods

The market mechanism has the unique capability to signal consumer demands for various goods and services. By offering to pay higher or lower prices for some goods, we express our preferences about WHAT to produce. However, this mode of communication works efficiently only if the benefits of consuming a particular good are available only to the individuals who purchase that product.

Consider doughnuts, for example. When you eat a doughnut, you alone get the satisfaction from its sweet, greasy taste—that is, you derive a private benefit. No one else benefits from your consumption of a doughnut: The doughnut you purchase in the market is yours alone to consume; it's a **private good.** Accordingly, your decision to purchase the doughnut will be determined only by your anticipated satisfaction, your income, and your opportunity costs.

private good: A good or service whose consumption by one person excludes consumption by others.

you have control over how much is made

No Exclusion. Most of the goods and services produced in the public sector are different from doughnuts—and not just because doughnuts look, taste, and smell different from "star wars" missile shields. When you buy a doughnut, you exclude others from consumption of that product. If Dunkin' Donuts sells you a particular pastry, it can't supply the same pastry to someone else. If you devour it, no one else can. In this sense, the transaction and product are completely private.

The same exclusiveness is not characteristic of national defense. If you buy a missile defense system to thwart enemy attacks, there's no way you can exclude your neighbors from the protection your system provides. Either the missile shield deters would-be attackers or it doesn't. In the former case, both you and your neighbors survive happily ever after; in the latter case, we're all blown away together. In that sense, you and your neighbors consume the benefits of a missile shield *jointly*. National defense isn't a divisible service. There's no such thing as exclusive consumption here. The consumption of nuclear defenses is a communal feat, no matter who pays for them. Accordingly, national defense is regarded as a **public good** in the sense that *consumption of a public good by one person doesn't preclude consumption of the same good by another person.* By contrast, a doughnut is a private good because if I eat it, no one else can consume it.

public good: A good or service whose consumption by one person does not exclude consumption by others.

- *national defense*
- *public roads*

free rider: An individual who reaps direct benefits from someone else's purchase (consumption) of a public good.

The Free-Rider Dilemma. The communal nature of public goods creates a dilemma. If you and I will *both* benefit from nuclear defenses, which one of us should buy the missile shield? I'd prefer that *you* buy it, thereby giving me protection at no direct cost. Hence, I may profess no desire for a missile shield, secretly hoping to take a **free ride** on your market purchase. Unfortunately, you too have an incentive to conceal your desire for national defenses. As a consequence, neither one of us may step forward to demand a missile shield in the marketplace. We'll both end up defenseless.

Flood control is also a public good. No one in the valley wants to be flooded out. But each landowner knows that a flood-control dam will protect *all* the landowners, regardless of who pays. Either the entire valley is protected or no one is. Accordingly, individual farmers and landowners may say they don't *want* a dam and aren't willing to *pay* for it. Everyone is waiting and hoping that someone else will pay for flood control. In other words, everyone wants a *free ride.* Thus, if we leave it to market forces, no one will *demand* flood control and all the property in the valley will be washed away.

The difference between public goods and private goods rests on *technical considerations* not political philosophy. The central question is whether we have the technical capability to exclude nonpayers. In the case of national defense or flood control, we simply don't have that capability. Even city streets have the characteristics of public goods. Although theoretically we could restrict the use of streets to those who paid to use them, a tollgate on every corner would be exceedingly expensive and impractical. Here again, joint or public consumption appears to be the only feasible alternative. As the following News on music downloads emphasizes, the technical capability to exclude nonpayers is the key factor in identifying "public goods."

IN THE NEWS

Paying for Tunes

Shawn Fanning had a brilliant idea for getting more music: download it from friends' computers to the Internet. So he wrote software in 1999 that enabled online file-sharing of audio files. This peer-to-peer (P2P) online distribution system became an overnight sensation: in 2000–01 nearly 60 million consumers were using Napster's software to acquire recorded music.

At first blush, Napster's service looked like a classic "public good." The service was free, and one person's consumption did not impede another person from consuming the same service. Moreover, the distribution system was configured in such a way that nonpayers could not be excluded from the service.

The definition of "*public good*" relies, however, on whether nonpayers *can* be excluded, not whether they *are* excluded. In other words, technology is critical in classifying goods as "public" or "private." In Napster's case, encryption technology that could exclude nonpayers was available, but the company had *chosen* not to use it. After being sued by major recording companies for copyright infringement, Napster changed its tune. In July 2001, it shut down its free download service. Two years later it re-opened with a *fee-based* service that could exclude nonpayers. Although free downloads are still available from offshore companies (e.g., Kazaa), fee-based services have sprung up all over (e.g., Apple's iTunes Music Store, Wal-Mart). For most consumers, music downloads are now a private good.

> **Analysis:** A product is a "public good" only if nonpayers *cannot* be excluded from its consumption. Napster had the technical ability to exclude nonpayers but initially chose not to do so. Fee-based music downloads are a private good.

web analysis

For examples of public goods, in addition to those considered in the accompanying paragraphs, visit **www.econlib.org** and search "public goods."

To the list of public goods we could add snow removal, the administration of justice (including prisons), the regulation of commerce, the conduct of foreign relations, airport security, and even Fourth of July fireworks. These services—which cost tens of *billions* of dollars and employ thousands of workers—provide benefits to everyone, no matter who pays for them. In each instance it's technically impossible or prohibitively expensive to exclude nonpayers from the services provided.

Underproduction of Public Goods. The free riders associated with public goods upset the customary practice of paying for what you get. If I can get all the national defense, flood control, and laws I want without paying for them, I'm not about to complain. I'm perfectly happy to let you pay for the services while we all consume them. Of course, you may feel the same way. Why should you pay for these services if you can consume just as much of them when your neighbors foot the whole bill? It might seem selfish not to pay your share of the cost of providing public goods. But you'd be better off in a material sense if you spent your income on doughnuts, letting others pick up the tab for public services.

Because the familiar link between paying and consuming is broken, public goods can't be peddled in the supermarket. People are reluctant to buy what they can get free. Hence, *if public goods were marketed like private goods, everyone would wait for someone else to pay.* The end result might be a total lack of public services. This is the kind of dilemma Robert Heilbroner had in mind when he spoke of the market's "deaf ear" (see quote at the beginning of this chapter).

The production possibilities curve in Figure 4.2 illustrates the dilemma created by public goods. Suppose that point *A* represents the optimal mix of private and public goods. It's the mix of goods and services we'd select if everyone's preferences were known and reflected in production decisions. The market mechanism won't lead us to point *A*, however, because the *demand* for public goods will be hidden. If we rely on the market, nearly everyone will withhold demand for public goods, waiting for a free ride to point *A*. As a result, we'll get a smaller quantity of public goods than we really want. The market mechanism will leave

FIGURE 4.2
Underproduction of Public Goods

Suppose point *A* represents the optimal mix of output, that is, the mix of private and public goods that maximizes society's welfare. Because consumers won't demand purely public goods in the marketplace, the price mechanism won't allocate so many resources to their production. Instead, the market will tend to produce a mix of output like point *B*, which includes fewer public goods (0*R*) than is optimal (0*S*).

us at point *B*, with few, if any, public goods. Since point *A* is assumed to be optimal, point *B* must be *suboptimal* (inferior to point *A*). The market fails: We can't rely on the market mechanism to allocate enough resources to the production of public goods, no matter how much they might be desired.

Note that we're using the term "public good" in a peculiar way. To most people, "public good" refers to any good or service the government produces. In economics, however, the meaning is much more restrictive. The term "public good" refers only to those nonexcludable goods and services that must be consumed jointly, both by those who pay for them and by those who don't. Public goods can be produced by either the government or the private sector. Private goods can be produced in either sector as well. The problem is that ***the market tends to underproduce public goods and overproduce private goods.*** If we want more public goods, we need a *nonmarket* force—government intervention—to get them. The government will have to force people to pay taxes, then use the tax revenues to pay for the production of national defense, flood control, snow removal, and other public goods.

Externalities

The free-rider problem associated with public goods is one justification for government intervention. It's not the only justification, however. Further grounds for intervention arise from the tendency of costs or benefits of some market activities to "spill over" onto third parties.

Consider the case of cigarettes. The price someone is willing to pay for a pack of cigarettes reflects the amount of satisfaction a smoker anticipates from its consumption. If that price is high enough, tobacco companies will produce the cigarettes demanded. That is how market-based price signals are supposed to work. In this case, however, the price paid isn't a satisfactory signal of the product's desirability. The smoker's pleasure is offset in part by nonsmokers' *dis*pleasure. In this case, smoke literally spills over onto other consumers, causing them discomfort and possibly even ill health (see News below). Yet their loss isn't reflected in the market price: The harm caused to nonsmokers is *external* to the market price of cigarettes.

IN THE NEWS

U.S. Details Dangers of Secondhand Smoking

Secondhand smoke dramatically increases the risk of heart disease and lung cancer in non-smokers and can be controlled only by making indoor spaces smoke-free, according to a comprehensive report issued yesterday by U.S. Surgeon General Richard H. Carmona.

"The health effects of secondhand smoke exposure are more pervasive than we previously thought," Carmona said. "The scientific evidence is now indisputable: Secondhand smoke is not a mere annoyance. It is a serious health hazard that can lead to disease and premature death in children and nonsmoking adults."

According to the report, the government's most detailed statement ever on secondhand smoke, exposure to smoke at home or work increases the nonsmokers' risk of developing heart disease by 25 to 30 percent and lung cancer by 20 to 30 percent. It is especially danger-ous for children living with smokers and is known to cause sudden infant death syndrome, respiratory problems, ear infections and asthma attacks in infants and children. . . .

The report does not present new scientific data but is an analysis of the best research on secondhand smoke. It said, for instance, that the Centers for Disease Control and Prevention estimated last year that exposure to secondhand smoke kills more than 3,000 nonsmokers from lung cancer, approximately 46,000 from coronary heart disease, and as many as 430 new-borns from sudden infant death syndrome.

—Marc Kaufman

Source: *The Washington Post*, June 28, 2006, p. 1. © 2006, The Washington Post. Used with permission by PARS International Corp.

Analysis: The health risks imposed on nonsmokers via "passive smoke" represent external costs. The market price of cigarettes doesn't reflect these costs borne by third parties.

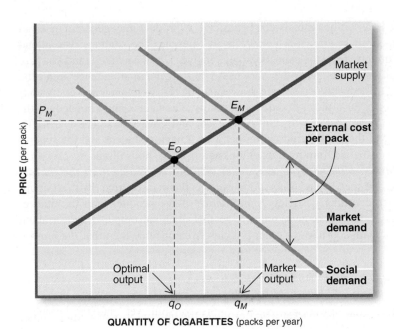

Second-hand Smokers pay for the problems.

FIGURE 4.3
Externalities

The market responds to consumer demands, not externalities. Smokers demand q_M cigarettes. But external costs on nonsmokers imply that the *social* demand for cigarettes is less than (below) *market* demand. The socially optimal level of output is q_O, less than the market output q_M.

*Figure labels:* PRICE (per pack); P_M; Market supply; E_M; E_O; External cost per pack; Market demand; Optimal output; Market output; Social demand; q_O; q_M; QUANTITY OF CIGARETTES (packs per year)

The term **externalities** refers to all costs or benefits of a market activity borne by a third party, that is, by someone other than the immediate producer or consumer. ***Whenever externalities are present, market prices aren't a valid measure of a good's value to society.*** As a consequence, the market will fail to produce the right mix of output. Specifically, ***the market will underproduce goods that yield external benefits and overproduce those that generate external costs.***

External Costs. Figure 4.3 shows how external costs cause the market to overproduce cigarettes. The market demand curve includes only the wishes of smokers, that is, people who are willing and able to purchase cigarettes. The forces of market demand and supply result in an equilibrium at E_M in which q_M cigarettes are produced and consumed. The market price P_M reflects the value of those cigarettes to smokers.

The well-being of *non*smokers isn't reflected in the market equilibrium. To take the *non*smoker's interests into account, we must subtract the external costs imposed on *them* from the value that *smokers* put on cigarettes. In general,

$$\text{Social demand} = \text{market demand} \pm \text{externalities}$$

In this case, the externality is a *cost,* so we must *subtract* the external cost from market demand to get a full accounting of social demand. The "social demand" curve in Figure 4.3 reflects this computation. To find this curve, we subtract the amount of external cost from every price on the market demand curve. What the *social* demand curve tells us is how much society would be willing and able to pay for cigarettes if the preferences of *both* smokers and nonsmokers were taken into account.

The social demand curve in Figure 4.3 creates a social equilibrium at E_O. At this juncture, we see that the socially *optimal* quantity of cigarettes is q_O, not the larger market-generated level at q_M. In this sense, the market produces too many cigarettes.

Externalities also exist in production. A power plant that burns high-sulfur coal damages the surrounding environment. Yet the damage inflicted on neighboring people, vegetation, and buildings is external to the cost calculations of the firm. Because the cost of such pollution is not reflected in the price of electricity, the firm will tend to produce more electricity (and pollution) than is socially desirable. To reduce this imbalance, the government has to step in and change market outcomes.

externalities: Costs (or benefits) of a market activity borne by a third party; the difference between the social and private costs (benefits) of a market activity.

External Benefits. Externalities can also be beneficial. A product may generate external *benefits* rather than external *costs*. Your college is an example. The students who attend your school benefit directly from the education they receive. That's why they (and you) are willing to *pay* for tuition, books, and other services. The students in attendance aren't the only beneficiaries of this educational service, however. The research that a university conducts may yield benefits for a much broader community. The values and knowledge students acquire may also be shared with family, friends, and co-workers. These benefits would all be *external* to the market transaction between a paying student and the school. Positive externalities also arise from immunizations against infectious diseases.

If a product yields external benefits, the social demand is greater than the market demand. In this case, the social value of the good *exceeds* the market price (by the amount of external benefit). Accordingly, society wants *more* of the product than the market mechanism alone will produce at any given price. To get that additional output, the government may have to intervene with subsidies or other policies. We conclude then that *the market fails by*

* *Overproducing goods that have external costs.*
* *Underproducing goods that have external benefits.*

If externalities are present, the market won't produce the optimal mix of output. To get that optimal mix, we need government intervention.

Market Power

In the case of both public goods and externalities, the market fails to achieve the optimal mix of output because the price signal is flawed. The price consumers are willing and able to pay for a specific good doesn't reflect all the benefits or cost of producing that good.

The market may fail, however, even when the price signals are accurate. The *response* to price signals, rather than the signals themselves, may be flawed.

Restricted Supply. Market power is often the cause of a flawed response. Suppose there were only one airline company in the world. This single seller of airline travel would be a **monopoly**—that is, the only producer in that industry. As a monopolist, the airline could charge extremely high prices without worrying that travelers would flock to a competing airline. At the same time, the high prices paid by consumers would express the importance of that service to society. Ideally, such prices would act as a signal to producers to build and fly more planes—to change the mix of output. But a monopolist doesn't have to cater to every consumer's whim. It can limit airline travel and obstruct our efforts to achieve an optimal mix of output.

Monopoly is the most severe form of **market power.** More generally, market power refers to any situation in which a single producer or consumer has the ability to alter the market price of a specific product. If the publisher (McGraw-Hill) charges a high price for this book, you'll have to pay the tab. McGraw-Hill has market power because there are relatively few economics textbooks and your professor has required you to use this one. You don't have power in the textbook market because your decision to buy or not won't alter the market price of this text. You're only one of the million students who are taking an introductory economics course this year.

The market power McGraw-Hill possesses is derived from the copyright on this text. No matter how profitable textbook sales might be, no one else is permitted to produce or sell this particular book. Patents are another common source of market power because they also preclude others from making or selling a specific product. Market power may also result from control of resources, restrictive production agreements, or efficiencies of large-scale production.

Whatever the source of market power, the direct consequence is that one or more producers attain discretionary power over the market's response to price signals. They may use that discretion to enrich themselves rather than to move the economy toward the optimal mix of output. In this case, the market will again fail to deliver the most desired goods and services.

monopoly: A firm that produces the entire market supply of a particular good or service.

market power: The ability to alter the market price of a good or a service.

The mandate for government intervention in this case is to prevent or dismantle concentrations of market power. That's the basic purpose of **antitrust** policy. Another option is to regulate market behavior. This was one of the goals of the antitrust case against Microsoft. The government was less interested in breaking Microsoft's near monopoly on operating systems than in changing the way Microsoft behaved.

In some cases, it may be economically efficient to have one large firm supply an entire market. Such a situation arises in **natural monopoly,** where a single firm can achieve economies of scale over the entire range of market output. Utility companies, local telephone service, subway systems, and cable all exhibit such scale (size) efficiencies. In these cases, a monopoly *structure* may be economically desirable. The government may have to regulate the *behavior* of a natural monopoly, however, to ensure that consumers get the benefits of that greater efficiency.

Public goods, externalities, and market power all cause resource misallocations. Where these phenomena exist, the market mechanism will fail to produce the optimal mix of output in the best-possible way.

Beyond the questions of WHAT and HOW to produce, we're also concerned about FOR WHOM output is produced. The market answers this question by distributing a larger share of total output to those with the most income. Although this result may be efficient, it's not necessarily equitable. As we saw in Chapter 2, the market mechanism may enrich some people while leaving others to seek shelter in abandoned cars. If such outcomes violate our vision of equity, we may want the government to change the market-generated distribution of income.

Taxes and Transfers. The tax-and-transfer system is the principal mechanism for redistributing incomes. The idea here is to take some of the income away from those who have "too much" and give it to those whom the market has left with "too little." Taxes are levied to take back some of the income received from the market. Those tax revenues are then redistributed via transfer payments to those deemed needy, such as the poor, the aged, the unemployed. **Transfer payments** are income payments for which no goods or services are exchanged. They're used to bolster the incomes of those for whom the market itself provides too little.

Merit Goods. Often, our vision of what is "too little" is defined in terms of specific goods and services. There is a widespread consensus in the United States that everyone is entitled to some minimum levels of shelter, food, and health care. These are regarded as **merit goods,** in the same sense that everyone merits at least some minimum provision of such goods. When the market does not distribute that minimum provision, the government is called on to fill in the gaps. In this case, the income transfers take the form of *in-kind* transfers (e.g., food stamps, housing vouchers, Medicaid) rather than *cash* transfers (e.g., welfare checks, Social Security benefits).

Some people argue that we don't need the government to help the poor—that private charity alone will suffice. Unfortunately, private charity alone has never been adequate. One reason private charity doesn't suffice is the "free-rider" problem. If I contribute heavily to the poor, you benefit from safer streets (fewer muggers), a better environment (fewer slums and homeless people), and a clearer conscience (knowing fewer people are starving). In this sense, the relief of misery is a *public* good. Were I the only taxpayer to benefit substantially from the reduction of poverty, then charity would be a private affair. As long as income support substantially benefits the public at large, then income redistribution is a *public* good, for which public funding is appropriate. This is the *economic* rationale for public income-redistribution activities. To this rationale one can add such moral arguments as seem appropriate.

The micro failures of the marketplace imply that we're at the wrong point on the production possibilities curve or inequitably distributing the output produced. There's another basic question we've swept under the rug, however. How do we get to the production

antitrust: Government intervention to alter market structure or prevent abuse of market power.

natural monopoly: An industry in which one firm can achieve economies of scale over the entire range of market supply.

Inequity

transfer payments: Payments to individuals for which no current goods or services are exchanged, like Social Security, welfare, and unemployment benefits.

merit good: A good or service society deems everyone is entitled to some minimal quantity of.

Macro Instability

unemployment: The inability of labor force participants to find jobs.

possibilities curve in the first place? To reach the curve, we must utilize all available resources and technology. Can we be confident that the invisible hand of the marketplace will use all available resources? That confidence was shattered in 2008–9 when total output contracted and **unemployment** soared. Millions of people who were willing and able to work but unable to find jobs demanded that the government intervene to increase output and create more jobs. The market had failed.

And what about prices? Price signals are a critical feature of the market mechanism. But the validity of those signals depends on some stable measure of value. What good is a doubling of salary when the price of everything you buy doubles as well? Generally, rising prices will enrich people who own property and impoverish people who rent. That's why we strive to avoid **inflation**—a situation in which the *average* price level is increasing.

inflation: An increase in the average level of prices of goods and services.

Historically, the marketplace has been wracked with bouts of both unemployment and inflation. These experiences have prompted calls for government intervention at the macro level. *The goal of macro intervention is to foster economic growth—to get us on the production possibilities curve (full employment), maintain a stable price level (price stability), and increase our capacity to produce (growth).*

GROWTH OF GOVERNMENT

The potential micro and macro failures of the marketplace provide specific justifications for government intervention. The question then turns to how well the activities of the public sector correspond to these implied mandates.

Federal Growth

Until the 1930s the federal government's role was largely limited to national defense (a public good), enforcement of a common legal system (also a public good), and provision of postal service (equity). The Great Depression of the 1930s spawned a new range of government activities, including welfare and Social Security programs (equity), minimum wage laws and workplace standards (regulation), and massive public works (public goods and externalities). In the 1950s the federal government also assumed a greater role in maintaining macroeconomic stability (macro failure), protecting the environment (externalities), and safeguarding the public's health (externalities and equity).

These increasing responsibilities have greatly increased the size of the public sector. In 1902 the federal government employed fewer than 350,000 people and spent a mere $650 *million.* Today the federal government employs nearly 4 million people and spends nearly $4 *trillion* a year.

Direct Expenditure. Figure 4.4 summarizes the growth of the public sector since 1930. World War II caused a massive increase in the size of the federal government. Federal purchases of goods and services for the war accounted for over 40 percent of total output during the 1943–44 period. The federal share of total U.S. output fell abruptly after World War II, rose again during the Korean War (1950–53), and has declined slightly since then.

The decline in the federal share of total output is somewhat at odds with most people's perception of government growth. This discrepancy is explained by two phenomena. First, people see the *absolute* size of the government growing every year. But we're focusing here on the *relative* size of the public sector. Since the 1950s the public sector has grown a bit more slowly than the private sector, slightly reducing its relative size.

web analysis

Information on government expenditures and national economic output for different countries can be found at **www.cia.gov.** Visit the "World Factbook" link.

Income Transfers. Second, Figure 4.4 depicts only government spending on goods and services, not *all* public spending. Direct expenditure on goods and services absorbs real resources, but income transfers don't. Hence, income transfers don't directly alter the mix of output. Their effect is primarily *distributional* (the FOR WHOM question), not *allocative* (the WHAT question). Were income transfers included, the relative size and growth of the federal government would be larger than Figure 4.4 depicts. This is because *most of the growth in federal spending has come from increased income transfers, not purchases of goods and services.* Income transfers now account for over half of federal spending.

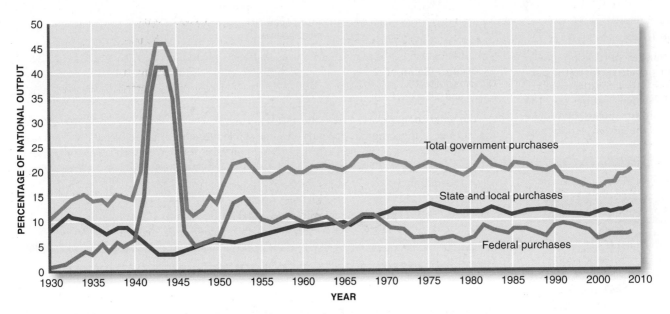

FIGURE 4.4
Government Growth

During World War II the public sector purchased nearly half of total U.S. output. Since the early 1950s the public-sector share of total output has been closer to 20 percent. Within the public sector, however, there's been a major shift: State and local claims on resources have grown, while the federal share has declined significantly.

Source: U.S. Bureau of Economic Analysis.

State and local spending on goods and services has followed a very different path from federal expenditure. Prior to World War II, state and local governments dominated public-sector spending. During the war, however, the share of total output going to state and local governments fell, hitting a low of 3 percent in that period (Figure 4.4).

State and local spending caught up with federal spending in the mid-1960s and has exceeded it ever since. Today *more than 80,000 state and local government entities buy much more output than Uncle Sam and employ five times as many people.* Education is a huge expenditure at lower levels of government. Most direct state spending is on colleges; most local spending is for elementary and secondary education. The fastest-growing areas for state expenditure are prisons (public safety) and welfare. At the local level, sewage and trash services are claiming an increasing share of budgets.

State and Local Growth

TAXATION

Whatever we may think of any specific government expenditure, we must recognize one basic fact of life: We pay for government spending. We pay not just in terms of tax *dollars* but in the more fundamental form of a changed mix of output. Government expenditures on goods and services absorb factors of production that could be used to produce consumer goods. The mix of output changes toward *more* public services and *less* private goods and services. Resources used to produce missile shields, operate elementary schools, or journey to Mars aren't available to produce cars, houses, or restaurant meals. In real terms, *the cost of government spending is measured by the private-sector output sacrificed when the government employs scarce factors of production.*

The **opportunity costs** of public spending aren't always apparent. We don't directly hand over factors of production to the government. Instead, we give the government part of

opportunity costs: The most desired goods or services that are forgone in order to obtain something else.

FIGURE 4.5
Federal Taxes

Taxes transfer purchasing power from the private sector to the public sector. The largest federal tax is the individual income tax. The second-largest source of federal revenue is the Social Security payroll tax.

Source: Office of Management and Budget, FY2010 data.

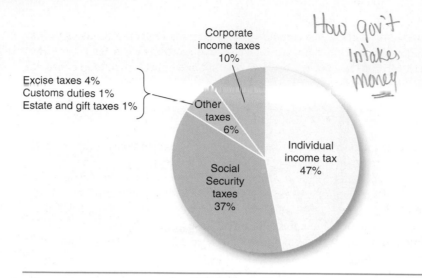

How gov't intakes money

web analysis

For the most recent budget information, visit the Office of Management and Budget Web site (**www.whitehouse.gov/omb**), and click on the "Budget Fact Sheets" link.

our income in the form of taxes. Those dollars are then used to buy factors of production or goods and services in the marketplace. Thus, ***the primary function of taxes is to transfer command over resources (purchasing power) from the private sector to the public sector.*** Although the government also borrows dollars to finance its purchases, taxes are the primary source of government revenues.

Federal Taxes

As recently as 1902, much of the revenue the federal government collected came from taxes imposed on alcoholic beverages. The federal government didn't have authority to collect income taxes. As a consequence, *total* federal revenue in 1902 was only $653 million.

Income Taxes. All that has changed. The Sixteenth Amendment to the U.S. Constitution, enacted in 1915, granted the federal government authority to collect income taxes. The government now collects over $1 *trillion* in that form alone. Although the federal government still collects taxes on alcoholic beverages, the individual income tax has become the largest single source of government revenue (see Figure 4.5).

progressive tax: A tax system in which tax rates rise as incomes rise.

In theory, the federal income tax is designed to be **progressive**—that is, to take a larger *fraction* of high incomes than of low incomes. In 2008, for example, a single person with less than $8,025 of taxable income was taxed at 10 percent. People with incomes of $32,550–$78,850 confronted a 25 percent tax rate on their additional income. The marginal tax rate got as high as 35 percent for people earning more than $350,000 in income. Thus ***people with high incomes not only pay more taxes but also pay a larger*** fraction ***of their income in taxes.***

Social Security Taxes. The second major source of federal revenue is the Social Security payroll tax. People working now transfer part of their earnings to retired workers by making "contributions" to Social Security. There's nothing voluntary about these "contributions"; they take the form of mandatory payroll deductions. In 2009, each worker paid 7.65 percent of his or her wages to Social Security and employers contributed an equal amount. As a consequence, the government collected nearly $1 trillion from this tax.

proportional tax: A tax that levies the same rate on every dollar of income.

At first glance, the Social Security payroll tax looks like a **proportional tax,** that is, a tax that takes the *same* fraction of every taxpayer's income. But this isn't the case. The Social Security (FICA) tax isn't levied on every payroll dollar. Incomes above a certain ceiling ($106,800 in 2009) aren't taxed. As a result, workers with *really* high salaries turn over a smaller fraction of their incomes to Social Security than do low-wage workers. This makes the Social Security payroll tax a **regressive tax.**

regressive tax: A tax system in which tax rates fall as incomes rise.

FICA only takes first $106,800 of income to tax.

Corporate Taxes. The federal government taxes the profits of corporations as well as the incomes of consumers. But there are far fewer corporations (less than 4 million) than consumers (310 million), and their profits are small in comparison to total consumer income. In 2008, the federal government collected only $250 billion in corporate income taxes, despite the fact that it imposed a top tax rate of 35 percent on corporate profits.

Excise Taxes. The last major source of federal revenue is excise taxes. Like the early taxes on whiskey, excise taxes are sales taxes imposed on specific goods and services. The federal government taxes not only liquor ($13.50 per gallon) but also gasoline (18.4 cents per gallon), cigarettes (39 cents per pack), air fares, firearms (10–11 percent), gambling (0.25 percent), and a variety of other goods and services. Such taxes not only discourage production and consumption of these goods—by raising their price and thereby reducing the quantity demanded—they also raise a substantial amount of revenue.

Taxes. State and local governments also levy taxes on consumers and businesses. In general, cities depend heavily on property taxes, and state governments rely heavily on sales taxes. Although nearly all states and many cities also impose income taxes, effective tax rates are so low (averaging less than 2 percent of personal income) that income tax revenues are much less than sales and property tax revenues.

Like the Social Security payroll tax, state and local taxes tend to be *regressive*—that is, they take a larger share of income from the poor than from the rich. Consider a 4 percent sales tax, for example. It might appear that a uniform tax rate like this would affect all consumers equally. But people with lower incomes tend to spend most of their income on goods and services. Thus, most of their income is subject to sales taxes. By contrast, a person with a high income can afford to save part of his or her income and thereby shelter it from sales taxes. A family that earns $40,000 and spends $30,000 of it on taxable goods and services, for example, pays $1,200 in sales taxes when the tax rate is 4 percent. In effect, then, they are handing over 3 percent of their *income* ($1,200 ÷ $40,000) to the state. By contrast, the family that makes only $12,000 and spends $11,500 of it for food, clothing, and shelter pays $460 in sales taxes in the same state. Their total tax is smaller, but it represents a much larger *share* (3.8 versus 3.0 percent) of their income.

Local property taxes are also regressive because poor people devote a larger portion of their incomes to housing costs. Hence, a larger share of a poor family's income is subject

State and Local Revenues

[handwritten note: Higher up in tax bracket are taxed less.]

"I can't find anything wrong here, Mr. Truffle . . . you just seem to have too much left after taxes."

Analysis: Taxes are a financing mechanism that enable the government to purchase scarce resources. Higher taxes imply less private-sector purchases.

Perpetuating Poverty: Lotteries Prey on the Poor

A recently released Gallup survey confirms the fears of many who oppose government-promoted gambling: the poorest among us are contributing much more to lottery revenues than those with higher incomes. The poll found that people who played the lottery with an income of less than $20,000 annually spent an average of $46 per month on lottery tickets. That comes out to more than $550 per year and it is nearly double the amount spent in any other income bracket.

The significance of this is magnified when we look deeper into the figures. Those with annual incomes ranging from $30,000 to $50,000 had the second-highest average—$24 per month, or $288 per year. A person making $20,000 spends three times as much on lottery tickets on average than does someone making $30,000. And keep in mind that these numbers represent average spending. For every one or two people who spend just a few bucks a year on lotteries, others spend thousands.

—Jordan Ballor

Source: Action Institute. March 3, 2004. From "Perpetuating Poverty: Lotteries Prey on the Poor" by Jordan Ballor, **www.action.org.** Used with permission by the author.

Analysis: Poor people spend a larger percentage of their income on lottery tickets than do rich people. This makes lotteries a regressive source of government revenue.

to property taxes. State lotteries are also regressive, for the same reason (see News). Low-income players spend 1.4 percent of their incomes on lottery tickets while upper-income players devote only 0.1 percent of their income to lottery purchases.

GOVERNMENT FAILURE

Some government intervention in the marketplace is clearly desirable. The market mechanism can fail for a variety of reasons, leaving a laissez-faire economy short of its economic goals. But how much government intervention is desirable? Communist nations once thought that complete government control of production, consumption, and distribution decisions was the surest path to utopia. They learned the hard way that *not only markets but governments as well can fail.* In this context, **government failure** means that government intervention fails to move us closer to our economic goals.

In Figure 4.6, the goal of government intervention is to move the mix of output from point *M* (failed market outcome) to point *X* (the social optimum). But government intervention

government failure: Government intervention that fails to improve economic outcomes.

FIGURE 4.6
Government Failure

When the market produces a suboptimal mix of output (point *M*), the goal of government is to move output to the social optimum (point *X*). A move to G_4 would be an improvement in the mix of output. But government intervention *may* move the economy to points G_1, G_2, or G_3—all reflecting government failure.

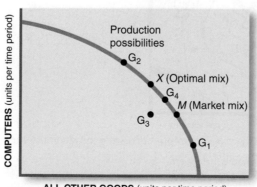

might unwittingly move us to point G_1, making matters worse. Or the government might overreact, sending us to point G_2. Red tape and onerous regulation might even force us to point G_3, *inside* the production possibilities curve (with less total output than at point M). All those possibilities (G_1, G_2, G_3) represent government failure. Government intervention is desirable only to the extent that it *improves* market outcomes (e.g., G_4). Government intervention in the FOR WHOM question is desirable only if the distribution of income gets better, not worse, as a result of taxes and transfers. Even when outcomes improve, government failure may occur if the costs of government intervention exceeded the benefits of an improved output mix, cleaner production methods, or a fairer distribution of income.

Perceptions of Waste

Taxpayers seem to have strong opinions about government failure. When asked whether the government "wastes" their tax dollars or uses them well, the majority see waste in government (see News on "Persistent Doubts"). The average taxpayer now believes that state governments waste 29 cents out of each dollar, while the federal government wastes 42 cents out of each tax dollar!

Makes me very happy when paying taxes ... not

Persistent Doubts about Government Waste

Question: Do you think that people in government waste a lot of the money we pay in taxes, waste some of it, or don't waste very much of it?

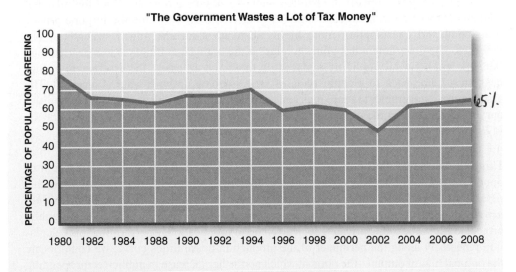

"The Government Wastes a Lot of Tax Money"

65%

Source: American National Election Studies (**www.electionstudies.org**).

Analysis: Market failure justifies government intervention. If the government wastes resources, however, it too may fail to satisfy our economic goals.

web analysis

For more public opinion on the role of government, visit the American National Election Studies Web site at **www.electionstudies.org**.

Government "waste" implies that the public sector isn't producing as many services as it could with the resources at its disposal. Such inefficiency implies that we're producing somewhere *inside* our production possibilities curve rather than on it (e.g., point G_3 in Figure 4.6). If the government is wasting resources this way, we can't possibly be producing the optimal mix of output.

Affects the PPC!

Opportunity Cost

Even if the government weren't wasting resources, it might still be guilty of government failure. As important as efficiency in government may be, it begs the larger question of how many government services we really want. In reality, *the issue of government waste encompasses two distinct questions:*

- *Efficiency:* Are we getting as much service as we could from the resources we allocate to government?
- *Opportunity cost:* Are we giving up too many private-sector goods in order to get those services?

If the government is producing goods inefficiently, we end up *inside* the production possibilities curve, with less output than attainable. Even if the government is efficient, however, the *mix* of output may not be optimal, as points G_1 and G_2 in Figure 4.6 illustrate. *Everything the government does entails an opportunity cost.* The more police officers or schoolteachers employed by the public sector, the fewer workers available to private producers and consumers. Similarly, the more computers, pencils, and paper consumed by government agencies, the fewer accessible to individuals and private companies.

When assessing government's role in the economy, *we must consider not only what governments do but also what we give up to allow them to do it.* The theory of public goods tells us only what activities are appropriate for government, not the proper *level* of such activity. National defense is clearly a proper function of the public sector. Not so clear, however, is how much the government should spend on tanks, aircraft carriers, and missile shields. The same is true of environmental protection or law enforcement.

The concept of opportunity costs puts a new perspective on the whole question of government size. Before we can decide how big is "too big," we must decide what we're willing to give up to support the public sector. A military force of 1.4 million men and women is "too big" from an economic perspective only if we value the forgone private production and consumption more highly than we value the added strength of our defenses. The government has gone "too far" if the highway it builds is less desired than the park and homes it implicitly replaced. In these and all cases, the assessment of bigness must come back to a comparison of what is given up with what is received. The assessment of government failure thus comes back to points on the production possibilities curve. Has the government moved us closer to the optimal mix of output (e.g., point G_4 in Figure 4.6) or not?

Cost-Benefit Analysis

This is a tough question to answer in the abstract. We can, however, use the concept of opportunity cost to assess the effectiveness of specific government interventions. From this perspective, *additional public-sector activity is desirable only if the benefits from that activity exceed its opportunity costs.* In other words, we compare the benefits of a public project to the value of the private goods given up to produce it. By performing this calculation repeatedly along the perimeter of the production possibilities curve, we could locate the optimal mix of output—the point at which no further increase in public-sector spending activity is desirable.

Valuation Problems. Although the principles of cost-benefit analysis are simple enough, they're deceptive. How are we to measure the potential benefits of improved police services, for example? Should we estimate the number of robberies and murders prevented, calculate the worth of each, and add up the benefits? And how are we supposed to calculate the worth of a saved life? By a person's earnings? value of assets? number of friends? And what about the increased sense of security people have when they know the police are patrolling in their neighborhood? Should this be included in the benefit calculation? Some people will attach great value to this service; others will attach little. Whose values should be the standard?

When we're dealing with (private) market goods and services, we can gauge the benefits of a product by the amount of money consumers are willing to pay for it. This price signal isn't available for most public services, however, because of externalities and the nonexclusive nature of pure public goods (the free-rider problem). Hence, *the value (benefits) of public services must be estimated because they don't have (reliable) market prices.* This opens the door to endless political squabbles about how beneficial any particular government activity is.

The same problems arise in evaluating the government's efforts to redistribute incomes. Government transfer payments now go to retired workers, disabled people, veterans, farmers, sick people, students, pregnant women, unemployed people, poor people, and a long list of other recipients. To pay for all these transfers, the government must raise tax revenues. With so many people paying taxes and receiving transfer payments, the net effects on the distribution of income aren't easy to figure out. Yet we can't determine whether this government intervention is worth it until we know how the FOR WHOM answer was changed and what the tax-and-transfer effort cost us.

In practice, we rely on political mechanisms, not cost-benefit calculations, to decide what to produce in the public sector and how to redistribute incomes. *Voting mechanisms substitute for the market mechanism in allocating resources to the public sector and deciding how to use them.* Some people have even suggested that the variety and volume of public goods are determined by the most votes, just as the variety and volume of private goods are determined by the most dollars. Thus, governments choose that level and mix of output (and related taxation) that seem to command the most votes.

Ballot Box Economics

By your votes you will try to determine the future of your nation

Sometimes the link between the ballot box and output decisions is very clear and direct. State and local governments, for example, are often compelled to get voter approval before building another highway, school, housing project, or sewage plant. *Bond referenda* are direct requests by a government unit for voter approval of specific public-spending projects (e.g., roads, schools). In 2008, for example, governments sought voter approval for $20 billion of new borrowing to finance public expenditure; over 70 percent of those requests were approved.

Bond referenda are more the exception than the rule. Bond referenda account for less than 1 percent of state and local expenditures (and none of federal expenditures). As a consequence, voter control of public spending is typically much less direct. Although federal agencies must receive authorization from Congress for all expenditures, consumers get a chance to elect new representatives only every 2 years. Much the same is true at state and local levels. Voters may be in a position to dictate the general level and pattern of public expenditures but have little direct influence on everyday output decisions. In this sense, the ballot box is a poor substitute for the market mechanism.

Even if the link between the ballot box and allocation decisions were stronger, the resulting mix of output might not be optimal. A democratic vote, for example, might yield a 51 percent majority for approval of new local highways. Should the highways then be built? The answer isn't obvious. After all, a large minority (49 percent) of the voters have stated that they don't want resources used this way. If we proceed to build the highways, we'll make those people worse off. Their loss may be greater than what proponents gain. Hence, the basic dilemma is really twofold. *We don't know what the real demand for public services is, and votes alone don't reflect the intensity of individual demands.* Moreover, real-world decision making involves so many choices that a stable consensus is impossible.

Public-Choice Theory

In the midst of all this complexity and uncertainty, another factor may be decisive—namely, self-interest. In principle, government officials are supposed to serve the people. It doesn't take long, however, before officials realize that the public is indecisive about what it wants and takes very little interest in government's day-to-day activities. With such latitude, government officials can set their own agendas. Those agendas may give higher priority to personal advancement than to the needs of the public. Agency directors may foster new programs that enlarge their mandate, enhance their visibility, and increase their prestige or income. Members of Congress may likewise pursue legislative favors like tax breaks for supporters more diligently than they pursue the general public interest. In such cases, the probability of attaining the socially optimal mix of output declines.

> **public choice:** Theory of public-sector behavior emphasizing rational self-interest of decision makers and voters.

The theory of **public choice** emphasizes the role of self-interest in public decision making. Public-choice theory essentially extends the analysis of market behavior to political behavior. Public officials are assumed to have specific personal goals (for example, power, recognition, wealth) that they'll pursue in office. *A central tenet of public-choice theory is that bureaucrats are just as selfish (utility maximizing) as everyone else.*

Public-choice theory provides a neat and simple explanation for public-sector decision making. But critics argue that the theory provides a woefully narrow view of public servants. Some people do selflessly pursue larger, public goals, such critics argue, and ideas can overwhelm self-interest. Steven Kelman of Harvard, for example, argues that narrow self-interest can't explain the War on Poverty of the 1960s, the tax revolt of the 1970s, or the deregulation movement of the 1980s. These tidal changes in public policy reflect the power of ideas, not simple self-interest.

Although self-interest can't provide a complete explanation of public decision making, it adds important perspectives on the policy process. James Buchanan of George Mason University (Virginia) won the 1986 Nobel Prize in Economics for helping develop this public-choice perspective. It adds a personal dimension to the faceless mechanics of ballot box economics, cost-benefit analysis, and other "objective" mechanisms of public-sector decision making.

THE ECONOMY TOMORROW

DOWNSIZING GOVERNMENT?

The Great Depression of the 1930s devastated the world economy. For many people, it was compelling evidence that the market alone couldn't be trusted to answer the WHAT, HOW, and FOR WHOM questions. With unemployment, hunger, and homelessness at record levels, people everywhere turned to government for help. In the United States, Franklin Roosevelt's New Deal envisioned a more activist government, restoring full employment and assuring everyone some minimal level of economic security. In Eastern Europe, the Communist Party advanced the notion that outright government *control* of the economy was the only sure way to attain economic justice for all.

Confidence in the ability of government to resolve core economic issues continued to increase in the post–World War II era. Securing national defenses during the Cold War (1948–89) justified the maintenance of a large military establishment, both in the United States and elsewhere. The War on Poverty that began in the mid-1960s brought about a huge increase in government social programs and income transfers. As the U.S. population has aged, the government's health care and retirement programs (e.g., Social Security, Medicare) have grown rapidly. In each case, there was a political consensus that expanded public services would enhance society's welfare. That consensus helped grow *total* federal spending (including purchases and income transfers) from 17 percent of GDP in 1965 to over 23 percent in 1982.

Public opinion didn't keep pace with the growth of government. Opinion polls revealed that people weren't convinced that government intervention was the surest way to resolve economic problems. President Reagan campaigned successfully on the promise of *reducing* government interference in the marketplace. With massive tax cuts and deregulation he tried to curb government growth in social programs.

The end of the Cold War created a unique opportunity to reduce military spending as well. Between 1991 and 1998 military spending declined every year and the armed forces shrank by nearly 500,000 personnel. In the process, the federal share of output gradually declined (see Figure 4.4). By 2000 total government spending had declined to 18 percent of GDP.

The decline in government spending wasn't confined to the United States. The collapse of the Soviet Union motivated market-oriented reforms throughout eastern Europe and Asia. In Europe and Latin America governments downsized by privatizing government-owned railroads, airlines, telephone service, and even postal service. In the process, the global economy became more market-driven and less government-directed.

The Post-9/11 Defense Buildup. The terrorist attacks of 9/11 reversed the slow downtrend in U.S. government spending. Defense expenditures increased by 50 percent in only 3 years (2002–4). Homeland security and the war in Iraq also expanded the government's claim on the economy's resources.

The global recession of 2008–9 expanded the government's share of total output yet further. Governments around the world expanded public-works spending and income-transfer programs as part of their economic recovery programs. President Obama also sought more permanent expansion of the government's role in health care and alternative energy supplies.

The longer-run trend in government growth isn't clear. Despite lingering doubts about government performance (see News), the worldwide war against terrorism is likely to keep defense expenditures at a high level for many years. The aging of the population in the United States, Europe, and Asia will also increase demands for public pensions and health care. Accordingly, governments aren't likely to resume shrinking. Whatever the size of the public sector turns out to be, the continuing challenge will be to promote optimal WHAT, HOW, and FOR WHOM outcomes in the economy tomorrow.

IN THE NEWS

Little Confidence in Government

Public-opinion polls reveal that Americans have little confidence in government, as the following responses illustrate.

Question: How much of the time do you think you can trust the government in Washington to do what is right—just about always, most of the time, or only some of the time?

Answers	
Just about always	5%
Most of the time	25%
Some of the time	68%
Never (vol.)	2%

Source: American National Election Studies, 2008 (**www.electionstudies.org**).

Analysis: In principle, governments intervene to remedy market failure. But the public has little confidence in government performance.

SUMMARY

- Government intervention in the marketplace is justified by market failure, that is, suboptimal market outcomes. LO1
- The micro failures of the market originate in public goods, externalities, market power, and an inequitable distribution of income. These flaws deter the market from achieving the optimal mix of output or distribution of income. LO1
- Public goods are those that can't be consumed exclusively; they're jointly consumed regardless of who pays. Because everyone seeks a free ride, no one demands public goods in the marketplace. Hence, the market underproduces public goods. LO1
- Externalities are costs (or benefits) of a market transaction borne by a third party. Externalities create a divergence between social and private costs or benefits, causing suboptimal market outcomes. The market overproduces goods with external costs and underproduces goods with external benefits. LO1
- Market power enables a producer to thwart market signals and maintain a suboptimal mix of output. Antitrust policy seeks to prevent or restrict market power. The government may also regulate the behavior of powerful firms. LO1
- The market-generated distribution of income may be unfair. This inequity may prompt the government to intervene with taxes and transfer payments that redistribute incomes. LO1

- The macro failures of the marketplace are reflected in unemployment and inflation. Government intervention is intended to achieve full employment and price stability. LO1
- The federal government expanded greatly after 1930. More recent growth has been in transfer payments, defense spending, and health programs. LO2
- State and local governments purchase more output (12 percent of GDP) than the federal government (7 percent) and employ five times as many workers. LO2
- Income and payroll taxes provide most federal revenues. States get most revenue from sales taxes; local governments rely on property taxes. LO2
- Government failure occurs when intervention moves us away from rather than toward the optimal mix of output (or income). Failure may result from outright waste (operational inefficiency) or from a misallocation of resources. LO3
- All government activity must be evaluated in terms of its opportunity cost, that is, the *private* goods and services forgone to make resources available to the public sector. LO2
- Allocation decisions within the public sector may be based on cost-benefit analysis or votes. The self-interests of government agents may also affect decisions of when and how to intervene. LO2

Key Terms

optimal mix of output	monopoly	inflation
market mechanism	market power	opportunity cost
market failure	antitrust	progressive tax
private good	natural monopoly	proportional tax
public good	transfer payments	regressive tax
free rider	merit good	government failure
externalities	unemployment	public choice

Questions for Discussion

1. Why should taxpayers subsidize public colleges and universities? What external benefits are generated by higher education? LO1
2. If everyone seeks a free ride, what mix of output will be produced in Figure 4.2? Why would anyone voluntarily contribute to the purchase of public goods like flood control or snow removal? LO1
3. Could local fire departments be privately operated, with their services sold directly to customers? What problems would be involved in such a system? LO1
4. Why might Fourth of July fireworks be considered a public good? Who should pay for them? What about airport security? LO1

5. What is the specific market-failure justification for government spending on (*a*) public universities, (*b*) health care, (*c*) trash pickup, (*d*) highways, (*e*) police? Would a purely private economy produce any of these services? LO1

6. If smoking generates external costs, should smoking simply be outlawed? How about cars that pollute? LO1

7. The government now spends over $700 billion a year on Social Security benefits. Why don't we leave it to individuals to save for their own retirement? LO1

8. What government actions might cause failures like points G_1, G_2, and G_3 in Figure 4.6? Can you give examples? LO3

9. How does XM Satellite deter nonsubscribers from listening to its transmissions? Does this make radio programming a private good or a public good? LO1

10. Should the government be downsized? Which functions should be cut back? LO2

web activities to accompany this chapter can be found on the Online Learning Center:
http://www.mhhe.com/schiller12e

LO1   1. In Figure 4.2, by how much is the market
        (a) Overproducing private goods?   (u) _____
        (b) Underproducing public goods?   (b) _____

LO1   2. Use Figure 4.3 to illustrate on the accompanying production
        possibilities curve
        (a) The market mix of output (M).
        (b) The optimal mix of output (X).

LO1   3. Assume that the product depicted below generates external
        costs in consumption of $4 per unit.
        (a) Draw the social demand curve.
        (b) What is the socially optimal output?   (b) _____
        (c) By how much does the market overproduce this good?   (c) _____

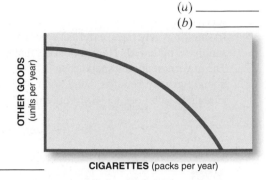

OTHER GOODS (units per year)

CIGARETTES (packs per year)

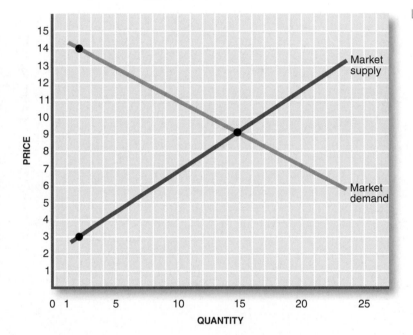

LO1   4. In the previous problem's
        market equilibrium, what is
        (a) The market value of
            the good?   _____
        (b) The social value of
            the good?   _____

LO1   5. If the average adult produces $75,000 of output per year, how much output is lost as a result of
        deaths from secondhand smoke, according to the News on page 70? $ _____

LO2   6. (a) Assuming a 10 percent sales tax is levied on all consumption, complete the following table:

Income	Consumption	Sales Tax	Percent of Income Paid in Taxes
$10,000	$12,000	_____	_____
20,000	18,000	_____	_____
40,000	32,000	_____	_____
80,000	60,000	_____	_____

        (b) Is the sales tax progressive or regressive?   _____

LO2 7. If a new home can be constructed for $150,000, what is the opportunity cost of federal defense spending, measured in terms of private housing? (Assume a defense budget of $600 billion.) _____

LO1 8. Suppose the following data represent the market demand for college education:

Tuition (per year)	$1,000	2,000	3,000	4,000	5,000	6,000	7,000	8,000
Enrollment demanded (in millions per year)	8	7	6	5	4	3	2	1

(a) If tuition is set at $4,000, how many students will enroll? _____

Now suppose that society gets an external benefit of $1,000 for every enrolled student.

(b) Draw the social and market demand curves for this situation on the graph below (left).
(c) What is the socially optimal level of enrollments at the same tuition price of $4,000? _____
(d) How large of a subsidy is needed to achieve this optimal outcome? _____

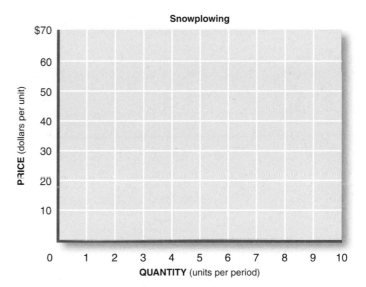

LO1 9. Suppose the following data represent the prices that each of three consumers is willing to pay for snowplowing:

Quantity	Consumer A	Consumer B	Consumer C
1	$50	$40	$30
2	30	20	20
3	20	15	10

(a) Construct the market demand curve for snowplowing on the graph above (right).
(b) If the market price of snowplowing were $40, how many units would be demanded? _____
(c) Now suppose that this is a public good, in the sense that all consumers receive satisfaction from the good even if only one person buys it. Under these conditions, what is the social value of the
  (i) First unit? _____
  (ii) Second unit? _____

LO2 10. According to the News on page 78, what percent of income is spent on lottery tickets by
(a) A poor family with income of $18,000 per year? _____
(b) An affluent family with income of $40,000 per year? _____

GDP - with a
nations borders
_____ be given
same period

GNP ___ output ___
produced by ___
___

PART 2

Measuring Macro Outcomes

Macroeconomics focuses on the performance of the entire economy rather than on the behavior of individual participants (a micro concern). The central concerns of macroeconomics are (1) the short-term business cycle and (2) long-term economic growth. In the long run, the goal is to expand the economy's capacity to produce goods and services, thereby raising future living standards. In the short run, the emphasis is on fully using available capacity, thereby maximizing output and minimizing unemployment. Chapters 5 through 7 focus on the measurement tools used to gauge the nation's macroeconomic performance (both short run and long run). Also examined are the social and economic damage caused by the problems of unemployment and inflation.

National-Income Accounting

5

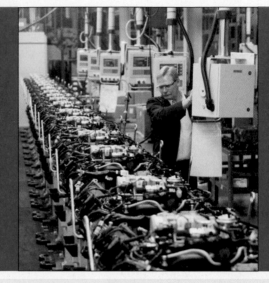

A favorite cliché of policymakers in Washington is that government likes to tackle only those problems it can measure. Politicians need visible results. They want to be able to brag to their constituents about the miles of new highways built, the number of students who graduated, the number of families that left welfare, and the number of unemployed workers who found jobs. To do this, they must be able to measure economic outcomes.

The Great Depression of the 1930s was an object lesson in the need for better measures of economic performance. There were plenty of anecdotes about factories closing, farms failing, and people selling apples on the streets. But nobody knew the dimensions of the nation's economic meltdown until millions of workers had lost their jobs. The need for more timely information about the health of the national economy was evident. From that experience a commitment to **national-income accounting**—the measurement of aggregate economic activity—emerged. During the 1930s the economist Simon Kuznets (who later received a Nobel Prize for his work) and the U.S. Department of Commerce developed an accounting system that gauges the economy's health. That national-accounting system now churns out reams of data that are essential to tracking the economy's performance. They answer such questions as

- **How much output is being produced? What is it being used for?**
- **How much income is being generated in the marketplace?**
- **What's happening to prices and wages?**

It's tempting, of course, to ignore all these measurement questions, especially since they tend to be rather dull. But if we avoid measurement problems, we severely limit our ability to understand how the economy works or how well (or poorly) it's performing. We also limit our ability to design policies for improving economic performance.

National-income accounting also provides a useful perspective on the way the economy works. It shows how factor markets relate to product markets, how output relates to income, and how consumer spending and business investment relate to production. It also shows how the flow of taxes and government spending may alter economic outcomes.

MEASURES OF OUTPUT

The array of goods and services we produce is truly massive, including everything from professional baseball to guided-missile systems. All these things are part of our total output; the problem is to find a summary measure.

Itemizing the amount of each good or service produced each year won't solve our measurement problems. The resulting list would be so long that it would be both unwieldy and meaningless. We couldn't even add it up, since it would contain diverse goods measured in a variety of units (e.g., miles, packages, pounds, quarts). Nor could we compare one year's output to another's. Suppose that last year we produced 2 billion oranges, 2 million bicycles, and 700 rock concerts, whereas this year we produced 3 billion oranges, 4 million bicycles, and 600 rock concerts. Which year's output was larger? With more of some goods, but less of others, the answer isn't obvious.

To facilitate our accounting chores, we need some mechanism for organizing annual output data into a more manageable summary. The mechanism we use is price. *Each good and service produced and brought to market has a price. That price serves as a measure of value for calculating total output.* Consider again the problem of determining how much output was produced this year and last. There's no obvious way to answer this question in physical terms alone. But once we know the price of each good, we can calculate the *value* of output produced. The total dollar value of final output produced each year is called the **gross domestic product (GDP).** GDP is simply the sum of all final goods and services produced for the market in a given time period, with each good or service valued at its market price.

Table 5.1 illustrates the use of prices to value total output in two hypothetical years. If oranges were 20 cents each last year and 2 billion oranges were produced, then the *value* of orange production last year was $400 million ($0.20 × 2 billion). In the same manner, we can determine that the value of bicycle production was $100 million and the value of rock

national-income accounting: The measurement of aggregate economic activity, particularly national income and its components.

Gross Domestic Product

Simon Kuznitz

gross domestic product (GDP): The total market value of all final goods and services produced within a nation's borders in a given time period.

Output	Amount
a. Last Year's Output	
In physical terms:	
Oranges	2 billion
Bicycles	2 million
Rock concerts	700
Total	?
In monetary terms:	
2 billion oranges @ $0.20 each	$ 400 million
2 million bicycles @ $50 each	100 million
700 rock concerts @ $1 million each	700 million
Total	$1,200 million
b. This Year's Output	
In physical terms:	
Oranges	3 billion
Bicycles	4 million
Rock concerts	600
Total	?
In monetary terms:	
3 billion oranges @ $0.20 each	$ 600 million
4 million bicycles @ $50 each	200 million
600 rock concerts @ $1 million each	600 million
Total	$1,400 million

TABLE 5.1
The Measurement of Output

It's impossible to add up all output when output is counted in *physical* terms. Accordingly, total output is measured in *monetary* terms, with each good or service valued at its market price. GDP refers to the total market value of all goods and services produced in a given time period. According to the numbers in this table, the total *value* of the oranges, bicycles, and rock concerts produced "last" year was $1.2 billion and $1.4 billion "this" year.

concerts was $700 million. By adding these figures, we can say that the value of last year's production—last year's GDP—was $1,200 million (Table 5.1*a*).

Now we're in a position to compare one year's output to another's. Table 5.1*b* shows that the use of prices enables us to say that the *value* of this year's output is $1,400 million. Hence, *total output* has increased from one year to the next. ***The use of prices to value market output allows us to summarize output activity and to compare the output of one period with that of another.***

GDP vs. GNP. The concept of GDP is of relatively recent use in U.S. national-income accounts. Prior to 1992, most U.S. statistics focused on gross *national* product or G*N*P. Gross *national* product refers to the output produced by American-owned factors of production regardless of where they're located. Gross *domestic* product refers to output produced within America's borders. Thus, GNP would include some output from an Apple computer factory in Singapore but exclude some of the output produced by a Honda factory in Ohio. In an increasingly global economy, where factors of production and ownership move easily across international borders, the calculations of GNP became ever more complex. It also became a less dependable measure of the nation's economic health. ***GDP is geographically focused, including all output produced within a nation's borders regardless of whose factors of production are used to produce it.*** Apple's output in Singapore ends up in Singapore's GDP; the cars produced at Honda's Ohio plant are counted in America's GDP.

International Comparisons. The geographic focus of GDP facilitates international comparisons of economic activity. Is Japan's output as large as that of the United States'? How could you tell? Japan produces a mix of output different from ours, making *quantity*-based comparisons difficult. We can compare the *value* of output produced in each country, however. The World View "Comparative Output" in Chapter 2 (p. 28) shows that the value of America's GDP is three times larger than Japan's.

GDP per capita Total GDP divided by total population; average GDP.

GDP per Capita. International comparisons of total output are even more vivid in *per capita terms*. **GDP per capita** relates the total value of annual output to the number of people who share that output; it refers to the average GDP per person. In 2008, America's total GDP of $14 trillion was shared by 300 million citizens. Hence, our average, or *per capita,* GDP was nearly $47,000. By contrast, the average GDP for the rest of the world's inhabitants was only $10,000. In these terms, America's position as the richest country in the world clearly stands out.

Statistical comparisons of GDP across nations are abstract and lifeless. They do, however, convey very real differences in the way people live. The following World View examines some everyday realities of living in a poor nation, compared with a rich nation. Disparities in per capita GDP mean that people in low-income countries have little access to telephones, televisions, paved roads, or schools. They also die a lot younger than do people in rich countries.

But even the World View fails to fully convey how tough life is for people at the *bottom* of the income distribution in both poor and rich nations. Per capita GDP isn't a measure of what every citizen is getting. In the United States, millions of individuals have access to far more goods and services than our *average* per capita GDP, while millions of others must get by with much less. Although per capita GDP in Kuwait is three times larger than that of Brazil's, we can't conclude that the typical citizen of Kuwait is three times as well off as the typical Brazilian. The only thing these figures tell us is that the average Kuwaiti *could have* almost three times as many goods and services each year as the average Brazilian *if* GDP were distributed in the same way in both countries. ***Measures of per capita GDP tell us nothing about the way GDP is actually distributed or used: they're only a statistical average.*** When countries are quite similar in structure, institutions, and income distribution, however—or when historical comparisons are made within a country—per capita GDP can be viewed as a rough-and-ready measure of relative living standards.

WORLD VIEW

Global Inequalities

The 1.3 billion residents of the world's low-income nations have comparatively few goods and services. Their average income (per capita GDP) is only $1,500 a year, a mere 4 percent of the average income in high-income nations such as the United States, Japan, and Germany. It's not just a colossal *income* disparity; it's also a disparity in the quality and even the duration of life. Some examples:

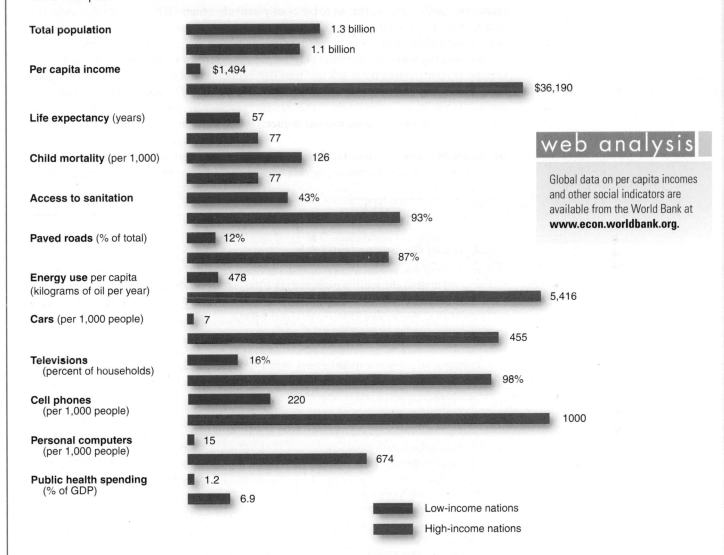

	Low-income nations	High-income nations
Total population	1.3 billion	1.1 billion
Per capita income	$1,494	$36,190
Life expectancy (years)	57	77
Child mortality (per 1,000)	126	77
Access to sanitation	43%	93%
Paved roads (% of total)	12%	87%
Energy use per capita (kilograms of oil per year)	478	5,416
Cars (per 1,000 people)	7	455
Televisions (percent of households)	16%	98%
Cell phones (per 1,000 people)	220	1000
Personal computers (per 1,000 people)	15	674
Public health spending (% of GDP)	1.2	6.9

web analysis

Global data on per capita incomes and other social indicators are available from the World Bank at **www.econ.worldbank.org.**

Source: From *World Development Report, 2009,* and *World Development Indicators, 2009.* **www.worldbank.org.**

Analysis: Hidden behind dry statistical comparisons of per capita GDP lie very tangible and dramatic differences in the way people live. Low GDP per capita reflects a lot of deprivation.

Nonmarket Activities. Although the methods for calculating GDP and per capita GDP are straightforward, they do create a few problems. For one thing, *GDP measures exclude most goods and services that are* produced *but not* sold *in the market.* This may appear to be a trivial point, but it isn't. Vast quantities of output never reach the market. For example, the homemaker who cleans, washes, gardens, shops, and cooks definitely contributes to the output of goods and services. Because she's not paid a market wage for these services,

Measurement Problems

however, her efforts are excluded from the calculation of GDP. At the same time, we do count the efforts of those workers who sell identical homemaking services in the marketplace. This seeming contradiction is explained by the fact that a homemaker's services aren't sold in the market and therefore carry no explicit, market-determined value.

The exclusion of homemakers' services from the GDP accounts is particularly troublesome when we want to compare living standards over time or between countries. In the United States, for example, most women now work outside the home. As a result households make greater use of *paid* domestic help (e.g., child care, house cleaning). Accordingly, a lot of housework and child care that were previously excluded from GDP statistics (because they were unpaid family help) are now included (because they're done by paid help). In this respect, our historical GDP figures may exaggerate improvements in our standard of living.

Homemaking services aren't the only output excluded. If a friend helps you with your homework, the services never get into the GDP accounts. But if you hire a tutor or engage the services of a term paper–writing agency, the transaction becomes part of GDP. Here again, the problem is simply that we have no way to determine how much output was produced until it enters the market and is purchased.[1]

Unreported Income. The GDP statistics also fail to capture market activities that aren't reported to tax or census authorities. Many people work "off the books," getting paid in

IN THE NEWS

A Lot Going On under the Table

- Percentage of households making untaxed or unmeasured "underground" purchases: 83
- Estimated unreported income per person in 2000, excluding illegal activities: $4,300
- Percentage of unreported income from wages and salaries: 18
- Percentage of unreported income from capital gains: 13
- Unreported income as a percentage of GDP: 12
- Taxes lost from unreported income in 2000: $195 billion

The underground economy—transactions that are untaxed or unaccounted for in GDP—involves a lot more than nannies and drug deals.

	Estimated Percentage of Services Supplied by the Underground Economy
Lawn maintenance	90
Domestic help	83
Child care	49
Home repair/improvements	34
Laundry/sewing services	25
Appliance repair	17
Car repairs	13
Haircuts/beauty service	8
Catering	8

Data from University of Michigan Institute for Social Research, U.S. Department of Labor.

Source: U.S. Internal Revenue Service. **www.irs.gov.**

Analysis: GDP statistics include only the value of reported market transactions. Unreported transactions in the underground economy can't be counted and may therefore distort perceptions of economic activity.

---

[1]The U.S. Commerce Department does, however, *estimate* the value of some nonmarket activities (e.g., food grown by farmers for their own consumption, the rental value of homeownership) and includes such estimates in GDP calculations.

unreported cash. This so-called underground economy is motivated by tax avoidance and the need to conceal illegal activities. Although illegal activities capture most of the headlines, tax evasion on income earned in otherwise legal pursuits accounts for most of the underground economy. The Internal Revenue Service estimates that over two-thirds of underground income comes from legitimate wages, salaries, profits, interest, and pensions that simply aren't reported. As the previous News indicates, unreported income is particularly common in the service sector. People who mow lawns, clean houses, paint walls, or provide child care services are apt to get paid in cash that isn't reported. The volume of such mundane transactions greatly exceeds the underground income generated by drug dealers, prostitutes, or illegal gambling.

[handwritten: people don't claim: ~ lottery winnings ~ tips / gratuities ~ babysitting $]

Value Added

Not every reported market transaction gets included at full value in GDP statistics. If it did, the same output would get counted over and over. The problem here is that the production of goods and services typically involves a series of distinct stages. Consider the production of a bagel, for example. For a bagel to reach Einstein's or some other bagel store, the farmer must grow some wheat, the miller must convert it to flour, and the baker must make bagels with it. Table 5.2 illustrates this chain of production.

Notice that each of the four stages of production depicted in Table 5.2 involves a separate market transaction. The farmer sells to the miller (stage 1), the miller to the baker (stage 2), the baker to the bagel store (stage 3), and finally, the store to the consumer (stage 4). If we added up the separate value of each market transaction, we'd come to the conclusion that $1.75 of output had been produced. In fact, though, only one bagel has been produced, and it's worth only 75 cents. Hence, we should increase GDP—the value of output—only by 75 cents.

To get an accurate measure of GDP we must distinguish between *intermediate* goods and *final* goods. **Intermediate goods** are goods purchased for use as input in further stages of production. Final goods are the goods produced at the end of the production sequence, for use by consumers (or other market participants).

> **intermediate goods:** Goods or services purchased for use as input in the production of final goods or in services.

We can compute the value of *final* output in one of two ways. The easiest way would be to count only market transactions entailing final sales (stage 4 in Table 5.2). To do this, however, we'd have to know who purchased each good or service in order to know when we had reached the end of the process. Such a calculation would also exclude any output produced in stages 1, 2, and 3 in Table 5.2 but not yet reflected in stage 4.

Another way to calculate GDP is to count only the **value added** at each stage of production. Consider the miller, for example. He doesn't really contribute $0.28 worth of production to total output, but only $0.16. The other $0.12 reflected in the price of his flour represents the contribution of the farmer who grew the wheat. By the same token, the baker *adds* only $0.32 to the value of output, as part of his output was purchased from the miller. By considering only the value *added* at each stage of production, we eliminate double counting. We don't count twice the *intermediate* goods and services that producers buy from other producers, which are then used as inputs. As Table 5.2 confirms, we can determine that value of final output by summing up the value added at each stage of production. (Note that $0.75 is also the price of a bagel.)

> **value added:** The increase in the market value of a product that takes place at each stage of the production process.

Stages of Production	Value of Transaction	Value Added
1. Farmer grows wheat, sells it to miller	$0.12	$0.12
2. Miller converts wheat to flour, sells it to baker	0.28	0.16
3. Baker bakes bagel, sells it to bagel store	0.60	0.32
4. Bagel store sells bagel to consumer	0.75	0.15
Total	$1.75	$0.75

TABLE 5.2

Value Added in Various Stages of Production

The value added at each stage of production represents a contribution to total output. Value added equals the market value of a product minus the cost of intermediate goods.

Real vs. Nominal GDP

Although prices are a convenient measure of market value, they can also distort perceptions of real output. Imagine what would happen to our calculations of GDP if all prices were to double from one year to the next. Suppose that the price of oranges, as shown in Table 5.1, rose from $0.20 to $0.40, the price of bicycles to $100, and the price of rock concerts to $2 million each. How would such price changes alter measured GDP? Obviously, the price increases would double the dollar *value* of final output. Measured GDP would rise from $1,400 million to $2,800 million.

Such a rise in GDP doesn't reflect an increase in the *quantity* of goods and services available to us. We're still producing the same quantities shown in Table 5.1; only the prices of those goods have changed. Hence, **changes in GDP brought about by changes in the price level give us a distorted view of real economic activity.** Surely we wouldn't want to assert that our standard of living had improved just because price increases raised measured GDP from $1,400 million to $2,800 million.

To distinguish increases in the *quantity* of goods and services from increases in their *prices,* we must construct a measure of GDP that takes into account price-level changes. We do so by distinguishing between *real* GDP and *nominal* GDP. **Nominal GDP** is the value of final output measured in *current* prices, whereas **real GDP** is the value of output measured in *constant* prices. **To calculate real GDP, we adjust the market value of goods and services for changing prices.**

Note, for example, that in Table 5.1 prices were unchanged from one year to the next. When prices in the marketplace are constant, interyear comparisons of output are simple. But if prices change, the comparison becomes more complicated. As we just saw, if all prices doubled from last year to this year, this year's nominal GDP would rise to $2,800 million. But these price increases wouldn't alter the quantity of goods produced. In other words, *real* GDP, valued at constant prices, would remain at $1,400 million. Thus, **the distinction between nominal and real GDP is important whenever the price level changes.**

Because the price level does change every year, both real and nominal GDP are regularly reported. Nominal GDP is computed simply by adding the *current* dollar value of production. Real GDP is computed by making an adjustment for changes in prices from year to year.

Consider the GDP statistics for 2005 and 2006, as displayed in Table 5.3. The first row shows *nominal* GDP in each year: Nominal GDP increased by $789 billion between 2005 and 2006 (row 2). This 6.3 percent increase looks impressive. However, some of that gain was fueled by higher prices, not increased output. Row 3 indicates that the price level rose by 3.3 percent from one year to the next.

Row 4 in Table 5.3 adjusts the GDP comparison for the change in prices. We represent the price increase as an index, with a base of 100. Thus, a price increase of 3.3 percent raises the base of 100 to 103.3. So the price-level change can be expressed as 103.3/100.0, or 1.033.

To convert the *nominal* value of GDP in 2006 to its *real* value, we only need a little division. As row 4 of Table 5.3 shows, we divide the nominal GDP of $13,245 by the indexed price change (1.033) and discover that *real* GDP in 2006 was only $12,822 billion. Hence, *real* GDP increased by only $366 billion in 2006 (row 5), not by the larger inflation-exaggerated amount in row 2.

nominal GDP The value of final output produced in a given period, measured in the prices of that period (current prices).

real GDP The value of final output produced in a given period, adjusted for changing prices.

TABLE 5.3
Computing Real GDP

Real GDP is the inflation-adjusted value of nominal GDP. Between 2005 and 2006, *nominal* GDP increased by $789 billion (row 2). Some of this gain was due to rising prices (row 3). After adjusting for inflation, *real* GDP increased by only $366 billion (row 5).

		2005	2006
1.	Nominal GDP (in billions)	$12,456	$13,245
2.	Change in nominal GDP		+$789
3.	Change in price level, 2005 to 2006		3.3%
4.	Real GDP in 2005 dollars $\left(= \dfrac{\text{Nominal GDP}}{\text{Price index}} \right)$	$12,456	$12,822 $\left(= \dfrac{\$13,245}{1.033} \right)$
5.	Change in real GDP		+$366

Notice in Table 5.3 that in 2005 real and nominal GDP are identical because we're using that year as the basis of comparison. We're comparing performance in 2006 to that of the 2005 **base year.** Real GDP can be expressed in the prices of any particular year; whatever year is selected serves as the base for computing price-level and output changes. In Table 5.3 we used 2005 as the base year for computing real GDP in subsequent years. The general formula for computing real GDP is

base year: The year used for comparative analysis; the basis for indexing price changes.

$$\text{Real GDP in year } t = \frac{\text{nominal GDP in year } t}{\text{price index}}$$

This is the formula we used in row 4 of Table 5.3 to compute real GDP in 2006, valued at 2005 base-year prices.

The distinction between nominal and real GDP becomes critical when more distant years are compared. Between 1933 and 2006, for example, prices rose by 1,300 percent: Table 5.4 shows how such price-level changes can distort our views of how living standards have changed since the Great Depression: In *nominal* terms, our per capita income

Suppose we want to determine how much better off the average American was in 2006, as measured in terms of new goods and services, than people were during the Great Depression. To do this, we'd compare GDP per capita in 2006 with GDP per capita in 1933. The following data make that comparison.

	Nominal GDP	Population	Nominal Per Capita GDP
1933	$ 56 billion	126 million	$ 444
2006	13,245 billion	299 million	44,298

In 1933, the nation's nominal GDP of $56 billion was shared by 126 million Americans, yielding a *per capita* GDP of $444. By contrast, nominal GDP in 2006 was over 200 times larger, at $13,245 billion, as we saw in Table 5.3. This vastly larger GDP was shared by 299 million people, giving us a per capita GDP of $44,298. Hence, it would appear that our standard of living in 2006 was nearly 100 times higher than the standard of 1933.

But this increase in *nominal* GDP vastly exaggerates the gains in our material well-being. The average price of goods and services—the *price level*—increased by 1,300 percent between 1933 and 2006. The goods and services you might have bought for $1 in 1933 cost $14 in 2006. In other words, we needed a lot more dollars in 2006 to buy any given combination of real goods and services.

To compare our *real* GDP in 2006 with the real GDP of 1933, we have to adjust for this tremendous jump in prices (inflation). We do so by measuring both years' output in terms of *constant* prices. Since prices went up, on average, fourteenfold between 1933 and 2006, we simply divide the 2006 *nominal* output by 14. The calculation is

$$\begin{array}{c}\text{Real GDP}\\\text{in 2006}\\\text{(in 1933 prices)}\end{array} = \frac{\text{nominal 2006 GDP}}{\text{price index}}$$

By arbitrarily setting the level of prices in the base year 1933 at 100 and noting that prices have increased fourteenfold since then, we can calculate

$$\begin{array}{c}\text{Real GDP}\\\text{in 2006}\\\text{(1933 prices)}\end{array} = \frac{\$13,245}{14.0}$$
$$= \$946 \text{ billion}$$

With a population of 299 million, this left us with real GDP per capita of $3,164 in 2006—as measured in base-year 1933 dollars. This was more than seven times the *real* per capita GDP of the depression ($444), but not nearly so great an increase as comparisons of *nominal* GDP suggest.

TABLE 5.4
Real vs. Nominal GDP: A Historical View

FIGURE 5.1

Changes in GDP: Nominal vs. Real

Increases in *nominal* GDP reflect higher prices as well as more output. Increases in *real* GDP reflect more output only. To measure these real changes, we must value each year's output in terms of common base prices. In this figure the base year is 2000. Nominal GDP rises faster than real GDP as a result of inflation.

Source: U.S. Bureau of Economic Analysis.

web analysis

If you want to see comprehensive charts on United States GDP and other economic statistics, visit the Bureau of Economic Analysis Web site at **www.bea.gov.**

inflation: An increase in the average level of prices of goods and services.

has risen a whopping 100 times over; in *real* terms, however, the income gain is a much less spectacular 7 times over.

Figure 5.1 shows how nominal and real GDP have changed just since 1995. Real GDP is calculated here on the basis of the level of prices prevailing in 2000. So 2000 is the *base year* in this case. (Note that real and nominal GDP are identical in that base year.) The dollar value of output produced each year has risen considerably faster than the quantity of output, reflecting persistent increases in the price level—that is, **inflation.**

Notice also how inflation can obscure actual *declines* in real output. Real GDP actually declined in 1991 (by 0.2 percent), though nominal GDP kept rising (by 3.3 percent). Although the dollar *value* of final output continued to rise in that year, the actual production of goods and services was falling; nominal and real GDP moved in opposite directions (see data on inside front cover).

Chain-Weighted Price Adjustments. Although the distinction between real and nominal GDP is critical in measuring the nation's economic health, the procedure for making inflation adjustments isn't perfect. When we use the prices of a specific year as the base for computing real GDP, we're implicitly freezing *relative* prices as well as *average* prices. Over time, however, relative prices change markedly. Computer prices, for example, have fallen sharply in recent years in both absolute and relative terms. During the same period, unit sales of computers have increased by 20 to 25 percent a year. If we used the higher computer prices of 5 years ago to compute that sales growth, we'd greatly exaggerate the *value* of today's computer output. If we use today's prices, however, we'll underestimate the value of output produced in the past. To resolve this problem, the U.S. Department of Commerce uses a *chain-weighted* price index to compute real GDP. Instead of using the prices of a *single* base year to compute real GDP, *chain-weighted indexes use a moving average of price levels in consecutive years as an inflation adjustment.* When chain-weighted price adjustments are made, real GDP still refers to the inflation-adjusted value of GDP but isn't expressed in terms of the prices prevailing in any specific base year. All official estimates of real GDP are now based on chain-weighted price indexes.

Changes in real GDP from one year to the next tell us how much the economy's output is growing. Some of that growth, however, may come at the expense of future output. Recall that our **production possibilities** determine how much output we can produce with available factors of production and technology. If we use up some of these resources to produce this year's output, future production possibilities may shrink. *Next year we won't be able to produce as much output unless we replace factors of production we use this year.*

We routinely use up plant and equipment (capital) in the production process. To maintain our production possibilities, therefore, we have to at least replace what we've used. The value of capital used up in producing goods and services is commonly called **depreciation.**[2] In principle, it's the amount of capital worn out by use in a year or made obsolete by advancing technology. In practice, the amount of capital depreciation is estimated by the U.S. Department of Commerce.

By subtracting depreciation from GDP we get **net domestic product (NDP).** This is the amount of output we could consume without reducing our stock of capital and therewith next year's production possibilities.

The distinction between GDP and NDP is mirrored in a distinction between *gross* investment and *net* **investment. Gross investment** is positive as long as some new plant and equipment are being produced. But *the stock of capital—the total collection of plant and equipment—won't grow unless gross investment exceeds depreciation.* That is, the *flow* of new capital must exceed depreciation, or our *stock* of capital will decline. Whenever the rate of gross investment exceeds depreciation, **net investment** is positive.

Notice that net investment can be negative as well; in such situations we're wearing out plant and equipment faster than we're replacing it. When net investment is negative, our capital stock is shrinking. This was the situation during the Great Depression. Gross investment fell so sharply in 1932–34 (see front endpaper of book) that it wasn't even replacing used-up machinery and structures. As a result, the economy's ability to produce goods and services declined.

THE USES OF OUTPUT

The role of investment in maintaining or expanding our production possibilities helps focus attention on the uses to which GDP is put. It's not just the total value of annual output that matters, it's also the use that we make of that output. *The GDP accounts also tell us what mix of output we've selected, that is, society's answer to the core issue of WHAT to produce.*

The major uses of total output conform to the four sets of market participants we encountered in Chapter 2, namely, consumers, business firms, government, and foreigners. Those goods and services used by households are called *consumption goods* and range all the way from doughnuts to wireless computer services. Included in this category are all goods and services households purchase in product markets. Presently, all this consumer spending claims over two-thirds of our annual output.

Investment goods represent another use of GDP. Investment goods are the plant, machinery, and equipment we produce. Net changes in business inventories and expenditures for residential construction are also counted as investment. To produce any of these investment goods, we must use scarce resources that could be used to produce something else. Investment spending claims about one-sixth of our total output.

The third major use of GDP is the *public sector*. Federal, state, and local governments purchase resources to police the streets, teach classes, write laws, and build highways. The

Net Domestic Product

production possibilities: The alternative combinations of final goods and services that could be produced in a given time period with all available resources and technology.

depreciation: The consumption of capital in the production process; the wearing out of plant and equipment.

net domestic product (NDP): GDP less depreciation.

investment: Expenditures on (production of) new plant, equipment, and structures (capital) in a given time period, plus changes in business inventories.

gross investment: Total investment expenditure in a given time period.

net investment: Gross investment less depreciation.

Consumption

Investment
• savings

Government Spending

---

[2]The terms *depreciation, capital consumption allowance,* and *consumption of fixed capital* are used interchangeably. The depreciation charges firms commonly make, however, are determined in part by income tax regulations and thus may not accurately reflect the amount of capital consumed.

Net Exports

exports: Goods and services sold to international buyers.

imports: Goods and services purchased from international sources.

exports – imports
* were –

net exports: The value of exports minus the value of imports.

GDP Components

resources purchased by the government sector are unavailable for either consumption or investment purposes. At present, government spending on goods and services (*not* income transfers) claims roughly one-fifth of total output.

Finally, remember that some of the goods and services we produce each year are used abroad rather than at home. That is, we **export** some of our output to other countries, for whatever use they care to make of it. Thus, GDP—the value of output produced—will be larger than the sum of our own consumption, investment, and government purchases to the extent that we succeed in exporting goods and services.

We **import** goods and services as well. A flight to London on British Air is an imported service; a Jaguar is an imported good. These goods and services aren't part of America's GDP since they weren't produced within our borders. In principle, these imports never enter the GDP accounts. In practice, however, it's difficult to distinguish imports from domestic-made products, especially when goods include value added from both foreign and domestic producers. Even "American-made" cars typically incorporate parts manufactured in Japan, Mexico, Thailand, Britain, Spain, or Germany, with final assembly here in the United States. Should that car be counted as an "American" product or as an import? Rather than try to sort out all these products and parts, the U.S. Commerce Department simply subtracts the value of all imports from the value of total spending. Thus, exports are *added* to GDP and *imports* are subtracted. The difference between the two expenditure flows is called **net exports.**

Once we recognize the components of output, we discover a simple method for computing GDP. ***The value of GDP can be computed by adding up the expenditures of market participants.*** Specifically, we note that

$$ GDP = C + I + G + (X - M) $$

where C = consumption expenditure
  I = investment expenditure
  G = government expenditure
  X = exports
  M = imports

• to increase income, we need to increase
one of these 4

This approach to GDP accounting emphasizes the fact that ***all the output produced in the economy must be claimed by someone.*** If we know who's buying our output, we know how much was produced and what uses were made of it.

MEASURES OF INCOME

There's another way of looking at GDP. Instead of looking at who's *buying* our output, we can look at who's *being paid* to produce it. Like markets themselves. ***GDP accounts have two sides: One side focuses on expenditure (the demand side), the other side focuses on income (the supply side).***

We've already observed (see Figure 3.1) that every market transaction involves an *exchange* of dollars for a good or resource. Moreover, the *value* of each good or resource is measured by the amount of money exchanged for it (its market price). Hence, ***the total value of market incomes must equal the total value of final output, or GDP.*** In other words, one person's expenditure always represents another person's income.

Figure 5.2 illustrates the link between spending on output and incomes. This is a modified version of the circular flow we saw in Chapter 3. The spending that flows into the product market gets funneled into the factor market, where resources are employed to produce the goods people want. The expenditure then flows into the hands of business owners, workers, landlords, and other resource owners. With the exception of sales taxes and depreciation, all spending on output becomes income to factors of production.

The equivalence of output and income isn't dependent on any magical qualities possessed by money. Were we to produce only one product—say, wheat—and pay everyone in bushels and pecks, total income would still equal total output. People couldn't receive in income more wheat than we produced. On the other hand, all the wheat produced would go to *someone*. Hence, one could say that the production possibilities of the economy define

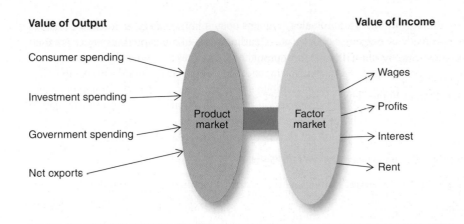

Value of Output

- Consumer spending
- Investment spending
- Government spending
- Net exports

Product market → Factor market

Value of Income

- Wages
- Profits
- Interest
- Rent

FIGURE 5.2
Output = Income

The spending that establishes the value of output also determines the value of incomes. With minor exceptions, the market value of income must equal the market value of output.

not only the limits to *output,* but also the limits to real *income.* The amount of income actually generated in any year depends on the production and expenditure decisions of consumers, firms, and government agencies.

Table 5.5 shows the actual flow of output and income in the U.S. economy during 2008. Total output is made up of the familiar components of GDP: consumption, investment, government goods and services, and net exports. The figures on the left side of Table 5.5 indicate that consumers spent over $10 trillion, businesses spent almost $2 trillion on plant and equipment, governments spent nearly $3 trillion, and net imports were $670 billion. Our total output value (GDP) was thus more than $14 trillion in 2008.

The right-hand side of Table 5.5 indicates who received the income generated from these markets transactions. ***Every dollar spent on goods and services provides income to someone.*** It may go to a worker (as wage or salary) or to a business firm (as profit and depreciation allowance). It may go to a landlord (as rent), to a lender (as interest), or to government (as taxes on production and imports). None of the dollars spent on goods and services disappears into thin air.

Although it may be exciting to know that we collectively received over $14 trillion of income in 2008, it might be of more interest to know who actually got all that income. After all, in addition to the 300 million pairs of outstretched palms among us, millions of businesses and government agencies were also competing for those dollars and the goods and services they represent. By charting the flow of income through the economy, we can see FOR WHOM our output was produced.

National Income

Depreciation. The annual income flow originates in product-market sales. Purchases of final goods and services create a flow of income to producers and, through them, to factors of

Expenditure		Income	
C: Consumer goods and services	$10,058	Wages and salaries	$ 8,062
I: Investment in plant,		Corporate profits	1,092
equipment, and		Proprietors' income	1,072
inventory	1,994	Rents	64
G: Government goods		Interest	929
and services	2,883	Taxes on output and imports	1,034
X: Exports	1,859	Depreciation	1,832
M: Imports	(2,529)	Miscellaneous	46
		Statistical discrepancy	134
GDP: Total value of output	$14,265 =	Total value of income	$14,265

Source: U.S. Department of Commerce (2008 data).

TABLE 5.5

The Equivalence of Expenditure and Income (in billions of dollars)

The value of total expenditure must equal the value of total income. Why? Because every dollar spent on output becomes a dollar of income for someone.

production. But a major diversion of sales revenues occurs immediately, as a result of depreciation charges made by businesses. As we noted earlier, some of our capital resources are used up in the process of production. For the most part, these resources are owned by business firms that expect to be compensated for such investments. Accordingly, they regard some of the sales revenue generated in product markets as reimbursement for wear and tear on capital plant and equipment. They therefore subtract *depreciation charges* from gross revenues in calculating their incomes. Depreciation charges reduce GDP to the level of *net* domestic product (NDP) before any income is available to current factors of production. As we saw earlier,

$$NDP = GDP - depreciation$$

Net Foreign Factor Income. Remember that some of the income generated in U.S. product markets belongs to foreigners. Wages, interest, and profits paid to foreigners are not part of U.S. income. So we need to subtract that outflow.

Recall also that U.S. citizens own factors of production employed in other nations (e.g., a Ford plant in Mexico; a McDonald's outlet in Singapore). This creates an *in*flow of income to U.S. households. To connect the value of U.S. output to U.S. incomes, we must add back in the net inflow of foreign factor income.

Once depreciation charges are subtracted from GDP and net foreign factor income added, we're left with **national income (NI),** which is the total income earned by U.S. factors of production. Thus,

$$NI = NDP + net\ foreign\ factor\ income$$

As Table 5.6 illustrates, our national income in 2008 was $12.4 trillion, nearly 90 percent of GDP.

national income (NI): Total income earned by current factors of production: GDP less depreciation, plus net foreign factor income.

Personal Income

There are still more revenue diversions as the GDP flow makes its way to consumer households.

Indirect Business Taxes. Another major diversion of the income flow occurs at its point of origin. When goods are sold in the marketplace, their purchase price is typically encumbered with some sort of sales tax. Thus, some of the revenue generated in product markets disappears before any factor of production gets a chance to claim it. These taxes on production and imports—often referred to as *indirect business taxes*—must be deducted from national income because they don't represent payment to factors of production.

TABLE 5.6
The Flow of Income, 2008

The revenue generated from market transactions passes through many hands. Households end up with disposable income equal to about 70 percent of GDP, after depreciation and taxes are taken out and net interest and transfer payments are added back in. Disposable income is either spent (consumption) or saved by households.

Income Flow	Amount (in billions)
Gross domestic product (GDP)	$14,265
Less depreciation	(1,832)
Net domestic product (NDP)	12,433
Plus net foreign factor income	133
Less statistical discrepancy	(136)
National income (NI)	12,430
Less indirect business taxes*	(983)
Less corporate profits	(1,477)
Less interest and misc payments	(778)
Less Social Security taxes	(996)
Plus transfer payments	1,869
Plus capital income	2,038
Personal income (PI)	12,103
Less personal taxes	(1,461)
Disposable income (DI)	10,642

*Taxes on production and imports.
Source: U.S. Department of Commerce.

Corporate Profits. Theoretically, all the income corporations receive represents income for their owners—the households who hold stock in the corporations. But the flow of income through corporations to stockholders is far from complete. First, corporations may pay taxes on their profits. Accordingly, some of the income received on behalf of a corporation's stockholders goes into the public treasury rather than into private bank accounts. Second, corporate managers typically find some urgent need for cash. As a result, part of the profits is retained by the corporation rather than passed on to the stockholders in the form of dividends. For convenience all corporate profits are substracted, then that part of profits paid out to households is later added back in under "capital income."

Payroll Taxes and Transfers. Still another deduction must be made for *Social Security taxes*. Nearly all people who earn a wage or salary are required by law to pay Social Security "contributions." In 2009, the Social Security tax rate for workers was 7.65 percent of the first $106,800 of earnings received in the year. Workers never see this income because it is withheld by employers and sent directly to the U.S. Treasury. Thus, the flow of national income is reduced considerably before it becomes **personal income (PI),** the amount of income received by households before payment of personal taxes.

> **personal income (PI):** Income received by households before payment of personal taxes.

Not all of our adjustments to national income are negative. Households receive income in the form of transfer payments from the public treasury. More than 50 million people receive monthly Social Security checks, for example, and another 14 million receive some form of public welfare. These income transfers represent income for the people who receive them.

Capital Income. People also receive interest payments and dividend checks. These forms of capital income provide another source of personal income. Accordingly, our calculation of personal income is as follows:

> *National income* (= income earned by factors of production)
> *less*   indirect business taxes
>   corporate profits
>   interest and misc. payments
>   Social Security taxes
> *plus*   transfer payments
>   capital income
> *Equals **personal income*** (= income received by households)

As you can see, the flow of income generated in production is significantly reduced before it gets into the hands of individual households. But we haven't yet reached the end of the reduction process. We have to set something aside for personal income taxes. To be sure we don't forget about our obligations, Uncle Sam and his state and local affiliates usually arrange to have their share taken off the top. Personal income taxes are withheld by the employer, who thus acts as a tax collector. Accordingly, to calculate **disposable income (DI),** which is the amount of income consumers may themselves spend (dispose of), we reduce personal income by the amount of personal taxes:

> **disposable income (DI):** After-tax income of households; personal income less personal taxes.

$$\text{Disposable income} = \text{personal income} - \text{personal taxes}$$

Disposable income is the end of the accounting line. As Table 5.6 shows, households end up with roughly 70 percent of the revenues generated from final market sales (GDP). Once consumers get this disposable income in their hands, they face two choices. They may choose to *spend* their disposable income on consumer goods and services. Or they may choose to *save* it. These are the only two choices in GDP accounting. **Saving,** in this context, simply refers to disposable income that isn't spent on consumption. In the analysis of income and saving flows, we don't care whether savings are hidden under a mattress, deposited in the bank, or otherwise secured. All we want to know is whether disposable income is spent. Thus, ***all disposable income is, by definition, either consumed or saved; that is,***

> **saving:** That part of disposable income not spent on current consumption; disposable income less consumption.

$$\text{Disposable income} = \text{consumption} + \text{saving}$$

THE FLOW OF INCOME

Figure 5.3 summarizes the relationship between expenditure and income. The essential point again is that every dollar spent on goods and services flows into somebody's hands. Thus, *the dollar value of output will always equal the dollar value of income.* Specifically, total income (GDP) ends up distributed in the following way:

- To *households,* in the form of disposable income.
- To *business,* in the form of retained earnings and depreciation allowances.
- To *government,* in the form of taxes.

Income and Expenditure

The annual flow of income to households, businesses, and government is part of a continuing process. Households rarely stash their disposable income under the mattress; they spend most of it on consumption. This spending adds to GDP in the next round of activity, thereby helping to keep the flow of income moving.

Business firms also have a lot of purchasing power tied up in retained earnings and depreciation charges. This income, too, may be recycled—returned to the circular flow—in the form of business investment.

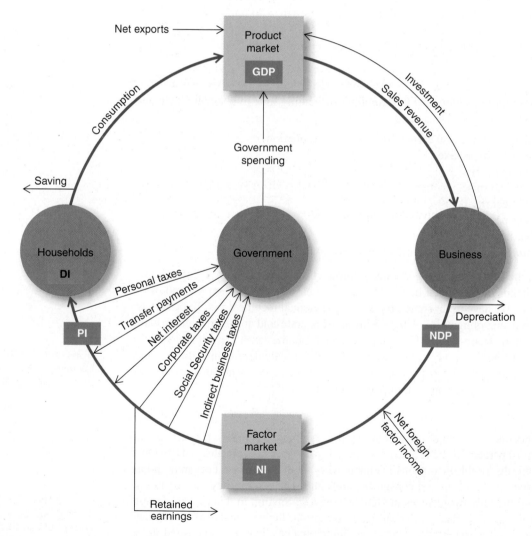

FIGURE 5.3

The Circular Flow of Spending and Income

GDP represents the dollar value of final output sold in the product market. The revenue stream flowing from GDP works its way through NDP, NI, and PI before reaching households in the form of smaller DI. DI is in turn either spent or saved by consumers. This consumption, plus investment, government spending, and net exports, continues the circular flow.

Even the income that flows into public treasuries finds its way back into the marketplace, as government agencies hire police officers, soldiers, and clerks, or they buy goods and services. Thus, ***the flow of income that starts with GDP ultimately returns to the market in the form of new consumption (C), investment (I), and government purchases (G).*** A new GDP arises, and the flow starts all over. In later chapters we examine in detail these *expenditure* flows, with particular emphasis on their ability to keep the economy producing at its full potential.

THE ECONOMY TOMORROW

THE QUALITY OF LIFE

Money, money, money—it seems that's all we talk about. Why don't we talk about important things like beauty, virtue, or the quality of life? Will the economy of tomorrow be filled with a glut of products but devoid of real meaning? Do the GDP accounts—either the expenditure side or the income side—tell us anything we really want to know about the quality of life? If not, why should we bother to examine them?

Intangibles. All the economic measures discussed in this chapter are important indexes of individual and collective welfare; they tell us something about how well people are living. They don't, however, capture the completeness of the way in which we view the world or the totality of what makes our lives satisfying. A clear day, a sense of accomplishment, even a smile can do more for a person's sense of well-being than can favorable movements in the GDP accounts. Or, as the economist John Kenneth Galbraith put it, "In a rational lifestyle, some people could find contentment working moderately and then sitting by the street—and talking, thinking, drawing, painting, scribbling, or making love in a suitably discreet way. None of these requires an expanding economy."[3]

The emphasis on economic outcomes arises not from ignorance of life's other meanings but from the visibility of the economic outcomes. We all realize that well-being arises from both material and intangible pleasures. But the intangibles tend to be elusive. It's not easy to gauge individual happiness, much less to ascertain the status of our collective satisfaction. We have to rely on measures we can see, touch, and count. As long as the material components of our environment bear some positive relation to our well-being, they at least serve a useful purpose.

Analysis: GDP includes *everything* produced and sold in the product market, no matter how much each good or service contributes to our social well-being.

[3]Cited in Leonard Silk, *Nixonomics,* 2nd ed. (New York: Praeger, 1973), p. 163.

In some situations, however, more physical output may actually worsen our collective welfare. If increased automobile production raises congestion and pollution levels, the rise in GDP occasioned by those additional cars is a misleading index of society's welfare. In such a case, the rise in GDP might actually mask a *decrease* in the well-being of the population. We might also wonder whether more casinos, more prisons, more telemarketing, more divorce litigation, and more Prozac—all of which contribute to GDP growth—are really valid measures of our well-being (see previous cartoon). Exclusive emphasis on measurable output would clearly be a mistake in many cases.

What is true of automobile production might also be true of other outputs. Increased development of urban areas may diminish social welfare if that development occurs at the expense of space, trees, and tranquillity. Increased mechanization on the farm may raise agricultural output but isolate and uproot farmers. So, too, increased productivity in factories and offices might contribute to a sense of alienation. These ill effects of increased output needn't occur; but if they do, indexes of output tell us less about social or individual well-being.

Index of Well-Being. Researchers at Fordham University devised an alternative index of well-being. Their Index of Social Health includes a few economic parameters (such as unemployment and weekly earnings) but puts more emphasis on sociological behavior (such as child abuse, teen suicides, crime, poverty, and inequality). They claim that this broader view offers a more meaningful guidepost to everyday life than GDP measures of material wealth (see News below).

Not everyone would accept Fordham's dour view of our collective social health. Their index, however, does underscore the fact that *social welfare* and *economic welfare* aren't

web analysis

The United Nations has constructed a Human Development Index that offers a broader view of social well-being than GDP alone. For details and country rankings, visit **www.undp.org.** Also check the Genuine Progress Indicator at **www.rprogress.org.**

IN THE NEWS

Material Wealth vs. Social Health

National-income accounts are regularly reported and widely quoted. They do not, however, adequately reflect the nation's *social* performance. To measure more accurately the country's social health, a Fordham University team of social scientists devised an Index of Social Health with 16 indicators, including infant mortality, drug abuse, health-insurance coverage, and poverty among the aged. According to this index, America's social health increased only 13.5 percent from 1990 to 2006, despite a 33.1 percent increase in real GDP per capita.

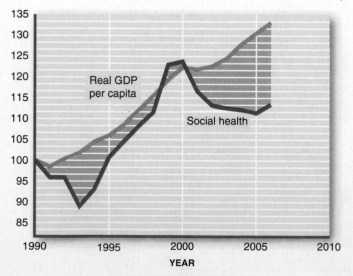

Source: Institute for Innovation in Social Policy (**miringoff.vassar.edu**).

Analysis: The national-income accounts emphasize material well-being. They are an important, but not a complete, gauge of our societal welfare.

always synonymous. The GDP accounts tell us whether our economic welfare has increased, as measured by the value of goods and services produced. They don't tell us how highly we value additional goods and services relative to nonmarket phenomena. Nor do they even tell us whether important social costs were incurred in the process of production. These judgments must be made outside the market; they're social decisions.

Finally, note that any given level of GDP can encompass many combinations of output. Choosing WHAT to produce is still a critical question, even after the goal of *maximum* production has been established. The quality of life in the economy tomorrow will depend on what specific mix of goods and services we include in GDP.

SUMMARY

- National-income accounting measures annual output and income flows. The national-income accounts provide a basis for assessing our economic performance, designing public policy, and understanding how all the parts of the economy interact.   LO1
- The most comprehensive measure of output is gross domestic product (GDP), the total market value of all final goods and services produced within a nation's borders during a given time period.   LO1
- In calculating GDP, we include only the value added at each stage of production. This procedure eliminates the double counting that results when business firms buy intermediate goods from other firms and include those costs in their selling price.   LO1
- To distinguish physical changes in output from monetary changes in its value, we compute both nominal and real GDP. Nominal GDP is the value of output expressed in *current* prices. Real GDP is the value of output expressed in *constant* prices (the prices of some *base year*).   LO1
- Each year some of our capital equipment is worn out in the process of production. Hence, GDP is larger than the amount of goods and services we could consume without reducing our production possibilities. The amount of capital used up each year is referred to as *depreciation*.   LO3
- By subtracting depreciation from GDP we derive net domestic product (NDP). The difference between NDP and GDP is also equal to the difference between *gross*

investment—the sum of all our current plant and equipment expenditures—and *net* investment—the amount of investment over and above that required to replace worn out capital.   LO3
- All the income generated in market sales (GDP) is received by someone. Therefore, the value of aggregate output must equal the value of aggregate income.   LO2
- The sequence of flows involved in this process is

GDP
less depreciation
equals **NDP**
plus net foreign factor income
equals national income (**NI**)
less indirect business taxes,
    corporate profits,
    interest payments, and
    Social Security taxes
plus transfer payments and
    capital income
equals personal income (**PI**)
less personal income taxes
equals disposable income (**DI**)   LO2

- The incomes received by households, business firms, and governments provide the purchasing power required to buy the nation's output. As that purchasing power is spent, further GDP is created and the circular flow continues.   LO3

Key Terms

national-income accounting	inflation	imports
gross domestic product (GDP)	production possibilities	net exports
GDP per capita	depreciation	national income (NI)
intermediate goods	net domestic product (NDP)	personal income (PI)
value added	investment	disposable income (DI)
nominal GDP	gross investment	saving
real GDP	net investment	
base year	exports	

Questions for Discussion

1. The manuscript for this book was typed for free by a friend. Had I hired a secretary to do the same job GDP would have been higher, even though the amount of output would have been identical. Why is this? Does this make sense?   LO1

2. GDP in 1981 was $2.96 trillion. It grew to $3.07 trillion in 1982, yet the quantity of output actually decreased. How is this possible?   LO1

3. If gross investment is not large enough to replace the capital that depreciates in a particular year, is net investment greater or less than zero? What happens to our production possibilities?   LO3

4. Can we increase consumption in a given year without cutting back on either investment or government services? Under what conditions?   LO3

5. Why is it important to know how much output is being produced? Who uses such information?   LO1

6. What jobs are likely part of the underground economy?   LO1

7. How might the quality of life be adversely affected by an increase in GDP? Cite specific examples.   LO1

8. Is the Fordham Index of Social Health, discussed in the News on page 106, a better barometer of well-being than GDP? What are its relative advantages or disadvantages?   LO1

9. Over 4 million Web sites sell a combined $70 billion of pornography a year. Should these sales be included in (a) GDP and (b) an index of social welfare?   LO1

10. Are you better off today than a year ago? How do you measure the change?   LO1

 web activities to accompany this chapter can be found on the Online Learning Center: **http://www.mhhe.com/schiller12e**

PROBLEMS FOR CHAPTER 5   Name: _____

connect
|ECONOMICS

LO1   1. Suppose that furniture production encompasses the following stages:

Stage 1: Trees sold to lumber company	$ 800
Stage 2: Lumber sold to furniture company	$1,500
Stage 3: Furniture company sells furniture to retail store	$2,800
Stage 4: Furniture store sells furniture to consumer	$5,400

  (a) What is the value added at each stage?

  Stage 1: _____

  Stage 2: _____

  Stage 3: _____

  Stage 4: _____

  (b) How much does this output contribute to GDP?   _____

  (c) How would answer (b) change if the lumber were imported from Canada?   _____

LO1   2. If real GDP increases by 3 percent next year and the price level goes up by 2 percent, what will happen to nominal GDP?   _____

LO1   3. What was real per capita GDP in 1933 measured in 2006 prices? (Use the data in Table 5.4 to compute your answer.)   _____

LO3   4. (a) Calculate national income from the following figures:

Consumption	$200 billion
Depreciation	20
Retained earnings	12
Gross investment	30
Imports	40
Exports	50
Net foreign factor income	10
Government purchases	60

  NI: _____

  (b) If there were 75 million people in this country, what would the GDP per capita be?   _____

  (c) If all prices were to double overnight, what would be the

   (i) Change in real GDP: _____

   (ii) Change in nominal GDP: _____

LO3   5. What is the value of net investment in Problem 4?   _____

LO3   6. What share of total income consists of
   (a) Wages and salaries   _____
   (b) Corporate profits   _____
   (Note: See Table 5.5 for data)

LO1   7. (a) Compute real GDP for 2005 using average prices of 1995 as the base year. (On the inside covers of this book you'll find data for GDP and the GDP "price deflator" used to measure inflation.)
   (b) By how much did real GDP increase between 1995 and 2005?   _____
   (c) By how much did nominal GDP increase between 1995 and 2005?   _____

LO3   8. Suppose all the dollar values in Problem 4 were in 2000 dollars. Use the Consumer Price Index shown on the end cover of this book to convert the numbers to 2008 dollars. What is the value of that income in 2008 dollars? (You'll be converting the figures from their nominal to their real values, with 2008 as the base year.)   _____

LO1   9. According to the data in Table 5.3 what is
   (a) Real GDP in 2006, at prices of 2005?   _____
   (b) Real GDP in 2005, at prices of 2006?   _____

LO1 10. On the accompanying graph, illustrate (*A*) nominal per capita GDP and (*B*) real per capita GDP
for each year. (The necessary data appear on the endpapers of this book.)
    (*a*) By what percent did nominal per capita GDP increase in the 1990s?   _____
    (*b*) By what percent did real per capita GDP increase in the 1990s?   _____
    (*c*) In how many years did nominal per capita GDP decline?   _____
    (*d*) In how many years did real per capita GDP decline?   _____

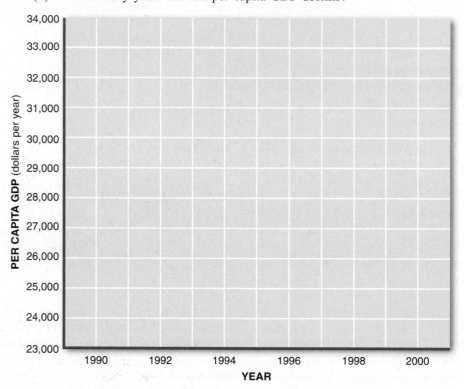

LO1 11. According to the News on page 106, do per capita GDP data overstate or understate the rise in
U.S. well-being since 1990?   _____

6

Unemployment

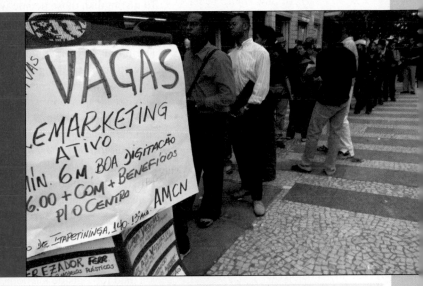

George H. had worked at the Chrysler factory in South St. Louis for 18 years. Now he was 46 years old, with a wife and three children. With his base salary of $48,200 and the performance bonus he received nearly every year, he was doing pretty well. He had his own home, two cars, company-paid health insurance for the family, and a growing nest egg in the company's pension plan. The H. family wasn't rich, but they were comfortable and secure.

Or so they thought. Overnight the H. family's comfort was shattered. The plant was closed on October 31, 2008. George H., along with 1,700 fellow workers, was permanently laid off. The weekly paychecks stopped immediately; the pension nest egg was in doubt. Within a few weeks, George H. was on the street looking for a new job—an experience he hadn't had since high school. The unemployment benefits the state and union provided didn't come close to covering the mortgage payment, groceries, insurance, and other necessities. The H. family quickly used up its savings, including the $5,000 they'd set aside for the children's college education.

George H. stayed unemployed for months. His wife found a part-time waitressing job, and his oldest son went to work rather than college. George himself ultimately found a ware-housing job that paid only half as much as his previous job.

In the recession of 2008–9 and its aftermath over 5 *million* workers lost their jobs as companies "downsized," "restruc-tured," or simply closed. Not all these displaced workers fared as badly as George H. and his family. But the job loss was a painful experience for every one of those displaced workers. That's the human side of an economic downturn.

The pain of joblessness is not confined to those who lose their jobs. In recessions, students discover that jobs are hard to find in the summer. No matter how good their grades are or how nice their résumés look, some graduates just don't get any job offers in a recession. Even people with jobs feel some economic pain: Their paychecks shrink when hours or wages are scaled back.

In this chapter we take a closer look at the problem of unemployment, focusing on the following questions:

- **When is a person "unemployed"?**
- **What are the costs of unemployment?**
- **What's an appropriate policy goal for "full employment"?**

As we answer these questions, we'll develop a sense of why full employment is a major goal of macro policy and begin to see some of the obstacles we face in achieving it.

THE LABOR FORCE

To assess the dimensions of our unemployment problems, we first need to decide who wants a job. Millions of people are jobless, yet they're not part of our unemployment problem. Full-time students, young children playing with their toys, and older people living in retirement are all jobless. We don't expect them to be working, so we don't regard them as part of the unemployment problem. We're not trying to get *everybody* a job, just those people who are ready and willing to work.

To distinguish those people who want a job from those who don't, we separate the entire population into two distinct groups. One group consists of *labor-force participants;* the other group encompasses all *nonparticipants.*

The **labor force** includes everyone age 16 and older who is actually working plus all those who aren't working but are actively seeking employment. Individuals are also counted as employed in a particular week if their failure to work is due to vacation, illness, labor dispute (strike), or bad weather. All such persons are regarded as "with a job but not at work." Also, unpaid family members working in a family enterprise (farming, for example) are counted as employed. ***Only those people who are either employed or actively seeking work are counted as part of the labor force.*** People who are neither employed *nor* actively looking for a job are referred to as *nonparticipants.* As Figure 6.1 shows, only half the U.S. population participates in the labor force.

Note that our definition of labor-force participation excludes most household and volunteer activities. People who choose to devote their energies to household responsibilities or to unpaid charity work aren't counted as part of the labor force, no matter how hard they work. Because they are neither in paid employment nor seeking such employment in the marketplace, they are regarded as outside the labor market (nonparticipants). But if they decide to seek a paid job outside the home, we'd say that they are "entering the labor force." Students too are typically out of the labor force until they leave school. They *"enter"* the labor force when they go looking for a job, either during the summer or after graduation. People *"exit"* the labor force when they go back to school, return to household activities, go to prison, or retire. These entries and exits keep changing the size and composition of the labor force.

Since 1960, the U.S. labor force has more than doubled in size. As Figure 6.2 indicates, this labor-force growth has come from two distinct sources: population growth and a rising **labor-force participation rate.** The U.S. population has increased by only 70 percent since 1960, while the labor force has more than doubled. The difference is explained by the rapid increase in the labor-force participation of women. Notice in Figure 6.2 that only 1 out of

labor force: All persons age 16 and over who are either working for pay or actively seeking paid employment.

[handwritten: Discouraged workers – not looking for employment aren't included in unemployment]

labor-force participation rate: The percentage of the working-age population working or seeking employment.

FIGURE 6.1
The Labor Force, 2008

Only half the total U.S. population participates in the civilian labor force. The rest of the population is too young, in school, at home, retired, or otherwise unavailable.

Unemployment statistics count only those participants who aren't currently working but are actively seeking paid employment. Nonparticipants are neither employed nor actively seeking employment.

Source: U.S. Bureau of Labor Statistics.

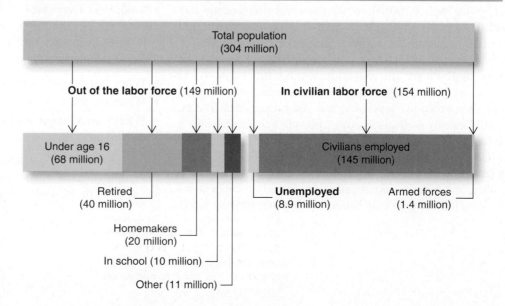

Total population (304 million)

Out of the labor force (149 million)   **In civilian labor force** (154 million)

Under age 16 (68 million)   Civilians employed (145 million)

Retired (40 million)   **Unemployed** (8.9 million)   Armed forces (1.4 million)

Homemakers (20 million)

In school (10 million)

Other (11 million)

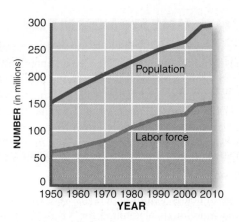

Participation Rates (age 16 and older)		
Year	Men	Women
1950	86.4	33.9
1960	83.3	37.7
1970	79.7	43.3
1980	77.4	51.5
1990	76.4	57.5
2000	74.7	60.0
2008	73.0	59.5

FIGURE 6.2
A Growing Labor Force

The labor force expands as births and immigration increase. A big increase in the participation rate of women after 1950 also added to labor-force growth.

Source: *Economic Report of the President,* 2009.

production possibilities: The alternative combinations of final goods and services that could be produced in a given time period with all available resources and technology.

3 women participated in the labor force in 1950–60, whereas 6 out of 10 now do so. The labor-force participation of men actually declined during the same period, even though it remains higher than that of women.

The labor force continues to grow each year along with population increases and con-
tinuing immigration. These sources add more than 2 million persons to the labor force every year. This is both good news and bad news. The good news is that labor-force growth expands our **production possibilities,** enabling us to produce more output with each passing year. The bad news is that we've got to create at least 2 million *more* jobs every year to assure that labor-force participants can find a job. If we don't, we'll end up *inside* the production possibilities curve, as at point *F* in Figure 6.3.

Labor-Force Growth

If we end up inside the production possibilities curve, we are not producing at capacity. We're also not using all available resources, including labor-force participants. This gives rise to the problem of **unemployment:** people who are willing and able to work aren't being hired. At point *F* in Figure 6.3 would-be workers are left unemployed; potential output isn't produced. Everybody suffers.

Unemployment

unemployment: The inability of labor-force participants to find jobs.

Okun's Law; Lost Output. Arthur Okun quantified the relationship between unemployment and the production possibilities curve. According to the original formulation of **Okun's Law,** each additional 1 percent of unemployment translated into a loss of 3 percent in real output. More recent estimates of Okun's Law put the ratio at about 1 to 2, largely due to the changing composition of both the labor force (more women and teenagers) and output (more services). Using that 1-to-2 ratio allows us to put a dollar value on the aggregate cost of unemployment. In 2008, high unemployment left us $600 billion short of our production possibilities. That output shortfall implied a loss of $2,000 of goods and services for every American.

Okun's Law: 1 percent more unemployment results in 2 percent less output. (GDP)

° use in an example

the production possibility curve moves up · represents economic growth

FIGURE 6.3
Labor-Force Growth

Labor-force growth increases production possibilities.

The amount of labor available for work—the *labor force*—is a prime determinant of a nation's production possibilities. As the labor force grows, so does the capacity to produce. To produce at capacity, however, the labor force must be fully employed. At point *F*, resources are unemployed.

MEASURING UNEMPLOYMENT

To determine how many people are actually unemployed, the U.S. Census Bureau surveys about 60,000 households each month. The Census interviewers first determine whether a person is employed—that is, worked for pay in the previous week (or didn't work due to illness, vacation, bad weather, or a labor strike). If the person isn't employed, he or she is either *unemployed* or *out of the labor force*. To make that distinction, the Census interviewers ask whether the person actively looked for work in the preceding 4 weeks. ***If a person is not employed and actively seeking a job, he or she is counted as unemployed.*** Individuals neither employed nor actively seeking a job are counted as outside the labor force (nonparticipants).

The Unemployment Rate

unemployment rate: The proportion of the labor force that is unemployed.

In 2008, an average of nearly 9 million persons were counted as unemployed in any month. These unemployed individuals accounted for 5.8 percent of our total labor force in that year. Accordingly, the average **unemployment rate** in 2008 was 5.8 percent.

$$\text{Unemployment rate} = \frac{\text{number of unemployed people}}{\text{labor force}}$$

$$\text{in } 2008 = \frac{8,924,000}{154,287,000} = 5.78\%$$

web analysis

Data on unemployment by race and gender from 1948 to the present are available from the Bureau of Labor Statistics at **www.bls.gov**.

The monthly unemployment figures indicate not only the total amount of unemployment in the economy but also which groups are suffering the greatest unemployment. Typically, teenagers just entering the labor market have the greatest difficulty finding (or keeping) jobs. They have no job experience and relatively few marketable skills. Employers are reluctant to hire them, especially if they must pay the federal minimum wage. As a consequence, teenage unemployment rates are typically three times higher than adult unemployment rates (see Figure 6.4).

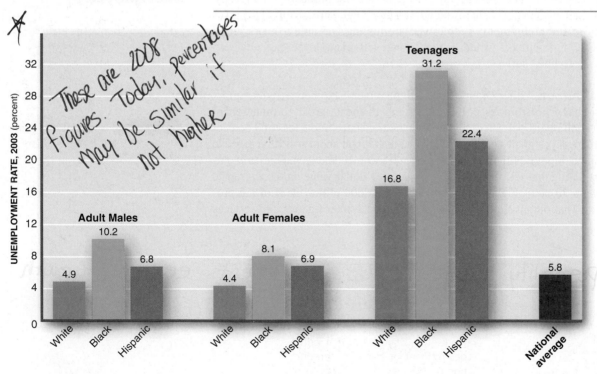

(handwritten note: These are 2008 figures. Today, percentages may be similar if not higher)

FIGURE 6.4
Unemployment Varies by Race and Sex

Minority groups, teenagers, and less-educated individuals experience higher rates of unemployment. Teenage unemployment rates are particularly high, especially for black and other minority youth.

Source: U.S. Department of Labor (2008 data).

(handwritten note in left margin: Why do people hire the 2-3 year mark of being unemployed?)

Duration	Percent of Unemployed
Less than 5 weeks	32.8%
5 to 14 weeks	31.4
15 to 26 weeks	16.0
27 weeks or more	19.7
Median duration	9.4 weeks

Source: U.S. Bureau of Labor Statistics (2008 data).

TABLE 6.1
Duration of Unemployment

The severity of unemployment depends on how long the spell of joblessness lasts. About one-third of unemployed workers return to work quickly, but many others remain unemployed for 6 months or longer.

Minority workers also experience above-average unemployment. Notice in Figure 6.4 that black and hispanic unemployment rates are much higher than white worker's unemployment rates.

Education. Education also affects the chances of being unemployed. If you graduate from college, your chances of being unemployed drop sharply, regardless of gender or race. Advancing technology and a shift to services from manufacturing have put a premium on better-educated workers. Very few people with master's or doctoral degrees stand in unemployment lines.

The Duration of Unemployment

Although high school dropouts are more likely to be unemployed than college graduates, they don't *stay* unemployed. in fact, most people who become unemployed remain jobless for a relatively brief period of time. As Table 6.1 indicates, the median spell of unemployment in 2008 was 9 weeks. Less than one out of five unemployed individuals had been jobless for as long as 6 months (27 weeks or longer). People who lose their jobs do find new ones. ***When the economy is growing, both unemployment rates and the average duration of unemployment decline.*** Recessions have the opposite effect—raising the costs of unemployment significantly.

Reasons for Unemployment

The reason a person becomes unemployed also affects the length of time the person stays jobless. A person just entering the labor market might need more time to identify job openings and develop job contacts. By contrast, an autoworker laid off for a temporary plant closing can expect to return to work quickly. Figure 6.5 depicts these and other reasons for unemployment. In 2008, over half the unemployed were job losers (laid off or fired), and only 1 in 10 were job leavers (quit). The rest were new entrants (primarily teenagers) or reentrants (primarily mothers returning to the workforce). Like the duration of unemployment, the reasons for joblessness are very sensitive to economic conditions. In really bad years like 2008–9, most of the unemployed are job losers, and they remain out of work a long time.

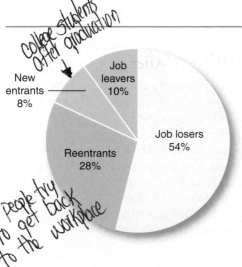

(handwritten note: College students after graduation)

(handwritten note: People try to get back to the workplace)

FIGURE 6.5
Reasons for Unemployment

People become unemployed for various reasons. Over half of the unemployed in 2008 were job losers. About 40 percent of the unemployed were entering or reentering the labor market in search of a job. In recessions, the proportion of job losers shoots up.

Source: U.S. Labor Department.

"I've stopped looking for work, which, I believe, helps the economic numbers."

Analysis: People who stop searching for a job but want one aren't officially counted as "unemployed." They are called "discouraged workers."

Discouraged Workers

discouraged worker: An individual who isn't actively seeking employment but would look for or accept a job if one were available.

Unemployment statistics don't tell the complete story about the human costs of a sluggish economy. When unemployment persists, job seekers become increasingly frustrated. After repeated rejections, job seekers often get so discouraged that they give up the search and turn to their families, friends, or public welfare for income support. When the Census Bureau interviewer asks whether they're actively seeking employment, such **discouraged workers** are apt to reply no. Yet they'd like to be working, and they'd probably be out looking for work if job prospects were better.

Discouraged workers aren't counted as part of our unemployment problem because they're technically out of the labor force (see cartoon above). The Labor Department estimates that nearly 500,000 individuals fell into this uncounted class of discouraged workers in 2008. In years of higher unemployment, this number jumps sharply.

Underemployment

underemployment: People seeking full-time paid employment who work only part-time or are employed at jobs below their capability.

Some people can't afford to be discouraged. Many people who become jobless have family responsibilities and bills to pay: They simply can't afford to drop out of the labor force. Instead, they're compelled to take some job—any job—just to keep body and soul together. The resultant job may be part-time or full-time and may pay very little. Nevertheless, any paid employment is sufficient to exclude the person from the count of the unemployed, though not from a condition of **underemployment.**

Underemployed workers represent labor resources that aren't being fully utilized. They're part of our unemployment problem, even if they're not officially counted as *unemployed.* In 2008, over 5 million workers were underemployed in the U.S. economy (see News, p. 123).

The Phantom Unemployed

Although discouraged and underemployed workers aren't counted in official unemployment statistics, some of the people who *are* counted probably shouldn't be. Many people report that they're actively seeking a job even when they have little interest in finding employment. To some extent, public policy actually encourages such behavior. For example, welfare recipients are often required to look for a job, even though some welfare mothers would prefer to spend all their time raising their children. Their resultant job search is likely to be perfunctory at best. Similarly, most states require people receiving unemployment benefits (see following News) to provide evidence that they're looking for a job, even though some recipients may prefer a brief period of joblessness. Here again, reported unemployment may conceal labor-force nonparticipation. More generous benefits in European nations are thought to create similar problems (see the following World View).

IN THE NEWS

Unemployment Benefits Not for Everyone

In 2008, more than 9 million people collected unemployment benefits averaging $295 per week. But don't rush to the state unemployment office yet—not all unemployed people are eligible. To qualify for weekly unemployment benefits you must have worked a substantial length of time and earned some minimum amount of wages, both determined by your state. Furthermore, you must have a "good" reason for having lost your last job. Most states will not provide benefits to students (or their professors!) during summer vacations, to professional athletes in the off-season, or to individuals who quit their last jobs.

If you qualify for benefits, the amount of benefits you receive each week will depend on your previous wages. In most states the benefits are equal to about one-half of the previous weekly wage, up to a state-determined maximum. The maximum benefit in 2008 ranged from $210 in Mississippi to a high of $900 in Massachusetts.

Unemployment benefits are financed by a tax on employers and can continue for as long as 26 weeks. During periods of high unemployment, eligibility may be extended another 13 weeks or more by the U.S. Congress, as happened twice in 2008.

Source: U.S. Employment and Training Administration. **www.workforcesecurity.doleta.gov**

Analysis: Some of the income lost due to unemployment is replaced by unemployment insurance benefits. Not all unemployed persons are eligible, however, and the duration of benefits is limited.

web analysis

For the latest information on unemployment benefit outlays by the federal government, visit the Department of Labor Web site (**www.dol.gov**).

WORLD VIEW

Europe's Unemployment Woes

Years of sluggish economic growth (low demand) raised unemployment rates in Europe to levels rarely seen in the United States. Generous unemployment benefits cushion the personal losses from this joblessness, however. Those same benefits also discourage European workers from accepting new jobs (less supply).

Japan	Australia	Canada	United Kingdom	United States	Italy	Germany	France
4.1	4.2	5.3	5.9	6.0	6.7	7.4	8.0

(Handwritten note: Figures are higher today, as the European unemployment rate is higher than the US.)

(Handwritten note: Also, Europe is trying to bail out the Greece bonds & protect bonds & the economy.)

web analysis

Compare unemployment rates of different countries at **stats.bls.gov.** Click on the "International" link.

Source: U.S. Department of Labor (2008 data). **http://stats.bls.gov/fls.**

Analysis: Unemployment rates are typically significantly higher in Europe than in the United States. Analysts blame both sluggish economic growth and high unemployment benefits.

THE HUMAN COSTS

Although our measures of unemployment aren't perfect, they're a reliable index to a serious macro problem. Unemployment statistics tell us that millions of people are jobless. That may be all right for a day or even a week, but if you need income to keep body and soul together, prolonged unemployment can hurt.

Lost Income. The most visible impact of unemployment on individuals is the loss of income. For workers who've been unemployed for long periods of time, such losses can spell financial disaster. Typically, an unemployed person must rely on a combination of savings, income from other family members, and government unemployment benefits for financial support. After these sources of support are exhausted, public welfare is often the only legal support left.

Lost Confidence. Not all unemployed people experience such a financial disaster, of course. College students who fail to find summer employment are unlikely to end up on welfare the following semester. Similarly, teenagers and others looking for part-time employment won't suffer great economic losses from unemployment. Nevertheless, the experience of unemployment—of not being able to find a job when you want one—can still be painful. This sensation isn't easily forgotten, even after one has finally found employment.

Social Stress. It is difficult to measure all the intangible effects of unemployment on individual workers. Studies have shown, however, that joblessness causes more crime, more health problems, more divorces, and other problems (see News below). Such findings

web analysis

John Steinbeck's novel *The Grapes of Wrath* depicts the toll of the Great Depression upon unemployed farmers. Visit **video.nytimes.com** to learn more about this classic piece of literature.

IN THE NEWS

How Unemployment Affects the Family

Percentages of unemployed adults who reported that the following had occurred in their family since they were last employed.

—Stephanie Armour

Increased family stress — 77%
Postponed medical care for financial reasons — 57%
Cut back spending on food — 56%
Reduced spending on children — 46%
Other family member started job or increased hours — 26%
Interrupted education — 23%
Lost telephone service — 22%
Had to stop paying for child care or elder care — 12%

Source: USA TODAY. June 27, 2003. Reprinted with Permission.

Analysis: The cost of unemployment is not measured in lost wages alone. Prolonged unemployment also impairs health, social relationships, and productivity.

underscore the notion that prolonged unemployment poses a real danger. Like George H., the worker discussed at the beginning of this chapter, many unemployed workers simply can't cope with the resulting stress. Thomas Cottle, a lecturer at Harvard Medical School, stated the case more bluntly: "I'm now convinced that unemployment is *the* killer disease in this country—responsible for wife beating, infertility, and even tooth decay."

Ill Health. German psychiatrists have also observed that unemployment can be hazardous to your health. They estimate that the anxieties and other nervous disorders that accompany 1 year of unemployment can reduce life expectancy by as much as 5 years. In Japan, the suicide rate jumped by more than 50 percent when the economy plunged into recession. In New Zealand, suicide rates are twice as high for unemployed workers than for employed ones.

DEFINING FULL EMPLOYMENT

In view of the economic and social losses associated with unemployment, it's not surprising that *full employment* is one of our basic macroeconomic goals. You may be surprised to learn, however, that *"full"* employment isn't the same thing as *"zero"* unemployment. There are in fact several reasons for regarding some degree of unemployment as inevitable and even desirable.

Some joblessness is virtually inevitable as long as we continue to grow crops, build houses, or go skiing at certain seasons of the year. At the end of each such season, thousands of workers must go searching for new jobs, experiencing some **seasonal unemployment** in the process.

Seasonal fluctuations also arise on the supply side of the labor market. Teenage unemployment rates, for example, rise sharply in the summer as students look for temporary jobs. To avoid such unemployment completely, we'd either have to keep everyone in school or ensure that all students went immediately from the classroom to the workroom. Neither alternative is likely, much less desirable.[1]

There are other reasons for expecting a certain amount of unemployment. Many workers have sound financial or personal reasons for leaving one job to look for another. In the process of moving from one job to another, a person may well miss a few days or even weeks of work without any serious personal or social consequences. On the contrary, people who spend more time looking for work may find *better* jobs.

The same is true of students first entering the labor market. It's not likely that you'll find a job the moment you leave school. Nor should you necessarily take the first job offered. If you spend some time looking for work, you're more likely to find a job you like. The job-search period gives you an opportunity to find out what kinds of jobs are available, what skills they require, and what they pay. Accordingly, a brief period of job search may benefit labor market entrants and the larger economy. The unemployment associated with these kinds of job searches is referred to as **frictional unemployment.**

Three factors distinguish frictional unemployment from other kinds of unemployment. First, enough jobs exist for those who are frictionally unemployed—that is, there's adequate *demand* for labor. Second, those individuals who are frictionally unemployed have the skills required for available jobs. Third, the period of job search will be relatively short. Under these conditions, frictional unemployment resembles an unconventional game of musical chairs. There are enough chairs of the right size for everyone, and people dance around them for only a brief period of time.

Seasonal Unemployment

seasonal unemployment: Unemployment due to seasonal changes in employment or labor supply.

- Its forecastable

Frictional Unemployment

frictional unemployment: Brief periods of unemployment experienced by people moving between jobs or into the labor market.

- Good situation b/c they find a better job

is not a problem

---

[1] Seasonal variations in employment and labor supply not only create some unemployment in the annual averages but also distort monthly comparisons. Unemployment rates are always higher in February (when farming and housing construction come to a virtual standstill) and June (when a mass of students goes looking for summer jobs). The Labor Department adjusts monthly unemployment rates according to this seasonal pattern and reports "seasonally adjusted" unemployment rates for each month. Seasonal adjustments don't alter *annual* averages, however.

No one knows for sure just how much of our unemployment problem is frictional. Most economists agree, however, that friction alone is responsible for an unemployment rate of 2 to 3 percent. Accordingly, our definition of *"full employment"* should allow for at least this much unemployment.

Structural Unemployment

For many job seekers, the period between jobs may drag on for months or even years because they don't have the skills that employers require. Imagine, for example, the predicament of steelworkers. During the 1980s, the steel industry contracted as consumers demanded fewer and lighter-weight cars and as construction of highways, bridges, and buildings slowed. In the process, over 300,000 steelworkers lost their jobs. Most of these workers had a decade or more of experience and substantial skill. But the skills they'd perfected were no longer in demand. They couldn't perform the jobs available in computer software, biotechnology, or other expanding industries. Although there were enough job vacancies in the labor market, the steelworkers couldn't fill them: These workers were victims of **structural unemployment.** ~don't have skills needed~

structural unemployment:
Unemployment caused by a mismatch between the skills (or location) of job seekers and the requirements (or location) of available jobs.

retraining + moving

The same kind of structural displacement hit the defense industry in the 1990s. Cutbacks in national defense spending forced weapons manufactures, aerospace firms, and electronics companies to reduce output and lay off thousands of workers. The displaced workers soon discovered that their highly developed skills weren't immediately applicable in non-defense industries.

Teenagers from urban slums also suffer from structural unemployment. Most poor teenagers have an inadequate education, few job-related skills, and little work experience. For them, almost all decent jobs are "out of reach." As a consequence, they remain unemployed far longer than can be explained by frictional forces.

Structural unemployment violates the second condition for frictional unemployment: that the job seekers can perform the available jobs. Structural unemployment is analogous to a musical chairs game in which there are enough chairs for everyone, but some of them are too small to sit on. It's a more serious concern than frictional unemployment and incompatible with any notion of full employment.

Cyclical Unemployment

The fourth type of unemployment is **cyclical unemployment**—joblessness that occurs when there simply aren't enough jobs to go around. Cyclical unemployment exists when the number of workers demanded falls short of the number of persons supplied (in the labor force). This isn't a case of mobility between jobs (frictional unemployment) or even of job seekers' skills (structural unemployment). Rather, it's simply an inadequate level of demand for goods and services and thus for labor. Cyclical unemployment resembles the most familiar form of musical chairs, in which the number of chairs is always less than the number of players.

cyclical unemployment:
Unemployment attributable to a lack of job vacancies, that is, to an inadequate level of aggregate demand.

The Great Depression is the most striking example of cyclical unemployment. The dramatic increase in unemployment rates that began in 1930 (see Figure 6.6) wasn't due to any increase in friction or sudden decline in workers' skills. Instead, the high rates of unemployment that persisted for a *decade* were caused by a sudden decline in the market demand for goods and services. How do we know? Just notice what happened to our unemployment rate when the demand for military goods and services increased in 1941!

Slow Growth. Cyclical unemployment can emerge even when the economy is expanding. Keep in mind that the labor force is always growing, due to population growth and continuing immigration. If these additional labor-force participants are to find jobs, the economy must grow. Specifically, *the economy must grow at least as fast as the labor force to avoid cyclical unemployment.* When economic growth slows below this threshold, unemployment rates start to rise.

The Full-Employment Goal

In later chapters we examine the causes of cyclical unemployment and explore some potential policy responses. At this point, however, we just want to establish a macro policy goal. In the Employment Act of 1946, Congress committed the federal government to pursue a goal of "maximum" employment but didn't specify exactly what that rate was. Presumably,

FIGURE 6.6
The Unemployment Record

Unemployment rates reached record heights (25 percent) during the Great Depression. In more recent decades, the unemployment rate has varied from 4 percent in full-employment years to over 10 percent in recession years. Keeping the labor force fully employed is a primary macro policy goal.

Source: U.S. Department of Labor.

---

this meant avoiding as much cyclical and structural unemployment as possible while keeping frictional unemployment within reasonable bounds. As guidelines for public policy, these perspectives are a bit vague.

Inflationary Pressures. The first attempt to define *full employment* more precisely was undertaken in the early 1960s. At that time the Council of Economic Advisers (itself created by the Employment Act of 1946) decided that our proximity to full employment could be gauged by watching *prices*. As the economy approached its production possibilities, labor and other resources would become increasingly scarce. As market participants bid for these remaining resources, wages and prices would start to rise. Hence, **rising prices are a signal that employment is nearing capacity.**

After examining the relationship between unemployment and inflation, the Council of Economic Advisers decided to peg full employment at 4 percent unemployment. The unemployment rate could fall below 4 percent. If it did, however, price levels would begin to rise. Thus, 4 percent unemployment was regarded as an acceptable compromise of our employment and price goals.

Changes in Structural Unemployment. During the 1970s and early 1980s, this view of our full-employment potential was considered overly optimistic. Unemployment rates stayed far above 4 percent, even when the economy expanded. Moreover, inflation began to accelerate at higher levels of unemployment. Critics suggested that structural barriers to full employment had intensified due to

- *More youth and women.* Between 1956 and 1979, the proportion of teenagers and adult women in the labor force grew tremendously (see Figure 6.2). Their relative lack of work experience increased frictional and structural unemployment.
- *Liberal transfer payments.* Higher benefits and easier rules for unemployment insurance, food stamps, welfare, and Social Security made unemployment less painful. As a result, more people were willing and able to stay unemployed rather than work.
- *Structural changes in demand.* Changes in consumer demand, technology, and trade shrank the markets in steel, textiles, autos, and other industries. The workers dislocated from these industries couldn't be absorbed fast enough in new high-tech and other service industries.

"I don't like six-per-cent unemployment, either. But I can live with it."

Analysis: So-called full employment entails a compromise between employment and inflation goals. That compromise doesn't affect everyone equally.

In view of these factors, the Council of Economic Advisers later raised the level of unemployment thought to be compatible with price stability. In 1983, the Reagan administration concluded that the "inflation-threshold" unemployment rate was between 6 and 7 percent (see cartoon above).

Declining Structural Pressures. The structural barriers that intensified inflationary pressures in the 1970s and early 1980s receded in the 1990s. The number of teenagers declined by 3 million between 1981 and 1993. The upsurge in women's participation in the labor force also leveled off. High school and college attendance and graduation rates increased. And welfare programs were reformed in ways that encouraged more work. All these structural changes made it easier to reduce unemployment rates without increasing inflation. In 1991, the first Bush administration concluded that **full employment** was equivalent to 5.5 percent unemployment. In 1999, the Clinton administration suggested the full-employment threshold might have dropped even further, to 5.3 percent. In reality, the national unemployment rate stayed below even that benchmark for 4 years (Figure 6.6) without any upsurge in inflation. In 2004 the Bush administration set the full-employment threshold at 5.1 percent. The Obama administration left that threshold intact.

The ambiguity about which rate of unemployment might trigger an upsurge in inflation has convinced some analysts to abandon the inflation-based concept of full employment. They prefer to specify a "natural" rate of unemployment that doesn't depend on inflation trends. In this view, the natural rate of unemployment consists of frictional and structural components only. It's the rate of unemployment that will prevail in the long run. In the short run, both the unemployment rate and the inflation rate may go up and down. However, the economy will tend to gravitate toward the long-run **natural rate of unemployment.**

Although the natural rate concept avoids specifying a short-term inflation trigger, it too is subject to debate. As we've seen, the *structural* determinants of unemployment (e.g., age

full employment: The lowest rate of unemployment compatible with price stability; variously estimated at between 4 percent and 6 percent unemployment.

The "Natural" Rate of Unemployment

natural rate of unemployment: Long-term rate of unemployment determined by structural forces in labor and product markets.

and composition of the labor force) change over time. When structural forces change, the level of natural unemployment presumably changes as well.

Although most economists agree that an unemployment rate of 4 to 6 percent is consistent with either natural or full employment, Congress has set tougher goals for macro policy. According to the Full Employment and Balanced Growth Act of 1978 (commonly called the Humphrey-Hawkins Act), our national goal is to attain a 4 percent rate of unemployment. The act also requires a goal of 3 percent inflation. There was an escape clause, however. In the event that both goals couldn't be met, the president could set higher, provisional definitions of full employment.

Congressional Targets

THE HISTORICAL RECORD

Our greatest failure to achieve full employment occurred during the Great Depression. As Figure 6.6 shows, as much as one-fourth of the labor force was unemployed in the 1930s.

Unemployment rates fell dramatically during World War II. In 1944, virtually anyone who was ready and willing to work quickly found a job: The civilian unemployment rate hit a rock-bottom 1.2 percent.

Since 1950, the unemployment rate has fluctuated from a low of 2.8 percent during the Korean War (1953) to a high of 10.8 percent during the 1981–82 recession. From 1982 to 1989 the unemployment rate receded, but it shot up again in the 1990–91 recession. During the last half of the 1990s the unemployment rate fell steadily and hit the low end of the full-employment range in 2000. Slow GDP growth in 2000–2001 and the economic stall caused by the September 11, 2001, terrorist attacks pushed the unemployment rate sharply higher in late 2001. The subsequent recovery of the U.S. economy pushed the unemployment rate down into the "full-employment" range again in 2006–7. But the credit crisis of 2008 wiped out that gain, sending the unemployment rate sharply higher (see News below).

3.9%

IN THE NEWS

Job Loss: Worst in 34 Years

Employers Slashed 598,000 More Jobs in January as Unemployment Rate Climbed to 7.6%

NEW YORK (CNNMoney.com)—Employers slashed another 598,000 jobs off of U.S. payrolls in January, taking the unemployment rate up to 7.6%, according to the latest government reading on the nation's battered labor market.

The latest job loss is the worst since December 1974, and brings job losses to 1.8 million in just the last three months, or half of the 3.6 million jobs that have been lost since the beginning of 2008.

As bad as the unemployment rate was, it only tells part of the story for people struggling to find jobs. Friday's report also showed that 2.6 million people have now been out of work for more than six months, the most long-term unemployed since 1983.

And that number only counts those still looking for work. The so-called underemployment rate, which includes those who have stopped looking for work and people working only part-time that want full-time positions, climbed to 13.9% from 13.5% in December. That is the highest rate for this measure since the Labor Department first started tracking it in 1994.

—Chris Isidore

Analysis: A slowdown in economic growth causes the unemployment rate to rise—sometimes sharply.

THE ECONOMY TOMORROW

OUTSOURCING JOBS

outsourcing: The relocation of production to foreign countries.

To keep unemployment rates low in the economy tomorrow, job growth in U.S. product markets must exceed labor-force growth. As we've observed, this will require at least 2 million *new* jobs every year. Achieving that net job growth is made more difficult when U.S. firms shut down their U.S. operations and relocate production to Mexico, China, and other foreign nations. Even in the absence of plant shutdowns, **outsourcing** of U.S. production to workers in India, Poland, Malaysia, and elsewhere can limit U.S. job growth.

Cheap Labor. Low wages are the primary motivation for all this outsourcing. As the accompanying World View documents, telephone operators and clerks in India are paid a tenth that of their U.S. counterparts. Indian accountants and paralegals get paid less than half that of their U.S. counterparts. Polish workers are even cheaper. With cheap, high-speed telecommunications, that offshore labor is an attractive substitute for U.S. workers. Over the next 10 years, over 3 million U.S. jobs are expected to move offshore in response to such wage differentials.

Small Numbers. In the short run, outsourcing clearly worsens the U.S. employment outlook. But there's a lot more to the story. To begin with, the total number of outsourced jobs averages less than 300,000 per year. That amounts to only .002 of all U.S. jobs, and only 3–5 percent of total U.S. *un*employment. So even in the worst case, outsourcing can't be a major explanation for U.S. unemployment.

Insourcing. We also have to recognize that outsourcing of U.S. jobs has a counterpart in the "insourcing" of foreign production. The German BMW company builds cars in Alabama to reduce production and distribution costs. In the process German autoworkers lose some jobs to U.S. autoworkers. In addition to this direct investment, foreign nations and firms hire U.S. workers to design, build, and deliver a wide variety of products. In other

WORLD VIEW

Salary Gap

Programmers' Pay

A Hungarian computer programmer starts at a salary of $4,800 per year; an American programmer begins at $60,000.

Average Salaries of Computer Programmers

Country	Salary Range
Poland and Hungary	$4,800–8,000
India	$5,880–11,000
Philippines	$6,564
Malaysia	$7,200
Russian Federation	$5,000–7,500
China	$8,952
Canada	$28,174
Ireland	$23,000–34,000
Israel	$15,000–38,000
United States	$60,000–80,000

Wages, India versus U.S.

Wages in the United States in some occupations are twice as high as in India, and in others 12 times as high.

Hourly Wages for Selected Occupations, U.S. and India, 2002–2003

Occupation	U.S.	India
Telephone Operator	$12.57	Under $1.00
Health Record Technologist/ Medical Transcriptionist	$13.17	$1.50–2.00
Payroll Clerk	$15.17	$1.50–2.00
Legal Assistant/Paralegal	$17.86	$6.00–8.00
Accountant	$23.35	$6.00–15.00
Financial Researcher/Analyst	$33.00–35.00	$6.00–15.00

Source: Ashok Deo Bardhan and Cynthia Kroll, "The New Wave of Outsourcing" (November 2, 2003). *Fisher Center for Real Estate and Urban Economics. Fisher Center Reports*: Report # 1103. **http://repositories. cdlib.org/iber/fcrene/reports/1103.**

Analysis: Cheap foreign labor is a substitute for U.S. labor. These and similar salary gaps encourage U.S. firms to relocate production offshore.

words, *trade in both products and labor resources is a two-way street.* Looking at the flow of jobs in only one direction distorts the jobs picture.

Productivity and Growth. Even the gross flow of outsourced jobs is not all bad. The cost savings realized by U.S. firms due to outsourcing increases U.S. profits. Those profits may finance new investment or consumption in U.S. product markets, thereby creating new jobs. The accompanying News suggests more jobs are gained than lost as a result. Outsourcing routine tasks to foreign workers also raises the productivity of U.S. workers by allowing U.S. workers to focus on more complex and high-value tasks. In other words, outsourcing promotes specialization and higher productivity both here and abroad. *Production possibilities expand, not contract, with outsourcing.*

IN THE NEWS

Outsourcing May Create U.S. Jobs

Higher Productivity Allows For Investment in Staffing, Expansion, a Study Finds

WASHINGTON—U.S. companies sending computer-systems work abroad yielded higher productivity that actually boosted domestic employment by 90,000 across the economy last year, according to an industry-sponsored study. . . .

Expected to be released today, the study's premise is that U.S. companies' use of foreign workers lowers costs, increases labor productivity and produces income that companies can use to expand both in the U.S. and abroad. . . .

The study claims that twice the number of U.S. jobs are created than displaced, producing wage increases in various sectors. . . .

Demand for U.S. exports is expected to increase due to the relatively lower prices of U.S.-produced goods and services and higher incomes in foreign countries where U.S. work is done.

—Michael Schroeder

Source: *The Wall Street Journal*, March 30, 2004. Copyright 2004 by Dow Jones & Company, Inc. Reproduced with permission of Dow Jones & Company, Inc. in the format Textbook via Copyright Clearance Center.

More Jobs

Estimated New U.S. Jobs Created from Outsourcing Abroad, According to an Industry Study

	2003	2008
Natural Resources & Mining	1,046	1,182
Construction	19,815	75,757
Manufacturing	3,078	25,010
Wholesale Trade	20,456	43,359
Retail Trade	12,552	30,931
Transportation & Utilities	18,895	63,513
Publishing, Software & Communications	−24,860	−50,043
Financial Services	5,604	32,066
Professional & Business Services	14,667	31,623
Education & Health Services	18,015	47,260
Leisure, Hospitality & Other Services	4,389	12,506
Government	−3,393	4,203
Total Employment	**90,264**	**317,367**

Source: Global Insight and North American Industry Classification System.

Analysis: Outsourcing increases U.S. productivity and profits while reducing U.S. production costs and prices. These outcomes may increase demand for U.S. jobs by more than the immediate job loss.

Firms that outsource may increase profits

Repatriation Tax

a second tax paid to US on goods manufactured outside of the US

Creating Jobs. Greater efficiency and expanded production possibilities don't guarantee jobs in the economy tomorrow. The challenge is still to *use* that expanded capacity to the fullest. To do so, we have to use macroeconomic tools to keep output growing faster than the labor force. Stopping the outsourcing of jobs won't achieve that goal—and may even worsen income and job prospects in the economy tomorrow.

SUMMARY

- To understand unemployment, we must distinguish the labor force from the larger population. Only people who are working (employed) or spend some time looking for a job (unemployed) are participants in the labor force. People neither working nor looking for work are outside the labor force.   LO1

- The labor force grows every year due to population growth and immigration. This growth increases production possibilities but also necessitates continued job creation.   LO1

- The economy (output) must grow at least as fast as the labor force to keep the unemployment rate from rising. Unemployment implies that we're producing inside the production possibilities curve rather than on it.   LO1

- The macroeconomic loss imposed by unemployment is reduced output of goods and services. Okun's Law suggests that 1 percentage point in unemployment is equivalent to a 2 percentage point decline in output.   LO1

- The human cost of unemployment includes not only financial losses but social, physical, and psychological costs as well.   LO1

- Unemployment is distributed unevenly; minorities, teenagers, and the less educated have much higher rates of unemployment. Also hurt are discouraged workers—those who've stopped looking for work at part-time or menial jobs because they can't find full-time jobs equal to their training or potential.   LO1

- There are four types of unemployment: seasonal, frictional, structural, and cyclical.   LO2

- Because some seasonal and frictional unemployment is inevitable and even desirable, full employment is not defined as zero unemployment. These considerations, plus fear of inflationary consequences, result in full employment being defined as an unemployment rate of 4 to 6 percent.   LO3

- The natural rate of unemployment is based on frictional and structural forces, without reference to short-term price (inflation) pressures.   LO1

- Unemployment rates got as high as 25 percent in the 1930s. Since 1960, the unemployment rate has ranged from 3.4 to 10.8 percent.   LO1

- Outsourcing of U.S. production directly reduces domestic employment. But the indirect effects of higher U.S. productivity, profits, and global competitiveness may create even more jobs.   LO1

Key Terms

labor force	unemployment rate	structural unemployment
labor-force participation rate	discouraged worker	cyclical unemployment
production possibilities	underemployment	full employment
unemployment	seasonal unemployment	natural rate of unemployment
Okun's Law	frictional unemployment	outsourcing

Questions for Discussion

1. Is it possible for unemployment rates to increase at the same time that the number of employed persons is increasing? How?   LO1

2. If more teenagers stay in school longer, what happens to (*a*) production possibilities? (*b*) unemployment rates?   LO1

3. What factors might explain (*a*) the rising labor-force participation rate of women and (*b*) the declining participation of men? (See Figure 6.2 for trends.)   LO1

4. Why might job (re)entrants have a harder time finding a job than job losers?   LO2

5. If the government guaranteed some income to all unemployed persons, how might the unemployment rate be affected? Who should get unemployment benefits? (See News, p. 117.)   LO2

6. When the Chrysler plant in South St. Louis closed (p. 111), whose jobs and incomes were affected?   LO2

7. Why is frictional unemployment deemed desirable?   LO2

8. Why do people expect inflation to heat up when the unemployment rate approaches 4 percent?   LO3

9. Identify (*a*) two jobs at your school that could be outsourced and (*b*) two jobs that would be hard to outsource.   LO3

10. How can the outsourcing of U.S. computer jobs generate new U.S. jobs in construction or retail trade? (See News, p. 125.)   LO3

web activities to accompany this chapter can be found on the Online Learning Center:

http://www.mhhe.com/schiller12e

LO1   1. According to Figure 6.1, what percent of the civilian labor force was
       (a) Employed?   _____%
       (b) Unemployed?   _____%
       (c) What percent of the *population* was employed in civilian jobs?   _____%

LO1   2. Between 2000 and 2007, by how much did
       (a) The labor force increase?   _____
       (b) Total employment increase?   _____
       (c) Total unemployment change?   _____
       (d) Total output (real GDP) increase?   _____
       (e) The national unemployment rate change?   _____
       (*Note:* Data on inside covers of the text.)

LO1   3. If the labor force is growing by 1.5 percent per year, how many new jobs have to be created each
       month to keep unemployment from increasing?   _____
       Web query: By how much did U.S. employment actually increase last month (**www.bls.gov**)?   _____

LO1   4. Between 1980 and 2008, by how much did the labor-force participation rate (Figure 6.2) of
       (a) Men fall?   _____%
       (b) Women rise?   _____%

LO1   5. According to Okun's Law, how much output (real GDP) was lost in 2008 when the nation's
       unemployment rate increased from 4.6 percent to 5.8 percent? $_____

LO1   6. Suppose the following data describe a nation's population:

	Year 1	Year 2
Population	200 million	204 million
Labor force	120 million	123 million
Unemployment rate	6 percent	6 percent

       (a) How many people are unemployed in each year?   Year 1:   _____
                                                                   Year 2:   _____
       (b) How many people are employed in each year?   Year 1:   _____
                                                                   Year 2:   _____
       (c) Compute the employment rate (i.e., number employed ÷ population) in each year.   Year 1:   _____
                                                                   Year 2:   _____

LO1   7. Based on the data in the previous problem, what happens ("up" or "down") to each of
       the following numbers in Year 2 when 1 million jobseekers become "discouraged
       workers"?
       (a) Number of unemployed persons.   _____
       (b) Unemployment rate.   _____
       (c) Employment rate.   _____

LO2   8. According to the data in the News on page 123, how high was the underemployment rate
       in January 2009?   _____

LO1   9. In 2008, how many of the 800,000 black teenagers who participated in the labor market
       (a) Were unemployed?   _____
       (b) Were employed?   _____
       (c) Would have been employed if they had the same unemployment rate as
           white teenagers?   _____
       (See Figure 6.4 for needed info.)

LO3 10. On the accompanying graph, illustrate both the unemployment rate and the percentage change in real
     GDP (output) for each year. (The data required for this exercise are on the inside cover of this book.)
     (*a*) In how many years was "full employment" achieved? (Use current benchmark.)   _____
     (*b*) Unemployment and growth rates tend to move in opposite directions. Which appears to
            change direction first?   _____
     (*c*) In how many years does the unemployment rate increase even when output is expanding?   _____

Inflation

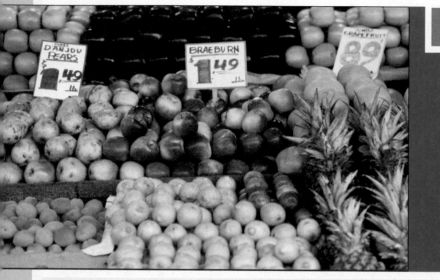

7

After reading this chapter, you should be able to:

LO1. Illustrate how inflation is measured.

LO2. Explain how inflation redistributes income and wealth.

LO3. Discuss the meaning of "price stability."

Germany set a record in 1923 that no other nation wants to beat. In that year, prices in Germany rose a *trillion* times over. Prices rose so fast that workers took "shopping breaks" to spend their twice-a-day paychecks before they became worthless. Menu prices in restaurants rose while people were still eating! Accumulated savings became worthless, as did outstanding loans. People needed sacks of currency to buy bread, butter, and other staples. With prices more than doubling every *day,* no one could afford to save, invest, lend money, or make long-term plans. In the frenzy of escalating prices, production of goods and services came to a halt, unemployment rose tenfold, and the German economy all but collapsed.

Hungary had a similar episode of runaway inflation in 1946, as did Japan. More recently, Russia, Bulgaria, Brazil, Zaire, Yugoslavia, Argentina, and Uruguay have all witnessed at least a tenfold jump in prices in a single year. Zimbabwe came close to breaking Germany's record in 2008, with an inflation rate of *231 million* percent (see News, p. 136).

The United States has never experienced such a price frenzy. During the Revolutionary War, prices did double in 1 year, but that was a singular event. In the last decade, U.S. prices have risen just 1 to 4 percent a year. Despite this enviable record, Americans still *worry* a lot about inflation. In response to this anxiety, every president since Franklin Roosevelt has expressed a determination to keep prices from rising. In 1971, the Nixon administration took drastic action to stop inflation.

With prices rising an average of only 3 percent, President Nixon imposed price controls on U.S. producers to keep prices from rising any faster. For 90 days all wages and prices were frozen by law—price increases were prohibited. For 3 more years, wage and price increases were limited by legal rules.

In 1990, U.S. prices were rising at a 6 percent clip—twice the pace that triggered the 1971–74 wage and price controls. Calling such price increases "unacceptable," Federal Reserve Chairman Alan Greenspan set a goal of *zero* percent inflation. In pursuit of that goal, the Fed slowed economic growth so much that the economy fell into a recession. The Fed did the same thing again in early 2000.

In later chapters we'll examine how the Fed and other policymakers slow the economy down or speed it up. Before looking at the levers of macro policy, however, we need to examine our policy goals. Why is inflation so feared? How much inflation is unacceptable? To get a handle on this basic issue, we'll ask and answer the following questions:

- **What kind of price increases are referred to as** *inflation*?
- **Who is hurt (or helped) by inflation?**
- **What is an appropriate goal for** *price stability*?

As we'll discover, inflation is a serious problem, but not for the reasons most people cite. We'll also see why deflation—falling prices—isn't so welcome either.

WHAT IS INFLATION?

Most people associate **inflation** with price increases on specific goods and services. The economy isn't necessarily experiencing an inflation, however, every time the price of a cup of coffee goes up. We must distinguish the phenomenon of inflation from price increases for specific goods. *Inflation is an increase in the average level of prices, not a change in any specific price.*

Suppose you wanted to know the average price of fruit in the supermarket. Surely you wouldn't have much success in seeking out an average fruit—nobody would be quite sure what you had in mind. You might have some success, however, if you sought out the prices of apples, oranges, cherries, and peaches. Knowing the price of each kind of fruit, you could then compute the average price of fruit. The resultant figure wouldn't refer to any particular product but would convey a sense of how much a typical basket of fruit might cost. By repeating these calculations every day, you could then determine whether fruit prices, *on average,* were changing. On occasion, you might even notice that apple prices rose while orange prices fell, leaving the *average* price of fruit unchanged.

The same kinds of calculations are made to measure inflation in the entire economy. We first determine the average price of all output—the average price level—then look for changes in that average. A rise in the average price level is referred to as inflation.

The average price level may fall as well as rise. A decline in average prices—a **deflation**—occurs when price decreases on some goods and services outweigh price increases on all others. This happened in Japan in 1995, and again in 2003. Such deflations are rare, however: The United States has not experienced any general deflation since 1940.

Because inflation and deflation are measured in terms of average price levels, it's possible for individual prices to rise or fall continuously without changing the average price level. We already noted, for example, that the price of apples can rise without increasing the average price of fruit, so long as the price of some other fruit, such as oranges, falls. In such circumstances, **relative prices** are changing, but not *average* prices. An increase in the *relative* price of apples simply means that apples have become more expensive in comparison with other fruits (or any other goods or services).

Changes in relative prices may occur in a period of stable average prices, or in periods of inflation or deflation. In fact, in an economy as vast as ours—in which literally millions of goods and services are exchanged in the factor and product markets—*relative prices are always changing.* Indeed, relative price changes are an essential ingredient of the market mechanism. Recall from Chapter 3 what happens when the market price of Web-design services rises relative to other goods and services. This (relative) price rise alerts Web architects (producers) to increase their output, cutting back on other production or leisure activities.

A general inflation—an increase in the average price level—doesn't perform this same market function. If all prices rise at the same rate, price increases for specific goods are of little value as market signals. In less extreme cases, when most but not all prices are rising, changes in relative prices do occur but aren't so immediately apparent. Table 7.1 reminds us that some prices do fall even during periods of general inflation.

REDISTRIBUTIVE EFFECTS OF INFLATION

The distinction between relative and average prices helps us determine who's hurt by inflation—and who's helped. Popular opinion notwithstanding, it's simply not true that everyone is worse off when prices rise. *Although inflation makes some people worse off, it makes other people better off.* Some people even get rich when prices rise! The micro consequences of inflation are reflected in redistributions of income and wealth, not general declines in either measure of our economic welfare. These redistributions occur because people buy different combinations of goods and services, own different assets,

---

inflation: An increase in the average level of prices of goods and services

• too much aggrigate demand

The Average Price

deflation: A decrease in the average level of prices of goods and services.

Relative Prices vs. the Price Level

relative price: The price of one good in comparison with the price of other goods.

TABLE 7.1

Prices That Have Fallen

Inflation refers to an increase in the average price level. It doesn't mean that *all* prices are rising. In fact, many prices fall, even during periods of general inflation.

Item	Early Price	2009 Price
Long-distance telephone call (per minute)	$ 6.90 (1915)	$ 0.03
Pocket electronic calculator	200.00 (1972)	1.99
Digital watch	2,000.00 (1972)	1.99
Pantyhose	2.16 (1967)	1.29
Ballpoint pen	0.89 (1965)	0.29
DVD player	800.00 (1997)	59.00
Laptop computer	3,500.00 (1986)	400.00
Airfare (New York–Paris)	490.00 (1958)	328.00
Microwave oven	400.00 (1972)	69.00
Contact lenses	275.00 (1972)	39.00
Television (19-inch, color)	469.00 (1980)	169.00
Compact disk player	1,000.00 (1985)	29.00
Digital camera	748.00 (1994)	117.00
Digital music player	399.00 (2001)	89.00
Cell phone	3,595.00 (1983)	59.95
Mobile e-mail (BlackBerry)	400.00 (1999)	100.00

and sell distinct goods or services (including labor). The impact of inflation on individuals therefore depends on how prices change for the goods and services each person actually buys or sells.

Price Effects

Price changes are the most visible consequence of inflation. If you've been paying tuition, you know how painful a price hike can be. Ten years ago, the average tuition at public colleges and universities was $1,000 per year. Today the average tuition exceeds $6,500. At private universities, tuition has increased eightfold in the past 10 years, to over $25,000 (see News below). You don't need a whole course in economics to figure out the implications of these tuition hikes. To stay in college, you (or your parents) must forgo increasing amounts of other goods and services. You end up being worse off since you can't buy as many goods and services as you could before tuition went up.

IN THE NEWS

College Tuition Just Keeps Climbing

Tuition and fees at four-year public colleges and universities rose faster than those of private schools, yet again outpacing the rate of inflation, the College Board said in a report released Oct. 29.

. . . this year's College Board report shows hikes of 6.4% for public in-state tuitions and 5.9% for private colleges. The consumer price index rose 5.6% between July 2007 and July 2008, the College Board said. . . .

According to the College Board report, the average in-state tuition and fees at four-year public colleges for the 2008–09 academic year are $6,585, up $394 from last year. Those numbers don't include room and board, which adds on about $8,000. . . .

Costs at private universities were also on the upswing, with published tuition and fees for this school year averaging $25,143, a $1,398 increase over last year.

—Alison Damast

Source: Reprinted from October 29, 2008, issue of *BusinessWeek* by special permission. Copyright © 2008 by The McGraw-Hill Companies, Inc.

Analysis: Tuition increases reduce the real income of students. How much you suffer from inflation depends on what happens to the prices of the products you purchase.

The effect of tuition increases on your economic welfare is reflected in the distinction between nominal income and real income. **Nominal income** is the amount of money you receive in a particular time period; it's measured in current dollars. **Real income,** by contrast, is the purchasing power of that money, as measured by the quantity of goods and services your dollars will buy. If the number of dollars you receive every year is always the same, your *nominal income* doesn't change— but your *real income* will rise or fall with price changes.

Suppose your parents agree to give you $6,000 a year while you're in school. Out of that $6,000 you must pay for your tuition, room and board, books, and everything else. The budget for your first year at school might look like this:

nominal income: The amount of money income received in a given time period, measured in current dollars.

real income: Income in constant dollars; nominal income adjusted for inflation.

FIRST YEAR'S BUDGET

Nominal income	$6,000
Consumption	
Tuition	$3,000
Room and board	2,000
Books	300
Everything else	700
Total	$6,000

After paying for all your essential expenses, you have $700 to spend on clothes, entertainment, or anything else you want. That's not exactly living high, but it's not poverty.

Now suppose tuition increases to $3,500 in your second year, while all other prices remain the same. What will happen to your nominal income? Nothing. Unless your parents take pity on you, you'll still be getting $6,000 a year. Your nominal income is unchanged. Your *real* income, however, will suffer. This is evident in the second year's budget:

SECOND YEAR'S BUDGET

Nominal income	$6,000
Consumption	
Tuition	$3,500
Room and board	2,000
Books	300
Everything else	200
Total	$6,000

You now have to use more of your income to pay tuition. This means you have less income to spend on other things. Since room and board and books still cost $2,300 per year, there's only one place to cut: the category of "everything else." After tuition increases, you can spend only $200 per year on movies, clothes, pizzas, and dates—not $700, as in the "good old days." This $500 reduction in purchasing power represents a *real* income loss. Even though your *nominal* income is still $6,000, you have $500 less of "everything else" in your second year than you had in the first.

Although tuition hikes reduce the real income of students, nonstudents aren't hurt by such price increases. In fact, if tuition *doubled,* nonstudents really wouldn't care. They could continue to buy the same bundle of goods and services they'd been buying all along. Tuition increases reduce the real incomes only of people who go to college.

Two basic lessons about inflation are to be learned from this sad story:

- *Not all prices rise at the same rate during an inflation.* In our example, tuition increased substantially while other prices remained steady. Hence, the "average" price increase wasn't representative of any particular good or service. Typically, some prices rise rapidly, others only modestly, and some actually fall.

TABLE 7.2
Price Changes in 2008

The average rate of inflation conceals substantial differences in the price changes of specific products. The impact of inflation on individuals depends in part on which goods and services are consumed. People who buy goods whose prices are rising fastest lose more real income. In 2008, bus riders and college students were particularly hard-hit by inflation.

Prices That Rose (%)		Prices That Fell (%)	
Bananas	+15.8%	New cars	−1.1%
Bread	+12.5	Eggs	−9.1
Bus fares	+8.2	Computers	−11.5
Textbooks	+7.5	Televisions	−19.4
College tuition	+5.5	Gasoline	−44.0
	Average inflation rate: +3.8%		

Source: U.S. Bureau of Labor Statistics.

Income Effects

Wealth Effects

• *Not everyone suffers equally from inflation.* This follows from our first observation. Those people who consume the goods and services that are rising faster in price bear a greater burden of inflation; their real incomes fall further. Other consumers bear a lesser burden, or even none at all, depending on how fast the prices rise for the goods they enjoy.

Table 7.2 illustrates some of the price changes that occurred in 2008. The average rate of inflation was only 3.8 percent. This was little solace to college students, however, who confronted tuition increases of 5.5 percent, and 7.5 percent price hikes on textbooks (sorry!). On the other hand, price reductions on televisions and computers spared consumers of these products from the pain of the *average* inflation rate.

Even if all prices rose at the *same* rate, inflation would still redistribute income. The redistributive effects of inflation originate not only in *expenditure* patterns but also *income* patterns. Some people have fixed incomes that *don't* go up with inflation. Fixed-income groups include those retired people who depend primarily on private pensions and workers with multiyear contracts that fix wage rates at preinflation levels. Lenders (like banks) that have lent funds at fixed interest rates also suffer real income losses when price levels rise. They continue to receive interest payments fixed in *nominal* dollars that have increasingly less *real* value. All these market participants experience a declining share of real income (and output) in inflationary periods.

Not all market participants suffer a real income decline when prices rise. Some people's nominal income rises *faster* than average prices, thereby boosting their *real* incomes. Keep in mind that there are two sides to every market transaction. **What looks like a price to a buyer looks like an income to a seller.** If students pay higher tuition, the university will take in more income. When the nominal incomes colleges receive rise faster than average prices, they actually *benefit* from inflation. They end up being able to buy *more* goods and services (including faculty, buildings, and library books) after a period of inflation than they could before. Their real income rises. When the price of this textbook goes up, my *nominal* income goes up. If the text price rises faster than other prices, my *real* income increases as well. In either case, you lose (sorry!).

Once we recognize that nominal incomes and prices don't all increase at the same rate, it makes no sense to say that "inflation hurts everybody." **If prices are rising, incomes must be rising too.** In fact, on *average,* incomes rise just as fast as prices (see Figure 7.1). That fact is of little comfort, however, to those who end up losing real income in the inflation game.

Still more winners and losers of the inflation game are selected on the basis of the assets they hold. Suppose you deposit $100 in a savings account on January 1, where it earns 5 percent interest. At the end of the year you'll have more nominal wealth ($105) than you started with ($100). But what if all prices have doubled in the meantime? In that case, your $105 will buy you no more at the end of the year than $52.50 would have bought you at the

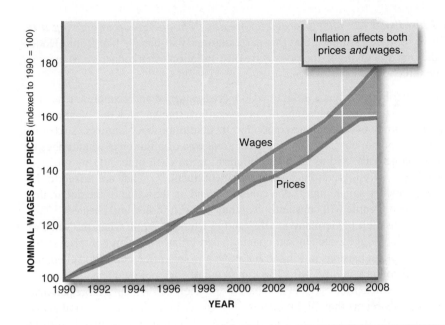

Inflation affects both prices *and* wages.

FIGURE 7.1
Nominal Wages and Prices

Inflation implies not only higher prices but higher incomes as well. Hence, inflation can't make *everyone* worse off. In fact, average wages increase along with average prices. They rise even faster than prices when productivity increases. Wages rise slower than prices when fringe benefits or payroll taxes are increasing.

Source: *Economic Report of the President, 2009.*

beginning. Inflation in this case reduces the *real* value of your savings, and you end up worse off than those individuals who spent all their income earlier in the year!

Table 7.3 shows how the value of various assets has changed. Between 1991 and 2001, the average price level increased 32 percent. The average value of stocks, diamonds, and homes rose much faster than the price level, increasing the *real* value of those assets. Farmland prices rose too, but just a bit more than average prices. People who owned bonds, silver, and gold weren't so lucky; their *real* wealth declined.

By altering relative prices, incomes, and the real value of wealth, inflation turns out to be a mechanism for redistributing incomes and wealth. ***The redistributive mechanics of inflation include:***

Redistributions

- ***Price effects.*** People who buy products that are increasing in price the fastest end up worse off.
- ***Income effects.*** People whose nominal incomes rise more slowly than the rate of inflation end up worse off.
- ***Wealth effects.*** People who own assets that are declining in real value end up worse off.

On the other hand, people whose nominal incomes increase faster than inflation end up with larger shares of total output. The same thing is true of those who enjoy goods that are rising slowest in price or who hold assets whose real value is increasing. In this sense,

Asset	Change in Value (%), 1991–2001
Stocks	+250%
Diamonds	+71
Oil	+66
Housing	+56
U.S. farmland	+49
Average price level	+32
Silver	+22
Bonds	+20
Stamps	−9
Gold	−29

TABLE 7.3
The Real Story of Wealth

Households hold their wealth in many different forms. As the value of various assets changes, so does a person's wealth. Between 1991 and 2001, inflation was very good to people who held stocks. By contrast, the real value of bonds, gold, and silver fell.

inflation acts just like a tax, taking income or wealth from one group and giving it to another. But we have no assurance that this particular tax will behave like Robin Hood, taking from the rich and giving to the poor. In reality, inflation often redistributes income in the opposite direction.

Social Tensions

Because of its redistributive effects, inflation also increases social and economic tensions. Tensions—between labor and management, between government and the people, and among consumers—may overwhelm a society and its institutions. As Gardner Ackley of the University of Michigan observed, "A significant real cost of inflation is what it does to morale, to social coherence, and to people's attitudes toward each other." "This society," added Arthur Okun, "is built on implicit and explicit contracts. . . . They are linked to the idea that the dollar means something. If you cannot depend on the value of the dollar, this system is undermined. People will constantly feel they've been fooled and cheated."[1] This is how the middle class felt in Germany in 1923 and in China in 1948, when the value of their savings was wiped out by sudden and unanticipated inflation. A surge in prices also stirred social and political tensions in Russia as it moved from a price-controlled economy to a market-driven economy in the 1990s. The same kind of sociopolitical tension arose in Zimbabwe in 2008–9 when prices skyrocketed (see World View below). On a more personal level, psychotherapists report that "inflation stress" leads to more frequent marital spats, pessimism, diminished self-confidence, and even sexual insecurity. Some people turn to crime as a way of solving the problem.

WORLD VIEW

Zimbabwe Introduces $50 Billion Note

HARARE, Zimbabwe (CNN)—Zimbabwe's central bank will introduce a $50 billion note—enough to buy just two loaves of bread—as a way of fighting cash shortage amid spiraling inflation. . . .

Zimbabwe is grappling with hyperinflation now officially estimated at 231 million percent, and its currency is fast losing its value. As of Friday, one U.S. dollar was trading at around ZW$25 billion.

When the government issued a $10 billion note just three weeks ago, it bought 20 loaves of bread. That note now can purchase less than half of one loaf.

Realizing the worthlessness of the currency, the RBZ has allowed most goods and services to be charged in foreign currency. As a result, grocery purchases, government hospital bills, property sales, rent, vegetables and even mobile phone recharge cards are now paid for in foreign currency, as the worthless Zimbabwe dollar virtually ceases to be legal tender. . . .

John Robertson, an economist in Zimbabwe, said he's puzzled by the introduction of the $50 billion and $20 billion notes. "I am not really sure what these notes would be for," he said, "No one now accepts the local currency. It is a waste of resources to print Zimbabwe dollar notes now. Who accepts a currency that loses value by almost 100 percent daily?"

Source: Excerpted from CNN.com, January 13, 2009. Used with permission.

Analysis: Hyperinflation forces market participants to focus on the very short run and increases sociopolitical tensions.

Money Illusion

Even those people whose nominal incomes keep up with inflation often feel oppressed by rising prices. People feel that they *deserve* any increases in wages they receive. When they later discover that their higher (nominal) wages don't buy any additional goods, they feel cheated. They feel worse off, even though they haven't suffered any actual loss of real income. This phenomenon is called **money illusion.** People suffering from money illusion are forever reminding us that they used to pay only $5 to see a movie or $20 for a textbook. What they forget is that nominal *incomes* were also a lot lower in the "good old days" than they are today.

money illusion: The use of nominal dollars rather than real dollars to gauge changes in one's income or wealth.

[1] Quoted in *BusinessWeek,* May 22, 1978, p. 118.

MACRO CONSEQUENCES

Although microeconomic redistributions of income and wealth are the primary consequences of inflation, inflation has *macroeconomic* effects as well.

One of the most immediate consequences of inflation is uncertainty. When the average price level is changing significantly in either direction, economic decisions become more difficult. As the accompanying cartoon suggests, even something as simple as ordering a restaurant meal is more difficult if menu prices are changing (as they did during Germany's 1923 runaway inflation). In Zimbabwe, postponing bread purchases cost a *billion* Zimbabwean dollars a day (see previous World View)!

Inflation makes longer-term decisions even more difficult. Should you commit yourself to 4 years of college, for example, if you aren't certain that you or your parents will be able to afford the full costs? In a period of stable prices you can be fairly certain of what a college education will cost. But if prices are rising, you can't be sure how large the bill will be. Under such circumstances, some individuals may decide not to enter college rather than risk the possibility of being driven out later by rising costs.

Price uncertainties affect production decisions as well. Imagine a firm that wants to build a new factory. Typically, the construction of a factory takes 2 years or more, including planning, site selection, and actual construction. If construction costs change rapidly, the firm may find that it's unable to complete the factory or to operate it profitably. Confronted with this added uncertainty, the firm may decide not to build a new plant. This deprives the economy of new investment and expanded production possibilities.

Inflation threatens not only to reduce the level of economic activity but to change its very nature. If you really expect prices to rise, it makes sense to buy goods and resources now for resale later. If prices rise fast enough, you can make a handsome profit. These are the kinds of thoughts that motivate people to buy houses, precious metals, commodities, and other assets. But such speculation, if carried too far, can detract from the production process. If speculative profits become too easy, few people will engage in production; instead, everyone will be buying and selling existing goods. People may even be encouraged to withhold resources from the production process, hoping to sell them later at higher prices. Such speculation may fuel **hyperinflation,** as spending accelerates and production declines. This happened in Germany in the 1920s, China in 1948–49, in Russia in the early 1990s and in Zimbabwe in 2007–9. No one wanted to hold Zimbabwean dollars or trade for them. Farmers preferred to hold their crops rather than sell them. With the price of a loaf of bread increasing by a billion Zimbabwean dollars a day, why would a baker want to *sell* his

Uncertainty

Speculation

> hyperinflation: Inflation rate in excess of 200 percent, lasting at least 1 year.

Affects both the factor market & the product market.

" DO I HAVE YOUR ASSURANCE THAT PRICES WILL NOT BE INCREASED BEFORE WE ARE SERVED ? "

From *The Wall Street Journal.* Permission, Cartoon Features Syndicate.

Analysis: The uncertainty caused by rising prices causes stress and may alter consumption and investment decisions.

Today, trying to reduce the Bracket payments

Bracket Creep

bracket creep: The movement of taxpayers into higher tax brackets (rates) as nominal incomes grow.

Deflation Dangers

Brackets are adjusted for inflation so you are not paying higher taxes on less income.

Consumer Price Index

Consumer Price Index (CPI): A measure (index) of changes in the average price of consumer goods and services.

inflation rate: The annual percentage rate of increase in the average price level.

bread?! Producers chose to hold rather than sell their products. The resulting contraction in supply caused a severe decline in output.

Another reason that savings, investment, and work effort decline when prices rise is that taxes go up, too. Federal income tax rates are *progressive;* that is, tax rates are higher for larger incomes. The intent of these progressive rates is to redistribute income from rich to poor. However, inflation tends to increase *everyone's* income. In the process, people are pushed into higher tax brackets and confront higher tax rates. The process is referred to as **bracket creep.** In recent years, bracket creep has been limited by the inflation indexing of personal income tax rates and a reduction in the number of tax brackets. However, Social Security payroll taxes and most state and local taxes aren't indexed.

Ironically, a *falling* price level—a deflation—might not make people happy either. In fact, a falling price level can do the same kind of harm as a rising price level. When prices are falling, people on fixed incomes and long-term contracts gain more *real* income. Lenders win and creditors lose. People who hold cash or bonds win: Homeowners and stamp collectors lose. A deflation simply reverses the kinds of redistributions caused by inflation.

A falling price level also has similar macro consequences. Time horizons get shorter. Businesses are more reluctant to borrow money or to invest. People lose confidence in themselves and public institutions when declining price levels deflate their incomes and assets.

MEASURING INFLATION

In view of the macro and micro consequences of price-level changes, the measurement of inflation serves two purposes: to gauge the average rate of inflation and to identify its principal victims.

The most common measure of inflation is the **Consumer Price Index (CPI).** As its name suggests, the CPI is a mechanism for measuring changes in the average price of consumer goods and services. It's analogous to the fruit price index we discussed earlier. The CPI doesn't refer to the price of any particular good but to the average price of all consumer goods.

By itself, the "average price" of consumer goods isn't a very useful number. But once we know the average price of consumer goods, we can observe whether that average rises— that is, whether inflation is occurring. By observing the extent to which prices increase, we can calculate the **inflation rate.**

We can get a better sense of how inflation is measured by observing how the CPI is constructed. The process begins by identifying a market basket of goods and services the typical consumer buys. For this purpose, the Bureau of Labor Statistics surveys a large sample of families every year to determine what goods and services consumers actually buy. Figure 7.2 summarizes the results of the 2007 survey, which reveal that 34.1 cents out of every consumer dollar is spent on housing (shelter, furnishings, and utilities), 12.4 cents on food, and another 17.6 cents on transportation. Only 5.4 cents of every consumer dollar is spent on entertainment.

Within these broad categories of expenditure, the Bureau of Labor Statistics itemizes specific goods and services. The details of the expenditure survey show, for example, that private expenditures for reading and education account for only 3 percent of the typical consumer's budget, less than is spent on alcoholic beverages, tobacco, and gambling. It also shows that we spend 7 cents out of every dollar on fuel, to drive our cars (3.2 cents) and to heat and cool our houses (3.8 cents).

Once we know what the typical consumer buys, it's relatively easy to calculate the average price of a market basket. The Bureau of Labor Statistics actually goes shopping in 85 cities across the country, recording the prices of the 184 items that make up the typical market basket. Approximately 19,000 stores are visited, and 60,000 landlords, renters, and homeowners are surveyed—every month!

As a result of these massive, ongoing surveys, the Bureau of Labor Statistics can tell us what's happening to consumer prices. Suppose, for example, that the market basket cost

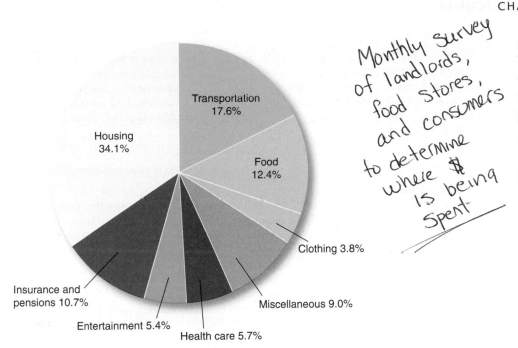

Monthly survey of landlords, food stores, and consumers to determine where $ is being spent

FIGURE 7.2
The Market Basket

To measure changes in average prices, we must first know what goods and services consumers buy. This diagram, based on consumer surveys, shows how the typical urban consumer spends each dollar. Housing, transportation, and food account for over two-thirds of consumer spending.

Source: U.S. Bureau of Labor Statistics, Consumer Expenditure Survey (2007 data).

$100 last year and that the same basket of goods and services cost $110 this year. On the basis of those two shopping trips, we could conclude that consumer prices had risen by 10 percent in 1 year.

In practice, the CPI is usually expressed in terms of what the market basket cost in a specific **base year.** The price level in the base year is arbitrarily designated as 100. In the case of the CPI, the average price level for the period 1982–84 is usually used as the base for computing price changes. Hence, the price index for that base year is set at 100. In January 2009, the CPI registered 212. In other words, it cost $212 in 2009 to buy the same market baskets that cost only $100 in the base year. Prices had increased by an average of 112 percent over that period. Each month the Bureau of Labor Statistics updates the CPI, telling us how the current cost of that same basket compares to its cost between 1982 and 1984.

Table 7.4 illustrates how changes in the official CPI are computed. Notice that all price changes don't have the same impact on the inflation rate. Rather, ***the effect of a specific price change on the inflation rate depends on the product's relative importance in consumer budgets.***

The relative importance of a product in consumer budgets is reflected in its **item weight,** which refers to the percentage of a typical consumer budget spent on the item. Table 7.4 shows the item weights for college tuition and housing. College tuition may loom very large in your personal budget, but only 1.5 percent of *all* consumer expenditure is spent on college tuition. Hence, the item weight for college tuition in the *average* consumer budget is only 0.0152.

Housing costs absorb a far larger share of the typical consumer budget. As was first observed in Figure 7.2, the item weight for housing is 0.341. Accordingly, rent increases have a much larger impact on the CPI than do tuition hikes. Notice in Table 7.4 how a 20 percent hike in tuition has a tiny impact on average inflation, whereas a 20 percent hike in housing prices adds a lot to the CPI.

The Core Rate. Every month the Labor Department reports the results of its monthly price surveys. In its news releases, the department distinguishes changes in the "core" price level from the broader, all-inclusive CPI. The **core inflation rate** excludes changes in food and energy prices, which have a lot of month-to-month variation. A freeze in California or Florida can cause a temporary spike in produce prices; a hurricane in the Gulf can do the

base year: The year used for comparative analysis: the basis for indexing, for example, of price changes.

item weight: The percentage of total expenditure spent on a specific product; used to compute inflation indexes.

core inflation rate: Changes in the CPI, excluding food and energy prices.

TABLE 7.4

Computing Changes in the CPI

The impact of any price change on the average price level depends on the importance of an item in the typical consumer budget.

web analysis

The importance of housing prices is emphasized in Steven Cecchetti's "Inflation Updates" at **http:// people.brandeis.edu/~cecchett.**

The Consumer Expenditure Survey of 2007 revealed that the average household spends 1.52 cents of every consumer dollar on college tuition. Households without college students don't pay any tuition, of course. And your family probably devotes more than 1.52 cents of each consumer dollar to tuition. On *average,* however, 1.52 cents is the proportion of each dollar spent on tuition. This figure is the *item weight* of tuition in computing the CPI.

The impact on the CPI of a price change for a specific good is calculated as follows:

Item weight × percentage change in price of item = percentage change in CPI

Suppose that tuition prices suddenly go up 20 percent. What impact will this single price increase have on the CPI? In this case, where tuition is the only price that increases, the impact on the CPI will be only 0.30 percent (0.0152 × 20) as illustrated below. Thus, a very large increase in the price of tuition (20 percent) has a tiny impact (0.30 percent) on the *average* price level.

Housing, on the other hand, accounts for 34.1 percent of consumer expenditure. Thus if housing prices increase 20 percent, and housing is the only price that increases, the impact on the CPI will be 6.82 percent, as shown below.

The relative importance of an item in consumer budgets—its item weight—is a key determinant of its inflationary impact.

Item	Item Weight	×	Price Increase for the Item	=	Impact on the CPI
College tuition	0.0152		20%		0.30%
Housing	0.341		20		6.82

same thing to oil prices. These temporary price shocks, however, may not reflect price trends. By excluding volatile food and energy prices from the core rate, we hope to get a more accurate monthly reading of consumer price trends.

Producer Price Indexes

In addition to the Consumer Price Index, there are three Producer Price Indexes (PPIs). The PPIs keep track of average prices received by *producers.* One index includes crude materials, another covers intermediate goods, and the last covers finished goods. The three PPIs don't include all producer prices but primarily those in mining, manufacturing, and agriculture. Like the CPI, changes in the PPIs are identified in monthly surveys.

Over long periods of time, the PPIs and the CPI generally reflect the same rate of inflation. In the short run, however, the PPIs usually increase before the CPI, because it takes time for producers' price increases to be reflected in the prices that consumers pay. For this reason, the PPIs are watched closely as a clue to potential changes in consumer prices.

The GDP Deflator

GDP deflator: A price index that refers to all goods and services included in GDP.

nominal GDP: The value of final output produced in a given period, measured in the prices of that period (current prices).

real GDP: The value of final output produced in a given period, adjusted for changing prices.

The broadest price index is the GDP deflator. The GDP deflator covers all output, including consumer goods, investment goods, and government services. Unlike the CPI and PPIs, the **GDP deflator** isn't based on a fixed "basket" of goods or services. Rather, it allows the contents of the basket to change with people's consumption and investment patterns. The GDP deflator therefore isn't a pure measure of price change. Its value reflects both price changes and market responses to those price changes, as reflected in new expenditure patterns. Hence, the GDP deflator typically registers a lower inflation rate than the CPI.

Real vs. Nominal GDP. The GDP deflator is the price index used to adjust nominal GDP statistics for changing price levels. Recall that **nominal GDP** refers to the *current-*dollar value of output, whereas **real GDP** denotes the *inflation-adjusted* value of output. These two measures of output are connected by the GDP deflator:

$$\text{Real GDP} = \frac{\text{nominal GDP}}{\text{GDP deflator}} \times 100$$

The nominal values of GDP were $10 trillion in 2000 and $5.7 trillion in 1990. At first blush, this would suggest that output had increased by 75 percent. However, the price level rose by 24 percent between those years. Hence, *real* GDP in 2000 in the base-year prices of 1990 was

$$\begin{array}{c}\text{2000 real GDP}\\\text{(in 1990 prices)}\end{array} = \frac{\text{nominal GDP}}{\text{price deflator}} = \frac{\$10\text{ trillion}}{\dfrac{124}{100}} = \frac{\$10\text{ trillion}}{1.24} = \$8.06\text{ trillion}$$

In reality, then, output increased by only 41 percent (from $5.7 trillion to $8.06 trillion) in the 1990s. Changes in real GDP are a good measure of how output and living standards are changing. Nominal GDP statistics, by contrast, mix up output and price changes.

THE GOAL: PRICE STABILITY

In view of the inequities, anxieties, and real losses caused by inflation, it's not surprising that price stability is a major goal of economic policy. As we observed at the beginning of this chapter, every U.S. president since Franklin Roosevelt has decreed price stability to be a foremost policy goal. Unfortunately, few presidents (or their advisers) have stated exactly what they mean by "price stability." Do they mean *no* change in the average price level? Or is some upward creep in the price index acceptable?

A Numerical Goal

An explicit numerical goal for **price stability** was established for the first time in the Full Employment and Balanced Growth Act of 1978. According to that act, the goal of economic policy is to hold the rate of inflation under 3 percent.

Unemployment Concerns

Why did Congress choose 3 percent inflation rather than zero inflation as the benchmark for price stability? One reason was concern about unemployment. To keep prices from rising, the government might have to restrain spending in the economy. Such restraint could lead to cutbacks in production and an increase in joblessness. In other words, there might be a trade-off between declining inflation and rising unemployment. From this perspective, a little bit of inflation might be the "price" the economy has to pay to keep unemployment rates from rising.

price stability: The absence of significant changes in the average price level; officially defined as a rate of inflation of less than 3 percent.

Recall how the same kind of logic was used to define the goal of full employment. The fear there was that price pressures would increase as the economy approached its production possibilities. This suggested that some unemployment might be the "price" the economy has to pay for price stability. Accordingly, the goal of "full employment" was defined as the lowest rate of unemployment *consistent with stable prices*. The same kind of thinking is apparent here. The amount of inflation regarded as tolerable depends in part on the effect of anti-inflation strategies on unemployment rates. After reviewing our experiences with both unemployment and inflation, Congress concluded that 3 percent inflation was a safe target.

Quality Changes

The second argument for setting our price-stability goal above zero inflation relates to our measurement capabilities. The Consumer Price Index isn't a perfect measure of inflation. In essence, the CPI simply monitors the price of specific goods over time. Over time, however, the goods themselves change, too. Old products become better as a result of *quality improvements*. A plasma TV set costs more today than a TV did in 1955, but today's television also delivers a bigger, clearer picture, in digital sound and color, and with a host of on-screen programming options. Hence, increases in the price of TV sets tend to exaggerate the true rate of inflation: Most of the higher price represents more product.

The same is true of automobiles. The best-selling car in 1958 (a Chevrolet Bel Air) had a list price of only $2,618. That makes a 2008 Ford Taurus look awfully expensive at $20,605. The quality of today's cars is much better, however. Improvements since 1958 include seat belts, air bags, variable-speed windshield wipers, electronic ignitions, rear-window defrosters, radial tires, antilock brakes, emergency flashers, remote-control mirrors, crash-resistant bodies, a doubling of fuel mileage, a 100-fold decrease in exhaust pollutants, and global positioning systems. As a result, today's higher car prices also buy cars that are safer, cleaner, and more comfortable.

The U.S. Bureau of Labor Statistics does adjust the CPI for quality changes. Such adjustments inevitably entail subjective judgments, however. Critics are quick to complain that the CPI overstates inflation because quality improvements are undervalued.

New Products   The problem of measuring quality improvements is even more difficult in the case of new products. The computers and word processors used today didn't exist when the Census Bureau conducted its 1972–73 survey of consumer expenditure. The 1982–84 expenditure survey included those products but not still newer ones such as the cellular phone. As the News below explains, the omission of cellular phones caused the CPI to overstate the rate of inflation. The consumer expenditure survey of 1993–95 included cell phones but not digital cameras, DVD players, flat-screen TVs, or MP3 players—all of which have had declining prices. As a result, there's a significant (though unmeasured) element of error in the CPI insofar as it's intended to gauge changes in the average prices paid by consumers. The goal of 3 percent inflation allows for such errors.

IN THE NEWS

Ignoring Cell Phones Biases CPI Upward

Cellular telephones have been in commercial operation in the United States for 13 years. Beginning in Chicago in late 1983, and then at the Los Angeles Olympic Games in 1984, cellular telephone usage spread first to the top 30 Metropolitan Statistical Areas (MSAs), then to the other 300 or so MSAs, and finally to rural areas. At year-end 1996, there were over 40 million cellular subscribers in the United States. . . .

Yet the cellular telephone will not be included in the calculation of the Consumer Price Index (CPI) until 1998 or 1999. "This neglect of new goods leads to an upward bias in the CPI," NBER Research Associate Jerry Hausman concludes.

The CPI estimates that since 1988, telecommunications prices have increased by 8.5 percent, or 1.02 percent per year. A corrected index that includes cellular service decreased 1.28 percent per year since 1988, Hausman figures. "Thus, the bias in the BLS [Bureau of Labor Statistics] telecommunications services CPI equals approximately 2.3 percentage points per year."

Source: National Bureau of Economic Research, *NBER Digest,* June 1997. **www.nber.org/digest.**

Analysis: Since the CPI tracks prices for a fixed basket of goods, it misses the effects of falling prices on new goods that appear between survey periods.

THE HISTORICAL RECORD

In the long view of history, the United States has done a good job of maintaining price stability. On closer inspection, however, our inflation performance is very uneven. Table 7.5 summarizes the long view, with data going back to 1800. The base period for pricing the market basket of goods is again 1982–84. Notice that the same market basket cost only $17 in 1800. Consumer prices increased 500 percent in 183 years. But also observe how frequently the price level *fell* in the 1800s and again in the 1930s. These recurrent deflations held down the long-run inflation rate. Because of these periodic deflations, average prices in 1945 were at the same level as in 1800!

what I'd pay $17 for an item in 1800, I'd pay $100 for it in 1982-84

Year	CPI	Year	CPI	Year	CPI	Year	CPI
1800	17.0	1900	8.3	1940	14.0	1980	82.4
1825	11.3	1915	10.1	1950	24.1	1982–84	100.0
1850	8.3	1920	20.0	1960	29.6	1990	130.5
1875	11.0	1930	16.7	1970	38.8	2000	172.8

Note: Data from 1915 forward reflect the official all-items Consumer Price Index, which used the pre-1983 measure of shelter costs. Estimated indexes for 1800 through 1900 are drawn from several sources.

Source: U.S. Bureau of Labor Statistics.

TABLE 7.5
Two Centuries of Price Changes

Before World War II, the average level of prices rose in some years and fell in others. Since 1945, prices have risen continuously. The Consumer Price Index has more than doubled since 1980.

Figure 7.3 provides a closer view of our more recent experience with inflation. In this figure we transform annual changes in the CPI into percentage rates of inflation. The CPI increased from 72.6 to 82.4 during 1980. This 9.8-point jump in the CPI translates into a 13.5 percent rate of inflation (9.8 ÷ 72.6 = 0.135). This inflation rate, represented by point A in Figure 7.3, was the highest in a generation. Since then, prices have continued to increase, but at much slower rates. These low rates of inflation in the United States are far below the pace in most nations.

web analysis

At the U.S. Bureau of Labor Statistics, **www.bls.gov,** you can find the CPI for the most recent month and the same month last year.

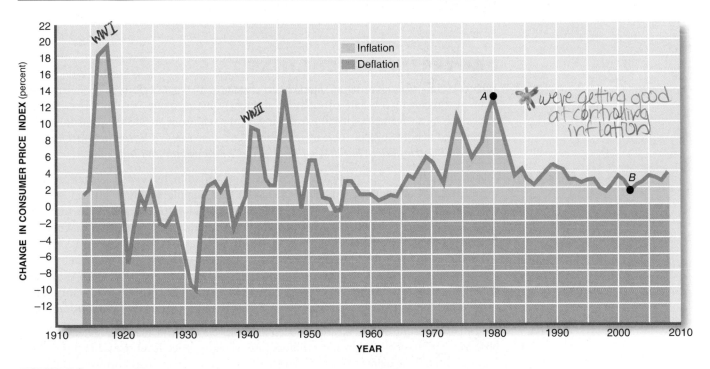

we're getting good at controlling inflation

FIGURE 7.3
Annual Inflation Rates

During the 1920s and 1930s, consumer prices fell significantly, causing a general deflation. Since the Great Depression, however, average prices have risen almost every year. But the annual rate of price increases has varied widely: The highest rate of inflation was 13.5 percent in 1980 (point A); the lowest rate (1.6 percent) occurred in 2002 (point B).

Source: U.S. Bureau of Labor Statistics.

CAUSES OF INFLATION

The evident variation in year-to-year inflation rates requires explanation. So do the horrifying bouts of hyperinflation that have erupted in other nations at various times. What causes price levels to rise or fall?

In the most general terms, this is an easy question to answer. Recall that all market transactions entail two converging forces, namely, *demand* and *supply*. Accordingly, any explanation of changing price levels must be rooted in one of these two market forces.

Demand-Pull Inflation

Excessive pressure on the demand side of the economy is often the cause of inflation. Suppose the economy was already producing at capacity but that consumers were willing and able to buy even more goods. With accumulated savings or easy access to credit, consumers could end up trying to buy more output than the economy was producing. This would be a classic case of "too much money chasing too few goods." As consumers sought to acquire more goods, store shelves (inventory) would begin to empty. Seeing this, producers would begin raising prices. The end result would be a demand-driven rise in average prices, or demand-pull inflation.

Cost-Push Inflation

The pressure on prices could also originate on the supply side. When hurricanes Katrina and Rita destroyed oil-producing facilities in the Gulf (August 2005), oil prices increased abruptly, raising transportation and production costs in a broad array of industries. To cover these higher costs, producers raised output prices. When a tsunami devastated Sri Lanka in December 2004, it destroyed a huge portion of that country's production capacity, including its vital fishing industry. As market participants scurried for the remaining output, prices rose across the board.

Inflationary pressures could also originate in higher wages. If labor unions were able to abruptly push up wage rates, the costs of production would increase, putting pressure on product prices.

PROTECTIVE MECHANISMS

Whatever the *causes* of inflation, market participants don't want to suffer the consequences. Even at a relatively low rate of inflation, the real value of money declines over time. If prices rise by an average of just 4 percent a year, the real value of $1,000 drops to $822 in 5 years and to only $676 in 10 years (see Table 7.6). ***Low rates of inflation don't have the drama of hyperinflation, but they still redistribute real wealth and income.***

COLAs

Market participants can protect themselves from inflation by *indexing* their nominal incomes, as is done with Social Security benefits, for example. In any year that the rate of inflation exceeds 3 percent, Social Security benefits go up *automatically* by the same percentage as the inflation rate. This **cost-of-living adjustment (COLA)** ensures that nominal benefits keep pace with the rising prices.

> **cost-of-living adjustment (COLA):** Automatic adjustments of nominal income to the rate of inflation.

Landlords often protect their real incomes with COLAs as well, by including in their leases provisions that automatically increase rents by the rate of inflation. COLAs are also common in labor union agreements, government transfer programs (like food stamps), and many other contracts. In every such case, ***a COLA protects real income from inflation.***

ARMs

Cost-of-living adjustments have also become more common in loan agreements. As we observed earlier, debtors win and creditors lose when the price level rises. Suppose a loan requires interest payments equal to 5 percent of the amount (principal) borrowed. If the rate of inflation jumps to 7 percent, prices will be rising faster than interest is accumulating. Hence, the **real interest rate**—the inflation-adjusted rate of interest—will actually be negative. The interest payments made in future years will buy fewer goods than can be bought today.

> **real interest rate:** The nominal interest rate minus the anticipated inflation rate.

The real rate of interest is calculated as

$$\text{Real interest rate} = \text{nominal interest rate} - \text{anticipated rate of inflation}$$

Year	Annual Inflation Rate				
	2%	4%	6%	8%	10%
2010	$1,000	$1,000	$1,000	$1,000	$1,000
2011	980	962	943	926	909
2012	961	925	890	857	826
2013	942	889	840	794	751
2014	924	855	792	735	683
2015	906	822	747	681	621
2016	888	790	705	630	564
2017	871	760	665	584	513
2018	853	731	627	540	467
2019	837	703	592	500	424
2020	820	676	558	463	386

TABLE 7.6
Inflation's Impact, 2010–2020

In the past 20 years, the U.S. rate of inflation ranged from a low of 1.6 percent to a high of 13.5 percent. Does a range of 12 percentage points really make much difference? One way to find out is to see how a specific sum of money will shrink in real value in a decade.

Here's what would happen to the real value of $1,000 from January 1, 2010, to January 1, 2020, at different inflation rates. At 2 percent inflation, $1,000 held for 10 years would be worth $820. At 10 percent inflation that same $1,000 would buy only $386 worth of goods in the year 2020.

web analysis

The United States Treasury offers a bond that protects one's principle against inflation. For information on the Treasury Inflation Protected Security, visit **www.savingsbonds.gov**.

In this case, the nominal interest rate is 5 percent and inflation is 7 percent. Hence, the *real* rate of interest is *minus* 2 percent.

The distinction between real and nominal interest rates isn't too important if you're lending or borrowing money for just a couple of days. But the distinction is critical for long-term loans like home mortgages. Mortgage loans typically span a period of 25 to 30 years. If the inflation rate stays higher than the nominal interest rate during this period, the lender will end up with less *real* wealth than was initially lent.

To protect against such losses, the banking industry offers home loans with adjustable interest rates. An **adjustable-rate mortgage (ARM)** stipulates an interest rate that changes during the term of the loan. A mortgage paying 5 percent interest in a stable (3 percent inflation) price environment may later require 9 percent interest if the inflation rate jumps to 7 percent. Such an adjustment would keep the real rate of interest at 2 percent. These and other inflation-indexing mechanisms underscore the importance of measuring price changes accurately.

adjustable-rate mortgage (ARM): A mortgage (home loan) that adjusts the nominal interest rate to changing rates of inflation.

THE ECONOMY TOMORROW

THE END OF INFLATION?

The earth spins, the sun shines, prices rise: two generations have grown up believing that inflation is an unalterable fact of life. No wonder. A dollar today is worth only 13 cents in 1945 money; a pound is worth only 6p. Much of the damage was done in the 1970s and early 1980s, and much has improved since then. In the OECD countries inflation is now hovering around its 1960s level of 3–4 percent. That gives governments the best chance they have had for decades to kill it off and achieve price stability. Sadly, they may fluff it.

Historical Stability. Price stability is not as extraordinary as it sounds. It does not mean that all prices stay the same: some will fall, others rise, but the average price level remains constant. Anyway, inflation, in the sense of continuously rising prices, is historically the exception, not the rule. On the eve of the first world war, prices in Britain were on average no higher than at the time of the fire of London in 1666. . . . During those 250 years, the

Zero & inflation not been seen in a long, long time

longest unbroken run of rising prices was six years. Since 1946, by contrast, prices in Britain have risen every year, and the same is true of virtually every other OECD country.

It is easy to say that double-digit inflation is bad, but harder to agree on the ideal rate. Should governments aim for 5 percent, 3 percent, or 0 percent? Some claim that the extra benefits of zero inflation are tiny and would be outweighed by the short-term cost—lost output, lost jobs—of pushing inflation lower. A little bit of inflation, they say, acts like a lubricant, helping relative prices and wages to adjust more efficiently, since all wages and most prices are hard to cut in absolute terms. But a little inflation sounds like "a little drink" for an alcoholic. It can too easily accelerate. That is the lesson of the past 40 years—that and the fact that the economies with the lowest inflation have tended to be the ones with the least unemployment. Beyond the short term governments cannot choose to have a bit faster growth in exchange for a bit more inflation. The choice does not exist.

The Virtue of Zero. The rewards of reducing inflation from 5 percent to 0 percent may be smaller than those from crunching inflation from 5,000 percent to 5 percent, but they are still highly desirable. The best inflation rate is one that least affects the behaviour of companies, investors, shoppers and workers. That means zero, because anything higher interferes with the most fundamental function of prices—their ability to provide information about relative scarcities. If prices in general are rising by 5 percent a year, the fact that the price of one particular product rises by 8 percent goes largely unnoticed. Yet that product's relative 3 percent increase ought to attract the attention of potential new producers, and to encourage buyers to look elsewhere—in short, to set in train the changes that maximize economic efficiency. It would do that if the 3 percent rise was like a hillock in an otherwise flat landscape; but, in the mountains of generalized inflation, nobody notices a crag. Even with an annual inflation rate of 5 percent, the general price level doubles every 14 years, obscuring changes in relative prices.

Now imagine a world without inflation. Once it was believable, it would transform the way people behave. Companies would be confident about borrowing long-term money, and lenders confident about providing it. Real interest rates would fall. Firms would invest more because the probable pay-out would be clearer; the same would be true of individuals investing time and money on their education. Governments could budget for infrastructural projects, knowing that their plans would not be derailed by unexpected surges in prices. In general, everyone would think more about the long term because the long term would be easier to see.

Source: *The Economist,* January 22, 1992. © 1992 The Economist Newspaper Limited, London. All Rights Reserved. Reprinted with permission.

SUMMARY

- Inflation is an increase in the average price level. Typically it's measured by changes in a price index such as the Consumer Price Index (CPI). LO1
- At the micro level, inflation redistributes income by altering relative prices, income, and wealth. Because not all prices rise at the same rate and because not all people buy (and sell) the same goods or hold the same assets, inflation doesn't affect everyone equally. Some individuals actually gain from inflation, whereas others suffer a loss of real income or wealth. LO2
- At the macro level, inflation threatens to reduce total output because it increases uncertainties about the future and

thereby inhibits consumption and production decisions. Fear of rising prices can also stimulate spending, forcing the government to take restraining action that threatens full employment. Rising prices also encourage speculation and hoarding, which detract from productive activity. LO2
- Fully anticipated inflation reduces the anxieties and real losses associated with rising prices. However, few people can foresee actual price patterns or make all the necessary adjustments in their market activity. LO1
- The U.S. goal of price stability is defined as an inflation rate of less than 3 percent per year. This goal recognizes potential conflicts between zero inflation and full employment as well

as the difficulties of measuring quality improvements and new products. LO3

- From 1800 to 1945, prices both rose and fell, leaving the average price level unchanged. Since then, prices have risen nearly every year but at widely different rates. LO3
- Inflation is caused by either excessive demand (demand-pull inflation) or structural changes in supply (cost-push inflation). LO1

- Cost-of-living adjustments (COLAs) and adjustable-rate mortgages (ARMs) help protect real incomes from inflation. Universal indexing, however, wouldn't eliminate inflationary redistributions of income and wealth. LO2
- Worldwide inflation rates have diminished in recent years. Experience with inflation and changing patterns of asset ownership are creating political pressure for greater price stability. LO3

Key Terms

inflation	bracket creep	nominal GDP
deflation	Consumer Price Index (CPI)	real GDP
relative price	inflation rate	price stability
nominal income	base year	cost-of-living adjustment (COLA)
real income	item weight	real interest rate
money illusion	core inflation rate	adjustable-rate mortgage (ARM)
hyperinflation	GDP deflator	

Questions for Discussion

1. Why would farmers rather store their output than sell it during periods of hyperinflation? How does this behavior affect prices? LO2
2. How might rapid inflation affect college enrollments? LO2
3. Who gains and who loses from rising house prices? LO2
4. Who gained and who lost from the price changes in Table 7.2? LO2
5. Whose real wealth (see Table 7.3) declined in the 1990s? Who else might have lost real income or wealth? Who gained as a result of inflation? LO2
6. If *all* prices increased at the same rate (i.e., no *relative* price changes), would inflation have any redistributive effects? LO2
7. Would it be advantageous to borrow money if you expected prices to rise? Would you want a fixed-rate loan or one with an adjustable interest rate? LO2
8. Are people worse off when the price level rises as fast as their income? Why do people often feel worse off in such circumstances? LO2
9. Identify two groups that benefit from deflation and two that lose. LO2
10. Could demand-pull inflation occur before an economy was producing at capacity? How? LO3
11. How much do higher gasoline prices contribute to inflation? LO1

---

 web activities to accompany this chapter can be found on the Online Learning Center:
http://www.mhhe.com/schiller12e

LO1 1. According to the World View on page 136, how much did a loaf of bread cost in Zimbabwe
    (a) At the beginning of the 3-week period?   _____
    (b) At the end of the 3-week period?   _____

LO2 2. If tuition keeps increasing at the same rate as in 2008–9 (see News, p. 132), what will it cost to
    attend a 4-year private college in 4 years?   _____

LO1 3. Suppose you'll have an annual nominal income of $40,000 for each of the next 3 years, and
    the inflation rate is 4 percent per year.
    (a) Find the real value of your $40,000 salary for each of the next 3 years.

    Year 1: _____
    Year 2: _____
    Year 3: _____

    (b) If you have a COLA in your contract, and the inflation rate is 4 percent, what is the real
        value of your salary for each year?

    Year 1: _____
    Year 2: _____
    Year 3: _____

LO2 4. Suppose you borrow $1,000 of principal that must be repaid at the end of 2 years, along with
    interest of 5 percent a year. If the annual inflation rate turns out to be 10 percent,
    (a) What is the real rate of interest on the loan?   _____
    (b) What is the real value of the principal repayment?   _____
    (c) Who loses, the debtor or the creditor?   _____

LO1 5. Assuming that the following table describes a typical consumer's complete budget,
    compute the item weights for each product.

Item	Quantity	Unit Price		Item Weight:
Coffee	20 pounds	$ 5		_____
Tuition	1 year	4,000		_____
Pizza	100 pizzas	8		_____
DVD rental	75 days	5		_____
Vacation	2 weeks	450	Total:	_____

LO1 6. Suppose the prices listed in the table for Problem 5 changed from one year to the next, as
    shown below. Use the rest of the table to compute the average inflation rate.

Item	Unit Price Last Year	This Year	Percent Change in Price	×	Item Weight	=	Inflation Impact
Coffee	$ 5	$ 6	_____		_____		_____
Tuition	4,000	7,000	_____		_____		_____
Pizza	8	10	_____		_____		_____
DVD rental	5	10	_____		_____		_____
Vacation	450	500	_____		_____		_____
					Average inflation:		_____

LO1 7. Use the item weights in Figure 7.2 to determine the percentage change in the CPI that would
    result from a
    (a) 10 percent increase in entertainment prices.   _____
    (b) 6 percent decrease in transportation costs.   _____
    (c) Doubling of clothing prices.   _____
    (Note: Review Table 7.4 for assistance.)

PROBLEMS FOR CHAPTER 7 (cont'd)   Name: _____

LO1   8. Use the GDP deflator data on the inside cover of this book to compute real GDP in 2000 at
2008 prices.   _____

LO1   9. According to Table 7.3, what happened during the period shown to the
(a) Nominal price of gold?   _____
(b) Real price of gold?   _____

LO3   10. Using the information of page 139 and Table 7.5, by how much did the price level increase
(a) Between 1982–84 and 2009?   _____
(b) Between 2000 and 2009?   _____

LO3   11. On the accompanying graph, illustrate for each year (A) the nominal interest rate (use the prime
rate of interest), (B) the CPI inflation rate, and (C) the real interest rate (adjusted for same-year
CPI inflation). The required data appear on the inside cover of the book.
(a) In what years was the official goal of price stability met?   _____
(b) In what years was the inflation rate lowest?   _____
(c) In the most recent of those years, what was the
  (i) Nominal interest rate?   _____
  (ii) Real interest rate?   _____
(d) What was the range of rates during this period for
  (i) Nominal interest rates?   _____
  (ii) Real interest rates?   _____
(e) On a year-to-year basis which varies more, nominal or real interest rates?   _____

PART 3

Cyclical Instability

One of the central concerns of macroeconomics is the short-run business cycle—recurrent bouts of expansion and contraction of the nation's output. These cycles affect jobs, prices, economic growth, and international trade and financial balances. Chapters 8 through 10 focus on the nature of the business cycle and the underlying market forces that can cause both macroeconomic gain and macroeconomic pain.

The Business Cycle

8

LEARNING OBJECTIVES

After reading this chapter, you should be able to:

LO1. Distinguish the major macro outcomes and their determinants.

LO2. Describe the nature of aggregate demand (AD) and aggregate supply (AS).

LO3. Assess how changes in AD and AS affect market outcomes.

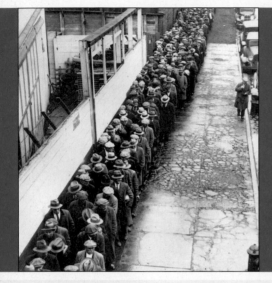

In 1929 it looked as though the sun would never set on the U.S. economy. For 8 years in a row, the U.S. economy had been expanding rapidly. During the Roaring Twenties, the typical American family drove its first car, bought its first radio, and went to the movies for the first time. With factories running at capacity, virtually anyone who wanted to work found a job readily.

Everyone was optimistic. In his Acceptance Address in November 1928, President-elect Herbert Hoover echoed this optimism by declaring: "We in America today are nearer to the final triumph over poverty than ever before in the history of any land. . . . We shall soon with the help of God be in sight of the day when poverty will be banished from this nation."

The booming stock market seemed to confirm this optimistic outlook. Between 1921 and 1927 the stock market's value more than doubled, adding billions of dollars to the wealth of U.S. households and businesses. The stock market boom accelerated in 1927, causing stock prices to double again in less than 2 years. The roaring stock market made it look easy to get rich in America.

The party ended abruptly on October 24, 1929. On what came to be known as Black Thursday, the stock market crashed. In a few short hours, the market value of U.S. corporations tumbled, in the most frenzied selloff ever seen (see News on the next page). The next day President Hoover tried to assure America's stockholders that the economy was "on a sound and prosperous basis." But despite his assurances and the efforts of leading bankers to stem the decline, the

stock market continued to plummet. The following Tuesday (October 29) the pace of selling quickened. By the end of the year, more than $40 billion of wealth had vanished in the Great Crash. Rich men became paupers overnight; ordinary families lost their savings, their homes, and even their lives.

The devastation was not confined to Wall Street. The financial flames engulfed the farms, the banks, and industry. Between 1930 and 1935, millions of rural families lost their farms. Automobile production fell from 4.5 million cars in 1929 to only 1.1 million in 1932. So many banks were forced to close that newly elected President Roosevelt had to declare a "bank holiday" in March 1933 to stem the outflow of cash to anxious depositors.

Throughout these years, the ranks of the unemployed continued to swell. In October 1929, only 3 percent of the workforce was unemployed. A year later the total was over 9 percent, and millions of additional workers were getting by on lower wages and shorter hours. But things got worse. By 1933, over one-fourth of the labor force was unable to find work. People slept in the streets, scavenged for food, and sold apples on Wall Street.

The Great Depression seemed to last forever. In 1933, President Roosevelt lamented that one-third of the nation was ill-clothed, ill-housed, and ill-fed. Thousands of unemployed workers marched to the Capitol to demand jobs and aid. In 1938, 9 years after Black Thursday, nearly 20 percent of the workforce was still idle.

IN THE NEWS

Market in Panic As Stocks Are Dumped in 12,894,600 Share Day; Bankers Halt It

Effect Is Felt on the Curb and throughout Nation—Financial District Goes Wild

The stock markets of the country tottered on the brink of panic yesterday as a prosperous people, gone suddenly hysterical with fear, attempted simultaneously to sell a record-breaking volume of securities for whatever they would bring.

The result was a financial nightmare, comparable to nothing ever before experienced in Wall Street. It rocked the financial district to its foundations, hopelessly overwhelmed its mechanical facilities, chilled its blood with terror.

In a society built largely on confidence, with real wealth expressed more or less inaccurately by pieces of paper, the entire fabric of economic stability threatened to come toppling down.

Into the frantic hands of a thousand brokers on the floor of the New York Stock Exchange poured the selling orders of the world. It was sell, sell, sell—hour after desperate hour until 1:30 P.M.

—Laurence Stern

Source: *The World*, October 25, 1929.

Analysis: Stock markets are a barometer of confidence in the economy. If people have doubts about the economy, they're less willing to hold stocks. The crash of 1929 mirrored and worsened consumer confidence.

The Great Depression shook not only the foundations of the world economy but also the self-confidence of the economics profession. No one had predicted the Depression, and few could explain it. The ensuing search for explanations focused on three central questions:

- **How stable is a market-driven economy?**
- **What forces cause instability?**
- **What, if anything, can the government do to promote steady economic growth?**

The basic purpose of **macroeconomics** is to answer these questions—to *explain* how and why economies grow and what causes the recurrent ups and downs of the economy that characterize the **business cycle.** In this chapter we introduce the theoretical model economists use to describe and explain the short-run business cycle. We'll also preview some of the policy options the government might use to dampen those cycles, including the slew of actions taken in 2008–9 to stem another macro downturn.

macroeconomics: The study of aggregate economic behavior, of the economy as a whole.

business cycle: Alternating periods of economic growth and contraction.

STABLE OR UNSTABLE?

Prior to the 1930s, macro economists thought there could never be a Great Depression. The economic thinkers of the time asserted that a market-driven economy was inherently stable. There was no need for government intervention.

This **laissez-faire** view of macroeconomics seemed reasonable at the time. During the nineteenth century and the first 30 years of the twentieth, the U.S. economy experienced some bad years in which the nation's output declined and unemployment increased. But most of these episodes were relatively short-lived. The dominant feature of the Industrial Era was *growth:* an expanding economy, with more output, more jobs, and higher incomes nearly every year.

A Self-Regulating Economy. In this environment, classical economists, as they later became known, propounded an optimistic view of the macro economy. *According to the classical view, the economy "self-adjusts" to deviations from its long-term growth trend.*

Classical Theory

laissez faire: The doctrine of "leave it alone," of nonintervention by government in the market mechanism.

do nothing, doesn't work

supply creates its own demand

every things going to get sold

law of demand: The quantity of a good demanded in a given time period increases as its price falls, *ceteris paribus.*

Say's Law: Supply creates its own demand.

Producers might occasionally reduce their output and throw people out of work, but these dislocations would cause little damage. If output declined and people lost their jobs, the internal forces of the marketplace would quickly restore prosperity. Economic downturns were viewed as temporary setbacks, not permanent problems.

The cornerstones of classical optimism were flexible prices and flexible wages. If producers couldn't sell all their output at current prices, they had two choices. They could reduce the rate of output and throw some people out of work, or they could reduce the price of their output, thereby stimulating an increase in the quantity demanded. According to the **law of demand,** price reductions cause an increase in unit sales. If prices fall far enough, all the output produced can be sold. Thus, flexible prices—prices that would drop when consumer demand slowed—virtually guaranteed that all output could be sold. No one would have to lose a job because of weak consumer demand.

Flexible prices had their counterpart in factor markets. If some workers were temporarily out of work, they'd compete for jobs by offering their services at lower wages. As wage rates declined, producers would find it profitable to hire more workers. Ultimately, flexible wages would ensure that everyone who wanted a job would have a job.

These optimistic views of the macro economy were summarized in Say's Law. **Say's Law**—named after the nineteenth-century economist Jean-Baptiste Say—decreed that "supply creates its own demand." Whatever was produced would be sold. All workers who sought employment would be hired. *Unsold goods and unemployed labor could emerge in this classical system, but both would disappear as soon as people had time to adjust prices and wages.* There could be no Great Depression—no protracted macro failure—in this classical view of the world.

Macro Failure. The Great Depression was a stunning blow to classical economists. At the onset of the Depression, classical economists assured everyone that the setbacks in production and employment were temporary and would soon vanish. Andrew Mellon, Secretary of the U.S. Treasury, expressed this optimistic view in January 1930, just a few months after the stock market crash. Assessing the prospects for the year ahead, he said: "I see nothing. . . . in the present situation that is either menacing or warrants pessimism. . . . I have every confidence that there will be a revival of activity in the spring and that during the coming year the country will make steady progress."[1] Merrill Lynch, one of the nation's largest brokerage houses, was urging that people should buy stocks. But the Depression deepened. Indeed, unemployment grew and persisted *despite* falling prices and wages (see Figure 8.1). The classical self-adjustment mechanism simply didn't work.

The Keynesian Revolution

The Great Depression effectively destroyed the credibility of classical economic theory. As the British economist John Maynard Keynes pointed out in 1935, classical economists

were apparently unmoved by the lack of correspondence between the results of their theory and the facts of observation:—a discrepancy which the ordinary man has not failed to observe. . . .

The celebrated optimism of [classical] economic theory . . . is . . . to be traced, I think, to their having neglected to take account of the drag on prosperity which can be exercised by an insufficiency of effective demand. For there would obviously be a natural tendency towards the optimum employment of resources in a Society which was functioning after the manner of the classical postulates. It may well be that the classical theory represents the way in which we should like our Economy to behave. But to assume that it actually does so is to assume our difficulties away.[2]

Inherent Instability. Keynes went on to develop an alternative view of the macro economy. Whereas the classical economists viewed the economy as inherently stable, *Keynes asserted that a market-driven economy is inherently unstable.* Small disturbances in output, prices, or unemployment were likely to be magnified, not muted, by the invisible hand

[1]David A. Shannon, *The Great Depression* (Englewood Cliffs, NJ: Prentice Hall, 1960), p. 4.
[2]John Maynard Keynes, *The General Theory of Employment, Interest and Money* (London: Macmillan, 1936), pp. 33–34.

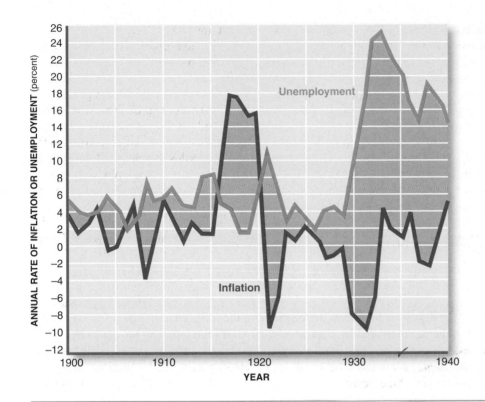

FIGURE 8.1
Inflation and Unemployment, 1900–1940

In the early 1900s, falling price levels (deflation) appeared to limit increases in unemployment. Periods of high unemployment also tended to be brief. These experiences bolstered the confidence of classical economists in the stability of the macro economy. Say's Law seemed to work.

In the 1930s, unemployment rates rose to unprecedented heights and stayed high for a decade. Falling wages and prices did not restore full employment. This macro failure prompted calls for new theories and policies to control the business cycle.

Source: U.S. Bureau of the Census, *The Statistics of the United States,* 1957.

of the marketplace. The Great Depression was not a unique event, Keynes argued, but a calamity that would recur if we relied on the market mechanism to self-adjust.

Government Intervention. In Keynes's view, the inherent instability of the marketplace required government intervention. When the economy falters, we can't afford to wait for some assumed self-adjustment mechanism but must instead intervene to protect jobs and income. The government can do this by "priming the pump": buying more output, employing more people, providing more income transfers, and making more money available. When the economy overheats, the government must cool it down with higher taxes, spending reductions, and less money.

Keynes's denunciation of classical theory didn't end the macroeconomic debate. On the contrary, economists continue to wage fierce debates about the inherent stability of the economy. Those debates—which became intense again in 2008–9—fill the pages of the next few chapters. But before examining them, let's first take a quick look at the economy's actual performance since the Great Depression.

HISTORICAL CYCLES

The upswings and downturns of the business cycle are gauged in terms of changes in total output. An economic upswing, or expansion, refers to an increase in the volume of goods and services produced. An economic downturn, or contraction, occurs when the total volume of production declines. Changes in employment typically mirror these changes in production.

Figure 8.2 depicts the stylized features of a business cycle. Over the long run, the output of the economy grows at roughly 3 percent per year. There's a lot of year-to-year variation around this growth trend, however. The short-run cycle looks like a roller coaster, climbing steeply, then dropping from its peak. Once the trough is reached, the upswing starts again.

In reality, business cycles aren't as regular or as predictable as Figure 8.2 suggests. The U.S. economy has experienced recurrent upswings and downswings, but of widely varying length, intensity, and frequency.

FIGURE 8.2
The Business Cycle

The model business cycle resembles a roller coaster. Output first climbs to a peak, then decreases. After hitting a trough, the economy recovers, with real GDP again increasing.

A central concern of macroeconomic theory is to determine whether a recurring business cycle exists and, if so, what forces cause it.

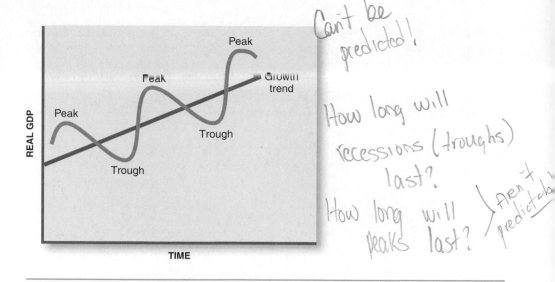

Handwritten notes: Can't be predicted!; How long will recessions (troughs) last?; How long will peaks last? Aren't predictable

real GDP: The value of final output produced in a given period, adjusted for changing prices.

Figure 8.3 illustrates the actual performance of the U.S. economy since 1929. Changes in total output are measured by changes in **real GDP,** the inflation-adjusted value of all goods and services produced. From a long-run view, the growth of real GDP has been impressive: Real GDP today is 15 times larger than it was in 1929. Americans now consume a vastly greater variety of goods and services, and in greater quantities, than earlier generations ever dreamed possible.

Our long-term success in raising living standards is clouded, however, by a spate of short-term macro setbacks. On closer inspection, *the growth path of the U.S. economy isn't a smooth, rising trend but a series of steps, stumbles, and setbacks.* This short-run

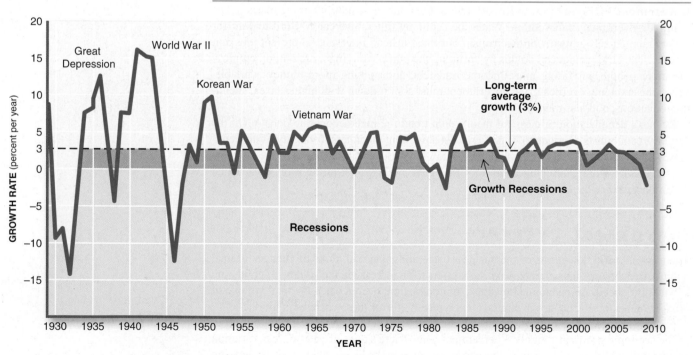

FIGURE 8.3
The Business Cycle in U.S. History

From 1929 to 2009, real GDP increased at an average rate of 3 percent a year. But annual growth rates have departed widely from that average. Years of above-average growth seem to alternate with years of sluggish growth (*growth recessions*) and actual decreases in total output (*recessions*).

Source: U.S. Department of Commerce (2009).

instability is evident in Figure 8.3. The dashed horizontal line across the middle of the chart represents the long-term *average* growth rate of the U.S. economy. From 1929 through 2009, the U.S. economy expanded at an average rate of 3 percent per year. But Figure 8.3 clearly shows that we didn't grow so nicely every year. There were lots of years when real GDP grew by less than 3 percent. Worse still, there were many years of *negative* growth, with real GDP *declining* from one year to the next. These successive short-run contractions and expansions are the essence of the business cycle.

The most prolonged departure from our long-term growth path occurred during the Great Depression. Between 1929 and 1933, total U.S. output steadily declined. Notice in Figure 8.3 how the growth rate is negative in each of these years. During these 4 years of negative growth, real GDP contracted a total of nearly 30 percent. Investments in new plant and equipment virtually ceased. Economies around the world came to a grinding halt (see World View below).

The Great Depression

WORLD VIEW

Global Depression

The Great Depression wasn't confined to the U.S. economy. Most other countries suffered substantial losses of output and employment over a period of many years. Between 1929 and 1932, industrial production around the world fell 37 percent. The United States and Germany suffered the largest losses, while Spain and the Scandinavian countries lost only modest amounts of output.

Some countries escaped the ravages of the Great Depression altogether. The Soviet Union, largely insulated from Western economic structures, was in the midst of Stalin's forced industrialization drive during the 1930s. China and Japan were also relatively isolated from world trade and finance and so suffered less damage from the Depression.

Country	Decline in Industrial Output
Chile	−22%
France	−31
Germany	−47
Great Britain	−17
Japan	−2
Norway	−7
Spain	−12
United States	−46

web analysis

J. Bradford DeLong provides a thorough account of the Great Depression on his webpage at **econ161.berkeley.edu.** Search for "Great Depression."

Analysis: International trade and financial flows tie nations together. When the U.S. economy tumbled in the 1930s, other nations lost export sales. Such interactions made the Great Depression a worldwide calamity.

The U.S. economy rebounded in April 1933 and continued to expand for 3 years (see positive growth rates in Figure 8.3). By 1937, however, the rate of output was still below that of 1929. Then things got worse again. During 1938 and 1939 output again contracted and more people lost their jobs. At the end of the decade GDP per capita was lower than it had been in 1929.

World War II greatly increased the demand for goods and services and ended the Great Depression. During the war years, real GDP grew at unprecedented rates—almost 19 percent in a single year (1942). Virtually everyone was employed, either in the armed forces or in the factories. Throughout the war, America's productive capacity was strained to the limit.

World War II

After World War II, the U.S. economy resumed a pattern of alternating growth and contraction. The contracting periods are called *recessions*. Specifically, we use the term **recession** to mean a decline in real GDP that continues for at least two successive quarters. As Table 8.1 indicates, there have been 12 recessions since 1944. The most severe postwar recession occurred immediately after World War II ended. Sudden cutbacks in defense production caused GDP to decline sharply in 1945. That postwar recession was relatively

6 months

The Postwar Years

recession: A decline in total output (real GDP) for two or more consecutive quarters.

TABLE 8.1
Business Slumps

The U.S. economy has experienced 14 business slumps since 1929. In the post–World War II period, these downturns have been much less severe. The typical recession lasts around 10 months.

Dates	Duration (months)	Percentage Decline in Real GDP	Peak Unemployment Rate
Aug. '29–Mar. '33	43	53.4%	24.9%
May '37 –June '38	13	32.4	20.0
Feb. '45 –Oct. '45	8	38.3	4.3
Nov. '48–Oct. '49	11	9.9	7.9
July '53–May '54	10	10.0	6.1
Aug. '57–Apr. '58	8	14.3	7.5
Apr. '60–Feb. '61	10	7.2	7.1
Dec. '69–Nov. '70	11	8.1	6.1
Nov. '73–Mar. '75	16	14.7	9.0
Jan. '80–July '80	6	8.7	7.6
July '81–Nov. '82	16	12.3	10.8
July '90–Feb. '91	8	2.2	6.5
Mar. '01–Nov. '01	8	0.6	5.6
Dec 07–	?	?	?

web analysis

To better understand the causes of the 1973–75 recession, visit **web.mit.edu/newsoffice** and search "oil crisis."

brief, however. Pent-up demand for consumer goods and a surge in investment spending helped restore full employment.

The 1980s

growth recession: A period during which real GDP grows, but at a rate below the long-term trend of 3 percent.

The 1980s started with two recessions, the second lasting 16 months (July 1981–November 1982). Despite the onset of a second recession at midyear, real GDP actually increased in 1981. But the growth rate was so slow (1.9 percent) that the number of unemployed workers actually rose that year. This kind of experience is called a **growth recession**—the economy grows, but at a slower rate than the long-run (3 percent) average: Thus,

- *A growth recession occurs when the economy expands too slowly.*
- *A recession occurs when real GDP actually contracts.* A depression is an extremely deep and long recession—or when you don't even get socks for Christmas (see cartoon).

In November 1982, the U.S. economy began an economic expansion that lasted over 7 years. During that period, real GDP increased by over $1 trillion and nearly 20 million new jobs were created.

Analysis: Recessions occur when total output in the economy declines. In recessions, household income and spending fall.

The 1990s started poorly. Beginning in July 1990, real GDP started declining again. Although the recession officially ended 8 months later (February 1991), subsequent growth was so slow that unemployment kept increasing. By the end of 1991, the recession had destroyed 2 million jobs and reduced total output by nearly 2 percent.

The 1990s

Economic growth accelerated in the late 1990s, again creating millions of new jobs. In the fall of 2000, the national unemployment rate fell to 3.9 percent, the lowest in over three decades.

2000–2009

Recession. The record low unemployment recorded in September 2000 didn't last long. The stock market dropped sharply that year, reducing people's wealth and confidence. Spending growth slowed, as did economic growth. By March 2001, real GDP was contracting and the economy was in another recession. The 9/11 terrorist attacks only added to the negative trend. By the end of 2001 the unemployment rate was up to 5.8 percent.

Recovery. The recession of 2001 was short-lived. Positive economic growth resumed and accelerated for the next 6 years. The national unemployment rate dropped from 6.3 percent in June 2003 to the full-employment level of 4.4 in March 2007. Real GDP increased by over *$1.5 trillion* in those 4 years, bringing the average U.S. family another $1,300 of goods and services per year. The good times were back.

Recession. The pendulum swung back yet again in 2008. Falling home and stock prices again sapped consumer wealth and confidence. A credit crisis made loans hard to obtain. Sales of homes, autos, and other big-ticket items plummeted, causing GDP to again contract (see News below). The Great Recession of 2008–9 was the worst since 1981–82.

IN THE NEWS

Economy Shrank Last Quarter

WASHINGTON—Signaling what could be the start of a prolonged recession, the government said Thursday that the U.S. economy shrank in the July–September quarter as consumers slashed spending and businesses pulled back.

The Commerce Department said gross domestic product, the broadest measure of goods and services produced in the USA, fell at a 0.3% annual rate in the third quarter. Consumer spending, two-thirds of economic activity, plummeted at a 3.1% rate—the steepest fall since 1980. The overall decline was the worst since the 2001 recession.

—Sue Kirchhoff

Source: USA TODAY, October 31, 2008, B1. Reprinted with Permission.

Analysis: Everyone agrees that the macro economy can contract on occasion. The debate is whether such contractions self-correct or require government intervention.

A MODEL OF THE MACRO ECONOMY

The bumpy growth record of the U.S. economy lends some validity to the notion of a recurring business cycle. Every decade seems to contain at least one boom or bust cycle. But the historical record doesn't really answer our key questions. Are business cycles *inevitable?* Can we do anything to control them? ***Keynes and the classical economists weren't debating whether business cycles occur but whether they're an appropriate target for government intervention.*** That debate continues.

To determine whether and how the government should try to control the business cycle, we first need to understand its origins. What causes the economy to expand or contract? What market forces dampen (self-adjust) or magnify economic swings?

Determinants

[handwritten: population growth, spending]

Internal market forces

[handwritten: terrorist attacks, war, natural disasters, trade problems]

External shocks

[handwritten: Fiscal/monetary policies]

Policy levers

Macro Economy

Outcomes

Output

Jobs

Prices

Growth

International balances

FIGURE 8.4
The Macro Economy

The primary outcomes of the macro economy are output of goods and services (GDP), jobs, prices, economic growth, and international balances (trade, currency). These outcomes result from the interplay of internal market forces such as population growth, innovation, and spending patterns; external shocks such as wars, weather, and trade disruptions; and policy levers such as tax, budget, and regulatory decisions.

Figure 8.4 sets the stage for answering these questions. This diagram provides a bird's-eye view of how the macro economy works. This basic macro model emphasizes that the performance of the economy depends on a surprisingly small set of determinants.

On the right side of Figure 8.4 the primary measures of macroeconomic performance are arrayed. These basic *macro outcomes include*

- *Output:* total value of goods and services produced (real GDP).
- *Jobs:* levels of employment and unemployment.
- *Prices:* average price of goods and services (inflation).
- *Growth:* year-to-year expansion in production capacity.
- *International balances:* international value of the dollar; trade and payment balances with other countries.

These macro outcomes define our economic welfare; we measure our economic well-being in terms of the value of output produced, the number of jobs created, price stability, and rate of economic expansion. We also seek to maintain a certain balance in our international trade and financial relations. The economy's performance is rated by the "scores" on these five macro outcomes.

On the left side of Figure 8.4 three very broad forces that shape macro outcomes are depicted. These *determinants of macro performance are*

- *Internal market forces:* population growth, spending behavior, invention and innovation, and the like.
- *External shocks:* wars, natural disasters, terrorist attacks, trade disruptions, and so on.
- *Policy levers:* tax policy, government spending, changes in the availability of money, and regulation, for example.

In the absence of external shocks or government policy, an economy would still function: It would still produce output, create jobs, develop prices, and maybe even grow. The U.S. economy operated with minimal government intervention for much of its history. Even today, many less developed countries operate in relative isolation from government or international events. In these situations, macro outcomes depend exclusively on internal market forces.

The crucial macro controversy is whether pure, market-driven economies are inherently stable or unstable. The GDP contraction described in the preceding News wouldn't have surprised classical economists. They knew the economy could sometimes stumble, but they believed the economy would quickly recover from any such setbacks. They saw no need for the box in Figure 8.4 labeled "Policy levers." Keynes, by contrast, argued that policy levers were both effective and necessary. Without such intervention, Keynes believed, the economy was doomed to bouts of repeated macro failure.

Modern economists hesitate to give policy intervention that great a role. Nearly all economists recognize that policy intervention affects macro outcomes. But there are great arguments about just how effective any policy lever is. Some economists even echo the classical notion that policy intervention may be either ineffective or, worse still, inherently *de*stabilizing.

AGGREGATE DEMAND AND SUPPLY

To determine which views of economic performance are valid, we need to examine the inner workings of the macro economy. All Figure 8.4 tells us is that macro outcomes depend on certain identifiable forces. But the figure doesn't reveal *how* the determinants and outcomes are connected. What's in the mysterious circle labeled "Macro Economy" at the center of Figure 8.4?

When economists peer into the mechanics of the macro economy they see the forces of supply and demand at work. All the macro outcomes depicted in Figure 8.4 are the result of market transactions—an interaction between supply and demand. Hence, ***any influence on macro outcomes must be transmitted through supply or demand.***

By conceptualizing the inner workings of the macro economy in supply and demand terms, economists have developed a remarkably simple model of how the economy works.

Economists use the term *aggregate demand* to refer to the collective behavior of all buyers in the marketplace. Specifically, **aggregate demand** refers to the various quantities of output (real GDP) that all people, taken together, are willing and able to buy at alternative price levels in a given period. Our view here encompasses the collective demand for *all* goods and services rather than the demand for any single good.

Aggregate Demand

> aggregate demand: The total quantity of output (real GDP) demanded at alternative price levels in a given time period, *ceteris paribus*.

To understand the concept of aggregate demand better, imagine that everyone is paid on the same day. With their incomes in hand, people then enter the product market. The question becomes: How much output will people buy?

To answer this question, we have to know something about prices. If goods and services are cheap, people will be able to buy more with their available income. On the other hand, high prices will limit both the ability and willingness to purchase goods and services. Note that we're talking here about the *average* price level, not the price of any single good.

Figure 8.5 illustrates this simple relationship between average prices and real spending. The horizontal axis depicts the various quantities of (real) output that might be purchased. The vertical axis shows various price levels that might exist.

The aggregate demand curve illustrates how the real value of purchases varies with the average level of prices. The downward slope of the aggregate demand curve suggests that with a given (constant) level of income, people will buy more goods and services at lower price levels. Why would this be the case? ***Three separate reasons explain the downward slope of the aggregate demand curve:***

- ***The real-balances effect.***
- ***The foreign-trade effect.***
- ***The interest-rate effect.***

Real-Balances Effect. The most obvious explanation for the downward slope of the aggregate demand curve is that cheaper prices make dollars more valuable. Suppose you had

FIGURE 8.5
Aggregate Demand

Aggregate demand refers to the total output (real GDP) demanded at alternative price levels, *ceteris paribus.* The vertical axis measures the average level of all prices rather than the price of a single good. Likewise, the horizontal axis refers to the real value of all goods and services, not the quantity of only one product.

The downward slope of the aggregate demand curve is due to the real-balances, foreign-trade, and interest-rate effects.

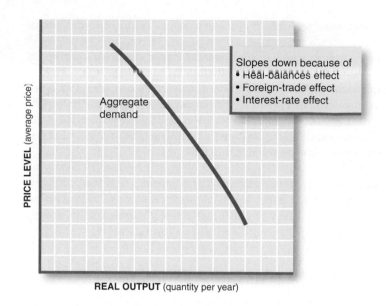

FIGURE 8.5
Aggregate Demand

Aggregate demand refers to the total output (real GDP) demanded at alternative price levels, *ceteris paribus.* The vertical axis measures the average level of all prices rather than the price of a single good. Likewise, the horizontal axis refers to the real value of all goods and services, not the quantity of only one product.

The downward slope of the aggregate demand curve is due to the real-balances, foreign-trade, and interest-rate effects.

$1,000 in your savings account. How much output could you buy with that savings balance? That depends on the price level. At current prices, you could buy $1,000 worth of output. But what if the price level rose? Then your $1,000 wouldn't stretch as far. *The real value of money is measured by how many goods and services each dollar will buy.* When the *real* value of your savings declines, your ability to purchase goods and services declines as well.

Suppose inflation pushes the price level up by 25 percent in a year. What will happen to the real value of your savings balance? At the end of the year, you'll have

$$\frac{\text{Real value of savings}}{\text{at year-end}} = \frac{\text{savings balance}}{\frac{\text{price level at year-end}}{\text{price level at year-start}}}$$

$$= \frac{\$1,000}{\frac{125}{100}} = \frac{\$1,000}{1.25}$$

$$= \$800$$

In effect, inflation has wiped out a chunk of your purchasing power. At year's end, you can't buy as many goods and services as you could have at the beginning of the year. The quantity of output you demand will decrease. In Figure 8.5 this would be illustrated by a movement up the aggregate demand curve.

A declining price level (deflation) has the opposite effect. Specifically, lower price levels make you "richer": *The cash balances you hold in your pocket, in your bank account, or under your pillow are worth more when the price level falls.* As a result, you can buy *more* goods, even though your *nominal income* hasn't changed.

Lower price levels increase the purchasing power of other dollar-denominated assets as well. Bonds, for example, rise in value when the price level falls. This may tempt consumers to sell some bonds and buy more goods and services. With greater real wealth, consumers might also decide to save less and spend more of their current income. In either case, the quantity of goods and services demanded at any given income level will increase. These real-balances effects create an inverse relationship between the price level and the real value of output demanded—that is, a downward-sloping aggregate demand curve.

Foreign-Trade Effect. The downward slope of the aggregate demand curve is reinforced by changes in imports and exports. Consumers have the option of buying either domestic or foreign goods. A decisive factor in choosing between them is their relative price. If the average price of U.S.-produced goods is rising, Americans may buy more imported goods and fewer domestically produced products. Conversely, falling price levels in the United States may convince consumers to buy more "Made in the USA" output and fewer imports.

International consumers are also swayed by relative price levels. When U.S. price levels decline, overseas tourists flock to Disney World. Global consumers also buy more U.S. wheat, airplanes, and computers when our price levels decline. Conversely, a rise in the relative price of U.S. products deters foreign buyers. These changes in import and export flows contribute to the downward slope of the aggregate demand curve.

Interest-Rate Effect. Changes in the price level also affect the amount of money people need to borrow. At lower price levels, consumer borrowing needs are smaller. As the demand for loans diminishes, interest rates tend to decline as well. This "cheaper" money stimulates more borrowing and loan-financed purchases. These interest-rate effects reinforce the downward slope of the aggregate demand curve, as illustrated in Figure 8.5.

Although lower price levels tend to increase the volume of output demanded, they have the opposite effect on the aggregate quantity *supplied.* As we observed, our production possibilities are defined by available resources and technology. Within those limits, however, producers must decide how much output they're *willing* to supply. Their supply decisions are influenced by changes in the price level.

Profit Effect. The primary motivation for supplying goods and services is the chance to earn a profit. Producers can earn a profit so long as the prices they receive for their output exceed the costs they pay in production. Hence, *changing price levels will affect the profitability of supplying goods.*

If the price level declines, profits tend to drop. In the short run, producers are saddled with some relatively constant costs like rent, interest payments, negotiated wages, and inputs already contracted for. If output prices fall, producers will be hard-pressed to pay these fixed costs, much less earn a profit. Their response will be to reduce the rate of output.

Higher output prices have the opposite effect. Because many costs are relatively constant in the short run, higher prices for goods and services tend to widen profit margins. As profit margins widen, producers will want to produce and sell more goods. Thus, *we expect the rate of output to increase when the price level rises.* This expectation is reflected in the upward slope of the aggregate supply curve in Figure 8.6. **Aggregate supply** reflects the

Aggregate Supply

aggregate supply: The total quantity of output (real GDP) producers are willing and able to supply at alternative price levels in a given time period, *ceteris paribus.*

web analysis

The slope of the aggregate supply curve depends in part on what producers pay for their inputs. Find out about producer prices at **www.bls.gov/ppi.**

FIGURE 8.6
Aggregate Supply

Aggregate supply is the real value of output (real GDP) producers are willing and able to bring to the market at alternative price levels, *ceteris paribus.* The upward slope of the aggregate supply curve reflects both profit effects (the lure of widening profit margins) and cost effects (increasing cost pressures).

PRICE LEVEL (average price)

Aggregate supply

Slopes up because:
• Profit effect
• Cost effect

REAL OUTPUT (quantity per year)

various quantities of real output that firms are willing and able to produce at alternative price levels, in a given time period.

Cost Effect The upward slope of the aggregate supply curve is also explained by rising costs. The profit effect depends on some costs remaining constant when the average price level rises. Not all costs will remain constant, however. Producers may have to pay overtime wages, for example, to increase output, even if *base* wages are constant. Tight supplies of other inputs may also unleash cost increases. Such cost pressures tend to multiply as the rate of output increases. As time passes, even costs that initially stayed constant may start creeping upward.

All these cost pressures will make producing output more expensive. Producers will be willing to supply additional output only if prices rise at least as fast as costs.

The upward slope of the aggregate supply curve in Figure 8.6 illustrates this cost effect. Notice how the aggregate supply curve is practically horizontal at low rates of aggregate output and then gets increasingly steeper. At high output levels the aggregate supply curve almost turns straight up. This changing slope reflects the fact that *cost pressures are minimal at low rates of output but intense as the economy approaches capacity.*

Macro Equilibrium

When all is said and done, what we end up with here is two rather conventional-looking supply and demand curves. But these particular curves have special significance. Instead of describing the behavior of buyers and sellers in a single product market, *aggregate supply and demand curves summarize the market activity of the whole (macro) economy.* These curves tell us what *total* amount of goods and services will be supplied or demanded at various price levels.

These graphic summaries of buyer and seller behavior provide some important clues about the economy's performance. The most important clue is point E in Figure 8.7, where the aggregate demand and supply curves intersect. This is the only point at which the behavior of buyers and sellers is compatible. We know from the aggregate demand curve that people are willing and able to buy the quantity Q_E when the price level is at P_E. From the aggregate supply curve we know that businesses are prepared to sell quantity Q_E at the price level P_E. Hence, buyers and sellers are willing to trade exactly the same quantity (Q_E) at that price level. We call this situation **macro equilibrium**—the unique combination of prices and output compatible with both buyers' and sellers' intentions.

Disequilibrium. To appreciate the significance of macro equilibrium, suppose that another price or output level existed. Imagine, for example, that prices were higher, at the

equilibrium (macro): The combination of price level and real output that is compatible with both aggregate demand and aggregate supply.

FIGURE 8.7
Macro Equilibrium

The aggregate demand and supply curves intersect at only one point (E). At that point, the price level (P_E) and output (Q_E) combination is compatible with both buyers' and sellers' intentions. The economy will gravitate to those equilibrium price (P_E) and output (Q_E) levels. At any other price level (e.g., P_1), the behavior of buyers and sellers is incompatible.

(3) Say's Law states that supply creates its own demand.

(4) The determinants of the macro economy are internal market forces, external shock, and policy levers.

13) Say's Law states that supply creates its own demand

14) The determinants of the macro economy are internal market forces, external shock, and policy levers.

-3.5 16
-4 in
—————
17.5
Tot· 16   17.5
Tot· in 17 3/4

⑦ Humphrey-Hawkins act of 1978 called for an
unemployment rate of 4% because while full
employment would be nice to reach there is
always going to be groups of people unemployed
for different reasons. This represents the
natural unemployment rate.

Concerned about rising costs

⑧ Inflation - an increase in the average level
of prices of goods & services.

⑨ The redistributive mechanics of inflation
are: reflected in a person's income and wealth.
Because incomes and wealth fluctuate and
vary person to person; price, income, wealth, are
the mechanisms used to redistribute income
and wealth, as a result of inflation.

increase/ decrease/ higher/ lower

⑩ Two significant measurements excluded from
the core rate of inflation are change in food
prices and change in energy.

⑪ Two protective mechanisms against inflation
are COLAs - Cost of Living Adjustment and
ARMs - Adjustable Rate Mortgages.

⑫ Cost-Push Inflation - cost of goods in production
go up then you are pushing the cost of
selling up.

Review Quiz

① Difference between GDP & NPD is: GDP represents all goods & services manufactured w/i a nation's borders during a given time.
GDP = C + I + 6 + (X-M)
NDP is the subtraction of depreciation charges from gross revenues when calculating income
NDP = GDP - depreciation

don't replace depreciation, you can't make the same amount of production

② The significance of this difference between the GDP and NPD is because the values of assets used to make goods decreases over time you are given a more accurate measurement by taking into account depreciation.

③ To convert nominal GDP to real GDP you must divide the nominal GDP by the price index.

$$Real\ GDP = \frac{nominal\ GDP}{price\ index}$$

Doesn't give an accurate count

④ This conversion from nominal to real GDP is important because real GDP adjusts for the changing prices of goods/services

⑤ Okun's Law states for each additional 1% of unemployment results into a loss of ~~gross~~ 3% (originally 3% then changed to 2%) of real output (GDP)

⑥ unemployment rate = $\frac{\#\ of\ unemployed}{labor\ force}$ $\frac{40,000,000}{160,000,000} = 25\%$

level P_1 in Figure 8.7. How much output would people want to buy at that price level? How much would business want to produce and sell?

The aggregate demand curve tells us that people would want to buy only the quantity D_1 at the higher price level P_1. In contrast, business firms would want to sell a larger quantity, S_1. This is a *dis*equilibrium situation in which the intentions of buyers and sellers are incompatible. The aggregate *quantity supplied* (S_1) exceeds the aggregate *quantity demanded* (D_1). Accordingly, a lot of goods will remain unsold at price level P_1.

To sell these goods, producers will have to reduce their prices. As prices drop, producers will decrease the volume of goods sent to market. At the same time, the quantities that consumers seek to purchase will increase. This adjustment process will continue until point E is reached and the quantities demanded and supplied are equal. At that point, the lower price level P_E will prevail.

The same kind of adjustment process would occur if a lower price level first existed. At lower prices, the aggregate quantity demanded would exceed the aggregate quantity supplied. The resulting shortages would permit sellers to raise their prices. As they did so, the aggregate quantity demanded would decrease, and the aggregate quantity supplied would increase. Eventually, we would return to point E, where the aggregate quantities demanded and supplied are equal.

Equilibrium is unique; it's the only price-level-output combination that is mutually compatible with aggregate supply and demand. In terms of graphs, it's the only place the aggregate supply and demand curves intersect. At point E there's no reason for the level of output or prices to change. The behavior of buyers and sellers is compatible. By contrast, any other level of output or prices creates a *dis*equilibrium that requires market adjustments. All other price and output combinations, therefore, are unstable. They won't last. Eventually, the economy will return to point E.

There are two potential problems with the macro equilibrium depicted in Figure 8.7. The *two potential problems with macro equilibrium are*

- *Undesirability:* The equilibrium price or output level may not satisfy our macroeconomic goals.
- *Instability:* Even if the designated macro equilibrium is optimal, it may not last long.

Undesirability. The macro equilibrium depicted in Figure 8.7 is simply the intersection of two curves. All we know for sure is that people want to buy the same quantity of output that businesses want to sell at the price level P_E. This quantity (Q_E) may be more or less than our full-employment capacity. This contingency is illustrated in Figure 8.8. The output level Q_F represents our **full-employment GDP** potential. It is the rate of output that would be produced if we were fully employed. In Figure 8.8, however, we are producing only the smaller quantity Q_E. In this case, the equilibrium rate of output (Q_E) falls far short of capacity production Q_F. We've failed to achieve our goal of full employment.

Macro Failures

full-employment GDP: The total market value of final goods and services that could be produced in a given time period at full employment; potential GDP.

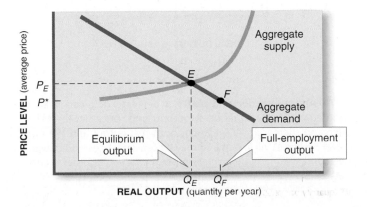

FIGURE 8.8
An Undesired Equilibrium

Equilibrium establishes only the level of prices and output that are compatible with both buyers' and sellers' intentions. These outcomes may not satisfy our policy goals. In this case, the equilibrium price level (P_E) is too high (above P^*) and the equilibrium output rate (Q_E) falls short of full employment (Q_F).

inflation: An increase in the average level of prices of goods and services.

Similar problems may arise from the equilibrium price level. Suppose that P^* represents the most desired price level. In Figure 8.8, we see that the equilibrium price level P_E exceeds P^*. If market behavior determines prices, the price level will rise above the desired level. The resulting increase in the average level of prices is what we call **inflation.**

It could be argued, of course, that our apparent macro failures are simply an artifact. We could have drawn the aggregate supply and demand curves to intersect at point F in Figure 8.8. At that intersection we'd have both price stability and full employment. Why didn't we draw them there, instead of intersecting at point E?

On the graph we can draw curves anywhere we want. In the real world, however, *only one set of aggregate supply and demand curves will correctly express buyers' and sellers' behavior.* We must emphasize here that these real-world curves may *not* intersect at point F, thus denying us price stability or full employment, or both. That is the kind of economic outcome illustrated in Figure 8.8.

Instability. Figure 8.8 is only the beginning of our macro worries. Suppose, just suppose, that the real-world AS and AD curves actually intersected in the perfect spot (point F). That is, imagine that macro equilibrium yielded the optimal levels of both employment and prices. If this happened, could we stop fretting about the state of the economy?

Unhappily, even a "perfect" macro equilibrium doesn't ensure a happy ending. Real-world AS and AD curves aren't permanently locked into their respective positions. They can *shift*—and they will, whenever the behavior of buyers and sellers changes.

AS Shifts. Suppose the Organization of Petroleum Exporting Countries (OPEC) increased the price of oil, as it did in early 2008. These oil price hikes directly increased the cost of production in a wide range of U.S. industries, making producers less willing and able to supply goods at prevailing prices. Thus, the aggregate supply curve *shifted to the left,* as in Figure 8.9a.

FIGURE 8.9
Macro Disturbances

(a) **Aggregate supply shifts** A decrease (leftward shift) of the aggregate-supply curve tends to reduce real GDP and raise average prices. When supply shifts from AS_0 to AS_1, the equilibrium moves from F to G. At G, output is lower and prices are higher than at F. Such a supply shift may result from higher import prices, natural disasters, changes in tax policy, or other events.

(b) **Aggregate demand shifts** A decrease (leftward shift) in aggregate demand reduces output and price levels. When demand shifts from AD_0 to AD_1, both real output and the price level decline. A fall in demand may be caused by decreased export demand, changes in expectations, higher taxes, or other events.

- consumer savings
- inadequate business
- govn. spending (insufficient)

The September 11, 2001, terrorist strikes against the World Trade Center and Pentagon also caused a leftward shift of aggregate supply. Physical destruction and fear of further terrorism kept some producers out of the market. Intensified security of transportation systems and buildings also increased the costs of supplying goods and services to the market.

The impact of a leftward AS shift on the economy is evident in Figure 8.9. Whereas macro equilibrium was originally located at the optimal point *F*, the new equilibrium is located at point *G*. At point *G*, less output is produced and prices are higher. Full employment and price stability have vanished before our eyes.

AD Shifts. A shift of the aggregate demand curve could do similar damage. In the wake of the September 11, 2001, terrorist attacks, Americans were worried about their physical and economic security. Consumers were afraid to go shopping at the mall, and even more afraid to board airplanes. Businesses were also fearful of starting new projects. As a result, the AD curve shifted left, as illustrated in Figure 8.9*b*.

The AD curve shifted left again in 2008. Falling home and stock prices reduced consumer wealth. Feeling poorer, consumers were less willing to buy goods and services at the prevailing price level. This AD decline led to a drop in equilibrium GDP (see News, p. 159).

Multiple Shifts. The situation gets even crazier when the aggregate supply and demand curves shift repeatedly in different directions. A leftward shift of the AD curve can cause a recession, as the rate of output falls. A later rightward shift of the AD curve can cause a recovery, with real GDP (and employment) again increasing. Shifts of the aggregate supply curve can cause similar upswings and downswings. Thus, *business cycles are likely to result from recurrent shifts of the aggregate supply and demand curves.*

COMPETING THEORIES OF
SHORT-RUN INSTABILITY

Figures 8.8 and 8.9 hardly inspire optimism about the macro economy. Figure 8.8 suggests that the odds of the market generating an equilibrium at full employment and price stability are about the same as finding a needle in a haystack. Figure 8.9 suggests that if we're lucky enough to find the needle, we'll probably drop it again.

The classical economists had no such worries. As we saw earlier, they believed that the economy would gravitate toward full employment. Keynes, on the other hand, worried that the macro equilibrium might start out badly and get worse in the absence of government intervention.

The AS/AD model doesn't really settle this controversy. It does, however, provide a convenient framework for comparing these and other theories about how the economy works. Essentially, *macro controversies focus on the shape of aggregate supply and demand curves and the potential to shift them.* With the right shape— or the correct shift—any desired equilibrium could be attained. As we'll see, there are differing views as to whether and how this happy outcome might come about. These differing views can be classified as demand-side explanations, supply-side explanations, or some combination of the two.

Keynesian Theory. Keynesian theory is the most prominent of the demand-side theories. Keynes argued that a deficiency of spending would tend to depress an economy. This deficiency might originate in consumer saving, inadequate business investment, or insufficient government spending. Whatever its origins, the lack of spending would leave goods unsold and production capacity unused. This contingency is illustrated in the News on page 159 and

**Demand-Side
Theories**

FIGURE 8.10
Demand-Side Theories

Inadequate demand may cause unemployment. In part (a), the demand AD$_1$ creates an equilibrium at E$_1$. The resulting output Q$_1$ falls short of full employment Q$_F$.

In part (b), excessive aggregate demand causes inflation. The price level rises from P$_0$ to P$_2$ when aggregate demand expands to AD$_2$. Demand-side theories emphasize how inadequate or excessive AD can cause macro failures.

Recessionary cycle

Too much demand Inflationary Cycle

(a) Inadequate demand

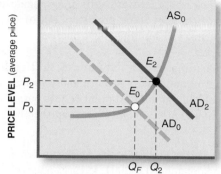

(b) Excessive demand

• *big hike in govt. spending*

here by point E$_1$ in Figure 8.10a. Notice that the equilibrium at E$_1$ leaves the economy at Q$_1$, below its full-employment potential (Q$_F$). Thus, **Keynes concluded that inadequate aggregate demand would cause persistently high unemployment.**

Keynes developed his theory during the Great Depression, when the economy seemed to be stuck at a very low level of equilibrium output, far below full-employment GDP. The only way to end the Depression, he argued, was for someone to start demanding more goods. He advocated a big hike in government spending—a rightward AD shift—to start the economy moving toward full employment. At the time his advice was largely ignored. When the United States mobilized for World War II, however, the sudden surge in government spending shifted the aggregate demand curve sharply to the right, restoring full employment (e.g., a reverse shift from AD$_1$ to AD$_0$ in Figure 8.10a). In times of peace, Keynes also advocated changing government taxes and spending to shift the aggregate demand curve in whatever direction is desired.

Monetary Theories. Another demand-side theory emphasizes the role of money in financing aggregate demand. Money and credit affect the ability and willingness of people to buy goods and services. If credit isn't available or is too expensive, consumers won't be able to buy as many cars, homes, or other expensive products. "Tight" money might also curtail business investment. In these circumstances, aggregate demand might prove to be inadequate, as illustrated in Figure 8.10a. In this case, an increase in the money supply and/or lower interest rates might help shift the AD curve into the desired position.

Both the Keynesian and monetarist theories also regard aggregate demand as a prime suspect for inflationary problems. In Figure 8.10b, the curve AD$_2$ leads to an equilibrium at E$_2$. At first blush, that equilibrium looks desirable, as it offers more output (Q$_2$) than the full-employment threshold (Q$_F$). Notice, however, what's happening to prices: The price level rises from P$_0$ to P$_2$. Hence, **excessive aggregate demand may cause inflation.**

The more extreme monetary theories attribute all our macro successes and failures to management of the money supply. According to these *monetarist* theories, the economy will tend to stabilize at something like full-employment GDP. Thus, only the price level will be affected by changes in the money supply and resulting shifts of aggregate demand. We'll examine the basis for this view in a moment. At this juncture we simply note that **both Keynesian and monetarist theories emphasize the potential of aggregate-demand shifts to alter macro outcomes.**

Supply-Side Theories

Figure 8.11 illustrates an entirely different explanation of the business cycle. Notice that the aggregate *supply* curve is on the move in Figure 8.11. The initial equilibrium is again at point E$_0$. This time, however, aggregate demand remains stationary, while aggregate supply shifts. The resulting decline of aggregate supply causes output and employment to decline (to Q$_3$ from Q$_F$).

FIGURE 8.11
Supply-Side Theories

Inadequate supply can keep the economy below its full-employment potential and cause prices to rise as well. AS_1 leads to equilibrium output Q_3 and increases the price level from P_0 to P_3. Supply-side theories emphasize how AS shifts can worsen or improve macro outcomes.

shortage of oil

The U.S. Bureau of Economic Analysis compiles data on gross domestic product. Using data from its Web site at **www.bea.doc. gov,** calculate the U.S. GDP growth rate for each of the last six quarters. What supply or demand shifts might explain recent quarterly fluctuations in real GDP?

Figure 8.11 tells us that aggregate supply may be responsible for downturns as well. Our failure to achieve full employment may result from the unwillingness of producers to provide more goods at existing prices. That unwillingness may originate in simple greed, in rising costs, in resource shortages, or in government taxes and regulation. Inadequate investment in infrastructure (e.g., roads, sewer systems) or skill training may also limit supply potential. Whatever the cause, if the aggregate supply curve is AS_1 rather than AS_0, full employment will not be achieved with the demand AD_0.

The inadequate supply illustrated in Figure 8.11 causes not only unemployment but inflation as well. At the equilibrium E_3, the price level has risen from P_0 to P_3. Hence, a decrease in aggregate supply can cause multiple macro problems. On the other hand, an increase—a rightward shift—in aggregate supply can move us closer to both our price-stability and full-employment goals. Chapter 16 examines the many ways of inducing such a shift.

Not everyone blames either the demand side or the supply side exclusively. *The various macro theories tell us that either AS or AD can cause us to achieve or miss our policy goals.* These theories also demonstrate how various shifts of the aggregate supply and demand curves can achieve any specific output or price level. One could also shift *both* the AS and AD curves to explain unemployment, inflation, or recurring business cycles. Such eclectic explanations of macro failure draw from both sides of the market.

Eclectic Explanations

demand side
supply side
AD+trying to maintain full employment

LONG-RUN SELF-ADJUSTMENT

Some economists argue that these various theories of short-run instability aren't only confusing but also pointless. As they see it, what really matters is the *long*-run trend of the economy, not *short*-run fluctuations around those trends. In their view, month-to-month or quarter-to-quarter fluctuations in real output or prices are just statistical noise. The *long*-term path of output and prices is determined by more fundamental factors.

This emphasis on long-term outcomes is reminiscent of the classical theory: the view that the economy will self-adjust. A decrease in aggregate demand is only a *temporary* problem. Once producers and workers make the required price and wage adjustments, the economy will return to its long-run equilibrium growth path.

The monetarist theory we encountered a moment ago has a similar view of long-run stability. According to the monetarist theory, the supply of goods and services is determined by institutional factors such as the size of the labor force and technology. These factors determine a "natural" rate of output that's relatively immune to short-run fluctuations in aggregate demand. If this argument is valid, the long-run aggregate supply curve is vertical, not sloped.

FIGURE 8.12
The "Natural" Rate of Output

Monetarists and neoclassical theorists assert that the level of output is fixed at the natural rate Q_N by the size of the labor force, technology, and other institutional factors. As a result, fluctuations in aggregate demand affect the price level but not real output.

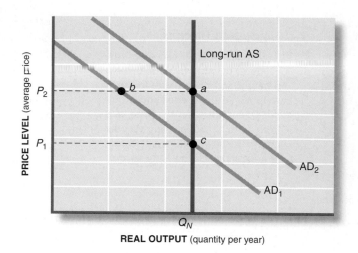

REAL OUTPUT (quantity per year)

Figure 8.12 illustrates the classical/monetarist view of long-run stability. The vertical long-run AS curve is anchored at the natural rate of output Q_N. The natural rate Q_N is itself determined by demographics, technology, market structure, and the institutional infrastructure of the economy.

If the long-run AS curve is really vertical, as the classical and monetarist theories assert, some startling conclusions follow. The most startling implication is that **shifts of the aggregate demand curve affect prices but not output in the long run.** Notice in Figure 8.12 how the shift from AD_1 to AD_2 raises the price level (from P_1 to P_2) but leaves output anchored at Q_N.

What has happened here? Didn't we suggest earlier that an increase in aggregate demand would spur producers to increase output? And aren't rising prices an extra incentive for doing so?

Monetarists concede that *short-run* price increases tend to widen profit margins. This profit effect is an incentive to increase the rate of output. In the *long run,* however, costs are likely to catch up with rising prices. Workers will demand higher wages, landlords will increase rents, and banks will charge higher interest rates as the price level rises. Hence, a rising price level has only a *temporary* profit effect on supply behavior. In the *long run,* cost effects will dominate. In the *long run,* a rising price level will be accompanied by rising costs, giving producers no special incentive to supply more output. Accordingly, output will revert to its natural rate Q_N.

Classical economists use the vertical AS curve to explain also how the economy self-adjusts to temporary setbacks. If AD declines from AD_2 to AD_1 in Figure 8.12, the economy may move from point *a* to point *b*, leaving a lot of unsold output. As producers respond with price cuts, however, the volume of output demanded increases as the economy moves from point *b* to point *c*. At point *c*, full employment is restored. Thus flexible prices (and wages) enable the economy to maintain the natural rate of output Q_N.

Short- vs. Long-Run Perspectives

All this may well be true. But as Keynes pointed out, it's also true that "in the long run we are all dead." How long are we willing to wait for the promised "self-adjustment"? In the Great Depression, people waited for 10 years—and still saw no self-adjustment.

Whatever the long run may hold, it's in the short run that we must consume, invest, and find a job. However stable and predictable the long run might be, short-run variations in macro outcomes will determine how well we fare in any year. Moreover, **the short-run aggregate supply curve is likely to be upward-sloping,** as shown in our earlier graphs. This implies that both aggregate supply and aggregate demand influence short-run macro outcomes.

By distinguishing between short-run and long-run aggregate supply curves, competing economic theories achieve a standoff. Theories that highlight the necessity of policy intervention emphasize the importance of short-run macro outcomes. People *care* about short-run changes in job prospects and prices. If inflation or unemployment is too high, voters insist that "Washington" fix the problem—now.

Theories that emphasize the "natural" stability of the market point to the predictability of long-run outcomes. They prefer to let the economy self-adjust rather than risk government intervention that might worsen macro outcomes. Even if true, however, the duration of acceptable "short-" and "long-" run periods remains controversial.

THE ECONOMY TOMORROW

COPING WITH RECESSION: 2008–9

The AS/AD model is a convenient summary of how the macro economy works. A market-driven economy will gravitate to an equilibrium that is compatible with the behavior of both buyers (AD) and sellers (AS). As we've observed, however, that short-run macro equilibrium may not be consistent with our economic goals. That was certainly the case in 2008–9, when the equilibrium rate of output was less than full-employment output. People expected newly elected President Obama—the new Economist in Chief—to do something about it. What *could* he do?

Policy Strategies. The beauty of the AS/AD model is that it highlights the strategic options for coping with a recession. In the AS/AD framework, there are really only *three strategy options for macro policy:*

- *Shift the aggregate demand curve to the right.* Find and use policy tools that will stimulate total spending.
- *Shift the aggregate supply curve to the right.* Find and implement policy levers that reduce the cost of production or otherwise stimulate more output at every price level.
- *Laissez faire.* Don't interfere with the market; let markets self-adjust.

The first two strategies assume some form of government intervention is needed to end a recession. The third strategy places more faith in the market's ability to self-adjust.

Selecting Policy Tools. There are a host of different policy tools available for implementing any given AS/AD strategy, as President Obama discovered.

Classical Laissez Faire. The laissez-faire strategy advocated by classical economists requires no tools, of course. Classical economists count on the self-adjustment mechanisms of the market—flexible prices and wages—to bring a quick end to recessions. Falling home prices would ultimately spur more sales; declining wages would encourage more hiring. In this view, AS and AD curves "naturally" shift back into an optimal position, where full-employment (Q_F) prevails.

—Ron Paul

Fiscal Policy. Keynes rejected this hands-off approach. He advocated using the federal budget as a policy tool. The government can shift the AD curve to the right by spending more money. Or it can cut taxes, leaving consumers with more income to spend. These budgetary tools are the hallmark of fiscal policy. Specifically, **fiscal policy** is the use of government tax and spending powers to alter economic outcomes.

fiscal policy: The use of government taxes and spending to alter macroeconomic outcomes.

Monetary Policy. The budget isn't the only tool in the interventionist toolbox. Interest rates and the money supply can also shift the AD curve. Lower interest rates encourage consumers to buy more big-ticket items like cars, homes, and appliances—purchases typically financed with loans. Businesses also take advantage of lower interest rates to buy more loan-financed plant and equipment. **Monetary policy** refers to the use of money and credit controls to alter economic outcomes.

monetary policy: The use of money and credit controls to influence macroeconomic outcomes.

> **supply-side policy:** The use of tax incentives, (de)regulation, and other mechanisms to increase the ability and willingness to produce goods and services.

Supply-Side Policy. Fiscal and monetary tools are used to fix the AD side of the macro economy. **Supply-side policy** pursues a different strategy: It uses tools that shift the aggregate supply curve. Tax incentives that encourage more work, saving, or investment are in the supply-side toolbox. So are deregulation actions that make it easier or cheaper to supply products.

Trade Policy. International trade and money flows offer yet another option for shifting aggregate supply and demand. A reduction in trade barriers makes imports cheaper and more available. This shifts the aggregate supply to the right, reducing price pressures at every output level. Reducing the international value (exchange rate) of the dollar lowers the relative price of U.S.-made goods, thereby encouraging foreigners to buy more U.S. exports. Hence, trade policy is another tool in the macroeconomic toolbox.

Getting It Right. The array of tools in the macro-policy toolbox is impressive. But there are still heated arguments about which tool—if any—to use in any given situation. From the outset of his presidency, Obama was under intense pressure to do *something*—something BIG—to end the recession he inherited. In the following chapters we'll examine his policy options in more detail. We'll look at the policy tools he used, how they were supposed to work, and how the economy tomorrow was expected to respond.

SUMMARY

- The long-term growth rate of the U.S. economy is approximately 3 percent a year. But output doesn't increase 3 percent every year. In some years, real GDP grows much faster; in other years growth is slower. Sometimes GDP actually declines.   LO1

- These short-run variations in GDP growth are a central focus of macroeconomics. Macro theory tries to explain the alternating periods of growth and contraction that characterize the business cycle; macro policy attempts to control the cycle.   LO1

- The primary outcomes of the macro economy are output, prices, jobs, and international balances. The outcomes result from the interplay of internal market forces, external shocks, and policy levers.   LO1

- All the influences on macro outcomes are transmitted through aggregate supply or aggregate demand. Aggregate demand refers to the rates of output people are willing to purchase at various price levels. Aggregate supply is the rate of output producers are willing to supply at various price levels.   LO3

- Aggregate supply and demand determine the equilibrium rate of output and prices. The economy will

gravitate to that unique combination of output and price levels.   LO3

- The market-driven macro equilibrium may not satisfy our employment or price goals. Macro failure occurs when the economy's equilibrium isn't optimal.   LO1

- Macro equilibrium may be disturbed by changes in aggregate supply (AS) or aggregate demand (AD). Such changes are illustrated by shifts of the AS and AD curves, and they lead to a new equilibrium.   LO2

- Competing economic theories try to explain the shape and shifts of the aggregate supply and demand curves, thereby explaining the business cycle. Specific theories tend to emphasize demand or supply influences.   LO2

- In the long run the AS curve tends to be vertical, implying that changes in aggregate demand affect prices but not output. In the short run, however, the AS curve is sloped, making macro outcomes sensitive to both supply and demand.   LO3

- Macro policy options range from laissez faire (the classical approach) to various strategies for shifting either the aggregate demand curve or the aggregate supply curve.   LO1

Key Terms

macroeconomics	recession	full-employment GDP
business cycle	growth recession	inflation
laissez faire	aggregate demand	fiscal policy
law of demand	aggregate supply	monetary policy
Say's Law	equilibrium (macro)	supply-side policy
real GDP		

Questions for Discussion

1. If business cycles were really inevitable, what purpose would macro policy serve?   LO1
2. What events might prompt consumers to demand fewer goods at current prices?   LO2
3. If equilibrium is compatible with both buyers' and sellers' intentions, how can it be undesirable?   LO1
4. How did the decline in U.S. home prices in 2006–8 affect aggregate demand?   LO2
5. What exactly did Say mean when he said "supply creates its own demand"?   LO1
6. What's wrong with the classical theory of self-adjustment? Why didn't sales and employment increase in 1929–33 in response to declining prices and wages (see Figure 8.1)?   LO2
7. What might have caused real GDP to decline so dramatically in (*a*) 1929 and (*b*) 1946 (see Figure 8.3)? What caused output to increase again in each case?   LO3
8. How would a sudden jump in U.S. prices affect (*a*) imports from Mexico, (*b*) exports to Mexico, and (*c*) U.S. aggregate demand?   LO3
9. Why might rising prices stimulate short-run production but have no effect on long-run production?   LO3
10. Could President Obama have pursued the classical policy strategy?   LO3

 web activities to accompany this chapter can be found on the Online Learning Center:
http://www.mhhe.com/schiller12e

connect
|ECONOMICS

LO1 1. (a) How much output is unsold at the price level P_1 in Figure 8.7?   _____

(b) At what price level is all output produced sold?   _____

LO2 2. In Figure 8.8, what price level will induce people to buy all the output produced at full employment?   _____

LO1 3. Suppose you have $500 in savings when the price level index is at 100.

(a) If inflation pushes the price level up by 10 percent, what will be the real value of your savings?   _____

(b) What is the real value of your savings if the price level *declines* by 10 percent?   _____

LO2 4. Use the following information to draw aggregate demand (AD) and aggregate supply (AS) curves on the graph below. Both curves are assumed to be straight lines.

Price Level	Output Demanded	Output Supplied
1,000	0	$1,000
100	$900	100

(a) At what price level does equilibrium occur?   _____

(b) What curve (AD or AS) would have shifted if a new equilibrium were to occur at an output level of 700 and a price level of 700?   _____

(c) What curve would have shifted if a new equilibrium were to occur at an output level of 700 and price level of 500?   _____

(d) What curve would have shifted if a new equilibrium were to occur at an output level of 700 and a price level of 300?   _____

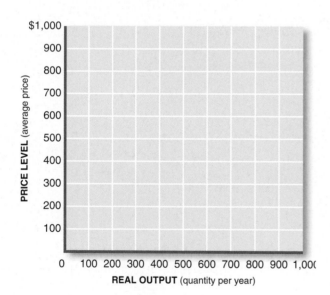

LO1 5. According to the News on page 159,

(a) By what percent did GDP decline?   _____

(b) How much output was lost in the $14 trillion economy?   _____

(c) How much income did this represent for each of the 300 million U.S. citizens?   _____

(d) What was the largest GDP decline in a postwar U.S. recession? (See Table 8.1.)   _____

LO3 6. If the AS curve shifts to the right, what happens ("increases" or "decreases") to

(a) The equilibrium rate of output?   _____

(b) The equilibrium price level?   _____

LO3 7. If the AD curve shifts to the right, what happens ("increases" or "decreases") to
    (*a*) The equilibrium rate of output?   _____
    (*b*) The equilibrium price level?   _____

LO3 8. Assume that the accompanying graph depicts aggregate supply and demand conditions in
    an economy. Full employment occurs when $6 trillion of real output is produced.
    (*a*) What is the equilibrium rate of output?   _____
    (*b*) How far short of full employment is the equilibrium rate of output?   _____
    (*c*) Illustrate a shift of aggregate demand that would change the equilibrium rate of output
        to $6 trillion. Label the new curve AD_2.   _____
    (*d*) What is the price level at this full-employment equilibrium?   _____
    (*e*) Illustrate a shift of aggregate supply (AS_2) that would, when combined with AD_1,
        move equilibrium output to $6 trillion.   _____
    (*f*) What is the price level at this new equilibrium?   _____

Aggregate Demand

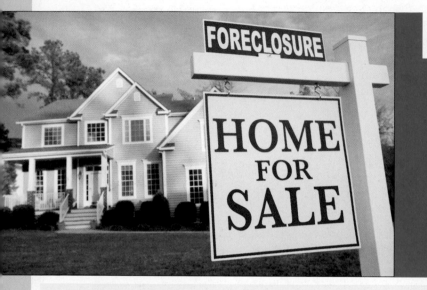

The last quarter of 2008 was a terrible one for the U.S. economy. Between Labor Day and New Years Eve, nearly *2 million* workers lost their jobs. A dozen auto plants closed in response to a dramatic decline in car and truck sales. The housing industry continued its downward spiral as millions of homeowners fell behind on their mortgage payments and were faced with foreclosure. Even Christmas failed to bring much economic cheer in 2008; U.S. consumers weren't spending as much as usual on holiday gifts. Clearly, the U.S. economy was in a recession—a recession caused primarily by weak aggregate demand.

As we've observed, President Obama's first priority was to help restore the U.S. economy. We've also seen what this requires, namely, shifting the AD curve to the right. But exactly how does an Economist in Chief make that happen?

To answer that question, we've got to know more about the details of aggregate demand. In this and the next two chapters we delve into those details. We confront the same questions President Obama's economic advisers had to consider, namely:

- **What are the components of aggregate demand?**
- **What determines the level of spending for each component?**
- **Will there be enough demand to maintain full employment?**

By working through the demand side of the macro economy, we'll get a better view of what might cause business cycles and what might cure them. Later on we'll examine the aggregate supply side more closely as well.

MACRO EQUILIBRIUM

In Chapter 8 we got a bird's-eye view of how macro equilibrium is established. Producers have some notion of how much output they're willing and able to produce at various price levels. Likewise, consumers, businesses, governments, and foreign buyers have some notion of how much output they're willing and able to buy at different price levels. These forces of **aggregate demand** and **aggregate supply** confront each other in the marketplace. Eventually, buyers and sellers discover that only one price level and output combination is acceptable to *both* sides. This is the price-output combination we designate as **(macro) equilibrium.** At equilibrium, the aggregate quantity of goods demanded exactly equals the aggregate quantity supplied. In the absence of macro disturbances, the economy will gravitate toward equilibrium.

Figure 9.1 illustrates again this general view of macro equilibrium. In the figure, aggregate supply (AS) and demand (AD$_1$) establish an equilibrium at E_1. At this particular equilibrium, the value of real output is Q_E, significantly short of the economy's full-employment potential at Q_F. Accordingly, the economy depicted in Figure 9.1 is saddled with excessive unemployment. This is the kind of situation the U.S. economy confronted in 2008–9.

All economists recognize that such a *short-run* macro failure is possible. We also realize that the unemployment problem depicted in Figure 9.1 would disappear if either the AD or AS curve shifted rightward. A central macro debate is over whether the curves *will* shift on their own (self-adjust). If not, the government might have to step in and do some heavy shifting.

To assess the possibilities for self-adjustment, we need to examine the nature of aggregate demand more closely. Who's buying the output of the economy? What factors influence their purchase decisions?

We can best understand the nature of aggregate demand by breaking it down into its various components. *The four components of aggregate demand are*

- *Consumption (C)*
- *Investment (I)*
- *Government spending (G)*
- *Net exports (X − M)*

Each of these components represents a stream of spending that contributes to aggregate demand. What we want to determine is how these various spending decisions are made. We also want to know what factors might *change* the level of spending, thereby *shifting* aggregate demand.

aggregate demand: The total quantity of output demanded at alternative price levels in a given time period, *ceteris paribus.*

aggregate supply: The total quantity of output producers are willing and able to supply at alternative price levels in a given time period, *ceteris paribus.*

The Desired Adjustment

equilibrium (macro): The combination of price level and real output that is compatible with both aggregate demand and aggregate supply.

Components of Aggregate Demand

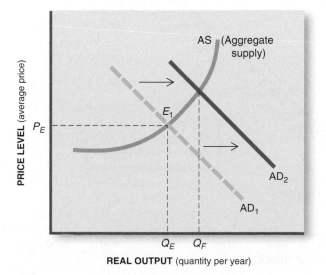

FIGURE 9.1
Escaping a Recession

Aggregate demand (AD) might be insufficient to ensure full employment (Q_F), as illustrated by the intersection of AD$_1$ and the aggregate supply curve. The question is whether and how AD will increase—that is, *shift* rightward—say, to AD$_2$. To answer these questions, the components or demand must be examined.

CONSUMPTION

Consider first the largest component of aggregate demand, namely, **consumption.** Consumption refers to expenditures by households (consumers) on final goods and services. As we observed in Chapter 2, *consumer expenditures account for over two-thirds of total spending.* Hence, whatever factors alter consumer behavior are sure to have an impact on aggregate demand.

consumption: Expenditure by consumers on final goods and services.

Income and Consumption

The aggregate demand curve tells us that consumers will buy more output at lower price levels with a *given* amount of income. But what if *incomes* themselves were to change? If incomes were to increase, consumers would have *more* money to spend at any given *price* level. This could cause a rightward *shift* of the AD curve, exactly the kind of move a recessionary economy (e.g., Figure 9.1) needs.

As far as the British economist John Maynard Keynes was concerned, this was a no-brainer. Experience shows that *consumers tend to spend most of whatever income they have.* This is apparent in Figure 9.2: Year after year, consumer spending has risen in tandem with income. Hence, with *more* income, we expect *more* spending at any given price level.

Disposable income is the key concept here. As noted in Chapter 5, **disposable income** is the amount of income consumers actually take home after all taxes have been paid, transfers (e.g., Social Security benefits) have been received, and depreciation charges and retained earnings have been subtracted (see Table 5.6).

disposable income: After-tax income of consumers; personal income less personal taxes.

whats left over after taxes; check amount

saving: That part of disposable income not spent on current consumption; disposable income less consumption.

What will consumers do with their disposable income? There are only two choices: They can either spend their disposable income on consumption, or they can save (not spend) it. At this point we don't care what form household **saving** might take (e.g., cash under the mattress, bank deposits, stock purchases); all we want to do is distinguish that share of disposable income spent on consumer goods and services from the remainder that is *not*

FIGURE 9.2
U.S. Consumption and Income

The points on the graph indicate the actual rates of U.S. disposable income and consumption for the years 1980–2000. By connecting these dots, we can approximate the long-term consumption function. Clearly, consumption rises with income. Indeed, consumers spend almost every extra dollar they receive.

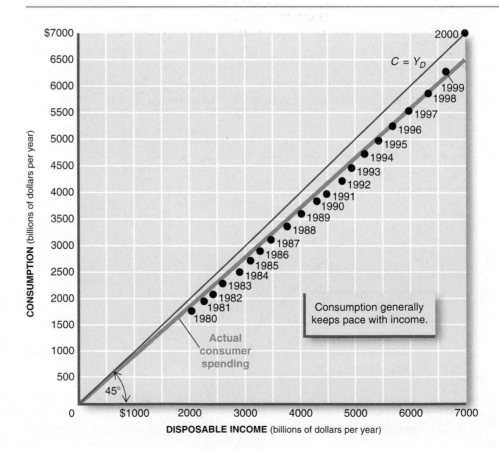

spent. By definition, then, ***all disposable income is either consumed (spent) or saved (not spent);*** that is,

$$\text{Disposable income} = \text{consumption} + \text{saving}$$
$$(Y_D) \qquad\qquad (C) \qquad (S)$$

To figure out how much consumer spending will add to aggregate demand, we need to know what fraction of disposable income will be consumed and how much will be saved. There are two ways of looking at this decision: first, in terms of *averages;* then in terms of *marginal* decisions.

APC. The proportion of *total* disposable income spent on consumer goods and services is referred to as the **average propensity to consume (APC).** To determine the APC, we simply observe how much consumers spend in a given time period out of that period's disposable income. In 2007, for example, the disposable income of U.S. households amounted to more than $10 *trillion*. Out of this amount, consumers spent nearly every available dollar, saving a measly $57 *billion*. Accordingly, we may calculate the *average* propensity to consume as

$$\text{APC} = \frac{\text{total consumption}}{\text{total disposable income}} = \frac{C}{Y_D}$$

For 2007 this works out to

$$\text{APC} = \frac{\$10{,}113 \text{ billion}}{\$10{,}170 \text{ billion}} = 0.994$$

In other words, U.S. consumers spent just about every penny they received in 2007. Specifically, consumers spent, on average, 99.4 cents out of every dollar of income. Less than a penny out of every disposable dollar was saved. (How much do *you* save?)

The relatively high APC in the United States distinguishes our consumer-oriented economy. In recent years, the U.S. APC has even *exceeded* 1.0 on occasion, forcing U.S. households to finance some of their consumption with credit or past savings. Prior to 9/11, a lot of U.S. households were doing exactly that, as the accompanying News reports. The APC can exceed 1.0 when consumers finance their purchases with both current income and credit.

Consumption vs. Saving

IN THE NEWS

Livin' Large

Some 40% of Americans admit they live beyond their means. Seniors are the most likely to match their spending to their income, while young adults are most likely to overspend.

Source: *BusinessWeek,* August 27, 2001. Reprinted by permission. Copyright 2001 by The McGraw-Hill Companies.

Data: Lutheran Brotherhood/Yankelovich Partners Survey of 1,010 Adults in January 2001.

PERCENTAGE OF ADULTS WHO SAY THEY SPEND MORE THAN THEY EARN

| 49 | 40 | 33 | 32 |
| 18–34 | 35–49 | 50–64 | 65–and over |

Analysis: When consumer spending exceeds disposable income, consumer saving is negative; households are *dis*saving. Dissaving is financed with credit or prior savings.

If the APC can change from year to year, then consumers aren't always spending the same fraction of every dollar received (the APC is just an average). This led Keynes to develop a second measure of consumption behavior, called the *marginal* propensity to consume. The

The Marginal Propensity to Consume

marginal propensity to consume (MPC): The fraction of each additional (marginal) dollar of disposable income spent on consumption; the change in consumption divided by the change in disposable income.

marginal propensity to consume (MPC) tells us how much consumer expenditure will *change* in response to *changes* in disposable income. With the delta symbol, Δ, representing "change in," MPC can be written as

$$MPC = \frac{\text{change in consumption}}{\text{change in disposable income}} = \frac{\Delta C}{\Delta Y_D}$$

To calculate the marginal propensity to consume, we could ask how consumer spending in 2007 was affected by the *last* dollar of disposable income. That is, how did consumer spending change when disposable income increased from $10,169,999,999 to $10,170,000,000? If consumer spending increased by 80 cents when this last $1.00 was received, we'd calculate the *marginal* propensity to consume as

$$MPC = \frac{\Delta C}{\Delta Y_D} = \frac{\$0.80}{\$1.00} = 0.8$$

Notice that the MPC in this particular case (0.8) is lower than the APC (0.994). Suppose we had incorrectly assumed that consumers would always spend $0.994 of every dollar's income. Then we'd have expected the rate of consumer spending to rise by 99.4 cents as the last dollar was received. In fact, however, the rate of spending increased by only 80 cents. In other words, consumers responded to an *increase* in their income differently than past averages implied.

No one would be upset if our failure to distinguish the APC from the MPC led to an error of only 19.4 cents in forecasts of consumer spending. After all, the rate of consumer spending in the U.S. economy now exceeds $10 *trillion* per year! But those same trillion-dollar dimensions make the accuracy of the MPC that much more important. Annual *changes* in disposable income entail hundreds of billions of dollars. When we start playing with those sums—the actual focus of economic policymakers—the distinction between APC and MPC is significant.

web analysis

To understand how our economy's marginal propensity to consume influences the effectiveness of federal tax cut stimulus plans, see Paul Krugman's New York Times column at **www.nytimes.com** (search "Bang for the Buck").

The Marginal Propensity to Save

marginal propensity to save (MPS): The fraction of each additional (marginal) dollar of disposable income not spent on consumption; 1 − MPC.

Once we know how much of their income consumers will spend, we also know how much they'll save. Remember that all **disposable income is, by definition, either consumed (spent on consumption) or saved.** Saving is just whatever income is left over after consumption expenditures. Accordingly, if the MPC is 0.80, then 20 cents of each additional dollar are being saved and 80 cents are being spent (see Figure 9.3). The **marginal propensity to save (MPS)**—the fraction of each additional dollar saved (that is, *not* spent)—is simply

$$MPS = 1 - MPC$$

As Table 9.1 illustrates, if we know how much of their income consumers spend, we also know how much of it they save.

FIGURE 9.3
MPC and MPS

The marginal propensity to consume (MPC) tells us what portion of an extra dollar of income will be spent. The remaining portion will be saved. The MPC and MPS help us predict consumer behavior.

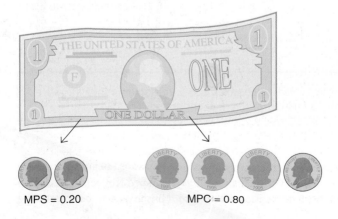

MPS = 0.20   MPC = 0.80

MPC. The marginal propensity to consume (MPC) is the *change* in consumption that accompanies a *change* in disposable income; that is,

$$MPC = \frac{\Delta C}{\Delta Y_D}$$

MPS. The marginal propensity to *save* (MPS) is the fraction of each additional (marginal) dollar of disposable income *not* spent—that is, saved. This is summarized as

$$MPS = \frac{\Delta S}{\Delta Y_D}$$

MPS equals 1− MPC, since every additional dollar is either spent (consumed) or not spent (saved).

APC. The *average* propensity to consume is the proportion of *total* disposable income that's spent on consumption. It is computed:

$$APC = \frac{C}{Y_D}$$

APS. The average *propensity* to save is $\frac{S}{Y_D}$ and must equal $1 - APC$.

TABLE 9.1
Average and Marginal Propensities

web analysis

Go to the U.S. Bureau of Economic Activity (BEA) Web site at **www.bea.gov,** and determine the rate of disposable income and consumer spending in the most recent two quarters. What was the APC in the most recent quarter? What was the MPC between the two quarters?

THE CONSUMPTION FUNCTION

The MPC, MPS, APC, and APS are simply statistical measures of observed consumer behavior. What we really want to know is what drives these measures. If we know, then we'll be in a position to *predict* rather than just *observe* consumer behavior. This ability would be of immense value in anticipating and controlling short-run business cycles. President Obama certainly could have used it.

Keynes had several ideas about the determinants of consumption. Although he observed that consumer spending and income were highly correlated (Figure 9.2), he knew consumption wasn't *completely* determined by current income. In extreme cases, this is evident. People who have no income in a given period continue to consume goods and services. They finance their purchases by dipping into their savings accounts (*past* income) or using credit (*future* income) instead of spending *current* income. We also observe that people's spending sometimes *changes* even when income doesn't, suggesting that income isn't the *only* determinant of consumption. Other, *non*income determinants of consumption include

- *Expectations:* People who anticipate a pay raise, a tax refund, or a birthday check often start spending that money even before they get it. Conversely, workers who anticipate being laid off tend to save more and spend less than usual. Hence, *expectations* may alter consumer spending before income itself changes.
- *Wealth effects:* The amount of wealth an individual owns also affects a person's ability and willingness to consume. A homeowner may take out a home equity loan to buy a flat-screen TV, a vacation, or a new car. In this case, consumer spending is being financed by wealth, not current income. *Changes* in wealth will also *change* consumer behavior. When the stock market rises, stockholders respond by saving less and spending more of their current income. This **wealth effect** was particularly evident in the late 1990s, when a persistent rise in the stock market helped fuel a consumption spree (and a negative savings rate). When the stock market reversed direction in 2000, consumers cut back their spending.

  Changes in housing prices have a similar effect. A 4-year surge in housing prices made consumers feel rich in 2002–5. Many homeowners tapped into those higher prices with home-equity loans in order to increase their consumption. When housing

Autonomous Consumption

wealth effect: A change in consumer spending caused by a change in the value of owned assets.

prices started declining in 2006, this source of consumer finance dried up. As we've already noted, this negative wealth effect contributed to the 2008–9 recession.

- *Credit:* The availability of credit allows people to spend more than their current income. Here again *changes* in credit availability or cost (interest rates) may alter consumer behavior. When banks curtailed credit in 2008, consumers had to stop buying cars and homes.
- *Taxes:* Taxes are the wedge between *total* income and *disposable* income. The tax cuts enacted in 2001–3 put more income into consumer hands immediately (via tax rebates) and left them with more income from future paychecks (via tax-rate cuts). Tax rebates in early 2008 had the same effect: These tax reductions stimulated more aggregate demand at existing price levels. Were income taxes to go up, disposable incomes and consumer spending would decline.

Income-Dependent Consumption

• be able to calculate

In recognition of these many determinants of consumption, Keynes distinguished between two kinds of consumer spending: (1) spending *not* influenced by current income and (2) spending that *is* determined by current income. This simple categorization is summarized as

$$\text{Total consumption} = \frac{\text{autonomous}}{\text{consumption}} + \text{income-dependent consumption}$$

where *autonomous* consumption refers to that consumption spending independent of current income. The level of autonomous spending depends instead on expectations, wealth, credit, taxes, and other nonincome influences.

These various determinants of consumption are summarized in an equation called the **consumption function,** which is written as

$$C = a + bY_D$$

> **consumption function:** A mathematical relationship indicating the rate of desired consumer spending at various income levels.

where C = current consumption
a = autonomous consumption
b = marginal propensity to consume
Y_D = disposable income

At first blush, the consumption function is just a mathematical summary of consumer behavior. It has important *predictive* power, however: ***The consumption function tells us:***

- ***How much consumption will be included in aggregate demand at the prevailing price level.***
- ***How the consumption component of AD will change (shift) when incomes change.***

One Consumer's Behavior

To see how the consumption function works, consider the plight of Justin, a college freshman who has no income. How much will Justin spend? Obviously he must spend *something,* otherwise he'll starve to death. At a very low rate of income—in this case, zero—consumer spending depends less on current income than on basic survival needs, past savings, and credit. The a in the consumption function expresses this autonomous consumption: Let's assume it's $50 per week. Thus, the weekly rate of consumption expenditure in this case is

$$C = \$50 + bY_D$$

Now suppose that Justin finds a job and begins earning $100 per week. Will his spending be affected? The $50 per week he'd been spending didn't buy much. Now that he's earning a little income, Justin will want to improve his lifestyle. That is, *we expect consumption to rise with income.* The marginal propensity to consume tells us how fast spending will rise.

Suppose Justin responds to the new-found income by increasing his consumption from $50 per week to $125. The *change* in his consumption is therefore $75. Dividing this *change* in his consumption ($75) by the *change* in income ($100) reveals that his marginal propensity to consume is 0.75.

Predictive Power. Once we know the level of autonomous consumption ($50 per week) and the marginal propensity to consume (0.75), we can predict consumer behavior with uncanny accuracy. In this case, Justin's consumption function is

$$C = \$50 + 0.75Y_D$$

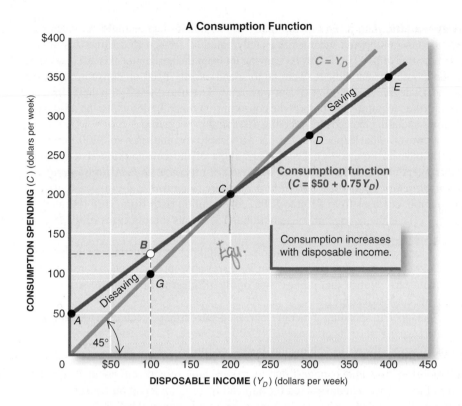

A Consumption Function

$C = Y_D$

Saving

E

D

Consumption function
$(C = \$50 + 0.75 Y_D)$

C

Consumption increases
with disposable income.

B

Dissaving

G

A

45°

CONSUMPTION SPENDING (C) (dollars per week)

DISPOSABLE INCOME (Y_D) (dollars per week)

FIGURE 9.4
A Consumption Function

The rate of consumer spending (C) depends on disposable income (Y_D). The marginal propensity to consume indicates how much consumption will increase with each added dollar of income. In this case, when disposable income rises from $100 to $200, consumption increases by $75 (from point B to point C). The MPC = 0.75.

The consumption function can be expressed in an equation, a table, or a graph. Point B on the graph, for example, corresponds to row B in the table. Both indicate that this consumer desires to spend $125 per week when his income is $100 per week. The difference between income and consumption equals (dis)saving.

		Consumption ($C = \$50 + 0.75\ Y_D$)		
	Disposable Income (Y_D)	Autonomous Consumption	+ Income Dependent Consumption =	Total Consumption
A	$ 0	$50	$ 0	$ 50
B	100	50	75	125
C	200	50	150	200
D	300	50	225	275
E	400	50	300	350
F	500	50	375	425

With these numerical values we can advance from simple *observation* (what he's spending now) to *prediction* (what he'll spend at *different* income levels). Figure 9.4 summarizes this predictive power.

We've already noted that Justin will spend $125 per week when his income is only $100. This observation is summarized in row B of the table in Figure 9.4 and by point B on the graph. Notice that his spending exceeds his income by $25 at this point. The other $25 is still being begged, borrowed, or withdrawn from savings. Without peering further into Justin's personal finances, we simply say that he's **dissaving** $25 per week. ***Dissaving occurs whenever current consumption exceeds current income.*** As the News on page 179 revealed, dissaving is common in the United States, especially among younger people who are "livin' large."

If Justin's income continues to rise, he'll stop dissaving at some point. Perhaps he'll even start saving enough to pay back all the people who have sustained him through these difficult months. Figure 9.4 shows just how and when this will occur.

dissaving: Consumption expenditure in excess of disposable income; a negative saving flow.

The 45-Degree Line. The green line in Figure 9.4, with a 45-degree angle, represents all points where consumption and income are exactly equal ($C = Y_D$). Recall that Justin currently has an income of $100 per week. By moving up from the horizontal axis at $Y_D = \$100$, we see all his consumption choices. Were he to spend exactly $100 on consumption, he'd end up on the 45-degree line at point G. But we already know he doesn't stop there. Instead, he proceeds further, to point B. At point B the consumption function lies *above* the 45-degree line, so Justin's spending exceeds his income; dissaving is occurring.

Observe, however, what happens when his disposable income rises to $200 per week (row C in the table in Figure 9.4). The upward slope of the consumption function (see graph) tells us that consumption spending will rise with income. In fact, ***the slope of the consumption function equals the marginal propensity to consume.*** In this case, we see that when income increases from $100 to $200, consumption rises from $125 (point B) to $200 (point C). Thus the *change* in consumption ($75) equals three-fourths of the *change* in income. The MPC is still 0.75.

Point C has further significance. At an income of $200 per week Justin is no longer dissaving; instead he is now breaking even—that is, disposable income equals consumption, so saving equals zero. Notice that point C lies on the 45-degree line, where current consumption equals current income.

What would happen to spending if income increased still further? According to Figure 9.4, Justin will start *saving* once income exceeds $200 per week. To the right of point C, the consumption function always lies below the 45-degree line.

The Aggregate Consumption Function

Repeated studies of consumers suggest that there's nothing remarkable about Justin. The consumption function we've constructed for him can be used to depict all consumers simply by changing the numbers involved. Instead of dealing in hundreds of dollars per week, we now play with trillions of dollars per year. But the basic relationship is the same. As we observed earlier in Figure 9.2, we can predict consumer spending if we know how much income consumers have. That's why there are no surprises in the following News, which confirms that both U.S. consumption and disposable income increased in January 2009. (What was the MPC?)

IN THE NEWS

News Release: Personal Income and Outlays

Personal Income and Outlays: January 2009

Personal income increased $20 billion, or 0.17 percent, and disposable personal income (DPI) increased $165 billion, or 1.6 percent, in January, according to the Bureau of Economic Analysis. Personal consumption expenditures (PCE) increased $95 billion, or 1.0 percent.

	December 2008	January 2009
Personal income................................	12,082	12,102
Disposable personal income.............	10,602	10,767
Personal outlays................................	9,831	9,926
Personal savings................................	408	478

Source: U.S. Bureau of Economic Analysis, March 2, 2009.

Analysis: When household incomes increase, consumer spending increases as well. The marginal propensity to consume summarizes this relationship.

Shifts of the Consumption Function

Although the consumption function is a handy device for predicting consumer behavior, it's not infallible. People change their behavior. Neither autonomous consumption (the *a* in the consumption function) nor the marginal propensity to consume (the *b* in $C = a + bY_D$) is set in stone. Whenever one of these parameters changes, the entire consumption function moves.

IN THE NEWS

Consumer Confidence Index at All-Time Low

NEW YORK (CNNMoney.com)—A key measure of consumer confidence fell to an all-time low in December amid a dismal job market and uncertain outlook for the new year.

The Conference Board, a New York-based business research group, said Tuesday that its Consumer Confidence Index fell to 38 in December from the downwardly revised 44.7 in November. . . .

Job Market Concerns

Perhaps most unsettling for Americans is the deteriorating job market. Layoffs and income cuts were widespread this year. The number of Americans filing for first-time unemployment benefits rose to a 26-year high for the week ended Dec. 20.

Nearly 2 million jobs were lost in 2008, and the slumped stock market means some nest eggs have shrunk considerably. . . .

2009 Outlook

Consumers anticipating business conditions to worsen over the next six months increased to 32.8% from 28.3% in November, the report said. . . .

The Consumer Confidence Survey is based on a representative sample of 5,000 U.S. households.

—Julianne Pepitone

Source: CNNMoney.com, December 30, 2008.

Analysis: When consumer confidence declines, autonomous spending drops and the consumption function shifts downward (as in Figure 9.5). This causes a leftward shift of the AD curve (as in Figure 9.6).

web analysis

For the latest U.S. Consumer Confidence Index value, visit **www.conference-board.org.**

A change in "a" **shifts** *the consumption function up or down; a change in "b" alters* **the** *slope of the function.*

Consider first the value for a. We noted earlier that autonomous consumption depends on wealth, credit, expectations, taxes, and price levels. If any of these nonincome determinants changes, the value of the a in the consumption function will change as well.

The plunge in consumer confidence that occurred in December 2008 illustrates how consumer behavior can change abruptly. The continued decline in home prices, mounting job losses, and a declining stock market all weighed heavily on consumer confidence. As the above News relates, 1 out of 3 consumers expected the economy to worsen further in 2009. With such dismal expectations, they weren't prepared to keep spending all their income. The value of autonomous consumption declined from a_1 to a_2 in Figure 9.5, *shifting* the consumer function downward.

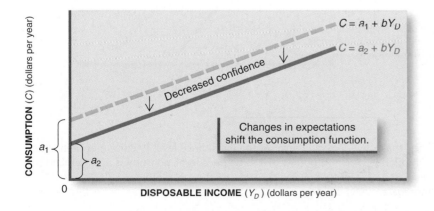

FIGURE 9.5

A Shift in the Consumption Function

Consumers' willingness to spend current income is affected by their confidence in the future. If consumers become more worried or pessimistic, autonomous consumption may decrease from a_1 to a_2. This change will shift the entire consumption function downward.

Shifts of Aggregate Demand. Shifts of the consumption function are reflected in shifts of the aggregate demand curve. Consider again the December 2008 downward shift of the consumption function. A decrease in consumer spending at any given income level implies a decrease in aggregate demand as well. Recall that the aggregate demand curve depicts how much real output will be demanded at various price levels, *with income held constant.* When the consumption function shifts downward, households spend less of their income. Hence, less real output is demanded at any given price level. To summarize,

- *A downward shift of the consumption function implies a leftward shift of the aggregate demand curve.*
- *An upward shift of the consumption function implies an increase (a rightward shift) in aggregate demand.*

These relationships are illustrated in Figure 9.6.

AD Shift Factors

Keep in mind what we're doing here. Our goal is to predict consumer spending. We want to know how much consumer spending will contribute to AD at any given price level. We get that information from the consumption function. That information helps us position the AD curve correctly. Then we want to know what might cause the AD curve to *shift*. We now know that *the AD curve will shift if consumer incomes change, if autonomous consumption changes,* or if the MPC changes. Hence, *the AD curve will shift in response to,*

- *Changes in income.*
- *Changes in expectations* (consumer confidence).
- *Changes in wealth.*
- *Changes in credit conditions.*
- *Changes in tax policy.*

As we've seen, a recession can change incomes quickly. Consumer confidence can change even more abruptly. A decline in home prices can reduce household wealth enormously. Between 2006 and 2008 home equity declined by roughly 2 trillion dollars. The stock market decline of 2008 further eroded consumer wealth. All these forces combined to shift the AD curve to the left.

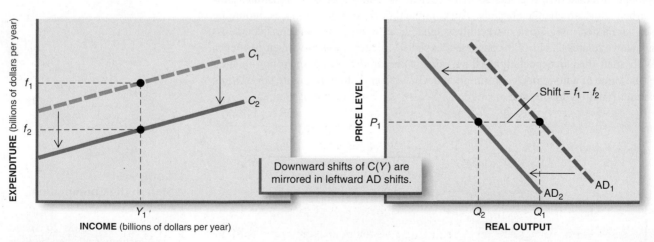

FIGURE 9.6
AD Effects of Consumption Shifts

A downward shift of the consumption function implies that households want to spend less of their income. Here consumption at the income level Y_1 decreases from f_1 to f_2. This decreased expenditure is reflected in a leftward shift of the aggregate demand curve. At the initial price level P_1 consumers demanded Q_1 output. At that same price level, consumers now demand less output, Q_2 [$= Q_1 - (f_1 - f_2)$].

Clearly, shifts of aggregate demand can be a cause of macro instability. As we first observed in Chapter 8, recurrent shifts of aggregate demand may cause real output to alternately expand and contract, thereby giving rise to short-run business cycles. What we've observed here is that those aggregate demand shifts may originate in consumer behavior. Changes in consumer confidence, in wealth, or in credit conditions alter the rate of consumer spending. If consumer spending increases abruptly, demand-pull inflation may follow. If consumer spending slows abruptly, a recession may occur.

Knowing that consumer behavior *might* cause macro problems is a bit worrisome. But it's also a source of policy power. What if we *want* AD to increase in order to achieve full employment? Our knowledge of consumer-based AD shift factors gives us huge clues about which macro policy tools to look for.

Shifts and Cycles

INVESTMENT

Consumption is only one of four AD components. To determine where AD is and when it might shift, we need to examine the other components of spending as well.

As we observed in Chapter 5, investment spending accounts for roughly 15 percent of total output. That spending includes not only expenditures on new plant, equipment, and business software (all referred to as *fixed investment*) but also spending on inventories (called *inventory investment*). Residential construction is also counted in investment statistics because houses and apartment buildings continue to produce housing services for decades. All these forms of **investment** represent a demand for output.

Expectations. Expectations play a critical role in investment decisions. No firm wants to purchase new plant and equipment unless it is convinced people will later buy the output produced by that plant and that equipment. Nor do producers want to accumulate inventories of goods unless they expect consumers to eventually buy them. Thus, *favorable expectations of future sales are a necessary condition for investment spending.*

Interest Rates. A second determinant of investment spending is the rate of interest. Business firms typically borrow money in order to purchase plant and equipment. The higher the rate of interest, the costlier it is to invest. Accordingly, *we anticipate a lower rate of investment spending when interest rates are high, more investment at lower rates,* ceteris paribus.

Technology and Innovation. A third determinant of investment is changes in technology and innovation. When scientists learned how to miniaturize electronic circuitry, an entire new industry of electronic calculators, watches, and other goods sprang to life. In this case, the demand for investment goods shifted to the right as a result of improved miniaturized circuits and imaginative innovation (the use of the new technology in pocket calculators). More recently, technological advances and cost reductions have stimulated an investment spree in digital music players, laptop computers, cellular phones, video conferencing, fiber-optic networks, and anything associated with the Internet.

The curve I_1, in Figure 9.7, depicts the general shape of the investment function. To find the rate of investment spending in this figure, we first have to know the rate of interest. At an interest rate of 8 percent, for example, we expect to see $150 billion of investment (point A in Figure 9.7). At 6 percent interest, we'd expect $300 billion of investment (point B).

As was the case with consumer spending, predicting investment spending isn't quite as easy as it first appears. Any specific investment function (like I_2 in Figure 9.7) is based on a specific set of investor expectations about future sales and profits. Those expectations can change, however.

Altered Expectations. Business expectations are essentially a question of confidence in future sales. An upsurge in current consumer spending could raise investor expectations for

Determinants of Investment

investment: Expenditures on (production of) new plant, equipment, and structures (capital) in a given time period, plus changes in business inventories.

not stocks + bonds

Shifts of Investment

FIGURE 9.7
Investment Demand

The rate of desired investment depends on expectations, the rate of interest, and innovation. A *change* in expectations will *shift* the investment-demand curve. With given expectations, a change in the rate of interest will lead to *movements* along the existing investment-demand curve. In this case, an increase in investment beyond $150 billion per year (point *A*) may be caused by lower interest rates (point *B*) or improved expectations (point *C*).

PLANNED INVESTMENT SPENDING (billions of dollars per year)

future sales, shifting the investment function rightward (to I_2). New business software might induce a similar response. New business tax breaks might have the same effect. If any of these things happened, businesses would be more eager to invest. They'd borrow *more* money at any given interest rate (e.g., point *C* in Figure 9.7) and use it to buy more plant, equipment, and inventory.

Business expectations could worsen as well. Imagine you were the CEO of a company contemplating a major expansion. Then you read a story about plunging consumer confidence, as in the News on page 185. Would you rethink your plans? Probably. That's what Panasonic's president did in January 2009 (see World View below). When *business* expectations worsen, investments get postponed or canceled. Suddenly, there's less investment spending at any given interest rate. This investment shift is illustrated by the curve I_3 in Figure 9.7.

WORLD VIEW

Panasonic Slashes Spending

Hurt by sliding consumer spending around the world, electronics giant Panasonic Corp. said it will slash spending on flat-panel-television operations and pull out of unspecified money-losing businesses.

President Fumio Ohtsubo said Friday the company will reduce planned investments in two Japanese factories making flat panels for TV sets by 23%, or about $1.5 billion, in the fiscal year beginning April 1. . . .

Panasonic now will spend 445 billion yen ($4.88 billion) on the plants through 2012, rather than 580 billion yen budgeted earlier.

—Yuzo Yamaguchi and Yoshio Takahashi

Analysis: Business investment is based more on expected future sales than on current sales and income. When expectations for future sales growth diminish, investment spending on plant, equipment, and inventory drops.

AD Shifts. As was the case with consumer behavior, we are looking at investor behavior to help us understand aggregate demand. From Figure 9.7 we see that knowledge of investor expectations and interest rates will tell us how much investment will be included in aggregate demand at the current price level. We also see that a change in expectations will alter investment behavior and thereby *shift* the AD curve. **When investment spending declines, the aggregate demand curve shifts to the left.**

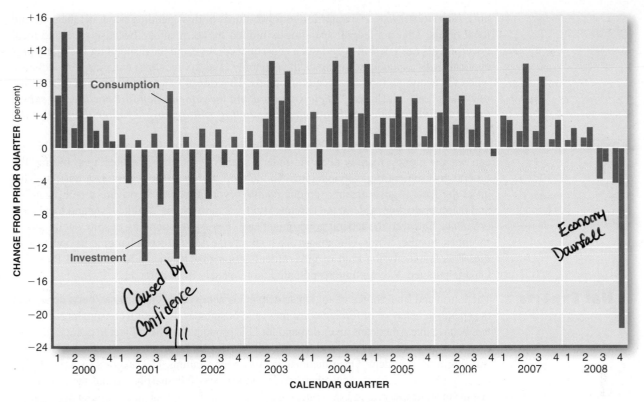

FIGURE 9.8
Volatile Investment Spending

Investment spending fluctuates more than consumption. Shown here are the quarter-to-quarter changes in the real rate of spending for fixed investment (excluding residential construction and inventory changes) and total consumption. Notice the sharp drops in investment spending just prior to the recession that began in March 2001 and again after the 9/11 attacks, and once more in the fourth quarter of 2008.

Source: *U.S. Bureau of Economic Analysis* (quarterly data seasonally adjusted).

Empirical Instability. Figure 9.8 shows that unstable investment is more than just a theoretical threat to macro stability. What is depicted here are the quarter-to-quarter changes in both consumer spending and investor spending for the years 2000–2006. Quarterly changes in *consumer* spending never exceeded 6.5 percent and never became negative. By contrast, *investment* spending plummeted by 13.3 percent in the post-9/11 quarter and jumped by over 14 percent in three other quarters. Those abrupt changes in investment (and related AD shifts) were a major cause of the 2001 recession and also an important source of subsequent recovery.

GOVERNMENT AND NET EXPORT SPENDING

The apparent volatility of investment spending heightens rather than soothes anxiety about short-run macro instability. Together, consumption and investment account for over 80 percent of total output. As we have seen, the investment component of aggregate demand can be both uncertain and unstable. The consumption component of aggregate demand may shift abruptly as well. Such shifts can sow the seeds of macro failure. Will the other components of aggregate demand improve the odds of macro success? What determines the level of government and net export spending? How stable are they?

At present, the government sector (federal, state, and local) spends over $2 trillion on goods and services, all of which is part of aggregate demand (unlike income transfers, which are

web analysis

To view the volatility of investment expenditures from quarter to quarter, visit **http://research.stlouisfed.org** and search "gross private domestic investment."

Government Spending

not). As we observed in Chapter 2, about two-thirds of this spending occurs at the state and local levels. That nonfederal spending is limited by tax receipts, because state and local governments can't deficit-spend. As a consequence, state and local spending is slightly pro-cyclical, with expenditure rising as the economy (and tax receipts) expands and declining when the economy (and tax receipts) slumps. This doesn't auger well for macro stability, much less "self-adjustment." *If consumption and investment spending decline, the subsequent decline in state-local government spending will aggravate rather than offset the leftward shift of the AD curve.*

Federal spending on goods and services isn't so constrained by tax receipts. Uncle Sam can *borrow* money, thereby allowing federal spending to exceed tax receipts. In fact, the federal government typically operates "in the red," with large annual budget deficits. This gives the federal government a unique *counter*-cyclical power. If private-sector spending and incomes decline, federal tax revenues will fall in response. Unlike state and local governments, however, the federal government can *increase* its spending despite declining tax revenues. In other words, Uncle Sam can help reverse AD shifts by changing its own spending. This is exactly the kind of government action that Keynes advocated and President Obama pursued. We examine its potential more closely in Chapter 11.

Net Exports

The fourth and final source of aggregate demand is net exports. Our gross exports depend on the spending behavior of foreign consumers and businesses. If foreign consumers and investors behave like Americans, their demand for U.S. products will be subject to changes in *their* income, expectations, wealth, and other factors. In the Asian currency crisis of 1997–99, this was alarmingly evident: Once incomes in Asia began falling, U.S. exports to Asia of rice, corn, lumber, computers, and other goods and services fell sharply. So did the number of Asian students applying to U.S. colleges (a demand for U.S.-produced educational services). This decline in export spending represented a leftward shift of U.S. aggregate demand.

Imports, too, can be unstable, and for the same reasons. Most U.S. imports are consumer goods and services. Imports, therefore, just get caught up in the ebb and flow of consumer spending. When consumer confidence slips or the stock market dips, import spending declines along with the rest of consumption (and investment). As a consequence, *net* exports can be both uncertain and unstable, creating further shifts of aggregate demand.

The AD Curve Revisited

Figure 9.9 illustrates how the four components of spending come together to determine aggregate demand. From the consumption function we determine how much output consumers

---

FIGURE 9.9

Building an AD Curve

The quantity of output demanded at the prevailing price level originates in the spending decisions of consumers (C), investors (I), government (G), and net exports ($X - M$). By adding up the intended spending of these market participants we can see how much output (Q_O) will be demanded at the current price level (P_O). Thus, point d is the first building block in the construction of the AD curve.

The slope of the AD curve above and below point d is based on the real-balances, interest-rate, and foreign-trade responses to changing price levels (see pp. 161–163).

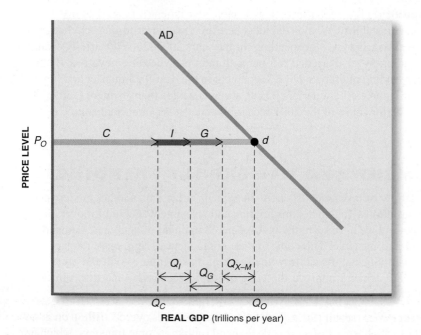

will demand at the prevailing price level P_O. In this case, they demand Q_C of output. To that amount, we add investment demand Q_I, as revealed in Figure 9.7 and investor surveys. Local, state, and federal budgets will tell us how much output (Q_G) the government intends to buy. Net exports complete the computation. When we add them all up, we see that output Q_O will be demanded at the prevailing price level P_O. The answer in this case is reflected at point d. Point d, therefore, is the initial building block in constructing the AD curve. It tells us how much output will be demanded at the current price level.

We know that the AD curve must go through point d. But how much output will be demanded at other price levels? The rest of the AD curve reflects how the quantity of output demanded will change if the price level rises or falls (i.e., the real-balances, interest-rate, and foreign-trade effects discussed in Chapter 8).

MACRO FAILURE

In principle, the construction of the AD curve is simple. In practice, it requires an enormous amount of information about the intentions and behavior of market participants. Let's assume for the moment, however, that we have all that information and can therefore accurately depict the AD curve. What then?

Once we know the shape and position of the AD curve we can put it together with the AS curve and locate macro equilibrium. Here's where our macro problems may emerge. As we noted earlier, *there are two chief concerns about macro equilibrium, namely,*

1. *The market's macro equilibrium might not give us full employment or price stability.*
2. *Even if the market's macro equilibrium were perfectly positioned (i.e., with full employment and price stability), it might not last.*

Figure 9.10*a* depicts the perfect macro equilibrium that everyone hopes for. Aggregate demand and aggregate supply intersect at E_1. At that macro equilibrium we get both full employment (Q_F) and price stability (P^*)—an ideal situation.

Undesired Equilibrium

(a) Macro success: "perfect AD"
(b) Cyclical unemployment: "too little AD"
(c) Demand-pull inflation: "too much AD"

FIGURE 9.10
Macro Failures

Keynesian theory emphasizes that the combined spending decisions of consumers, investors, governments, and net exporters may not be compatible with the desired full employment (Q_F)–price stability (P^*) equilibrium (as they are in Figure *a*). Aggregate demand may be too small (Figure *b*) or too great (Figure *c*) causing cyclical unemployment (*b*) or demand-pull inflation (*c*). Worse yet, even a desirable macro equilibrium (*a*) may be upset by abrupt *shifts* of aggregate demand.

Keynes didn't think such a perfect outcome was likely. Why should aggregate demand intersect with aggregate supply exactly at point E_1? As we've observed, consumers, investors, government, and foreigners make independent spending decisions, based on many influences. Why should all these decisions add up to just the right amount of aggregate demand? Keynes didn't think they would. ***Because market participants make independent spending decisions, there's no reason to expect that the sum of their expenditures will generate exactly the right amount of aggregate demand.*** Instead, there's a high likelihood that we'll confront an imbalance between desired spending and full-employment output levels—that is, too much or too little aggregate demand.

Recessionary GDP Gap. Figure 9.10b illustrates one of the undesired equilibriums that Keynes worried about. **Full-employment GDP** is still at Q_F and stable prices are at the level P^*. In this case, however, the rate of output demanded at price level P^* is only Q_2, far short of full-employment GDP (Q_F). How could this happen? Quite simple: The spending plans of consumers, investors, government, and export buyers don't generate enough aggregate demand at current (P^*) prices.

The economy depicted in Figure 9.10b is in trouble. At full employment, a lot more output would be produced than market participants would be willing to buy. As unsold inventories rose, production would get cut back, workers would get laid off, and prices would decline. Eventually, the economy would settle at E_2, where AD_2 and AS intersect. **Equilibrium GDP** would be equal to Q_{E2} and the equilibrium price level would be at P_2.

E_2 is clearly not a happy equilibrium. What particularly concerned Keynes was the **recessionary GDP gap,** the amount by which equilibrium GDP falls short of full-employment GDP. In Figure 9.10b, the recessionary GDP gap equals Q_F minus Q_{E2}. This gap represents unused productive capacity: lost GDP and unemployed workers. It is the breeding ground of **cyclical unemployment,** the kind of situation President Obama confronted in 2009.

Figure 9.11 illustrates this dilemma with more numerical details on aggregate demand. The table depicts the demand for GDP at different price levels by consumers, investors, government, and net export buyers. Full-employment GDP is set at $10 trillion and the price level at 100. Producers are hoping to sell all the output produced, as indicated by point *a* on the graph. As is evident, however, the quantity of output demanded at that price level is only $8 trillion (point *b* in Figure 9.11). This shortfall of aggregate demand will lead to output and price reductions, pushing the economy downward to the equilibrium GDP at point *E*. At that AS = AD intersection, the *equilibrium* GDP is at $9 trillion, with a price level of 90. The recessionary GDP gap is therefore $1 trillion ($Q_F - Q_E$). This recessionary gap spells job losses and economic misery.

Inflationary GDP Gap. Aggregate demand won't always fall short of potential output. But Keynes saw it as a distinct possibility. He also realized that aggregate demand might even *exceed* the economy's full-employment/price stability capacity. This contingency is illustrated in Figure 9.10c.

In Figure 9.10c, the AD_3 curve represents the combined spending plans of all market participants. According to this aggregate demand curve, market participants demand more output (Q_3) at current prices than the economy can produce (Q_F). To meet this excessive demand, producers will use overtime shifts and strain capacity. This will push prices up. The economy will end up at the macro equilibrium E_3. At E_3 the price level is higher (inflation) and short-run output exceeds sustainable levels.

What we end up with in Figure 9.10c is another undesirable equilibrium. In this case we have an **inflationary GDP gap,** wherein equilibrium GDP (Q_{E3}) exceeds full-employment GDP (Q_F). This is a fertile breeding ground for **demand-pull inflation.**

The GDP gaps illustrated in Figure 9.10b and c are clearly troublesome. In a nutshell,

- *The goal is to produce at full employment, but*
- *Equilibrium GDP may be greater or less than full-employment GDP.*

---

full-employment GDP: The value of total output (real GDP) produced at full employment.

equilibrium GDP: The value of total output (real GDP) produced at macro equilibrium (AS = AD).

recessionary GDP gap: The amount by which equilibrium GDP falls short of full-employment GDP.

cyclical unemployment: Unemployment attributable to a lack of job vacancies; that is, to inadequate aggregate demand.

inflationary GDP gap: The amount by which equilibrium GDP exceeds full-employment GDP.

demand-pull inflation: An increase in the price level initiated by excessive aggregate demand.

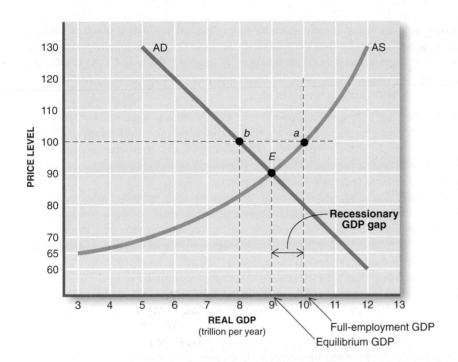

FIGURE 9.11
A Recessionary GDP Gap

The level of aggregate demand depends on the spending behavior of market participants. In this case, the level of GDP demanded at current prices ($P = 100$) ($8 trillion) is less than full-employment GDP ($10 trillion). More output is being produced (point a) than purchased (point b) at prevailing prices. This results in a lower equilibrium GDP ($9 trillion) and a recessionary GDP gap ($1 trillion). The price level also declines from 100 to 90.

Price Level	Real GDP Demanded (in $ trillions) by:					Aggregate Supply
	Consumers +	Investors +	Government +	Net Exports =	Aggregate Demand	
130	3.0	0.25	1.5	0.25	5.0	12.0
120	3.5	0.50	1.5	0.50	6.0	11.5
110	4.0	0.75	1.5	0.75	7.0	11.0
100	4.5	1.00	1.5	1.0	8.0	10.0
90	5.0	1.25	1.5	1.25	9.0	9.0
80	5.5	1.50	1.5	1.50	10.0	7.0
70	6.0	1.75	1.5	1.75	11.0	5.0
60	6.5	2.0	1.5	2.0	12.0	3.0

(Handwritten annotations to the right of the table: "Recessionary Debt", "Equilibrium", "Inflationary")

Unstable Equilibrium

Whenever equilibrium GDP differs from full-employment GDP, we confront a macro failure (unemployment or inflation).

Things need not always work out so badly. Although Keynes thought it improbable, the spending plans of market participants *might* generate the perfect amount of aggregate demand, leaving the economy at the desired macro equilibrium depicted in Figure 9.10a. In Figure 9.10a, equilibrium GDP equals full-employment GDP. Unfortunately, that happy outcome might not last.

As we've observed, market participants may change their spending behavior abruptly. The stock market may boom or bust, shifting the consumption component of aggregate demand. Changed sales forecasts (expectations) may alter investment plans. Crises in foreign economies may disrupt export sales. A terrorist attack or outbreak of war may rock everybody's boat. Any of these events will cause the aggregate demand curve to shift. When this happens, the AD curve will get knocked out of its "perfect" position in Figure 9.10a, sending us to undesirable outcomes like 9.10b and 9.10c. Recurrent shifts of aggregate demand could even cause a **business cycle.**

business cycle: Alternating periods of economic growth and contraction.

Macro Failures   Economies can get into macro trouble from the supply side of the market place as well, as we'll see later (Chapter 16). Keynes's emphasis on demand-side inadequacies serves as an early warning of potential macro failure, however. ***If aggregate demand is too little, too great, or too unstable, the economy will not reach and maintain the goals of full employment and price stability.***

Self-Adjustment?   As we noted earlier, not everyone is as pessimistic as Keynes was about the prospects for macro bliss. The critical question is not whether undesirable outcomes might *occur* but whether they'll *persist.* In other words, the seriousness of any short-run macro failure depends on how markets *respond* to GDP gaps. If markets self-adjust, as classical economists asserted, then macro failures would be temporary.

How might markets self-adjust? If investors stepped up *their* spending whenever consumer spending faltered, the right amount of aggregate demand could be maintained. Such self-adjustment requires that some components of aggregate demand shift in the right direction at just the right time. In other words, self-adjustment requires that any shortfalls in one component of aggregate demand be offset by spending in another component. If such offsetting shifts occurred, then the desired macro equilibrium in Figure 9.10*a* could be maintained. Keynes didn't think that likely, however, for reasons we'll explore in the next chapter.

THE ECONOMY TOMORROW

ANTICIPATING AD SHIFTS

The Index of Leading Indicators. Keynes's theory of macro failure gave economic policymakers a lot to worry about. If Keynes was right, abrupt changes in aggregate demand could ruin even the best of economic times. Even if he was wrong about the ability of the economy to self-adjust, sudden shifts of aggregate demand could cause a lot of temporary pain. To minimize such pain, policymakers need some way of peering into the future—to foresee shifts of aggregate demand. With such a crystal ball, they might be able to take defensive actions and keep the economy on track.

Market participants have developed all kinds of crystal balls for anticipating AD shifts. The Foundation for the Study of Cycles has identified 4,000 different crystal balls people use to foretell changes in spending. They include the ratio of used-car to new-car sales (it rises in economic downturns); the number of divorce petitions (it rises in bad times); animal population cycles (they peak just before economic downturns); and even the optimism/pessimism content of popular music (a reflection of consumer confidence).

One of the more conventional crystal balls is the Index of Leading Indicators (ILI). The Index includes 10 gauges that are supposed to indicate in what direction the economy is moving. What's appealing about the ILI is the plausible connection between its components and future spending. Equipment orders, for example, is one of the leading indicators (number 5 in Table 9.2). This seems eminently reasonable, since businesses don't order equipment unless they later plan to buy it. The same is true of building permits (indicator 6); people obtain permits only if they plan to build something. Hence, both indicators appear to be dependable signs of future investment.

Unfortunately, the Leading Indicators aren't a perfect crystal ball. Equipment orders are often canceled. Building plans get delayed or abandoned. Hence, shifts of aggregate demand still occur without warning. No crystal ball could predict a terrorist strike or the timing and magnitude of a natural disaster. Compared to other crystal balls, however, the ILI has a pretty good track record—and a very big audience. It helps investors and policymakers foresee what aggregate demand in the economy tomorrow might look like.

if these items change in the desired direction, then the economy is likely to warm up & grow.

Indicator	Expected Impact
1. Average workweek	Hours worked per week typically increase when greater output and sales are expected.
2. Unemployment claims	Initial claims for unemployment benefits reflect changes in industry layoffs.
3. New orders	New orders for consumer goods trigger increases in production and employment.
4. Delivery times	The longer it takes to deliver ordered goods, the greater the ratio of demand to supply.
5. Equipment orders	Orders for new equipment imply increased production capacity and higher anticipated sales.
6. Building permits	A permit represents the first step in housing construction.
7. Stock prices	Higher stock prices reflect expectations of greater sales and profits.
8. Money supply *Controlled by Fed.*	Faster growth of the money supply implies a pickup in aggregate demand.
9. Interest rates	Larger differences between long- and short-term rates indicate faster growth.
10. Consumer confidence	Optimism spurs more consumer spending.

TABLE 9.2
The Leading Economic Indicators

Everyone wants a crystal ball to foresee economic events. In reality, forecasters must reckon with very crude predictors of the future. One of the most widely used predictors is the Index of Leading Economic Indicators, which includes 10 factors believed to predict economic activity 3 to 6 months in advance. Changes in the leading indicators are used to forecast changes in GDP.

The leading indicators rarely move in the same direction at the same time. They're weighted together to create the index. Up-and-down movements of the index are reported each month by the nonprofit Conference Board.

SUMMARY

- Macro failure occurs when the economy fails to achieve full employment and price stability.   LO3
- Too much or too little aggregate demand, relative to full employment, can cause macro failure. Too little aggregate demand causes cyclical unemployment; too much aggregate demand causes demand-pull inflation.   LO3
- Aggregate demand reflects the spending plans of consumers (C), investors (I), government (G), and foreign buyers (net exports = $X - M$).   LO1
- Consumer spending is affected by nonincome (autonomous) factors and current income, as summarized in the consumption function: $C = a + bY_D$.   LO1
- Autonomous consumption (a) depends on wealth, expectations, taxes, credit, and price levels. Income-dependent consumption depends on the marginal propensity to consume (MPC), the b in the consumption function.   LO1

- Consumer saving is the difference between disposable income and consumption (that is, $S = Y_D - C$). All disposable income is either spent (C) or saved (S).   LO1
- The consumption function shifts up or down when autonomous influences such as wealth and expectations change.   LO1
- The AD curve shifts left or right whenever the consumption function shifts up or down.   LO2
- Investment spending depends on interest rates, expectations for future sales, and innovation. *Changes* in investment spending will also shift the AD curve.   LO2
- Government spending and net exports are influenced by a variety of cyclical and noncyclical factors and may also change abruptly.   LO1
- Even a "perfect" macro equilibrium may be upset by abrupt shifts of spending behavior. Recurrent shifts of the AD curve may cause a business cycle.   LO1

Key Terms

aggregate demand	marginal propensity to consume (MPC)	equilibrium GDP
aggregate supply	marginal propensity to save (MPS)	recessionary GDP gap
equilibrium (macro)	wealth effect	cyclical unemployment
consumption	consumption function	inflationary GDP gap
disposable income	dissaving	demand-pull inflation
saving	investment	business cycle
average propensity to consume (APC)	full-employment GDP	

Questions for Discussion

1. What percentage of last month's income did you spend? How much more would you spend if you won a $1,000 lottery prize? Why might your average and marginal propensities to consume differ? LO1

2. Why do rich people have a higher marginal propensity to save than poor people? LO1

3. How do households dissave? Where do they get the money to finance their extra consumption? Can everyone dissave at the same time? LO1

4. Why would an *employed* consumer cut spending when other workers were being laid off (see News, p. 185)? LO2

5. According to the World View on page 188, why did Panasonic cut investment spending in 2009? Was this a rational response? LO2

6. How should home builders respond when they see home prices falling? LO2

7. What factors influence the level of (a) U.S. exports to Mexico and (b) U.S. imports from Mexico? LO2

8. Why wouldn't market participants always want to buy all the output produced? LO3

9. If an inflationary GDP gap exists, what will happen to business inventories. How will producers respond? LO3

10. How might a "perfect" macro equilibrium (Figure 9.10a) be affected by (a) a stock market crash, (b) the death of a president, (c) a recession in Canada, and (d) a spike in oil prices? LO3

---

 web activities to accompany this chapter can be found on the Online Learning Center: http://www.mhhe.com/schiller12e

---

APPENDIX

THE KEYNESIAN CROSS

The Keynesian view of the macro economy emphasizes the potential instability of the private sector and the undependability of a market-driven self-adjustment. We have illustrated this theory with shifts of the AD curve and resulting real GDP gaps. The advantage of the AS/AD model is that it illustrates how both real output and the price level are simultaneously affected by AD shifts. At the time Keynes developed his theory of instability, however, inflation was not a threat. In the Great Depression prices were *falling*. With unemployment rates reaching as high as 25 percent, no one worried that increased aggregate demand would push price levels up. The only concern was to get back to full employment.

Because inflation was not seen as an immediate threat, early depictions of Keynesian theory didn't use the AS/AD model. Instead, they used a different graph, called the "Keynesian cross." *The Keynesian cross focuses on the relationship of total spending to the value of total output, without an explicit distinction between price levels and real output.* As we'll see, the Keynesian cross doesn't change any conclusions we've come to about macro instability. It simply offers an alternative, and historically important, framework for explaining macro outcomes.

aggregate expenditure: The rate of total expenditure desired at alternative levels of income, *ceteris paribus*.

Focus on Aggregate Expenditure

Keynes said that in a really depressed economy we could focus exclusively on the rate of *spending* in the economy, without distinguishing between real output and price levels. All he worried about was whether **aggregate expenditure**—the sum of consumer, investor, government, and net export buyers' spending plans—would be compatible with the dollar value of full-employment output.

Keynes: Market is unstable

Classical view: market can self-adjustment

Say's Law - Supply creates its own demand

acts of production will create a reward
   for the acts of production

* If you produce, you create by your production
   the ability to buy other goods.

Same chapter
as buy: Unemployment Rate = $\frac{\# \text{ of Unemployed people}}{\text{total labor force}}$

McArdle
law of
markets

Q_E on the left of Q_F : Recessionary Gap
Q_F on the left of Q_E : Inflationary Gap

Determinants of the macro economy
    Internal Market Forces
    External Shock
    Policy Levers

* Consumption Function *
    Bonus of 10 pts!

$$C = a + bY_D$$
Consumption = Autonomous Consumption + (MPC · Disposable Income)

zero savings
all of the disposable income is } spent
(45° line) $C = Y_D$ MPC = 100

Real GDP
Nominal GDP- calculated without inflation

$$\text{Nominal GDP} = \frac{\text{Real GDP}}{\text{GDP Deflator}}$$ why is the conversion important?

Reasons for Unemployment:

Takes out the inflation factor
so that it is comparable
between nations

Seasonal change in season
Frictional entering WF for 1st time
Structural ppl don't have necessary requirements for jobs available
Cyclical not enough jobs available

AS

P

e₁

e

AD

Output   Q_F

to move from equilibrium to
equilibrium at e₁ (full
employment) you must
increase aggregate demand
(gov't injection)

P

A

B

Real Output

As the price drops the
real out increases

Natural Rate of unemployment 4-6%
As an unemployment rate reaches 0, then
the rate of inflation will increase

unemployment

inflation

unemployment

Phillips' Curve

Lower unemployment rate
can cause a
higher inflation
rate

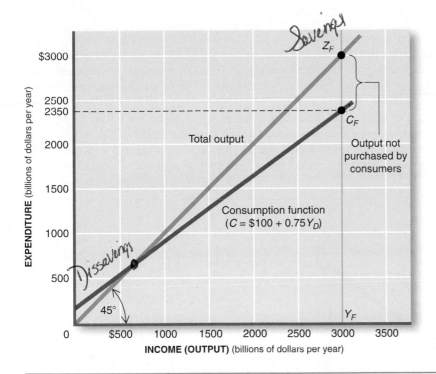

FIGURE 9A.1
The Consumption Shortfall

To determine how much output consumers will demand at full-employment output (Y_F), we refer to the consumption function. First locate full-employment output on the horizontal axis (at Y_F). Then move up until you reach the consumption function. In this case, the amount C_F (equal to $2,350 billion per year) will be demanded at full-employment output ($3,000 billion per year). This leaves $650 billion of output not purchased by consumers.

For Keynes, the critical question was how much each group of market participants would spend at different levels of nominal *income*. As we saw earlier, Keynes showed that consumer spending directly varies with the level of income. That's why the consumption function in Figure 9.4 had *spending* on the vertical axis and nominal *income* on the horizontal axis.

Figure 9A.1 puts the consumption function into the larger context of the macro economy. In this figure, the focus is exclusively on *nominal* incomes and spending. Y_F indicates the dollar value of full-employment output at current prices. In this figure, $3,000 billion is assumed to be the value of Y_F. The 45-degree line shows all points where total spending equals total income.

The consumption function in Figure 9A.1 is the same one we used before, namely

$$C = \$100 + 0.75(Y_D)$$

Notice again that consumers *dissave* at lower income levels but *save* at higher income levels.

What particularly worried Keynes was the level of intended consumption at full employment. At full employment, $3 trillion of income (output) is generated. But consumers plan to spend only

$$C = \$100 + 0.75(\$3,000 \text{ billion}) = \$2,350 \text{ billion}$$

and save the rest ($650 billion).[1] Were product-market sales totally dependent on consumers, this economy would be in trouble: Consumer spending falls short of full-employment output. In Figure 9A.1, this consumption shortfall is the vertical difference between points Z_F and C_F.

The Consumption Shortfall

---

[1]In principle, we first have to determine how much *disposable* income is generated by any given level of *total* income, then use the consumption function to determine how much consumption occurs. If Y_D is a constant percentage of Y, this two-step computation boils down to

$$Y_D = dY$$

where d = the share of total income received as disposable income, and

$$C = a + b(dY)$$
$$= a + (b \times d)Y$$

The term $(b \times d)$ is the marginal propensity to consume out of *total* income.

Nonconsumer Spending

The evident shortfall in consumer spending need not doom the economy to macro failure. There are other market participants, and their spending will add to aggregate expenditure. Keynes, however, emphasized that the spending decisions of investors, governments, and net export buyers are made independently. They *might* add up to just the right amount—or they might *not*.

To determine how much other market participants might spend, we'd have to examine their behavior. Suppose we did so and ended up with the information in Figure 9A.2. The data in that figure reveal how many dollars will be spent at various income levels. By vertically stacking these expenditure components, we can draw an *aggregate* (total) expenditure

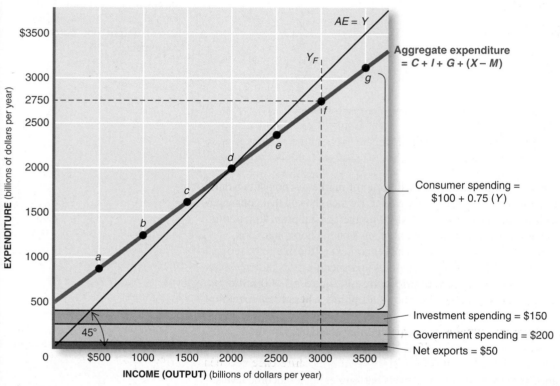

FIGURE 9A.2
Aggregate Expenditure

The aggregate expenditure curve depicts the desired spending of market participants at various income (output) levels. In this case, I, G, and $(X - M)$ don't vary with income, but C does. Adding these four components gives us total desired spending. If total income were $1,000 billion, desired spending would total $1,250 billion, as shown in row *b* in the table and by point *b* in the graph.

	At Income (output) of	Consumers Desire to Spend	+	Investors Desire to Spend	+	Governments Desire to Spend	+	Net Export Spending	=	Aggregate Expenditure
a	$ 500	$ 475		$150		$200		$50		$ 875
b	1,000	850		150		200		50		1,250
c	1,500	1,225		150		200		50		1,625
d	2,000	1,600		150		200		50		2,000
e	2,500	1,975		150		200		50		2,375
f	3,000	2,350		150		200		50		2,750
g	3,500	2,725		150		200		50		3,125

curve as in Figure 9A.2. The aggregate expenditure curve shows how *total* spending varies with income.

Keynes used the aggregate expenditure curve to assess the potential for macro failure. He was particularly interested in determining how much market participants would spend if the economy were producing at full-employment capacity.

With the information in Figure 9A.2, it is easy to answer that question. At full employment (Y_F), total income is $3,000 billion. From the table, we see that total spending at that income level is:

Consumer spending at	$Y_F = \$100 + 0.75(\$3,000)$	$= \$2,350$
Investment spending at	Y_F	$= 150$
Government spending at	Y_F	$= 200$
Net export spending at	Y_F	$= 50$
Aggregate spending at	Y_F	$= \$2,750$

In this case, we end up with less aggregate expenditure in product markets ($2,750 billion) than the value of full-employment output ($3,000 billion). This is illustrated in Figure 9A.2 by point *f* on the graph and row *f* in the table.

The economy illustrated in Figure 9A.2 is in trouble. If full employment were achieved, it wouldn't last. At full employment, $3,000 billion of output would be produced. But only $2,750 of output would be sold. There isn't enough aggregate expenditure at current price levels to sustain full employment. As a result, $250 billion of unsold output piles up in warehouses and on store shelves. That unwanted inventory pileup is a harbinger of trouble.

The difference between full-employment output and desired spending at full employment is called a **recessionary gap.** Not enough output is willingly purchased at full employment to sustain the economy. Producers may react to the spending shortfall by cutting back on production and laying off workers.

recessionary gap: The amount by which aggregate spending at full employment falls short of full-employment output.

A Single Equilibrium. You might wonder whether the planned spending of market participants would ever be exactly equal to the value of output. It will, but not necessarily at the rate of output we seek.

Figure 9A.3 illustrates where this **expenditure equilibrium** exists. Recall the significance of the 45-degree line in that figure. The 45-degree line represents all points where expenditure *equals* income. At any point on this line there would be no difference between total spending and the value of output.

expenditure equilibrium: The rate of output at which desired spending equals the value of output.

The juxtaposition of the aggregate expenditure function with the 45-degree line is called the Keynesian cross. *The Keynesian cross relates aggregate expenditure to total income (output), without explicit consideration of (changing) price levels.* As is evident in Figure 9A.3, the aggregate expenditure curve crosses the 45-degree line only once, at point *E*. At that point, therefore, desired spending is *exactly* equal to the value of output. In Figure 9A.3 this equilibrium occurs at an output rate of $2,000 billion. Notice in the accompanying table how much market participants desire to spend at that rate of output. We have

Consumer spending at	$Y_E = \$100 + 0.75(\$2,000)$	$= \$1,600$
Investment spending at	Y_E	$= 150$
Government spending at	Y_E	$= 200$
Net export spending at	Y_E	$= 50$
Aggregate spending at	Y_E	$= \$2,000$

At Y_E we have spending behavior that's completely compatible with the rate of production. At this equilibrium rate of output, no goods remain unsold. At that one rate of output where desired spending and the value of output are exactly equal, an expenditure equilibrium exists. *At macro equilibrium producers have no incentive to change the rate of output because they're selling everything they produce.*

FIGURE 9A.3
Expenditure Equilibrium

There's only one rate of output at which desired expenditure equals the value of output. This expenditure equilibrium occurs at point *E*, where the aggregate expenditure and 45-degree lines intersect. At this equilibrium, $2,000 billion of output is produced and willingly purchased.

At full-employment output ($Y_F =$ $3,000), aggregate expenditure is only $2,750 billion. This spending shortfall leaves $250 billion of output unsold. The difference between full-employment output (point *h*) and desired spending at full employment (point *f*) is called the recessionary gap.

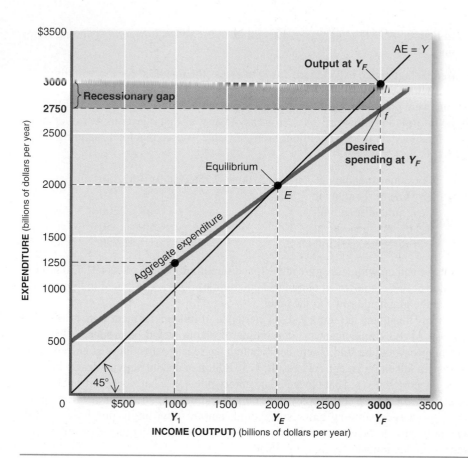

Macro Failure

Unfortunately, the equilibrium depicted in Figure 9A.3 isn't the one we hoped to achieve. At Y_E the economy is well short of its full-employment goal (Y_F).

The expenditure equilibrium won't always fall short of the economy's productive capacity. Indeed, market participants' spending desires could also *exceed* the economy's full-employment potential. This might happen if investors, the government, or foreigners wanted to buy more output or if the consumption function shifted upward. In such circumstances an **inflationary gap** would exist. An inflationary gap arises when market participants want to *spend more* income than can be produced at full employment. The resulting scramble for goods may start a bidding war that pushes price levels even higher. This would be another symptom of macro failure.

inflationary gap: The amount by which aggregate spending at full employment exceeds full-employment output.

Two Paths to the Same Conclusion

The Keynesian analysis of aggregate *expenditure* looks remarkably similar to the Keynesian analysis of aggregate *demand*. In fact, it is: Both approaches lead to the same conclusions about macro instability. The key difference between the "old" (expenditure) analysis and the "new" (AD) analysis is the level of detail about macro outcomes. In the old aggregate-expenditure analysis, the focus was simply on total spending, the product of output and prices. ***In the newer AD analysis, the separate effects of macro instability on prices and real output are distinguished.***[2] In a world where changes in both real output and price levels are important, the AD/AS framework is more useful.

---

[2]This distinction is reflected in the differing definitions for the traditional *recessionary gap* (the *spending* shortfall at full-employment income) and the newer *recessionary real GDP gap* (real output gap between full-employment GDP and equilibrium GDP).

LO1   1. From the information on pages 179–181 in 2007 what was
     (*a*) The APC?   _____
     (*b*) The APS?   _____
     (*c*) The MPC?   _____
     (*d*) The MPS?   _____

LO1   2. (*a*) What is the implied MPC in the News on page 184?   _____
     (*b*) What is the implied APC?   _____

LO1   3. On the accompanying graph, draw the consumption function $C = \$100 + 0.8Y_D$.
     (*a*) At what level of income do households begin to save?   _____
        Designate that point on the graph with the letter *A*.
     (*b*) By how much does consumption increase when income rises $200 beyond point *A*?
        Designate this new level of consumption with point *B*.   _____
     (*c*) Illustrate the impact on consumption of the change in consumer confidence described in the
        News on page 185.

LO2   4. Illustrate on the following two graphs the wealth effect from declining home prices (discussed on p. 186).

LO2   5. If every $1,000 increase in the real price of homes adds 5 cents to annual consumer spending (the "wealth effect"), by how much did consumption *decline* when home prices fell by $2 trillion in 2006–8?   _____

LO2   6. Illustrate on the following graphs the impact of Panasonic's changed investment plans (World View, p. 188).

LO2 7. What was the range, in absolute percentage points, of the variation in quarterly growth rates between 2000 and 2008 of
   (a) Consumer spending?
   (b) Investment spending?
   (*Note:* See Figure 9.8 for data.)

LO3 8. Complete the following table:

	Real Output Demanded (in $ billions) by:						
Price Level	Consumers	+ Investors	+ Government	+ Net Exports	=	Aggregate Demand	Aggregate Supply
120	80	15	20	10		—	320
110	92	16	20	12		—	260
100	104	17	20	14		—	210
90	116	18	20	16		—	170
80	128	19	20	18		—	135
70	140	20	20	20		—	100
60	154	21	20	22		—	80

   (a) What is the level of equilibrium GDP?
   (b) What is the equilibrium price level?
   (c) If full employment occurs at real GDP = $200 billion, what kind of GDP gap exists? _____
   (d) How large is that gap?
   (e) Which macro problem exists here (unemployment or inflation)? _____

LO3 9. On the graph below, draw the AD and AS curves with these data:

Price level	140	130	120	110	100	90	80	70	60	50
Real output										
Demanded	600	700	800	900	1,000	1,100	1,200	1,300	1,400	1,500
Supplied	1,200	1,150	1,100	1,050	1,000	950	900	800	600	400

   (a) What is the equilibrium
       (i) Real output level?
       (ii) Price level?

Suppose net exports decline by $150 at all price levels, but all other components of aggregate demand remain constant.
   (b) Draw the new AD curve.
   (c) What is the new equilibrium
       (i) Output level?
       (ii) Price level?
   (d) What macro problem has arisen in this economy? _____

10

Self-Adjustment or Instability?

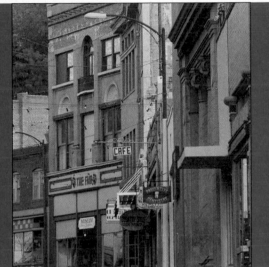

After reading this chapter, you should be able to:

LO1. Identify the sources of circular flow leakages and injections.

LO2. Describe what the multiplier is and how it works.

LO3. Explain how recessionary and inflationary GDP gaps arise.

John Maynard Keynes took a dim view of a market-driven macro economy. He emphasized that (1) macro failure is likely to occur in such an economy, and, worse yet, (2) macro failure isn't likely to go away. As noted earlier, the first prediction wasn't all that controversial. The classical economists had conceded the possibility of occasional recession or inflation. In their view, however, the economy would quickly self-adjust, restoring full employment and price stability. Keynes's second proposition challenged this view. The most distinctive, and frightening, proposition of Keynes's theory was that there'd be no automatic self-adjustment; the economy could stagnate in *persistent* unemployment or be subjected to *continuing* inflation.

President Herbert Hoover was a believer in the market's ability to self-adjust. So was President George H. Bush. As Hoover and Bush Sr. waited for the economy to self-adjust, however, they both lost their reelection bids. President George W. Bush wasn't willing to take that chance. As soon as he was elected, he pushed tax cuts through Congress that boosted consumer disposable incomes and helped bolster a sagging economy. After the terrorist attacks of September 11, 2001, he

called for even greater government intervention. Yet when the economy slowed down in his final year, he seemed willing to await the self-correcting forces of the marketplace.

President Obama embraced the Keynesian perspective from day 1. He explicitly rejected the "worn-out dogma" of classical theory and insisted that only dramatic government intervention could keep a bad economic situation from getting worse. He advocated massive spending programs to jump-start the recession-bound economy of 2008–9.

These different presidential experiences don't resolve the self-adjustment debate; rather, they emphasize how important the debate is. In this chapter we'll focus on the *adjustment process,* that is, how markets *respond* to an undesirable equilibrium. We're especially concerned with the following questions:

- **Why does anyone think the market might self-adjust (returning to a desired equilibrium)?**
- **Why might markets *not* self-adjust?**
- **Could market responses actually *worsen* macro outcomes?**

LEAKAGES AND INJECTIONS

Chapter 9 demonstrated how the economy could end up at the wrong macro equilibrium—with too much or too little aggregate demand. Such an undesirable outcome might result from an initial imbalance between **aggregate demand** at the current price level and full-employment GDP. Or the economy could fall into trouble from a shift in aggregate demand that pushes the economy out of a desirable full-employment–price-stability equilibrium. Whatever the sequence of events might be, the bottom line is the same: Total spending doesn't match total output at the desired full-employment–price-stability level.

The Circular Flow. The circular flow of income illustrates how such an undesirable outcome comes about. Recall that all income originates in product markets, where goods and services are sold. If the economy were producing at **full-employment GDP,** then enough income would be available to buy everything a fully employed economy produces. As we've seen, however, aggregate demand isn't so certain. It could happen that market participants opt *not* to spend all their income, leaving some goods unsold. Alternatively, they might try to buy *more* than full-employment output, pushing prices up.

To see how such imbalances might arise, Keynes distinguished *leakages* from the circular flow and *injections* into that flow, as illustrated in Figure 10.1.

As we observed in Chapter 9, consumers typically don't spend *all* the income they earn in product markets; they *save* some fraction of it. This is the first leak in the circular flow. Some income earned in product markets isn't being instantly converted into spending. This circular flow **leakage** creates the potential for a spending shortfall.

Suppose the economy were producing at full employment, with $3,000 billion of output at the current price level, indexed at $P = 100$. This initial output rate is marked by point F in Figure 10.2. Suppose further that *all* of the income generated in product markets went to consumers. In that case, would consumers *spend* enough to *maintain* full employment? We already observed in Chapter 9 that such an outcome is unlikely. Typically, consumers *save* a small fraction of their incomes.

aggregate demand (AD): The total quantity of output demanded at alternative price levels in a given time period, *ceteris paribus*.

full-employment GDP: The value of total output (real GDP) produced at full employment.

Consumer Saving

leakage: Income not spent directly on domestic output but instead diverted from the circular flow, for example, saving, imports, taxes.

FIGURE 10.1
Leakages and Injections

The income generated in production doesn't return completely to product markets in the form of consumer spending. Consumer saving, imports, taxes, and business saving all leak from the circular flow, reducing aggregate demand. If this leakage isn't offset, some of the output produced will remain unsold.

Business investment, government purchases of goods and services, and exports inject spending into the circular flow, adding to aggregate demand. The focus of macro concern is whether desired injections will offset desired leakage at full employment.

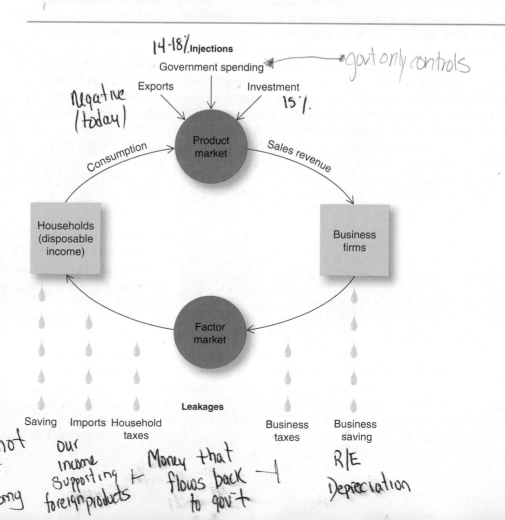

[handwritten annotations: 14-18%; govt only controls; Negative (today); 15%; Money not being put back into economy; our income supporting foreign products; Money that flows back to govt; R/E Depreciation]

Injections: Government spending, Exports, Investment → Product market → Sales revenue → Business firms

Consumption → Product market

Households (disposable income) → Factor market

Leakages

Saving Imports Household taxes   Business taxes Business saving

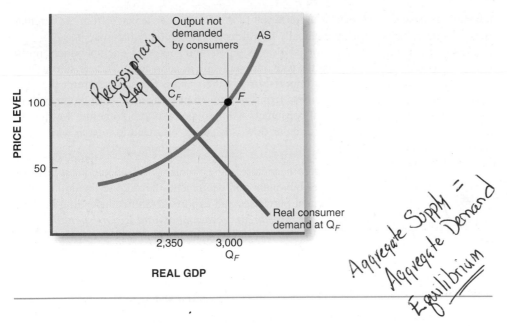

REAL GDP

Handwritten annotations on figure: Recessionary Gap; Aggregate Supply = Aggregate Demand Equilibrium; Q_F Quantity Full Employment

FIGURE 10.2
Leakage and AD

The disposable income consumers receive is only about 70 percent of total income (GDP), due to taxes and income held by businesses. Consumers also tend to save some of their disposable income and buy imported products. As a result of these leakages, consumers will demand less output at the current price level ($P = 100$) than the economy produces at full-employment GDP (Q_F). In this case, consumers demand only $2,350 billion of output at the price level $P = 100$ (point C_F) when $3,000 billion of output (income) is produced (point F).

If the consumption function were $C_F = \$100$ billion $+ 0.75Y$, consumers will spend only

$$C_F = \$100 \text{ billion} + 0.75 \,(\$3,000 \text{ billion})$$
$$= \$2,350 \text{ billion}$$

at the current price level. This consumption behavior is illustrated in Figure 10.2 by the point C_F. Consumers would demand more real output with their current income if prices were to fall. Hence, the consumption component of aggregate demand slopes downward from point C_F. Our immediate concern, however, focuses on how much (real) output consumers will purchase at the *current* price level. At the price level $P = 100$ consumers choose to save $650 billion, leaving consumption ($2,350 billion) far short of full-employment GDP ($3,000 billion).

The decision to save some fraction of household income isn't necessarily bad, but it does present a potential problem. Unless other market participants, such as business, government, and foreigners, buy this unsold output, goods will pile up on producers' shelves. As undesired inventory accumulates, producers will reduce the rate of output and unemployment will rise.

Saving isn't the only source of leakage. ***Imports also represent leakage from the circular flow.*** When consumers buy imported goods, their spending leaves (that is, leaks out of) the domestic circular flow and goes to foreign producers. As a consequence, income spent on imported goods and services is not part of the aggregate demand for domestic output.

In the real world, ***taxes are a form of leakage as well.*** A lot of revenue generated in market sales gets diverted into federal, state, and local government coffers. Sales taxes are taken out of the circular flow in product markets. Then payroll taxes and income taxes are taken out of paychecks. Households never get the chance to spend any of that income. They start with **disposable income,** which is much less than the total income generated in product markets. In 2008, disposable income was only $10.5 trillion while total income (GDP) was $14 trillion. Hence, consumers couldn't have bought everything produced that year with their current incomes even if they had saved nothing.

The business sector also keeps part of the income generated in product markets. Some revenue is set aside to cover the costs of maintaining, repairing, and replacing plant and equipment. The revenue held aside for these purposes is called a *depreciation allowance*. In addition, corporations keep some part of total profit (retained earnings) for continuing business uses rather than paying all profits out to stockholders in the form of dividends. The total value of depreciation allowances and retained earnings is called **gross business saving.** The

Imports and Taxes

Handwritten: Can either be Spent / Saved

disposable income: After-tax income of consumers; personal income less personal taxes.

Business Saving

gross business saving: Depreciation allowances and retained earnings.

income businesses hold back in these forms represents further leakage from the circular flow—income that doesn't automatically flow directly back into product markets.

Although leakage from the circular flow is a potential source of unemployment problems, we shouldn't conclude that the economy will sink as soon as consumers start saving some of their income, buy a few imports, or pay their taxes. Consumers aren't the only source of aggregate demand; business firms and government agencies also contribute to total spending. So do international consumers who buy our exports. So before we run out into the streets and scream, "The circular flow is leaking!" we need to look at what other market participants are doing.

Injections into the Circular Flow

injection: An addition of spending to the circular flow of income.

The top half of Figure 10.1 completes the picture of the circular flow by depicting **injections** of new spending. When businesses buy plant and equipment, they add to the dollar value of product market sales. Government purchases and exports also inject spending into the product market. These *injections of investment, government, and export spending help offset leakage from saving, imports, and taxes.* As a result, there may be enough aggregate demand to maintain full employment at the current price level, even if consumers aren't spending every dollar of income.

The critical issue for macro stability is whether spending injections will actually equal spending leakage at full employment. *Injections must equal leakages if all the output supplied is to equal the output demanded* (macro equilibrium). Ideally, the economy will satisfy this condition at full employment and we can stop worrying about short-run macro problems. If not, we've still got some work to do.

Self-Adjustment?

As we noted earlier, classical economists had no worries. They assumed that spending injections would always equal spending leakage. That was the foundation of their belief in the market's self-adjustment. The mechanism they counted on for equalizing leakages and injections was the interest rate.

Flexible Interest Rates. Ignore all other injections and leakages for the moment and focus on just consumer saving and business investment (Figure 10.3). If consumer saving (a leakage) exceeds business investment (an injection), unspent income must be piling up somewhere (in bank accounts, for example). These unspent funds will be a tempting lure for business investors. Businesses are always looking for funds to finance expansion or modernization. So they aren't likely to leave a pile of consumer savings sitting idle. Moreover, the banks and other institutions that are holding consumer savings will be eager to lend more funds as consumer savings pile up. To make more loans, they can lower the interest rate. As we observed in Chapter 9 (Figure 9.7), lower interest rates prompt businesses to borrow and invest more. Hence, *classical economists concluded that if interest rates fell far enough, business investment (injections) would equal consumer saving (leakage).* From this perspective, any spending shortfall would soon be closed by this self-adjustment of leakage and injection flows. Aggregate demand would be maintained at full-employment

web analysis

Check the U.S. Bureau of Economic Analysis (BEA) Web site at **www. bea.gov** to see how much investment varied in the last year. Click on "Gross Domestic Product," and then "Selected NIPA Tables."

Leakages	Injections
Consumer saving	Investment
Business saving	Government spending
Taxes	Exports
Imports	

FIGURE 10.3
Leakages and Injections

Macro equilibrium is possible only if leakages equal injections. Of these, consumer saving and business investment are the primary sources of (im)balance in a wholly private and closed economy. Hence the relationship between saving and investment reveals whether a market-driven economy will self-adjust to a full-employment equilibrium.

GDP, because investment spending would soak up all consumer saving. The *content* of AD would change (less *C*, more *I*), but the *level* would remain at full-employment GDP.

Changing Expectations. Keynes argued that classical economists ignored the role of expectations. As Figure 9.7 illustrated, the level of investment *is* sensitive to interest rates. But the whole investment function *shifts* when business expectations change. Keynes thought it preposterous that investment spending would *increase* in response to *declining* consumer sales. A decline in investment is more likely, Keynes argued.

Flexible Prices. The classical economists said self-adjustment was possible even without flexible interest rates. Flexible *prices* would do the trick. Look at Figure 10.2 again. It says consumers will demand only $2,350 billion of output *at the current price level.* But what if prices *fell*? Then consumers would buy more output. In fact, if prices fell far enough, consumers might buy *all* the output produced at full employment. In Figure 10.2, the price level *P* = 50 elicits such a response.

Expectations (again). Keynes again chided the classical economists for their naïveté. Sure, a nationwide sale might prompt consumers to buy more goods and services. But how would businesses react? They had planned on selling Q_F amount of output at the price level *P* = 100. If prices must be cut in half to move their merchandise, businesses are likely to rethink their production and investment plans. Keynes argued that declining (retail) prices were likely to prompt investment cutbacks. This was a real fear in 2008–9, as the accompanying News suggests.

IN THE NEWS

Deflation

There Are Bargains Everywhere. Here's Why That Could Be a Problem.

WASHINGTON—Everything is on sale. And that's not a good thing.

Consumer prices in October fell at the fastest pace in more than 60 years, sucked down by the rapidly deteriorating economy. The prices of oil, food, cars, clothing and electronics have all plunged. Home prices continue to swoon and so do stock prices.

As the early reports from the holiday shopping season suggest, the nationwide fire sale might seem like a boon for consumers. But it's increasing the risk that the economy could become mired in a dangerous deflationary spiral—a widespread, sustained reduction in prices. That's something that hasn't happened here since the Great Depression.

As prices fall, consumers eventually stop spending, either because they are worried about their jobs, or because they figure they can get lower prices later. Companies start laying off workers because lower prices have pushed down—or eliminated—their profits. That, in turn, means even less demand.

Ultimately, higher unemployment and lower demand create a self-reinforcing cycle that further depresses profits, growth, wages and prices.

President-elect Barack Obama cited the danger of deflation last month in calling for a massive stimulus bill to put millions to work in the next two years and boost economic activity. . . .

—John Waggoner, Sue Kirchhoff, and Barbara Hagenbaugh

Source: USA TODAY, December 3, 2008, IA. Reprinted with Permission.

Analysis: Deflation does make products cheaper for consumers. But declining prices also reduce business revenues, profits, and sales expectations.

THE MULTIPLIER PROCESS

Keynes not only rejected the classical notion of self-adjustment, he also argued that things were likely to get *worse,* not better, once a spending shortfall emerged. This was the scariest part of Keynes's theory.

FIGURE 10.4
AD Shift

When investment spending drops, aggregate demand shifts to the left. In the short run, this causes output and the price level to fall. The initial equilibrium at *F* is pushed to a new equilibrium at point *b*.

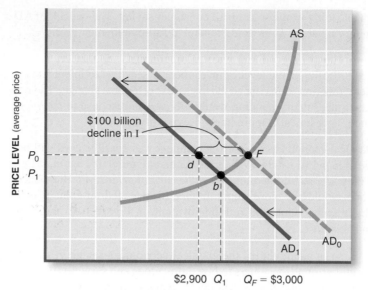

To understand Keynes's fears, imagine that the economy is initially at the desired full-employment GDP equilibrium, as represented again by point *F* in Figure 10.4. Included in that full-employment equilibrium GDP is

Consumption	=	$2,350 billion
Investment	=	400 billion
Government	=	150 billion
Net exports	=	100 billion
Aggregate demand at current price level	=	$3,000 billion

Everything looks good in this macro economy. This is pretty much how the U.S. economy looked in 2006–7.

The 2007:4 Spending Slowdown

In the fourth quarter of 2007, the U.S. economy took a turn for the worse. Housing prices began falling in 2006, eroding consumer wealth. By the end of 2007, the wealth effect caused consumers to start tightening their belts. As consumer spending slowed (see accompanying News),

IN THE NEWS

Consumer Spending Drops 1%

NEW YORK (CNNMoney.com)—Consumer spending fell dramatically in October, according to a government report released Wednesday, in another woeful sign that the economy will continue to contract.

The Commerce Department said spending by individuals fell by 1% last month, after declining 0.3% in September. It was the biggest decline since September 2001 and worse than the 0.7% drop economists surveyed by Briefing.com had forecast. . . .

That's an ominous sign ahead of the holiday shopping season. It's particularly worrisome for the economy since consumer spending accounts for about two-thirds of the nation's gross domestic product.

Source: CNNMoney.com, November 26, 2008.

Analysis: Declining wealth and confidence depress consumer spending. The decline in sales that results prompts businesses to cut back investment plans.

inventories of unsold goods started piling up. This worried investors so much that they actually *reduced* total investment. (Recall Panasonics' investment cutbacks from the News on p. 188).

Undesired Inventory. When business investment was cut back, unsold capital goods started piling up. Unsold houses, trucks, office equipment, machinery, and airplanes quickly reached worrisome levels.

Ironically, this additional inventory is counted as part of investment spending. (Recall that our definition of investment spending includes changes in business inventories.) This additional inventory is clearly undesired, however, as producers had planned on selling these goods.

To keep track of these unwanted changes in investment, we **distinguish** desired *(or planned) investment from* **actual** *investment. Desired* investment represents purchases of new plant and equipment plus any *desired* changes in business inventories. By contrast, *actual* investment represents purchases of new plant and equipment plus *actual* changes in business inventories, desired or otherwise. In other words,

$$\text{Actual investment} = \text{desired investment} + \text{undesired investment}$$

Falling Output and Prices. How are business firms likely to react when they see undesired inventory piling up on car lots and store shelves? They could regard the inventory pileup as a brief aberration and continue producing at full-employment levels. But the inventory pileup might also set off sales alarms, causing businesses to alter their pricing, production, and investment plans. If that happens, they're likely to start cutting prices in an attempt to increase the rate of sales. Producers are also likely to reduce the rate of new output.

Figure 10.4 illustrates these two responses. Assume that investment spending declines by $100 billion at the existing price level P_0. This shifts the aggregate demand curve leftward from AD_0 to AD_1 and immediately moves the economy from point F to point d. At d, however, excess inventories prompt firms to reduce prices. As prices fall, the economy gravitates toward a new **equilibrium GDP** at point b. At point b, the rate of output (Q_1) is less than the full-employment level (Q_F) and the price level has fallen from P_0 to P_1.

The decline in GDP depicted in Figure 10.4 isn't pretty. But Keynes warned that the picture would get uglier when *consumers* start feeling the impact of the production cutbacks.

So far we've treated the production cutbacks that accompany a GDP gap as a rather abstract problem. But the reality is that when production is cut back, people suffer. When producers decrease the rate of output, workers lose their jobs or face pay cuts, or both. Cutbacks in investment spending in 2007–8 led to layoffs among homebuilders, mortgage companies, banks, equipment manufacturers, auto companies, and even hi-tech companies like Hewlett-Packard, IBM, Yahoo!, and Google. A decline in travel caused layoffs at airlines and aircraft manufacturers. As workers get laid off or have their wages cut, household incomes decline. Thus, *a reduction in investment spending implies a reduction in household incomes.*

We saw in Chapter 9 the kind of threat a reduction in household income poses. Those consumers who end up with less income won't be able to purchase as many goods and services as they did before. As a consequence, aggregate demand will fall further, leading to still larger stocks of unsold goods, more job layoffs, and further reductions in income. It's this sequence of events—called the *multiplier process*—that makes a sudden decline in aggregate demand so frightening. **What starts off as a relatively small spending shortfall quickly snowballs into a much larger problem.**

We can see the multiplier process at work by watching what happens to a $100 billion decline in investment spending as it makes its way around the circular flow. The process starts at step 1 in Figure 10.5, when investment is cut back by $100 billion. At first (step 2), the only thing that happens is that unsold goods appear (in the form of undesired inventories). Producers adjust to this problem by cutting back on production and laying off workers or reducing wages and prices (step 3). In either case, consumer income falls $100 billion per year shortly after the investment cutbacks occur (step 4).

equilibrium GDP: The value of total output (real GDP) produced at macro equilibrium (AS = AD).

Household Incomes

Income-Dependent Consumption

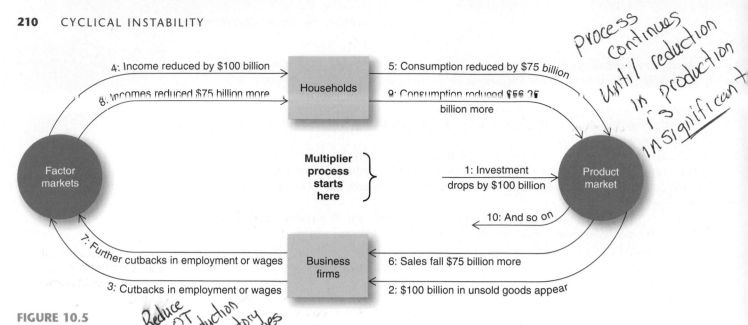

Process continues until reduction in production is insignificant

FIGURE 10.5
The Multiplier Process *Reduce OT production Inventory wages*

A decline in investment (step 1) will leave output unsold (step 2) and may lead to a cutback in production and income (step 3). A reduction in total income (step 4) will in turn lead to a reduction in consumer spending (step 5). These additional cuts in spending cause a further decrease in income, leading to additional spending reductions, and so on. This sequence of adjustments is referred to as the *multiplier process.*

---

marginal propensity to consume (MPC): The fraction of each additional (marginal) dollar of disposable income spent on consumption; the change in consumption divided by the change in disposable income.

How will consumers respond to this drop in disposable income? *If disposable income falls, we expect consumer spending to drop as well.* In fact, the consumption function tells us just how much spending will drop. The **marginal propensity to consume (MPC)** is the critical variable in this process. Since we've specified that $C = \$100$ billion $+ 0.75Y$, we expect consumers to reduce their spending by $0.75 for every $1.00 of lost income. In the present example, the loss of $100 billion of annual income will induce consumers to reduce their rate of spending by $75 billion per year ($0.75 \times \$100$ billion). This drop in spending is illustrated by step 5 in Figure 10.5.

The multiplier process doesn't stop here. A reduction in consumer spending quickly translates into more unsold output (step 6). As additional goods pile up on producers' shelves, we anticipate further cutbacks in production, employment, and disposable income (step 7).

As disposable incomes are further reduced by job layoffs and wage cuts (step 8), more reductions in consumer spending are sure to follow (step 9). Again the marginal propensity to consume (MPC) tells us how large such reductions will be. With an MPC of 0.75, we may expect spending to fall by another $56.25 billion per year ($0.75 \times \$75$ billion) in step 9.

The Multiplier

The multiplier process continues to work until the reductions in income and sales become so small that no one's market behavior is significantly affected. We don't have to examine each step along the way. As you may have noticed, all the steps begin to look alike once we've gone around the circular flow a few times. Instead of examining each step, we can look ahead to see where they are taking us. Each time the multiplier process works its way around the circular flow, the reduction in spending equals the previous drop in income multiplied by the MPC. Accordingly, by pressing a few keys on a calculator, we can produce a sequence of events like that depicted in Table 10.1 on page 212.

The impact of the multiplier is devastating. The ultimate reduction in real spending resulting from the initial drop in investment isn't $100 billion per year but $400 billion! Even if one is accustomed to thinking in terms of billions and trillions, this is a huge drop in demand. What the multiplier process demonstrates is that the dimensions of an initial spending gap greatly understate the severity of the economic dislocations that will follow in its wake. *The eventual decline in spending will be much larger than the initial (autonomous) decrease in aggregate demand.* This was evident in the recession of 2008–9, when layoffs snowballed from industry to industry (see following News), ultimately leaving millions of people unemployed.

IN THE NEWS

Job Losses Surge As U.S. Downturn Accelerates

Declines Extend beyond Construction and Manufacturing to Service Sectors

Rising unemployment across the nation reveals a pervasive downturn that is spreading at an accelerating pace.

In data released Friday by the Bureau of Labor Statistics, 12 states, including Florida, Idaho, North Carolina and Illinois, reported a rise of at least two percentage points in unemployment rates over the past year.

For many states, the pace of decline is more severe than during the 2001 recession. Job losses have spread beyond construction and manufacturing to service sectors such as tourism, hospitality and professional and business services.

"It's remarkable how fast the unemployment rate is increasing" in several states, said Luke Tilley, a senior economist at IHS Global Insight. "We are now seeing the full ripple effects."

In October, month-over-month unemployment rates increased in 38 states and the District of Columbia. Unemployment rates held steady in seven states and fell in five. Many economists forecast the national unemployment rate, currently at 6.5%, will top 8% in the next few months.

—Conor Dougherty

Source: *The Wall Street Journal*, November 22, 2008, p. A3. Copyright 2008 by Dow Jones & Company, Inc. Reproduced with permission of Dow Jones & Company, Inc. in the format Textbook via Copyright Clearance Center.

Analysis: Cutbacks in production cause employee layoffs. The newly unemployed workers curtail *their* spending, causing sequential layoffs in other industries. These ripple effects give rise to the multiplier.

web analysis

For the latest information on job loss in the United States, visit the Bureau of Labor Statistics mass layoff statistics page at **www. bls.gov/mls.**

The ultimate impact of an AD shift on total spending can be determined by computing the change in income and consumption at each cycle of the circular flow. This is the approach summarized in Table 10.1, with each row representing a spending cycle. The entire computation can be simplified considerably by using a single figure, the multiplier. The **multiplier** tells us the extent to which the rate of total spending will change in response to an initial change in the flow of expenditure. The multiplier summarizes the sequence of steps described in Table 10.1.[1] In its simplest form, the multiplier can be computed as:

$$\text{Multiplier} = \frac{1}{1 - \text{MPC}}$$

multiplier: The multiple by which an initial change in spending will alter total expenditure after an infinite number of spending cycles; $1/(1 - \text{MPC})$.

In our example, the initial change in aggregate demand occurs when investment drops by $100 billion per year at full-employment output ($3,000 billion per year). Table 10.1 indicates that this investment drop-off will lead to a $400 billion reduction in the rate of total spending at the current price level. Using the multiplier, we arrive at the same conclusion by observing that

$$\begin{aligned}
\frac{\text{Total change}}{\text{in spending}} &= \text{multiplier} \times \frac{\text{initial change}}{\text{in aggregate spending}} \\
&= \frac{1}{1 - \text{MPC}} \times \$100 \text{ billion per year} \\
&= \frac{1}{1 - 0.75} \times \$100 \text{ billion per year} \\
&= 4 \times \$100 \text{ billion per year} \\
&= \$400 \text{ billion per year}
\end{aligned}$$

In other words, *the cumulative decrease in total spending ($400 billion per year) resulting from a shortfall in aggregate demand at full employment is equal to the initial*

[1]The multiplier summarizes the geometric progression $1 + \text{MPC} + \text{MPC}^2 + \text{MPC}^3 + \cdots + \text{MPC}^n$, which equals $1/(1 - \text{MPC})$ when n becomes infinite.

TABLE 10.1
The Multiplier Cycles

The circular flow of income implies that an initial change in income will lead to cumulative changes in consumer spending and income. Here, an initial income loss of $100 billion (first cycle) causes a cutback in consumer spending in the amount of $75 billion (second cycle). At each subsequent cycle, consumer spending drops by the amount MPC × prior change in income. Ultimately, total spending (and income) falls by $400 billion, or $1/(1 - MPC) \times$ initial change in spending.

Spending Cycles	Change in This Cycle's Spending and Income (billions per year)	Cumulative Decrease in Spending and Income (billions per year)
First cycle: recessionary gap emerges	$100.00	$100.00 } Δ*I*
Second cycle: consumption drops by MPC × $100	75.00	175.00
Third cycle: consumption drops by MPC × $75	56.25	231.25
Fourth cycle: consumption drops by MPC × $56.25	42.19	273.44
Fifth cycle: consumption drops by MPC × $42.19	31.64	305.08 } Δ**C**
Sixth cycle: consumption drops by MPC × $31.64	23.73	328.81
Seventh cycle: consumption drops by MPC × $23.73	17.80	346.61
Eighth cycle: consumption drops by MPC × $17.80	13.35	359.95
⋮	⋮	⋮
*n*th cycle and beyond		400.00

shortfall ($100 billion per year) multiplied by the multiplier (4). More generally, we may observe that the larger the fraction (MPC) of income respent in each round of the circular flow, the greater the impact of any autonomous change in spending on cumulative aggregate demand. The cumulative process of spending adjustments can also have worldwide effects. As the accompanying World View illustrates, Asia's economic growth slowed when the U.S. economy slumped in 2008–9.

WORLD VIEW

Crisis in Europe and U.S. Hurts Asian Economies

HONG KONG—Sagging demand from recession-struck Europe and the United States is helping to brake Asian economic growth to a halt with extraordinary abruptness, according to fresh data from several of Asia's leading economies.

Japanese exports, which are crucial to corporate giants like Sony and Toyota, plummeted in December to a level 35 percent lower than a year earlier, the Japanese finance ministry reported. Meanwhile, the South Korean economy contracted sharply in the last quarter of 2008, with output down by 3–4 percent from a year earlier.

China's once-roaring economy slowed markedly in the last quarter as well, the government statistical office reported on Thursday. The annual growth rate, which hit 13 percent in 2007, fell to 6.8 percent in the fourth quarter and 9 percent for all of 2008.

The figures from Japan and South Korea, especially, were much worse than economists were expecting, and illustrated how difficult it has become to accurately forecast the effects of the global economic slowdown, which was brought on by the financial crisis stemming from trouble in American mortgage finance.

—Bettina Wassener

Source: *The New York Times*, January 22, 2009.

Analysis: Multiplier effects can spill over national borders. The 2008–9 recession in the United States reduced U.S. demand for Asian exports, setting off a sequence of spending cuts in Japan, Korea, China, and other Asian nations.

MACRO EQUILIBRIUM REVISITED

The key features of the Keynesian adjustment process are

* *Producers cut output and employment when output exceeds aggregate demand at the current price level (leakage exceeds injections).*
* *The resulting loss of income causes a decline in consumer spending.*
* *Declines in consumer spending lead to further production cutbacks, more lost income, and still less consumption.*

Figure 10.6 illustrates the ultimate impact of the multiplier process. Notice that the AD curve shifts *twice.* The first shift—from AD_0 to AD_1—represents the $100 billion drop in investment spending. As we saw earlier in Figure 10.4, this initial shift of aggregate demand will start the economy moving toward a new equilibrium at point *b.*

Along the way, however, the multiplier kicks in and things get worse. *The decline in household income caused by investment cutbacks sets off the multiplier process, causing a secondary shift of the AD curve.* We measure these multiplier effects at the initial price level of P_0. With a marginal propensity to consume of 0.75, we've seen that induced consumption declines by $300 billion when autonomous investment declines by $100 billion. In Figure 10.6 this is illustrated by the *second* shift of the aggregate demand curve, from AD_1 to AD_2. Notice that the horizontal distance between AD_1 and AD_2 is $300 billion.

Although aggregate demand has fallen (shifted) by $400 billion, real output doesn't necessarily drop that much. *The impact of a shift in aggregate demand is reflected in both output and price changes.* This is evident in Figure 10.7, which is a close-up view of Figure 10.6. When AD shifts from AD_0 to AD_2 the macro equilibrium moved down the sloped AS curve to point *c.* At point *c* the new equilibrium output is Q_E and the new price level is P_E.

Recessionary GDP Gap. As long as the aggregate supply curve is upward-sloping, the shock of any AD shift will be spread across output and prices. In Figure 10.7, the net effect on real output is shown as the real GDP gap. *The recessionary GDP gap equals the difference between equilibrium real GDP (Q_E) and full-employment real GDP (Q_F).* It represents the amount by which the economy is underproducing during a recession. As we noted in Chapter 9, this is a classic case of **cyclical unemployment.**

Sequential AD Shifts

Price and Output Effects

recessionary GDP gap: The amount by which equilibrium GDP falls short of full-employment GDP.

cyclical unemployment: Unemployment attributable to a lack of job vacancies, that is, to an inadequate level of aggregate demand.

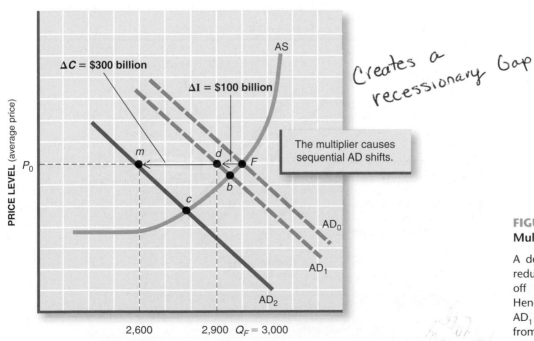

FIGURE 10.6
Multiplier Effects

A decline in investment spending reduces household income, setting off negative multiplier effects. Hence, the *initial* shift of AD_0 to AD_1 is followed by a *second* shift from AD_1 to AD_2. The second shift represents reduced consumption.

FIGURE 10.7
Recessionary GDP Gap

The real GDP gap is the difference between equilibrium GDP (Q_E) and full-employment GDP (Q_F). It represents the lost output due to a recession.

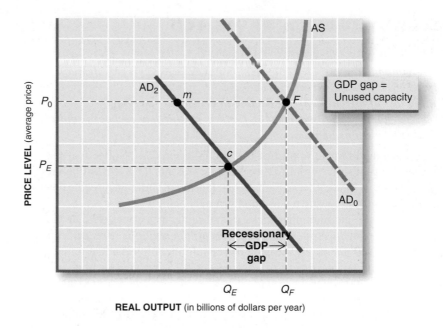

Short-Run Inflation-Unemployment Trade-Offs

Figure 10.7 not only illustrates how much output declines when AD falls but also provides an important clue about the difficulty of restoring full employment. Suppose the recessionary GDP gap were $200 billion, as illustrated in Figure 10.8. How much more AD would we need to get back to full employment?

Upward-Sloping AS. Suppose aggregate demand at the equilibrium price level (P_E) were to increase by exactly $200 billion (including multiplier effects), as illustrated by the shift to AD_3. Would that get us back to full-employment output? Not according to Figure 10.8. *When AD increases, both output and prices go up.* Because the AS curve is upward-sloping, the $200 billion shift from AD_2 to AD_3 moves the new macro equilibrium to point *g* rather than point *f*. We'd like to get to point *f* with full employment and price stability. But as demand picks up, producers are likely to raise prices. This leads us up the AS curve to point *g*. At point *g*, we're still short of full employment and have experienced a bit of

---

FIGURE 10.8
The Unemployment-Inflation Trade-Off

If the short-run AS curve is upward-sloping, an AD increase will raise output *and* prices. If AD increases by the amount of the recessionary GDP gap only (AD_2 to AD_3), full employment (Q_F) won't be reached. Macro equilibrium moves to point *g*, not point *f*.

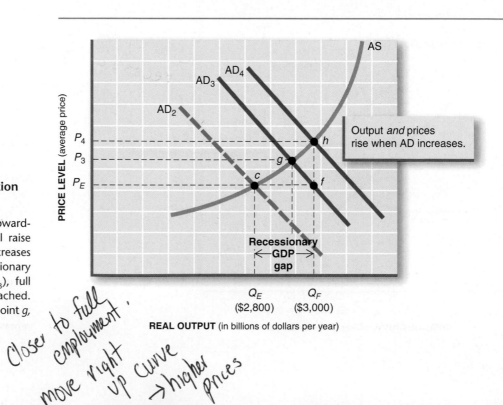

inflation (an increased price level). ***So long as the short-run AS is upward-sloping, there's a trade-off between unemployment and inflation.*** We can get lower rates of unemployment (more real output) only if we accept some inflation.

"Full" vs. "Natural" Unemployment. The short-term trade-off between unemployment and inflation is the basis for the definition of "full" employment. We don't define full employment as *zero* unemployment; we define it as the rate of unemployment *consistent with price stability.* As noted in Chapter 6, **full employment** is typically defined as a 4 to 6 percent rate of unemployment. What the upward-sloping AS curve tells us is that ***the closer the economy gets to capacity output, the greater the risk of inflation.*** To get back to full employment in Figure 10.8, aggregate demand would have to increase to AD_4, with the price level rising to P_4.

Not everyone accepts this notion of full employment. As we saw in Chapter 8, neoclassical and monetarist economists prefer to focus on *long*-run outcomes. In their view, the long-run AS curve is vertical (see Figure 8.12). In that long-run context, there's no unemployment-inflation trade-off: An AD shift doesn't change the "natural" (institutional) rate of unemployment but does alter the price level. We'll examine this argument in Chapters 16 and 17.

> **full employment:** The lowest rate of unemployment compatible with price stability; variously estimated at between 4 and 6 percent unemployment.

◦ frictional + structural
= 4 - 6% unemployment

ADJUSTMENT TO AN INFLATIONARY GDP GAP

As we've observed, ***a sudden shift in aggregate demand can have a cumulative effect on macro outcomes*** that's larger than the initial imbalance. This multiplier process works both ways: Just as a *decrease* in investment (or any other AD component) can send the economy into a recessionary tailspin, an *increase* in investment might initiate an inflationary spiral.

Figure 10.9 illustrates the consequences of a sudden jump in investment spending. We start out again in the happy equilibrium (point *F*), where full employment (Q_F) and price stability (P_0) prevail. Initial spending consists of

$$C = \$2,350 \text{ billion} \qquad G = \$150 \text{ billion}$$
$$I = \$400 \text{ billion} \qquad X - M = \$100 \text{ billion}$$

◦ nominal prices ↑

FIGURE 10.9
Demand-Pull Inflation

An increase in investment or other autonomous spending sets off multiplier effects shifting AD to the right. AD shifts to the right *twice*, first (AD_0 to AD_5) because of increased investment and then (AD_5 to AD_6) because of increased consumption. The increased AD moves the economy up the short-run AS curve, causing some inflation. How much inflation results depends on the slope of the AS curve.

Figure content labels:
AS
ΔC = $300 billion
ΔI = $100 billion
New spending causes sequential AD shifts and inflationary pressure.
P_6 w
P_0 r   F
AD_6
AD_5
AD_0
Inflationary ←GDP→ gap
PRICE LEVEL (average price)
Q_F Q_E
(= $3,000)
REAL OUTPUT (in billions of dollars per year)

Increased Investment

Then investors suddenly decide to step up the rate of investment. Perhaps their expectations for future sales have risen. Maybe new technology has become available that compels firms to modernize their facilities. Whatever the reason, investors decide to raise the level of investment from $400 billion to $500 billion at the current price level (P_0). This change in investment spending shifts the aggregate demand curve from AD_0 to AD_5 (a horizontal shift of $100 billion).

Inventory Depletion. One of the first things you'll notice when AD shifts like this is that available inventories shrink. Investors can step up their *spending* more quickly than firms can increase their *production*. A lot of the increased investment demand will have to be satisfied from existing inventory. The decline in inventory is a signal to producers that it might be a good time to raise prices a bit. Thus, *inventory depletion is a warning sign of impending inflation.* As the economy moves up from point F to point r in Figure 10.9, that inflation starts to become visible.

Household Incomes

Whether or not prices start rising quickly, household incomes will get a boost from the increased investment. Producers will step up the rate of output to rebuild inventories and supply more investment goods (equipment and structures). To do so, they'll hire more workers or extend working hours. The end result for workers will be fatter paychecks.

Induced Consumption

What will households do with these heftier paychecks? By now, you know what the consumer response will be. The marginal propensity to consume prompts an increase in consumer spending. Eventually, consumer spending increases by a *multiple* of the income change. In this case, the consumption increase is $300 billion (see Table 10.1).

Figure 10.9 illustrates the secondary shift of AD caused by multiplier-induced consumption. Notice how the AD curve shifts a second time, from AD_5 to AD_6.

A New Equilibrium

demand-pull inflation: An increase in the price level initiated by excessive aggregate demand.

The ultimate impact of the investment surge is reflected in the new equilibrium at point w. As before, the shift of AD has affected both real output and prices. Real output does increase beyond the full-employment level, but it does so only at the expense of accelerating inflation. This is a classic case of **demand-pull inflation.** The initial increase in investment was enough to kindle a little inflation. The multiplier effect worsened the problem by forcing the economy further along the ever-steeper AS curve. The **inflationary GDP gap** ends up as $Q_E - Q_F$.

Booms and Busts

inflationary GDP gap: The amount by which equilibrium GDP exceeds full-employment GDP.

The Keynesian analysis of leakages, injections, and the multiplier paints a fairly grim picture of the prospects for macro stability. *The basic conclusion of the Keynesian analysis is that the economy is vulnerable to abrupt changes in spending behavior and won't self-adjust to a desired macro equilibrium.* A shift in aggregate demand can come from almost anywhere. The September 2001 terrorist attack on the World Trade Center shook both consumer and investor confidence. Businesses starting cutting back production even *before* inventories started piling up. Worsened *expectations* rather than rising inventories caused investment demand to shift, setting off the multiplier process. In 2008, declining home and stock prices curtailed both confidence and spending, setting off a negative multiplier process.

When the aggregate demand curve shifts, macro equilibrium will be upset. Moreover, *the responses of market participants to an abrupt AD shift are likely to worsen rather than improve market outcomes.* As a result, the economy may gravitate toward an equilibrium of stagnant recession (point c in Figure 10.6) or persistent inflation (point w in Figure 10.9).

As Keynes saw it, the combination of alternating AD shifts and multiplier effects also causes recurring business cycles. A drop in consumer or business spending can set off a recessionary spiral of declining GDP and prices. A later increase in either consumer or business spending can set the ball rolling in the other direction. This may result in a series of economic booms and busts.

THE ECONOMY TOMORROW

MAINTAINING CONSUMER CONFIDENCE

This chapter emphasized how a sudden change in investment might set off the multiplier process. Investors aren't the only potential culprits, however. A sudden change in government spending or exports could just as easily start the multiplier ball rolling. In fact, the whole process could originate with a change in *consumer* spending.

Consumer Confidence. Recall the two components of consumption: *autonomous* consumption and *induced* consumption. These two components may be expressed as

$$C = a + bY$$

We've seen that autonomous consumption is influenced by *non*income factors, including consumer confidence. What's more, consumer confidence can change abruptly, as Figure 10.10 confirms. Notice how consumer confidence slipped at the end of 2007 and then plunged in 2008 as the economy worsened. When this happened, the values of both *a* and *b* in the consumption function declined and the consumption function shifted downward. According to a recent World Bank study, every 1 percent change in consumer confidence alters autonomous consumer spending by $1.1 billion.

The reverberation of a change in consumer confidence will cause *two* shifts of the AD curve. The first shift will be due to the effect of changed consumer confidence on *autonomous* consumption. The second shift will result from the multiplier effects on *induced* consumption. Ironically, when consumers try to cope with recession by cutting their spending

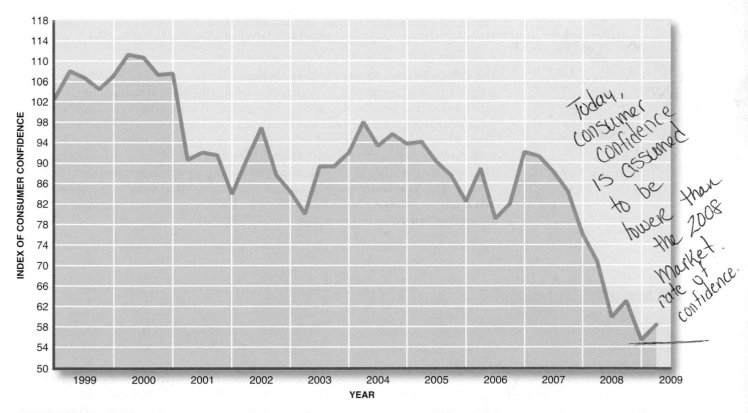

Today, consumer confidence is assumed to be lower than the 2008 market rate of confidence.

FIGURE 10.10
Consumer Confidence

Consumer confidence is affected by various financial, political, and international events. Changes in consumer confidence affect consumer behavior and thereby shift the AD curve.

Source: University of Michigan.

IN THE NEWS

Hard-Hit Families Finally Start Saving, Aggravating Nation's Economic Woes

BOISE, Idaho—Rick and Noreen Capp recently reduced their credit-card debt, opened a savings account and stopped taking their two children to restaurants. Jessica and Alan Muir have started buying children's clothes at steep markdowns, splitting bulk-food purchases with other families and gathering their firewood instead of buying it for $200 a cord.

As layoffs and store closures grip Boise, these two local families hope their newfound frugality will see them through the economic downturn. But this same thriftiness, embraced by families across the U.S., is also a major reason the downturn may not soon end. Americans, fresh off a decadeslong buying spree, are finally saving more and spending less—just as the economy needs their dollars the most.

Usually, frugality is good for individuals and for the economy. Savings serve as a reservoir of capital that can be used to finance investment, which helps raise a nation's standard of living. But in a recession, increased saving—or its flip side, decreased spending—can exacerbate the economy's woes. It's what economists call the "paradox of thrift."

—Kelly Evans

Source: *The Wall Street Journal*, January 6, 2009, p. 1. Copyright 2009 by Dow Jones & Company, Inc. Reproduced with permission of Dow Jones & Company, Inc. In the format Textbook via Copyright Clearance Center.

Analysis: When consumers become more pessimistic about their economy, they start saving more and spending less. This shifts AD leftward and deepens a recession.

[Handwritten note in margin: Today, people are still spending + still saving less, more keeping us in a recession. The large protests around the world country about the compensation of large executives; many are unemployed.]

and saving more of their incomes, they actually make matters worse (see News above). This "paradox of thrift" recognizes that what might make sense for an *individual* consumer doesn't necessarily make sense for *aggregate* demand.

The Official View: Always a Rosy Outlook. Because consumer spending vastly outweighs any other component of aggregate demand, the threat of abrupt changes in consumer behavior is serious. Recognizing this, public officials strive to maintain consumer confidence in the economy tomorrow, even when such confidence might not be warranted. That's why President Hoover, bank officials, and major brokerage houses tried to assure the public in 1929 that the outlook was still rosy. (Look back at the first few pages of Chapter 8.) The "rosy outlook" is still the official perspective on the economy tomorrow. The White House is always upbeat about prospects for the economy. If it weren't—if it were even to hint at the possibility of a recession—consumer and investor confidence might wilt. Then the economy might quickly turn ugly.

SUMMARY

- The circular flow of income has offsetting leakages (consumer saving, taxes, business saving, imports) and injections (autonomous consumption, investment, government spending, exports). LO1
- When desired injections equal leakage, the economy is in equilibrium (output demanded = output supplied at prevailing price level). LO3
- An imbalance of injections and leakages will cause the economy to expand or contract. An imbalance at full-employment GDP will cause cyclical unemployment or

demand-pull inflation. How serious these problems become depends on how the market responds to the initial imbalance. LO3
- Classical economists believed (flexible) interest rates and price levels would equalize injections and leakages (especially consumer saving and investment), restoring full-employment equilibrium. LO1, LO3
- Keynes showed that spending imbalances might actually *worsen* if consumer and investor expectations changed. LO2

- An abrupt change in autonomous spending (injections) shifts the AD curve, setting off a sequential multiplier process (further AD shifts) that magnifies changes in equilibrium GDP. LO2
- The multiplier itself is equal to 1/(1 − MPC). It indicates the cumulative change in demand that follows an initial (autonomous) disruption of spending flows. LO2
- As long as the short-run aggregate supply curve slopes upward, AD shifts will affect both real output and prices. LO2

- The recessionary GDP gap measures the amount by which equilibrium GDP falls short of full-employment GDP. LO3
- Sudden changes in consumer confidence would destabilize the economy. To avoid this, policymakers always maintain a rosy outlook. LO2, LO3

Key Terms

aggregate demand	injection	cyclical unemployment
full-employment GDP	equilibrium GDP	full employment
leakage	marginal propensity to consume (MPC)	demand-pull inflation
disposable income	multiplier	inflationary GDP gap
gross business saving	recessionary GDP gap	

Questions for Discussion

1. How might declining prices affect a firm's decision to borrow and invest? (See News, p. 207.) LO3
2. Why wouldn't investment and saving flows at full employment always be equal? LO1
3. When unwanted inventories pile up in retail stores, how is production affected? What are the steps in this process? LO3
4. How can equilibrium output exceed full-employment output (as in Figure 10.9)? LO3
5. How might construction-industry job losses affect incomes in the clothing and travel industries? LO2

6. Why was President Obama so concerned about the economy at the outset of his presidency? LO3
7. What forces might turn an economic bust into an economic boom? What forces might put an end to the boom? LO3
8. Why might "belt-tightening" by consumers in a recession be unwelcome? (See News, p. 218.) LO3
9. What is the "ripple effect" in the News on page 211? LO2
10. Will the price level always rise when AD increases? Why or why not? LO2

 web activities to accompany this chapter can be found on the Online Learning Center:
http://www.mhhe.com/schiller12e

LO1   1   From 1929 to 2008, in how many years did
    (a) Real consumption decline?   _____
    (b) Real investment decline?   _____
    (c) Real government spending increase at least $100 billion? (Data on end covers of text.)   _____

LO1   2. If the consumption function is $C = \$200$ billion $+ 0.9Y$,
    (a) How much do consumers spend with incomes of $3 trillion?   _____
    (b) How much do they save?   _____

LO2   3. If the marginal propensity to consume is 0.75,
    (a) What is the value of the multiplier?   _____
    (b) What is the marginal propensity to save?   _____

LO2   4. Suppose that investment demand increases by $100 billion in a closed and private economy
    (no government or foreign trade). Assume further that households have a marginal propensity to
    consume of 80 percent.
    (a) Compute four rounds of multiplier effects:

	Changes in This Cycle's Spending	Cumulative Change in Spending
First cycle	_____	_____
Second cycle	_____	_____
Third cycle	_____	_____
Fourth cycle	_____	_____

    (b) What will be the final cumulative impact on spending?   _____

LO3   5. Illustrate in the graph below the impact of a sudden decline in consumer confidence
    that reduces autonomous consumption by $50 billion at the price level P_F. Assume $MPC = 0.8$.
    (a) What is the new equilibrium level of real output? (Don't forget the multiplier.)   _____
    (b) How large is the real GDP gap?   _____
    (c) What has happened to average prices ("increased" or "decreased")?   _____

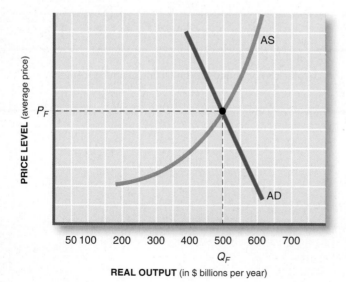

LO1   6. By how much did annualized consumption decline in November 2008 when GDP was
$14 trillion? (See News, p. 208.)   _____

LO2   7. If Korean exports to the U.S. decline by $15 billion (World View, p. 212) by how much will total
Korean spending drop if their MPC is 0.60?   _____

LO3   8. According to World Bank estimates (see p. 217), by how much did consumer spending decline as
a result of the 7-point drop in the index of consumer confidence at the end of 2007 (Figure 10.10)?   _____

LO3   9. How large is the inflationary GDP gap in Figurc 10.9?   _____

LO2   10. The accompanying graph depicts a macro equilibrium. Answer the questions based on the
LO3   information in the graph.
           (a) What is the equilibrium rate of GDP?   _____
           (b) If full-employment real GDP is $1,200, what problem does this economy have? _____
           (c) How large is the real GDP gap?   _____
           (d) If the multiplier were equal to 4, how much additional investment would be needed to
                increase aggregate demand by the amount of the initial GDP gap?   _____
           (e) Illustrate the changes in autonomous investment and induced consumption that occur in (d).
           (f) What happens to prices when aggregate demand increases by the amount of
                the initial GDP gap?   _____
           (g) Is full employment restored by the AD shift?   _____

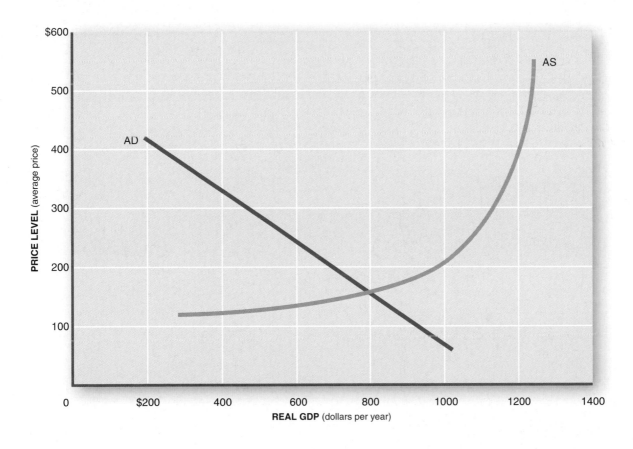

not at full
employment

Recessionary Gap

PART 4

Fiscal Policy Tools

The government's tax and spending activities influence economic outcomes. Keynesian theory emphasizes the market's lack of self-adjustment, particularly in recessions. If the market doesn't self-adjust, then the government may have to intervene. Specifically, the government may have to use its tax and spending power (fiscal policy) to stabilize the macro economy at its full-employment equilibrium. Chapters 11 and 12 look closely at the policy goals, strategies, and tools of fiscal policy.

Fiscal Policy

11

LEARNING OBJECTIVES

After reading this chapter, you should be able to:

LO1. Explain what the AD shortfall and AD excess measure.

LO2. Describe the tools of fiscal policy.

LO3. Predict how fiscal stimulus or restraint affects macro outcomes.

The **Keynesian theory** of macro instability is practically a mandate for government intervention. From a Keynesian perspective, too little aggregate demand causes unemployment; too much aggregate demand causes inflation. Since the market itself won't correct these imbalances, the federal government must. Keynes concluded that the government must intervene to manage the level of aggregate demand. This implies increasing aggregate demand when it's deficient and decreasing aggregate demand when it's excessive.

President Obama agreed completely with the Keynesian prescription for ending a recession. Even before taking office, he developed a spending and tax-cut package designed to stimulate aggregate demand and "get the country moving again." In this chapter we'll examine the fiscal-policy tools an Economist in Chief has available, which ones President Obama selected, and what impact they were expected to have. The basic questions we address are:

- **Can government spending and tax policies ensure full employment?**
- **What policy actions will help fight inflation?**
- **What are the risks of government intervention?**

As we'll see, the government's tax and spending activities affect not only the *level* of output and prices but the *mix* of output as well.

TAXES AND SPENDING

Article I of the U.S. Constitution empowers Congress "to lay and collect taxes, duties, imposts and excises, to pay the debts and provide for the common defense and general welfare of the United States." Up until 1915, however, the federal government collected few taxes and spent little. In 1902, the federal government employed fewer than 350,000 people and spent a mere $650 million. Today, the federal government employs over 4 million people and spends more than $3.5 trillion a year.

The tremendous expansion of the federal government started with the Sixteenth Amendment to the U.S. Constitution (1913), which extended the government's taxing power to *incomes*. Prior to that, most government revenue came from taxes on imports, whiskey, and tobacco. Once the federal government got the power to tax incomes, it had the revenue base to finance increased expenditure.

Today, the federal government collects nearly $3 trillion a year in tax revenues. Nearly half of that revenue comes from individual income taxes (see Figure 4.5). Social Security payroll taxes are the second-largest revenue source, followed at a distance by corporate income taxes. The customs, whiskey, and tobacco taxes on which the federal government depended in 1902 now count for very little.

In 1902, federal government expenditures mirrored tax revenues: Both were very small. Today, things are very different. The federal government now spends all of its much larger tax revenues—and more. Uncle Sam even borrows additional funds to pay for federal spending. In Chapter 12 we look at the implications of the budget deficits that help finance federal spending. In this chapter we focus on how government spending *directly* affects **aggregate demand.**

Purchases vs. Transfers. To understand how government spending affects aggregate demand, we must again distinguish between government *purchases* and *income transfers.* Government spending on defense, highways, and health care entails the purchase of real goods and services in product markets; they're part of aggregate demand. By contrast, the government doesn't buy anything when it mails out Social Security checks. Those checks simply transfer income from taxpayers to retired workers. **Income transfers** don't become part of aggregate demand until the transfer recipients decide to spend that income.

As we observed in Chapter 4, less than half of all federal government spending entails the purchase of goods and services. The rest of federal spending is either an income transfer or an interest payment on the national debt.

The federal government's tax and spending powers give it a great deal of influence over aggregate demand. ***The government can alter aggregate demand by***

- *Purchasing more or fewer goods and services.*
- *Raising or lowering taxes.*
- *Changing the level of income transfers.*

Fiscal policy entails the use of these various budget levers to influence macroeconomic outcomes. ***From a macro perspective, the federal budget is a tool that can shift aggregate demand and thereby alter macroeconomic outcomes.*** Figure 11.1 puts this tool into the framework of the basic AS/AD model.

Although fiscal policy can be used to pursue any of our economic goals, we begin our study by exploring its potential to ensure full employment. We then look at its impact on inflation. Along the way we also observe the potential of fiscal policy to alter the mix of output and the distribution of income.

Government Revenue

[handwritten margin note: progressive income taxes b/c everyone isn't treated equally now]

Government Expenditure

aggregate demand: The total quantity of output demanded at alternative price levels in a given time period, *ceteris paribus.*

income transfers: Payments to individuals for which no current goods or services are exchanged, such as Social Security, welfare, unemployment benefits.

Fiscal Policy

fiscal policy: The use of government taxes and spending to alter macroeconomic outcomes.

Determinants

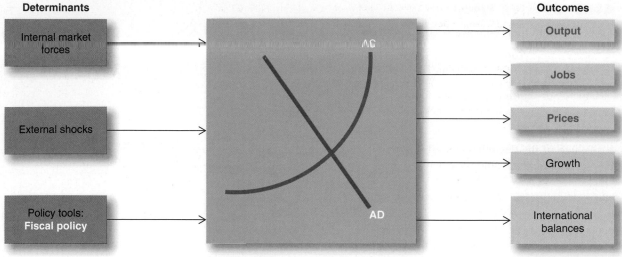

Outcomes

FIGURE 11.1
Fiscal Policy

Fiscal policy refers to the use of the government's tax and spending powers to alter macro outcomes. Fiscal policy works principally through shifts of the aggregate demand curve.

FISCAL STIMULUS

> **equilibrium (macro):** The combination of price level and real output that is compatible with both aggregate demand and aggregate supply.

The basic premise of fiscal policy is that the market's short-run macro equilibrium may not be a desirable one. This is clearly the case in Figure 11.2. **Macro equilibrium** occurs at Q_E, where $5.6 trillion of output is being produced. Full-employment GDP occurs at Q_F, where the real value of output is $6 trillion. Accordingly, the economy depicted in Figure 11.2 confronts a **recessionary GDP gap** of $400 billion. This is the kind of situation President Obama faced in 2009.

Keynesian Strategy

> **recessionary GDP gap:** The amount by which equilibrium GDP falls short of full-employment GDP.

The Keynesian model of the adjustment process helps us not only understand how an economy can get into such trouble but also see how it might get out. Keynes emphasized how the aggregate demand curve *shifts* with changes in spending behavior. He also emphasized how new injections of spending into the circular flow multiply into much larger changes in total spending via the multiplier process. *From a Keynesian perspective, the way out of recession is obvious: Get someone to spend more on goods and services.* Should desired

FIGURE 11.2
The Policy Goal

If the economy is in a recessionary equilibrium like point *a*, the policy goal is to increase output to full employment (Q_F). Keynes urged the government to use its tax and spending powers to shift the AD curve rightward.

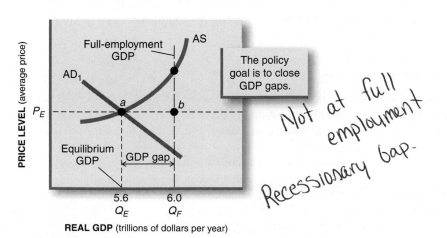

spending increase, the aggregate demand curve would *shift* to the right, leading the economy out of recession. That additional spending impetus could come from increased government purchases or from tax cuts that induce increased consumption or investment. Such a **fiscal stimulus** might propel the economy out of recession.

Although the general strategy for Keynesian fiscal policy is clear, the scope of desired intervention isn't so evident. Two strategic policy questions must be addressed:

- By how much do we want to shift the AD curve to the right?
- How can we induce the desired shift?

At first glance, the size of the desired AD shift might seem obvious. If the GDP gap is $400 billion, why not just increase aggregate demand by that amount?

How Large a Shift? Keynes thought that policy might just work. But it's not quite that simple, as Figure 11.3 illustrates. The intent of expansionary fiscal policy is to achieve full employment. In Figure 11.3, this goal would be attained at point *b*. So it looks like we could restore full employment simply by shifting AD to the right by $400 billion, as the curve AD_2 illustrates. The AD_2 curve does in fact pass through point *b*. That tells us that people would actually demand the full-employment output Q_F at the price level P_E.

But where is the *equilibrium* output associated with the AD_2 curve? Not at *b*, since the AS curve doesn't pass through that same point. Instead, AD_2 and **aggregate supply** (AS) intersect at point *c*. So the *equilibrium* output associated with AD_2 is less than Q_F. Hence, *a rightward AD shift equal to the real GDP gap will leave the economy short of full employment.*

Price-Level Changes. The failure of the AD_2 curve to restore full employment results from the upward slope of the AS curve. *When the AD curve shifts to the right, the economy moves up the aggregate supply (AS) curve, not horizontally to the right. As a result both real output and the price level change.*

Figure 11.3 illustrates the consequences of the upward-sloping aggregate supply curve. When the aggregate demand curve shifts from AD_1 to AD_2, the economy moves to the macro equilibrium at point *c*, not to point *b*. As demand picks up, we expect cost pressures to increase, pushing the price level up the upward-sloping AS curve. At point *c*, the AS and

The Fiscal Target

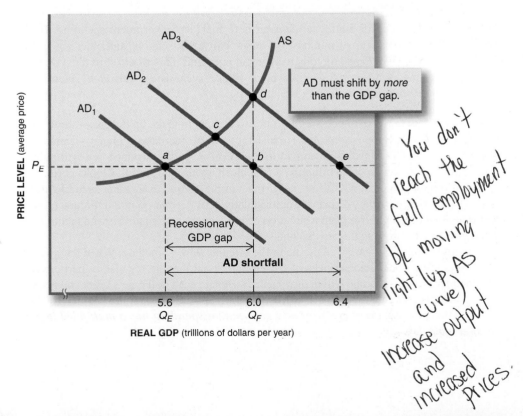

FIGURE 11.3
The AD Shortfall

If aggregate demand increased by the amount of the recessionary GDP gap, we would get a shift from AD_1 to AD_2. The new equilibrium would occur at point *c*, leaving the economy short of full employment (Q_F). (Some of the increased demand pushes up prices instead of output.)

To reach full-employment equilibrium (point *d*), the AD curve must shift to AD_3, thereby eliminating the entire AD shortfall. The AD shortfall—the horizontal distance between point *a* and point *e*—is the fiscal policy target for achieving full employment.

You don't reach the full employment b/c moving right (up AS curve) increase output and increased prices.

AD$_2$ curves intersect, establishing a new equilibrium. At that equilibrium, the price level is higher than it was initially (P_E). Real output is higher as well. But at point c we are still short of the full-employment target (Q_F).

The Naïve Keynesian Model. Under very special circumstances the job of restoring full employment wouldn't be that difficult. If there was no cost-push pressure as the economy expanded, the price level wouldn't rise when AD increased. In such an "inflation-free" environment the AS curve would be *horizontal* rather than upward-sloping. With a horizontal AS curve no rightward AD shifts would cause prices to rise. Keynes thought this was the case during the Great Depression, when prices were actually *falling* (see Figure 8.1). So he proposed shifting the AD curve by the amount of the recessionary GDP gap.

The assumption of a horizontal AS curve seems naïve in today's world. Although not every AD shift will raise prices, inflationary pressures do increase as AD expands. That is why the short-run AS curve has the upward slope.

The AD Shortfall. Although the naive Keynesian approach doesn't work, we needn't forsake fiscal policy. Figure 11.3 simply tells us that the naive Keynesian policy prescription (increasing AD by the amount of the GDP gap) probably won't cure all our unemployment ills. It also suggests, however, that a *larger* dose of fiscal stimulus might just work. *So long as the AS curve slopes upward, we must increase aggregate demand by more than the size of the recessionary GDP gap in order to achieve full employment.*

Figure 11.3 illustrates this new policy target. The **AD shortfall** is the amount of additional aggregate demand needed to achieve full employment *after allowing for price-level changes*. Notice in Figure 11.3 that full employment (Q_F) is achieved only when the AD curve intersects the AS curve at point d. To get there, the aggregate demand curve must shift from AD$_1$ all the way to AD$_3$. That third aggregate demand curve passes through point e as well. Hence, aggregate demand must increase until it passes through point e. **This horizontal distance between point a and point e in Figure 11.3 measures the AD shortfall.** Aggregate demand must increase (shift) by the amount of the AD shortfall in order to achieve full employment. Thus, *the AD shortfall is the fiscal target.* In Figure 11.3, the AD shortfall amounts to $800 billion ($0.8 trillion). That's how much *additional* aggregate demand is required to reach full employment (Q_F).

Were we to increase AD by enough to attain full employment, it's apparent in Figure 11.3 that prices would increase as well. We'll examine this dilemma later; for the time being we focus on the policy options for increasing aggregate demand by the desired amount.

More Government Spending

The simplest way to shift aggregate demand is to increase government spending. If the government were to step up its purchases of tanks, highways, schools, and other goods, the increased spending would add directly to aggregate demand. This would shift the AD curve rightward, moving us closer to full employment. Hence, *increased government spending is a form of fiscal stimulus.*

Multiplier Effects. It isn't necessary for the government to make up the entire shortfall in aggregate demand. Suppose that the fiscal target was to increase aggregate demand by $800 billion, the AD shortfall illustrated in Figure 11.3, by the distance between point e ($6.4 billion) and point a ($5.6 billion). At first blush, that much stimulus looks perfect for restoring full employment. But life is never that simple. Were government spending to increase by $800 billion, the AD curve would actually shift *beyond* point e in Figure 11.3. In that case we'd quickly move from a situation of *inadequate* aggregate demand (point a) to a situation of *excessive* aggregate demand.

The origins of this apparent riddle lie in the circular flow of income. When the government buys more goods and services, it creates additional income for market participants. The recipients of this income will in turn spend it. Hence, each dollar gets spent and respent many times. This is the multiplier adjustment process we encountered in Chapter 10. As a result of this process, *every dollar of new government spending has a multiplied impact on aggregate demand.*

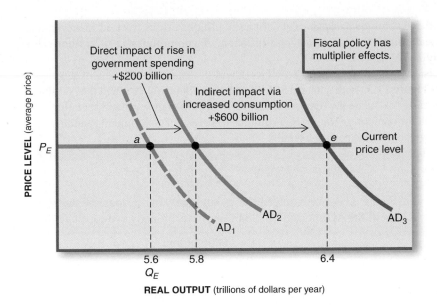

FIGURE 11.4
Multiplier Effects

Fiscal stimulus will set off the multiplier process. As a result of this, aggregate demand will increase (shift) in two distinct steps: (1) the initial fiscal stimulus (AD_1 to AD_2) and (2) induced changes in consumption (AD_2 to AD_3). In this case, a $200 billion increase in government spending causes an $800 billion increase in aggregate demand at the *existing* price level.

How much "bang" the economy gets for each government "buck" depends on the value of the **multiplier.** Specifically,

$$\text{Total change in spending} = \text{multiplier} \times \text{new spending injection}$$

The multiplier adds a lot of punch to fiscal policy. Suppose that households have a **marginal propensity to consume** equal to 0.75. In this case, the multiplier would have a value of 4 and each dollar of new government expenditure would increase aggregate demand by $4.

Figure 11.4 illustrates that leveraged impact of government spending. Aggregate demand shifts from AD_1 to AD_2 when the government buys an additional $200 billion of output. Multiplier effects then increase consumption spending by $600 billion more. This additional consumption shifts aggregate demand further, to AD_3. Thus, *the impact of fiscal stimulus on aggregate demand includes both the new government spending and all subsequent increases in consumer spending triggered by multiplier effects.* In Figure 11.4, the shift from AD_1 to AD_3 includes

AD_1 to AD_2: Shift due to $200 billion injection of new government spending.
AD_2 to AD_3: Shift due to multiplier-induced increase in consumption ($600 billion).

As a result of these initial and multiplier-induced shifts, aggregate demand at the current price level (P_E) increases by $800 billion. Thus,

$$\text{Cumulative increase (horizontal shift) in AD} = \begin{array}{c}\text{new spending injection}\\ \text{(fiscal stimulus)}\end{array} + \begin{array}{c}\text{induced increase}\\ \text{in consumption}\end{array}$$

$$= \text{multiplier} \times \begin{array}{c}\text{fiscal stimulus}\\ \text{(new spending injection)}\end{array}$$

The second equation is identical to the first but expressed in the terminology of fiscal policy. The "fiscal stimulus" is the "new spending injection" that sets the multiplier process in motion.

The Desired Stimulus. Multiplier effects make changes in government spending a powerful policy lever. The multiplier also increases the risk of error, however. Just as too little fiscal stimulus may leave the economy in a recession, too much can rapidly lead to excessive spending and inflation. This was the dilemma President Obama confronted in his first year.

multiplier: The multiple by which an initial change in aggregate spending will alter total expenditure after an infinite number of spending cycles; $1/(1 - MPC)$.

marginal propensity to consume (MPC): The fraction of each additional (marginal) dollar of disposable income spent on consumption; the change in consumption divided by the change in disposable income.

He wanted a fiscal stimulus package of at least $850 billion. Critics worried, however, that too much fiscal stimulus might accelerate inflation. A compromise ($787 billion) was struck in early 2009.

Policy decisions would be a lot easier if we knew the exact dimensions of aggregate demand, as in Figure 11.3. With such perfect information about AD, AS, and the AD shortfall, we could easily calculate the required increase in the rate of government spending. The general formula for computing the *desired* stimulus (increase in government spending) is a simple rearrangement of the earlier formula:

$$\text{Desired fiscal stimulus} = \frac{\text{AD shortfall}}{\text{the multiplier}}$$

In the economy in Figure 11.3, we assumed the policy goal was to increase aggregate demand by the amount of the AD shortfall ($800 billion). Accordingly, we conclude that

$$\text{Desired fiscal stimulus} = \frac{\$800 \text{ billion}}{4}$$

$$= \$200 \text{ billion}$$

In other words, a $200 billion increase in government spending at the current price level would be enough fiscal stimulus to close the $800 billion AD shortfall and achieve full employment.

In practice, we rarely know the exact size of the shortfall in aggregate demand. The multiplier is also harder to calculate when taxes and imports enter the picture. Nevertheless, the foregoing formula does provide a useful rule of thumb for determining how much fiscal stimulus is needed to achieve any desired increase in aggregate demand. Such calculations helped the Chinese government decide how much fiscal stimulus was needed in 2008 to keep its economy out of recession (see World View below).

WORLD VIEW

China Sets Big Stimulus Plan in Bid to Jump-Start Growth

BEIJING—China unveiled an economic stimulus program it billed as totaling $586 billion, aiming to bolster domestic demand and help avert a global recession. . . .

The plan includes spending in housing, infrastructure, agriculture, health care and social welfare, and features a tax deduction for capital spending by companies. . . .

If the stimulus package can help alleviate a slowdown in China's housing and investment boom, that could help cushion decreases in Chinese purchases of raw materials and goods from the U.S. and other developed nations. . . .

Based on recent trends and without a policy response, China could have seen 5% to 6% growth next year, according to Mr. Wang. With stimulus measures that include previous moves to cut interest rates and end caps on bank lending, he said China now has good odds of achieving the 8% to 9% growth in 2009 that officials still say they expect.

—Andrew Batson

Source: *The Wall Street Journal*, November 10, 2008, p. 1. Copyright 2008 by Dow Jones & Company, Inc. Reproduced with permission of Dow Jones & Company, Inc. in the format Textbook via Copyright Clearance Center.

Analysis: Fear of a pending decline in aggregate demand prompted China's government to increase government spending on roads, bridges, and telecom networks. The government hoped such a fiscal stimulus would offset a decline in export sales and avert recession.

web analysis

For more information on China's fiscal stimulus, search "Dr. Keynes's Chinese Patient" at **www. economist.com.**

Tax Cuts

There is no doubt that increased government spending can shift the AD curve to the right, helping to close a GDP gap. But increased government spending isn't the only way to get there. The increased demand required to raise output and employment levels from Q_E to Q_F could emerge from increases in autonomous consumption or investment as well as from increased government spending. An AD shift could also originate overseas, in the form of increased demand for our exports. In other words, any "Big Spender" would help, whether from the public sector or the private sector. Of course, the reason we're initially at Q_E instead of Q_F in Figure 11.3 is that consumers, investors, and export buyers have chosen *not* to spend as much as required for full employment.

Consumer and investor decisions are subject to change. Moreover, fiscal policy can encourage such changes. Congress not only buys goods and services but also levies taxes. By lowering taxes, the government increases the **disposable income** of the private sector. This was the objective of the 2008 Bush tax cuts, which gave all taxpayers a rebate of $300–600 in the summer of 2008. By putting $168 billion more after-tax income into the hands of consumers, Congress hoped to stimulate (shift) the consumption component of aggregate demand. President Obama used the same fiscal-policy tool as part of his 2009 stimulus package (see News below).

disposable income: After-tax income of consumers; personal income less personal taxes.

IN THE NEWS

$787b Stimulus Bill Approved

WASHINGTON—Less than one month after President Obama took office, Congress last night passed his flagship proposal, an unprecedented collection of tax cuts and new spending that Democrats say offers the country its best hope to stave off an impending depression.

After a frenzied month of legislating, the House and Senate produced an economic stimulus bill estimated yesterday to cost $787 billion, with $281 billion in new tax cuts and the remainder in one-time spending on infrastructure investments, expanded unemployment benefits, and other programs.

It passed both chambers on a largely party-line vote, winning the support of no Republicans in the House and three in the Senate.

—Sasha Issenberg

Source: *The Boston Globe*, February 14, 2009. © Copyright 2009, Globe Newspaper Co., Inc.

Analysis: President Obama's huge fiscal-stimulus package included both increased government spending and tax cuts. The package was intended to shift the AD curve substantially to the right.

Taxes and Consumption. A tax cut directly increases the disposable income of consumers. The question here, however, is how a tax cut affects *spending*. By how much will consumption increase for every dollar of tax cuts?

The answer lies in the marginal propensity to consume. Consumers won't spend every dollar of tax cuts; they'll *save* some of the cut and spend the rest. The MPC tells us how the tax-cut dollar will be split between saving and spending. If the MPC is 0.75, consumers will spend $0.75 out of every tax-cut $1.00. In other words,

$$\text{Initial increase in consumption} = \text{MPC} \times \text{tax cut}$$

If taxes were cut by $200 billion, the resulting spree would amount to

$$\text{Initial increase in consumption} = 0.75 \times \$200 \text{ billion}$$

$$= \$150 \text{ billion}$$

Hence, *the effect of a tax cut that increases disposable incomes is to stimulate consumer spending.* A tax cut therefore shifts the aggregate demand curve to the right.

Multiplier Effects. The initial consumption spree induced by a tax cut starts the multiplier process in motion. The new consumer spending creates additional income for producers and workers, who will then use the additional income to increase their own consumption. This will propel us along the multiplier path already depicted in Figure 11.4. The cumulative change in total spending will be

$$\text{Cumulative change in spending} = \text{multiplier} \times \text{initial change in consumption}$$

In this case, the cumulative change is

$$\text{Cumulative change in spending} = \frac{1}{1 - \text{MPC}} \times \$150 \text{ billion}$$

$$= 4 \times \$150 \text{ billion}$$

$$= \$600 \text{ billion}$$

Here again we see that the multiplier increases the impact on aggregate demand of a fiscal policy stimulus. There's an important difference here, though. When we increased government spending by $200 billion, aggregate demand increased by $800 billion. When we cut taxes by $200 billion, however, aggregate demand increases by only $600 billion. Hence, *a tax cut contains less fiscal stimulus than an increase in government spending of the same size.*

The lesser stimulative power of tax cuts is explained by consumer saving. Only part of a tax cut gets spent. Consumers save the rest. This is evident in Figure 11.5, which illustrates the successive rounds of the multiplier process. Notice that the tax cut is used to increase both consumption and saving, according to the MPC. Only that part of the tax cut that's used for consumption enters the circular flow as a spending injection. Hence, *the initial spending injection is less than the size of the tax cuts.* By contrast, every dollar of government purchases goes directly into the circular flow. Accordingly, tax cuts are less powerful than government purchases because the initial *spending* injection is smaller.

FIGURE 11.5
The Tax-Cut Multiplier

Only part of a tax cut is used to increase consumption; the remainder is saved. Accordingly, the initial spending injection is less than the tax cut. This makes tax cuts less stimulative than government purchases of the same size. The multiplier still goes to work on that new consumer spending, however.

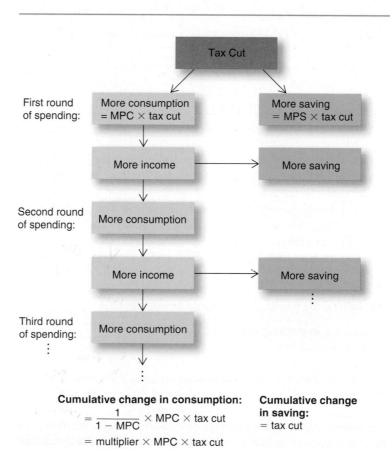

This doesn't mean we can't close the AD shortfall with a tax cut. It simply means that the desired tax cut must be larger than the required stimulus. It remains true that

$$\text{Desired fiscal stimulus} = \frac{\text{AD shortfall}}{\text{the multiplier}}$$

But now we're using a consumption shift as the fiscal stimulus rather than increased government spending. Hence, we have to allow for the fact that the initial surge in consumption (the fiscal stimulus) will be *less* than the tax cut. Specifically,

$$\text{Initial consumption injection} = \text{MPC} \times \text{tax cut}$$

Hence, if we want to use a consumer tax cut to close a GDP gap, we have

$$\text{Desired tax cut} = \frac{\text{desired fiscal stimulus}}{\text{MPC}}$$

In the economy in Figure 11.3, we assumed that the desired stimulus is $200 billion and the MPC equals 0.75. Hence, the desired tax cut is

$$\text{Desired tax cut} = \frac{\$200 \text{ billion}}{0.75} = \$267 \text{ billion}$$

By cutting taxes $267 billion, we directly increase disposable income by the same amount. Consumers then increase their rate of spending $200 billion (0.75 × $267 billion); they save the remaining $67 billion. As the added spending enters the circular flow, it starts the multiplier process, ultimately increasing aggregate demand by $800 billion per year.

This comparison of government purchases and tax cuts clearly reveals their respective power. What we've demonstrated is that *a dollar of tax cuts is less stimulative than a dollar of government purchases.* This doesn't mean that tax cuts are undesirable, just that they need to be larger than the desired injection of spending. The accompanying News shows that the 2008 tax cut boosted consumer spending by 3.5 percent, thereby shifting AD to the right and accelerating real GDP growth.

IN THE NEWS

Just How Stimulating Are Those Checks?

To get an idea of how much those government rebate checks have spurred spending—and who's benefiting from the buying—business school professors Jonathan Parker (Northwestern) and Christian Broda (University of Chicago) analyzed the spending of 30,000 rebate-receiving households. Using data provided by AC-Nielsen's Homescan, whose participants scan the barcodes on their purchases into a database, the researchers found the rebates "clearly have increased household spending," Parker says. Lower-income households boosted consumption most—spending 6% more, compared with a 3.5% rise across all households.

—Tara Kalwarski

Source: *BusinessWeek*, September 8, 2008, p. 14.

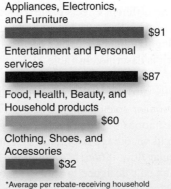

THE 2008 REBATE BOOST

Additional dollars spent due to stimulus checks*

Appliances, Electronics, and Furniture — $91

Entertainment and Personal services — $87

Food, Health, Beauty, and Household products — $60

Clothing, Shoes, and Accessories — $32

*Average per rebate-receiving household

Data: Christian Broda, University of Chicago; Jonathan Parker, Northwestern University

web analysis

To follow the ups and downs of Federal income tax as a percentage of GDP, go to the Congressional Budget Office at **www.cbo.gov** and choose "Historical Budget Data."

Analysis: The 2008 tax cuts were a form of fiscal stimulus that boosted consumption (personal spending), increased real GDP growth, and reduced unemployment.

TABLE 11.1

The Balanced Budget Multiplier

An increase in government spending paid for by a tax cut of equal size shifts aggregate demand. This box explains why.

Many taxpayers and politicians demand that any new government spending be balanced with new taxes. Such balancing at the margin, it's asserted, will keep the budget deficit from rising, while avoiding further economic stimulus.

However, changes in government spending (G) are more powerful than changes in taxes (T) or transfers. This implies that an increase in G seemingly "offset" with an equal rise in T will actually increase aggregate demand.

To see how this curious result comes about, suppose that the government decided to spend $50 billion per year on a new fleet of space shuttles and to pay for them by raising income taxes by the same amount. Thus

$$\text{Change in } G = +\$50 \text{ billion per year}$$
$$\text{Change in } T = +\$50 \text{ billion per year}$$
$$\text{Change in budget balance} = 0$$

How will this pay-as-you-go (balanced) budget initiative affect total spending?

The increase in the rate of government spending represents a new injection of $50 billion. But the higher taxes don't increase leakage by the same amount. Households will pay taxes by reducing *both* consumption and saving. The initial reduction in annual consumer spending equals only MPC × $50 billion.

The reduction in consumption is therefore less than the increase in government spending, implying a net increase in *aggregate* spending. The *initial* change in aggregate demand brought about by this balanced budget expenditure is

$$\text{Initial increase in government spending} = \$50 \text{ billion}$$
$$\underline{\text{less Initial reduction in consumer spending} = \text{MPC} \times \$50 \text{ billion}}$$
$$\text{Net initial change in total spending} = (1 - \text{MPC})\$50 \text{ billion}$$

Like any other changes in the rate of spending, this initial increase in aggregate spending will start a multiplier process in motion. The *cumulative* change in expenditure will be much larger, as indicated by the multiplier. In this case, the cumulative (ultimate) change in total spending is

$$\frac{\text{The}}{\text{multiplier}} \times \frac{\text{initial change}}{\text{in spending per year}} = \frac{\text{cumulative change}}{\text{in total spending}}$$

$$\frac{1}{1 - \text{MPC}} \times (1 - \text{MPC})\$50 \text{ billion} = \$50 \text{ billion}$$

Thus, the balanced budget multiplier is equal to 1. In this case, a $50 billion increase in annual government expenditure combined with an equivalent increase in taxes increases aggregate demand by $50 billion per year.

The different effects of tax cuts and increased government spending have an important implication for government budgets. Because some of the power of a tax cut "leaks" into saving, tax increases don't "offset" government spending of equal value. This unexpected result is described in Table 11.1.

Taxes and Investment. A tax cut may also be an effective mechanism for increasing *investment* spending. As we observed in Chapter 9, investment decisions are guided by expectations of future profit. If a cut in corporate taxes raises potential after-tax profits, it should encourage additional investment. Once additional investment spending enters the circular flow, it, too, has a multiplier effect.

Tax cuts designed to stimulate consumption (C) and investment (I) have been used frequently. In 1963, President John F. Kennedy announced his intention to reduce taxes in order to stimulate the economy, citing that the marginal propensity to consume for the average U.S. family at that time appeared to be exceptionally high.

In 1981, President Reagan convinced Congress to cut personal taxes $250 billion over a 3-year period and cut business taxes another $70 billion. The resulting increase in disposable income stimulated consumer spending and helped push the economy out of the 1981–82 recession. When the economy slowed down at the end of the 1980s, President George H. Bush

	2009	2010	2011	2012
Real GDP Acceleration (%)				
Low estimate	1.4	1.1	0.4	0.1
High estimate	3.8	3.4	1.2	0.5
Increase in Employment (million jobs)				
Low estimate	0.8	1.2	0.6	0.3
High estimate	2.3	3.6	1.8	0.7

Source: Congressional Budget Office.

TABLE 11.2
Projected Stimulus Impact

A stimulus program's success is measured by the implied impact on macroeconomic outcomes. The Congressional Budget Office projected significant 2009–2012 job creation and GDP acceleration from the Obama program.

proposed to cut the capital gains tax, hoping to stimulate investment. President Clinton also embraced the notion of tax incentives for investment. He favored a tax credit for new investments in plant and equipment to increase the level of investment and set off multiplier effects for many years.

President George W. Bush pulled out all the tax-cut stops. Immediately upon taking office in 2001, he convinced Congress to pass a $1.35 trillion tax cut for consumers, spread over several years. He followed that up with business tax cuts in 2002 and 2003. The cumulative impact of these tax cuts shifted AD significantly to the right and accelerated recovery from the 2001 recession. President Obama used the same tax-cut tactics to help push the economy out of recession in 2009.

A third fiscal policy option for stimulating the economy is to increase transfer payments. If Social Security recipients, welfare recipients, unemployment insurance beneficiaries, and veterans get larger benefit checks, they'll have more disposable income to spend. The resulting increase in consumption will boost aggregate demand. Thus, increases in unemployment benefits like those Congress approved in November 2008 not only help jobless workers but also boost the macro economy.

Increased Transfers

Increased transfer payments don't, however, increase injections dollar-for-dollar. Here again, we have to recognize that consumers will save some of their additional transfer payments; only part (MPC) of the additional income will be injected into the spending stream. Hence, *the initial fiscal stimulus (AD shift) of increased transfer payments is*

Initial fiscal stimulus (injection) = MPC $\times$ increase in transfer payments

This initial stimulus sets the multiplier in motion, shifting the aggregate demand curve further to the right.

As we've observed, the 2009 fiscal stimulus package (News, p. 231) included a mix of increased government spending, tax cuts, and increased income transfers. That fiscal stimulus, combined with subsequent multiplier effects, was intended to give a significant boost to aggregate demand. According to the Congressional Budget Office, that's exactly what happened. As Table 11.2 shows, real GDP was expected to increase by 1.4–3.8 percentage points in 2009, and to keep growing in subsequent years.

Impact of the 2009 Fiscal Stimulus

FISCAL RESTRAINT

The objective of fiscal policy isn't always to increase aggregate demand. At times the economy is already expanding too fast and **fiscal restraint** is more appropriate. In these circumstances, policymakers are likely to be focused on inflation, not unemployment. Their objective will be to *reduce* aggregate demand, not to stimulate it.

The means available to the federal government for restraining aggregate demand emerge again from both sides of the budget. The difference here is that we use the budget tools in reverse. We now want to *reduce* government spending, *increase* taxes, or *decrease* transfer payments.

fiscal restraint: Tax hikes or spending cuts intended to reduce (shift) aggregate demand.

FIGURE 11.6
Excess Aggregate Demand

Too much aggregate demand (AD_1) causes the price level to rise (P_E) above its desired level (P_F). To restore price stability, the AD curve must shift leftward by the entire amount of the excess AD (here shown as $Q_1 - Q_2$). In this case, the excess AD amounts to $400 billion. If AD shifts by that much (from AD_1 to AD_2), the excess AD is eliminated and equilibrium moves from E_1 to E_2.

[handwritten: losing stimulus & to price reduction in quantity]

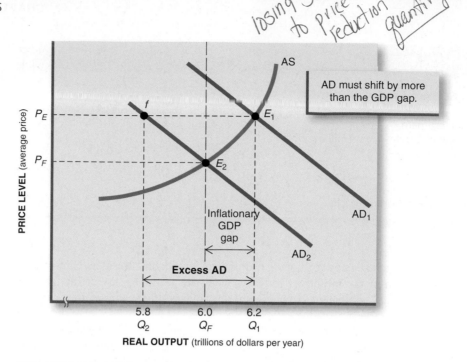

AD must shift by more than the GDP gap.

PRICE LEVEL (average price)

REAL OUTPUT (trillions of dollars per year)

The Fiscal Target

As before, our first task is to determine how much we want aggregate demand to fall. To determine this, we must consult Figure 11.6. The initial equilibrium in this case occurs at point E_1, where the AS and AD_1 curves intersect. At that equilibrium the unemployment rate falls below the rate consistent with full employment (Q_F) and we produce the output Q_1. The resulting strains on production push the price level to P_E, higher than we're willing to accept. Our goal is to maintain the price level at P_F, which is consistent with our notion of full employment *and* price stability.

In this case, we have an **inflationary GDP gap**—that is, equilibrium GDP exceeds full-employment GDP by the amount $Q_1 - Q_F$, or $200 billion (=$6.2 billion − $6.0 billion on the graph). If we want to restore price stability (P_F), however, we need to reduce aggregate demand by *more* than this GDP gap.

The **AD excess**—like its counterpart, the AD shortfall—takes into account potential changes in the price level. Observe that *the AD excess exceeds the inflationary GDP gap.* In Figure 11.6, the AD excess equals the horizontal distance from E_1 to point f, which amounts to $400 billion (=$6.2 billion − $5.8 billion). This excess aggregate demand is our fiscal policy target. To restore price stability, we must shift the AD curve leftward until it passes through point f. The AD_2 curve does this. The shift to AD_2 moves the economy to a new equilibrium at E_2. At E_2 we have less output but also a lower price level (less inflation).

Knowing the dimensions of excess aggregate demand, we can compute the desired fiscal restraint as

$$\frac{\text{Desired}}{\text{fiscal restraint}} = \frac{\text{excess AD}}{\text{the multiplier}}$$

In other words, first we determine how far we want to shift the AD curve to the left, that is, the size of the AD excess. Then we compute how much government spending or taxes must be changed to achieve the desired shift, taking into account multiplier effects.

> **inflationary GDP gap:** The amount by which equilibrium GDP exceeds full-employment GDP.

> **AD excess:** The amount by which aggregate demand must be reduced to achieve full-employment equilibrium after allowing for price-level changes.

Budget Cuts

The first option to consider is budget cuts. By how much should we reduce government expenditure on goods and services? The answer is simple in this case: We first calculate the desired fiscal restraint, as computed above. Then we cut government expenditure by that amount.

The Excess AD Target. The GDP gap in Figure 11.6 amounts to $200 billion ($Q_1 - Q_F$). If aggregate demand is reduced by that amount, however, some of the restraint will be dissipated in price-level reductions. To bring *equilibrium* GDP down to the full-employment (Q_F) level, even more of a spending reduction is needed. In this case, the excess AD amounts to $400 billion.

The Multiplier. Budget cuts of less than $400 billion will achieve the desired reduction in aggregate demand. If we assume a marginal propensity to consume of 0.75, the multiplier equals 4. In these circumstances, the desired fiscal restraint is

$$\frac{\text{Desired}}{\text{fiscal restraint}} = \frac{\text{excess AD}}{\text{the multiplier}}$$

$$= \frac{\$400 \text{ billion}}{4}$$

$$= \$100 \text{ billion}$$

What would happen to aggregate demand if the federal government cut that much spending out of, say, the defense budget? Such a military cutback would throw a lot of aerospace employees out of work. Thousands of workers would get smaller paychecks, or perhaps none at all. These workers would be forced to cut back on their own spending, thereby reducing the consumption component of aggregate demand. Hence, aggregate demand would take two hits: first a cut in government spending, then induced cutbacks in consumer spending. The accompanying News highlights the impact of this multiplier process.

IN THE NEWS

Economy Is Already Feeling the Impact of Federal Government's Spending Cuts

WASHINGTON—Skeptical about the federal government's pledge to tighten its belt? Consider this: It already has, and that's one reason the economy is so sluggish.

Federal purchases of goods and services dropped 3.3 percent in 1992, the first decline in three years and the largest in almost 20. Behind the decline were huge defense cutbacks: These purchases tumbled more than 6.0 percent during the year. . . .

The economy has felt the pinch. Kurl Karl of the WEFA Group, economic consultants based in suburban Philadelphia, estimates that cuts in purchases by the federal government knocked as much as 0.5 percentage point off the gross domestic product last year, costing roughly 400,000 jobs, and will probably do the same in 1993.

"Government cuts in defense spending have definitely been a drag" on the economy, says Jim O'Sullivan, economist with Morgan Guaranty in New York.

—Lucinda Harper

Source: *The Wall Street Journal*, August 18, 1993. Copyright 1993 by Dow Jones & Company, Inc. Reproduced with permission of Dow Jones & Company, Inc. in the format Textbook via Copyright Clearance Center.

Analysis: Reductions in governmental spending on goods and services directly decrease aggregate demand. Multiplier effects induce additional cutbacks in consumption, further reducing aggregate demand.

web analysis

To review the latest budget data, go to the Congressional Budget Office at **www.cbo.gov.** CNN (**www.cnn.com**) is a good source for budget news.

The marginal propensity to consume again reveals the power of the multiplier process. If the MPC is 0.75, the consumption of aerospace workers will drop by $75 billion when the government cutbacks reduce their income by $100 billion. (The rest of the income loss will be covered by a reduction in saving.)

From this point on the story should sound familiar. The $100 billion government cutback will ultimately reduce consumer spending by $300 billion. The total drop in spending is thus $400 billion. Like their mirror image, **budget cuts have a multiplied effect on aggregate demand.** The total impact is equal to

$$\text{Cumulative reduction in spending} = \text{multiplier} \times \text{initial budget cut (fiscal restraint)}$$

This cumulative reduction in spending would eliminate excess aggregate demand. We conclude, then, that **the budget cuts should equal the size of the desired fiscal restraint.**

Tax Hikes   Cuts in government spending aren't the only tool for restraining aggregate demand. Tax increases can also be used to shift the AD curve to the left. The direct effect of a tax increase is a reduction in disposable income. People will pay the higher taxes by reducing their consumption *and* saving less. Only the reduced consumption results in less aggregate demand. As consumers tighten their belts, they set off the multiplier process, leading again to a much larger, cumulative shift of aggregate demand.

Because people pay higher tax bills by reducing both consumption and saving (by MPC and MPS, respectively), **taxes must be increased more than a dollar to get a dollar of fiscal restraint.** This leads us to the following guideline:

$$\frac{\text{Desired increase}}{\text{in taxes}} = \frac{\text{desired fiscal restraint}}{\text{MPC}}$$

In other words, changes in taxes must always be larger than the desired change in leakages or injections. How much larger depends on the marginal propensity to consume. In this case

$$\frac{\text{Desired}}{\text{fiscal restraint}} = \frac{\text{excess AD}}{\text{the multiplier}}$$

Using the numbers from Figure 11.6 as an example, we see that

$$\frac{\text{Desired}}{\text{fiscal restraint}} = \frac{\$400 \text{ billion}}{4}$$

$$= \$100 \text{ billion}$$

Therefore, the appropriate tax increase is

$$\frac{\text{Desired}}{\text{tax hike}} = \frac{\text{desired fiscal restraint}}{\text{the multiplier}}$$

$$= \frac{\$100 \text{ billion}}{\text{MPC}}$$

$$= \frac{\$100 \text{ billion}}{0.75}$$

$$= \$133 \text{ billion}$$

Were taxes increased by this amount, consumers would reduce their consumption by $100 billion (= 0.75 × $133 billion). This cutback in consumption would set off the multiplier, leading to a cumulative reduction in spending of $400 billion. In Figure 11.6, aggregate demand would shift from AD_1 to AD_3.

Tax increases have been used to "cool" the economy on several occasions. In 1968, for example, the economy was rapidly approaching full employment and Vietnam War expenditures were helping to drive up prices. Congress responded by imposing a 10 percent surtax (temporary additional tax) on income, which took more than $10 billion in purchasing power away from consumers. Resultant multiplier effects reduced spending in 1969 over $20 billion and thus helped restrain price pressures.

In 1982 there was great concern that the 1981 tax cuts had been excessive and that inflation was emerging. To reduce that inflationary pressure, Congress withdrew some of its earlier tax cuts, especially those designed to increase investment spending. The net effect of the Tax Equity and Fiscal Responsibility Act of 1982 was to increase taxes

[signature]

① Shortfall : 2 billion
        MPC = 80%

inject
$$\frac{2,000,000,000}{5} = \$400,000,000$$

tax cut
$$\frac{400,000,000}{.80} = \$500,000,000$$

✓ No. ② Shortfall : 2 billion
        MPC = 90%

inject
$$\frac{2,000,000,000}{10} = \$200,000,000$$

tax cut
$$\frac{200,000,000}{.90} = \$222,222,222.2$$

✓ ③ National Debt is the total accumulated debt of the federal government. The deficit is a given time period in which government spending exceeds government revenue.

goes back to 1776

✓ ④ An injection is an addition of spending to the circular flow of income. Some examples of injections are : government spending, exports (+), and investments. They are significant because they help increase the GDP. A leakage is income not spent directly on output, but instead diverted from the circular flow. Examples include savings, imports, and taxes. They are significant because they attribute to a decrease in GDP.

✓ ⑤ Fiscal Policy is the use of government taxes & spending to alter macroeconomic outcomes. Fiscal Policy is controlled by the federal government.

Injections aren't affected by the MPC ✓ ⑥ A government injection into the economy is more powerful than a transfer payment because of the multiplier. Every dollar injected is multiplied by the multiplier.

✓ ⑦ Automatic fiscal stabilizers is designed to counter cyclical spending by federal expenditure/revenue item that automatically responds countercyclically to changes in national income.

beyond gov't control

✓ ⑧ Cyclical deficit is the portion of the budget balance attributable to short-run changes in economic conditions. While structural deficit is federal revenues at full employment minus expenditures at full employment under prevailing fiscal policy.

✓ ⑨ External debt is debt of the US government held by foreign households/institutions. 28% of all debt is external.

✓ ⑩ It is possible for the US to operate outside the production possibility curve because of external financing. Long-term implications of doing this is repayment. The US bonds will be wanted to turned in for cash and thus the US will have to export goods/services to pay off it's debt.

roughly $90 billion for the years 1983 to 1985. This shifted aggregate demand leftward, thus reducing price-level pressures.

The third option for fiscal restraint is to reduce transfer payments. *A cut in transfer payments works like a tax hike, reducing the disposable income of transfer recipients.* With less income, consumers spend less, as reflected in the MPC. The appropriate size of the transfer cut can be computed exactly as the desired tax increase in the preceding formula.

Although transfer cuts have the same fiscal impact as a tax hike, they're seldom used. An outright cut in transfer payments has a direct and very visible impact on recipients, including the aged, the poor, the unemployed, and the disabled. Hence, this policy option smacks of "balancing the budget on the backs of the poor." In practice, *absolute* cuts in transfer payments are rarely proposed. Instead, this lever is sometimes used to reduce the rate of increase in transfer benefits. Then only *future* benefits are reduced, and not so visibly.

FISCAL GUIDELINES

The essence of fiscal policy entails deliberate shifting of the aggregate demand curve. The steps required to formulate fiscal policy are straightforward:

- *Specify the amount of the desired AD shift* (excess AD or AD shortfall).
- *Select the policy tools needed to induce the desired shift.*

As we've seen, the fiscal policy toolbox contains a variety of tools for managing aggregate demand. When the economy is in a slump, the government can stimulate the economy with more government purchases, tax cuts, or an increase in transfer payments. When the economy is overheated, the government can reduce inflationary pressures by reducing government purchases, raising taxes, and cutting transfer payments. Table 11.3 summarizes the policy options and the desired use of each. As confusing as this list of options might at first

Macro Problem: Weak Economy (unemployment)
Policy Target: The AD Shortfall
Policy Strategy: Fiscal Stimulus (rightward AD shift)

$$\text{Desired fiscal stimulus} = \frac{\text{AD shortfall}}{\text{the multiplier}}$$

Policy Tools	Amount
• Increase government purchases	desired fiscal stimulus
• Cut taxes	$\dfrac{\text{desired fiscal stimulus}}{\text{MPC}}$
• Increase transfers	$\dfrac{\text{desired fiscal stimulus}}{\text{MPC}}$

Macro Problem: Overheated Economy (inflation)
Policy Target: The AD Excess
Policy Strategy: Fiscal Restraint (leftward AD shift)

$$\text{Desired fiscal restraint} = \frac{\text{AD excess}}{\text{the multiplier}}$$

Policy Tools	Amount
• Reduce government purchases	desired fiscal restraint
• Increase taxes	$\dfrac{\text{desired fiscal restraint}}{\text{MPC}}$
• Reduce transfer payments	$\dfrac{\text{desired fiscal restraint}}{\text{MPC}}$

TABLE 11.3
Fiscal Policy Primer

The goal of fiscal policy is to eliminate GDP gaps by shifting the AD curve rightward (to reduce unemployment) or leftward (to curb inflation). The desired shifts may be measured by the AD shortfall or the AD excess. In either case the size of the fiscal initiative is equal to the desired shift divided by the multiplier. Once the size of the desired stimulus or restraint is known, the appropriate policy response is easily calculated.

appear, the guidelines are pretty simple. To use them all one needs to know is the size of the AD shortfall or excess and the marginal prosperity to consume.

A Warning: Crowding Out

The fiscal policy guidelines in Table 11.3 are a useful guide. However, they neglect a critical dimension of fiscal policy. Notice that we haven't said anything about how the government is going to *finance* its expenditures. Suppose the government wanted to stimulate the economy with a $50 billion increase in federal purchases. How would it pay for those purchases? If the government raised taxes for this purpose, the fiscal stimulus would be largely offset by resultant declines in consumption and investment. If, instead, the government *borrows* the money from the private sector, less credit may be available to finance consumption and investment, again creating an offsetting reduction in private demand. In either case, government spending may "crowd out" some private expenditure. If this happens, some of the intended fiscal stimulus may be offset by the **crowding out** of private expenditure. We examine this possibility further in Chapter 12 when we look at the budget deficits that help finance fiscal policy.

> **crowding out:** A reduction in private-sector borrowing (and spending) caused by increased government borrowing.

Time Lags

Another limitation on fiscal policy is *time*. In the real world it takes time to recognize that the economy is in trouble. A blip in the unemployment or inflation rate may not signal a trend. Before intervening, we may want to be more certain that a recessionary or inflationary GDP gap is emerging. Then it will take time to develop a policy strategy and to get Congress to pass it. That's why President-elect Obama prepared a stimulus package even *before* he took office. He wanted Congress to authorize a stimulus program within weeks of his inauguration.

Once Congress authorizes fiscal-policy initiatives, it still takes time to implement the policy. An increase in government spending on infrastructure, for example, doesn't actually occur until bids are obtained, contracts are signed, permits are issued, and resources are assembled. That can take months. Although President Obama targeted "shovel-ready" projects in his stimulus proposals, few infrastructure projects can be cranked up instantly (see News p. 231). Even tax cuts can take months to implement.

Once fiscal stimulus actually hits the economy, we have to wait for the many steps in the multiplier process to unfold. In the best of circumstances, the fiscal policy rescue may not arrive for quite a while. In the meantime, the very nature of our macro problems could change if the economy is hit with other internal or external shocks.

Pork Barrel Politics

Congress responds to pressures rather than what should be done

└> interferes

Before putting too much faith in fiscal policy, we should also remember who designs and implements tax and spending initiatives: the U.S. Congress. Once a tax or spending plan arrives at the Capitol, politics take over. However urgent fiscal restraint might be, members of Congress are reluctant to sacrifice any spending projects in their own districts. And if taxes are to be cut, they want *their* constituents to get the biggest tax savings. And no one in Congress wants a tax hike or spending cut *before* the election. This kind of pork barrel politics can alter the content and timing of fiscal policy. We'll examine the *politics* of fiscal policy further in Chapters 12 and 18.

THE ECONOMY TOMORROW

THE CONCERN FOR CONTENT

The guidelines for fiscal policy don't say anything about how the government spends its revenue or whom it taxes. The important thing is that the right amount of spending take place at the right time. In other words, insofar as our stabilization objectives are concerned, the content of total spending is of secondary interest; the level of spending is the only thing that counts.

The "Second Crisis." But it does matter, of course, whether federal expenditures are devoted to military hardware, urban transit systems, or tennis courts. Our economic goals include not only full employment and price stability but also a desirable mix of output, an equitable distribution of income, and adequate economic growth. These other goals are directly affected by the content of total spending. The relative emphasis on, and sometimes exclusive concern for, stabilization objectives—to the neglect of related GDP content—has been designated by Joan Robinson as the "second crisis of economic theory." She explains:

> The first crisis arose from the breakdown of a theory which could not account for the *level* of employment. The second crisis arises from a theory that cannot account for the *content* of employment.
>
> Keynes was arguing against the dominant orthodoxy which held that government expenditure could not increase employment. He had to prove, first of all, that it could. He had to show that an increase in investment will increase consumption—that more wages will be spent on more beer and boots whether the investment is useful or not. He had to show that the secondary increase in real income [the multiplier effect] is quite independent of the object of the primary outlay. Pay men to dig holes in the ground and fill them up again if you cannot do anything else.
>
> There was an enormous orthodox resistance to this idea. The whole weight of the argument had to be on this one obvious point.
>
> The war was a sharp lesson in Keynesism. Orthodoxy could not stand up any longer. Government accepted the responsibility to maintain a high and stable level of employment. Then economists took over Keynes and erected the new orthodoxy. Once the point had been established the question should have changed. Now that we all agree that government expenditure can maintain employment, we should argue about what the expenditure should be for. Keynes did not *want* anyone to dig holes and fill them.[1]

The alternatives to paying people for digging and filling holes in the ground are virtually endless. With over $3 trillion to spend each year, the federal government has great influence not only on short-run prices and employment but also on the mix of output, the distribution of income, and the prospects for long-run growth. In other words, fiscal policy helps shape the dimensions of the economy tomorrow.

Public vs. Private Spending. One of the most debated issues in fiscal policy is the balance between the public and private sectors. Critics of Keynesian theory object to its apparent endorsement of government growth. They fear that using government spending to stabilize the economy will lead to an ever-larger public sector. They attribute the growth of the government's GDP share (from 10 percent in 1930 to 19 percent today) to the big-government bias of Keynesian fiscal policy.

In principle, this big-government bias doesn't exist. Keynes never said government spending was the only lever of fiscal policy. Even in 1934 he advised President Roosevelt to pursue only *temporary* increases in government spending. As we've seen, tax policy can be used to alter consumer and investor spending as well. Hence, fiscal policy can just as easily focus on changing the level of *private*-sector spending as on changing *public*-sector spending. In 1934, however, business confidence was so low that tax-induced increases in investment seemed unlikely. In less desperate times, the choice of which fiscal tool to use is a political decision, not a Keynesian mandate. President Clinton favored increased government spending to stimulate the economy, whereas President George W. Bush favored tax cuts to bolster private spending. President Obama reversed that course, with more emphasis on increased government spending (see News, p. 231).

Output Mixes within Each Sector. In addition to choosing whether to increase public or private spending, fiscal policy must also consider the specific content of spending within each sector. Suppose we determine that stimulation of the private sector is preferable to additional government spending as a means of promoting full employment. We still have many choices. We could, for example, cut corporate taxes, cut individual taxes, reduce excise taxes, or increase Social Security benefits. Each alternative implies a different mix of consumption and investment and a different distribution of income. Congressional Democrats, for example, characterized President George W. Bush's original 2001 tax-cut plan as

---

[1]From "The Second Crisis of Economic Theory," by Joan Robinson, *American Economic Review,* May 1972, p. 6. Used by permission of American Economic Association.

a "fat cat's tax break." They objected that too much of the tax cuts went to high-income taxpayers. They wanted a smaller tax cut for the rich, more tax relief for the poor, and more government spending on social programs. After months of negotiation, they got a compromise that altered both the mix of output and the distribution of income a bit more to their liking. President Obama had to make similar compromises. He believed only the government could get the economy out of recession. Initially, he wanted to focus on increased government spending and was even willing to *raise* taxes to pay for it. To get broader support for a stimulus package he had to compromise, scaling back spending plans and including tax cuts (see News, p. 231).

SUMMARY

- The economy's short-run macro equilibrium may not coincide with full employment and price stability. Keynes advocated government intervention to shift the AD curve to a more desirable equilibrium. LO1
- Fiscal policy refers to the use of the government's tax and spending powers to achieve desired macro outcomes. The tools of fiscal stimulus include increasing government purchases, reducing taxes, and raising income transfers. LO2
- Fiscal restraint may originate in reductions in government purchases, increases in taxes, or cuts in income transfers. LO2
- Government purchases add directly to aggregate demand; taxes and transfers have an indirect effect by inducing changes in consumption and investment. This makes changes in government spending more powerful per dollar than changes in taxes or transfers. LO3
- Fiscal policy initiatives have a multiplied impact on total spending and output. An increase in government

spending, for example, will result in more disposable income, which will be used to finance further consumer spending. LO3
- The objective of fiscal policy is to close GDP gaps. To do this, the aggregate demand curve must shift by *more* than the size of the GDP gap to compensate for changing price levels. The desired shift is equal to the AD shortfall (or AD excess). LO3
- Because of multiplier effects, the desired fiscal stimulus or restraint is always less than the size of the AD shortfall or AD excess. LO1
- Time lags in the design, authorization, and implementation of fiscal policy reduce its effectiveness. LO3
- Changes in government spending and taxes alter the content of GDP and thus influence what to produce. Fiscal policy affects the relative size of the public and private sectors as well as the mix of output in each sector. LO3

Key Terms

aggregate demand	fiscal stimulus	disposable income
income transfers	aggregate supply	fiscal restraint
fiscal policy	AD shortfall	inflationary GDP gap
equilibrium (macro)	multiplier	AD excess
recessionary GDP gap	marginal propensity to consume (MPC)	crowding out

Questions for Discussion

1. How can you tell if the economy is in equilibrium? How could you estimate the GDP gap? LO1
2. How did consumers spend their 2008 tax cut (News, p. 233)? Does it matter what they spend it on? Explain. LO3
3. What happens to aggregate demand when transfer payments and the taxes to pay them both rise by the same amount? LO3
4. Why are the AD shortfall and AD excess larger than their respective GDP gaps? Are they ever the same size as the GDP gap? LO1
5. Will consumers always spend the same percentage of any tax cut? Why might they spend more or less than usual? LO2

6. How does the slope of the AS curve affect the size of the AD shortfall? If the AS curve were horizontal, how large would the AD shortfall be in Figure 11.3? LO1

7. According to the World View on page 230, what prompted China's fiscal stimulus in 2008? Had the government not intervened, what might have happened? LO1

8. How quickly should Congress act to remedy an AD excess or AD shortfall? What are the risks of quick fiscal policy responses? LO2, LO3

9. Why do critics charge that fiscal policy has a "big-government bias"? LO2

10. When Barack Obama was campaigning for president in 2008, he proposed more government spending paid for with higher taxes on "the rich." What impact would those options have on macro equilibrium? LO3

11. What were the differences in size, content, and expected impact between the U.S.'s and China's 2009 stimulus packages? (World View, p. 230; News, p. 231, and Table 11.2.) LO2

web activities to accompany this chapter can be found on the Online Learning Center:
http://www.mhhe.com/schiller12e

LO2 1. In the tax-cut example on pages 231–233,
   (*a*) By how much does consumer saving increase initially? _____
   (*b*) How large is the initial spending injection? _____

LO2 2. Suppose the consumption function is

$$C = \$500 \text{ billion} + 0.9Y$$

and the government wants to stimulate the economy. By how much will aggregate demand at current prices shift initially (before multiplier effects) with
   (*a*) A $50 billion increase in government purchases? _____
   (*b*) A $50 billion tax cut? _____
   (*c*) A $50 billion increase in income transfers? _____

   What will the cumulative AD shift be for
   (*d*) The increased G? _____
   (*e*) The tax cut? _____
   (*f*) The increased transfers? _____

LO3 3. Suppose the government decides to increase taxes by $30 billion in order to increase Social Security benefits by the same amount. How will this combined tax-transfer policy affect aggregate demand at current prices? _____

LO1 4. On the accompanying graph, identify and label
   (*a*) Macro equilibrium.
   (*b*) The real GDP gap.
   (*c*) The AD excess or AD shortfall.
   (*d*) The new equilibrium that would occur with appropriate fiscal policy.

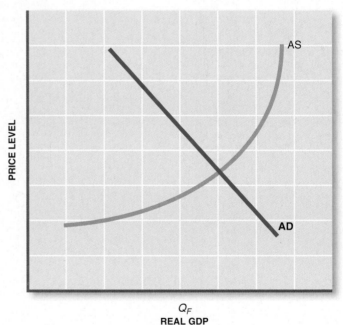

PRICE LEVEL

AS

AD

Q_F
REAL GDP

LO2 5. If the AD shortfall is $800 billion and the MPC is 0.8,
LO3   (*a*) How large is the desired fiscal stimulus? _____
   (*b*) How large an income tax cut is needed? _____
   (*c*) Alternatively, how much more government spending would achieve the target? _____

LO2 6. If the AD excess is $400 billion and the MPC is 0.9,
LO3   (*a*) How much fiscal restraint is desired? _____
   (*b*) By how much do income taxes have to be increased to get that restraint? _____

LO3 7. (*a*) According to the News on page 233, how much more did the average household spend on appliances, electronics, and furniture when it received the 2008 tax rebate? _____
   (*b*) If the MPC was 0.9, how much would cumulative spending increase as a result? _____

LO3   8. According to the World View on page 230,
    (*a*) How large was China's 2008 fiscal stimulus? $_____
    (*b*) How much faster was GDP expected to grow as a result?   _____
    (*c*) According to the News on page 231, and Table 11.2 how large was
         President Obama's proposed fiscal stimulus?   _____
    (*d*) How much faster was GDP expected to grow in 2011 as a result?   _____

LO3   9. According to the News on page 231, how much of a cumulative impact on spending could be expected
    from President Obama's
    (*a*) Increase in government spending?   _____
    (*b*) Tax cuts?   _____
    Assume an MPC of 0.8.

LO2 10. Suppose that an increase in income transfers rather than government spending was the preferred
    policy for stimulating the economy depicted in Figure 11.4. By how much would transfers have to
    increase to attain the desired shift of AD?   _____

LO3 11. If the marginal propensity to consume was 0.8, how large would each of the following need to be
    in order to restore a full-employment equilibrium in Figure 11.6?
    (*a*) A tax increase.   _____
    (*b*) A government spending cut.   _____
    (*c*) A cut in income transfers.   _____

LO1 12. Use the following data to answer the following questions:
LO3

Price level	10	20	30	40	50	60	70	80	90	100
Real GDP supplied	$500	600	680	750	820	880	910	940	960	970
Real GDP demanded	$960	920	880	840	800	760	720	680	640	600

    (*a*) If full employment occurs at a real output rate of $880, how large is the real GDP gap?   _____
    (*b*) How large is the AD shortfall?   _____
    (*c*) What will happen to prices if AD increases enough to restore full employment?   _____
    (*d*) Assuming MPC = 0.75, how will macro equilibrium change if the government purchases
         increase by $20?   _____

Deficits and Debt

LEARNING OBJECTIVES

After reading this chapter, you should be able to:

LO1. Distinguish between cyclical and structural deficits.
LO2. Explain how "crowding out" works.
LO3. Identify the burden of the national debt.

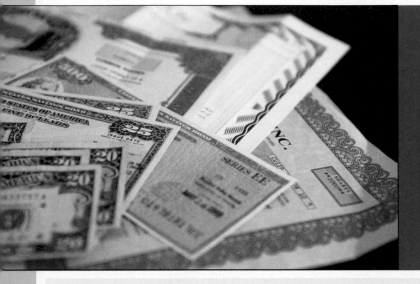

President Obama's massive 2009 stimulus package was designed to jump-start the recession-bound economy. Critics argued about both the content and size of that package. But the most biting critique of Obama's fiscal stimulus was that it would ultimately do more harm than good. Those critics argued that the massive deficits generated by Obama's "American Recovery and Reinvestment Act" (see News on the next page) would undermine America's financial stability. To pay those deficits off, the government would later be forced to *raise* taxes and *cut* spending, taking the wind out of the economy's sails. Whatever short-term boost the economy got from the fiscal stimulus would be reversed in later years.

How can this be?! Didn't we just show how tax cuts shift aggregate demand rightward, propelling the economy toward full employment? Why would anyone have misgivings about such beneficial intervention?

The core critique of fiscal stimulus focuses on the *budget* consequences of government pump-priming. Fiscal stimulus entails either tax cuts or increased government spending. Either option increases the size of the government's budget deficit. Hence, we need to ask how fiscal stimulus is *financed* before we close the books on fiscal policy. We start with these questions:

- **How do deficits arise?**
- **What harm, if any, do deficits cause?**
- **Who will pay off the accumulated national debt?**

As we'll see, the answers to these questions add an important dimension to fiscal policy debates.

Deficit Projected to Swell beyond Earlier Estimates

President Obama's ambitious plans to cut middle-class taxes, overhaul health care and expand access to college would require massive borrowing over the next decade, leaving the nation mired far deeper in debt than the White House previously estimated, congressional budget analysts said yesterday.

In the first independent analysis of Obama's budget proposal, the nonpartisan Congressional Budget Office concluded that Obama's policies would cause government spending to swell above historic levels even after costly programs to ease the recession and stabilize the nation's financial system have ended.

Tax collections, meanwhile, would lag well behind spending, producing huge annual budget deficits that would force the nation to borrow nearly $9.3 trillion over the next decade.

—Lori Montgomery

Source: *Washington Post*, March 21, 2009; p. 1.

Analysis: Fiscal stimulus widens budget deficits. The Obama $787 stimulus package caused a spike in the federal budget deficit and debt.

BUDGET EFFECTS OF FISCAL POLICY

Keynesian theory highlights the potential of **fiscal policy** to solve our macro problems. The guidelines are simple. Use fiscal stimulus—stepped-up government spending, tax cuts, increased transfers—to eliminate unemployment. Use fiscal restraint—less spending, tax hikes, reduced transfers—to keep inflation under control. From this perspective, the federal budget is a key policy tool for controlling the economy.

Use of the budget to stabilize the economy implies that federal expenditures and receipts won't always be equal. In a recession, for example, the government has sound reasons both to cut taxes and to increase its own spending. By reducing tax revenues and increasing expenditures simultaneously, however, the federal government will throw its budget out of balance. This practice is called **deficit spending,** a situation in which the government borrows funds to pay for spending that exceeds tax revenues. The size of the resulting **budget deficit** is equal to the difference between expenditures and receipts:

$$\text{Budget deficit} = \text{government spending} - \text{tax revenues} > 0$$

As Table 12.1 shows, the federal government had a huge budget deficit in 2008. In that year the government spent almost $3 trillion but had revenues of just over $2.5 trillion, leaving a budget deficit of $459 billion. That record was shattered in 2009 when the budget deficit skyrocketed to more than $1.8 *trillion!*

As Figure 12.1 illustrates, the 2008 deficit was the largest one in over 30 years. The figure also reveals, however, that budget deficits have been common. In fact, the few years (1998–2001) in which the government ran a **budget surplus** were a rare departure from the historical pattern.

fiscal policy: The use of government taxes and spending to alter macroeconomic outcomes.

Budget Surpluses and Deficits

deficit spending: The use of borrowed funds to finance government expenditures that exceed tax revenues.

budget deficit: Amount by which government spending exceeds government revenue in a given time period.

budget surplus: An excess of government revenues over government expenditures in a given time period.

Budget Total (in billions of dollars)	2004	2005	2006	2007	2008	2009	2010
Revenues	1,880	2,154	2,407	2,568	2,524	2,159	2,289
Outlays	−2,293	−2,472	−2,655	−2,729	−2,983	−4,004	−3,669
Surplus (deficit)	(413)	(318)	(248)	(161)	(459)	(1,845)	(1,380)

Source: Congressional Budget Office.

TABLE 12.1
Budget Deficits and Surpluses

Budget deficits arise when government outlays (spending) exceed revenues (receipts). When revenues exceed outlays, a budget surplus exists.

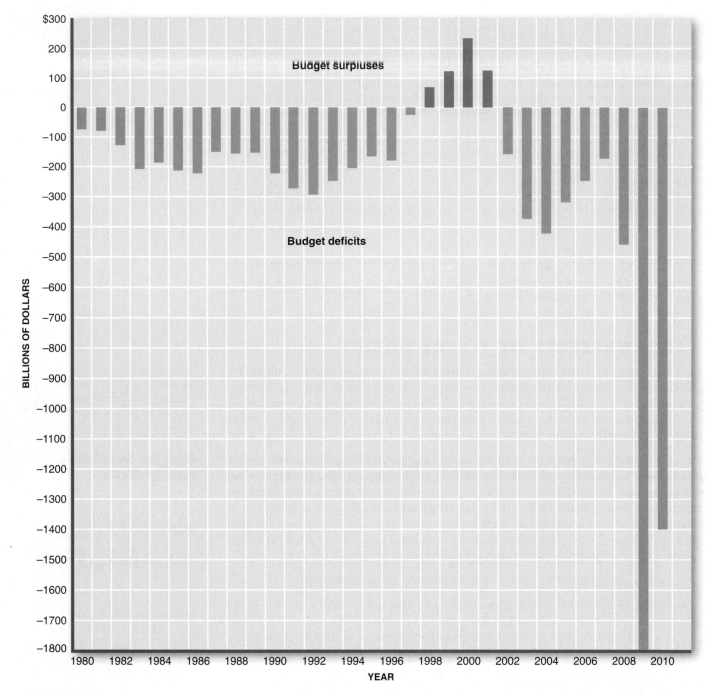

FIGURE 12.1
A String of Deficits

Budget deficits are overwhelmingly the rule, not the exception. A budget surplus was achieved in only 4 years (1998–2001) since 1970. Deficits result from both cyclical slowdowns and discretionary policies. Both forces contributed to the massive deficits of 2009–10.

Source: Congressional Budget Office.

Keynesian View. What made the budget deficits of 2003–9 so remarkable was not only their absolute size but also their sudden emergence after a brief string of budget surpluses (1998–2001). Keynes wouldn't have been too surprised by such a turnaround, however. As far as he was concerned, budget deficits and surpluses are just a routine by-product of countercyclical fiscal policy. Deficits can easily arise when the government uses fiscal stimulus to increase aggregate demand, just as fiscal restraint (tax hikes, spending cuts) may cause a budget surplus. As Keynes saw it, ***the goal of macro policy is not to balance the budget but to balance the economy (at full employment).*** If a budget deficit or surplus is needed to shift aggregate demand to the desired equilibrium, then so be it. In Keynes's view, a balanced budget would be appropriate only if all other injections and leakages were in balance and the economy was in full-employment equilibrium. As the accompanying World View confirms, other nations evidently subscribe to that conclusion as well.

WORLD VIEW

Budget Imbalances Common

Although U.S. budget deficits receive the most attention, budget imbalances are a common feature of fiscal policy. As these figures reveal, many nations had budget deficits in 2008; relatively few had budget surpluses.

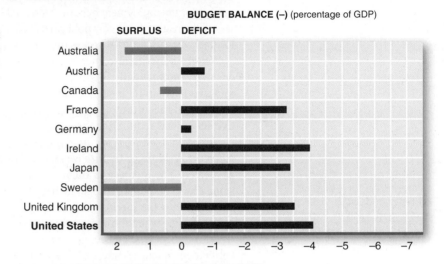

Source: International Monetary Fund. **www.imf.org.**

Analysis: To compare U.S. budget balances to those of other industrialized countries, we must adjust for differences in size by computing the *ratio* of deficits or surpluses to GDP. By this measure, U.S. budget imbalances haven't been that large in most years.

Theory aside, budget analysts tell us that Congress couldn't balance the federal budget every year even if it wanted to. Congress doesn't have as much control over spending and revenues as people assume. Hence, neither deficits nor surpluses are necessarily the result of fiscal policy decisions. To understand the limits of budget management, we have to take a closer look at how budget outlays and receipts are actually determined.

At the beginning of each year, the president and Congress put together a budget blueprint for the next **fiscal year (FY).** They don't start from scratch, however. Most budget line items reflect commitments made in earlier years. In FY 2008, for example, the federal budget included $586 billion in Social Security benefits. The FY 2008 budget also provided for $79 billion in veterans benefits, $253 billion for interest payments on the national debt, and many billions more for completion of projects begun in previous years. Short of repudiating all prior commitments, there's little that Congress or the president can do to alter these expenditures in any given year. ***To a large extent, current revenues and expenditures are the result of decisions made in prior years.*** In this sense, much of each year's budget is considered "uncontrollable."

At present, uncontrollables account for roughly 80 percent of the federal budget. This leaves only 20 percent for **discretionary fiscal spending**—that is, spending decisions not "locked in" by prior legislative commitments. In recent years, rising interest payments and increasing entitlements (Social Security, Medicare, civil service pensions, etc.) have reduced the discretionary share of the budget even further. This doesn't mean that discretionary fiscal policy is no longer important; it simply means that the potential for *changing* budget outlays in any year is much smaller than it might first appear. Yet, the ability to

Discretionary vs. Automatic Spending

fiscal year (FY): The 12-month period used for accounting purposes; begins October 1 for the federal government.

discretionary fiscal spending: Those elements of the federal budget not determined by past legislative or executive commitments.

fiscal restraint: Tax hikes or spending cuts intended to reduce (shift) aggregate demand.

fiscal stimulus: Tax cuts or spending hikes intended to increase (shift) aggregate demand.

income transfers: Payments to individuals for which no current goods or services are exchanged, such as Social Security, welfare, unemployment benefits.

automatic stabilizer: Federal expenditure or revenue item that automatically responds countercyclically to changes in national income, like unemployment benefits, income taxes.

counter cyclical spending

Cyclical Deficits

change tax or spending levels is the force behind Keynesian fiscal policy. Recall that deliberate changes in government spending or taxes are the essence of **fiscal restraint** and **fiscal stimulus.** If most of the budget is uncontrollable, those policy tools are less effective.

Automatic Stabilizers. Most of the uncontrollable line items in the federal budget have another characteristic that directly affects budget deficits: Their value *changes* with economic conditions. Consider unemployment insurance benefits. The unemployment insurance program, established in 1935, provides that persons who lose their jobs will receive some income (an average of $300 per week) from the government. The law establishes the *entitlement* to unemployment benefits but not the amount to be spent in any year. Each year's expenditure depends on how many workers lose their jobs and qualify for benefits. In 2002, for example, outlays for unemployment benefits increased by $17 billion. That increase in federal spending wasn't the result of any new policy decisions. Spending went up simply because more workers lost their jobs in the 2001 recession. The spending increase was *automatic,* not *discretionary*.

Welfare benefits also increased by $5 billion in 2002. This increase in spending also occurred automatically in response to worsened economic conditions. As more people lost jobs and used up their savings, they turned to welfare for help. They were *entitled* to welfare benefits according to eligibility rules already written; no new congressional or executive action was required to approve this increase in government spending.

Notice that **outlays for unemployment compensation and welfare benefits increase when the economy goes into recession.** This is exactly the kind of fiscal policy that Keynes advocated. The increase in **income transfers** helps offset the income losses due to recession. These increased transfers therefore act as **automatic stabilizers**—injecting new spending into the circular flow during economic contractions. Conversely, transfer payments *decline* when the economy is *expanding* and fewer people qualify for unemployment or welfare benefits. Hence, no one has to pull the fiscal policy lever to inject more or less entitlement spending into the circular flow; much of it happens automatically.

Automatic stabilizers also exist on the revenue side of the federal budget. Income taxes are an important stabilizer because they move up and down with the value of spending and output. As we've observed, if household incomes increase, a jump in consumer spending is likely to follow. The resultant multiplier effects might create some demand-pull inflation. The tax code lessens this inflationary pressure. When you get more income, you have to pay more taxes. Hence, income taxes siphon off some of the increased purchasing power that might have found its way to product markets. Progressive income taxes are particularly effective stabilizers, as they siphon off increasing proportions of purchasing power when incomes are rising and decreasing proportions when aggregate demand and output are falling.

Automatic stabilizers imply that policymakers don't have total control of each year's budget. In reality, *the size of the federal deficit or surplus is sensitive to expansion and contraction of the macro economy.*

Effects of GDP Growth. Table 12.2 shows just how sensitive the budget is to cyclical forces. When the GDP growth rate falls by 1 percent, tax revenues decline by $38 billion. As the economy slows, people also turn to the government for additional income support: Unemployment benefits and other transfer payments increase by $2 billion. As a consequence, the budget deficit increases by $40 billion. This is exactly what happened in FY 2002: The recession that began in March 2001 shrank the budget surplus by roughly $30 billion.

Effects of Inflation. Inflation also affects the budget. Because Social Security benefits are automatically adjusted to inflation, federal outlays increase as the price level rises. This added expenditure is offset, however, by inflation-swollen tax receipts. Both Social Security payroll taxes and corporate profit taxes rise automatically with inflation. These offsetting expenditure and revenue effects almost cancel each other out: Table 12.2 shows that a one-point increase in the inflation rate *shrinks* the budget deficit by only $7 billion.

The most important implication of Table 12.2 is that neither the president nor the Congress has complete control of the federal deficit. *Actual budget deficits and surpluses may*

- **Changes in Real GDP Growth**
When the GDP growth rate decreases by one percentage point:
1. Government spending (*G*) automatically increases for:
    Unemployment insurance benefits
    Food stamps
    Welfare benefits
    Social Security benefits
    Medicaid
    Total increase in outlays: +$2 billion
2. Government tax revenues (*T*) automatically decline for:
    Individual income taxes
    Corporate income taxes
    Social Security payroll taxes:
    Total decline in revenues: −$38 billion
3. **The deficit increases by $40 billion**

- **Changes in Inflation**
When the inflation rate increases by one percentage point:
1. Government spending (*G*) automatically increases for:
    Indexed retirement and Social Security benefits
    Higher interest payments
    Total increase in outlays: +$41 billion
2. Government tax revenues (*T*) automatically increase for:
    Corporate income taxes
    Social Security payroll taxes
    Total increase in revenues: +$48 billion
3. **The deficit shrinks by $7 billion**

Source: Congressional Budget Office (first-year effects).

TABLE 12.2
The Budget Impact of Cyclical Forces (in 2008 dollars)

Changes in economic conditions alter federal revenue and spending. When GDP growth slows, tax revenues decline and income transfers increase. This widens the budget deficit.

Higher rates of inflation increase both outlays and revenues but not equally.

The cyclical balance reflects these budget impacts.

arise from economic conditions as well as policy. Perhaps no one learned this better than President Reagan. In 1980 he campaigned on a promise to balance the budget. The 1981–82 recession, however, caused the actual deficit to soar. The president later had to admit that actual deficits aren't solely the product of big spenders in Washington.

President George H. Bush explained the persistence of huge deficits during his presidency on the same basis. During the recession of 1990–91, the nation's unemployment rate jumped by more than two percentage points. That setback alone added roughly $84 billion to the federal deficit.

President Clinton had more luck with the deficit. Although he increased discretionary spending in his first 2 years, the annual budget deficit *shrank* by over $90 billion between 1993 and 1995. Most of the deficit reduction was due to automatic stabilizers that kicked in as GDP growth accelerated and the unemployment rate fell. As the economy continued to grow sharply, the unemployment rate fell to 4 percent. That surge in the economy increased tax revenues, reduced income transfers, and propelled the 1998 budget into surplus. It was primarily the economy, not the president or the Congress, that produced the first budget surplus in a generation.

President Bush also benefited from GDP growth. From 2003–7, economic growth raised both incomes and tax payments. Notice in Table 12.1 how tax revenue jumped from $1,880 billion in 2004 to $2,568 billion in 2007. Tax *rates* weren't increased during those years; people were simply earning more money. The *automatic* increase in revenues helped shrink the deficit from $413 billion in 2004 to $161 in 2007.

The recession of 2008–9 reversed these favorable trends. Even before President Obama convinced Congress to cut taxes and increase government spending, the federal deficit was increasing. Tax receipts were declining as more and more workers lost paychecks. Federal

Fiscal Year	Budget Balance	=	Cyclical Component	+	Structural Component
2000	+236		+94		+142
2001	+128		+19		+109
2002	−158		−62		−96
2003	−378		−84		−294
2004	−413		−46		−367
2005	−318		−21		−297
2006	−248		−8		−240
2007	−161		−28		−133
2008	−459		−76		−383
2009	−1667		−310		−1357

Source: Congressional Budget Office (June 2009).

TABLE 12.3
Cyclical vs. Structural Budget Balances (in billions of dollars)

The budget balance includes both cyclical and structural components. Changes in the structural component result from policy changes; changes in the cyclical component result from changes in the economy. Between 2003 and 2006 the cyclical deficit shrank from $84 billion to $8 billion due to faster GDP growth. The cyclical deficit jumped again, however, when the economy fell into a recession.

web analysis

For more historical data on cyclical and structural deficits, visit the U.S. Congressional Budget Office Web site at **www.cbo.gov** and look for "Historical Budget Data."

spending was increasing as more workers sought unemployment benefits, welfare, and medical assistance.

That part of the federal deficit attributable to cyclical disturbances (unemployment and inflation) is referred to as the **cyclical deficit.** As we've observed,

cyclical deficit: That portion of the budget balance attributable to short-run changes in economic conditions.

- *The cyclical deficit widens when GDP growth slows or inflation decreases.*
- *The cyclical deficit shrinks when GDP growth accelerates or inflation increases.*

If observed budget balances don't necessarily reflect fiscal policy decisions, how are we to know whether fiscal policy is stimulative or restrictive? Clearly, some other indicator is needed.

Structural Deficits

To isolate the effects of fiscal policy, economists break down the actual budget balance into *cyclical* and *structural* components:

structural deficit: Federal revenues at full employment minus expenditures at full employment under prevailing fiscal policy.

$$\frac{\text{Total budget}}{\text{balance}} = \frac{\text{cyclical}}{\text{balance}} + \frac{\text{structural}}{\text{balance}}$$

The cyclical portion of the budget balance reflects the impact of the business cycle on federal tax revenues and spending. The **structural deficit** reflects fiscal policy decisions. Rather than comparing actual outlays to actual receipts, the structural deficit compares the outlays and receipts that would occur if the economy were at full employment.[1] This technique eliminates budget distortions caused by cyclical conditions. Any remaining changes in spending or outlays must be due to policy decisions. Hence, ***part of the deficit arises from cyclical changes in the economy; the rest is the result of discretionary fiscal policy.***

Table 12.3 shows how the total, cyclical, and structural balances have behaved in recent years. Consider what happened to the federal budget in 2000–2001. In 2000 the federal surplus was $236 billion. In 2001 the surplus shrank to $128 billion. The shrinking surplus suggests that the government was trying to stimulate economic activity with expansionary fiscal policies (tax cuts, spending hikes). But this wasn't the case. The primary reason for the smaller 2001 surplus was an abrupt halt in GDP growth. As the economy slipped into recession, the *cyclical* component shifted from a *surplus* of $94 billion in 2000 to only $19 billion in 2001. This $75 billion swing in the cyclical budget accounted for most of the decrease in

[1]The structural deficit is also referred to as the "full-employment," "high-employment," or "standardized" deficit.

the total budget surplus. By contrast, the *structural* surplus shrank only $33 billion, reflecting the absence of significant *discretionary* fiscal stimulus.

By distinguishing between the structural budget and the actual budget, we can evaluate fiscal policy more accurately. Only changes in the structural deficit are relevant. In fact, *only changes in the structural budget balance measure the dimensions of fiscal policy.* By this measure we categorize fiscal policy in the following ways:

- *Fiscal stimulus is measured by an increase in the structural deficit* (or shrinkage in the structural surplus).
- *Fiscal restraint is gauged by a decrease in the structural deficit* (or increase in the structural surplus).

According to this measure, fiscal policy was actually restrictive during the Great Depression, when fiscal stimulus was desperately needed (see accompanying News). Both Presidents

IN THE NEWS

Fiscal Policy in the Great Depression

In 1931 President Herbert Hoover observed, "Business depressions have been recurrent in the life of our country and are but transitory." Rather than proposing fiscal stimulus, Hoover complained that expansion of public-works programs had unbalanced the federal budget. In 1932 he proposed *cut-backs* in government spending and *higher* taxes. In his view, the "unquestioned balancing of the federal budget . . . is the first necessity of national stability and is the foundation of further recovery."

Franklin Roosevelt shared this view of fiscal policy. He criticized Hoover for not balancing the budget, and in 1933, warned Congress that "all public works must be considered from the point of view of the ability of the government treasury to pay for them."

As the accompanying figure shows, the budget deficit persisted throughout the Great Depression. But these deficits were the result of a declining economy, not stimulative fiscal policy. The structural deficit actually *decreased* from 1931 to 1933 (see figure), thereby restraining aggregate spending at a time when producers were desperate for increasing sales. Only when the structural deficit was expanded tremendously by spending during World War II did fiscal policy have a decidedly positive effect. Federal defense expenditures jumped from $2.2 billion in 1940 to $87.4 billion in 1944!

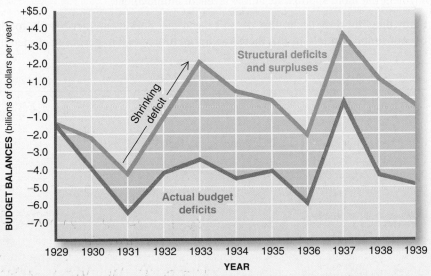

Source: Adapted from E. Cary Brown, "Fiscal Policy in the Thirties: A Reappraisal," *American Economic Review,* December 1956. Table 1. Used by permission of The American Economic Association.

Analysis: From 1931 to 1933, the structural deficit decreased from $4.5 billion to a $2 billion *surplus.* This fiscal restraint reduced aggregate demand and deepened the Great Depression.

Hoover and Roosevelt thought the government should rein in its spending when tax revenues declined, so as to keep the federal budget balanced. It took years of economic devastation before the fiscal policy lever was reversed. Also notice in Table 12.3 the abrupt shift from structural surplus (+$109) in 2001 to structural deficit (−$96) in 2002. This $205 billion swing in the structural balance reflects the fiscal stimulus of the initial Bush tax cuts and stepped-up defense spending. Nothing comes close, however, to the increase in the structural deficit caused by President Obama's fiscal-stimulus package in 2009–10.

ECONOMIC EFFECTS OF DEFICITS

No matter what the origins of budget deficits, most people are alarmed by them. Should they be? What are the *consequences* of budget deficits?

Crowding Out

> **crowding out:** A reduction in private-sector borrowing (and spending) caused by increased government borrowing.

We've already encountered one potential consequence of deficit financing: *If the government borrows funds to finance deficits, the availability of funds for private-sector spending may be reduced.* This is the **crowding-out** problem first noted in Chapter 11. If crowding out occurs, the increase in government expenditure will be at least partially offset by reductions in consumption and investment.

If the economy were operating at full employment, crowding out would be inevitable. At full employment, we'd be on the production possibilities curve, using all available resources. As Figure 12.2 reminds us, additional government purchases can occur only if private-sector purchases are reduced. In real terms, *crowding out implies less private-sector output.*

Crowding out is complete only if the economy is at full employment. If the economy is in recession, it's possible to get more public-sector output (like highways, schools, defense) without cutbacks in private-sector output. This possibility is illustrated by the move from point *c* to point *b* in Figure 12.2.

Tax cuts have crowding-out effects as well. The purpose of the 2001 tax cuts was to stimulate consumer spending. As the economy approaches full employment, however, how can more consumer output be produced? At the production possibilities limit, the added consumption will force cutbacks in either investment or government services.

What Figure 12.2 emphasizes is that *the risk of crowding out is greater the closer the economy is to full employment.* This implies that deficits are less appropriate at high levels of employment but more appropriate at low levels of employment.

> **opportunity cost:** The most desired goods or services that are forgone in order to obtain something else.

Opportunity Cost

Even if crowding out does occur, that doesn't mean that deficits are necessarily too big. Crowding out simply reminds us that there's an **opportunity cost** to government spending.

FIGURE 12.2
Crowding Out

If the economy is fully employed, an increase in public-sector expenditure (output) will reduce private-sector expenditure (output). In this case a deficit-financed increase in government expenditure moves the economy from point *a* to point *b*. In the process the quantity $h_1 - h_2$ of private-sector output is crowded out to make room for the increase in public-sector output (from g_1 to g_2). If the economy started at point *c*, however, with unemployed resources, crowding out need not occur.

We still have to decide whether the private-sector output crowded out by government expenditure is more or less desirable than the increased public-sector output.

President Clinton defended government expenditure on education, training, and infrastructure as public "investment." He believed that any resulting crowding out of private-sector expenditure wasn't necessarily an unwelcome trade-off. Public investments in education, health care, and transportation systems might even accelerate long-term economic growth.

President George W. Bush saw things differently. He preferred a mix of output that included less public-sector output and more private-sector output. Accordingly, he didn't regard any resulting crowding out of government spending as a real loss.

For his part, President Obama believes that government has to play a leading role in education, health care, infrastructure, and the development of alternative energy sources. He viewed a shift of resources from the private sector to the public sector as a necessity to promote both short-run stimulus and long-term growth. Crowding out, if it occurred, wasn't a bad thing from his perspective.

Although the production possibilities curve illustrates the inevitability of crowding out at full employment, it doesn't explain *how* the crowding out occurs. Typically, the mechanism that enforces crowding out is the rate of interest. When the government borrows more funds to finance larger deficits, it puts pressure on financial markets. That added pressure may cause interest rates to rise. If they do, households will be less eager to borrow more money to buy cars, houses, and other debt-financed products. Businesses, too, will be more hesitant to borrow and invest. Hence, *rising interest rates are both a symptom and a cause of crowding out.*

Interest-Rate Movements

Rising interests may also crowd out *government* spending in the wake of tax cuts. As interest rates rise, government borrowing costs rise as well. According to the Congressional Budget Office, a one-point rise in interest rates increases Uncle Sam's debt expenses by over $100 billion over 4 years. These higher interest costs leave less room in government budgets for financing new projects.

How much interest rates rise again depends on how close the economy is to its productive capacity. If there is lots of excess capacity, interest-rate–induced crowding out isn't very likely. This was the case in early 2009. Interest rates stayed low despite a run-up in government spending and the expectation of tax cuts. There was enough excess capacity in the economy to accommodate fiscal stimulus without crowding out. As capacity is approached, however, interest rates and crowding out are both likely to increase.

ECONOMIC EFFECTS OF SURPLUSES

Although budget deficits are clearly the norm, we might at least ponder the economic effects of budget *surpluses*. Essentially, they are the mirror image of those for deficits.

When the government takes in more revenue than it spends, it adds to leakage in the circular flow. But Uncle Sam doesn't hide the surplus under a mattress. And the sums involved (such as $236 billion in FY 2000) are too large to put in a bank. Were the government to buy corporate stock with the budget surplus, it would effectively be nationalizing private enterprises. So where does the surplus go?

Crowding In

There are really only four potential uses for a budget surplus, namely,

- *Spend it on goods and services.*
- *Cut taxes.*
- *Increase income transfers.*
- *Pay off old debt ("save it").*

The first three options effectively wipe out the surplus by changing budget outlays or receipts. There are important differences here, though. The first option—increased government spending—not only reduces the surplus but enlarges the public sector. Cutting taxes or increasing income transfers, by contrast, puts the money into the hands of consumers and enlarges the private sector.

crowding in: An increase in private-sector borrowing (and spending) caused by decreased government borrowing.

The fourth budget option is to use the surplus to pay off some of the debt accumulated from earlier deficits. This has a similar but less direct **crowding-in** effect. If Uncle Sam pays off some of his accumulated debt, households that were holding that debt (government bonds) will end up with more money. If they use that money to buy goods and services, then private-sector output will expand.

Even people who haven't lent any money to Uncle Sam will benefit from the debt reduction. When the government reduces its level of borrowing, it takes pressure off market interest rates. As interest rates drop, consumers will be more willing and able to purchase big-ticket items such as cars, appliances, and houses, thus changing the mix of output in favor of private-sector production.

Cyclical Sensitivity

Like crowding out, the extent of crowding in depends on the state of the economy. In a recession, a surplus-induced decline in interest rates isn't likely to stimulate much spending. If consumer and investor confidence are low, even a surplus-financed tax cut might not lift private-sector spending much. This was clearly the case in 2001. Taxpayers were slow to spend their tax-rebate checks and businesses were initially unpersuaded by low interest rates to increase their investment spending.

THE ACCUMULATION OF DEBT

national debt: Accumulated debt of the federal government.

Because the U.S. government has had many more years of budget deficits than budget surpluses, Uncle Sam has accumulated a large **national debt.** In fact, the United States started out in debt. The Continental Congress needed to borrow money in 1777 to continue fighting the Revolutionary War. The Congress tried to raise tax revenues and even printed new money (the Continental dollar) in order to buy needed food, tents, guns, and ammunition. But by the winter of 1777, these mechanisms for financing the war were failing. To acquire needed supplies, the Continental Congress plunged the new nation into debt.

Debt Creation

Treasury bonds: Promissory notes (IOUs) issued by the U.S. Treasury.

As with today's deficits, the Continental Congress acknowledged its loans by issuing bonds. Today the U.S. Treasury is the fiscal agent of the U.S. government. The Treasury collects tax revenues, signs checks for federal spending, and—when necessary—borrows funds to cover budget deficits. When the Treasury borrows funds, it issues **Treasury bonds;** these are IOUs of the federal government. People buy bonds—lend money to the U.S. Treasury— because bonds pay interest and are a very safe haven for idle funds.

The total stock of all outstanding bonds represents the national debt. It's equal to the sum total of our accumulated deficits, less net repayments in years when a budget surplus existed. In other words, *the national debt is a stock of IOUs created by annual deficit flows.* Whenever there's a budget deficit, the national debt increases. In years when a budget surplus exists, the national debt can be pared down.

Early History, 1776–1900

The United States began accumulating debt as soon as independence was declared. By 1783, the United States had borrowed over $8 million from France and $250,000 from Spain. Most of these funds were secretly obtained to help finance the Revolutionary War.

During the period 1790–1812, the United States often incurred debt but typically repaid it quickly. The War of 1812, however, caused a massive increase in the national debt. With neither a standing army nor an adequate source of tax revenues to acquire one, the U.S. government had to borrow money to repel the British. By 1816, the national debt was over $129 million. Although that figure seems tiny by today's standards, it amounted to 13 percent of national income in 1816.

1835–1836: Debt-Free! After the War of 1812, the U.S. government used recurrent budget surpluses to repay its debt. These surpluses were so frequent that the U.S. government was completely out of debt by 1835. In 1835 and again in 1836, the government had neither national debt nor a budget deficit. The dilemma in those years was how to use the budget *surplus!* Since there was no accumulated debt, the option of using the surplus to reduce the debt didn't exist. In the end, Congress decided simply to distribute the surplus funds to the states. That was the last time the U.S. government was completely out of debt.

The Mexican-American War (1846–48) necessitated a sudden increase in federal spending. The deficits incurred to fight that war caused a fourfold increase in the debt. That debt was pared down the following decade. Then the Civil War (1861–65) broke out, and both sides needed debt financing. By the end of the Civil War, the North owed over $2.6 billion, or approximately half its national income. The South depended more heavily on newly printed Confederate currency to finance its side of the Civil War, relying on bond issues for only one-third of its financial needs. When the South lost, however, neither Confederate currency nor Confederate bonds had any value.[2]

The Spanish-American War (1898) also increased the national debt. But all prior debt was dwarfed by World War I, which increased the national debt from 3 percent of national income in 1917 to 41 percent at the war's end.

Twentieth Century

The national debt declined during the 1920s because the federal government was consistently spending less revenue than it took in. Budget surpluses disappeared quickly when the economy fell into the Great Depression, however, and the cyclical deficit widened (see News, p. 253).

World War II. The most explosive jump in the national debt occurred during World War II, when the government had to mobilize all available resources. Rather than raise taxes to the fullest, the U.S. government restricted the availability of consumer goods. With consumer goods rationed, consumers had little choice but to increase their saving. Uncle Sam encouraged people to lend their idle funds to the U.S. Treasury by buying U.S. war bonds. The resulting bond purchases raised the national debt from 45 percent of GDP in 1940 to over 125 percent of GDP in 1946 (see Figure 12.3).

The 1980s. During the 1980s, the national debt jumped again—by nearly $2 *trillion*. This 10-year increase in the debt exceeded all the net debt accumulation since the country was founded. This time, however, the debt increase wasn't war-related. Instead, the debt explosion of the 1980s originated in recessions (1980–82 and 1990–91), massive tax cuts (1981–84), and increased defense spending. The recessions caused big jumps in the cyclical deficit while the Reagan tax cuts and military buildup caused the structural deficit to jump fourfold in only 4 years (1982–86).

The 1990s. The early 1990s continued the same trend. Discretionary federal spending increased sharply in the first 2 years of the George H. Bush administration. The federal government was also forced to bail out hundreds of failed savings and loan associations. Although taxes were raised a bit and military spending was cut back, the structural deficit was little changed. Then the recession of 1990–91 killed any chance of achieving smaller deficits. In only 4 years (1988–92) the national debt increased by another $1 trillion.

In 1993, the Clinton administration persuaded Congress to raise taxes, thereby reducing the structural deficit. Continuing recovery from the 1990–91 recession also reduced the cyclical deficit. Nevertheless, the budget deficits of 1993–96 pushed the national debt to over $5 trillion.

2000–. After a couple of years of budget surplus, the accumulated debt still exceeded $5.6 trillion in 2002. Then the Bush tax cuts and the defense buildup kicked in, increasing the structural deficit by nearly $300 billion in only 3 years (FY 2002–4) (Table 12.4). As a consequence, the national debt surged again. By January 2009—*before* the Obama stimulus plan was enacted—the debt exceeded $10 trillion, which works out to more than $37,000 of debt for every U.S. citizen.

---

[2]In anticipation of this situation, European leaders had forced the South to guarantee most of its loans with cotton. When the South was unable to repay its debts, these creditors could sell the cotton they had held as collateral. But most holders of Confederate bonds or currency received nothing.

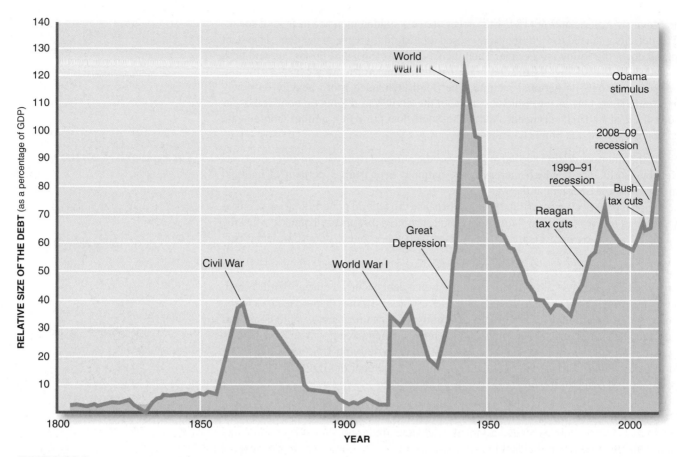

FIGURE 12.3
Historical View of the Debt/GDP Ratio

From 1790 to 1917, the national debt exceeded 10 percent of GDP during the Civil War years only. After 1917, however, the debt ratio grew sharply. World War I, the Great Depression, and World War II all caused major increases in the debt ratio. The tax cuts of 1981–84 and 2001–5 and the recessions of 1990–91, 2001, and 2008–9 caused further increases in the debt/GDP ratio. The Obama fiscal stimulus pushed the debt ratio still higher.

Source: Office of Management and Budget.

TABLE 12.4
The National Debt

It took nearly a century for the national debt to reach $1 trillion. Then the debt tripled in a mere decade. The accumulated debt now totals more than $11 trillion.

Year	Total Debt Outstanding (millions of dollars)	Year	Total Debt Outstanding (millions of dollars)
1791	75	1930	16,185
1800	83	1940	42,967
1810	53	1945	258,682
1816	127	1960	286,331
1820	91	1970	370,919
1835	0	1980	914,300
1850	63	1985	1,827,500
1865	2,678	1990	3,163,000
1900	1,263	2000	5,629,000
1915	1,191	2009	10,500,000
1920	24,299		

Source: Office of Management and Budget.

WHO OWNS THE DEBT?

To the average citizen, the accumulated national debt is both incomprehensible and frightening. Who can understand debts that are measured in *trillions* of dollars? Who can ever be expected to pay them?

The first thing to note about the national debt is that it represents not only a liability but an asset as well. When the U.S. Treasury borrows money, it issues bonds. Those bonds are a **liability** for the federal government since it must later repay the borrowed funds. But those same bonds are an **asset** to the people who hold them. Bondholders have a claim to future repayment. They can even convert that claim into cash by selling their bonds in the bond market. Therefore, *national debt creates as much wealth (for bondholders) as liabilities (for the U.S. Treasury).* Neither money nor any other form of wealth disappears when the government borrows money.

The fact that total bond assets equal total bond liabilities is of little consolation to taxpayers confronted with $11 trillion of national debt and worried about when, if ever, they'll be able to repay it. The fear that either the U.S. government or its taxpayers will be "bankrupted" by the national debt always lurks in the shadows. How legitimate is that fear?

Figure 12.4 shows who owns the bonds the U.S. Treasury has issued. The largest bondholder is the U.S. government itself: *Federal agencies hold almost half of all outstanding Treasury bonds.* The Federal Reserve System, an independent agency of the U.S. government, acquires Treasury bonds in its conduct of monetary policy (see Chapters 14 and 15). Other agencies of the U.S. government also purchase bonds. The Social Security Administration, for example, maintains a trust fund balance to cover any shortfall between monthly payroll tax receipts and retirement benefits. Most of that balance is held in the form of interest-bearing Treasury bonds. Thus, one arm of the federal government (the U.S. Treasury) owes another arm (the U.S. Social Security Administration) a significant part of the national debt. Because Social Security has been accumulating huge annual reserves in recent years, it's now the largest single holder of the national debt.

State and local governments hold another 5 percent of the national debt. This debt, too, arises when state and local governments use their own budget surpluses to purchase interest-bearing Treasury bonds.

The private sector owns only about 17 percent of the national debt. This private wealth is in the form of familiar U.S. savings bonds or other types of Treasury bonds. Much of this private wealth is held *indirectly* by banks, insurance companies, money market funds, corporations, and other institutions. All this wealth is ultimately owned by the people who have

Liabilities = Assets

liability: An obligation to make future payment; debt.

asset: Anything having exchange value in the marketplace; wealth.

Ownership of the Debt

FIGURE 12.4
Debt Ownership

The bonds that create the national debt represent wealth that's owned by bondholders. Half of that wealth is held by the U.S. government itself. The private sector in the United States holds only 17 percent of the debt, and foreigners own about 28 percent.

Source: U.S. Treasury Department (2008 data).

[handwritten annotations: Internal; 72% of the debt is internal debt; External]

Pie chart: Public Sector — Federal reserve 5%, Federal agencies 22%; Foreigners 28%; State and local governments 5%; Private Sector 17%

internal debt: U.S. government debt (Treasury bonds) held by U.S. households and institutions.

deposits at the bank or in money market funds, who own stock in corporations, or who are insured by companies that hold Treasury bonds. Thus, *U.S. households hold about one-sixth of the national debt, either directly or indirectly.*

All the debt held by U.S. households, institutions, and government entities is referred to as **internal debt.** As Figure 12.4 illustrates, 72 percent of the national debt is internal. In other words, *we owe most of the national debt to ourselves.*

The remaining 28 percent of the national debt is held by foreign banks, corporations, households, and governments. U.S. Treasury bonds are attractive to global participants because of their relative security, the interest they pay, and the general acceptability of dollar-denominated assets in world trade. Bonds held by foreign households and institutions are referred to as **external debt.**

external debt: U.S. government debt (Treasury bonds) held by foreign households and institutions.

BURDEN OF THE DEBT

It may be comforting to know that most of our national debt is owned internally, and much of it by the government itself. Figure 12.4 won't still the fears of most taxpayers, however, especially those who don't hold any Treasury bonds. From their perspective, the total debt still looks frightening.

refinancing: The issuance of new debt in payment of debt issued earlier.

Refinancing

How much of a "burden" the debt really represents isn't so evident. For nearly 30 years (1970–97), the federal government kept piling up more debt without apparent economic damage. The few years that the government had a budget surplus (1998–2001) weren't markedly different from the deficit years. As we saw earlier (Figure 12.3), deficits and debt stretched out over even longer periods in earlier decades without apparent economic damage.

How was the government able to pile debt upon debt? Quite simple: As debts have become due, the federal government has simply borrowed new funds to pay them off. New bonds have been issued to replace old bonds. This **refinancing** of the debt is a routine feature of the U.S. Treasury's debt management.

The ability of the U.S. Treasury to refinance its debt raises an intriguing question. What if the debt could be eternally refinanced? What if no one *ever* demanded to be paid off more than others were willing to lend Uncle Sam? Then the national debt would truly grow forever.

"**What's this I hear about you adults mortgaging my future?**"

Analysis: The fear that present generations are passing the debt burden to future generations is exaggerated.

Two things are worrisome about this scenario. First, eternal refinancing seems like a chain letter that promises to make everyone rich. In this case, the chain requires that people hold ever-larger portions of their wealth in the form of Treasury bonds. People worry that the chain will be broken and that they'll be forced to repay all the outstanding debt. Parents worry that the scheme might break down in the next generation, unfairly burdening their own children or grandchildren (see cartoon).

Aside from its seeming implausibility, the notion of eternal refinancing seems to defy a basic maxim of economics, namely, that "there ain't no free lunch." Eternal refinancing makes it look as though government borrowing has no cost, as though federal spending financed by the national debt is really a free lunch.

There are two flaws in this way of thinking. The first relates to the interest charges that accompany debt. The second, and more important, oversight relates to the real economic costs of government activity.

Debt Service

debt service: The interest required to be paid each year on outstanding debt.

With over $11 trillion in accumulated debt, the U.S. government must make enormous interest payments every year. **Debt service** refers to these annual interest payments. In FY 2009, the U.S. Treasury paid over $200 billion in interest charges. These interest payments force the government to reduce outlays for other purposes or to finance a larger budget each year. In this respect, *interest payments restrict the government's ability to balance the budget or fund other public-sector activities.*

Although the debt-servicing requirements may pinch Uncle Sam's spending purse, the real economic consequences of interest payments are less evident. Who gets the interest payments? What economic resources are absorbed by those payments?

As noted, most of the nation's outstanding debt is internal—that is, owned by domestic households and institutions. Therefore, most interest payments are made to people and institutions within the United States. ***Most debt servicing is simply a redistribution of income from taxpayers to bondholders.*** In many cases, the taxpayer and bondholder are the same person. In all cases, however, the income that leaks from the circular flow in the form of taxes to pay for debt servicing returns to the circular flow as interest payments. Total income is unchanged. Thus, debt servicing may not have any direct effect on the level of aggregate demand.

Debt servicing also has little impact on the real resources of the economy. The collection of additional taxes and the processing of interest payments require the use of some land, labor, and capital. But the value of the resources used for the processing of debt service is trivial—a tiny fraction of the interest payments themselves. This means that ***interest payments themselves have virtually no direct opportunity cost.*** The amount of goods and services available for other purposes is virtually unchanged as a result of debt servicing.

Opportunity Costs

If debt servicing absorbs few economic resources, can we conclude that the national debt really does represent a free lunch? Unfortunately not. But the concept of opportunity cost does provide a major clue about the true burden of the debt and who bears it.

Opportunity costs are incurred only when real resources (factors of production) are used. The amount of that cost is measured by the other goods and services that could have been produced with those resources, but weren't. As noted earlier, the *process* of debt servicing absorbs few resources and so has negligible opportunity cost. To understand the true burden of the national debt, we have to look at what that debt financed. ***The true burden of the debt is the opportunity cost of the activities financed by the debt.*** To assess that burden, we need to ask what the government did with the borrowed funds.

Government Purchases. Suppose Congress decides to upgrade our naval forces and borrows $10 billion for that purpose. What's the opportunity cost of that decision? The economic cost of the fleet upgrade is measured by the goods and services forgone in order to build more ships. The labor, land, and capital used to upgrade the fleet can't be used to produce something else. We give up the opportunity to produce another $10 billion worth of private goods and services when Congress upgrades the fleet.

The economic cost of the naval buildup is unaffected by the method of government finance. Whether the government borrows $10 billion or increases taxes by that amount, the forgone civilian output will still be $10 billion. ***The opportunity cost of government purchases is the true burden of government activity, however financed.*** The decision to finance such activity with debt rather than taxes doesn't materially alter that cost.

Transfer Payments. Suppose the government uses debt financing to pay for increased transfer payments rather than the purchase of real goods and services. What would be the burden of debt in this case?

Note first that transfer payments entail few real costs. Income transfers entail a redistribution of income from the taxpayer to the transfer recipient. The only direct costs of those transfer payments are the land, labor, and capital involved in the administrative process of making that transfer. Those direct costs are so trivial that they can be ignored. Whatever changes in output or prices occur because of transfer payments result from *indirect* behavioral responses. If taxpayers or transfer recipients respond to transfers by working, saving, or investing less, the economy may suffer. These important *indirect* effects must be distinguished from the *direct* cost of the transfers, which are minimal. As a result, the amount of income transferred isn't a meaningful measure of economic burden. Hence, the debt that originated in deficit-financed income transfers can't be viewed as a unique "burden" either.

The Real Trade-Offs

Although the national debt poses no special burden to the economy, the transactions it finances have a substantial impact on the basic questions of WHAT, HOW, and FOR WHOM to produce. The mix of output is influenced by how much deficit spending the government undertakes. The funds obtained by borrowing allow the federal government to bid for scarce resources. Private investors and consumers will have less access to loanable funds and be less able to acquire incomes or goods. The larger the deficit, the more the private sector gets crowded out. Hence, deficit financing allows the government to obtain more resources and change the mix of output. In general, *deficit financing tends to change the mix of output in the direction of more public-sector goods.*

As noted earlier, the deficits of the 1980s helped finance a substantial military buildup. The same result could have been financed with higher taxes. Taxes are more visible and always unpopular, however. By borrowing rather than taxing, the federal government's claim on scarce resources is less apparent. Either financing method allows the public sector to expand at the expense of the private sector. This resource reallocation reveals the true burden of the debt: *The burden of the debt is really the opportunity cost (crowding out) of deficit-financed government activity.* How large that burden is depends on how many unemployed resources are available and the behavioral responses of consumers and investors to increased government activity.

Notice also *when* that cost is incurred. If the military is upgraded this year, then the opportunity cost is incurred this year. It's only while resources are actually being used by the military that we give up the opportunity to use them elsewhere. Opportunity costs are incurred at the time a government activity takes place, not when the resultant debt is paid. In other words, *the primary burden of the debt is incurred when the debt-financed activity takes place.*

If the entire military buildup is completed this year, what costs are borne next year? None. The land, labor, and capital available next year can be used for whatever purposes are then desired. Once the military buildup is completed, no further resources are allocated to that purpose. The real costs of government projects can't be postponed until a later year. In other words, the real burden of the debt can't be passed on to future generations. On the contrary, future generations will benefit from the sacrifices made today to build ships, parks, highways, dams, and other public-sector projects. Future taxpayers will be able to *use* these projects without incurring the opportunity costs of their construction.

Economic Growth. Although future generations may benefit from current government spending, they may also be adversely affected by today's opportunity costs. Of particular concern is the possibility that government deficits might crowd out private investment. Investment is essential to enlarging our production possibilities and attaining higher living standards in the future. If federal deficits and debt-servicing requirements crowd our private investment, the rate of economic growth will slow, leaving future generations with less productive capacity than they would otherwise have. Thus, *if debt-financed government spending crowds out private investment, future generations will bear some of the debt burden.* Their burden will take the form of smaller-than-anticipated productive capacity.

There's no certainty that such crowding out will occur. Also, any reduction in private investment may be offset by public works (such as highways, schools, defense systems) that benefit future generations. So future generations may not suffer a net loss in welfare even if the national debt slows private investment and economic growth. From this perspective, *the whole debate about the burden of the debt is really an argument over the optimal mix of output.* If we permit more deficit spending, we're promoting more public-sector activity. On the other hand, limits on deficit financing curtail growth of the public sector. *Battles over deficits and debts are a proxy for the more fundamental issue of private versus public spending.*

Repayment. All this sounds a little too neat. Won't future generations have to pay interest on the debts we incur today? And might they even have to pay off some of the debt?

We've already observed that the collection of taxes and processing of interest payments absorb relatively few resources. Hence, the mechanisms of repayment entail little burden.

Notice also who *receives* future interest payments. When we die, we leave behind not only the national debt but also the bonds that represent ownership of that debt. Hence,

optimal mix of output: The most desirable combination of output attainable with existing resources, technology, and social values.

future grandchildren will be both taxpayers *and* bondholders. If interest payments are made 30 years from today, only people who are alive and holding bonds at that time will receive interest payments. ***Future interest payments entail a redistribution of income among taxpayers and bondholders living in the future.***

The same kind of redistribution occurs if and when our grandchildren decide to pay off the debt. Tax revenues will be used to pay off the debt. The debt payments will go to people then holding Treasury bonds. The entire redistribution will occur among people living in the future.

EXTERNAL DEBT

The nature of opportunity costs makes it difficult but not impossible to pass the debt burden on to future generations. The exception is the case of external debt.

When we borrow funds from abroad, we increase our ability to consume, invest, and finance government activity. In effect, other nations are lending us the income necessary to *import* more goods. If we can buy imports with borrowed funds (without offsetting exports), our real income will exceed our production possibilities. As Figure 12.5 illustrates, external borrowing allows us to enjoy a mix of output that lies *outside* our production possibilities curve. Specifically, ***external financing allows us to get more public-sector goods without cutting back on private-sector production (or vice versa).*** When we use external debt to finance government spending, we move from point *a* to point *d* in Figure 12.5. Imported goods and services eliminate the need to cut back on private-sector activity, a cutback that would otherwise force us to point *b*. External financing eliminates this opportunity cost. The move from point *a* to point *d* reflects the additional imports financed by external debt.

The imports needn't be public-sector goods. A tax cut at point *b* might increase consumption and imports by $h_1 - h_2$, moving the economy to point *d*. At *d* we have *more* consumption and *no less* government activity.

External financing appears to offer the proverbial free lunch. It would be a free lunch if foreign lenders were willing to accumulate U.S. Treasury bonds forever. They would then own stacks of paper (Treasury bonds), and we'd consume some of their output (our imports) each year. ***As long as outsiders are willing to hold U.S. bonds, external financing imposes no real cost.*** No goods or services are given up to pay for the additional output received.

Foreign investors may not be willing to hold U.S. bonds indefinitely. At some point they'll want to collect their bills. To do this, they'll cash in (sell) their bonds, then use the proceeds to buy U.S. goods and services. When this happens, the United States will be *exporting* goods and

No Crowding Out

Repayment

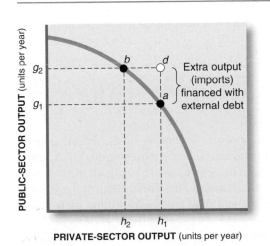

[handwritten: Increases gov't spending w/o decreasing output of the private sector]

FIGURE 12.5
External Financing

A closed economy must forsake some private-sector output in order to increase public-sector output (see Figure 12.2). External financing temporarily eliminates that opportunity cost. Instead of having to move from *a* to *b*, external borrowing allows us to move from *a* to *d*. At point *d* we have more public output and no less private output.

services to pay off its debts. Recall that the external debt was used to acquire imported goods and services. Hence, *external debt must be repaid with exports of real goods and services.*

DEFICIT AND DEBT LIMITS

Although external and internal debts pose very different problems, most policy discussions overlook these distinctions. In policy debates, the aggregate size of the national debt is usually the only concern. The key policy questions are whether and how to limit or reduce the national debt.

Deficit Ceilings

deficit ceiling: An explicit, legislated limitation on the size of the budget deficit.

The only way to stop the growth of the national debt is to eliminate the budget deficits that create debt. The first step in debt reduction, therefore, is a balanced annual budget. A balanced budget will at least stop the debt from growing further. **Deficit ceilings** are explicit limitations on the size of the annual budget deficit. A deficit ceiling of zero compels a balanced budget.

The Balanced Budget and Emergency Deficit Control Act of 1985—popularly referred to as the Gramm-Rudman-Hollings Act—was the first explicit attempt to force the federal budget into balance. The essence of the Gramm-Rudman-Hollings Act was simple:

* First, it set a lower ceiling on each year's deficit, until budget balance was achieved.
* Second, it called for automatic cutbacks in spending if Congress failed to keep the deficit below the ceiling.

The original Gramm-Rudman-Hollings law required Congress to pare the deficit from over $200 billion in FY 1985 to zero (a balanced budget) by 1991. But Congress wasn't willing to cut spending and increase taxes enough to meet those targets. And the Supreme Court declared that the "automatic" mechanism for spending cuts was unconstitutional.

In 1990, President George H. Bush and the Congress developed a new set of rules for reducing the deficit. They first acknowledged that they lacked total control of the deficit. At best, Congress could close the *structural* deficit by limiting discretionary spending or raising taxes. The Budget Enforcement Act (BEA) of 1990 laid out a plan for doing exactly this. The BEA set separate limits on defense spending, discretionary domestic spending, and international spending. It also required that any new spending initiative be offset with increased taxes or cutbacks in other programs—a process called "pay as you go," or simply "paygo."

The Budget Enforcement Act was successful in reducing the structural deficit somewhat. But the political pain associated with spending cuts and higher taxes was too great for elected officials to bear. Soon thereafter, legislated deficit ceilings proved to be more political ornaments than binding budget mandates.

Debt Ceilings

debt ceiling: An explicit, legislated limit on the amount of outstanding national debt.

Explicit **debt ceilings** are another mechanism for forcing Congress to adopt specific fiscal policies. A debt ceiling can be used either to stop the accumulation of debt or to force the federal government to start *reducing* the accumulated national debt. In effect, debt ceilings are a backdoor approach to deficit reduction. *Like deficit ceilings, debt ceilings are really just political mechanisms for forging compromises on how best to use budget deficits.*

THE ECONOMY TOMORROW

DIPPING INTO SOCIAL SECURITY

The Social Security Trust Fund has been a major source of funding for the federal government for over 25 years. Since 1985, the Trust Fund has collected more payroll (FICA) taxes each year than it has paid out in retirement benefits. As we noted already, all of those surpluses have been "invested" in Treasury securities, making the Social Security Trust Fund the U.S. Treasury's largest creditor. The Trust Fund now holds $2.5 trillion of Treasury securities and is still accumulating more. Between 2009 and 2014, the Trust Fund will acquire another $1.5 trillion in Treasury securities.

Year	Workers per Beneficiary	Year	Workers per Beneficiary
1950	16.5	2000	3.4
1960	5.1	2015	2.7
1970	3.7	2030	2.0

Source: U.S. Social Security Administration.

TABLE 12.5
Changing Worker-Retiree Ratios

Fifty years ago there were over 16 tax-paying workers for every retiree. Today there are only 3, and the ratio slips further when the Baby Boomers start retiring. This demographic change will convert Social Security surpluses into deficits, causing future budget problems.

Aging Baby Boomers. The persistent surpluses in the Social Security Trust Fund are largely the result of aging Baby Boomers. In the 15 years after World War II ended, birthrates soared. These Baby Boomers are now in their peak earning years (45–60) and paying lots of payroll taxes. This keeps the Social Security Trust Fund flush with cash.

As we peer into the economy tomorrow, however, the fiscal outlook is not so bright. The Baby Boomers are fast approaching retirement age. When they do retire, the Baby Boomers will throw the budget of the Social Security Trust Fund out of whack. Today, there are 3 active (tax-paying) workers for every retiree. By 2015, that worker-retiree ratio will slip to 2.7. By 2030, there'll be only 2 workers for every retiree (see Table 12.5). By then, the Trust Fund payroll-tax collections will be a lot smaller than the benefit promises made to retired Baby Boomers. When that happens, a primary source of government financing will disappear.

Social Security Deficits. In fact, the Trust Fund balance shifts from annual surpluses to annual deficits as soon as 2014. After that, Social Security will be able to pay promised benefits only if (1) the U.S. Treasury pays all interest due on bonds held by the Trust Fund and, ultimately, (2) the U.S. Treasury redeems the $4 trillion-plus of bonds the Trust Fund will then be holding. This is what scares aging Baby Boomers (and should worry you!).

The Baby Boomers wonder where the Treasury is going to get the funds needed to repay the Social Security Trust Fund. There really aren't many options. ***To pay back Social Security loans, the Congress will have to raise future taxes significantly, make substantial cuts in other (non–Social Security) programs or sharply increase budget deficits.*** None of these options is attractive. Worse yet, the budget squeeze created by the Social Security payback will severely limit the potential for discretionary fiscal policy.

When GDP growth slows in the economy tomorrow, it will be increasingly difficult to cut taxes or increase government spending while the U.S. Treasury is scurrying to repay Social Security Trust Fund loans. Aging Baby Boomers worry that Congress might instead cut their promised retirement benefits.

SUMMARY

- Budget deficits result from both discretionary fiscal policy (structural deficits) and cyclical changes in the economy (cyclical deficits).   LO1
- Fiscal restraint is measured by the reduction in the structural deficit; fiscal stimulus occurs when the structural deficit increases.   LO1
- Automatic stabilizers increase federal spending and reduce tax revenues during recessions. When the economy

expands, they have the reverse effect, thereby shrinking the cyclical deficit.   LO1
- Deficit financing of government expenditure may crowd out private investment and consumption. The risk of crowding out increases as the economy approaches full employment. If investment becomes the opportunity cost of increased government spending or consumer tax cuts, economic growth may slow.   LO2

- Crowding in refers to the increase in private-sector output made possible by a decline in government borrowing.   LO2
- Each year's deficit adds to the national debt. The national debt grew sporadically until World War II and then sky-rocketed. Tax cuts, recessions, and increased government spending since 1980 have increased the national debt to over $11 trillion.   LO1
- Budget surpluses may be used to finance tax cuts or more government spending, or used to reduce accumulated national debt.   LO2
- Every dollar of national debt represents a dollar of assets to the people who hold U.S. Treasury bonds. Most U.S. bonds are held by U.S. government agencies, U.S. households, and U.S. banks, insurance companies, and other institutions, and are thus "internal debt".   LO3

- The real burden of the debt is the opportunity cost of the activities financed by the debt. That cost is borne at the time the deficit-financed activity takes place. The benefits of debt-financed activity may extend into the future.   LO3
- External debt (bonds held by foreigners) permits the public sector to expand without reducing private-sector output. External debt also makes it possible to shift some of the real debt burden on to future generations.   LO3
- Deficit and debt ceilings are largely symbolic efforts to force consideration of real trade-offs, to restrain government spending, and to change the mix of output.   LO3
- The coming retirement of the Baby Boomers (born 1946–60) will transform Social Security surpluses into deficits, imposing severe constraints on future fiscal policy.   LO1

Key Terms

fiscal policy	automatic stabilizer	asset
deficit spending	cyclical deficit	internal debt
budget deficit	structural deficit	external debt
budget surplus	crowding out	refinancing
fiscal year (FY)	opportunity cost	debt service
discretionary fiscal spending	crowding in	optimal mix of output
fiscal restraint	national debt	deficit ceiling
fiscal stimulus	Treasury bonds	debt ceiling
income transfers	liability	

Questions for Discussion

1. Who paid for the Revolutionary War? Did the deficit financing initiated by the Continental Congress pass the cost of the war on to future generations?   LO3
2. When are larger deficits desirable?   LO2
3. Can you forecast next year's deficit without knowing how fast GDP will grow?   LO1
4. In what ways do *future* generations benefit from this generation's deficit spending? Cite three examples.   LO3
5. What's considered "too much" debt or "too large" a deficit? Are you able to provide any guidelines for deficit or debt ceilings?   LO2
6. If deficit spending "crowds out" some private investment, could future generations be worse off? If external financing eliminates crowding out, are future generations thereby protected?   LO2

7. A constitutional amendment has been proposed that would require Congress to balance the budget each year. Is it possible to balance the budget each year? Is it desirable?   LO1
8. By how much did defense spending increase in 1940 to 1944? (See back endpapers of this book.) What was crowded out?   LO2
9. How long would it take to pay off the national debt? How would the economy be affected?   LO3
10. Which of the following options do you favor for resolving future Social Security deficits? What are the advantages and disadvantages of each option? (a) cutting Social Security benefits, (b) raising payroll taxes, (c) cutting non–Social Security programs, and (d) raising income taxes.   LO1

 web activities to accompany this chapter can be found on the Online Learning Center:
http://www.mhhe.com/schiller12e

LO1   1. From 2006 to 2008 how did each of the following change?
    (*a*) Tax revenue   _____
    (*b*) Government spending   _____
    (*c*) Budget deficit   _____
    (*Note:* See Table 12.1.)

LO1   2. Since 1980, in how many years has the federal budget had a surplus? (See Figure 12.1.)   _____

LO1   3. What country had the largest budget deficit (as percent of GDP) in 2008?   _____

LO1   4. What would happen to the budget deficit if the
    (*a*) GDP growth rate jumped from 1 percent to 3 percent?   _____
    (*b*) Inflation rate increased by two percentage points?   _____
    (*Note:* See Table 12.2 for clues.)

LO1   5. Use Table 12.3 to determine how much fiscal stimulus or restraint occured between
    (*a*) 2003 and 2004.   _____
    (*b*) 2006 and 2007.   _____
    (*c*) 2008 and 2009.   _____

LO1   6. Suppose a government has no debt and a balanced budget. Suddenly it decides to spend $10 billion while raising only $8 billion worth of taxes.
    (*a*) What will be the government's deficit?   _____
    (*b*) If the government finances the deficit by issuing bonds, what amount of bonds will it issue?   _____
    (*c*) At a 10 percent rate of interest, how much interest will the government pay each year?   _____
    (*d*) Add the interest payment to the government's $10 billion expenditures for the next year, and assume that taxes remain at $8 billion. In the second year, compute the
      (*i*) Deficit.   _____
      (*ii*) Amount of new debt (bonds) issued.   _____
      (*iii*) Total debt, end of year.   _____
      (*iv*) Debt-service requirement.   _____
    (*e*) Repeat these calculations for the third, fourth, and fifth years, assuming that the government taxes at a rate of $8 billion each year and has noninterest expenditures of $10 billion annually.

	Year 3	Year 4	Year 5
Deficit	_____	_____	_____
New debt	_____	_____	_____
Total debt	_____	_____	_____
Debt service	_____	_____	_____

    (*f*) What is the ratio of interest payments, relative to the deficit, with each passing year?   _____

Year 2	Year 3	Year 4	Year 5
_____	_____	_____	_____

    (*g*) What will happen to the ratio of government debt to government expenditure with each passing year?   _____

LO1   7. (*a*) According to the News on page 253, how much fiscal restraint occurred between 1931 and 1933?   _____
    (*b*) By how much did this policy reduce aggregate demand if the MPC was 0.8?   _____

LO3 8. In Figure 12.5, what is the opportunity cost of increasing government spending from g_1 to g_2 if
    (a) No external financing is available?
    (b) Complete external financing is available?
    _____

LO3 9. (a) What percent of U.S. debt do foreigners hold? (See Figure 12.4.) _____
    (b) If the interest rate on U.S. Treasury debt is 4 percent, how much interest do foreigners
    collect each year from the U.S. Treasury? (Assume *total* debt of $10 trillion.) _____

LO1 10. Use the accompanying graph to illustrate *changes* in the structural and total deficits for fiscal years
    2002–2009 (data in Table 12.3).
    (a) In how many years do the two deficits change in *different* directions? _____
    (b) In how many years was the government pursuing fiscal restraint? _____

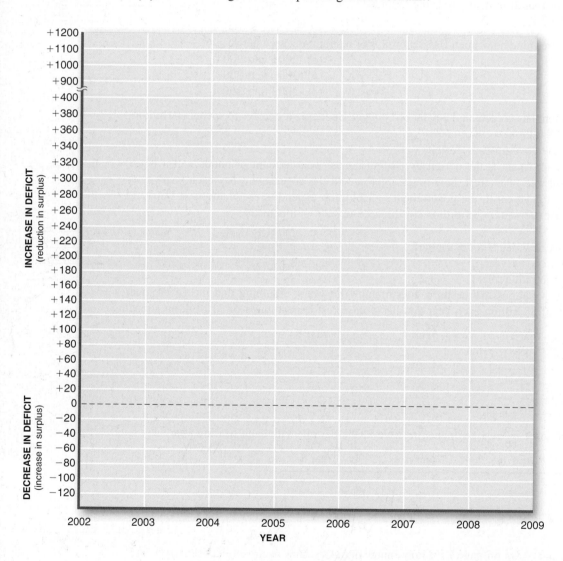

5 PART

Monetary Policy Options

Monetary policy tries to alter macro outcomes by managing the amount of money available in the economy. By changing the money supply and/or interest rates, monetary policy seeks to shift the aggregate demand curve in the desired direction. Chapters 13 through 15 illustrate how this policy tool works.

Money and Banks

13

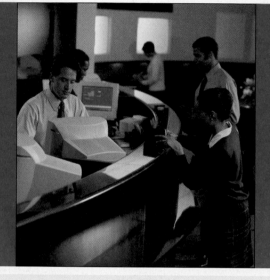

Sophocles, the ancient Greek playwright, had very strong opinions about the role of money. As he saw it, "Of evils upon earth, the worst is money. It is money that sacks cities, and drives men forth from hearth and home; warps and seduces native intelligence, and breeds a habit of dishonesty."

In modern times, people may still be seduced by the lure of money and fashion their lives around its pursuit. Nevertheless, it's hard to imagine an economy functioning without money. Money affects not only morals and ideals but also the way an economy works.

This and the following two chapters examine the role of money in the economy today. We begin with a very simple question:

- **What is money?**

As we'll discover, money isn't exactly what you might think it is. There's a lot more money in the economy than there is cash. And there's a lot more income around than money. So money is something quite different from either cash or income. Once we've established the characteristics of money, we go on to ask:

- **How is money created?**
- **What role do banks play in the circular flow of income and spending?**

In Chapter 14 we look at how the Federal Reserve System controls the amount of money created. In Chapter 15 we look at the implications for monetary policy, another tool in our macro policy toolbox.

WHAT IS "MONEY"?

To appreciate the significance of money for a modern economy, imagine for a moment that there were no such thing as money. How would you get something for breakfast? If you wanted eggs for breakfast, you'd have to tend your own chickens or go see Farmer Brown. But how would you pay Farmer Brown for his eggs? Without money, you'd have to offer him some goods or services that he could use. In other words, you'd have to engage in primitive **barter**—the direct exchange of one good for another—in order to get eggs for breakfast. You'd get those eggs only if Farmer Brown happened to want the particular goods or services you had to offer.

The use of money greatly simplifies market transactions. It's a lot easier to exchange money for eggs at the supermarket than to go into the country and barter with farmers every time you crave an omelet. Our ability to use money in market transactions, however, depends on the grocer's willingness to accept money as a *medium of exchange.* The grocer sells eggs for money only because he can use the same money to pay his help and buy the goods he himself desires. He too can exchange money for goods and services.

Without money, the process of acquiring goods and services would be much more difficult and time-consuming. This was evident when the value of the Russian ruble plummeted. Trading goods for Farmer Brown's eggs seems simple compared to the complicated barter deals Russian factories had to negotiate when paper money was no longer accepted (see World View below). And Russian workers certainly would've preferred to be paid in cash rather than in bras and coffins.

> **barter:** The direct exchange of one good for another, without the use of money.

[handwritten note: everyone is looking for something to trade that others want]

WORLD VIEW

The Cashless Society

Bartering Chokes Russian Economy

NARO-FOMINSK, RUSSIA—Natalya Karpova, a supervisor at a fabric factory here on the outskirts of Moscow, heard good news a couple of weeks ago. Three carloads of concrete utility poles had arrived at the train station.

This was a matter of utmost importance to Karpova, because her factory was a year behind on its electric bill and had no cash on hand. The electric company agreed to accept utility poles instead, but how to pay for utility poles with no rubles?

Simple. First, her factory shipped fabric 200 miles to a sewing factory in Nizhny Novgorod. In exchange for the fabric, that factory sewed shirts for the security guards who work at a nearby automobile manufacturer. In exchange for the shirts, the auto factory shipped a car and truck to a concrete plant. In exchange for the vehicles, the concrete plant delivered the poles to the electric company.

Thus did the Narfomsholk fabric factory pay for the power to run its dye machines.

But only for a while. "Now they want a steam shovel," said Karpova, with a little sigh.

This is how Karpova's factory and much of Russia's industry survives these days: barter. By some estimates, it accounts for almost three-fourths of all transactions.

Barter is poisoning the development of capitalism in Russia because it consumes huge amounts of time that would be better spent producing goods.

Many workers have no expectation of a real paycheck. Unpaid wages now amount to an estimated $11 billion. Instead of money, the workers are stuck with whatever the factory or farm is handing out, usually what it produces. The practice is so common now that only the more bizarre substitutes for wages draw notice, such as bras or coffins.

—Sharon LaFraniere

Source: *Washington Post,* September 3, 1998. © **1998, The Washington Post, excerpted with permission.** www.washingtonpost.com

Analysis: When the Russian ruble lost its value, people would no longer accept it in payment. Market transactions had to be bartered, a clumsy and inefficient process.

web analysis

Though bartering is inefficient, it is practiced at low levels even in countries with a stable currency. This is partly because bartering helps market participants lawfully avoid certain taxes. For a story of bartering activity in the U.S., visit **www.cnn.com** and search "barter."

THE MONEY SUPPLY

Many Types of Money

Although markets can't function well without money, they can get along without *dollars*. In the early days of colonial America, there were no U.S. dollars; a lot of business was conducted with Spanish and Portuguese gold coins. Later, people used Indian wampum, then tobacco, grain, fish, and furs as mediums of exchange. Throughout the colonies, gunpowder and bullets were frequently used for small change. These forms of money weren't as convenient as U.S. dollars, but they did the job.

This historical perspective on money highlights its essential characteristics. ***Anything that serves all the following purposes can be thought of as money:***

- *Medium of exchange:* is accepted as payment for goods and services (and debts).
- *Store of value:* can be held for future purchases.
- *Standard of value:* serves as a yardstick for measuring the prices of goods and services.

All the items used during the colonial days satisfied these conditions and were thus properly regarded as money.

After the colonies became an independent nation, the U.S. Constitution prohibited the federal government from issuing paper money. Money was instead issued by state-chartered banks. Between 1789 and 1865, over 30,000 different paper bills were issued by 1,600 banks in 34 states. People often preferred to get paid in gold, silver, or other commodities rather than in one of these uncertain currencies.

The first paper money the federal government issued consisted of $10 million worth of "greenbacks," printed in 1861 to finance the Civil War. The National Banking Act of 1863 gave the federal government permanent authority to issue money.

Modern Concepts

The "greenbacks" we carry around today aren't the only form of "money" we use. Most people realize this when they offer to pay for goods with a check rather than cash. People do distinguish between "cash" and "money," and for good reason. The "money" you have in a checking account can be used to buy goods and services or to pay debts, or it can be retained for future use. In these respects, your checking account balance is as much a part of your "money" as are the coins and dollars in your pocket or purse. You can access your balance by writing a check or using an ATM or debit card. Checks are more convenient than cash because they eliminate trips to the bank. Checks are also safer: Lost or stolen cash is gone forever; checkbooks and credit cards are easily replaced at little or no cost. We might use checks and debit cards even more frequently if everyone accepted them.

There's nothing unique about cash, then, insofar as the market is concerned. ***Checking accounts can and do perform the same market functions as cash.*** Accordingly, we must include checking account balances in our concept of **money.** The essence of money isn't its taste, color, or feel but, rather, its ability to purchase goods and services.

> **money:** Anything generally accepted as a medium of exchange.

Credit cards are another popular medium of exchange. People use credit cards for about one-third of all purchases over $100. This use is not sufficient, however, to qualify credit cards as a form of "money." Credit card balances must be paid by check or cash. The same holds true for balances in online electronic credit accounts ("e-cash"). Electronic purchases on the Internet or online services are ultimately paid by withdrawals from a bank account (by check or computer). Online payment mechanisms and credit cards are a payment *service,* not a final form of payment (credit card companies charge fees and interest for this service). The cards themselves are not a store of value, in contrast to cash or bank account balances.

The Diversity of Bank Accounts. To determine how much money is available to purchase goods and services, we need to count up all our coins and currency—as well as our bank account balances. This effort is complicated by the variety of bank accounts people have. In addition to simple no-interest checking accounts at full-service banks, people have bank accounts that pay interest, offer automatic transfers, require minimum holding periods, offer overdraft protection, or limit the number of checks that can be written. People also have "bank" accounts in credit unions, brokerage houses, and other nontraditional financial institutions.

[handwritten: 4x larger than M1]

M2
($8,223 billion)

$

Money market mutual funds and deposits — $1,098 billion

Savings account balances — $5,523 billion

M1
($1,602 billion)

$

Traveler's checks ($6 billion)
Transactions account balances — $776 billion / $776 billion
Currency in circulation — $820 billion / $820 billion

FIGURE 13.1
Composition of the Money Supply

Cash is only a part of the money supply. People also have easy access to transactions account balances and various savings account balances that are counted in measures of the money supply (M1 and M2). Because people hold so much money in money market mutual funds and savings (time-deposit) accounts, M2 is five times larger than M1.

Source: Federal Reserve (January 2009 data).

[handwritten: How much spending power is in the economy]

[handwritten: M1 + M2 = money supply]

Although all bank account balances can be spent, they're not all used the same way. People use regular checking accounts all the time to pay bills or make purchases. But consumers can't write checks on most savings accounts. And few people want to cash in a certificate of deposit just to go to the movies. Hence, *some bank accounts are better substitutes for cash than others.*

Several different measures of money have been developed to accommodate the diversity of bank accounts and other payment mechanisms. The narrowest definition of the **money supply** is designated **M1,** *which includes*

- *Currency in circulation.*
- *Transactions account balances.*
- *Traveler's checks.*

As Figure 13.1 indicates, the second largest component of this basic money supply (M1) is **transactions account** balances, which are the balances in bank accounts that are readily accessed by check. Most people refer to these simply as "checking accounts." The term "transactions account" is broader, however, including NOW accounts, ATS accounts, credit union share drafts, and demand deposits at mutual savings banks. *The distinguishing feature of all transactions accounts is that they permit direct payment to a third party (by check or debit card),* without requiring a trip to the bank to make a special withdrawal. Because of this feature, transactions accounts are the readiest substitutes for cash in market transactions. Traveler's checks issued by nonbank firms such as American Express can also be used directly in market transactions, just like good old-fashioned cash.

Transactions accounts aren't the only substitute for cash. People can and do dip into savings accounts on occasion. People sometimes even cash in their certificates of deposit in order to buy something, despite the interest penalty associated with early withdrawal. And banks have made it easy to transfer funds from one type of account to another. Savings accounts

M1: Cash and Transactions Accounts

money supply: (M1) Currency held by the public, plus balances in transactions accounts.
[handwritten: (checkbook money)]
[handwritten: • money that's used the most]

transactions account: A bank account that permits direct payment to a third party, for example, with a check or debit card.

M2: M1 + Savings Accounts, etc.

TABLE 13.1
Alternative Measures of the Money Supply

Measures of the money supply are intended to gauge the extent of purchasing power held by consumers. But the extent of purchasing power depends on how accessible assets are and how often people use them. The various money supply measures reflect variations in the liquidity and accessibility of assets.

Measure	Components
M1	Currency in circulation outside of bank vaults
	Demand deposits at commercial banks
	NOW and ATS accounts
	Credit union share drafts
	Demand deposits at mutual savings banks
	Traveler's checks (nonbank)
M2	M1 plus:
	Savings accounts
	Time deposits of less than $100,000
	Money market mutual funds
M3	M2 plus:
	Time deposits larger than $100,000
	Repurchase agreements
	Overnight Eurodollars
L	M3 plus other liquid assets, for example:
	Treasury bills
	U.S. savings bonds
	Bankers' acceptances
	Term Eurodollars
	Commercial paper

web analysis

Go to **www.frbatlanta.org** and search "The Story of Money" for a brief history of money.

M2 money supply: M1 plus balances in most savings accounts and money market mutual funds.

aggregate demand: The total quantity of output demanded at alternative price levels in a given time period, *ceteris paribus.*

can be transformed into transactions accounts with a phone call or computer instruction. As a result, *savings account balances are almost as good a substitute for cash as transactions account balances.*

Another popular way of holding money is to buy shares of money market mutual funds. Deposits into money market mutual funds are pooled and used to purchase interest-bearing securities such as Treasury bills. The interest rates paid on these funds are typically higher than those paid by banks. Moreover, the deposits made into the funds can often be withdrawn immediately, just like those in transactions accounts. When interest rates are high, deposits move out of regular transactions accounts into money market mutual funds in order to earn a higher return.

Additional measures of the money supply have been constructed to account for the possibility of using savings account balances, money market mutual funds, and various other deposits to finance everyday spending. The most widely watched money measure is **M2,** which includes all of M1 *plus* balances in savings accounts, money market mutual funds, and some CDs ("time deposits"). As Figure 13.1 shows, M2 is nearly five times as large as M1. Table 13.1 summarizes the content of these and two other measures of money.

Our concern about the specific nature of money stems from our broader interest in **aggregate demand.** What we want to know is how much purchasing power consumers have, since this will affect their ability to purchase goods and services. What we've observed, however, is that money isn't so easily defined. How much spending power people have depends not only on the number of coins in their pockets but also on their willingness to write checks, make trips to the bank, or convert other assets into cash.

In an increasingly complex financial system, the core concept of "money" isn't easy to pin down. Nevertheless, the official measures of the money supply (particularly M1 and M2) are fairly reliable benchmarks for gauging how much purchasing power market participants have.

CREATION OF MONEY

Once we've decided what money is, we still have to explain where it comes from. Part of the explanation is simple. Currency must be printed. Some nations use private printers for this purpose, but all U.S. currency is printed by the Bureau of Engraving and Printing in

BANK   DIRECT DEPOSIT DEPT.

YOU SEE, WITH DIRECT DEPOSIT OF YOUR PAYCHECK WE COMPLETELY DO AWAY WITH THE ILLUSION THAT YOU ACTUALLY EVER SEE ANY OF YOUR MONEY.

FRANK & ERNEST: © Thaves/Dist. by Newspaper Enterprise Association, Inc.

Analysis: People see very little of their money—most deposits and loans are computer entries in the banking system.

Washington, D.C. Coins come from the U.S. mints located in Philadelphia and Denver. As we observed in Figure 13.1, however, currency is only a fraction of our total money supply. So we need to look elsewhere for the origins of most money. Specifically, where do all the transactions accounts come from? How do people acquire transactions deposits? How does the total amount of such deposits—and therefore the money supply of the economy—change?

Most people assume that all transactions account balances come from cash deposits. But this isn't the case. Direct deposits of paychecks, for example, are carried out by computer, not by the movement of cash (see cartoon). Moreover, the employer who issues the paycheck probably didn't make any cash deposits. It's more likely that she covered those paychecks with customers' checks that she deposited or with loans granted by the bank itself.

The ability of banks to lend money opens up a whole new set of possibilities for creating money. *When a bank lends someone money, it simply credits that individual's bank account.* The money appears in an account just as it would with a cash deposit. And the owner of the account is free to spend that money as with any positive balance. Hence, *in making a loan, a bank effectively creates money because transactions account balances are counted as part of the money supply.*

To understand the origins of our money supply, then, we must recognize two basic principles:

- Transactions account balances are a large portion of the money supply.
- Banks can create transactions account balances by making loans.

The following two sections examine this process of **deposit creation** more closely. We determine how banks actually create deposits and what forces might limit the process of deposit creation.

Bank Regulation. Banks' deposit-creation activities are regulated by the government. The most important agency in this regard is the Federal Reserve System. "The Fed" puts limits on the amount of bank lending, thereby controlling the basic money supply. We'll discuss the structure and functions of the Fed in the next chapter; here we focus on the process of deposit creation itself.

There are thousands of banks, of various sorts, in the United States. To understand how banks create money, however, we'll make life simple. We'll assume for the moment that there's only one bank in town, University Bank. Imagine also that you've been saving some of your income by putting loose change into a piggy bank. Now, after months of saving, you break the bank and discover that your thrift has yielded $100. You immediately deposit this money in a new checking account at University Bank. How will this deposit affect the money supply?

Your initial deposit will have no immediate effect on the money supply. The coins in your piggy bank were already counted as part of the money supply (M1 and M2) because they represented cash held by the public. *When you deposit cash or coins in a bank, you're only changing the composition of the money supply, not its size.* The public (you) now holds

Deposit Creation

deposit creation: The creation of transactions deposits by bank lending.

A Monopoly Bank

$100 less of coins but $100 more of transactions deposits. Accordingly, no money is created by the demise of your piggy bank (the initial deposit). This accounting outcome is reflected in the following "T-account" of University Bank and the composition of the money supply:

University Bank		Money Supply	
Assets	Liabilities	Cash held by the public	−$100
		Transactions deposits at bank	+$100
+$100 in coins	+$100 in deposits	Change in M	0

The T-account on the left shows that your coins are now held by University Bank. Your coins are an "asset"—something of value—held now by the bank. In exchange for this asset, the bank has credited your checking account $100 ("deposits"). This balance is a liability for the bank since it must allow you to withdraw the deposit on demand.

The total money supply is unaffected by your cash deposit because two components of the money supply change in opposite directions (i.e., $100 less cash, $100 more bank deposits). This initial deposit is just the beginning of the money creation process, however. Banks aren't in business for your convenience; they're in business to earn a profit. To earn a profit on your deposit, University Bank will have to put your money to work. This means using your deposit as the basis for making a loan to someone who's willing to pay the bank interest for use of money. If the function of banks was merely to store money, they wouldn't pay interest on their accounts or offer free checking services. Instead, you'd have to pay them for these services. Banks pay you interest and offer free (or inexpensive) checking because ***banks can use your money to make loans that earn interest.***

The Initial Loan. Typically, a bank doesn't have much difficulty finding someone who wants to borrow money. Someone is always eager to borrow money. The question is: How much money can a bank lend? Can it lend your entire deposit? Or must University Bank keep some of your coins in reserve, in case you want to withdraw them? The answer will surprise you.

Suppose University Bank decided to lend the entire $100 to Campus Radio. Campus Radio wants to buy a new antenna but doesn't have any money in its own checking account. To acquire the antenna, Campus Radio must take out a loan.

When University Bank agrees to lend Campus Radio $100, it does so by crediting the account of Campus Radio. Instead of giving Campus Radio $100 cash, University Bank simply adds an electronic $100 to Campus Radio's checking account balance. That is, the loan is made with a simple bookkeeping entry as follows:

University Bank		Money Supply	
Assets	Liabilities	Cash held by the public	no change
$100 in coins	$100 your account balance	Transactions deposits at bank	+$100
		Change in M	+$100
$100 in loans	$100 Campus Radio account		

Notice that the bank's assets have increased. It now has your $100 in coins *plus* an IOU worth $100 from Campus Radio. On the right-hand side of the T-account, deposit liabilities now include $100 in your account and $100 in the Campus Radio account.

This simple bookkeeping procedure is the key to creating money. When University Bank lends $100 to the Campus Radio account, it "creates" money. Keep in mind that transactions deposits are counted as part of the money supply. Once the $100 loan is credited to its account, Campus Radio can use this new money to purchase its desired antenna, without worrying that its check will bounce.

Or can it? Once University Bank grants a loan to Campus Radio, both you and Campus Radio have $100 in your checking accounts to spend. But the bank is holding only $100 of reserves (your coins). In other words, the increased account balance obtained by Campus Radio doesn't limit *your* ability to write checks. There's been a net *increase* in the value of transactions deposits but no increase in bank reserves.

Secondary Deposits. What happens if Campus Radio actually spends the $100 on a new antenna? Won't this "use up all" the reserves held by the bank, endangering your check writing privileges? The answer is no.

Consider what happens when Atlas Antenna receives the check from Campus Radio. What will Atlas do with the check? Atlas could go to University Bank and exchange the check for $100 of cash (your coins). But Atlas may prefer to deposit the check in its own checking account at University Bank (still the only bank in town). This way, Atlas not only avoids the necessity of going to the bank (it can deposit the check by mail) but also keeps its money in a safe place. Should Atlas later want to spend the money, it can simply write a check. In the meantime, the bank continues to hold its entire reserves (your coins), and both you and Atlas have $100 to spend.

Fractional Reserves. Notice what's happened here. The money supply has increased by $100 as a result of deposit creation (the loan to Campus Radio). Moreover, the bank has been able to support $200 of transaction deposits (your account and either the Campus Radio or Atlas account) with only $100 of reserves (your coins). In other words, *bank reserves are only a fraction of total deposits.* In this case, University Bank's reserves (your $100 in coins) are only 50 percent of total deposits. Thus the bank's **reserve ratio** is 50 percent—that is,

$$\frac{\text{Reserve}}{\text{ratio}} = \frac{\text{bank reserves}}{\text{total deposits}}$$

The ability of University Bank to hold reserves that are only a fraction of total deposits results from two facts: (1) people use checks and debit cards for most transactions, and (2) there's no other bank. Accordingly, reserves are rarely withdrawn from this monopoly bank. In fact, if people *never* withdrew their deposits and *all* transactions accounts were held at University Bank, University Bank wouldn't need *any* reserves. In this most unusual case, University Bank could make as many loans as it wanted. Every loan it made would increase the supply of money.

In reality, many banks are available, and people both withdraw cash from their accounts and write checks to people who have accounts in other banks. In addition, bank lending practices are regulated by the Federal Reserve System. *The Federal Reserve System requires banks to maintain some minimum reserve ratio.* This reserve requirement directly limits banks' ability to grant new loans.

Required Reserves. The potential impact of Federal Reserve requirements on bank lending can be readily seen. Suppose that the Federal Reserve imposed a minimum reserve requirement of 75 percent on University Bank. Such a requirement would prohibit University Bank from lending $100 to Campus Radio. That loan would result in $200 of deposits, supported by only $100 of reserves. The actual ratio of reserves to deposits would be 50 percent ($100 of reserves ÷ $200 of deposits), which would violate the Fed's assumed 75 percent reserve requirement. A 75 percent reserve requirement means that University Bank must hold **required reserves** equal to 75 percent of *total* deposits, including those created through loans.

The bank's dilemma is evident in the following equation:

$$\frac{\text{Required}}{\text{reserves}} = \frac{\text{required reserve}}{\text{ratio}} \times \frac{\text{total}}{\text{deposits}}$$

To support $200 of total deposits, University Bank would need to satisfy this equation:

$$\frac{\text{Required}}{\text{reserves}} = 0.75 \times \$200 = \$150$$

bank reserves: Assets held by a bank to fulfill its deposit obligations.

reserve ratio: The ratio of a bank's reserves to its total transactions deposits.

required reserves: The minimum amount of reserves a bank is required to hold; equal to required reserve ratio times transactions deposits.

But the bank has only $100 of reserves (your coins) and so would violate the reserve requirement if it increased total deposits to $200 by lending $100 to Campus Radio.

University Bank can still issue a loan to Campus Radio. But the loan must be less than $100 in order to keep the bank within the limits of the required reserve formula. Thus, *a minimum reserve requirement directly limits deposit-creation (lending) possibilities.* It's still true, however, as we'll now illustrate, that the banking system, taken as a whole, can create multiple loans (money) from a single deposit.

A Multibank World

Table 13.2 illustrates the process of deposit creation in a multibank world with a required reserve ratio. In this case, we assume that legally required reserves must equal at least 20 percent of transactions deposits. Now when you deposit $100 in your checking account, University Bank must hold at least $20 as required reserves.[1]

Excess Reserves. The remaining $80 the bank obtains from your deposit is regarded as **excess reserves.** These reserves are "excess" because your bank is *required* to hold in reserve only $20 (equal to 20 percent of your initial $100 deposit):

> excess reserves: Bank reserves in excess of required reserves.

$$\frac{\text{Excess}}{\text{reserves}} = \frac{\text{total}}{\text{reserves}} - \frac{\text{required}}{\text{reserves}}$$

The $80 of excess reserves aren't required and may be used to support additional loans. Hence, the bank can now lend $80. In view of the fact that banks earn profits (interest) by making loans, we assume that University Bank will try to use these excess reserves as soon as possible.

To keep track of the changes in reserves, deposit balances, and loans that occur in a multibank world we'll have to do some bookkeeping. For this purpose we'll again use the same balance sheet, or "T-account," that banks themselves use. On the left side of the balance sheet, a bank lists all its assets. *Assets* are things of value the bank possesses, including cash held in a bank's vaults, IOUs (loan obligations) from bank customers, reserve credits at the Federal Reserve (essentially the bank's own deposits at the central bank), and securities (bonds) the bank has purchased.

On the right side of the balance sheet a bank lists all its liabilities. *Liabilities* are things the bank owes to others. The largest liability is represented by the deposits of bank customers. The bank owes these deposits to its customers and must return them "on demand."

Table 13.2 also shows the use of balance sheets. Notice how the balance of University Bank looks immediately after it receives your initial deposit (step 1, Table 13.2). Your deposit of coins is entered on *both* sides of University's balance sheet. On the left-hand side, your deposit is regarded as an asset, because your piggy bank's coins have an immediate market value and can be used to pay off the bank's liabilities. The coins now appear as *reserves.* The reserves these coins represent are further divided into required reserves ($20, or 20 percent of your deposit) and excess reserves ($80).

On the right-hand side of the balance sheet, the bank reminds itself that it has an obligation (liability) to return your deposit when you demand. Thus, the bank's accounts balance, with assets and liabilities being equal. In fact, *a bank's books must always balance because all the bank's assets must belong to someone (its depositors or the bank's owners).*

University Bank wants to do more than balance its books, however; it wants to earn profits. To do so, it will have to make loans—that is, put its excess reserves to work. Suppose that it lends $80 to Campus Radio.[2] As step 2 in Table 13.2 illustrates, this loan alters both sides of University Bank's balance sheet. On the right-hand side, the bank creates a new transactions deposit for (credits the account of) Campus Radio; this item represents an additional liability (promise to pay). On the left-hand side of the balance sheet, two things happen.

web analysis

Find the most recent data on total bank reserves, borrowed reserves, excess reserves, and required reserves at **www.federalreserve. gov.** Search for "aggregate reserves of depository institutions."

---

[1]The reserves themselves may be held in the form of cash in the bank's vault but are usually held as credits with one of the regional Federal Reserve banks.

[2]Because of the Fed's assumed minimum reserve requirement (20 percent), University Bank can now lend only $80 rather than $100, as before.

Step 1: You deposit cash at University Bank. The deposit creates $100 of reserves, $20 of which are designated as required reserves.

University Bank				Banking System	
Assets		Liabilities		Change in Transactions Deposits	Change in M
Required reserves	$ 20	Your deposit	$100	+$100	$0
Excess reserves	80				
Total	$100		100		

Step 2: The bank uses its excess reserves ($80) to make a loan to Campus Radio. Total deposits now equal $180. The money supply has increased.

University Bank				Banking System	
Assets		Liabilities		Δ Deposits	Δ M
Required reserves	$ 36	Your account	$100	+$80	+$80
Excess reserves	64	Campus Radio account	80		
Loans	80				
Total	$180	Total	$180		

Step 3: Campus Radio buys an antenna. This depletes Campus Radio's account but increases Atlas's balance. Eternal Savings gets $80 of reserves when the Campus Radio check clears.

University Bank				Eternal Savings				Banking System	
Assets		Liabilities		Assets		Liabilities		Δ Deposits	Δ M
Required reserves	$ 20	Your account	$100	Required reserves	$16	Atlas Antenna account	$80	$0	$0
Excess reserves	0	Campus Radio account	0	Excess reserves	64				
Loan	80								
Total	$100	Total	$100	Total	$80	Total	$80		

Step 4: Eternal Savings lends money to Herman's Hardware. Deposits, loans, and M all increase by $64.

University Bank				Eternal Savings				Banking System	
Assets		Liabilities		Assets		Liabilities		Change in Transaction Deposits	Change in M
Required reserves	$ 20	Your account	$100	Required reserves	$28.80	Atlas Antenna account	$ 80	+$64	+$64
Excess reserves	0	Campus Radio account	0	Excess reserves	51.20	Herman's Hardware account	64		
Loan	80			Loans	64				
Total	$100	Total	$100		$ 144		$144		
⋮		⋮		⋮		⋮		⋮	⋮
nth step: Some bank lends $1.00								+1	+1

Cumulative Change in Banking System

Bank Reserves	Transactions Deposits	Money Supply
+$100	+$500	+$400

TABLE 13.2

Deposit Creation

Excess reserves (step 1) are the basis of bank loans. When a bank uses its excess reserves to make a loan, it creates a deposit (step 2). When the loan is spent, a deposit will be made somewhere else (step 3). This new deposit creates additional excess reserves (step 3) that can be used for further loans (step 4, etc.). The process of deposit creation continues until the money supply has increased by a multiple of the initial deposit.

First, the bank notes that Campus Radio owes it $80 ("loans"). Second, the bank recognizes that it's now required to hold $36 in *required* reserves, in accordance with its higher level of transactions deposits ($180). (Recall we're assuming that required reserves are 20 percent of total transactions deposits.) Since its total reserves are still $100, $64 is left as *excess* reserves. Note again that ***excess reserves are reserves a bank isn't required to hold.***

Changes in the Money Supply. Before examining further changes in the balance sheet of University Bank, consider again what's happened to the economy's money supply during these first two steps. In the first step, you deposited $100 of cash in your checking account. This initial transaction didn't change the value of the money supply. Only the composition of the money supply (M1 or M2) was affected ($100 less cash held by the public, $100 more in transactions accounts).

Not until step 2—when the bank makes a loan—does all the excitement begin. In making a loan, the bank automatically increases the total money supply by $80. Why? Because someone (Campus Radio) now has more money (a transactions deposit) than it did before, *and no one else has any less.* And Campus Radio can use its money to buy goods and services, just like anybody else.

This second step is the heart of money creation. Money effectively appears out of thin air when a bank makes a loan. To understand how this works, you have to keep reminding yourself that money is more than the coins and currency we carry around. Transactions deposits are money too. Hence, ***the creation of transactions deposits via new loans is the same thing as creating money.***

More Deposit Creation. Suppose again that Campus Radio actually uses its $80 loan to buy an antenna. The rest of Table 13.2 illustrates how this additional transaction leads to further changes in balance sheets and the money supply.

In step 3, we see that when Campus Radio buys the $80 antenna, the balance in its checking account at University Bank drops to zero because it has spent all its money. As University Bank's liabilities fall (from $180 to $100), so does the level of its required reserves (from $36 to $20). (Note that required reserves are still 20 percent of its remaining transactions deposits.) But University Bank's excess reserves have disappeared completely! This disappearance reflects the fact that Atlas Antenna keeps *its* transactions account at another bank (Eternal Savings). When Atlas deposits the check it received from Campus Radio, Eternal Savings does two things: First it credits Atlas's account by $80. Second, it goes to University Bank to get the reserves that support the deposit.[3] The reserves later appear on the balance sheet of Eternal Savings as both required ($16) and excess ($64) reserves.

Observe that the money supply hasn't changed during step 3. The increase in the value of Atlas Antenna's transactions account balance exactly offsets the drop in the value of Campus Radio's transactions account. Ownership of the money supply is the only thing that has changed.

In step 4, Eternal Savings takes advantage of its newly acquired excess reserves by making a loan to Herman's Hardware. As before, the loan itself has two primary effects. First, it creates a transactions deposit of $64 for Herman's Hardware and thereby increases the money supply by the same amount. Second, it increases the required level of reserves at Eternal Savings. (To how much? Why?)

THE MONEY MULTIPLIER

By now it's perhaps obvious that the process of deposit creation won't come to an end quickly. On the contrary, it can continue indefinitely, just like the income multiplier process in Chapter 10. Indeed, people often refer to deposit creation as the money multiplier process,

---

[3]In actuality, banks rarely "go" anywhere; such interbank reserve movements are handled by bank clearinghouses and regional Federal Reserve banks. The effect is the same, however. The nature and use of bank reserves are discussed more fully in Chapter 14.

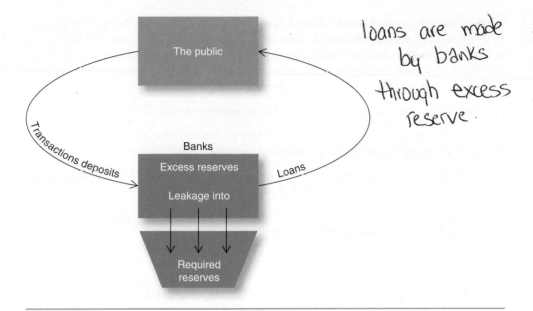

loans are made by banks through excess reserve.

FIGURE 13.2
The Money Multiplier Process

Part of every new bank deposit leaks into required reserves. The rest—excess reserves—can be used to make loans. These loans, in turn, become deposits elsewhere. The process of money creation continues until all available reserves become required reserves.

with the **money multiplier** expressed as the reciprocal of the required reserve ratio.[4] That is,

$$\text{Money multiplier} = \frac{1}{\substack{\text{required} \\ \text{reserve ratio}}}$$

money multiplier: The number of deposit (loan) dollars that the banking system can create from $1 of excess reserves; equal to $1 \div$ required reserve ratio.

Figure 13.2 illustrates the money multiplier process. When a new deposit enters the banking system, it creates both excess and required reserves. The required reserves represent leakage from the flow of money since they can't be used to create new loans. Excess reserves, on the other hand, can be used for new loans. Once those loans are made, they typically become transactions deposits elsewhere in the banking system. Then some additional leakage into required reserves occurs, and further loans are made. The process continues until all excess reserves have leaked into required reserves. Once excess reserves have completely disappeared, the total value of new loans will equal initial excess reserves multiplied by the money multiplier.

The potential of the money multiplier to create loans is summarized by the equation

$$\substack{\text{Excess} \\ \text{reserves} \\ \text{of banking} \\ \text{system}} \times \substack{\text{money} \\ \text{multiplier}} = \substack{\text{potential} \\ \text{deposit creation}}$$

Notice how the money multiplier worked in our previous example. The value of the money multiplier was equal to 5, since we assumed that the required reserve ratio was 0.20. Moreover, the initial level of excess reserves was $80, as a consequence of your original deposit (step 1). According to the money multiplier, then, the deposit-creation potential of the banking system was

$$\substack{\text{Excess reserves} \\ \text{($80)}} \times \substack{\text{money multiplier} \\ \text{(5)}} = \substack{\text{potential} \\ \text{deposit} \\ \text{creation ($400)}}$$

When all the banks fully utilized their excess reserves at each step of the money multiplier process, the ultimate increase in the money supply was in fact $400 (see the last row in Table 13.2).

---

[4]The money multiplier $(1/r)$ is the sum of the infinite geometric progression
$1 + (1 - r) + (1 - r)^2 + (1 - r)^3 + \cdots + (1 - r)^\infty$.

Excess Reserves as Lending Power

While you're struggling through Table 13.2, notice the critical role that excess reserves play in the process of deposit creation. A bank can make additional loans only if it has excess reserves. Without excess reserves, all of a bank's reserves are required, and no further liabilities (transactions deposits) can be created with new loans. On the other hand, a bank with excess reserves can make additional loans. In fact,

● *Each bank may lend an amount equal to its excess reserves and no more.*

As such loans enter the circular flow and become deposits elsewhere, they create new excess reserves and further lending capacity. As a consequence,

● *The entire banking system can increase the volume of loans by the amount of excess reserves multiplied by the money multiplier.*

By keeping track of excess reserves, then, we can gauge the lending capacity of any bank or, with the aid of the money multiplier, the entire banking system.

Table 13.3 summarizes the entire money multiplier process. In this case, we assume that all banks are initially "loaned up"—that is, without any excess reserves. The money multiplier process begins when someone deposits $100 in cash into a transactions account at

[handwritten note in margin: Process continues until all the money leaks out into the reserve.]

Required reserves = 0.20	Change in Transactions Deposits	Change in Total Reserves	Change in Required Reserves	Change in Excess Reserves	Change in Lending Capacity
If $100 in cash is deposited in Bank A, Bank A acquires	$100.00	$100.00	$20.00	$80.00	$80.00
If loan made and deposited elsewhere, Bank B acquires	80.00	80.00	16.00	64.00	64.00
If loan made and deposited elsewhere, Bank C acquires	64.00	64.00	12.80	51.20	51.20
If loan made and deposited elsewhere, Bank D acquires	51.20	51.20	10.24	40.96	40.96
If loan made and deposited elsewhere, Bank E acquires	40.96	40.96	8.19	32.77	32.77
If loan made and deposited elsewhere, Bank F acquires	32.77	32.77	6.55	26.27	26.22
If loan made and deposited elsewhere, Bank G acquires	26.22	26.22	5.24	20.98	20.98
. . .					
If loan made and deposited elsewhere, Bank Z acquires	0.38	0.38	0.08	0.30	0.30
Cumulative, through Bank Z	$498.80	$100.00	$99.76	$0.24	$398.80
. . .					
And if the process continues indefinitely	$500.00	$100.00	$100.00	$0.00	$400.00

Note: A $100 cash deposit creates $400 of new lending capacity when the required reserve ratio is 0.20. Initial excess reserves are $80 (= $100 deposit − $20 required reserves). The money multiplier is 5 (= 1 ÷ 0.20). New lending potential equals $400 (= $80 excess reserves × 5).

TABLE 13.3
The Money Multiplier at Work

The process of deposit creation continues as money passes through different banks in the form of multiple deposits and loans. At each step, excess reserves and new loans are created. The lending capacity of this system equals the money multiplier times excess reserves. In this case, initial excess reserves of $80 create the possibility of $400 of new loans when the reserve ratio is 0.20 (20 percent).

Bank A. If the required reserve ratio is 20 percent, this initial deposit creates $80 of excess reserves at Bank A while adding $100 to total transactions deposits.

If Bank A uses its newly acquired excess reserves to make a loan that ultimately ends up in Bank B, two things happen: Bank B acquires $64 in excess reserves (0.80 × $80), and total transactions deposits increase by $80 as well.

The money multiplier process continues with a series of loans and deposits. When the twenty-sixth loan is made (by bank Z), total loans grow by only $0.30 and transactions deposits by an equal amount. Should the process continue further, the *cumulative* change in loans will ultimately equal $400, that is, the money multiplier times initial excess reserves. The money supply will increase by the same amount.

BANKS AND THE CIRCULAR FLOW

The bookkeeping details of bank deposits and loans are rarely exciting and often confusing. But they do demonstrate convincingly that banks can create money. In that capacity, **banks perform two essential functions for the macro economy:**

- **Banks transfer money from savers to spenders by lending funds (reserves) held on deposit.** - main function of banks
- **The banking system creates additional money by making loans in excess of total reserves.**

In performing these two functions, banks change the size of the money supply—that is, the amount of purchasing power available for buying goods and services. Market participants may respond to these changes in the money supply by altering their spending behavior and shifting the aggregate demand curve.

Figure 13.3 is a simplified perspective on the role of banks in the circular flow. As before, income flows from product markets through business firms to factor markets and returns to consumers in the form of disposable income. Consumers spend most of their income but also save (don't spend) some of it.

The leakage represented by consumer saving is a potential source of stabilization problems, particularly unemployment. If additional spending by business firms, foreigners, or

Financing Injections

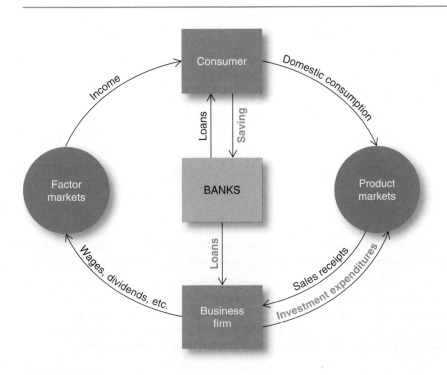

FIGURE 13.3
Banks in the Circular Flow

Banks help transfer income from savers to spenders by using their deposits to make loans to business firms and consumers who want to spend more money than they have. By lending money, banks help maintain any desired rate of aggregate demand.

governments doesn't compensate for consumer saving at full employment, a recessionary GDP gap will emerge, creating unemployment (see Chapters 9 and 10). Our interest here is in the role the banking system can play in encouraging such additional spending.

Suppose for the moment that *all* consumer saving was deposited in piggy banks rather than depository institutions (banks) and that no one used checks. Under these circumstances, banks couldn't transfer money from savers to spenders by holding deposits and making loans.

In reality, a substantial portion of consumer saving *is* deposited in banks. These and other bank deposits can be used as the basis of loans, thereby returning purchasing power to the circular flow. In fact, the primary economic function of banks isn't to store money but to transfer purchasing power from savers to spenders. They do so by lending money to businesses for new plant and equipment, to consumers for new homes or cars, and to government entities that desire greater purchasing power. Moreover, because the banking system can make *multiple* loans from available reserves, banks don't have to receive all consumer saving in order to carry out their function. On the contrary, *the banking system can create any desired level of money supply if allowed to expand or reduce loan activity at will.*

Constraints on Deposit Creation

There are four major constraints on the deposit creation of the banking system.

Deposits. The first constraint is the willingness of consumers and businesses to continue using and accepting checks rather than cash in the marketplace. If people preferred to hold cash rather than checkbooks, banks wouldn't be able to acquire or maintain the reserves that are the foundation of bank lending activity.

Willingness to Lend. Once banks are holding sufficient reserves, they must be willing to make new loans. In 2008–9, this condition was violated. Banks had accumulated huge losses on previous mortgage loans. In addition, the economy was sliding into a deepening recession. So banks were reluctant to make new loans that might not get paid. In more stable environments, however, banks know that new lending is the key to future profits.

Willingness to Borrow. The third constraint on deposit creation is the willingness of consumers, businesses, and governments to borrow the money that banks make available. The chain of events we've observed in deposit creation depends on the willingness of Campus Radio to borrow $80, of Herman's Hardware to borrow $64, and so on. If no one wanted to borrow any money, deposit creation would never begin. By the same reasoning, if all excess reserves aren't borrowed (lent), deposit creation won't live up to its theoretical potential.

Regulation. The fourth major constraint on deposit creation is the Federal Reserve System. As we've observed, the Fed may limit deposit creation by imposing reserve requirements. These and other tools of monetary policy are discussed in Chapter 14.

THE ECONOMY TOMORROW

WHEN BANKS FAIL

The power of banks to create money originates in the *fractional reserve* system. As we've observed, a bank holds reserves that are a small fraction of its liabilities, implying that *no bank could pay off its customers if they all sought to withdraw their deposits at one time.*

Bank Panics. In earlier times, banks did experience occasional "runs" when depositors would rush to withdraw their funds. Such depositor runs usually began when word spread that a particular bank was running low on cash and might close. Depositor runs became self-fulfilling confirmation of a bank's insolvency. The resulting bank closing wiped out customer deposits, curtailed bank lending, and often pushed the economy into recession.

During the Great Depression there was widespread fear that the U.S. banking system would collapse. Borrowers weren't able to repay their loans and depositors were withdrawing more cash. As their reserves dwindled, banks' ability to create money evaporated. Suddenly, a chunk of money (bank deposits and loans) just disappeared. With little cash coming in and a lot of cash flowing out, banks quickly ran out of cash reserves and had to shut their doors. Between 1930 and 1933, over 9,000 banks failed. To prevent total collapse of the banking system, newly elected president Franklin Roosevelt declared a "bank holiday" that closed all the nation's banks for 1 week.

Deposit Insurance. Congress used that opportunity to create a deposit insurance that would protect customer deposits. The Federal Deposit Insurance Corporation (FDIC) and the Federal Savings and Loan Insurance Corporation (FSLIC) were created in 1933 and 1934 to ensure depositors that they'd get their money back even if their bank failed. The guarantee of insured deposits eliminated the motivation for deposit runs. If a bank closed, the federal government would step in and repay deposits.

The S&L Crisis. Federal deposit insurance greatly increased public confidence in the banking system. It didn't, however, ward off bank failures. In some respects, deposit insurance even *contributed* to bank failures. By insuring deposits, the federal government eliminated a major risk for bank customers. Depositors no longer had to concern themselves with the soundness of a bank's lending practices; their deposits were insured. This created the opportunity for bank owners to engage in riskier loans that had greater profit potential.

During the 1970s, accelerating inflation pushed interest rates up. To attract deposits, banks had to offer higher rates of interest on customer deposits. Many of their loans, however, were already set at lower interest rates. This was particularly true for savings and loan associations (S&Ls), which traditionally lent most of their funds in long-term home mortgages. Suddenly, they were stuck earning low interest rates on long-term mortgages while paying high interest rates on short-term deposits. This was a recipe for failure.

The woes of the S&Ls were exacerbated by increased competition from new financial institutions (like money market mutual funds) that enticed deposits away from S&Ls. Sharp downturns in oil prices and real estate also weakened borrowers' ability to repay their loans. These and other forces caused more than half the S&Ls that existed in 1970 to disappear by 1990. In 1988, more banks failed (200) than in any year since the Great Depression. The 1990–91 recession pushed still more banks into insolvency.

The FSLIC and FDIC averted bank panics by paying off depositors in failed banks. So many S&Ls failed, however, that the FSLIC itself ran out of funds. Congress had to appropriate ever larger sums of money to bail out the banks. In 1992 alone, over $60 billion was spent on bank bailouts.

The 2008 Credit Crisis. In 2008, the U.S. was hit with another banking crisis. Once again, the problem originated in the housing industry. Banks had helped finance a surge in home buying that pushed home prices sharply higher in 2002–6. But then prices started to decline. As home prices fell, two things happened. First, homeowners fell behind on their mortgage payments. Second, the value of the mortgaged properties (an asset on the banks' balance sheets) tumbled. By 2008, some banks didn't have enough assets to pay all their liabilities. It was like a replay of the 1980s S&L crisis, only larger. This time the potential bank failures were so large that the whole process of deposit creation—the monetary foundation of aggregate demand growth—was threatened (see News on the next page).

Bank Bailouts. As in the earlier S&L crisis, the federal government had to step in again to "bail out" the banks. The FDIC helped avert a bank panic by increasing the limit on insured deposits to $250,000 (from $100,000) and extending that coverage to other forms of deposits. The Federal Reserve helped the banks by lending them more reserves. But the most dramatic action was taken by the U.S. Treasury. The Treasury agreed to guarantee deposits in money market funds, lend money to financial institutions at low interest rates, and even purchase ownership stakes in major banks (via the Troubled Asset Relief Program, or "TARP"). All told, hundreds of billions of government dollars were pumped

IN THE NEWS

WaMu's Failure Biggest in US Banks History

As the debate over a $700 billion bank bailout rages on in Washington, one of the nation's largest banks—Washington Mutual Inc.—has collapsed under the weight of its enormous bad bets on the mortgage market.

The Federal Deposit Insurance Corp. seized WaMu on Thursday, and then sold the thrift's banking assets to JPMorgan Chase & Co. for $1.9 billion.

Seattle-based WaMu, which was founded in 1889, is the largest bank to fail by far in the country's history. Its $307 billion in assets eclipse the $40 billion of Continental Illinois National Bank, which failed in 1984, and the $32 billion of IndyMac, which the government seized in July. . . .

WaMu "was under severe liquidity pressure," FDIC Chairman Sheila Bair told reporters in a conference call.

"For all depositors and other customers of Washington Mutual Bank, this is simply a combination of two banks," Bair said in a statement. "For bank customers, it will be a seamless transition. There will be no interruption in services and bank customers should expect business as usual come Friday morning."

—Madlen Read
AP Business Writer

Source: *New York Post,* September 26, 2008. Used with permission by The Associated Press.

> **Analysis:** Banks fail when they no longer have sufficient assets to meet deposit obligations. The government helps avert panic by guaranteeing deposits.

web analysis

To understand the commonalities between the savings and loan crisis of the late 1980s and the 2008 credit crisis, go to **www.nytimes.com** and search "savings and loan crisis."

into the banking system. The intent of the 2008–9 bailout was to restore faith in the banking system—thereby assuring that credit would continue to flow in the economy tomorrow— even from banks holding only fractional reserves.

SUMMARY

- In a market economy, money serves a critical function in facilitating exchanges and specialization, thus permitting increased output. LO1
- *Money* refers to any medium that's generally accepted in exchange, serves as a store of value, and acts as a standard of value. LO1
- Because people use bank account balances to buy goods and services (with checks or debit cards), such balances are also regarded as money. The money supply M1 includes cash plus transactions account (checkable) deposits. M2 adds savings account balances and other deposits to form a broader measure of the money supply. LO1
- Banks have the power to create money by making loans. In making loans, banks create new transactions deposits, which become part of the money supply. LO2
- A bank's ability to make loans—create money—depends on its reserves. Only if a bank has excess reserves—reserves greater than those required by federal regulation—can it make new loans. LO2

- As loans are spent, they create deposits elsewhere, making it possible for other banks to make additional loans. The money multiplier (1 ÷ required reserve ratio) indicates the total value of deposits that can be created by the banking system from excess reserves. LO3
- The role of banks in creating money includes the transfer of money from savers to spenders as well as deposit creation in excess of deposit balances. Taken together, these two functions give banks direct control over the amount of purchasing power available in the marketplace. LO2
- The deposit-creation potential of the banking system is limited by government regulation. It's also limited by the willingness of market participants to hold deposits or borrow money. LO3
- When banks fail, the federal government (FDIC) guarantees to pay deposits. In extreme cases the government may also lend banks more reserves, purchase depressed assets, or even acquire an ownership stake. LO2

Key Terms

barter	aggregate demand	required reserves
money	deposit creation	excess reserves
money supply (M1, M2)	bank reserves	money multiplier
transactions account	reserve ratio	

Questions for Discussion

1. Why are checking account balances, but not credit cards, regarded as "money"?   LO1

2. In what respects are modern forms of money superior to the colonial use of wampum as money?   LO1

3. How are an economy's production possibilities affected when workers are paid in bras and coffins rather than cash? (See World View, p. 271, about bartering in Russia.)   LO1

4. What percentage of your monthly bills do you pay with (*a*) cash, (*b*) check, (*c*) credit card, and (*d*) automatic transfers. How do you pay off the credit card balance? How does your use of cash compare with the composition of the money supply (Figure 13.1)?   LO1

5. If you can purchase airline tickets with online computer services, should your electronic account be counted in the money supply? Explain.   LO1

6. Does the fact that your bank keeps only a fraction of your account balance in reserve make you uncomfortable? Why don't people rush to the bank and retrieve their money? What would happen if they did?   LO2

7. If people never withdrew cash from banks, how much money could the banking system potentially create? Could this really happen? What might limit deposit creation in this case?   LO3

8. If all banks heeded Shakespeare's admonition "Neither a borrower nor a lender be," what would happen to the circular flow?   LO2

9. How does federal deposit insurance encourage greater risk-taking by banks? Could the banking system function without government deposit insurance? How?   LO2

10. Why is the failure of a major bank (News, p. 286) so frightening?   LO3

! **web activities** to accompany this chapter can be found on the Online Learning Center:

http://www.mhhe.com/schiller12e

LO1 1. If you cash a $100 traveler's check at a bank, by how much do(es)
LO2
                                           (*a*) M1 change? _____
                                           (*b*) M2 change? _____
                                           (*c*) bank reserves change? _____

If you deposit the traveler's check in your bank account, by how much do(es)
                                           (*d*) M1 change? _____
                                           (*e*) M2 change? _____
                                           (*f*) bank reserves change? _____

LO2 2. Suppose a bank's balance sheet looks as follows:

Assets		Liabilities	
Reserves	$450	Deposits	$5,000

and banks are required to hold reserves equal to 10 percent of deposits.
(*a*) How much excess reserves does the bank hold? (*a*) _____
(*b*) How much more can this bank lend? (*b*) _____

LO2 3. Suppose a bank's balance sheet looks like this:

Assets		Liabilities	
Reserves		Deposits	$500
Excess	$ 75		
Required	25		
Loans	400		
Total	$500	Total	$500

What is the required reserve ratio? _____

LO3 4. What is the value of the money multiplier when the required reserve ratio is
                                           (*a*) 5 percent? _____
                                           (*b*) 4 percent? _____

LO2 5. In December 1994, a man in Ohio decided to deposit all of the 8 *million* pennies he'd been saving for nearly 65 years. (His deposit weighed over 48,000 pounds!) With a reserve requirement of 5 percent, what will be the cumulative change for the banking system in
                                           (*a*) Transactions deposits? _____
                                           (*b*) Total reserves? _____
                                           (*c*) Lending capacity? _____

LO2 6. (*a*) When the reserve requirement changes, which of the following will change for an individual bank (answer "change" or "no change").
                                      Transactions deposits _____
                                      Total reserves _____
                                      Required reserves _____
                                      Excess reserves _____
                                      Lending capacity _____

      (*b*) When the reserve requirement changes, which of the following will change in the total banking system?
                                      Transactions deposits _____
                                      Total reserves _____
                                      Required reserves _____
                                      Excess reserves _____
                                      Lending capacity _____

LO2 7. In Table 13.2, how much unused lending capacity does Eternal Savings have at step 4? _____

LO2
LO3
8. Suppose that a lottery winner deposits $20 million in cash into her transactions account at the Bank of America (B of A). Assume a reserve requirement of 25 percent and no excess reserves in the banking system prior to this deposit.

(*a*) Use step 1 in the T-accounts below to show how her deposit affects the balance sheet at B of A.

(*b*) Has the money supply been changed by her deposit?   _____

(*c*) Use step 2 below to show the changes at B of A after the bank fully uses its new lending capacity.

(*d*) Has the money supply been changed in step 2?   _____

(*e*) In step 3 the new borrower(s) writes a check for the amount of the loan in step 2. That check is deposited at another bank, and B of A pays the other bank when the check clears. What does the B of A balance sheet look like now?

(*f*) After the entire banking system uses the lending capacity of the initial ($20 million) deposit, by how much will the following have changed?

Total reserves	_____
Total deposits	_____
Total loans	_____
Cash held by public	_____
The money supply	_____

Step 1: Winnings Deposited
Bank of America

Assets (in millions)		Liabilities (in millions)	
Reserves:		Deposits	_____
Required	_____		
Excess	_____		
Subtotal	_____		
Loans	_____		
Total assets	_____	Total liabilities	_____

Step 2: Loans Made
Bank of America

Assets (in millions)		Liabilities (in millions)	
Reserves:		Deposits	_____
Required	_____		
Excess	_____		
Subtotal	_____		
Loans	_____		
Total assets	_____	Total liabilities	_____

Step 3: Check Clears
Bank of America

Assets (in millions)		Liabilities (in millions)	
Reserves:		Deposits	_____
Required	_____		
Excess	_____		
Subtotal	_____		
Loans	_____		
Total assets	_____	Total liabilities	_____

The Federal Reserve System

14

We've seen how money is created with bank loans. We've also gotten a few clues about how the government limits money creation and thus aggregate demand. This chapter examines the mechanics of government control more closely. The basic issues addressed are

- **How does the government control the amount of money in the economy?**
- **Which government agency is responsible for exercising this control?**
- **How are banks and bond markets affected by the government's policies?**

Most people have a ready answer for the first question. The popular view is that the government controls the amount of money in the economy by printing more or fewer dollar bills. But we've already observed that the concept of "money" isn't so simple. In Chapter 13 we demonstrated that banks, not the printing presses, create most of our money. In making loans, banks create transactions deposits that are counted as part of the money supply.

Because bank lending activities are the primary source of money, the *government must regulate bank lending if it wants to control the amount of money in the economy.* That's exactly what the Federal Reserve System does. The Federal Reserve System—the "Fed"—not only limits the volume of loans that the banking system can make from available reserves; it can also alter the amount of reserves banks hold.

The Federal Reserve System's control over the supply of money is the key mechanism of **monetary policy.** The potential of this policy lever to alter macro outcomes (unemployment, inflation, etc.) is examined in Chapter 15. In this chapter, we focus on the *tools* of monetary policy.

STRUCTURE OF THE FED

In the absence of any government regulation, the supply of money would be determined by individual banks. Moreover, individual depositors would bear all the risks of bank failures. In fact, this is the way the banking system operated until 1914. The money supply was subject to abrupt changes, and consumers frequently lost their savings in recurrent bank failures.

A series of bank failures resulted in a severe financial panic in 1907. Millions of depositors lost their savings, and the economy was thrown into a tailspin. In the wake of this panic, a National Monetary Commission was established to examine ways of restructuring the banking system. The mandate of the commission was to find ways to avert recurrent financial crises. After 5 years of study, the commission recommended the creation of a Federal Reserve System. Congress accepted the commission's recommendations, and President Wilson signed the Federal Reserve Act in December 1913.

The core of the Federal Reserve System consists of 12 Federal Reserve banks. Each bank acts as a central banker for the private banks in its region. In this role, the regional Fed banks perform the following services:

- *Clearing checks between private banks.* Suppose the Bank of America in San Francisco receives a deposit from one of its customers in the form of a share draft written on the New York State Employees Credit Union. The Bank of America doesn't have to go to New York to collect the cash or other reserves that support that draft. Instead, the Bank of America can deposit the draft (check) at its account with the Federal Reserve Bank of San Francisco. The Fed then collects from the credit union. This vital clearinghouse service saves the Bank of America and other private banks a great deal of time and expense in processing the 40 *billion* checks that are written every year. (The Fed employs 5,000 people for this processing activity.)
- *Holding bank reserves.* Notice that the Fed's clearinghouse service was facilitated by the fact that the Bank of America and the New York Employees Credit Union had their own accounts at the Fed. As we noted in Chapter 13, banks are *required* to hold some minimum fraction of their deposits in reserve. Only a small amount of reserves is held as cash in a bank's vaults. The rest is held in reserve accounts at the regional Federal Reserve banks. These accounts not only provide greater security and convenience for bank reserves but also enable the Fed to monitor the actual level of bank reserves.
- *Providing currency.* Before every major holiday there's a great demand for cash. People want some pocket money during holidays and know that it's difficult to cash checks on weekends or holidays, especially if they're going out of town. So they load up on cash at their bank or ATMs. After the holiday is over, most of this cash is returned to the banks, typically by the stores, gas stations, and restaurants that benefited from holiday spending. Because banks hold very little cash in their vaults, they turn to the Fed to meet these sporadic cash demands. A private bank can simply call the regional Federal Reserve bank and order a supply of cash, to be delivered (by armored truck) before a weekend or holiday. The cash will be deducted from the bank's own account at the Fed. When all the cash comes back in after the holiday, the bank can reverse the process, sending the unneeded cash back to the Fed.
- *Providing loans.* The Federal Reserve banks may also loan reserves to private banks. This practice, called "discounting," is examined more closely in a moment.

At the top of the Federal Reserve System's organization chart (Figure 14.1) is the Board of Governors, which is responsible for setting monetary policy. The Board, located in Washington, D.C., consists of seven members ("governors"), appointed by the president of the United States and confirmed by the U.S. Senate. Board members are appointed for 14-year terms and can't be reappointed. Their exceptionally long appointments give the Fed governors a measure of political independence. They're not beholden to any elected official and will hold office longer than any president.

monetary policy: The use of money and credit controls to influence macroeconomic outcomes.

Federal Reserve Banks

The Board of Governors

FIGURE 14.1
Structure of the Federal Reserve System

The Fed's broad policies are determined by the seven-member Board of Governors. The 12 Federal Reserve banks provide central banking services to individual banks in their respective regions. The Federal Open Market Committee directs Federal Reserve transactions in the money market. Various committees offer formal and informal advice to the Board of Governors.

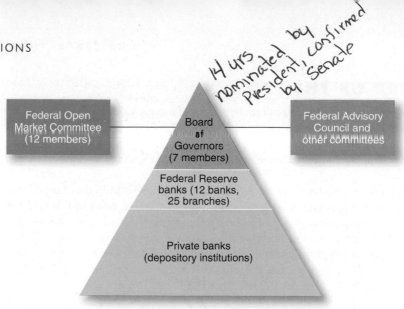

(handwritten: 4 yrs nominated by president, confirmed by Senate)

web analysis

Who runs the Fed? Read profiles of the governors at **www.federalreserve.gov/bios.**

(handwritten: daily →)

The Federal Open Market Committee (FOMC)

money supply (M1): Currency held by the public, plus balances in transactions accounts.

M2 money supply: M1 plus balances in most savings accounts and money market mutual funds.

Reserve Requirements

required reserves: The minimum amount of reserves a bank is required to hold; equal to required reserve ratio times transactions deposits.

The intent of the Fed's independence is to keep control of the nation's money supply beyond the immediate reach of politicians (especially members of Congress, elected for 2-year terms). The designers of the Fed system feared that political control of monetary policy would cause wild swings in the money supply and macro instability. Critics argue, however, that the Fed's independence makes it unresponsive to the majority will.

The president selects one of the governors to serve as chairman of the Board for 4 years. The current chairman, Ben Bernanke, was appointed by President Bush in January 2006 and may be reappointed by President Obama at the end of 2009. Previously he had been an economics professor at Princeton University and had served as chair of Bush's Council of Economic Advisers. Chairman Bernanke is the primary spokesperson for Fed policy and reports to Congress every 6 months on the conduct of monetary policy.

A key arm of the Board is the Federal Open Market Committee (FOMC), which is responsible for the Fed's daily activity in financial markets. The FOMC plays a critical role in setting short-term interest rates and the level of reserves held by private banks. The membership of the FOMC includes all seven governors and 5 of the 12 regional Reserve bank presidents. The FOMC meets in Washington, D.C., every 4 or 5 weeks throughout the year to review the economy's performance. It decides whether the economy is growing fast enough (or too fast) and then adjusts monetary policy as needed.

MONETARY TOOLS

Our immediate interest isn't in the structure of the Federal Reserve but the way the Fed is able to alter the **money supply.** The Fed's control of the money supply is exercised by use of three policy instruments:

- Reserve requirements *(handwritten: —isn't used frequently)*
- Discount rates
- Open market operations *(handwritten: —most important)*

The Fed's first policy tool focuses on reserve requirements. As noted in Chapter 13, the Fed requires private banks to keep some stated fraction of their deposits "in reserve." These **required reserves** are held either in the form of actual vault cash or, more commonly, as credits (deposits) in the bank's "reserve account" at a regional Federal Reserve bank. *By changing the reserve requirements, the Fed can directly alter the lending capacity of the banking system.*

Recall that the banking system's ability to make additional loans—create deposits—is determined by two factors: (1) the amount of excess reserves banks hold and (2) the money multiplier. Both factors are directly influenced by the Fed's required reserve ratio.

Computing Excess Reserves. Suppose, for example, that banks collectively hold $100 billion of deposits and total reserves of $30 billion. Assume too that the minimum reserve requirement is 20 percent. Under these circumstances, banks are holding more reserves than they have to. Recall that

$$\frac{\text{Required}}{\text{reserves}} = \frac{\text{required}}{\text{reserve ratio}} \times \frac{\text{total}}{\text{deposits}}$$

so, in this case

$$\frac{\text{Required}}{\text{reserves}} = 0.20 \times \$100 \text{ billion}$$
$$= \$20 \text{ billion}$$

Banks are *required* to hold $20 billion in reserve to meet Federal Reserve regulations on their deposit base ($100 billion). They're actually holding $30 billion of reserves, however. The $10 billion difference between actual and required reserves is **excess reserves**—that is,

$$\frac{\text{Excess}}{\text{reserves}} = \frac{\text{total}}{\text{reserves}} - \frac{\text{required}}{\text{reserves}}$$

The existence of excess reserves implies that banks aren't fully utilizing their lending powers. With $10 billion of excess reserves and the help of the **money multiplier** the banks *could* lend an additional $50 billion.

The potential for additional loans is calculated as

$$\frac{\text{Available lending capacity}}{\text{of banking system}} = \text{excess reserves} \times \text{money multiplier}$$

or, in this case,

$$\$10 \text{ billion} \times \frac{1}{0.20} = \$50 \text{ billion of unused lending capacity}$$

That is, the banking system could create another $50 billion of money (transactions account balances) without any additional reserves.

A simple way to confirm this—and thereby check your arithmetic—is to note what would happen to total deposits if the banks actually made further loans. Total deposits would increase to $150 billion in this case (the initial $100 billion of deposits plus the new loan-created deposits of $50 billion), an amount that could be supported with $30 billion in reserves (20 percent of $150 billion).

Soaking Up Excess Reserves. But what if the Fed doesn't want the money supply to increase this much? Maybe prices are rising and the Fed wants to restrain rather than stimulate total spending in the economy. Under such circumstances, the Fed would want to restrict the availability of credit (loans). Does it have the power to do so? Can the Fed reduce the lending capacity of the banking system?

The answer to both questions is clearly yes. *By raising the required reserve ratio, the Fed can immediately reduce the lending capacity of the banking system.*

Table 14.1 summarizes the impact of an increase in the required reserve ratio. In this case, the required reserve ratio is increased from 20 to 25 percent. Notice that this change

excess reserves: Bank reserves in excess of required reserves

money multiplier: The number of deposit (loan) dollars that the banking system can create from $1 of excess reserves; equal to 1 ÷ required reserve ratio.

	Required Reserve Ratio	
	20 Percent	**25 Percent**
1. Total deposits	$100 billion	$100 billion
2. Total reserves	30 billion	30 billion
3. Required reserves	20 billion	25 billion
4. Excess reserves	10 billion	5 billion
5. Money multiplier	5	4
6. Unused lending capacity	$ 50 billion	$ 20 billion

TABLE 14.1

The Impact of an Increased Reserve Requirement

An increase in the required reserve ratio reduces both excess reserves (row 4) and the money multiplier (row 5). As a consequence, changes in the reserve requirement have a substantial impact on the lending capacity of the banking system (row 6).

in the reserve requirement has no effect on the amount of deposits in the banking system (row 1, Table 14.1) or the amount of total reserves (row 2). They remain at $100 billion and $30 billion, respectively. What the increased reserve requirement does affect is the way those reserves can be used. Before the increase, only $20 billion in reserves were *required*, leaving $10 billion of *excess* reserves. Now, however, banks are required to hold $25 billion (0.25 × $100 billion) in reserves, leaving them with only $5 billion in excess reserves. Thus an increase in the reserve requirement immediately reduces excess reserves, as illustrated in row 4, Table 14.1.

There's also a second effect. Notice what happens to the money multiplier (1 ÷ reserve ratio). Previously it was 5(= 1 ÷ 0.20); now it's only 4(= 1 ÷ 0.25). Consequently, a higher reserve requirement not only reduces excess reserves but diminishes their lending power as well.

A change in the reserve requirement, therefore, hits banks with a triple whammy. *A change in the reserve requirement causes a change in*

- *Excess reserves.*
- *The money multiplier.*
- *The lending capacity of the banking system.*

These changes lead to a sharp reduction in bank lending power. Whereas the banking system initially had the power to increase the volume of loans by $50 billion ($10 billion of excess reserves × 5), it now has only $20 billion ($5 million × 4) of unused lending capacity, as noted in the last row in Table 14.1.

Changes in reserve requirements are a powerful tool for altering the lending capacity of the banking system. The Fed uses this tool sparingly, so as not to cause abrupt changes in the money supply and severe disruptions of banking activity. From 1970 to 1980, for example, reserve requirements were changed only twice, and then by only half a percentage point each time (for example, from 12.0 to 12.5 percent). The Fed last cut the reserve requirement from 12 to 10 percent in 1992 to increase bank profits and encourage more lending (see News below). Smaller banks have a lower reserve requirement (3 percent), which gives them a competitive advantage.

IN THE NEWS

Fed Cuts Deposit-Reserve Requirements

Reduction Is the Latest Bid to Bolster Bank Profits and Encourage Lending

WASHINGTON—The Federal Reserve Board, in another attempt to shore up bank profits so bankers will be more willing to lend, reduced the fraction of deposits that must be held as reserves.

The Fed cut to 10 percent from 12 percent the percentage of checking account deposits that banks are required to hold as reserves. Because reserves must be in cash or in accounts that don't pay any interest, the change will add between $300 million and $600 million to bank industry profits.

—David Wessel

Source: *The Walll Street Journal*, February 19, 1992. Copyright 1992 by Dow Jones & Company, Inc. Reproduced with permission of Dow Jones & Company, Inc. in the format Textbook via Copyright Clearance Center.

Analysis: A reduction in the reserve requirement transforms some of the banking system's required reserves into excess reserves, thus increasing potential lending activity and profits. It also increases the size of the money multiplier.

The Discount Rate

Banks have a tremendous incentive to maintain their reserves at or close to the minimum established by the Fed. Bank reserves held at the Fed earn lower rates of interest than banks could get from making loans or holding bonds. Hence, a profit-maximizing bank seeks to

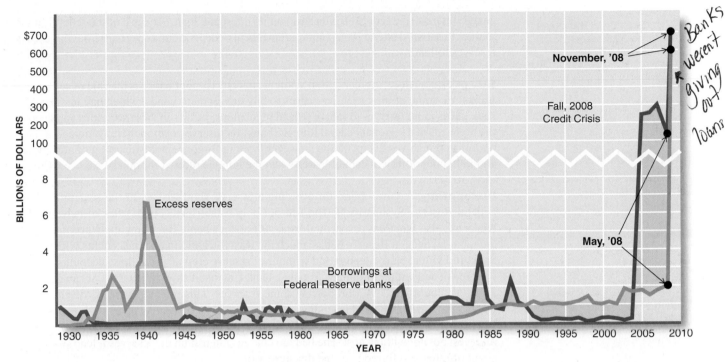

Banks weren't giving out loans

FIGURE 14.2
Excess Reserves and Borrowings

Excess reserves represent unused lending capacity. Hence, banks strive to keep excess reserves at a minimum. One exception to this practice occurred in the Great Depression, when banks were hesitant to make any loans. It happened again in the "Great Recession" of 2008–09, when bank assets lost value and new loans looked risky.

In more normal circumstances, banks try to minimize excess reserves, occasionally falling short of required reserves in the process. At such times they may borrow from other banks (the federal funds market), or they may borrow reserves from the Fed. Borrowing from the Fed is called "discounting."

web analysis

To update Figure 14.2, visit **www. federalreserve.gov** and search "reserves and borrowings."

keep its excess reserves as low as possible, preferring to put its reserves to better, more profitable work. In fact, banks have demonstrated an uncanny ability to keep their reserves close to the minimum federal requirement. As Figure 14.2 illustrates, the few times banks held huge excess reserves were in the Great Depression of the 1930s and during the 2008 credit crisis. The banks didn't want to make any more loans and were fearful of loan defaults and panicky customers withdrawing their deposits.

Because banks continually seek to keep excess reserves at a minimum, they run the risk of falling below reserve requirements. A large borrower may be a little slow in repaying a loan, or the rate of deposit withdrawals and transfers may exceed expectations, or as we saw in the 2008 credit crisis (Chapter 13), defaults and price declines may reduce the value of assets held by the bank. At such times, a bank may find that it doesn't have enough reserves to satisfy Fed requirements.

Banks could ensure continual compliance with reserve requirements by maintaining large amounts of excess reserves. But that's an unprofitable procedure, and a profit-maximizing bank will seek other alternatives.

The Federal Funds Market. A bank that finds itself short of reserves can turn to other banks for help. If a reserve-poor bank can borrow some reserves from a reserve-rich bank, it may be able to bridge its temporary deficit and satisfy the Fed. *Reserves borrowed by one bank from another are referred to as " federal funds" and are lent for short periods, usually overnight.* Although trips to the federal funds market—via telephone and computer—will usually satisfy Federal Reserve requirements, such trips aren't free. The lending bank will

federal funds rate: The interest rate for interbank reserve loans.

charge interest (the **federal funds rate**) on its interbank loan.[1] The use of the federal funds market to satisfy Federal Reserve requirements also depends on other banks having excess reserves to lend.

Sale of Securities. Another option available to reserve-poor banks is the sale of securities. Banks use some of their excess reserves to buy government bonds, which pay interest. If a bank needs more reserves to satisfy federal regulations, it can sell these securities and deposit the proceeds at a regional Federal Reserve bank. Its reserve position thereby increases. This option also involves distinct costs, however, both in forgone interest-earning opportunities and in the possibility of capital losses when the bond is offered for quick sale.

Discounting. A third option for avoiding a reserve shortage lies in the structure of the Federal Reserve System itself. The Fed not only establishes certain rules of behavior for banks but also functions as a central bank, or banker's bank. Banks maintain accounts with the regional Federal Reserve banks, much the way you and I maintain accounts with a local bank. Individual banks deposit and withdraw "reserve credits" from these accounts, just as we deposit and withdraw dollars. Should a bank find itself short of reserves, it can go to the Fed's "discount window" and borrow some reserves. This process is called **discounting.** Discounting means the Fed is lending reserves directly to private banks.[2]

discounting: Federal Reserve lending of reserves to private banks.

The Fed's discounting operation provides private banks with an important source of reserves, but not without cost. The Fed too charges interest on the reserves it lends to banks, a rate of interest referred to as the **discount rate.**

discount rate: The rate of interest the Federal Reserve charges for lending reserves to private banks.

The discount window is a mechanism for directly influencing the size of bank reserves. *By raising or lowering the discount rate, the Fed changes the cost of money for banks and therewith the incentive to borrow reserves.* At high discount rates, borrowing from the Fed is expensive. High discount rates also signal the Fed's desire to restrain the money supply and an accompanying reluctance to lend reserves. Low discount rates, on the other hand, make it profitable to acquire additional reserves and exploit one's lending capacity to the fullest. Low discount rates also indicate the Fed's willingness to support credit expansion.

Open Market Operations

Reserve requirements and discount window operations are important tools of monetary policy. But they don't come close to open market operations in day-to-day impact on the money supply. *Open market operations are the principal mechanism for directly altering the reserves of the banking system.* Since reserves are the lifeblood of the banking system, open market operations are of immediate and critical interest to private banks and the larger economy.

Portfolio Decisions. To appreciate the impact of open market operations, you have to think about the alternative uses for idle funds. All of us have some idle funds, even if they amount to just a few dollars in our pocket or a minimal balance in our checking account. Other consumers and corporations have great amounts of idle funds, even millions of dollars at any time. Here we're concerned with what people decide to do with such funds.

People (and corporations) don't hold all their idle funds in transactions accounts or cash. Idle funds are also used to purchase stocks, build up savings account balances, and purchase bonds. These alternative uses of idle funds are attractive because they promise some additional income in the form of interest, dividends, or capital appreciation, such as higher stock prices. Deciding where to place idle funds is referred to as the **portfolio decision.**

portfolio decision: The choice of how (where) to hold idle funds.

Hold Money or Bonds? The Fed's *open market operations focus on one of the portfolio choices people make: whether to deposit idle funds in bank accounts or purchase government bonds.* The Fed attempts to influence this choice by making bonds more or less attractive,

---

[1]An overnight loan of $1 million at 6 percent interest (per year) costs $165 in interest charges plus any service fees that might be added. Banks make multimillion-dollar loans in the federal funds market.

[2]In the past banks had to present loan notes to the Fed in order to borrow reserves. The Fed "discounted" the notes by lending an amount equal to only a fraction of their face value. Although banks no longer have to present loans as collateral, the term "discounting" endures.

FIGURE 14.3
Open Market Operations

People may hold assets in the form of bank deposits (money) or bonds. When the Fed buys bonds from the public, it increases the flow of deposits (and reserves) to the banks. When the Fed sells bonds, it diminishes the flow of deposits and therewith the banks' capacity to lend (create money).

---

as circumstances warrant. The Fed's goal is to encourage people to move funds from banks to bond markets or vice versa. In the process, reserves either enter or leave the banking system, thereby altering the lending capacity of banks.

Figure 14.3 depicts the general nature of the Fed's open market operations. As we first observed in Chapter 13 (Figure 13.2), the process of deposit creation begins when people deposit money in the banking system. But people may also hold their assets in the form of bonds. The Fed's objective is to alter this portfolio decision by buying or selling bonds. *When the Fed buys bonds from the public, it increases the flow of deposits (reserves) to the banking system. Bond sales by the Fed reduce the inflow.*

The Bond Market. To understand how open market operations work, let's look closer at the bond market. Not all of us buy and sell bonds, but a lot of consumers and corporations do: Daily volume in bond markets exceeds $1 *trillion*. What's being exchanged in this market, and what factors influence decisions to buy or sell?

In our discussion thus far, we've portrayed banks as intermediaries between savers and spenders. Banks aren't the only mechanism available for transferring purchasing power from nonspenders to spenders. Funds are lent and borrowed in bond markets as well. In this case, a corporation may borrow money directly from consumers or other institutions. When it does so, it issues a bond as proof of its promise to repay the loan. A **bond** is simply a piece of paper certifying that someone has borrowed money and promises to pay it back at some future date. In other words, *a bond is nothing more than an IOU.* In the case of bond markets, however, the IOU is typically signed by a giant corporation or a government agency rather than a friend. It's therefore more widely accepted by lenders.

Because most corporations and government agencies that borrow money in the bond market are well known and able to repay their debts, their bonds are actively traded. If I lend $1,000 to General Motors on a 10-year bond, for example, I don't have to wait 10 years to get my money back; I can resell the bond to someone else at any time. If I do, that person will collect the face value of the bond (plus interest) from GM when it's due. The actual purchase and sale of bonds take place in the bond market. Although a good deal of the action occurs on Wall Street in New York, the bond market has no unique location. Like other markets we've discussed, the bond market exists whenever and however (electronically) bond buyers and sellers get together.

Bond Yields. People buy bonds because bonds pay interest. If you buy a General Motors bond, GM is obliged to pay you interest during the period of the loan. For example, an 8 percent 2025 GM bond in the amount of $1,000 states that GM will pay the bondholder $80 interest annually (8 percent of $1,000) until 2025. At that point GM will repay the initial $1,000 loan (the "principal").

bond: A certificate acknowledging a debt and the amount of interest to be paid each year until repayment; an IOU.

yield: The rate of return on a bond; the annual interest payment divided by the bond's price

The current **yield** paid on a bond depends on the promised interest rate (8 percent in this case) and the actual purchase price of the bond. Specifically,

$$\text{Yield} = \frac{\text{annual interest payment}}{\text{price paid for bond}}$$

If you pay \$1,000 for the bond, then the current yield is

$$\text{Yield} = \frac{\$80}{\$1,000} = 0.08, \text{ or } 8\%$$

which is the same as the interest rate printed on the face of the bond. But what if you pay only \$900 for the bond? In this case, the interest rate paid by GM remains at 8 percent, but the *yield* jumps to

$$\text{Yield} = \frac{\$80}{\$900} = 0.089, \text{ or } 8.9\%$$

Buying a \$1,000 bond for only \$900 might seem like too good a bargain to be true. But bonds are often bought and sold at prices other than their face value (see accompanying News). In fact, *a principal objective of Federal Reserve open market activity is to alter the price of bonds, and therewith their yields.* By doing so, the Fed makes bonds a more or less attractive alternative to holding money.

IN THE NEWS

Treasury Prices Fall As Refunding Weighs

A fund-raising announcement from the Treasury Department and better-than-expected economic data pulled Treasury prices down. . . .

The Treasury on Wednesday said that it will sell a record \$67 billion of new securities in its quarterly refunding next week to refund \$36.3 billion in maturing issues and raise about \$30.7 billion. . . .

Late in New York, the 10-year note was down 21/32 point, or \$6.5625 per \$1,000 face value, at 107 2/32, to yield 2.914% up from 2.842% late Tuesday, as yields move inversely to prices. The 30-year bond was down 30/32 point, at 114 24/32, to yield 3.673%, up from 3.626% Tuesday.

—Deborah Lynn Blumberg

Source: *The Wall Street Journal*, February 5, 2009. Copyright 2009 by Dow Jones & Company, Inc. Reproduced with permission of Dow Jones & Company, Inc. in the format Textbook via Copyright Clearance Center.

Analysis: Bond prices and yields move in opposite directions. If the Fed sells bonds, bond prices fall and yields (interest rates) rise.

Open Market Activity. The basic premise of open market activity is that participants in the bond market will respond to changes in bond prices and yields. As we've observed, *the less you pay for a bond, the higher its yield.* Accordingly, the Fed can induce people to *buy* bonds by offering to sell them at a lower price (e.g., a \$1,000, 8 percent bond for only \$900). Similarly, the Fed can induce people to *sell* bonds by offering to buy them at higher prices. In either case, the Fed hopes to move reserves into or out of the banking system. In other words, **open market operations** entail the purchase and sale of government securities (bonds) for the purpose of altering the flow of reserves into and out of the banking system.

open market operations: Federal Reserve purchases and sales of government bonds for the purpose of altering bank reserves.

Open Market Purchases. Suppose the Fed's goal is to increase the money supply. Its strategy is to provide the banking system with additional reserves. To do so, it must persuade

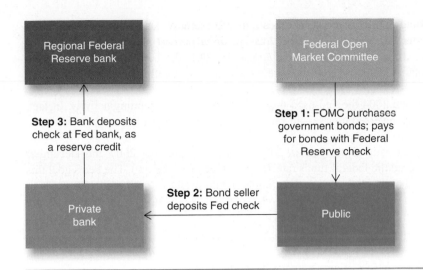

FIGURE 14.4
An Open Market Purchase

The Fed can increase bank reserves by buying bonds from the public. The Fed check used to buy bonds (step 1) gets deposited in a private bank (step 2). The bank returns the check to the Fed (step 3), thereby obtaining additional reserves. To decrease bank reserves, the Fed would sell bonds, thus reversing the flow of reserves.

people to deposit a larger share of their financial assets in banks and hold less in other forms, particularly government bonds. The tool for doing this is bond prices. *If the Fed offers to pay a higher price for bonds ("bids up bonds"), it will effectively lower bond yields and market interest rates.* The higher prices and lower yields will reduce the attractiveness of holding bonds. If the price offered by the Fed is high enough, people will sell some of their bonds to the Fed and deposit the proceeds of the sale in their bank accounts. This influx of money into bank accounts will directly increase bank reserves. Bingo, goal achieved.

Figure 14.4 illustrates the dynamics of open market operations in more detail. When the Fed buys a bond from the public, it pays with a check written on itself (step 1 in Figure 14.4). What will the bond seller do with the check? There really aren't any options. If the seller wants to use the proceeds of the bond sale, he or she will have to deposit the Fed check at a bank (step 2 in the figure). The bank, in turn, deposits the check at a regional Federal Reserve bank, in exchange for a reserve credit (step 3). The bank's reserves are directly increased by the amount of the check. Thus, *by buying bonds, the Fed increases bank reserves.* These reserves can be used to expand the money supply still further, as banks put their newly acquired reserves to work making loans.

Open Market Sales. Should the Fed desire to slow the growth in the money supply, it can reverse the whole process. Instead of offering to *buy* bonds, the Fed in this case will try to *sell* bonds. If the Fed "bids bonds down" (offers to sell them at low prices), bond yields will rise. In response, individuals, corporations, and government agencies will convert some of their transactions deposits into bonds. When they do so, they write a check, paying the Fed for the bonds.[3] The Fed then returns the check to the depositor's bank, taking payment through a reduction in the bank's reserve account. The reserves of the banking system are thereby diminished, as is the capacity to make loans. Thus, *by selling bonds, the Fed reduces bank reserves.*

A market signal of these changing reserve flows is provided by the federal funds rate. Recall that "fed funds" are excess reserves traded among banks. If the Fed pumps more reserves into the banking system (by buying bonds), the interest rate charged for overnight reserve loans—the federal funds rate—will decline. Conversely, if the Fed is reducing bank

The Fed Funds Rate

---

[3]In actuality, the Fed deals directly with only 36 "primary" bond dealers. These intermediaries then trade with each other, "secondary" dealers, financial institutions, and individuals. These additional steps don't significantly alter the flow of funds depicted here. Using electronic transactions rather than paper checks doesn't alter the flow of funds either.

reserves (by selling bonds), the federal funds rate will increase. Hence, ***the federal funds rate is a highly visible signal of Federal Reserve open market operations.*** When Alan Greenspan reduced the federal funds rate *11 times* in 2001, the Fed was underscoring the urgency of monetary stimulus to combat the recession and the aftereffects of the September 11 terrorist attacks.

Beginning in June 2004 the Fed used this same tool to *reduce* lending activity. In fact, the Fed completely reversed course and raised the fed funds rate *17 times* between June 2004 and June 2006.

The Fed changed course yet again in 2007. Between September 2007 and December 2008 the Fed lowered the federal funds rate *10 times* (see News below). The Fed's goal this time was to push bond yields so low that people would prefer to hold their idle funds in banks rather than buy bonds. The lower interest rates are also intended to encourage people to borrow and spend the increased reserves.

IN THE NEWS

U.S. Federal Reserve Cuts Interest Rates to Historic Low

U.S. Central Bank Decision Aimed at Reassuring Market, Stimulating Economy

Washington—The U.S. central bank on December 16 cut interest rates to an all-time low, a move aimed at reassuring financial markets and stimulating banks to lend money.

The Federal Reserve Board lowered the target federal funds rate to a range of 0 percent to 0.25 percent, the lowest level in the history of modern monetary policy. The federal funds rate is the rate at which banks lend to one another. The rate, historically, has an effect on the rates consumers are charged for home mortgage loans and other types of credit. . . .

A cut in the Fed's target rate lowers the interest rates consumers and businesses pay, making it more appealing for them to borrow money. When they spend that loaned cash, it boosts the economy by increasing the demand for goods, services and labor.

—Katherine Lewis

Source: **www.America.gov.** December 16, 2008.

Analysis: The Fed uses open market operations to change short-term interest rates. In this case the Fed intended to cut interest rates to near zero by aggressively buying Treasury bonds.

web analysis

How has the federal funds rate changed in the past 8 weeks? What does it signal about Federal Reserve activity? For data on the fed funds rate visit the Fed's Web site at **www.federalreserve.gov.**

When the Fed announces a change in the federal funds rate, it always refers to the "target" rate. The Fed doesn't actually *set* the fed funds rate. It only establishes a desired "target" rate. When the Fed lowers the target rate, it seeks to hit it by buying more bonds in the market.

Volume of Activity. To appreciate the significance of open market operations, you need a sense of the magnitudes involved. As we noted earlier, the volume of trading in U.S. bond markets exceeds $1 *trillion* a day. The Fed alone owned over $500 billion worth of government securities at the beginning of 2009 and bought or sold enormous sums daily. Thus, open market operations involve tremendous amounts of money and, by implication, potential bank reserves. Each $1 of reserves represents something like $10 of potential lending capacity (via the money multiplier). Thus, open market operations can have a profound impact on the money supply.

INCREASING THE MONEY SUPPLY

The three major tools of monetary policy are reserve requirements, discount rates, and open market operations. The Fed can use these tools individually or in combination to change the money supply. This section illustrates the use of each tool to attain a specific policy goal.

Item	Amount
1. Cash held by public	$100 billion
2. Transactions deposits	240 billion
3. Total money supply (M1)	$340 billion
4. Required reserves	$ 60 billion
5. Excess reserves	0
6. Total reserves of banks	$ 60 billion
7. U.S. bonds held by public	$460 billion
8. Discount rate	5%

TABLE 14.2
How to Increase the Money Supply

The accompanying data depict a banking system that has $340 billion of money (M1) and no further lending capacity (excess reserves = 0). To enlarge M1 to $400 billion, the Fed can (1) lower the required reserve ratio, (2) reduce the discount rate, or (3) buy bonds held by the public.

Suppose the policy goal is to increase the money supply from an assumed level of $340 billion to $400 billion. In surveying the nation's banks, the Fed discovers the facts shown in Table 14.2. On the basis of the facts presented in Table 14.2, it's evident that

- The banking system is "loaned up." Because excess reserves are zero (see row 5 in Table 14.2), there's no additional lending capacity.
- The required reserve ratio must be equal to 25 percent, because this is the current ratio of required reserves ($60 billion) to total deposits ($240 billion).

Accordingly, if the Fed wants to increase the money supply, it will have to pump additional reserves into the banking system or lower the reserve requirement. *To increase the money supply the Fed can*

- *Lower reserve requirements.*
- *Reduce the discount rate.*
- *Buy bonds.*

Lowering Reserve Requirements

Lowering the reserve requirements is an expedient way of increasing the lending capacity of the banking system. But by how much should the reserve requirement be reduced?

Recall that the Fed's goal is to increase the money supply from $340 billion to $400 billion, an increase of $60 billion. If the public isn't willing to hold any additional cash, this entire increase in money supply will have to take the form of added transactions deposits. In other words, total deposits will have to increase from $240 billion to $300 billion. These additional deposits will have to be *created* by the banks, in the form of new loans to consumers or business firms.

If the banking system is going to support $300 billion in transactions deposits with its *existing* reserves, the reserve requirement will have to be reduced from 25 percent; thus,

$$\frac{\text{Total reserves}}{\text{Desired level of deposits}} = \frac{\$60 \text{ billion}}{\$300 \text{ billion}} = 0.20$$

At the moment the Fed lowers the minimum reserve ratio to 0.20, *total* reserves won't change. The bank's potential lending power will change, however. Required reserves will drop to $48 billion (0.20 × $240 billion), and excess reserves will jump from zero to $12 billion. These new excess reserves imply an additional lending capacity:

$$\underset{(\$12\text{ billion})}{\text{Excess reserves}} \times \underset{(5)}{\text{money multiplier}} = \underset{(\$60\text{ billion})}{\text{unused lending capacity}}$$

If the banks succeed in putting all this new lending power to work—actually make $60 billion in new loans—the Fed's objective of increasing the money supply will be attained.

Lowering the Discount Rate

The second monetary tool available to the Fed is the discount rate. We assumed it was 5 percent initially (see row 8 in Table 14.2). If the Fed lowers this rate, it will become cheaper for banks to borrow reserves from the Fed. The banks will be more willing to borrow (cheaper) reserves so long as they can make additional loans to their own customers at higher interest rates. The profitability of discounting depends on the *difference* between the discount rate and the interest rate the bank charges its loan customers. The Fed increases this difference when it lowers the discount rate.

There's no way to calculate the appropriate discount rate without more detailed knowledge of the banking system's willingness to borrow reserves from the Fed. Nevertheless, we can determine how much reserves the banks *must* borrow if the Fed's money supply target is to be attained. The Fed's objective is to increase transactions deposits by $60 billion. If these deposits are to be created by the banks—and the reserve requirement is unchanged at 0.25—the banks will have to borrow an additional $15 billion of reserves ($60 billion divided by 4, the money multiplier).

Buying Bonds

The Fed can also get additional reserves into the banking system by buying U.S. bonds in the open market. As row 7 in Table 14.2 indicates, the public holds $460 billion in U.S. bonds, none of which are counted as part of the money supply. If the Fed can persuade people to sell some of these bonds, bank reserves will surely rise.

To achieve its money supply target, the Fed will offer to buy $15 billion of U.S. bonds. It will pay for these bonds with checks written on its own account at the Fed. The people who sold the bonds will deposit these checks in their own transactions accounts. As they do so, they'll directly increase bank deposits and reserves by $15 billion.

Is $15 billion of open market purchases enough? Yes. The $15 billion is a direct addition to transactions deposits, and therefore to the money supply. The additional deposits bring in $15 billion of reserves, only $3.75 billion of which is required (0.25 × $15 billion). Hence, the new deposits bring in $11.25 billion of excess reserves, which themselves create an additional lending capacity:

$$\begin{array}{ccc} \text{Excess reserves} & & \text{money multiplier} \\ (\$11.25\text{billion}) & \times & (4) \end{array} = \begin{array}{c} \text{unused lending capacity} \\ (\$45 \text{ billion}) \end{array}$$

Thus, the $15 billion of open market purchases will eventually lead to a $60 billion increase in M1 as a consequence of both direct deposits ($15 billion) and subsequent loan activity ($45 billion).

Federal Funds Rate. When the Fed starts bidding up bonds, bond yields and market interest rates will start falling. So will the federal funds rate. This will give individual banks an incentive to borrow any excess reserves available, thereby accelerating deposit (loan) creation.

DECREASING THE MONEY SUPPLY

All the tools used to increase the money supply can also be used to decrease it. *To reduce the money supply, the Fed can*

- *Raise reserve requirements.*
- *Increase the discount rate.*
- *Sell bonds.*

On a week-to-week basis the Fed does occasionally seek to reduce the total amount of cash and transactions deposits held by the public. These are minor adjustments, however, to broader policies. A growing economy needs a steadily increasing supply of money to finance market exchanges. Hence, the Fed rarely seeks an outright reduction in the size of the money supply. What it does do is regulate the *rate of growth* in the money supply. When the Fed wants to slow the rate of consumer and investor spending, it restrains the *growth* of money and credit. Although many people talk about "reducing" the money supply, they're really talking about slowing its rate of growth. More immediately, they expect to see *rising* interest rates. To slow economic growth (and potential price inflation) China pursued this sort of monetary restraint in 2007 (see World View on the next page).

WORLD VIEW

China Lifts Bank Reserves in Bid to Cool Growth

BEIJING—For the seventh time in less than a year, China's central bank raised the share of deposits banks must keep on reserve as the government struggles to soak up capital and keep the country's economy from overheating. . . .

The newly announced increase will bring the reserve-requirement ratio—the share of deposits that lenders must keep with the central bank—up half a percentage point to 11% for most banks. The increase, in theory, reduces the amount available to banks to lend, though in practice many Chinese banks already keep more than the minimum on reserve. . . .

China's consumer-price index rose 3.3% in March and 2.7% in the first quarter, compared with a year earlier. That pickup has sparked concerns that after muted inflation in recent years, rising production capacity might no longer be able to counterbalance demand, and a surge in prices could be ahead for the world's fastest-growing major economy.

—Rick Carew and J. R. Wu

Source: *The Wall Street Journal*, April 30, 2007. Copyright 2007 by Dow Jones & Company, Inc. Reproduced with permission of Dow Jones & Company, Inc. in the format Textbook via Copyright Clearance Center.

Analysis: Central banks raise required reserve ratios and slow lending activity when they sense inflationary pressures.

THE ECONOMY TOMORROW

IS THE FED LOSING CONTROL?

The policy tools at the Fed's disposal imply tight control of the nation's money supply. By altering reserve requirements, discount rates, or open market purchases, the Fed apparently has the ability to increase or decrease the money supply at will. But the Fed's control is far from complete. The nature of "money," as well as our notion of what a "bank" is, keeps changing. As a result, the Fed has to run pretty fast just to stay in place.

Monetary Control Act. Before 1980, the Fed's control of the money supply wasn't only incomplete but actually weakening. The Fed didn't have authority over all banks. Only one-third of all commercial banks were members of the Federal Reserve System and subject to its regulations. All savings and loan associations and other savings banks remained outside the Federal Reserve System. These banks were subject to regulations of state banking commissions and other federal agencies but not to Federal Reserve requirements. As a consequence, a substantial quantity of money and near-money lay beyond the control of the Fed.

To increase the Fed's control of the money supply, Congress passed the Depository Institutions Deregulation and Monetary Control Act of 1980. Commonly referred to simply as the Monetary Control Act, that legislation subjected *all* commercial banks, S&Ls, savings banks, and most credit unions to Fed regulation. All depository institutions now have to satisfy Fed reserve requirements. All depository institutions also enjoy access to the Fed's discount window. These reforms (phased in over a period of 7 years) obliterated the distinction between member and nonmember banks and greatly strengthened the Fed's control of the banking system.

Decline of Traditional Banks. Ironically, *as the Fed's control of the banks was increasing, the banks themselves were declining in importance.* Banks are part of a larger financial services industry that provides deposit, credit, and payment services. Many of these services are provided by financial institutions other than banks. These nonbank financial institutions have grown in importance while traditional banks have declined in number and importance.

Accepting and holding deposits is a core bank function. Consumers can also place idle funds in money market mutual funds (MMMF), however. MMMFs typically pay higher interest rates than traditional bank accounts and also permit limited check writing privileges. They thus serve as a potential substitute for traditional banks. Many brokerage houses also offer to hold idle cash in interest-earning accounts for their stock and bond customers.

Nonbanks are also competing against banks for loan business; 30 percent of all consumer loans are now made through credit cards. Banks themselves were once the primary source of credit cards. Now corporate giants like AT&T, GM, Sears, and American Airlines offer nonbank credit cards. Large corporations also offer loans to consumers who want to buy their products and even extend loans to unaffiliated businesses.

Insurance companies and pension funds also use their vast financial resources to make loans. The Teachers Insurance and Annuity Association (TIAA)—the pension fund for college professors—has lent over $10 billion directly to corporations. Many insurance companies provide long-term loans for commercial real estate.

Global Finance. Foreign banks, corporations, and pension funds may also extend credit to American businesses. They may also hold deposits of U.S. dollars abroad (for example, Eurodollars). As the accompanying World View illustrates, money—even terrorists' money—travels easily across national borders.

WORLD VIEW

Fighting Terror/Targeting Funds; Laws May Not Stop Flow of Terror Funds

Congress is expected to approve legislation as early as today aimed at crippling the ability of terrorists to send money around the world. But law enforcement officials say that the increased globalization of electronic money transfer systems has made it easier than ever to move cash and avoid detection. . . .

The question, money laundering specialists say, is whether any unilateral action Congress takes can do much to stop the flow of dirty money across the world's borders. "The technology is changing all the time that makes it easier to transfer funds anonymously and to send money through five or six countries in one day," said William Schroeder, former director of the FBI's legal forfeiture division. . . .

Bank cash machines hardly qualify as cutting edge, but ATMs help criminals, according to the Treasury Department's Financial Crimes Enforcement Network, by allowing them "to wire funds into accounts in the United States from other nations and almost instantaneously and virtually anonymously to withdraw those funds." . . .

"If you know what you're doing, you can send money from the US to Spain to Cyprus to the Cayman Islands to Peru in a matter of minutes," said Schroeder.

—Scott Bernard Nelson

Source: *Boston Globe,* October 24, 2001. © Copyright 2001 Globe Newspaper Company. Used with permission.

Analysis: Nearly two-thirds of all U.S. currency circulates outside the United States, and over $1.5 trillion is transmitted by bank wire every day. This globalization of money makes it hard not only to track terrorists' money but also to control the domestic money supply.

All this credit and deposit activity by global and nonbank institutions competes with traditional banks. And the nonbanks are winning the competition. In the past 20 years, the share of all financial institution assets held by banks has dropped from 37 percent to 27 percent, which means that banks are less important than they once were. This has made control of the money supply increasingly difficult.

Focus on Fed Funds Rate, Not Money Supply. Because of the difficulties in managing an increasingly globalized and electronic flow of funds, the Fed has shifted away from money-supply targets to interest rate targets. Although changes in the money supply and in interest rates are intrinsically related, interest rates are easier and faster to track. The Fed also has the financial power to change short-term interest rates through its massive open market operations. Last, but not least, the Fed recognizes that interest rates, not more obscure data on the money-supply or bank reserves, are the immediate concern in investment and big-ticket consumption decisions. As a result, the Fed will continue to use the federal funds rate as its primary barometer of monetary policy in the economy tomorrow.

SUMMARY

- The Federal Reserve System controls the nation's money supply by regulating the loan activity (deposit creation) of private banks (depository institutions).   LO2
- The core of the Federal Reserve System is the 12 regional Federal Reserve banks, which provide check-clearance, reserve deposit, and loan ("discounting") services to individual banks. Private banks are required to maintain minimum reserves on deposit at the regional Federal Reserve banks.   LO1
- The general policies of the Fed are set by its Board of Governors. The Board's chair is selected by the U.S. president and confirmed by the Senate. The chair serves as the chief spokesperson for monetary policy. The Fed's policy strategy is implemented by the Federal Open Market Committee (FOMC), which directs open market sales and purchase of U.S. bonds.   LO1
- The Fed has three basic tools for changing the money supply. By altering the reserve requirement, the Fed can immediately change both the quantity of excess reserves in the banking system and the money multiplier, which limits banks' lending capacity. By altering discount rates (the rate of interest charged by the Fed for reserve borrowing), the Fed can also influence the amount of reserves maintained by banks. Finally, and most important, the Fed can increase or decrease the reserves of the banking system by buying or selling government bonds, that is, by engaging in open market operations.   LO2
- When the Fed buys bonds, it causes an increase in bank reserves (and lending capacity). When the Fed sells bonds, it induces a reduction in reserves (and lending capacity).   LO3
- The federal funds (interest) rate is a market signal of Fed open market activity and intentions.   LO2
- In the 1980s, the Fed gained greater control of the banking system. Global and nonbank institutions such as pension funds, insurance companies, and nonbank credit services have grown in importance, however, making control of the money supply more difficult.   LO2

Key Terms

monetary policy	money multiplier	portfolio decision
money supply (M1, M2)	federal funds rate	bond
required reserves	discounting	yield
excess reserves	discount rate	open market operations

Questions for Discussion

1. Why do banks want to maintain as little excess reserves as possible? Under what circumstances might banks want to hold excess reserves? (*Hint:* See Figure 14.2.)   LO2
2. Why do people hold bonds rather than larger savings account or checking account balances? Under what circumstances might they change their portfolios, moving their funds out of bonds and into bank accounts?   LO3
3. What is the current price and yield of 10-year U.S. Treasury bonds? Of General Motors bonds? (Check the financial section of your daily newspaper.) What accounts for the difference?   LO3
4. Why did China raise reserve requirements in 2007? How did they expect consumers and businesses to respond? (See World View, p. 303.)   LO2
5. Why might the Fed want to decrease the money supply?   LO2
6. Why did bond prices decline at the February 2009 auction? (See News, p. 298.)   LO3
7. In early 2009, short-term bond yields in the United States fell to less than 0.5 percent. Yet, relatively few people moved their assets out of bonds into banks. How might this failure of open market operations be explained?   LO3
8. In 2008, the Fed reduced both the discount and federal fund rates dramatically. But bank loan volume didn't increase. What considerations might have constrained the market's response to Fed policy?   LO2
9. If bondholders expect the Fed to raise interest rates, what action might they take? How would this affect the Fed's goal?   LO3

---

 web activities to accompany this chapter can be found on the Online Learning Center:
http://www.mhhe.com/schiller12e

Name: _____

LO1 1. What is the money multiplier when the reserve requirement is:

                                        (*u*) 0.10   _____

                                        (*b*) 0.12   _____

LO2 2. In Table 14.1, what would the following values be if the required reserve ratio fell to 0.10?

                                    (*a*) Total deposits   _____

                                    (*b*) Total reserves   _____

                                    (*c*) Required reserves   _____

                                    (*d*) Excess reserves   _____

                                    (*e*) Money multiplier   _____

                                    (*f*) Unused lending capacity   _____

LO2 3. Assume that the following data describe the condition of the banking system:

Total reserves	$200 billion
Transactions deposits	$700 billion
Cash held by public	$100 billion
Reserve requirement	0.20

    (*a*) How large is the money supply (M1)?   (*a*) _____

    (*b*) How large are *required* reserves?   (*b*) _____

    (*c*) How large are *excess* reserves?   (*c*) _____

    (*d*) By how much could the banks increase their lending activity?   (*d*) _____

LO2 4. In Problem 3, suppose the Fed wanted to stop further lending activity. To do this, what reserve requirement should the Fed impose?   _____

LO2 5. According to the News on page 294, and World View on page 303, what was the money multiplier in

                                    (*a*) The United States?   _____

                                    (*b*) China?   _____

LO2 6. Assume the banking system contains

Total reserves	$ 80 billion
Transactions deposits	$800 billion
Cash held by public	$100 billion
Reserve requirement	0.10

    (*a*) Are the banks fully utilizing their lending capacity?   _____

    (*b*) What would happen to the money supply *initially* if the public deposited another $50 billion of cash in transactions accounts?   _____

    (*c*) What would the lending capacity of the banking system be after such a portfolio switch?   _____

    (*d*) How large would the money supply be if the banks fully utilized their lending capacity?   _____

    (*e*) What three steps could the Fed take to offset that potential growth in M1?   _____

                                      _____

                                      _____

LO3 7. Assume that a $1,000 bond issued in 2009 pays $100 in interest each year. What is the current yield on the bond if it can be purchased for

                                    (*a*) $1,200?   _____

                                    (*b*) $1,000?   _____

                                    (*c*) $800?   _____

LO3 8. Suppose a $1,000 bond pays $40 per year in interest.

    (*a*) What is the contractual interest rate on the bond?   _____

    (*b*) If market interest rates rise to 8 percent, what price will the bond sell for?   _____

LO3   9. What was the Fed's target for the fed funds rate in December 2008 (News, p. 300)   _____

LO3 10. If the GM bond described on pages 297–298 was resold for $1200, what would its yield be?   _____

LO3 11. Suppose a banking system with the following balance sheet has no excess reserves. Assume that banks will make loans in the full amount of any excess reserves that they acquire and will immediately be able to eliminate loans from their portfolio to cover inadequate reserves.

Assets (in billions)		Liabilities (in billions)	
Total reserves	$ 30	Transactions accounts	$300
Securities	90		
Loans	180		
Total	$300	Total	$300

(a) What is the reserve requirement?   _____

(b) Suppose the reserve requirement is changed to 5 percent. Reconstruct the balance sheet of the total banking system after all banks have fully utilized their lending capacity.

Assets (in billions)		Liabilities (in billions)	
Total reserves	_____	Transactions accounts	_____
Securities	_____		
Loans	_____		
Total	_____	Total	_____

(c) By how much has the money supply changed as a result of the lower reserve requirement (step b)?   _____

(d) Suppose the Fed now buys $10 billion of securities directly from the banks. What will the banks' books look like after this purchase?

Assets (in billions)		Liabilities (in billions)	
Total reserves	_____	Transactions accounts	_____
Securities	_____		
Loans	_____		
Total	_____	Total	_____

(e) How much excess reserves do the banks have now?   _____

(f) By how much can the money supply now increase?   _____

Monetary Policy

15

After reading this chapter, you should be able to:

LO1. Describe how monetary policy affects macro outcomes.

LO2. Summarize the constraints on monetary-policy impact.

LO3. Identify the differences between Keynesian and monetarist monetary theories.

So **what if** the Federal Reserve System controls the nation's money supply? Why is this significant? Does it matter how much money is available?

Vladimir Lenin thought so. The first communist leader of the Soviet Union once remarked that the best way to destroy a society is to destroy its money. If a society's money became valueless, it would no longer be accepted in exchange for goods and services in product markets. People would have to resort to barter, and the economy's efficiency would be severely impaired. Adolf Hitler tried unsuccessfully to use this weapon against Great Britain during World War II. His plan was to counterfeit British currency, then drop it from planes flying over England. He believed that the sudden increase in the quantity of money, together with its suspect origins, would render the British pound valueless.

Even in peacetime, the quantity of money in circulation influences its value in the marketplace. Moreover, interest rates and access to credit (bank loans) are basic determinants of spending behavior. As we witnessed in 2008, when credit becomes unavailable, the economy can grind to a halt. Consequently, control over the money supply is a critical policy tool for altering macroeconomic outcomes.

But how much influence does the money supply have on macro performance? Specifically,

- **What's the relationship between the money supply, interest rates, and aggregate demand?**
- **How can the Fed use its control of the money supply or interest rates to alter macro outcomes?**
- **How effective is monetary policy, compared to fiscal policy?**

Economists offer very different answers to these questions. Some argue that changes in the money supply directly affect macro outcomes; others argue that the effects of such changes are indirect and less certain.

Paralleling these arguments about *how* **monetary policy** works are debates over the relative effectiveness of monetary and fiscal policy. Some economists argue that monetary policy is more effective than fiscal policy; others contend the reverse is true. This chapter examines these different views of money and assesses their implications for macro policy.

THE MONEY MARKET

The best place to learn how monetary policy works is the money *market*. You must abandon any mystical notions you may harbor about money and view it like any other commodity that's traded in the marketplace. Like other goods, there's a supply of money and a demand for money. Together they determine the "price" of money, or the **interest rate.**

At first glance, it may appear strange to call interest rates the price of money. But when you borrow money, the "price" you pay is measured by the interest rate you're charged. When interest rates are high, money is "expensive." When interest rates are low, money is "cheap."

Even people who don't borrow must contend with the price of money. Money, as we've seen, comes in many different forms. A common characteristic of all money is that it can be held as a store of value. People hold cash and maintain positive bank balances for this purpose. Most of the money in our common measures of **money supply (M1, M2)** is in the form of bank balances. There's an opportunity cost associated with such money balances, however. Money held in transactions accounts earns little or no interest. Money held in savings accounts and money market mutual funds does earn interest but usually at relatively low rates. By contrast, money used to buy bonds or stocks or to make loans is likely to earn a higher rate of return, as Table 15.1 illustrates.

The Price of Money. The nature of the "price" of money should be apparent: People who hold *cash* are forgoing an opportunity to earn interest. So are people who hold money in checking accounts that pay no interest. In either case, *forgone interest is the opportunity cost (price) of money people choose to hold.* How high is that price? It's equal to the market rate of interest.

Money held in interest-paying bank accounts does earn some interest. In this case, the opportunity cost of holding money is the *difference* between the prevailing rate of interest and the rate paid on deposit balances. In Table 15.1 the opportunity cost of holding cash rather than Treasury bonds is 2.52 percent. As is the case with cash and regular checking accounts, opportunity cost is measured by the forgone interest.

Once we recognize that money does have a price, we can easily formulate a demand for money. As is the case with all goods, the **demand for money** is a schedule (or curve) showing the quantity of money demanded at alternative prices (interest rates).

So why would anyone want to "hold" money? The decision to hold (demand) money balances is the kind of **portfolio decision** we examined in Chapter 14. While at first glance it might seem irrational to hold money balances that pay little or no interest, there are many good reasons for doing so.

Transactions Demand. Even people who've mastered the principles of economics hold money. They do so because they want to buy goods and services. In order to transact business in product or factor markets, we need money in the form of either cash or a positive bank account balance. Debit cards and ATM cards don't work unless there's money in the bank. Payment by e-cash also requires a supporting bank balance. Even when we use credit cards, we're only postponing the date of payment by a few weeks or so. Some merchants won't even

Option	Interest Rate
Cash	0.00%
Checking accounts	0.35
6-month CD	1.53
10-yr. Treasury bond	2.52
Corporate bond	5.05

Source: Federal Reserve (February 2009 rates).

monetary policy: The use of money and credit controls to influence macroeconomic outcomes.

interest rate: The price paid for the use of money.

Money Balances

money supply (M1): Currency held by the public, plus balance in transactions accounts.

money supply (M2): M1 plus balances in most savings accounts and money market mutual funds.

The Demand for Money

demand for money: The quantities of money people are willing and able to hold at alternative interest rates, *ceteris paribus.*

portfolio decision: The choice of how (where) to hold idle funds.

TABLE 15.1
Portfolio Choices

Idle funds can be held in many forms. Holding funds in cash or checking accounts pays little or no interest. The "price" of holding money is the interest forgone from alternative portfolio choices. When that price is high, people hold (demand) less money.

transactions demand for money: Money held for the purpose of making everyday market purchases.

precautionary demand for money: Money held for unexpected market transactions or for emergencies.

speculative demand for money: Money held for speculative purposes, for later financial opportunities.

accept credit cards, especially for small purchases. Accordingly, we recognize the existence of a basic **transactions demand for money,** that is, money held for everyday purchases.

Precautionary Demand. Another reason people hold money is their fear of the proverbial rainy day. A sudden emergency may require money purchases over and above normal transactions needs. Such needs may arise when the banks are closed or in a community where one's checks aren't accepted. Also, future income is uncertain and may diminish unexpectedly. Therefore, people hold a bit more money (cash or bank account balances) than they anticipate spending. This **precautionary demand for money** is the extra money being held as a safeguard against the unexpected.

Speculative Demand. People also hold money for speculative purposes. Suppose you were interested in buying stocks or bonds but hadn't yet picked the right ones or regarded their present prices as too high. In such circumstances, you might want to hold some money so that you could later buy a "hot" stock or bond at a price you think attractive. Thus, you'd be holding money in the hope that a better financial opportunity would later appear. In this sense, you'd be *speculating* with your money balances, forgoing present opportunities to earn interest in the hope of hitting a real jackpot later. These money balances represent a **speculative demand for money.**

The Market Demand Curve. These three motivations for holding money combine to create a *market demand* for money. The question is, what shape does this demand curve take? Does the quantity of money demanded decrease sharply as the rate of interest rises? Or do people tend to hold the same amount of money, regardless of its price?

People do cut down on their money balances when interest rates rise. At such times, the opportunity cost of holding money is simply too high. This explains why so many people move their money out of transactions deposits (M1) and into money market mutual funds (M2) when interest rates are extraordinarily high (for example, in 1980–82). Corporations are even more careful about managing their money when interest rates rise. Better money management requires watching checking account balances more closely and even making more frequent trips to the bank, but the opportunity costs are worth it.

Figure 15.1 illustrates the total market demand for money. Like nearly all demand curves, the market demand curve for money slopes downward. The downward slope indicates that *the quantity of money people are willing and able to hold (demand) increases as interest rates fall* (ceteris paribus).

The Money Supply. The money supply curve is assumed to be a vertical line. As we saw in Chapter 13, the Federal Reserve has the power to regulate the money supply through its

FIGURE 15.1
Money Market Equilibrium

All points on the money demand curve represent the quantity of money people are willing to hold at a specific interest rate. The equilibrium interest rate occurs at the intersection (E_1) of the money supply and money demand curves. At that rate of interest, people are willing to hold as much money as is available. At any other interest rate (for example, 9 percent), the quantity of money people are *willing* to hold won't equal the quantity available, and people will adjust their portfolios.

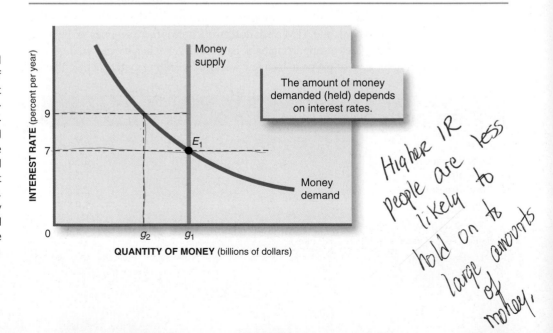

Higher IR people are less likely to hold on to large amounts of money.

reserve requirements, discount window, and open market operations. By using these policy tools, the Fed can target a specific quantity for the money supply (M1 or M2).

Once a money demand curve and a money supply curve are available, the action in money markets is easy to follow. Figure 15.1 summarizes this action. The money demand curve in Figure 15.1 reflects existing demands for holding money. The money supply curve is drawn at an arbitrary level of g_1. In practice, its position depends on Federal Reserve policy (Chapter 14), the lending behavior of private banks, and the willingness of consumers and investors to borrow money.

The intersection of the money demand and money supply curves (E_1) establishes an **equilibrium rate of interest.** Only at this interest rate is the quantity of money supplied equal to the quantity demanded. In this case, we observe that an interest rate of 7 percent equates the desires of suppliers and demanders.

At any rate of interest other than 7 percent, the quantity of money demanded wouldn't equal the quantity supplied. Look at the imbalance that exists, for example, when the interest rate is 9 percent. At that rate, the quantity of money supplied (g_1 in Figure 15.1) exceeds the quantity demanded (g_2). All the money (g_1) must be held by someone, of course. But the demand curve indicates that people aren't *willing* to hold so much money at that interest rate (9 percent). People will adjust their portfolios by moving money out of cash and bank accounts into bonds or other assets that offer higher returns. This will tend to lower interest rates (recall that buying bonds tends to lower their yields). As interest rates drop, people are willing to hold more money. Ultimately we get to E_1, where the quantity of money demanded equals the quantity supplied. At that equilibrium, people are content with their portfolio choices.

The equilibrium rate of interest is subject to change. As we saw in Chapter 14, the Federal Reserve System can alter the money supply through changes in reserve requirements, changes in the discount rate, or open market operations. By implication, then, *the Fed can alter the equilibrium rate of interest.*

Figure 15.2 illustrates the potential impact of monetary policy on the equilibrium rate of interest. Assume that the money supply is initially at g_1 and the equilibrium interest rate is 7 percent, as indicated by point E_1. The Fed then increases the money supply to g_3 by lowering the reserve requirement, reducing the discount rate, or, most likely, purchasing additional bonds in the open market. This expansionary monetary policy brings about a new equilibrium, at E_3. At this new intersection, the market rate of interest is only 6 percent. Hence, *by increasing the money supply, the Fed tends to lower the equilibrium rate of interest.* To put the matter differently, people are *willing* to hold larger money balances only at lower interest rates.

Equilibrium

> **equilibrium rate of interest:** The interest rate at which the quantity of money demanded in a given time period equals the quantity of money supplied.

Changing Interest Rates

FIGURE 15.2
Changing the Rate of Interest

Changes in the money supply alter the equilibrium rate of interest. In this case, an increase in the money supply (from g_1 to g_3) lowers the equilibrium rate of interest (from 7 percent to 6 percent).

Interest Rate	Type of Loan	Rate
Federal funds rate	Interbank reserves, overnight	0.20%
Discount rate	Reserves lent to banks by Fed	0.50
Prime rate	Bank loans to blue-chip corporations	3.25
Mortgage rate	Loans for house purchases; up to 30 years	5.06
Auto loan	Financing of auto purchases	7.80
Consumer installment credit	Loans for general purposes	12.49
Credit cards	Financing of unpaid credit card purchases	15.09

Source: Federal Reserve (January 2009 rates).

federal funds rate: The interest rate for interbank reserve loans.

Were the Fed to reverse its policy and *reduce* the money supply, interest rates would rise. You can see this result in Figure 15.2 by observing the change in the rate of interest that occurs when the money supply *shrinks* from g_3 to g_1.

Federal Funds Rate. As we noted in Chapter 14, the most visible market signal of the Fed's activity is the **federal funds rate.** When the Fed injects or withdraws reserves from the banking system (via open market operations), the interest rate on interbank loans is most directly affected. Any change in the federal funds rate, moreover, is likely to affect a whole hierarchy of interest rates (see Table 15.2). *The federal funds rate reflects the cost of funds for banks.* When that cost decreases, banks respond by lowering the interest rates *they* charge to businesses (the prime rate), home buyers (the mortgage rate), and consumers (e.g., auto loans, installment credit, and credit cards), as the accompanying News explains.

IN THE NEWS

Fed Cut Means Lower Rates for Consumers

The Federal Reserve took extraordinary actions Tuesday to revive the feeble U.S. economy. USA TODAY reporters **Sue Kirchhoff** *and* **John Waggoner** *answer questions about the Fed's moves:*

Q: What's the good news in the Fed's actions?
A: The Fed's decision to nudge its key fed funds rate to a range of zero to 0.25%—along with its plans to buy securities that are backed by mortgages—should mean lower consumer interest rates, particularly mortgage rates. Low mortgage rates mean that more people can afford to buy houses, which will help revive the moribund housing market. A drop in mortgage rates will also allow homeowners to refinance their loans at lower rates, easing some of the burdens of their debts.

Low rates also make it cheaper for companies to borrow and expand. That, in turn, is a powerful economic stimulus. Most major banks, including Bank of America and Wachovia, lowered their prime lending rate to 3.25% from 4% Tuesday.

Q: What is the Fed trying to do?
A: The Fed is pulling out all the stops to revive business and consumer lending and get the economy moving. The central bank is particularly focused on the wide difference, or spread, on interest rates between supersafe Treasury bills, for example, and market-based loans for autos, homes and other purchases.

Fed officials think the wide spreads are due to a lack of liquidity, as lenders pull back. They hope that by flooding markets with cash, using such strategies as buying mortgage-backed bonds, they can bring interest rates down and relieve such pressures.

Source: USA TODAY. December 17, 2008, 3B. Reprinted with Permission.

Analysis: The ultimate goal of monetary stimulus is to increase aggregate demand. By reducing the cost of money for banks, the Fed expects banks to reduce interest rates for consumers.

INTEREST RATES AND SPENDING

A change in the interest rate isn't the end of this story. The ultimate goal of monetary policy is to alter macroeconomic outcomes: prices, output, employment. This requires a change in aggregate demand. Hence, the next question is

* **How do changes in interest rates affect consumer, investor, government, and net export spending?**

Consider first a policy of monetary stimulus. The strategy of monetary stimulus is to increase **aggregate demand.** A tactic for doing so is to lower interest rates.

Investment. Will lower interest rates encourage spending? In Chapter 9 we observed that investment decisions are sensitive to the rate of interest. Specifically, we demonstrated that lower rates of interest reduce the cost of buying plant and equipment, making capital investment more profitable. Lower interest rates also reduce the opportunity cost of holding inventories. Accordingly, a lower rate of interest should result in a higher rate of desired investment spending, as shown by the movement down the investment-demand curve in step 2 of Figure 15.3.

Aggregate Demand. The increased investment brought about by lower interest rates represents an injection of new spending into the circular flow. That jump in spending will kick off multiplier effects and result in an even larger increase in aggregate demand. Step 3 in Figure 15.3 illustrates this increase by the rightward *shift* of the AD curve. Market participants, encouraged by lower interest rates, are now willing to buy more output at the prevailing price level.

Consumers too may change their behavior when interest rates fall. As interest rates fall, mortgage payments decline. Monthly payments on home equity and credit card balances may also decline. These lower interest changes free up billions of consumer dollars. This increased net cash flow and lower interest rates may encourage consumers to buy new cars, appliances, or other big-ticket items (see News on the following page). State and local governments may also conclude that lower interest rates increase the desirability of bond-financed public works. All such responses would add to aggregate demand.

Monetary Stimulus

aggregate demand: The total quantity of output demanded at alternative price levels in a given time period, *ceteris paribus*.

Step 1: An increase in the money supply lowers the rate of interest.

Step 2: Lower interest rates stimulate investment.

Step 3: More investment increases aggregate demand (including multiplier effects).

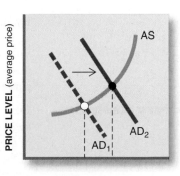

FIGURE 15.3
Monetary Stimulus

An increase in the money supply may reduce interest rates and encourage more investment. The increase in investment will trigger multiplier effects that increase aggregate demand by an even larger amount.

$\boxed{\text{IN THE NEWS}}$

Today, people have mortgages higher than what the house is worth.

More People Refinance to Wring Cash Out of Their Homes

McLEAN, Va.—Jay and Sharon Sebastian refinanced the mortgage on their 30-year-old home this month for the second time in less than a year. And, like millions of others, they took out some cold, hard cash that soon will be spent.

Not only did they reduce their 30-year fixed interest rate from 6⅝% to 6%, they upped the mortgage on their four-bedroom, three-bath home in this Washington, D.C., suburb to $300,000 from the previous $275,000 balance. The bank cut them a check for $25,000, which they're using to remodel their outdated kitchen with granite countertops, hardwood floors and stainless steel appliances. . . .

The extra cash, along with lower monthly mortgage payments from a raft of refinancings, is acting as a key source of spending as the U.S. economy struggles to stay on its feet, many economists say. . . .

An estimated $140 billion was cashed out last year. That helped boost consumer spending in a year that saw a recession, a falling stock market and the Sept. 11 attacks. . . .

The benefit to the economy doesn't stop at the first sale. If the Sebastians' contractor decides to use his cut to take his family on a trip to Disney World, which then hires a new person to play a dwarf and that person buys a new stereo, the economy has benefited three more times.

—Barbara Hagenbaugh

Source: USA TODAY. October 28, 2002, 3B. Reprinted with Permission.

Analysis: Lower interest rates encourage market participants to borrow and spend more money. This shifts the AD curve rightward, setting off multiplier effects.

From this perspective, ***the Fed's goal of stimulating the economy is achieved in three distinct steps:***

- *An increase in the money supply.*
- *A reduction in interest rates.*
- *An increase in aggregate demand.*

Quantitative Impact. Just how much stimulus can monetary policy create? According to former Fed Chairman Alan Greenspan, the impact of monetary policy can be impressive:

$$\text{Greenspan's policy guide:} \quad \frac{\text{1/10 point reduction in}}{\text{long-term interest rate}} = \frac{\text{\$10 billion}}{\text{fiscal stimulus}}$$

By this rule of thumb, a full-point reduction in long-term interest rates would increase aggregate demand just as much as a $100 billion injection of new government spending. This kind of stimulus was evident in 2002–3: low interest rates prompted a consumer-driven spending spree (see News above). This injection of new spending shifted the AD curve rightward, propelling the economy out of recession.

Monetary Restraint

Like fiscal policy, monetary policy is a two-edged sword, at times seeking to increase aggregate demand and at other times trying to restrain it. When inflation threatens, the goal of monetary policy is to reduce the rate of total spending, which puts the Fed in the position of "leaning against the wind." If successful, the resulting reduction in spending will keep aggregate demand from increasing inflationary pressures.

Higher Interest Rates. The mechanics of monetary policy designed to combat inflation are similar to those used to fight unemployment; only the direction is reversed. In this case, we seek to discourage spending by increasing the rate of interest. The Fed can push interest rates up by selling bonds, increasing the discount rate, or increasing the reserve requirement. All these actions reduce the money supply and help establish a new and higher equilibrium rate of interest.

IN THE NEWS

Fed Shifts Focus from Job Growth to Rising Prices

WASHINGTON—An unexpected quickening in the pace of price increases in the past two months is challenging the Federal Reserve's plan to raise short-term interest rates only slowly from today's 46-year lows.

The recent shift in prices is at odds with Fed officials' forecast that the combination of unemployment, unused industrial capacity and rapid growth in productivity would keep inflation very low for another year or two.

Fed officials, though not ready to abandon the forecast, acknowledge that their primary concern has shifted in the past few months from sluggish job growth to rising prices. If inflation moves higher in coming months, they are likely to reexamine their public assessment, made earlier this month, that rates will rise "at a pace that is likely to be measured."

"The flareup in inflation in the first quarter is a matter for concern," Fed Governor Ben Bernanke said yesterday in a speech in Seattle. "The inflation data bear close watching." . . .

The Fed is almost certain to raise its target for the federal-funds rate, charged on overnight loans between banks, from 1% at its late June meeting. Markets are assuming the rate will then rise rapidly to about 2% by the end of the year. . . .

—Greg Ip

Source: *The Wall Street Journal*, May 21, 2004. Copyright 2004 by Dow Jones & Company, Inc. Reproduced with permission of Dow Jones & Company, Inc. in the format Textbook via Copyright Clearance Center.

Analysis: When inflationary pressures build up, monetary restraint is appropriate. Higher interest rates may slow spending and restrain aggregate demand.

web analysis

For an official explanation of monetary policy, with links to relevant data, visit the "Monetary Policy" link at **www.federalreserve.org.**

The ultimate objective of a restrictive monetary policy is to reduce aggregate demand. For monetary restraint to succeed, spending behavior must be responsive to interest rates.

Reduced Aggregate Demand. Figure 15.3 showed the impact of interest rates on investment and aggregate demand. If the interest rate rises from 6 to 7 percent, investment declines from I_2 to I_1 and the AD curve shifts *leftward*. At higher rates of interest, many marginal investments will no longer be profitable. Likewise, many consumers will decide that they can't afford the higher monthly payments associated with increased interest rates; purchases of homes, cars, and household appliances will be postponed. State and local governments may also decide to cancel or postpone bond-financed projects. Thus, ***monetary restraint is achieved with***

- *A decrease in the money supply.*
- *An increase in interest rates.*
- *A decrease in aggregate demand.*

The resulting leftward shift of the AD curve lessens inflationary pressures.

Ironically, the monetary stimulus of 2001–2 was so effective that the Fed started worrying about inflation in mid-2004 (see News above). In June 2004, monetary policy switched to restraint, not stimulus. Over the next 2 years the Fed raised the federal-funds target rate 17 times.

POLICY CONSTRAINTS

The mechanics of monetary policy are simple enough. They won't always work as well as we might hope, however. Several constraints can limit the Fed's ability to alter the money supply, interest rates, or aggregate demand.

Short- vs. Long-Term Rates. One of the most visible constraints on monetary policy is the distinction between short-term interest rates and long-term interest rates. Greenspan's policy guide (p. 314) focuses on changes in *long-term* rates like mortgages and installment loans. Yet, the Fed's open market operations have the most direct effect on *short-term* rates (e.g., the overnight federal funds rate). As a consequence, ***the success of***

Constraints on Monetary Stimulus

Fed intervention depends in part on how well changes in long-term interest rates mirror changes in short-term interest rates.

In 2001, the Fed reduced the federal funds rate by three full percentage points between January and September, the biggest reduction in short-term rates since 1994. Long-term rates fell much less, however. The interest rate on 30-year mortgages, for example, fell less than half a percentage point in the first few months of monetary stimulus.

The same thing happened when the Fed reversed direction in 2004–6. The *short*-run fed funds rate was ratcheted up from 1.0 to 5.25 percent during that period. But *long*-term rates (e.g., 10-year Treasury bonds and home mortgages) rose only modestly. Fed Chairman Alan Greenspan characterized these disparate trends as a "conundrum."

The same "conundrum" frustrated Fed Chairman Bernanke in 2008. The Fed was successful in pushing the short-term federal funds rate down from 4.25 percent at the start of 2008 to near zero at year's end, but long-term mortgage and bond rates didn't drop nearly as much. Hence, the aggregate demand stimulus was less than hoped for.

Reluctant Lenders. There are several reasons why long-term rates might not closely mirror cuts in short-term rates. The first potential constraint is the willingness of private banks to increase their lending activity. The Fed can reduce the cost of funds to the banking system; the Fed can even reduce reserve requirements. But the money supply won't increase unless banks lend more money.

If the banks instead choose to accumulate excess reserves, the money supply won't increase as much as intended. We saw this happen in the Great Depression (Figure 14.2). This happened again in 2008, when the Fed was trying to stimulate the economy but banks were reluctant to increase their loan activity (see accompanying News). Banks were trying to shore up their own equity and were wary of making any new loans that might not get repaid in a weak economy. In such cases, long-term rates stay relatively high even when short-term rates are falling.

IN THE NEWS

Lending Drops at Big U.S. Banks

Lending at many of the nation's largest banks fell in recent months, even after they received $148 billion in taxpayer capital that was intended to help the economy by making loans more readily available.

Ten of the 13 big beneficiaries of the Treasury Department's Troubled Asset Relief Program, or TARP, saw their outstanding loan balances decline by a total of about $46 billion, or 1.4%, between the third and fourth quarters of 2008.

Credit Constraints

The fourth-quarter decline in overall loan volume at the 13 banks coincides with an industry-wide retreat from broad swaths of consumer lending. Banks have scaled back on mortgage lending, canceled or substantially reduced many home-equity and credit-card lines and, in some cases, simply stopped making certain types of loans unless they're guaranteed by the U.S. government.

Recession Woes

Scott Silvestri, a Bank of America spokesman, said the Charlotte, N.C., bank's loan balances declined in part because more borrowers have been paying off their debts. In addition, "there were fewer opportunities to make high-quality loans because of the recession," he said.

—David Enrich

Source: *The Wall Street Journal*, January 26, 2009. Copyright 2009 by Dow Jones & Company, Inc. Reproduced with permission of Dow Jones & Company, Inc. in the format Textbook via Copyright Clearance Center.

Analysis: If banks are reluctant to make new loans in an depressed economy, new bank reserves created by the Fed won't bolster more spending.

Liquidity Trap. There are circumstances in which even *short-term* rates may not fall when the Fed wants them to. The possibility that interest rates may not respond to changes in the money supply is illustrated by the "liquidity trap." When interest rates are low, the opportunity cost of holding money is cheap. At such times people may decide to hold all the money they can get, waiting for income-earning opportunities to improve. Bond prices, for example, may be high and their yields low. Buying bonds at such times entails the risk of capital losses (when bond prices fall) and little reward (since yields are low). Accordingly, market participants may decide just to hold any additional money the Fed supplies. At this juncture—a phenomenon Keynes called the **liquidity trap**—further expansion of the money supply has no effect on the rate of interest. The horizontal section of the money demand curve in Figure 15.4*a* portrays this situation.

What happens to interest rates when the initial equilibrium falls into this trap? Nothing at all. Notice that the equilibrium rate of interest doesn't fall when the money supply is increased from g_1 to g_2 (Figure 15.4*a*). People are willing to hold all that additional money without a reduction in the rate of interest.

Low Expectations. Even if both short- and long-term interest rates do fall, we've no assurance that aggregate demand will increase as expected. Keynes put great emphasis on *expectations*. Recall that investment decisions are motivated not only by interest rates but by expectations as well. During a recession—when unemployment is high and the rate of spending low—corporations have little incentive to expand production capacity. With little expectation of future profit, investors are likely to be unimpressed by "cheap money" (low interest rates) and may decline to use the lending capacity that banks make available.

> **liquidity trap:** The portion of the money demand curve that is horizontal; people are willing to hold unlimited amounts of money at some (low) interest rate.

(a) A liquidity trap can stop interest rates from falling.

(b) Inelastic investment demand can also impede monetary policy.

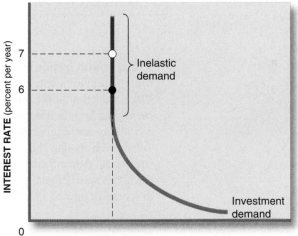

FIGURE 15.4
Constraints on Monetary Stimulus

(a) Liquidity Trap   If people are willing to hold unlimited amounts of money at the prevailing interest rate, increases in the money supply won't push interest rates lower. A liquidity trap—the horizontal segment of the money demand curve—prevents interest rates from falling.

(b) Inelastic Demand   A lower interest rate won't always stimulate investment. If investors have unfavorable expectations for future sales, small reductions in interest rates may not alter their investment decisions. Here the rate of investment remains constant when the interest rate drops from 7 to 6 percent. This kind of situation blocks the second step in the Keynesian approach to monetary policy (see Figure 15.3*b*).

Investment demand that's slow to respond to the stimulus of cheap money is said to be *inelastic* because it won't expand. Consumers too are reluctant to borrow when current and future income prospects are uncertain or distinctly unfavorable. Accordingly, even if the Fed is successful in lowering interest rates, there's no assurance that lower interest rates will stimulate borrowing and spending. Such a reluctance to spend was evident in 2008–9. Although the Fed managed to push interest rates down to historic lows, investors and consumers preferred to pay off old debts rather than incur new ones (see News below). Expectations, not interest rates, dominated spending decisions.

IN THE NEWS

Consumer Borrowing Dips More than Expected in Feb.

WASHINGTON (AP)—Consumer borrowing plunged more than expected in February as Americans cut back their use of credit cards by a record amount.

The Federal Reserve said Tuesday that consumer borrowing dropped at an annual rate of $7.48 billion in February, or 3.5 percent, from January.

"Consumers don't want to borrow as much, they want to build up their savings," said Zach Pandl, an economist at Nomura Securities International. "People are adjusting to new spending habits."

Consumer spending accounts for about 70 percent of U.S. economic activity. It fell by 4.3 percent in the final quarter of 2008, the largest drop in more than 28 years. That decline contributed to the economy's steep 6.3 percent contraction during that period.

—Christopher S. Rugaber

Source: *San Jose Mercury News*, April 7, 2009. Used with permission by The Associated Press. All rights reserved.

Analysis: Interest rate cuts are supposed to stimulate investment and consumption. But gloomy expectations may deter people from borrowing and spending.

The vertical portion of the investment demand curve in Figure 15.4*b* illustrates the possibility that investment spending may not respond to changes in the rate of interest. Notice that a reduction in the rate of interest from 7 percent to 6 percent doesn't increase investment spending. In this case, businesses are simply unwilling to invest any more funds. As a consequence, aggregate spending doesn't rise. The Fed's policy objective remains unfulfilled, even though the Fed has successfully lowered the rate of interest. Recall that the investment demand curve may also *shift* if expectations change. If expectations worsened, the investment demand curve would shift to the left and might result in even *less* investment at 6 percent interest (see Figure 15.4*b*).

Time Lags. Even when expectations are good, businesses won't respond *instantly* to changes in interest rates. Lower interest rates make investments more profitable. But it still takes time to develop and implement new investments. Hence, ***there is always a time lag between interest rate changes and investment responses.***

The same is true for consumers. Consumers don't rush out the door to refinance their homes or buy new ones the day the Fed reduces interest rates. They might start *thinking* about new financing, but aren't likely to *do* anything for a while. As the News on the next page suggests, it may take 6–12 months before market behavior responds to monetary policy. It took at least that long before investors and consumers responded to the monetary stimulus of 2001–2 and 2008–9.

IN THE NEWS

Lag Time Is a Variable to Watch in Fed Rate Cut

NEW YORK—Here is a New Economy paradox: Thanks to the increasingly free flow of information, it takes less time than ever for companies and individuals to adjust to changes in the economy. Yet shifts in monetary policy, while perhaps having a faster impact than in the past, can still take between six and 12 months to make their presence really felt.

"We're not going to see growth any stronger tomorrow than it was yesterday," says Bruce Steinberg, chief economist at Merrill Lynch & Co. In fact, he says, "It is going to be the second half of the year at the soonest," before the economy feels the full impact of the half percentage-point decline in interest rates that the Federal Reserve pushed through on Wednesday.

Why such a long lag? Economists say that makets and information may be traveling at supercharged speeds, but simple decisions about how to invest in stocks, whether to buy a new home and when's the right time to upgrade business equipment, travel at very human speeds—and can take months to play out.

—Jon E. Hilsenrath

Source: *The Wall Street Journal,* January 5, 2000. Copyright 2000 by Dow Jones & Company, Inc. Reproduced with permission of Dow Jones & Company, Inc. in the format Textbook via Copyright Clearance Center.

Analysis: It takes time for consumers and businesses to develop and implement new loan and expenditure decisions. This creates a time lag for monetary-policy effects.

web analysis

To get a global view of how interest rates and inflation move together, visit Australia (their central bank) at **www.rba.gov.au.**

Limits on Monetary Restraint

Expectations. Time lags and expectations could also limit the effectiveness of monetary restraint. In pursuit of "tight" money, the Fed could drain bank reserves and force interest rates higher. Yet market participants might continue to borrow and spend if high expectations for rising sales and profits overwhelm high interest rates in investment decisions. Consumers too might believe that future incomes will be sufficient to cover larger debts and higher interest charges. Both groups might foresee accelerating inflation that would make even high interest rates look cheap in the future. This was apparently the case in Britain in 2004, as the World View below documents.

WORLD VIEW

Rising Rates Haven't Thwarted Consumers

THE BANK OF ENGLAND continued its tightening of monetary policy on June 10. And with the British economy still expanding at a decent clip, more hikes are on the way.

As expected by most economists, the BOE raised its lending rate by a quarter-point, to 4.5%. It was the fourth bump up since November, 2003. In explaining the move, the BOE's statement pointed to above-trend output growth, strong household, business, and public spending, as well as a labor market that "has tightened further." . . .

The BOE is the first of the world's major central banks to raise rates, but the moves have done little to curb borrowing, especially by consumers. Home buying remains robust. . . .

The easy access to credit and the strong labor markets are boosting consumer spending.

Source: Reprinted from June 28, 2004, issue of *BusinessWeek* by special permission. Copyright © 2004 by The McGraw-Hill Companies, Inc.

Analysis: Strong expectations and rising incomes may fuel continued spending even when interest rates are rising.

Global Money. Market participants might also tap global sources of money. If money gets too tight in domestic markets, business may borrow funds from foreign banks or institutions. GM, Disney, ExxonMobil, and other multinational corporations can borrow funds from foreign subsidiaries, banks, and even bond markets. As we saw in Chapter 14, market participants can also secure funds from nonbank sources in the United States. These nonbank and global lenders make it harder for the Fed to restrain aggregate demand.

How Effective? In view of all these constraints on monetary policies, some observers have concluded that monetary policy is an undependable policy lever. Keynes, for example, emphasized that monetary policy wouldn't be very effective in ending a deep recession. He believed that the combination of reluctant bankers, the liquidity trap, and low expectations would render monetary stimulus ineffective. Using monetary policy to stimulate the economy in such circumstances would be akin to "pushing on a string." Alan Greenspan came to much the same conclusion in September 1992 when he said that further Fed stimulus would be ineffective in accelerating a recovery from the 1990–91 recession. He believed, however, that earlier cuts in interest rates would help stimulate spending once banks, investors, and consumers gained confidence in the economic outlook. The same kind of problem existed in 2001: The Fed's actions to reduce interest rates (11 times in as many months!) weren't enough to propel the economy forward in 2001–2. Market participants had to recover their confidence in the future before they would start spending "cheap" money. The same lack of confidence limited the effectiveness of monetary stimulus in 2008–9.

The limitations on monetary restraint aren't considered as serious. The Fed has the power to reduce the money supply. If the money supply shrinks far enough, the rate of spending will have to slow down.

THE MONETARIST PERSPECTIVE

The Keynesian view of money emphasizes the role of interest rates in fulfilling the goals of monetary policy. *In the Keynesian model, changes in the money supply affect macro outcomes primarily through changes in interest rates.* The three-step sequence of (1) money supply change, (2) interest rate movement, and (3) aggregate demand shift makes monetary policy subject to several potential uncertainties. As we've seen, the economy doesn't always respond as expected to Fed policy.

An alternative view of monetary policy seizes on those occasional failures to offer another explanation of how the money supply affects macro outcomes. The so-called monetarist school dismisses changes in short-term interest rates (e.g., the federal funds rate) as unpredictable and ineffective. They don't think real output levels are affected by monetary stimulus. As they see it, only the price level is affected by Fed policy, and then only by changes in the money supply. Monetarists conclude that monetary policy isn't an effective tool for fighting short-run business cycles, but it is a powerful tool for managing inflation.

The Equation of Exchange

equation of exchange: Money supply (M) times velocity of circulation (V) equals level of aggregate spending (P × Q).

income velocity of money (V): The number of times per year, on average, a dollar is used to purchase final goods and services; PQ ÷ M.

Monetarists assert that the potential of monetary policy can be expressed in a simple equation called the **equation of exchange,** written as

$$MV = PQ$$

where M refers to the quantity of money in circulation and V to its **velocity** of circulation. Total spending in the economy is equal to the average price (P) of goods times the quantity (Q) of goods sold in a period. This spending is financed by the supply of money (M) times the velocity of its circulation (V).

Suppose, for example, that only two participants are in the market and that the money supply consists of one crisp $20 bill. What's the limit to total spending in this case? If you answer "$20," you haven't yet grasped the nature of the circular flow. Suppose I begin the circular flow by spending $20 on eggs, bacon, and a gallon of milk. The money I spend ends up in Farmer Brown's pocket because he is the only other market participant. Once in possession of the money, Farmer Brown may decide to satisfy his long-smoldering desire to learn something about economics and buy one of my books. If he acts on that decision, the $20 will return to me. At that point, both Farmer Brown and I have sold $20 worth of goods. Hence, $40 of total spending has been financed with one $20 bill.

As long as we keep using this $20 bill to buy goods and services from each other, we can continue to do business. Moreover, the faster we pass the money from hand to hand during any period of time, the greater the value of sales each of us can register. If the money is passed from hand to hand eight times, then I'll be able to sell $80 worth of textbooks and Farmer Brown will be able to sell $80 worth of produce during that period, for a total nominal output of $160. ***The quantity of money in circulation and the velocity with which it travels (changes hands) in product markets will always be equal to the value of total spending and income (nominal GDP).*** The relationship is summarized as

$$M \times V = P \times Q$$

In this case, the *equation of exchange* confirms that

$$\$20 \times 8 = \$160$$

The value of total sales for the year is $160.

Monetarists use the equation of exchange to simplify the explanation of how monetary policy works. There's no need, they argue, to follow the effects of changes in M through the money markets to interest rates and further to changes in total spending. The basic consequences of monetary policy are evident in the equation of exchange. The two sides of the equation of exchange must always be in balance. Hence, we can be absolutely certain that ***if* M *increases, prices* (P) *or output* (Q) *must rise, or* V *must fall.***

The equation of exchange is an incontestable statement of how the money supply is related to macro outcomes. The equation itself, however, says nothing about *which* variables will respond to a change in the money supply. The *goal* of monetary policy is to change the macro outcomes on the right side of the equation. It's *possible,* however, that a change in V might be offset with a reverse change in V, leaving P and Q unaffected. Or it could happen that the *wrong* macro outcome is affected. Prices (P) might rise, for example, when we're trying to increase real output (Q).

Monetarists add some important assumptions to transform the equation of exchange from a simple identity to a behavioral *model* of macro performance. The first assumption is that the velocity of money (V) is stable. How fast people use their money balances depends on the institutional structure of money markets and people's habits. Neither the structure of money markets nor people's habits are likely to change in the short run. Accordingly, a short-run increase in M won't be offset by a reduction in V. Instead, the impact of an increased money supply will be transmitted to the right-hand side of the equation of exchange, which means that ***total spending must rise if the money supply* (M) *grows and* V *is stable.***

Stable Velocity

From a monetarist perspective, there's no need to trace the impacts of monetary policy through interest rate movements. The focus on interest rates is a uniquely Keynesian perspective. Monetarists claim that interest rate movements are secondary to the major thrust of monetary policy. ***As monetarists see it, changes in the money supply must alter total spending, regardless of how interest rates move.***

A monetarist perspective leads to a whole different strategy for the Fed. Because interest rates aren't part of the monetarist explanation of how monetary policy works, the Fed shouldn't try to manipulate interest rates; instead, it should focus on the money supply itself. Monetarists also argue that the Fed can't really control interest rates well since they depend on both the supply of and the demand for money. What the Fed *can* control is the supply of money, and the equation of exchange clearly shows that money matters.

Money Supply Focus

Some monetarists add yet another perspective to the equation of exchange. They assert that not only V but Q as well is stable. If this is true, then changes in the money supply (M) would affect only prices (P).

What does it mean for Q to be stable? The argument here is that the quantity of goods produced is primarily dependent on production capacity, labor market efficiency, and other

"Natural" Unemployment

Analysis: If the money supply shrinks (or its growth rate slows), price levels will rise less quickly.

natural rate of unemployment: long-term rate of unemployment determined by structural forces in labor and product markets.

"structural" forces. These structural forces establish a **"natural" rate of unemployment** that's fairly immune to short-run policy intervention. This is the *long-run* aggregate supply curve we first encountered in Chapter 8. From this perspective, there's no reason for producers to depart from this "natural" rate of output when the money supply increases. Producers are smart enough to know that both prices and costs will rise when spending increases. Hence, rising prices won't create any new profit incentives for increasing output. Firms will just continue producing at the "natural" rate with higher (nominal) prices and costs. As a result, increases in aggregate spending—whether financed by more *M* or faster *V*—aren't likely to alter real output levels. *Q* will stay constant.

If the quantity of real output is in fact stable, then *P* is the only thing that can change. Thus, ***the most extreme monetarist perspective concludes that changes in the money supply affect prices only.*** As the "simple economics" in the accompanying cartoon suggests, a decrease in *M* should directly reduce the price level. When *M increases,* total spending rises, but the higher nominal value of spending is completely absorbed by higher prices. In this view, monetary policy affects only the rate of inflation. This is the kind of money-driven inflation that bedeviled George Washington's army (see News on the next page).

Figure 15.5 illustrates the extreme monetarist argument in the context of aggregate supply and demand. The assertion that real output is fixed at the natural rate of unemployment is reflected in the vertical, long-run aggregate supply curve. With real output stuck at Q^*, any increase in aggregate demand directly raises the price level.

Monetarist Policies

At first glance, the monetarist argument looks pretty slick. Keynesians worry about how the money supply affects interest rates, how interest rates affect spending, and how spending affects output. By contrast, monetarists point to a simple equation ($MV = PQ$) that produces straightforward responses to monetary policy.

FIGURE 15.5
The Monetarist View

Monetarists argue that the rate of real output is set by structural factors. Furthermore, firms aren't likely to be fooled into producing more just because prices are rising since costs are likely to rise just as much. Hence, long-run aggregate supply remains at the "natural" level Q^*. Any monetary-induced increases in aggregate demand, therefore, raise the price level (inflation) but not output.

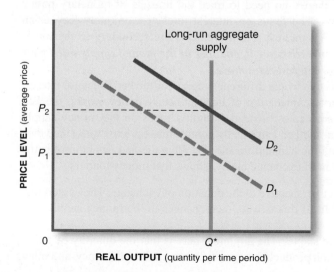

IN THE NEWS

"Not Worth a Continental": The U.S. Experience with Hyperinflation

The government of the United States had no means to pay for the Revolutionary War. Specifically, the federal government had no power to levy taxes that might transfer resources from the private sector to the public sector. Instead, it could only request the states to levy taxes of their own and contribute them to the war effort. The states were not very responsive, however: state contributions accounted for only 6 percent of federal revenues during the war years.

To pay for needed weapons and soldiers, the federal government had only two other options, either (1) borrow money or (2) create new money. When loans proved to be inadequate, the Continental Congress started issuing new paper money—the "Continental" dollar—in 1775. By the end of 1779, Congress had authorized issuance of over $250 million in Continental dollars.

At first the paper money enabled George Washington's troops to acquire needed supplies, ammunition, and volunteers. But soon the flood of paper money inundated product markets. Wholesale prices of key commodities skyrocketed. Commodity prices *doubled* in 1776, in 1777, and again in 1778. Then prices increased *tenfold* in the next two years.

Many farmers and storekeepers refused to sell goods to the army in exchange for Continental dollars. Rapid inflation had taught them that the paper money George Washington's troops offered was nearly worthless. The expression "not worth a Continental" became a popular reference to things of little value.

The states tried price controls and even empowered themselves to seize needed war supplies. But nothing could stop the inflation fueled by the explosive increase in the money supply. Fortunately, the war ended before the economy collapsed. After the war, the U.S. Congress established a new form of money, and in 1787 it empowered the federal government to levy taxes and mint gold and silver coins.

—Sidney Ratner, James H. Soltow, and Richard Sylla

Source: *The Evolution of the American Economy,* 2nd ed. (1993). © 1979 Sidney Ratner Estate. Reprinted by permission of the authors.

Analysis: Rapid expansion of the money supply will push the price level up. As inflation accelerates, money becomes less valuable.

web analysis

For an essay on hyperinflation in Germany after World War I, search "hyperinflation" at **www.pbs.org.**

There are fundamental differences between the two schools here, not only about how the economy works but also about how successful macro policy might be. To appreciate those differences, consider monetarist responses to inflationary and recessionary gaps.

Fighting Inflation. Consider again the options for fighting inflation. The policy goal is to reduce aggregate demand. From a Keynesian perspective, the way to achieve this reduction is to shrink the money supply and drive up interest rates. But monetarists argue that nominal interest rates are already likely to be high. Furthermore, if an effective anti-inflation policy is adopted, interest rates will come *down,* not go up. Yes, interest rates will come *down,* not go up, when the money supply is tightened, according to monetarists.

Real vs. Nominal Interest. To understand this monetarist conclusion, we have to distinguish between *nominal* interest rates and *real* ones. Nominal interest rates are the ones we actually see and pay. When a bank pays 5½ percent interest on your bank account, it's quoting (and paying) a nominal rate.

Real interest rates are never actually seen and rarely quoted. These are "inflation-adjusted" rates. Specifically, the **real interest rate** equals the nominal rate *minus* the anticipated rate of inflation; that is,

$$\begin{matrix} \text{Real} & & \text{nominal} & & \text{anticipated} \\ \text{interest} & = & \text{interest} & - & \text{inflation} \\ \text{rate} & & \text{rate} & & \text{rate} \end{matrix}$$

real interest rate: The nominal rate of interest minus anticipated inflation rate.

Recall what inflation does to the purchasing power of the dollar: As inflation continues, each dollar purchases fewer goods and services. As a consequence, dollars borrowed today are of less real value when they're paid back later. The real rate of interest reflects this inflation adjustment.

Suppose you lend someone $100 at the beginning of the year, at 8 percent interest. You expect to get more back at the end of the year than you start with. That "more" you expect refers to *real* goods and services, not just dollar bills. Specifically, you anticipate that when the loan is repaid with interest at the end of the year, you'll be able to buy more goods and services than you could at the beginning. This expectation of a *real* gain is at least part of the reason for making a loan.

Your expected gain won't materialize, however, if all prices rise by 8 percent during the year. If the inflation rate is 8 percent, you'll discover that $108 buys you no more at the end of the year than $100 would have bought you at the beginning. Hence, you'd have given up the use of your money for an entire year without any real compensation. In such circumstances, the *real* rate of interest turns out to be zero; that is,

$$\begin{matrix} \text{Real} \\ \text{interest} \\ \text{rate} \end{matrix} = \begin{matrix} 8\% \text{ nominal} \\ \text{interest} \\ \text{rate} \end{matrix} - \begin{matrix} 8\% \text{ inflation} \\ \text{rate} \end{matrix}$$

$$= 0\%$$

The nominal rate of interest, then, really has two components: (1) the real rate of interest, and (2) an inflation adjustment. If the real rate of interest was 4 percent and an inflation rate of 9 percent was expected, the nominal rate of interest would be 13 percent. If inflationary expectations *declined*, the *nominal* interest rate would *fall*. This is evident in the rearranged formula:

$$\frac{\text{Nominal}}{\text{interest rate}} = \frac{\text{real}}{\text{interest rate}} + \frac{\text{anticipated rate}}{\text{of inflation}}$$

If the real interest rate is 4 percent and anticipated inflation falls from 9 to 6 percent, the nominal interest rate would decline from 13 to 10 percent.

A central assumption of the monetarist perspective is that the real rate of interest is fairly stable. This is a critical point. ***If the real rate of interest is stable, then changes in the nominal interest rate reflect only changes in anticipated inflation.*** From this perspective, high nominal rates of interest are a symptom of inflation, not a cure. Indeed, high nominal rates may even look cheap if inflationary expectations are worsening faster than interest rates are rising. This was the case in Zimbabwe in 2008, when the nominal interest rate rose above 400 percent (see World View, p. 136).

Consider the implications of all this for monetary policy. Suppose we want to close an inflationary GDP gap. Monetarists and Keynesians alike agree that a reduced money supply (*M*) will deflate total spending. But Keynesians rely on a "quick fix" of *higher* interest rates to slow consumption and investment spending. Monetarists, by contrast, assert that nominal interest rates will *fall* if the Fed tightens the money supply. Once market participants are convinced that the Fed is going to reduce money supply growth, inflationary expectations diminish. When inflationary expectations diminish, nominal interest rates will begin to fall.

Short- vs. Long-Term Rates (again). The monetarist argument helps resolve the "conundrum" that puzzled former Fed Chairman Alan Greenspan and bedeviled his successor, Ben Bernanke, that is, the contradictory movements of short-term and long-term interest rates. As we observed earlier, short-run rates (like the federal funds rate) are very responsive to Fed intervention. But long-term rates are much slower to respond. This suggests that banks and borrowers look beyond current economic conditions in making long-term financial commitments.

If the Fed is reducing money-supply growth, short-term rates may rise quickly. But long-term rates won't increase unless market participants expect inflation to worsen. Given the pivotal role of long-term rates in investment decisions, the Fed may have to stall GDP growth—even spark a recession—to restrain aggregate demand enough to stop prices from rising. Rather than take such risks, ***monetarists advocate steady and predictable changes in the money supply.*** Such a policy, they believe, would reduce uncertainties and thus stabilize both long-term interest rates and GDP growth.

Fighting Unemployment. The link between anticipated inflation and nominal interest rates also constrains expansionary monetary policy. The Keynesian cure for a recession is to expand M and lower interest rates. But monetarists fear that an increase in M will lead—via the equation of exchange—to higher P. If everyone believed this would happen, then an unexpectedly large increase in M would immediately raise people's inflationary expectations. Even if short-term interest rates fell, long-term interest rates might actually rise. This would defeat the purpose of monetary stimulus.

From a monetarist perspective, expansionary monetary policies aren't likely to lead us out of a recession. On the contrary, such policies might heap inflation problems on top of our unemployment woes. All monetary policy should do, say the monetarists, is ensure a stable and predictable rate of growth in the money supply. Then people could concentrate on real production decisions without worrying so much about fluctuating prices.

THE CONCERN FOR CONTENT

Monetary policy, like fiscal policy, can affect more than just the *level* of total spending. We must give some consideration to the impact of Federal Reserve actions on the *content* of the GDP if we're going to be responsive to the "second crisis" of economic theory.[1]

The Mix of Output

Both Keynesians and monetarists agree that monetary policy will affect nominal interest rates. When interest rates change, not all spending decisions will be affected equally. High interest rates don't deter consumers from buying pizzas, but they do deter purchases of homes, cars, and other big-ticket items typically financed with loans. Hence, the housing and auto industries bear a disproportionate burden of restrictive monetary policy. Accordingly, when the Fed pursues a policy of tight money—high interest rates and limited lending capacity—it not only restrains total spending but reduces the share of housing and autos in that spending. Utility industries, public works projects, and state and local finances are also disproportionately impacted by monetary policy.

In addition to altering the content of demand and output, monetary policy affects the competitive structure of the market. When money is tight, banks must ration available credit among loan applicants. Large and powerful corporations aren't likely to run out of credit because banks will be hesitant to incur their displeasure and lose their business. Thus, General Motors and IBM stand a much better chance of obtaining tight money than does the corner grocery store. Moreover, if bank lending capacity becomes too small, GM and IBM can always resort to the bond market and borrow money directly from the public. Small businesses seldom have such an alternative.

Income Redistribution

Monetary policy also affects the distribution of income. When interest rates fall, borrowers pay smaller interest charges. On the other hand, lenders get smaller interest payments. Hence, a lower interest rate redistributes income from lenders to borrowers. When interest rates declined sharply in 2008–9, homeowners refinanced their mortgages and saved billions of dollars in interest payments. The decline in interest rates, however, *reduced* the income of retired persons, who depend heavily on interest payments from certificates of deposit, bonds, and other assets.

---

[1]See the quotation from Joan Robinson in Chapter 11, calling attention to the exclusive focus of economists on the *level* of economic activity (the "first crisis"), to the neglect of content (the "second crisis").

WHICH LEVER TO PULL?

Our success in managing the macro economy of tomorrow depends on pulling the right policy levers at the right time. But which levers should be pulled? Keynesians and monetarists offer very different prescriptions for treating an ailing economy. Can we distill some usable policy guidelines from this discussion for policy decisions in the economy tomorrow?

The Policy Tools. The equation of exchange is a convenient summary of the differences between Keynesian and monetarist perspectives. There's no disagreement about the equation itself: Aggregate spending ($M \times V$) *must* equal the value of total sales ($P \times Q$). **What Keynesians and monetarists argue about is which of the policy tools—M or V—is likely to be effective in altering aggregate spending.**

- *Monetarists* point to changes in the money supply (M) as the principal lever of macroeconomic policy. They assume V is reasonably stable.
- *Keynesian* fiscal policy *must* rely on changes in the velocity of money (V) because tax and expenditure policies have no direct impact on the money supply.

Crowding Out. The extreme monetarist position that *only* money matters is based on the assumption that the velocity of money (V) is constant. **If V is constant, changes in total spending can come about only through changes in the money supply.** There are no other policy tools on the left side of the equation of exchange.

Think about an increase in government spending designed to stimulate the economy. How does the government pay for this fiscal policy stimulus? Monetarists argue that there are only two ways to pay for this increased expenditure (G): The government must either raise additional taxes or borrow more money. If the government raises taxes, the disposable income of consumers will be reduced, and private spending will fall. On the other hand, if the government *borrows* more money to pay for its expenditures, there will be less money available for loans to private consumers and investors. In either case, more government spending (G) implies less private spending (C or I). Thus, *increased G* effectively **"crowds out"** some C or I, leaving total spending unchanged. From this viewpoint, fiscal policy is ineffective; it can't even shift the aggregate demand curve. At best, fiscal policy can change the composition of demand and thus the mix of output. Only changes in M (monetary policy) can shift the aggregate demand curve.

Milton Friedman, formerly of the University of Chicago, championed the monetarist view with this argument:

> I believe that the state of the government budget matters; matters a great deal—for some things. The state of the government budget determines what fraction of the nation's income is spent through the government and what fraction is spent by individuals privately. The state of the government budget determines what the level of our taxes is, how much of our income we turn over to the government. The state of the government budget has a considerable effect on interest rates. If the federal government runs a large deficit, that means the government has to borrow in the market, which raises the demand for loanable funds and so tends to raise interest rates.
>
> If the government budget shifts to a surplus, that adds to the supply of loanable funds, which tends to lower interest rates. It was no surprise to those of us who stress money that enactment of the surtax was followed by a decline in interest rates. That's precisely what we had predicted and what our analysis leads us to predict. But—and I come to the main point—in my opinion, the state of the budget by itself has no significant effect on the course of nominal income, on inflation, on deflation, or on cyclical fluctuations.[2]

Keynesians reply that the alleged constant velocity of money is a monetarist's pipe dream. Some even argue that the velocity of money is so volatile that changes in V can completely offset changes in M, leaving us with the proposition that money doesn't matter.

The liquidity trap illustrates the potential for V to change. Keynes argued that people tend to accumulate money balances—slow their rate of spending—during recessions. *A slowdown in spending implies a reduction in the velocity of money.* Indeed, in the extreme

---

crowding out: A reduction in private-sector borrowing (and spending) caused by increased government borrowing.

---

[2]Milton Friedman and Walter W. Heller, *Monetary vs. Fiscal Policy* (New York: Norton, 1969), pp. 50–51.

TABLE 15.3
How Fiscal Policy Matters:
Monetarist vs. Keynesian Views

Do Changes in G or T Affect:	Monetarist View	Keynesian View
1. Aggregate demand?	No (stable V causes crowding out)	Yes (V changes)
2. Prices?	No (aggregate demand not affected)	Maybe (if at capacity)
3. Real output?	No (aggregate demand not affected)	Yes (output responds to demand)
4. Nominal interest rates?	Yes (crowding out)	Maybe (may alter demand for money)
5. Real interest rates?	No (determined by real growth)	Yes (real growth and expectations may vary)

Monetarists and Keynesians have very different views on the impact of fiscal policy. Monetarists assert that changes in government spending (G) and taxes (T) don't alter the velocity of money (V). As a result, fiscal policy alone can't alter total spending. Keynesians reject this view, arguing that V is changeable. They claim that tax cuts and increased government spending increase the velocity of money and so alter total spending.

case of the liquidity trap, the velocity of money falls toward zero. Under these circumstances, changes in M (monetary policy) won't influence total spending. The velocity of money falls as rapidly as M increases. On the other hand, increased government spending (fiscal policy) can stimulate aggregate spending by putting idle money balances to work (thereby increasing V). Changes in fiscal policy will also influence consumer and investor expectations, and thereby further alter the rate of aggregate spending.

How Fiscal Policy Works: Two Views. Tables 15.3 and 15.4 summarize these different perspectives on fiscal and monetary policy. The first table evaluates fiscal policy from both Keynesian and monetarist viewpoints. The central issue is whether and how a change in government spending (G) or taxes (T) will alter macroeconomic outcomes. Keynesians assert that aggregate demand will be affected as the velocity of money (V) changes. Monetarists say no, because they anticipate an unchanged V.

If aggregate demand isn't affected by a change in G or T, then fiscal policy won't affect prices (P) or real output (Q). Thus, monetarists conclude that fiscal policy isn't a viable tool for combating either inflation or unemployment. By contrast, Keynesians believe V *will* change and that output and prices will respond accordingly.

Insofar as interest rates are concerned, monetarists recognize that nominal interest rates will be affected (read Friedman's quote again) but *real* rates won't be. Real interest

TABLE 15.4
How Money Matters:
Monetarist vs. Keynesian Views

Do Changes in M Affect:	Monetarist View	Keynesian View
1. Aggregate demand?	Yes (V stable)	Maybe (V may change)
2. Prices?	Yes (V and Q stable)	Maybe (V and Q may change)
3. Real output?	No (rate of unemployment determined by structural forces)	Maybe (output responds to demand)
4. Nominal interest rates?	Yes (but direction unknown)	Maybe (liquidity trap)
5. Real interest rates?	No (depends on real growth)	Maybe (real growth may vary)

(handwritten note: up/down)

Because monetarists believe that V is stable, they assert that changes in the money supply (M) must alter total spending. But all the monetary impact is reflected in prices and nominal interest rates; *real* output and interest rates are unaffected.

Keynesians think that V is variable and thus that changes in M might *not* alter total spending. If monetary policy does alter aggregate spending, however, Keynesians expect all outcomes to be affected.

rates depend on real output and growth, both of which are seen as immune to fiscal policy. Keynesians see less impact on nominal interest rates and more on real interest rates.

What all this boils down to is this: Fiscal policy, by itself, will be effective only if it can alter the velocity of money. *How well fiscal policy works depends on how much the velocity of money can be changed by government tax and spending decisions.*

How Monetary Policy Works: Two Views. Table 15.4 offers a similar summary of monetary policy. This time the positions of monetarists and Keynesians are reversed, or nearly so. Monetarists say a change in M must alter total spending ($P \times Q$) because V is stable. Keynesians assert that V may vary, so they aren't convinced that monetary policy will always work. The heart of the controversy is again the velocity of money. Monetary policy works as long as V is stable, or at least predictable. *How well monetary policy works depends on how stable or predictable* **V** *is.*

Once the central role of velocity is understood, everything else falls into place. Monetarists assert that prices but not output will be directly affected by a change in M because the right-hand side of the equation of exchange contains only two variables (P and Q), and one of them (Q) is assumed unaffected by monetary policy. Keynesians, by contrast, aren't so sure prices will be affected by M or that real output won't be. It all depends on V and the responsiveness of P and Q to changes in aggregate spending.

Finally, monetarists predict that nominal interest rates will respond to changes in M, although they're not sure in what direction. It depends on how inflationary expectations adapt to changes in the money supply. Keynesian economists aren't so sure nominal interest rates will change but are sure about the direction if they do.

Is Velocity Stable? Tables 15.3 and 15.4 highlight the velocity of money as a critical determinant of policy impact. The critical question appears to be whether V is stable. Why hasn't someone answered this simple question and resolved the debate over fiscal versus monetary policy?

Long-Run Stability. The velocity of money (V) turns out, in fact, to be quite stable over long periods of time. Over the past 30 years the velocity of money (M2) has averaged about 1.64, as Figure 15.6 illustrates. Moreover, the range of velocity has been fairly narrow, extending from a low of 1.56 in 1987 to a high of 2.05 in 1997. Monetarists conclude that the historical pattern justifies the assumption of a stable V.

Short-Run Instability. Keynesians reply that monetarists are farsighted and so fail to see significant short-run variations in V. The difference between a velocity of 1.56 and velocity of 2.05 translates into hundreds of billions of dollars in aggregate demand. Moreover, there's a pattern to short-run variations in V: Velocity tends to decline in recessions (see Figure 15.6). These are precisely the situations in which fiscal stimulus (increasing V) would be appropriate.

Money Supply Targets. The differing views of monetarists and Keynesians clearly lead to different conclusions about which policy lever to pull.

Monetarist Advice. The monetarists' policy advice to the Fed is straightforward. *Monetarists favor fixed money supply targets.* They believe that V is stable in the long run and unpredictable in the short run. Hence, the safest course of action is to focus on M. All the Fed has to do is announce its intention to increase the money supply by some fixed amount (such as 3 percent per year), then use its central banking powers to hit that money growth target.

Interest Rate Targets. Keynesian Advice. *Keynesians reject fixed money supply targets,* favoring more flexibility in control of the money supply. In their view, a fixed money supply target would render monetary policy useless in combating cyclical swings of the economy. Keynesians prefer the risks of occasional policy errors to the straitjacket of a fixed money supply target. *Keynesians advocate targeting interest rates, not the money supply.* Keynesians also advocate liberal use of the fiscal policy lever.

Inflation Targeting. In the past, the Fed has tried both monetarist and Keynesian strategies for managing aggregate demand, depending on the needs of the economy and the convictions of the Fed chairman. The current chairman, Ben Bernanke, isn't committed to either the monetarist or Keynesian perspective. Instead, he tries to walk a thin line between these perspectives. Like his predecessors, Bernanke believes that price stability is the Fed's primary

Ratio of GDP to M2

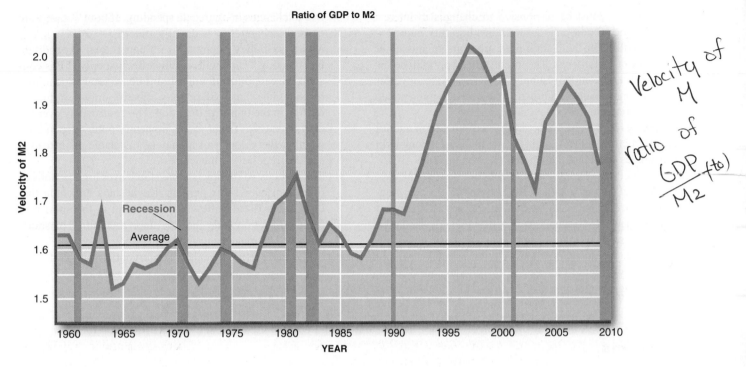

Velocity of M
ratio of
$$\frac{GDP \; (to)}{M2}$$

FIGURE 15.6
The Velocity of M2

The velocity of money (the ratio of GDP to M2) averages about 1.64. However, *V* appears to decline in recessions. Keynes urged the use of fiscal stimulus to boost *V*. Monetarists caution that short-run changes in *V* are too unpredictable.

Source: Federal Reserve.

goal. So long as inflation stays below a certain benchmark, there is no reason for the Fed to adjust its policy levers—autopilot will do just fine. When inflation rises above the inflation "target" (currently, 2–3 percent), however, the Fed must mobilize its policy tools.

What market participants like about this **inflation targeting** strategy is that it appears to offer greater predictability about whether and how the Fed will act. Critics point out, though, that *future* inflation, not *past* inflation, is the central policy concern. Because today's price movements may or may not be precursors of future inflation, the decision to pull monetary levers is still a judgment call. Former Chairman Alan Greenspan recognized this when he said, "The Federal Reserve specializes in precision guesswork." As Fed Chairman Bernanke peers into the economy tomorrow, he will certainly need that same skill.

> **inflation targeting:** The use of an inflation ceiling ("target") to signal the need for monetary policy adjustments.

SUMMARY

- The essence of monetary policy lies in the Federal Reserve's control over the money supply. By altering the money supply, the Fed can determine the amount of purchasing power available. LO1
- There are sharp disagreements about how monetary policy works. Keynesians argue that monetary policy works indirectly, through its effects on interest rates and spending. Monetarists assert that monetary policy has more direct and more certain impacts, particularly on price levels. LO3
- In the Keynesian view, the demand for money is important. This demand reflects desires to hold money (in cash or bank balances) for transactions, precautionary, and speculative purposes. The interaction of money supply and money demand determines the equilibrium rate of interest. LO1
- From a Keynesian perspective, the impact of monetary policy on the economy occurs in three distinct steps: (1) changes in the money supply alter interest rates; (2) changes in interest rates alter the rate of expenditure; and (3) the change in desired expenditure alters (shifts) aggregate demand. LO1
- For Keynesian monetary policy to be fully effective, interest rates must be responsive to changes in the money supply,

and spending must be responsive to changes in interest rates. Neither condition is assured. In a liquidity trap, people are willing to hold unlimited amounts of money at some low rate of interest. The interest rate won't fall below this level as the money supply increases. Also, investor expectations of sales and profits may override interest rate considerations in investment decisions. LO2

- Fed policy has the most direct impact on short-term interest rates, particularly the overnight federal funds rate. Long-term rates are less responsive to open market operations. LO2

- The monetarist school emphasizes long-term linkages. Using the equation of exchange ($MV = PQ$) as a base, monetarists assert that the velocity of money (V) is stable, so that changes in M must influence ($P \times Q$). Monetarists focus on the money supply; Keynesians, on interest rates. LO3

- Some monetarists also argue that the level of real output (Q) is set by structural forces, as illustrated by the vertical, long-run aggregate supply curve. Q is therefore insensitive to changes in aggregate spending. If both V and Q are constant, changes in M directly affect P. LO1

- Monetary policy attempts to influence total expenditure by changing M and will be fully effective only if V is constant. Fiscal policy attempts to influence total expenditure by changing V and will be fully effective only if M doesn't change in the opposite direction. The controversy over the effectiveness of fiscal versus monetary policy depends on whether the velocity of money (V) is stable or instead is subject to policy influence. LO3

- The velocity of money is more stable over long periods of time than over short periods. Keynesians conclude that this makes fiscal policy more powerful in the short run. Monetarists conclude that the unpredictability of short-run velocity makes any short-run policy risky. LO3

- Inflation targeting signals Fed intervention when inflation rises above a policy-set ceiling ("target"), currently 2–3 percent. LO1

Key Terms

monetary policy	precautionary demand for money	equation of exchange
interest rate	speculative demand for money	income velocity of money (V)
money supply (M1, M2)	equilibrium rate of interest	natural rate of unemployment
demand for money	federal funds rate	real interest rate
portfolio decision	aggregate demand	crowding out
transactions demand for money	liquidity trap	inflation targeting

Questions for Discussion

1. What proportions of your money balance are held for transactions, precautionary, and speculative purposes? Can you think of any other purposes for holding money? LO1

2. Why do high interest rates so adversely affect the demand for housing and yet have so little influence on the demand for pizzas? LO1

3. If the Federal Reserve banks mailed everyone a brand-new $100 bill, what would happen to prices, output, and income? Illustrate your answer by using the equation of exchange. LO1

4. Can there be any inflation without an increase in the money supply? How? LO3

5. How might the existence of multiplier effects increase the risk of inflation when interest rates are cut? LO1

6. When prices started doubling (see News, p. 323), why didn't the Continental Congress print even *more* money so Washington's army could continue to buy supplies? What brings an end to such "inflation financing"? LO3

7. Could long-term interest rates rise when short-term rates are falling? What would cause such a pattern? LO3

8. In the News on p. 314, what starts the multiplier process? When will it stop? LO1

9. Why were banks reluctant to use their lending capacity in 2008? (See News, p. 316.) What did they do with their increased reserves? LO2

10. If mortgage rates fell to 0 percent ("free money"), why might consumers still hesitate to borrow money to buy a home? LO2

11. Does inflation targeting resolve uncertainties about Fed policy? LO1

web activities to accompany this chapter can be found on the Online Learning Center:
http://www.mhhe.com/schiller12e

LO1   1. In Table 15.1, what is the implied price of holding money in a checking account rather than in
Treasury bonds?   _____

LO1   2. Suppose homeowners owe $6 trillion in mortgage loans.
(a) If the mortgage interest rate is 8 percent, approximately how much are homeowners paying
in annual mortgage interest?   _____
(b) If the interest rate drops to 7 percent, by how much will annual interest payments decline? _____

LO1   3. If all of the "cash out" described in the News on page 314 was spent on consumption, by how much
did AD shift

(a) initially?   _____
(b) cumulatively?   _____

LO1   4. Illustrate the effects on investment of:
(a) An interest-rate hike (point A).
(b) An interest-rate hike accompanied by increased
sales expectations (point B).

LO2   5. Is the value of the short-term multiplier in the
News on page 314 greater or less than 1.0?   _____

LO2   6. Suppose that an economy is characterized by
LO3
$$M = \$6,000 \text{ billion}$$
$$V = 2.5$$
$$P = 100$$
(a) What is the real value of output (Q)?   _____

Now assume that the Fed increases the money supply by 10 percent and velocity remains
unchanged.
(b) If the price level remains constant, by how much will real output increase?   _____ %
(c) If, instead, real output is fixed at the natural level of unemployment, by
how much will prices rise?   _____ %
(d) By how much would V have to fall to offset the increase in M?   _____

LO1   7. If the nominal rate of interest is 7 percent and the real rate of interest is 3 percent, what rate of
inflation is anticipated?   _____

LO1   8. Suppose the Fed decided to purchase $30 billion worth of government securities in the
LO2   open market. What impact would this action have on the economy? Specifically, answer the
following questions:
(a) How will M1 be affected initially?   _____
(b) By how much will the banking system's lending capacity increase if the reserve requirement is
25 percent?   _____
(c) Must interest rates rise or fall to induce investors to utilize this expanded
lending capacity?   _____
(d) By how much will aggregate demand increase if investors borrow and spend
all the newly available credit?   _____
(e) Under what circumstances ("recession" or "inflation") would the Fed be
pursuing such an open market policy?   _____
(f) To attain those same objectives, what should the Fed do ("increase" or "decrease")
with the
(i) Discount rate?   _____
(ii) Reserve requirement?   _____

LO1
LO2   9. According to Greenspan's rule of thumb, how much fiscal stimulus would be equivalent to a 2-point reduction in long-term interest rates?   _____

LO2   10. The following data describe market conditions:
LO3

Money supply (in billions)	$100	$200	$300	$400	$ 500	$ 600	$ 700
Interest rate	8.0	7.5	7.0	6.5	6.0	5.5	5.5
Rate of investment (in billions)	$ 12	$ 12	$ 15	$ 16	$16.5	$16.5	$16.5

    (*a*) At what rate of interest does the liquidity trap emerge?   _____

    (*b*) At what rate of interest does investment demand become totally inelastic?   _____

LO3   11. Use the accompanying graphs to show what happens in the economy when *M* increases from $300 billion to $400 billion.

    (*a*) By how much does *PQ* change if *V* is constant?   _____

    (*b*) If aggregate supply were fixed (vertical) at the initial output level, what would happen to the price level?   _____

    (*c*) What is the value of *V*?   _____

  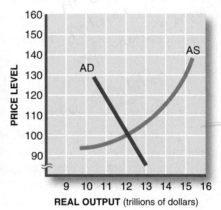

LO2   12. Use the data on the end covers of this text to determine for 2008:

    (*a*) The interest rate on 10-year Treasury bonds.   _____

    (*b*) The U.S. inflation rate.   _____

    (*c*) The real rate of interest.   _____

PART 6

Supply-Side Options

Fiscal and monetary policies attempt to alter macro outcomes by managing aggregate demand. Supply-side policies focus instead on possibilities for shifting the aggregate *supply* curve. In the short run, any increase in aggregate supply promotes more output and less inflation. Supply-siders also emphasize how rightward shifts of aggregate supply are critical to long-run economic growth. Chapter 16 focuses on short-run supply-side options; Chapter 17 takes the long-run view.

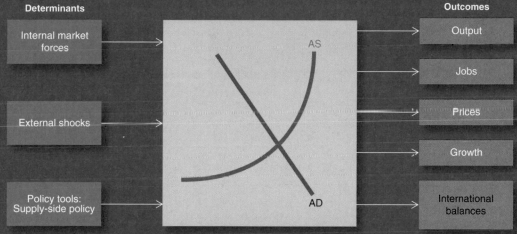

Determinants

- Internal market forces
- External shocks
- Policy tools: Supply-side policy

Outcomes

- Output
- Jobs
- Prices
- Growth
- International balances

Supply Side Policy:
Short-Run Options

16

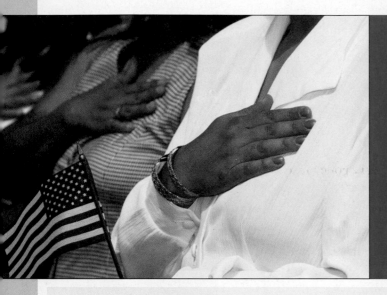

Fiscal and monetary policies focus on the *demand* side of the macro economy. The basic premise of both approaches is that macro goals can be achieved by shifting the aggregate demand curve to a desirable macro equilibrium. The aggregate demand curve isn't the only game in town, however; there's an aggregate supply curve as well. Why not focus instead on possibilities for shifting the aggregate *supply* curve?

Any policies that alter the willingness or ability to supply goods at various price levels will shift the aggregate supply curve. This chapter identifies some of those policy options and examines how they affect macro outcomes. The focus is on two questions:

- **How does the aggregate supply curve affect macro outcomes?**
- **How can the aggregate supply curve be shifted?**

As we'll see, the aggregate supply curve plays a critical role in determining how difficult it is to achieve the goals of full employment and price stability.

AGGREGATE SUPPLY

The impetus for examining the supply side of the macro economy sprang up in the stagflation of the 1970s. **Stagflation** occurs when both unemployment *and* inflation increase at the same time. From 1973 to 1974, for example, consumer price inflation surged from 8.7 to 12.3 percent. At the same time, the unemployment rate jumped from 4.9 to 5.6 percent. How could this happen? ***No shift of the aggregate demand curve can increase inflation and unemployment at the same time.*** If aggregate demand increases (shifts right), the price level may rise but unemployment should decline with increased output. If aggregate demand decreases (shifts left), inflation should subside but unemployment increase. In other words, most demand-side theories predict that inflation and unemployment move in *opposite* directions in the short run. When this didn't happen, an alternative explanation was sought. The explanation was found on the supply side of the macro economy. Two critical clues were (1) the shape of the **aggregate supply** curve and (2) potential AS shifts.

stagflation: The simultaneous occurrence of substantial unemployment and inflation.

SHAPE OF THE AS CURVE

As we've seen, the basic short-run objective of fiscal and monetary policy is to attain full employment and price stability. The strategy is to shift the aggregate demand curve to a more favorable position. Now the question turns to the *response* of producers to an aggregate demand shift. Will they increase real output? Raise prices? Or some combination of both?

The answer depends on the shape of the aggregate supply curve: ***The response of producers to an AD shift is expressed in the slope and position of the aggregate supply curve.*** Until now we've used a generally upward-sloping AS curve to depict aggregate supply. Now we'll consider a range of different supply responses.

aggregate supply: The total quantity of output producers are willing and able to supply at alternative price levels in a given time period, *ceteris paribus*.

Figure 16.1 illustrates three very different supply behaviors.

Three Views of AS

Keynesian AS. Part (*a*) depicts what we've called the "naive" Keynesian view. Recall that Keynes was primarily concerned with the problem of unemployment. He didn't think there was much risk of inflation in the depths of a recession. He expected producers to increase output, not prices, when aggregate demand expanded. This expectation is illustrated by a *horizontal* AS curve. When fiscal or monetary stimulus shifts the AD curve rightward (e.g., AD_1 to AD_2 in Figure 16.1), output (Q) rises but not the price level (P). Only when capacity (Q^*) is reached do prices start rising abruptly (AD_2 to AD_3).

Monetarist AS. The monetarist view of supply behavior is very different. In the most extreme monetarist view, real output remains at its "natural" rate, regardless of fiscal or monetary interventions. Rising prices don't entice producers to increase output because costs are likely to rise just as fast. They instead make output decisions based on more fundamental factors like technology and market size. The monetarist AS curve is *vertical* because output doesn't respond to changing price levels. (This is the long-run AS curve we first encountered in Chapter 8.) With a vertical AS curve, only prices can respond to a shift in aggregate demand. In Figure 16.1*b*, the AS curve is anchored at the natural rate of unemployment Q_N. When aggregate demand increases from AD_4 to AD_5, the price level (P) rises, but output (Q) is unchanged.

Hybrid AS. Figure 16.1*c* blends these Keynesian and monetarist perspectives into a hybrid AS curve. At low rates of output, the curve is nearly horizontal; at high rates of output, the AS curve becomes nearly vertical. In the broad middle of the AS curve, the curve slopes gently upward. In this area, shifts of aggregate demand affect *both* prices and output. The message of this hybrid AS curve is that the outcomes of fiscal and monetary policy depend on how close the economy is to full employment. ***The closer we are to capacity, the greater the risk that fiscal or monetary stimulus will spill over into price inflation.***

FIGURE 16.1
Contrasting Views of Aggregate Supply

The effectiveness of fiscal and monetary policy depends on the shape of the AS curve. Some possibilities include:

(a) Keynesian AS In the simple Keynesian model, the rate of output responds fully and automatically to increases in demand until full employment (Q*) is reached. If demand increases from AD_1 to AD_2, equilibrium GDP will expand from Q_1 to Q*, without any inflation. Inflation becomes a problem only if demand increases beyond capacity—to AD_3, for example.

(b) Monetarist AS Monetarists assert that changes in the money supply affect prices but not output. They regard aggregate supply as a fixed quantum, at the long-run, natural rate of unemployment (here noted as Q_N). Accordingly, a shift of demand (from AD_4 to AD_5) can affect only the price level (from P_4 to P_5).

(c) Hybrid AS The consensus view incorporates Keynesian and monetarist perspectives but emphasizes the upward slope that dominates the middle of the AS curve. When demand increases, both price levels and the rate of output increase. Hence, the slope and position of the AS curve limit the effectiveness of fiscal and monetary policies.

[handwritten: Closer you get to full employment, higher risk of inflation.]

The Inflation-Unemployment Trade-Off

(a) The Keynesian view

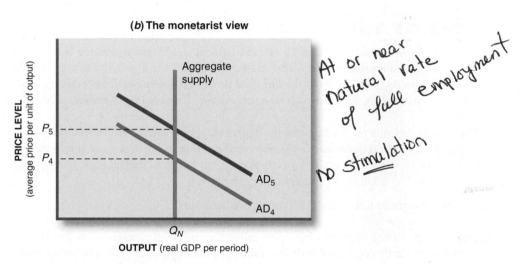

(b) The monetarist view

[handwritten: At or near natural rate of full employment — no stimulation]

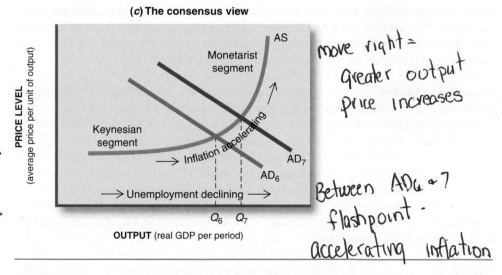

(c) The consensus view

[handwritten: move right = greater output price increases]

[handwritten: Between AD_6 & 7 flashpoint - accelerating inflation]

Because Figure 16.1c allows for varying output/price responses at different levels of economic activity, that AS curve is regarded as the most realistic for short-run outcomes. However, the upward-sloping section of the AS curve in Figure 16.1c has some disturbing implications. Because both prices and output respond to demand-side shifts, the economy can't reduce both unemployment and inflation at the same time—at least not with fiscal

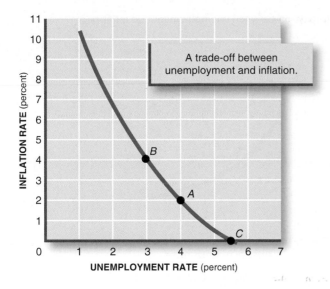

A trade-off between unemployment and inflation.

FIGURE 16.2
The Phillips Curve

The Phillips curve illustrates a trade-off between full employment and price stability. In the 1960s it appeared that efforts to reduce unemployment rates below 5.5 percent (point C) led to increasing rates of inflation (points A and B). Inflation threatened to reach unacceptable heights long before everyone was employed.

and monetary policies. To see why this is the case, consider the simple geometry of policy stimulus and restraint.

Demand Stimulus. Monetary and fiscal stimulus shift the aggregate demand curve rightward. This demand-side effect is evident in all three graphs in Figure 16.1. However, *all rightward shifts of the aggregate demand curve increase both prices and output if the aggregate supply curve is upward-sloping.* This implies that fiscal and monetary efforts to reduce unemployment will also cause some inflation. How much inflation depends on the slope of the AS curve.

Demand Restraint. Monetary and fiscal restraint shift the aggregate demand curve leftward. *If the aggregate supply curve is upward-sloping, leftward shifts of the aggregate demand curve cause both prices and output to fall.* Therefore, fiscal and monetary efforts to reduce inflation will also increase unemployment. How much unemployment depends again on the slope of the AS curve.

The Phillips Curve. The message of the upward-sloping aggregate supply curve is clear: *Demand-side policies alone can never succeed completely; they'll always cause some unwanted inflation or unemployment.*

Our macro track record provides ample evidence of this dilemma. Consider, for example, our experience with unemployment and inflation during the 1960s, as shown in Figure 16.2. This figure shows a **Phillips curve,** indicating that prices (*P*) generally started rising before the objective of expanded output (*Q*) had been completely attained. Inflation struck before full employment was reached.

The Phillips curve was developed by a New Zealand economist, Alban W. Phillips, to summarize the relationship between unemployment and inflation in England for the years 1826–1957.[1] The Phillips curve was raised from the status of an obscure graph to that of a policy issue by the discovery that the same kind of relationship apparently existed in other countries and at other times. Paul Samuelson and Robert Solow of the Massachusetts Institute of Technology were among the first to observe that the Phillips curve was a reasonable

wrote an article

Phillips curve: A historical (inverse) relationship between the rate of unemployment and the rate of inflation; commonly expresses a trade-off between the two.

---

[1] A. W. Phillips. "The Relationship between Unemployment and the Rate of Change of Money Wage Rates in the United Kingdom, 1826–1957," *Economica* (November 1958). Phillips's paper studied the relationship between unemployment and *wage* changes rather than *price* changes; most later formulations (and public policy) focus on prices.

(a) Increases in aggregate demand cause . . .

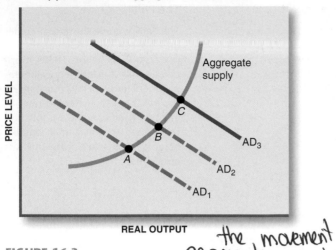

(b) A trade-off between unemployment and inflation.

FIGURE 16.3
The Phillips Curve Trade-Off

[handwritten annotation: the movement of aggregate supply curve to the right will cause unemployment to drop, but also inflation to rise]

If the aggregate supply curve slopes upward, increases in aggregate demand always cause both prices and output to rise. Thus, higher inflation becomes a cost of achieving lower unemployment. In (a), increased demand moves the economy from point A to point B. At B, unemployment is lower, but prices are higher. This trade-off is illustrated on the Phillips curve in (b). Each point on the Phillips curve represents a different AS/AD equilibrium from the graph on the left.

description of U.S. economic performance for the years 1900–1960. For the post–World War II years in particular, Samuelson and Solow noted that an unemployment rate of 4 percent was likely to be accompanied by an inflation rate of approximately 2 percent. This relationship is expressed by point *A* in Figure 16.2. By contrast, lower rates of unemployment were associated with higher rates of inflation, as at point *B*. Alternatively, complete price stability appeared attainable only at the cost of an unemployment rate of 5.5 percent (point *C*). A seesaw kind of relationship existed between inflation and unemployment: When one went up, the other fell.

The trade-off between unemployment and inflation originates in the upward-sloping AS curve. Figure 16.3*a* illustrates this point. Suppose the economy is initially at equilibrium *A*, with fairly stable prices but low output. When aggregate demand expands to AD_2, prices rise along with output, so we end up with higher inflation but less unemployment. This is also shown in Figure 16.3*b* by the move from point *a* to point *b* on the Phillips curve. The move from point *a* to point *b* indicates a decline in unemployment (more output) but an increase in inflation (higher price level). If demand is increased further, to AD_3, a still lower unemployment rate is achieved but at the cost of higher inflation (point *c*).

The Inflationary Flashpoint. The Phillips curve reminds us that there is bound to be a trade-off between unemployment and inflation at some point in economic expansions and contractions. But is there a *specific* point at which the trade-off becomes particularly worrisome? With the Keynesian AS curve (Figure 16.1*a*) there is *no* trade-off until full employment (Q^*) is reached, then inflation rockets upwards. Hence, the output level Q^* represents the **inflationary flashpoint**—the point at which inflationary pressures intensify—on the Keynesian AS curve.

The hybrid AS curve in Figure 16.1*a* doesn't have such a sharp flashpoint. The slope of the curve seems pretty smooth. In fact, however, inflationary pressures could bubble up as the economy expands. If that were to happen, the AS curve wouldn't be quite so smooth. Instead,

inflationary flashpoint: The rate of output at which inflationary pressures intensify; point of inflection on AS curve.

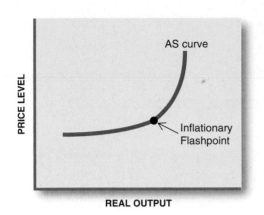

FIGURE 16.4
The Inflationary Flashpoint

As the economy approaches capacity, inflationary pressures intensify. The point at which inflation noticeably accelerates is the "inflationary flashpoint"—a juncture policymakers want to avoid.

its slope would have a noticeable point of inflection as in Figure 16.4. That inflationary flashpoint represents the rate of output at which inflation begins to accelerate significantly. It is a point policymakers don't want to cross.

SHIFTS OF THE AS CURVE

The unemployment-inflation trade-off implied by the upward-sloping AS curve is not etched in stone. Nor is the inflationary flashpoint unmovable. Many economists argue that the economy can attain lower levels of unemployment *without* higher inflation. This certainly appeared to be the case in the 1990s: Unemployment rates fell sharply from 1992 to 2000 and again from 2002–8 without any increase in inflation. How could this have happened? There's no AD shift in any of part of Figure 16.3 that would reduce both unemployment *and* inflation.

Only a rightward shift of the AS curve can reduce unemployment and inflation at the same time. When aggregate supply increases from AS_1 to AS_2 in Figure 16.5, macro equilibrium moves from E_1 to E_2. At E_2 real output is higher, so the unemployment rate must be lower. At E_2 the price level is also lower, indicating reduced inflation. Hence, a rightward shift of the AS curve offers the best of two worlds—something aggregate *demand* shifts (Figure 16.1) can't do.

Rightward AS Shifts: All Good News

[handwritten margin notes:]
more goods = less competition ∴ decreased pricing

Shift R
Drive up production
Increase output
decrease price

FIGURE 16.5
Shifts of Aggregate Supply

A rightward AS shift (AS_1 to AS_2) reduces both unemployment and inflation. A leftward shift has the opposite effect, creating stagflation.

*[Figure 16.5 graph: PRICE LEVEL (average price per unit of output) vertical axis, OUTPUT (real GDP per period) horizontal axis. Curves AS_1, AS_2, AD_1 with equilibrium points E_1 and E_2. Callout: "Rightward AS shifts reduce unemployment *and* inflation."]*

FIGURE 16.6
A Phillips Curve Shift

If the Phillips curve shifts leftward, the short-run unemployment inflation trade-off eases. With PC₁, 5 percent unemployment ignites 4 percent inflation (point a). With PC₂, 5 percent unemployment causes only 2 percent inflation (point b).

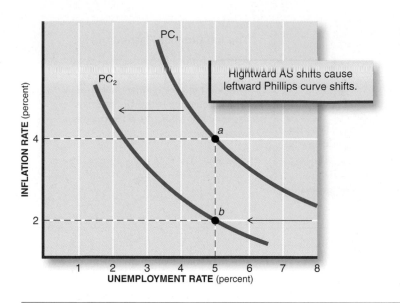

Rightward AS shifts cause leftward Phillips curve shifts.

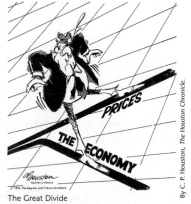

The Great Divide

Analysis: Leftward shifts of the aggregate supply curve push price levels up and output down. The remedy for such stagflation is a rightward shift of aggregate supply.

By C. P. Houston, *The Houston Chronicle.*

**Leftward AS Shifts:
All Bad News**

Phillips Curve Shift. As we saw in Figure 16.3, the Phillips curve is a direct by-product of the AS curve. Accordingly, *When the AS curve shifts, the Phillips curve shifts as well.* As Figure 16.6 illustrates, the Phillips curve shifts to the left, the opposite of the AS shift in Figure 16.5. No new information is conveyed here. The Phillips curve simply focuses more directly on the implied change in the unemployment-inflation trade-off. *When the Phillips curve shifts to the left, the unemployment-inflation trade-off eases.*

The Misery Index. To keep track of simultaneous changes in unemployment and inflation, Arthur Okun developed the "misery index"—a simple sum of the inflation and unemployment rates. As the News feature on the next page illustrates, macro misery diminished substantially during the first Reagan administration (1981–84). President Clinton also benefited from a leftward shift of the Phillips curve through 1998, but saw the misery index climb in 1999–2000. President George W. Bush experienced a sharp increase in the misery index during the recession of 2001. The misery index didn't recede until 2004, when strong output growth reduced the unemployment rate. The index jumped again in 2008–9 when the high jobless rate made everybody miserable.

Whereas rightward AS shifts appear to be a dream come true, leftward AS shifts are a real nightmare. Imagine in Figure 16.5 that the AS shift is reversed, that is, from AS₂ to AS₁. What would happen? Output would decrease and prices would rise, exactly the kind of dilemma depicted in the previous cartoon. In other words, nothing would go in the right direction. This would be rampant stagflation.

A natural disaster can trigger a leftward shift of the AS curve, especially in smaller nations. When a tsunami washed over nations in the Indian Ocean in December 2004, over 200,000 people were killed. In Sri Lanka, 80 percent of the fishing fleet was destroyed, along with port facilities, railroads, highways, and communications systems. The huge loss of human and physical capital reduced Sri Lanka's production possibilities. This was reflected in a leftward shift of the AS curve.

In an economy as large as United States', leftward shifts of aggregate supply are less dramatic. But Mother Nature can still push the AS curve around. Hurricanes Katrina and Rita, for example, destroyed vast amounts of production, transportation, and communications infrastructure in August 2005. The resulting delays and cost increases (see

IN THE NEWS

The Misery Index

Unemployment is a problem and so is inflation. Being burdened with both problems at the same time is real misery.

The late Arthur Okun proposed measuring the extent of misery by adding together the inflation and unemployment rates. He called the sum of the two rates the "discomfort index". Political pundits quickly renamed it the "misery index".

In essence, the misery index is a measure of stagflation—the simultaneous occurrence of inflation and unemployment. In 1980, the misery index peaked at 19.6 percent as a result of high inflation (12.5 percent) as well as high unemployment (7.1 percent). Stagflation—and the misery it causes—has since receded markedly.

Source: *Economic Report of the President, 2009.*

Analysis: Stagflation refers to the simultaneous occurrence of inflation and unemployment. The "misery index" combines both problems into a single measure of macro performance.

News on the next page) were reflected in a leftward shift of the AS curve and an uptick in the misery index in 2005 (see News above).

The September 11, 2001, terrorist attacks on the World Trade Center and Pentagon were another form of external shock. The attacks directly destroyed some production capacity (office space, telecommunications links, and transportation links). But they took an even greater toll on the *willingness* to supply goods and services. In the aftermath of the attacks businesses, perceiving new risks to investment and production, held back from making new commitments. Increased security measures also made transporting goods more expensive. All of these responses shifted the AS curve leftward and the Phillips curve rightward, adding to macro misery.

From the supply side of macro markets, the appropriate response to negative external shocks is clear: Shift the AS curve rightward. As the foregoing graphs have demonstrated, *rightward shifts of the aggregate supply curve always generate desirable macro outcomes.* The next question, of course, is how to shift the aggregate supply curve in the desired (rightward) direction. Supply-side economists look for clues among the forces that influence the supply-side response to changes in demand. Among

Policy Tools

– what supply side is all about

IN THE NEWS

Hurricane Damage to Gulf Ports Delays Deliveries, Raises Costs

The damage to important Gulf Coast ports and waterways from Hurricanes Katrina and Rita is delaying deliveries, sharply boosting shipping costs and will complicate rebuilding efforts in areas devastated by the storms.

The rising costs could put more downward pressure on growth, particularly for industries dependent on key products that typically flow through the region. Bringing imported steel through substitute ports could add to the prices paid by U.S. manufacturers, said John Martin, president of Martin Associates, a maritime-transportation consulting firm in Lancaster, Pa. The rising cost of forest products like lumber could add to the mounting price tag for rebuilding the region, while grain companies could see their exports become less competitive.

Ports from Houston to Mobile, Ala., that handle more than a third of U.S. cargo by tonnage were battered by the hurricanes, along with nearby shipping terminals, warehouses, navigation channels, roads and rail lines. . . .

Barge-tariff rates—the rates paid by grain companies for transportation outside longer-term shipping contracts—to move grain from St. Louis to New Orleans for export have soared by 60% to 100% since Katrina hit.

—Daniel Machalaba

Source: *The Wall Street Journal*, October 3, 2005, p. A8. Copyright 2005 by Dow Jones & Company, Inc. Reproduced with permission of Dow Jones & Company, Inc. in the format Textbook via Copyright Clearance Center.

Analysis: A natural disaster that destroys both human and physical capital shifts the aggregate supply curve to the left, reducing output and raising price levels.

web analysis

To understand the effect of oil supply shocks on economic conditions, visit **www.eia.doe.gov** and search "oil supply shocks."

those forces, the following policy options for shifting the AS curve rightward have been emphasized:

- Tax incentives for saving, investment, and work.
- Human capital investment.
- Deregulation.
- Trade liberalization. *— more competition, lower prices*
- Infrastructure development. *— new highways etc.*

All these policies have the potential to change supply decisions *independently* of any changes in aggregate demand. If they're effective, they'll result in a rightward shift of the AS curve and an *improved* trade-off between unemployment and inflation.

TAX INCENTIVES

The most renowned supply-side policy option for improving the unemployment-inflation trade-off was the "supply-side" tax cuts of the early 1980s. Tax cuts are of course a staple of Keynesian economics. But tax cuts take on a whole new role on the supply side of the economy. *In Keynesian economics, tax cuts are used to increase aggregate demand.* By putting more disposable income in the hands of consumers, Keynesian economists seek to increase expenditure on goods and services. Output is expected to increase in response. From a Keynesian perspective, the form of the tax cut is not very important, as long as disposable income increases.

The supply side of the economy encourages a different view of taxes. *Taxes not only alter disposable income but also affect the incentives to work and produce.* High tax rates destroy incentives to work and produce, so they end up reducing total output. Low tax rates, by contrast, allow people to keep more of what they earn and so stimulate greater output. *The direct effects of taxes on the supply of goods are the concern of supply-side economists.* Figure 16.7 shows the difference between demand-side and supply-side perspectives on tax policy.

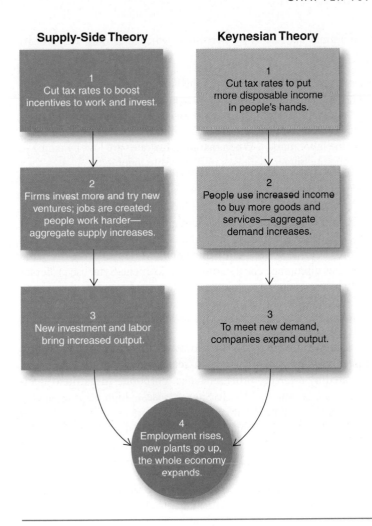

Supply-Side Theory

1
Cut tax rates to boost incentives to work and invest.

2
Firms invest more and try new ventures; jobs are created; people work harder—aggregate supply increases.

3
New investment and labor bring increased output.

Keynesian Theory

1
Cut tax rates to put more disposable income in people's hands.

2
People use increased income to buy more goods and services—aggregate demand increases.

3
To meet new demand, companies expand output.

4
Employment rises, new plants go up, the whole economy expands.

FIGURE 16.7
Two Theories for Getting the Economy Moving

Keynesians and supply-siders both advocate cutting taxes to reduce unemployment. But they have very different views on the kind of tax cuts required and the impact of any cuts enacted.

Supply-side theory places special emphasis on *marginal* tax rates. The **marginal tax rate** is the tax rate imposed on the last (marginal) dollar of income received. In our progressive income tax system, marginal tax rates increase as more income is received. Uncle Sam takes a larger share out of each additional dollar earned. In 2009, the highest marginal tax rate on personal income was 35 percent. That top tax rate was far below the 91 percent rate that existed in 1944, but it was also a lot higher than the 12 percent tax rate imposed in 1914 (see Figure 16.8).

In view of the wild history of tax rates, one might wonder whether the rate selected matters. Specifically, does the marginal tax rate affect supply decisions? Will people work and

Marginal Tax Rates

> **marginal tax rate:** The tax rate imposed on the last (marginal) dollar of income.

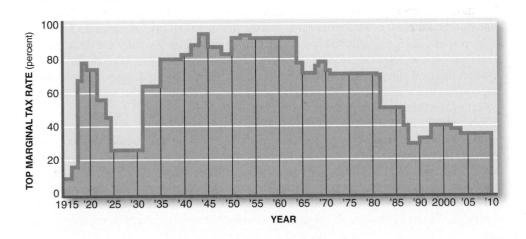

FIGURE 16.8
Changes in Marginal Tax Rates since 1915

The top marginal tax rate on income has varied from a low of 12 percent in 1914 to a high of 91 percent in 1944. Supply-side theory emphasizes how these varying tax rates affect work, investment, and production decisions, that is, aggregate supply.

invest as much when the marginal tax rate is 91 percent as when it is only 12 percent? Doesn't seem likely, does it.

Labor Supply. The marginal tax rate directly changes the financial incentive to *increase* one's work. *If the marginal tax rate is high, there's less incentive to work more*—Uncle Sam will get most of the added income. Confronted with high marginal tax rates, workers may choose to stay home rather than work an extra shift. Families may decide that it doesn't pay to send both parents into the labor market. When marginal tax rates are low, by contrast, those extra work activities generate bigger increases in disposable income.

Entrepreneurship. Marginal tax rates affect not only labor-supply decisions but also decisions on whether to start or expand a business. Most small businesses are organized as sole proprietorships or partnerships and subject to *personal,* not *corporate,* tax rates. Hence, a decline in personal tax rates will affect the risk/reward balance for potential entrepreneurs. Columbia Business School professors William Gentry and Glenn Huber have demonstrated that progressive marginal tax rates discourage entry into self-employment. Syracuse professor Douglas Holtz-Eakin and Princeton economist Harvey Rosen have shown that the growth rate, investment, and employment of small businesses are also affected by marginal tax rates. As Holtz-Eakin concluded, "taxes matter."

Investment. Taxes matter for corporations too. Corporate entities account for nearly 90 percent of business output and 84 percent of business assets. Like small proprietorships, corporations, too, are motivated by *after*-tax profits. Hence, corporate **investment** decisions will be affected by corporate tax rates. If Uncle Sam imposes a high tax rate on corporate profits, the payoff to investors will be diminished. Potential investors may decide to consume their income or to purchase tax-free bonds rather than invest in plant and equipment. If that happens, total investment will decline and output will suffer. Accordingly, *if high tax rates discourage investment, aggregate supply will be constrained.*

investment: Expenditures on (production of) new plant, equipment, and structures (capital) in a given time period, plus changes in business inventories.

Tax-Induced Supply Shifts

If tax rates affect supply decisions, then *changes* in tax rates will shift aggregate supply. Specifically, supply-siders conclude that *a reduction in marginal tax rates will shift the aggregate supply curve to the right.* The increased supply will come from three sources: more work effort, more entrepreneurship, and more investment. This increased willingness to produce will reduce the rate of unemployment. The additional output will also help reduce inflationary pressures. Thus we end up with less unemployment *and* less inflation.

From a supply-side perspective, the form of the tax cut is critical. For example, **tax rebates** are a one-time windfall to consumers and have no effect on marginal tax rates. As a consequence, disposable income rises, but not the incentives for work or production. Rebates directly affect only the demand side of the economy.

tax rebate: A lump-sum refund of taxes paid.

To stimulate aggregate *supply,* tax *rates* must be reduced, particularly at the margin. These cuts can take the form of reductions in personal income tax rates or reductions in the marginal tax rates imposed on businesses. In either case, the lower tax rates will give people a greater incentive to work, invest, and produce. This was the motivation for the Reagan tax cuts of 1981–84. Shifting the aggregate supply curve rightward was also the goal of President George W. Bush's 2001 proposal to cut the top marginal tax rate from 39.6 percent to 33 percent. Congress ultimately adopted a package of supply-side and demand-side incentives. In the 2009 debate over President Obama's stimulus program, the distinction between demand-side stimulus and supply-side incentives surfaced again. Supply-siders emphasized that supply-oriented tax cuts were critical to reducing the potential inflation impact of increased government spending.

Table 16.1 illustrates the distinction between Keynesian and supply-side tax cuts. Under both tax systems (A and B), a person earning $200 pays $80 in taxes before the tax cut and $60 after the tax cut. But under system A, the marginal tax rate is always 50 percent, which means that Uncle Sam is getting half of every dollar earned above $100. By contrast, system B imposes a marginal tax rate of only 30 percent—$0.30 of every dollar above $100 goes to the government. Under system B, people have a greater incentive to earn *more* than

| Initial Alternatives | | | | | |
| Tax System | Initial Tax Schedule | Tax on Income of $200 | Tax Rate | | Disposable Income |
			Average	Marginal	
A	$30 + 50% of income over $100	$80	40%	50%	$120
B	$50 + 30% of income over $100	$80	40%	30%	$120

TABLE 16.1
Average vs. Marginal Tax Rates

The same amount of taxes can be raised via two very different systems. Here a person earning $200 pays $80 in taxes under either system (A or B). Thus, the *average* tax rate (total tax ÷ total income) is the same in both cases ($80 ÷ $200 = 40%). The *marginal* tax rates are very different, however. System A has a high marginal rate (50%), whereas system B has a low marginal tax rate (30%). System B provides a greater incentive for people to earn over $100.

| Alternative Forms of Tax Cut | | | | | |
| Tax System | Revised Tax Schedule | Tax on Income of $200 | Tax Rate | | Disposable Income |
			Average	Marginal	
A	$10 + 50% of income over $100	$60	30%	50%	$140
B	$30 + 30% of income over $100	$60	30%	30%	$140

The average tax rate could be cut to 30 percent under either system. Under both systems, the revised tax would be $60 and disposable income would be increased to $140. Keynesians would be happy with either form of tax cut. But supply-siders would favor system B because the lower marginal tax rate gives people more incentive to earn higher incomes.

$100. Although both systems raise the same amount of taxes, system B offers greater incentives to work extra hours and produce more output.

All economists agree that tax rates influence people's decisions to work, invest, and produce. But the policy-relevant question is, *how much* influence do taxes have? Do reductions in the marginal tax rate shift the aggregate supply curve far to the right? Or are the resultant shifts quite small?

The response of labor and capital to a change in tax rates is summarized by the **tax elasticity of supply.** Like other elasticities, this one measures the proportional response of supplies to a change in price (in this case, a tax *rate*). Specifically, the tax elasticity of supply is the percentage change in quantity supplied divided by the percentage in tax rates, that is,

$$\text{Tax elasticity of supply} = \frac{\%\ \text{change in quantity supplied}}{\%\ \text{change in tax rate}}$$

Normally we expect quantity supplied to go up when tax rates go down. Elasticity (E) is therefore negative, although it's usually expressed in absolute terms (without the minus sign). The (absolute) value of E must be greater than zero, since we expect *some* response to a tax cut. The policy issue boils down to the question of how large E actually is.

If the tax elasticity of supply were large enough, a tax cut might actually *increase* tax revenues. Suppose the tax elasticity were equal to 1.5. In that case a tax cut of 10 percent would cause output supplied to increase by 15 percent (= 1.5 × 10%). Such a large increase in the tax base (income) would result in *more* taxes being paid even though the tax *rate* was reduced. One of President Reagan's economic advisers, Arthur Laffer, actually thought such an outcome was possible. He predicted that tax revenues would *increase* after the Reagan supply-side tax cuts were made. In reality, the tax elasticity of supply turned out to

Tax Elasticity of Supply

tax elasticity of supply: The percentage change in quantity supplied divided by the percentage change in tax rates.

be much smaller (around 0.15) and tax revenues fell substantially. The aggregate supply curve *did* shift to the right, but not very far, when marginal tax rates were cut.

The evidently low tax elasticity of supply helped President Clinton convince Congress to *increase* marginal tax rates in 1993. Although opponents objected that higher tax rates would reduce work and investment, the Clinton administration pointed out that any leftward shift of aggregate supply was likely to be small. President George W. Bush reversed that shift with the 2001–4 marginal tax-rate cuts. According to a 2006 study by the Congressional Research Service, those tax-rate cuts elicited a 0.20 tax elasticity of supply.

Savings Incentives

Supply-side economists emphasize the importance of *long-run* responses to changed tax incentives. On the demand side, an increase in income translates very quickly into increased spending. On the supply side, things don't happen so fast. It takes time to construct new plants and equipment. People are also slow to respond to new work and investment incentives. Hence, the full benefits of supply-side tax cuts—or the damage done by tax hikes—won't be immediately visible.

> **saving:** That part of disposable income not spent on current consumption; disposable income less consumption.

Of particular concern to supply-side economists is the rate of saving in the economy. Demand-side economists emphasize spending and tend to treat **saving** as a leakage problem. Supply-siders, by contrast, emphasize the importance of saving for financing investment and economic growth. At full employment, a greater volume of investment is possible only if the rate of consumption is cut back. In other words, additional investment requires additional saving. Hence, *supply-side economists favor tax incentives that encourage saving as well as greater tax incentives for investment.* This kind of perspective contrasts sharply with the Keynesian emphasis on stimulating consumption, as the accompanying cartoon emphasizes.

Investment Incentives

An alternative lever for shifting aggregate supply is to offer tax incentives for investment. The 1981 tax cuts focused on *personal* income tax rates. By contrast, President George H. Bush advocated cutting capital gains taxes. These are taxes levied on the increase in the value of property, such as land, buildings, and corporate stock, when it's sold. Lower capital gains taxes, Bush argued, would encourage people to start businesses or invest in them.

President Clinton also emphasized the need for investment incentives. His very first proposal for stimulating the economy was a temporary investment tax credit. People who invested in new plant and equipment would receive a tax credit equal to 10 percent of their investment. In effect, Uncle Sam would pay for part of any new investment by collecting less taxes. Because the credit is available only to those who make new investments, it's a particularly

> **web analysis**
>
> The U.S. Bureau of Economic Analysis maintains data on the personal saving rate of U.S. households. To view this information, visit **www.bea.gov** and search "Overview of the U.S. Economy."

Analysis: In the short run, consumer saving may reduce aggregate demand. However, saving also finances increased investment, which is essential to long-run growth.

efficient lever for shifting the aggregate supply curve. President Clinton withdrew the investment-credit proposal, however, when he decided that deficit reduction was a higher priority.

President George W. Bush pulled this supply-side lever more firmly. After securing the huge *personal* tax cuts in 2001, Bush sought *business* tax cuts. In 2002 Congress approved larger capital expensing, which reduced the after-tax cost of new investments. In 2003, tax rates on dividends and capital gains were reduced, making investment still more profitable. During the 2008 campaign, Barack Obama vowed to reverse the Bush "tax-cuts for the rich" by *raising* marginal income tax rates as well as capital-gains and inheritance taxes. By the time he took office, however, the economy was deep into a recession and these *left*ward AS shifts were abandoned temporarily. Obama continued to pursue these tax-code changes, however, after the 2009 stimulus package was enacted.

HUMAN CAPITAL INVESTMENT

A nation's ability to supply goods and services depends on its *human* capital as well as its *physical* capital. If the size of the labor force increased, more output could be produced in any given price level. Similarly, if the *quality* of the workforce were to increase, more output could be supplied at any given price level. In other words, increases in **human capital**—the skills and knowledge of the workforce—add to the nation's potential output.

A mismatch between the skills of the workforce and the requirements of new jobs is a major cause of the unemployment-inflation trade-off. When aggregate demand increases, employers want to hire more workers. But the available (unemployed) workers may not have the skills employers require. This is the essence of **structural unemployment.** The consequence is that employers can't increase output as fast as they'd like to. Prices, rather than output, increase.

The larger the skills gap between unemployed workers and the requirements of emerging jobs, the worse will be the Phillips curve trade-off. To improve the trade-off, the skills gap must be reduced. This is another supply-side imperative. ***Investments in human capital reduce structural unemployment and shift the aggregate supply curve rightward.***

The tax code is a policy tool for increasing human capital investment as well as physical capital investment. In this case tax credits are made available to employers who offer more worker training. Such credits reduce the employer's after-tax cost of training.

President Clinton proposed even stronger incentives for employer-based training. He wanted to *require* employers to spend at least 1.5 percent of their total payroll costs on training activities. Those employers who didn't provide training activities directly would have to pay an equivalent sum into a public training fund. This "play-or-pay" approach would force employers to invest in the human capital of their employees.

Although the "play-or-pay" concept is intriguing, it might actually shift the aggregate supply curve the *wrong* way. The *costs* of employing workers would rise in the short run as employers shelled out more money for training or taxes. Hence, the aggregate supply curve would shift *leftward* in the short run, worsening the unemployment-inflation trade-off. Only later might AS shift rightward, and then only to the extent that training actually improved **labor productivity.**

Another way to increase human capital is to expand and improve the efficacy of the education system. President George H. Bush encouraged local school systems to become more competitive. He suggested they experiment with vouchers that would allow students to attend the school of their choice. Schools would then have to offer services that attracted voucher-carrying students. Those schools that didn't compete successfully wouldn't have enough funds (vouchers) to continue.

President Clinton advocated a more conventional approach. He urged Congress to allocate more funds to the school system, particularly programs for preschoolers, like Head Start, and for disadvantaged youth. He acknowledged that vouchers might increase school quality but wanted to limit their use to public schools.

President George W. Bush characterized himself as the "education President." He increased federal spending on education and improved tax incentives for college-savings accounts and

human capital: The knowledge and skills possessed by the workforce.

Structural Unemployment

structural unemployment: Unemployment caused by a mismatch between the skills (or location) of job seekers and the requirements (or location) of available jobs.

Worker Training

Education Spending

labor productivity: Amount of output produced by a worker in a given period of time; output per hour.

tuition payments. His No Child Left Behind program also increased school accountability for human capital development. President Obama also emphasized educational improvements as a key to long-run growth. None of these educational tools generate a quick AS-curve shift. Rather, any improvements in labor productivity are likely to emerge many years later.

Affirmative Action

Lack of skills and experience aren't the only reasons it's sometimes hard to find the "right" workers. The mismatch between employed workers and jobs is often less a matter of skills than of race, gender, or age. In other words, discrimination can create an artificial barrier between job seekers and available job openings.

If discrimination tends to shift the aggregate supply curve leftward, then reducing discriminatory barriers should shift it to the right. Equal opportunity programs are thus a natural extension of a supply-side approach to macro policy. However, critics are also quick to point out the risks inherent in government regulation of hiring decisions. From a supply-side perspective, laws that forbid discrimination are welcome and should be enforced. But aggressive affirmative action programs that require employers to hire specific numbers of women or minority workers limit productive capabilities and can lead to excessive costs.

Transfer Payments

transfer payments: Payments to individuals for which no current goods or services are exchanged, like Social Security, welfare, unemployment benefits.

Welfare programs also discourage workers from taking available jobs. Unemployment and welfare benefits provide a source of income when a person isn't working. Although these **transfer payments** are motivated by humanitarian goals, they also inhibit labor supply. Transfer recipients must give up some or all of their welfare payments when they take a job, which makes working less attractive and therefore reduces the number of available workers. The net result is a leftward shift of the aggregate supply curve.

In 1996, Congress reformed the nation's core welfare program. The supply-side emphasis of that reform was manifest in the very title of the reform legislation: the Personal Responsibility and Work Opportunity Act. Congress set time limits on how long people can draw welfare benefits. The act also required recipients to engage in job-related activities like job search and training while still receiving benefits.

The 1996 reforms had a dramatic effect on recipient behavior. Nationally, over 5 million adults left welfare between 1996 and 2001. Over half of these ex-welfare recipients entered the labor force, thereby shifting the AS curve rightward.

Recognizing that income transfers reduce aggregate supply doesn't force us to eliminate all welfare programs. Welfare programs are also intended to serve important social needs. The AS/AD framework reminds us, however, that the structure of such programs will affect aggregate supply. With over 60 million Americans receiving income transfers, the effect on aggregate supply can be significant.

DEREGULATION

Government intervention affects the shape and position of the aggregate supply curve in other ways. The government intervenes directly in supply decisions by *regulating* employment and output behavior. In general, such regulations limit the flexibility of producers to respond to changes in demand. Government regulation also tends to raise production costs. The higher costs result not only from required changes in the production process but also from the expense of monitoring government regulations and filling out endless government forms. Thomas Hopkins, a Rochester Institute of Technology economist, estimates that the total costs of regulation exceed $700 billion a year. These added costs of production shift the aggregate supply curve to the left.

Factor Markets

Government intervention in factor markets increases the cost of supplying goods and services in many ways.

Minimum Wages. Minimum wage laws are one of the most familiar forms of factor-market regulation. The Fair Labor Standards Act of 1938 required employers to pay workers a minimum of 25 cents per hour. Over time, Congress has increased the coverage of that act and the minimum wage itself repeatedly.

The goal of the minimum wage law is to ensure workers a decent standard of living. But the law has other effects as well. By prohibiting employers from using lower-paid workers, it limits the ability of employers to hire additional workers. Teenagers, for example, may not have enough skills or experience to merit the federal minimum wage. Employers may have to rely on more expensive workers rather than hire unemployed teenagers.

Here again the issue is not whether minimum wage laws serve any social purposes but how they affect macro outcomes. By shifting the aggregate supply curve leftward, minimum wage laws make it more difficult to achieve full employment with stable prices.

Mandatory Benefits. Government-directed fringe benefits have the same kind of effect on aggregate supply. One of the first bills President Clinton signed into law was the Family and Medical Leave Act, which requires all businesses with 50 or more employees to grant leaves of absence for up to 12 weeks. The employer must continue to pay health benefits during such absences and must also incur the costs of recruiting and training temporary replacements. The General Accounting Office estimated these benefits add nearly $700 million per year to payroll costs. These added payroll costs add to the costs of production, making producers less willing to supply output at any given price level.

Occupational Health and Safety. Government regulation of factor markets extends beyond wages and benefits. The government also sets standards for workplace safety and health. The Occupational Safety and Health Administration (OSHA), for example, issued new rules in November 2000 to reduce ergonomic injuries at work. The rules would have required employers to redesign workplaces (assembly lines, computer workstations) to accommodate individual workers. The rules would have also required employers to pay higher health care costs and grant more injury-related leave. OSHA itself estimated that the new regulations would cost employers $4.5 billion a year. Employers said the ergonomics regulations would cost *far* more that—up to $125 billion a year. Concern over the implied upward shift of aggregate supply prompted Congress to rescind the new ergonomics rules in early 2001, before they took effect.

Product Markets

The government's regulation of factor markets tends to raise production costs and inhibit supply. The same is true of regulations imposed directly on product markets, as the following examples illustrate.

Transportation Costs. At the federal level, various agencies regulate the output and prices of transportation services. Until 1984, the Civil Aeronautics Board (CAB) determined which routes airlines could fly and how much they could charge. The Interstate Commerce Commission (ICC) has had the same kind of power over trucking, interstate bus lines, and railroads. The routes, services, and prices for ships (in U.S. coastal waters and foreign commerce) have been established by the Federal Maritime Commission. In all these cases, the regulations constrained the ability of producers to respond to increases in demand. The rate of output was kept too low and prices too high.

Similar problems continue to inflate intrastate trucking costs. All but eight states limit the routes, the loads, and the prices of intrastate trucking companies. These regulations promote inefficient transportation and protect producer profits. The net cost to the economy is at least $8 billion, or about $128 a year for a family of four.

Many cities and counties also limit the number of taxicabs and regulate their prices. The net effect of such regulation is to limit competition and drive up the cost of transportation.

Food and Drug Standards. The Food and Drug Administration (FDA) has a broad mandate to protect consumers from dangerous products. In fulfilling this responsibility, the FDA sets health standards for the content of specific foods. The FDA also sets standards for the testing of new drugs and evaluates the test results.

The goal of FDA regulation is to minimize health risks to consumers. Like all regulation, however, the FDA standards entail real costs. The tests required for new drugs are expensive and time-consuming. Getting a new drug approved for sale can take years of effort and require a huge investment. The net results are that (1) fewer new drugs are brought to market and (2) those that do reach the market are more expensive than they would have been in the absence of regulation. In other words, the aggregate supply of goods is shifted to the left.

Other examples of government regulation are commonplace. The Environmental Protection Agency (EPA) regulates auto emissions, the discharge of industrial wastes, and water pollution. The U.S. Congress restricts foreign imports and raises their prices. The Federal Trade Commission (FTC) limits firms' freedom to increase their output or advertise their products.

Reducing Costs

Many—perhaps most—of these regulatory activities are beneficial. In fact, all were originally designed to serve specific public purposes. As a result of such regulation, we get safer drugs, cleaner air, and less deceptive advertising. We must also consider the costs involved, however. All regulatory activities impose direct and indirect costs. These costs must be compared to the benefits received. ***The basic contention of supply-side economists is that regulatory costs are now too high.*** To improve our economic performance, they assert, we must *deregulate* the production process, thereby shifting the aggregate supply curve to the right again.

EASING TRADE BARRIERS

Government regulation of international trade also influences the shape and position of aggregate supply. Trade flows affect both factor and product markets.

Factor Markets

In factor markets, U.S. producers buy raw materials, equipment parts, and components from foreign suppliers. Tariffs (taxes on imported goods) make such inputs more expensive, thereby increasing the cost of U.S. production. Regulations or quotas that make foreign inputs less accessible or more expensive similarly constrain the U.S. aggregate supply curve. The quota on imported sugar, for example, increases the cost of U.S.-produced soda, cookies, and candy. Just that one trade barrier has cost U.S. consumers over $2 billion in higher prices.

Product Markets

The same kind of trade barriers affect product markets directly. With completely unrestricted ("free") trade, foreign producers would be readily available to supply products to U.S. consumers. If U.S. producers were approaching capacity or incurring escalating cost pressures, foreign suppliers would act as a safety valve. By increasing the quantity of output available at any given price level, foreign suppliers help flatten out the aggregate supply curve.

Despite the success of the North American Free Trade Agreement (NAFTA) and the World Trade Organization (WTO) in reducing trade barriers, half of all U.S. imports are still subject to tariffs. Nontariff barriers (regulation, quotas, and so forth) also still constrain aggregate supply. This was evident in the multiyear battle over Mexican trucking. Although NAFTA authorized Mexican trucking companies to compete freely in the United States by 2000, U.S. labor unions (Teamsters) and trucking companies vigorously protested their entry, delaying the implied reduction in transportation costs for 7 years.

Immigration

Another global supply-side policy lever is immigration policy. Skill shortages in U.S. labor markets can be overcome with education and training. But even faster relief is available in the vast pool of foreign workers. In 2000, Congress increased the quota for software engineers and other high-tech workers by 70 percent, to 195,000 workers. The intent was to relieve the skill shortage in high-tech industries and with it, the cost pressures that were increasing the slope of the aggregate supply curve. Temporary visas for farm workers also help avert cost-push inflation in the farm sector. By regulating the flow of immigrant workers, Congress has the potential to alter the shape and position of the short-run AS curve.

INFRASTRUCTURE DEVELOPMENT

Another way to reduce the costs of supplying goods and services is to improve the nation's **infrastructure,** that is, the transportation, communications, judicial, and other systems that bind the pieces of the economy into a coherent whole. The interstate highway system, for example, enlarged the market for producers looking for new sales opportunities. Improved air traffic controls and larger airports have also made international markets and factors of production readily accessible. Without interstate highways and international airports, the process of supplying goods and services would be more localized and much more expensive.

It's easy to take infrastructure for granted until you have to make do without it. In recent years, U.S. producers have rushed into China, Russia, and eastern Europe looking for new profit opportunities. What they discovered is that even simple communication is difficult where Internet access and even telephones are often scarce. Outside the major cities business facilities and accommodations are often equally scarce. There are few established clearinghouses for marketing information, and labor markets are fragmented and localized. Getting started sometimes requires doing everything from scratch.

Although the United States has a highly developed infrastructure, it too could be improved. There are roads and bridges to repair, more airports to be built, faster rail systems to construct, and space-age telecommunications networks to install. Spending on this kind of infrastructure will not only increase aggregate demand (fiscal stimulus) but also shift aggregate supply. That is why President Obama made infrastructure spending the centerpiece of his 2009 stimulus program (see News below). The *spending* would boost aggregate demand; the finished projects would increase aggregate supply.

infrastructure: The transportation, communications, education, judicial, and other institutional systems that facilitate market exchanges.

IN THE NEWS

Can Infrastructure Spending Rev Up the Economy?

President-elect Barack Obama said over the weekend that he would lead the biggest government infrastructure investment since the interstate highway system was launched in the 1950s. He is also planning to boost government spending in other areas in hopes of spurring both short- and long-term economic growth.

Every $1 billion the federal government commits to roads, bridges and other infrastructure helps to support some 35,000 jobs.

Jump-Starting the Economy

Obama said this weekend that he would focus on projects that get the money moving quickly.

"I think we can get a lot of work done fast. When I met with the governors, all of them have projects that are shovel-ready," Obama said on NBC's *Meet the Press.*

The president-elect also hopes to use the economic stimulus package to fund initiatives that are valuable in their own right, such as making medical records available electronically and retrofitting buildings to make them more energy efficient.

"The key for us is making sure that we jump-start that economy in a way that doesn't just deal with the short term, doesn't just create jobs immediately, but also puts us on a glide path for long-term, sustainable economic growth," he said.

—Scott Horsley

Source: National Public Radio. December 8, 2008.

Analysis: Spending on infrastructure not only creates fiscal stimulus (AD), but also increases the capacity to produce (AS).

EXPECTATIONS

Last, but not least, we must again take expectations into account. Expectations play a crucial role not only in consumer expenditure decisions but in production and investment decisions as well. Hence, expectations will influence the shape of the short-run aggregate supply curve—the *willingness* and ability to supply output at various prices. If producers expect more "business-friendly" government policies they will be more willing to invest in new plant, equipment, and software. By contrast, the prospect of increasing government regulation or higher taxes deters investors from expanding production capacity. *Because investment is always a bet on future economic conditions, expectations directly affect the shape of the AS curve.*

THE ECONOMY TOMORROW

REBUILDING AMERICA

The output of the U.S. economy depends not only on *private* investment but on *public* investment as well. The infrastructure of transportation, communications, and environmental systems affects the nation's production possibilities. As we look to the future, we have to wonder whether that infrastructure will satisfy the needs of the economy tomorrow. If it doesn't, it will become increasingly difficult and costly to increase output. Inadequate infrastructure would not only worsen short-term macro outcomes but also impair our ability to compete in world markets.

Declining Infrastructure Investment. The United States has over $2 trillion worth of public, nonmilitary infrastructure, including highways, bridges, sewage systems, buildings, hospitals, and schools. Like private capital (business plant, equipment, and structures), this *public* capital contributes to our production possibilities.

Investment in public infrastructure slowed down in the 1970s and 1980s. The rate of infrastructure investment peaked at around 3.5 percent of GDP in the mid-1960s. It then declined steadily to a low of about 0.5 percent of GDP in the early 1980s. As a result of this decline in spending, the United States has barely been able to *maintain* existing infrastructure, much less *expand* it. Studies by Alan Aschauer and others suggest that *declining infrastructure investment has reduced actual and potential output.* In other words, crumbling infrastructure has shifted the aggregate supply curve leftward.

Not everyone agrees that the nation's infrastructure is actually crumbling. Accident rates on the roads, rails, and in the air have been declining. Moreover, the quality of interstate roads—including the 155,000-mile national highway system—has improved significantly since 1980. But everyone agrees that *the transportation system isn't keeping up with a growing economy.* Highway traffic is increasing at 2.5 percent a year, while airline passenger traffic is rising at closer to 4 percent a year. To accommodate this growth, we need more and better transportation systems.

The Cost of Delay. The failure to expand the infrastructure could prove costly. The U.S. Department of Transportation estimates that people now spend nearly 3.5 *billion* hours a year in traffic delays. If the nation's highways don't improve, those delays will skyrocket to more than 4 *billion* hours a year a decade from now. That's a lot of labor resources to leave idle. Moreover, cars stuck on congested highways waste a lot of gasoline: nearly 4 billion gallons a year.

Delays in air travel impose similar costs. The Federal Aviation Administration says air travel delays increase airline operating costs by over $2 billion a year and idle over $3 billion worth of passenger time. That time imposes a high opportunity cost in forgone business transactions and shortened vacations. Ultimately, all these costs are reflected in lower productivity, reduced output, and higher prices.

The Rebuilding Process. To alleviate these constraints on aggregate supply, Congress voted to accelerate infrastructure spending. The Transportation Equity Act of 2000 raised federal spending to over $600 billion in this decade. Among the public investments:

* *Highways:* Highway construction and rehabilitation.
* *Air traffic control:* Modernization of the air traffic control system.

- *Weather service:* Modernization of the weather service (new satellites, a super-computer).
- *Maglev trains:* Research on magnetically levitated ("maglev") trains that can travel at 300 miles per hour and are environmentally clean.
- *Smart cars and highways:* Research and testing of cars and highways outfitted with radar, monitors, and computers to reduce congestion and accidents.

Other legislation authorized more spending on sewage systems, access to space (for example, the space shuttle), modernization of the postal service, and construction of more hospitals, prisons, and other buildings. To this list President Obama added development of alternative energy sources, expansion of broadband access, an improved electrical grid, and energy-saving retooling of public buildings (see News, p. 351). He also added a couple of hundred billion dollars to this task. All these infrastructure improvements increase aggregate supply, improving both short- and long-run economic outcomes. In the process, they create more potential for economic growth without inflation in the economy tomorrow.

SUMMARY

- Fiscal and monetary policies seek to attain full employment and price stability by altering the level of aggregate demand. Their success depends on microeconomic responses, as reflected in the price and output decisions of market participants.   LO1
- The market's response to shifts in aggregate demand is reflected in the shape and position of the aggregate supply curve. If the AS curve slopes upward, a trade-off between unemployment and inflation exists. The Phillips curve illustrates the trade-off.   LO2
- The inflationary flashpoint is the rate of output where inflation accelerates—where the unemployment-inflation trade-off becomes acute.   LO2
- If the AS curve shifts to the left, the trade-off between unemployment and inflation worsens. Stagflation—a combination of substantial inflation and unemployment—results. This is illustrated by rightward shifts of the Phillips curve.   LO2
- Supply-side policies attempt to alter price and output decisions directly. If successful, they'll shift the aggregate supply curve to the right. A rightward AS shift implies less inflation *and* less unemployment.   LO3

- Marginal tax rates are a major concern of supply-side economists. High tax rates discourage extra work, investment, and saving. A reduction in marginal tax rates should shift aggregate supply to the right.   LO3
- The tax elasticity of supply measures the response of quantity supplied to changes in tax rates. Empirical evidence suggests that tax elasticity is low and that short-run shifts of the aggregate supply curve are therefore small.   LO3
- Investments in human capital increase productivity and therefore shift aggregate supply also. Workers' training and education enhancement are policy tools.   LO3
- Government regulation often raises the cost of production and limits output. Deregulation is intended to reduce costly restrictions on price and output behavior, thereby shifting the AS curve to the right.   LO3
- Public infrastructure is part of the economy's capital resources. Investments in infrastructure (such as transportation systems) facilitate market exchanges and expand production possibilities.   LO3
- Trade barriers shift the AS curve leftward by raising the cost of imported inputs and the price of imported products. Lowering trade barriers increases aggregate supply.   LO3

Key Terms

stagflation	investment	structural unemployment
aggregate supply	tax rebate	labor productivity
Phillips curve	tax elasticity of supply	transfer payments
inflationary flashpoint	saving	infrastructure
marginal tax rate	human capital	

Questions for Discussion

1. Why might prices rise when aggregate demand increases? What factors might influence the extent of price inflation? LO1

2. What were the unemployment and inflation rates last year? Where would they lie on Figure 16.6? Can you explain the implied shift from curve PC₂? LO2

3. Why would a Gulf Coast hurricane have *national* impact on aggregate supply? (News, p. 342). LO1

4. Which of the following groups are likely to have the highest tax elasticity of labor supply? (*a*) college students, (*b*) single parents, (*c*) primary earners in two-parent families, and (*d*) secondary earners in two-parent families. Why are there differences? LO3

5. How is the aggregate supply curve affected by (*a*) minimum wage laws, and (*b*) Social Security payroll taxes and retirement benefits? LO3

6. OSHA predicted that its proposed ergonomics rules (text, p. 349) would have cut repetitive-stress injuries by 50 percent. Was Congress correct in repealing those rules? LO1

7. If all workplace-safety regulations both (*a*) improve workers' well-being and (*b*) raise production costs, how should the line between "good" regulations and "bad" regulations be drawn? LO3

8. How do each of the following infrastructure items affect aggregate supply? (*a*) highways, (*b*) schools, (*c*) sewage systems, and (*d*) courts and prisons. LO3

9. How would the volume and timing of capital investments be affected by (*a*) a permanent cut in the capital-gains tax, and (*b*) a temporary 10-percent tax credit? LO3

10. How might the inflationary flashpoint affect policy decisions? How would you represent the flashpoint on the Phillips curve? LO2

11. Why would anyone object to President Obama's proposed infrastructure spending? LO2

! **web activities** to accompany this chapter can be found on the Online Learning Center:
http://www.mhhe.com/schiller12e

PROBLEMS FOR CHAPTER 16   Name: _____

LO1   1. On the graph below, draw the (A) Keynesian, (B) monetarist, and (C) hybrid AS curves, all
      intersecting AD at point E. If AD shifts rightward, which AS curve (A, B, or C) generates

      (a) The biggest increase in output?   _____

      (b) The biggest increase in prices?   _____

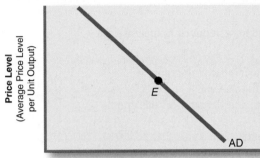

Output (Real GDP per Period)

LO1   2. Which AS curve (a, b, or c) in Figure 16.1 causes the least unemployment when fiscal or monetary
      restraint is pursued?   _____

LO1   3. The Economy Tomorrow section provides estimates of time spent in traffic delays. If the average
      worker produces $80 of output per hour, what is the opportunity cost of

      (a) Current traffic delays? $_____

      (b) Estimated delays in 10 years? $_____

LO3   4. Suppose taxpayers are required to pay a base tax of $50 plus 30 percent on any income over
      $100, as in the initial tax system B in Table 16.1. Suppose further that the taxing authority
      wishes to raise by $20 the taxes of people with incomes of $200.

      (a) If marginal tax rates are to remain unchanged, what will the new base tax have to be? $_____

      (b) If the base tax of $50 is to remain unchanged, what will the marginal tax rate have to be?   _____%

LO3   5. Suppose households supply 430 billion hours of labor per year and have a tax elasticity of supply of
      0.20. If the tax rate is increased by 10 percent, by how many hours will the supply of labor decline?   _____

LO3   6. By how much did the disposable income of rich people increase as a result of the 2001–4
      reduction in the top marginal tax rate from 39.6 to 35 percent? Assume they have $1 trillion of
      income in the highest bracket.   _____

LO2   7. According to Figure 16.6, what inflation rate would occur if the unemployment rate rose to 6 percent, with

      (a) PC_1?   _____

      (b) PC_2?   _____

LO2   8. On the following graph, plot the unemployment and inflation rates for the years 2000–2008. Is
      there any evidence of a Phillips curve trade-off?   _____

LO3   9. If the tax elasticity of labor supply is 0.20, by how much will the quantity of labor supplied increase in response to
    (*a*) A $500 per person income-tax rebate?
    (*b*) A 4-percent reduction in marginal tax rates?   _____

LO3   10. If the tax elasticity of supply is 0.10, by how much do tax rates have to be reduced to increase the labor supply by 2 percent?   _____

LO3   11. Suppose an economy is characterized by the AS/AD curves in the accompanying graph. A decision is then made to increase infrastructure spending by $10 billion a year.
    (*a*) Illustrate the direct impact of the increased spending on aggregate demand on the graph (ignore multiplier effects).
    (*b*) If AS is unaffected, what is the new equilibrium rate of output?   _____
    (*c*) What is the new equilibrium price level?   _____
    (*d*) Now assume that the infrastructure investments increase aggregate supply by $20 billion a year (from the initial equilibrium). Illustrate this effect on the graph.
    (*e*) After both demand and supply adjustments occur, what is the final equilibrium
      (*i*) Rate of output?
      (*ii*) Price level?   _____

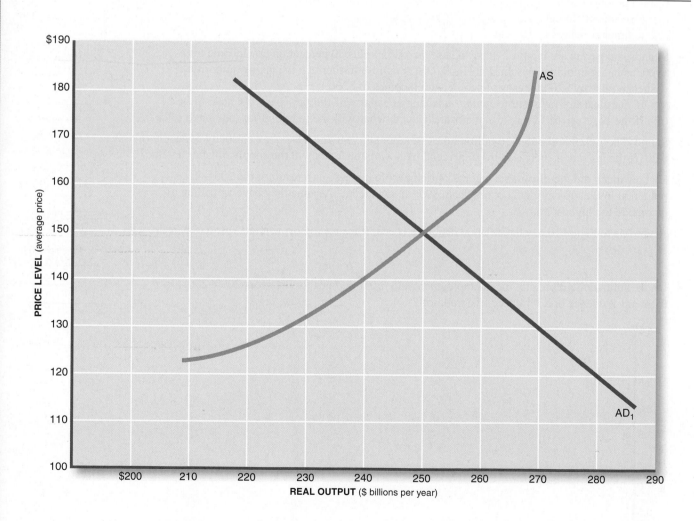

17

Growth and Productivity:
Long-Run Possibilities

> Economic growth is the fundamental determinant of the long-run success of any nation, the basic source of rising living standards, and the key to meeting the needs and desires of the American people.
>
> —*Economic Report of the President, 1992*

Imagine a world with no fax machines, no cell phones, no satellite TV, and no digital sound. Such a world actually existed—and only 30 years ago! At the time, personal computers were still on the drawing board, and laptops weren't even envisioned. Web sites were a place where spiders gathered, not locations in the Internet. Home video hadn't been seen, and no one had yet popped any microwave popcorn. Biotechnology hadn't yet produced any blockbuster drugs, and people wore the same pair of athletic shoes for a wide variety of sports.

New products are evidence of economic progress. Over time, we produce not only *more* goods and services but also *new* and *better* goods and services. In the process, we get richer: Our material living standards rise.

Rising living standards aren't inevitable, however. According to World Bank estimates, almost 3 *billion* people—nearly half the world's population—continue to live in abject poverty (with incomes of less than $2 per day). Worse still, living standards in many of the poorest countries have *fallen* in the last decade.

This chapter takes a longer-term view of economic performance. Chapters 8 to 16 were concerned with the business cycle—that is, *short-run* variations in output and prices. This chapter looks at the prospects for *long-run* growth and considers three questions:

- **How important is economic growth?**
- **How does an economy grow?**
- **Is continued economic growth possible? Is it desirable?**

We develop answers to these questions by first examining the nature of economic growth and then examining its sources and potential limits.

THE NATURE OF GROWTH

Economic growth refers to increases in the output of goods and services. But there are two distinct ways in which output increases, and they have very different implications for our economic welfare.

Short-Run Changes in Capacity Utilization

production possibilities: The alternative combinations of final goods and services that could be produced in a given time period with all available resources and technology.

Long-Run Change in Capacity

economic growth: An increase in output (real GDP); an expansion of production possibilities.

The easiest kind of growth comes from increased use of our productive capabilities. In any given year there's a limit to an economy's potential output. This limit is determined by the quantity of resources available and our technological know-how. We've illustrated these short-run limits with a **production possibilities** curve, as in Figure 17.1a. By using all our available resources and our best expertise, we can produce any combination of goods and services on the production possibilities curve.

We don't always take full advantage of our productive capacity. The economy often produces a mix of output that lies *inside* our production possibilities, like point A in Figure 17.1a. When this happens, a major *short-run* goal of macro policy is to achieve full employment—to move us from point A to some point on the production possibilities curve (such as point B). In the process, we produce more output.

Once we're fully utilizing our productive capacity, further increases in output are attainable only if we *expand* that capacity. To do so we have to *shift* the production possibilities curve outward as in Figure 17.1b. Such shifts imply an increase in *potential* GDP—that is, our productive capacity.

Over time, increases in capacity are critical. Short-run increases in the utilization of existing capacity can generate only modest increases in output. Even high unemployment rates, such as 7 percent, leave little room for increased output. ***To achieve large and lasting increases in output we must push our production possibilities outward.*** For this reason, economists often define **economic growth** in terms of changes in *potential* GDP.

The unique character of economic growth can also be illustrated with aggregate supply and demand curves. Figure 17.2 depicts both a sloped, *short-run* AS curve and a vertical, *long-run*

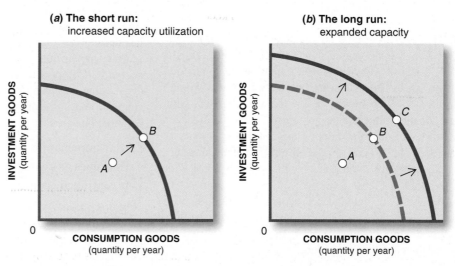

FIGURE 17.1
Two Types of Growth

Increases in output result from increased use of existing capacity or from increases in that capacity itself. In part *a* the mix of output at point A doesn't make full use of production possibilities. We can get additional output by employing more of our available resources or using them more efficiently. This is illustrated by point B (or any other point on the curve).

Once we're on the production possibilities curve, we can get more output only by *increasing* our productive capacity. This is illustrated by the outward *shift* of the production possibilities curve in part *b*.

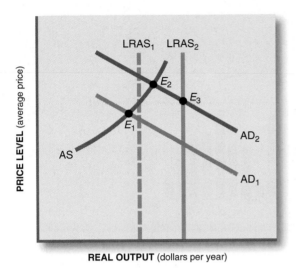

PRICE LEVEL (average price)

REAL OUTPUT (dollars per year)

FIGURE 17.2
Shifts of Long-Run Supply

Macro stabilization policies try to shift the aggregate demand curve (e.g., from AD$_1$ to AD$_2$) to achieve greater output and employment. The vertical long-run AS curve implies that these efforts will have no lasting impact on the natural rate of output, however. To achieve economic growth, the long-run aggregate supply curve must be shifted to the right (e.g., from LRAS$_1$ to LRAS$_2$).

aggregate supply curve

AS curve. In the short run, macro stabilization policies try to shift the AD curve to a more desirable price-output equilibrium. Such demand-side policies are unlikely to change the country's long-run capacity to produce, however. At best they move the macro equilibrium to a more desirable point on the *short-run* AS curve (for example, from E_1 to E_2 in Figure 17.2).

Our productive capacity may increase nevertheless. If it does, the "natural" long-run AS curve will also shift. In this framework, *economic growth implies a rightward shift of the long-run aggregate supply curve.* Should that occur, the economy will be able to produce still more output with less inflationary pressure (e.g., as at E_3 in Figure 17.2).

Notice we refer to *real* GDP, not *nominal* GDP, in our concept of economic growth. Nominal GDP can rise even when the quantity of goods and services falls, as was the case in 1991. The total quantity of goods and services produced in 1991 was less than the quantity produced in 1990. Nevertheless, prices rose enough in 1991 to keep nominal GDP growing.

Real GDP refers to the actual quantity of goods and services produced. Real GDP avoids the distortions of inflation by adjusting for changing prices. By using 2000 prices as a **base year,** we observe that real GDP fell from $7,113 billion in 1990 to only $7,101 billion in 1991 (see inside cover). Since then real GDP has increased nearly 70 percent—an impressive growth achievement.

Nominal vs. Real GDP

real GDP: The value of final output produced in a given period, adjusted for changing prices.

base year: The time period used for comparative analysis; the basis for indexing, e.g., of price changes.

MEASURES OF GROWTH

Typically, changes in real GDP are expressed in percentage terms, as a growth *rate*. The **growth rate** is simply the change in real output between two periods divided by total output in the base period. The percentage decline in real output during 1991 was thus $12 billion ÷ $7,113 billion, or less than 0.2 percent. By contrast, real output grew in 1992 by 3.3 percent.

Figure 17.3 illustrates the recent growth experience of the U.S. economy. In the 1960s, real GDP grew by an average of 4.1 percent per year. Economic growth slowed to only 2.8 percent in the 1970s, however, with actual output declines in 3 years. The steep recession of 1982, as seen in Figure 17.3, reduced GDP growth in the 1980s to an even lower rate: 2.5 percent per year. The 1990s started out even worse, with negligible growth in 1990 and a recession in 1991. The economy performed a lot better after that, however. From 1997 to 2000, real GDP grew by more than 4.5 percent a year. That acceleration of the growth rate was so impressive that observers began to talk about a "New Economy," in which faster growth would be the norm (see News on the next page).

The notion of a fast-growth New Economy was badly shaken in 2001. In the first quarter of 2001, GDP fell by 0.2 percent and then by 0.6 percent in the second quarter. In the third

The Growth Rate

growth rate: Percentage change in real output from one period to another.

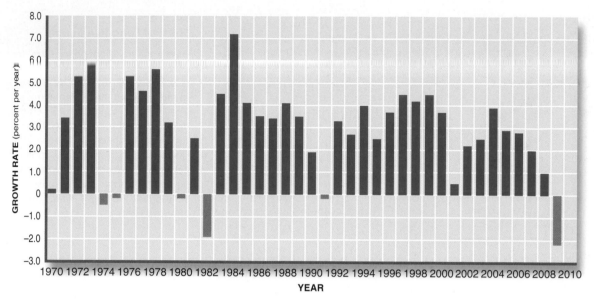

FIGURE 17.3
Recent U.S. Growth Rates

Total output typically increases from one year to another. The focus of policy is on the growth *rate,* that is, how fast real GDP increases from one year to the next. Annual growth rates since 1970 have ranged from a high of 7.2 percent (1984) to a low of *minus* 1.9 percent (1982).

Source: *Economic Report of the President, 2009.*

web analysis

The U.S. Bureau of Economic Analysis (BEA) maintains quarterly data on real GDP growth. Visit **www.bea.gov** and search "Overview of the U.S. Economy."

quarter (which included the Sept. 11 terrorist attacks), real GDP again declined by 1.3 percent. The recession of 2008-9 dealt another blow to the "New Economy" thesis. People feared that the economy was imploding and might *never* recover. People were praying for *zero* growth (i.e., no more declines in output), not the more remote goals of "fast track" growth in the 3–4 percent range.

IN THE NEWS

The New Economy

The U.S. economy today displays several exceptional features. The first is its strong rate of productivity growth. . . . A second is its unusually low levels of both inflation and unemployment. . . . A third is the disappearance of Federal budget deficits. . . . A fourth is the strength of the U.S. economy's performance relative to other industrial economies. . . . These developments reveal profound changes in economic trends that justify the term "New Economy."

Three interrelated factors lie behind these extraordinary economic gains: technological innovation, organizational changes in business, and public policy. . . . The interactions among these three factors have created a virtuous cycle in which developments in one area reinforce and stimulate developments in another. The result is an economic system in which the whole is greater than the sum of the parts. . . .

This Report defines the New Economy by the extraordinary gains in performance—including rapid productivity growth, rising incomes, low unemployment, and moderate inflation—that have resulted from this combination of virtually reinforcing advances in technologies, business practices, and economic policies.

Source: *Economic Report of the President, 2001,* pp. 22–23.

Analysis: The successes of the late 1990s spawned the hope of continuing rapid gains in productivity and GDP growth—a "new" economy. The recession of 2001, coupled with widespread "dot.com" failures, shed doubt on this concept.

The Exponential Process. Although the implications of *negative* growth (e.g., job layoffs, smaller paychecks, home foreclosures) become evident in a recession, the implications of variations in *positive* growth rates aren't so immediately apparent. Indeed, the whole subject of economic growth looks rather dull when you discover that "big" gains in economic growth are measured in fractions of a percent. However, this initial impression isn't fair. First, even 1 year's "low" growth implies lost output. If we had just *maintained* output in 2009 at its 2008 level—that is, "achieved" a *zero* growth rate rather than an outright decline—we would have had $280 billion more worth of goods and services, which works out to over $900 worth of goods and services per person. In today's $14 trillion economy, each 1 percent of GDP growth translates into almost $500 more output per person. Lots of people would like that extra output.

Second, economic growth is a *continuing* process. Gains made in one year accumulate in future years. It's like interest you earn at the bank: If you leave your money in the bank for several years, you begin to earn interest on your interest. Eventually you accumulate a nice little bankroll.

The process of economic growth works the same way. Each little shift of the production possibilities curve broadens the base for future GDP. As shifts accumulate over many years, the economy's productive capacity is greatly expanded. Ultimately we discover that those "little" differences in annual growth rates generate tremendous gains in GDP.

This cumulative process, whereby interest or growth is compounded from one year to the next, is called an "exponential process." At growth rates of 2.5 percent, GDP doubles in 28 years. With 3.5 percent growth, GDP doubles in only 20 years. In a single generation the *difference* between 2.5 percent growth and 3.5 percent growth amounts to roughly $10 trillion of output a year. That *difference* is roughly two-thirds of this year's total output. From this longer-term perspective, the difference between 2.5 percent and 3.5 percent growth begins to look very meaningful.

The exponential process looks even more meaningful when we translate it into *per capita* terms. We can do so by looking at GDP *per capita* rather than total GDP. **GDP per capita** is simply total output divided by total population. In 2008, the total output of the U.S. economy was $14.3 trillion. Since there were 300 million of us to share that output, GDP per capita was

$$\text{GDP per capita} \atop (2008) = \frac{\$14.3 \text{ trillion of output}}{300 \text{ million people}} = \$47,666$$

This does not mean that every man, woman, and child in the United States received $47,666 worth of goods and services in 2008; it simply indicates how much output was potentially available to the "average" person. GDP per capita is often used as a basic measure of our standard of living.

Growth in GDP per capita is attained only when the growth of output exceeds population growth. In the United States, this condition is usually achieved. Even when *total* GDP growth slowed in the 1970s and 1980s, *per capita* GDP kept rising because the U.S. population was growing by only 1 percent a year. Hence, even relatively slow economic growth of 2.5 percent a year was enough to keep raising living standards.

The developing nations of the Third World aren't so fortunate. Many of these countries bear both slower *economic* growth and faster *population* growth. They have a difficult time *maintaining* living standards, much less increasing them. Madagascar, for example, is one of the poorest countries in the world, with GDP per capita of roughly $900. Yet its population continues to grow rapidly (2.8 percent per year), putting constant pressure on living standards. In recent years, Madagascar's GDP grew at a slower rate of only 2.0 percent. As a consequence, GDP per capita *declined* nearly 0.8 percent per year. As we'll see in Chapter 36, many other poor nations are in similarly dire straits.

By comparison with these countries, the United States has been most fortunate. Our GDP per capita has more than doubled since the 1980s, despite several recessions. This means that the average person today has twice as many goods and services as the average person had a generation ago.

GDP per Capita: A Measure of Living Standards

GDP per capita: Total GDP divided by total population; average GDP.

measure for standard of living

TABLE 17.1
The Rule of 72

Small differences in annual growth rates cumulate into large differences in GDP. Shown here are the number of years it would take to double GDP per capita at various net growth rates. *"Net"* growth refers to the GDP growth rate minus the population growth rate.

Doubling times can be approximated by the "rule of 72." Seventy-two divided by the growth rate equals the number of years it takes to double.

Net Growth Rate (%)	Doubling Time (years)
0.0%	Never
0.5	140 years
1.0	70
1.5	47
2.0	35
2.5	30
3.0	24
3.5	20
4.0	18

web analysis

To understand why the rule of 72 works, visit **http://mathworld.wolfram.com** and search "rule of 72."

GDP per Worker: A Measure of Productivity

labor force: All persons over age 16 who are either working for pay or actively seeking paid employment.

employment rate: The percentage of the adult population that is employed.

What about the future? Will we continue to enjoy substantial gains in living standards? Many Americans harbor great doubts. A 2008 poll revealed that 4 out of 10 adults believe their children's living standards will be no higher than today's. That would happen only if population growth outstrips or equals GDP growth. That seems most unlikely. Table 17.1 displays more optimistic scenarios in which GDP continues to grow faster than the population. If GDP *per capita* continues to grow at 2 percent per year—as it did in the 1990s—it will take 35 years to double our standard of living. If GDP per capita grows just half a percent faster, say, by 2.5 percent per year, our standard of living will double in only 30 years. Would you like to have that extra output when you're middle-aged?

The potential increases in living standards depicted in Table 17.1 won't occur automatically. Someone is going to have to produce more output if we want GDP per capita to rise. One reason our living standard rose in the 1980s is that the labor force grew faster than the population. Those in the World War II baby boom had reached maturity and were entering the **labor force** in droves. At the same time, more women took jobs outside the home, a trend that continued into the 1990s (see Figure 6.2). As a consequence, the **employment rate** increased significantly, as Figure 17.4 shows. With the number of workers growing faster than the population, GDP per capita was sure to rise.

The employment rate can't increase forever. At the limit, everyone would be in the labor market, and no further workers could be found. As Figure 17.4 reveals, the employment rate peaked in 2000. Further increases in GDP per capita can only come from increases in output *per worker*.

FIGURE 17.4
A Rising Employment Rate

The entry of Baby Boomers (born 1946–60) into the labor force and increased labor-force attachment of women caused the ratio of workers to total population (the employment rate) to rise from 1975 to 2000. This boosted per capita GDP.

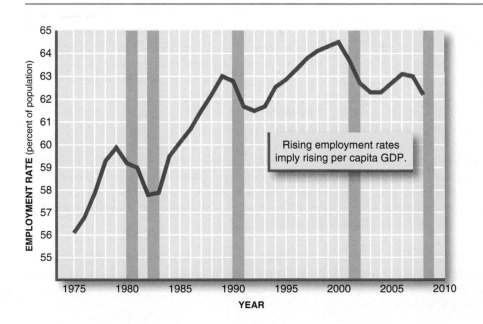

Rising employment rates imply rising per capita GDP.

The most common measure of **productivity** is output per labor-hour, which is simply the ratio of total output to the number of hours worked. As noted earlier, total GDP in 2008 was $14.3 trillion. In that same year 145,362,000 workers were employed. Hence, the average worker's productivity was

$$\frac{\text{Labor}}{\text{productivity}} = \frac{\text{total output}}{\text{total employment}}$$

$$= \frac{\$14.3 \text{ trillion}}{145{,}362{,}000 \text{ workers}}$$

$$= \$98{,}375$$

This is a *lot* of output per worker! China has many more workers (850 million) but they produce much less output ($10,000) each. So Chinese living standards are far below American standards.

The *increase* in our GDP per capita in recent decades is directly related to the *rising* productivity of the average U.S. worker. The average worker today produces twice as many goods and services as the average worker did in 1980.

The Productivity Turnaround. For economic growth to continue, the productivity of the average U.S. worker must rise still further. Will it? As Figure 17.5 reveals, productivity grew at an average pace of 1.4 percent from 1973 to 1995. Along the way, however, there were many years (e.g., 1978–84) in which productivity advances slowed to a snail's pace. This productivity slowdown constrained GDP growth.

> **productivity:** Output per unit of input, for example, output per labor-hour.

web analysis

The U.S. Bureau of Labor Statistics (BLS) maintains quarterly data on labor productivity at **www.bls. gov/data.**

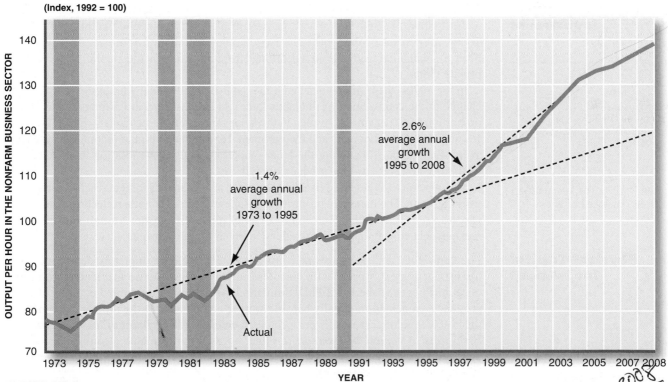

(Index, 1992 = 100)

1.4% average annual growth 1973 to 1995

2.6% average annual growth 1995 to 2008

Actual

FIGURE 17.5
Productivity Gains

Increasing productivity (output per worker) is the critical factor in raising per capita GDP over time. Productivity advances slowed in 1978–84 but accelerated sharply in 1995–2008.

Note: Shaded areas indicate recessions.

Source: *U.S. Department of Commerce.*

1995–2008 average workers are putting out more work than they have in past.

After 1995, productivity advances accelerated sharply, as seen in Figure 17.5. This productivity jump was so impressive that it raised hopes for a "New Economy" (see News, p. 360), in which technological breakthroughs, better management, and enlightened public policy would keep both productivity and GDP growing at faster rates. Although the economy did stumble into a short-run recession in 2008, worker productivity—and thus, *potential* output—kept increasing at a fast clip.

SOURCES OF GROWTH

The arithmetic of economic growth is simple. But what keeps the arithmetic so positive? Future output growth depends on two factors:

$$\frac{\text{Growth rate of}}{\text{total output}} = \frac{\text{growth rate of}}{\text{labor force}} + \frac{\text{growth rate of}}{\text{productivity}}$$

Accordingly, how fast GDP increases in the future depends on how fast the labor force grows and how fast productivity advances. Since the long-run growth of the labor force has stabilized at around 1.1 percent, the real uncertainty about future economic growth originates in the unpredictability of productivity advances. Can worker productivity continue to increase at such a fast clip? Forever?

To assess the potential for future productivity gains, we need to examine the sources of productivity improvement. *The sources of productivity gains include*

- *Higher skills*—an increase in labor skills.
- *More capital*—an increase in the ratio of capital to labor.
- *Technological advance*—the development and use of better capital equipment and products.
- *Improved management*—better use of available resources in the production process.

Human-Capital Investment

Continuing advances in education and skills training have greatly increased the quality of U.S. labor. In 1950, less than 8 percent of all U.S. workers had completed college. Today, 30 percent of the workforce has completed 4 years of college. There has also been a substantial increase in vocational training, both in the public sector and by private firms.

In the 1970s, these improvements in the quality of individual workers were offset by a change in the composition of the labor force. As we observed in Chapters 6 and 16, the proportion of teenagers and women in the labor force grew tremendously in the 1960s and 1970s. These Baby Boomers and their mothers contributed to higher output. Because teenagers and women (re)entering the labor market generally have less job experience than adult men, however, *average* productivity fell.

human capital: The knowledge and skills possessed by the workforce.

This phenomenon reversed itself in the 1990s, as the Baby Boomers reached their prime working years. The increased productivity of the workforce is not a reflection of the aging process itself. Rather, the gains in productivity reflect the greater **human-capital** investment associated with more schooling and more on-the-job learning.

Physical-Capital Investment

The knowledge and skills a worker brings to the job don't completely determine his or her productivity. A worker with no tools, no computers, and no machinery won't produce much even if she has a PhD. Similarly, a worker with outmoded equipment won't produce as much as an equally capable worker equipped with the newest machines and the best technology. From this perspective, *a primary determinant of labor productivity is the rate of capital investment.* In other words, improvements in output per *worker* depend in large part on increases in the quantity and quality of *capital* equipment (see World View on the next page).

The efforts of the average U.S. worker are presently augmented with over $100,000 of invested capital. This huge capital endowment is a prime source of high productivity. To *increase* productivity, however, the quality and quantity of capital available to the average worker must continue to increase. That requires capital spending to increase faster

WORLD VIEW

High Investment = Fast Growth

Investment in new plant and equipment is essential for economic growth. In general, countries that allocate a larger share of output to investment will grow more rapidly. In recent years, China has had one of the world's fastest GDP growth rates and one of the highest investment rates.

Country	Gross Investment as Percentage of GDP	Growth Rate of GDP (average, 2000–2007)
China	44	10.2
India	38	7.8
Vietnam	35	7.8
United States	19	2.7
Ivory Coast	10	0.2

Source: World Bank. **www.worldbank.org.**

Analysis: Investment increases production possibilities. Countries that devote a larger share of output to investment tend to grow faster.

[Handwritten margin notes: Gross Investment = total investment; why only .2? → other skills! - management - human capital/skills]

than the labor force. With the labor force growing at 1.1 percent a year, that's not a hard standard to beat. How *much* faster capital investment grows is nevertheless a decisive factor in productivity gains. In the 1980s, investment growth was slow and erratic. In the 1990s, however, capital investment accelerated markedly. Investment in information technology (computers, software, and telecommunications equipment) was exceedingly robust, reaching growth rates as high as 25 percent. In the process, workers got "smarter," communications improved, and productivity jumped. The Council of Economic Advisers credited this boom in information-technology investment with nearly one-third of *all* the 1995–99 GDP growth.

Saving and Investment Rates. The dependence of productivity gains on capital investment puts a new perspective on consumption and saving. In the short run, the primary concern of macroeconomic policy is to balance aggregate demand and aggregate supply. In this context, savings are a form of leakage that requires offsetting injections of investment or government spending. From the longer-run perspective of economic growth, saving and investment take on added importance. ***Savings aren't just a form of leakage but a basic source of investment financing.*** If we use all our resources to produce consumer, export, and public-sector goods, there won't be any investment. In that case, we might not face a short-run stabilization problem—our productive capacity might be fully utilized—but we'd confront a long-run *growth* problem. Indeed, if we consumed our entire output, our productive capacity would actually shrink since we wouldn't even be replacing worn-out plant and equipment. We must have at least enough savings to finance **net investment**.

net investment: Gross investment less depreciation.

Household and Business Saving. Household saving rates in the United States have been notoriously low and falling since the early 1980s. In 2000 and again in 2006, U.S. households actually *dis*saved—spending more on consumption than their disposable incomes. Despite the meager flow of household saving, investment growth actually accelerated in the late 1990s. Virtually all of that investment was financed with *business saving* and *foreign investment*. The retained earnings and depreciation allowances that create business savings generated a huge cash flow for investment in the 1990s.

Foreign Investment. In addition to this business-saving flow, foreign investors poured money into U.S. plant, equipment, software, and financial assets. These two income flows more than compensated for the virtual absence of household saving. Many people worry, though, that foreign investments may get diverted elsewhere and that business saving will drop when profits diminish. Then continued investment growth will be more dependent on a flow of funds from household saving.

Management Training

The accumulation of more and better capital equipment does not itself guarantee higher productivity or faster GDP growth. The human factor is still critical: How well resources are organized and managed will affect the rate of growth. Hence, entrepreneurship and the quality of continuing management are also major determinants of economic growth.

It's difficult to characterize differences in management techniques or to measure their effectiveness. However, much attention has been focused in recent years on the alleged shortsightedness of U.S. managers. U.S. firms, it is said, focus too narrowly on short-run profits, neglecting long-term productivity. There is little evidence of such a failure, however. The spreading use of stock options in management ranks ties executives' compensation to multiyear performance. Moreover, productivity trends in the United States have not only accelerated in recent years but also have consistently surpassed productivity gains in other industrial nations (see World View below). To maintain that advantage, U.S. corporations spend billions of dollars each year on continuing management training. Accordingly, the charge of shortsightedness is better regarded as a precautionary warning than an established fact.

WORLD VIEW

U.S. Workers Compete Well

U.S. workers are the most productive in the world, producing close to $100,000 of output per year. In manufacturing, the U.S. productivity lead continues to widen. Among the 16 industrial nations tracked by the Bureau of Labor Statistics, only three had faster productivity growth than the United States since 2000.

Growth Rate of Manufactured Output per Hour, 2000–2007

Korea	7.6%
Taiwan	6.4%
Sweden	5.6%
United States	4.6%
United Kingdom	3.9%
Japan	3.8%
Germany	3.8%
Norway	3.7%
Denmark	2.5%
France	2.5%
Australia	2.1%
Spain	2.1%
Canada	1.1%
Italy	−0.2%

Source: U.S. Bureau of Labor Statistics.

Analysis: U.S. productivity gains are among the fastest of industrial nations. These gains are fueled by research and development and investment spending.

Research and Development

A fourth and vital source of productivity advance is research and development (R&D), a broad concept that includes scientific research, product development, innovations in production techniques, and the development of management improvements. R&D activity may be a specific, identifiable activity such as in a research lab, or it may be part of the process of learning by doing. In either case, the insights developed from R&D generally lead to new products and cheaper ways of producing them. Over time, R&D is credited with the greatest contributions to economic growth. In his study of U.S. growth during the period 1929–82, Edward Denison concluded that 26 percent of *total* growth was due to "advances in knowledge." Gordon Moore, the co-founder of Intel, doesn't see an end to research-based productivity advance. His "Moore's Law" predicts a *doubling* of computer power every 18 months. As the accompanying News suggests, he may not be wrong.

IN THE NEWS

Intel Reveals Major Chip-Design Advance

Intel announced yesterday that it had mastered a new design that makes computing more powerful, less expensive and so much more efficient that mobile devices like cellphones may soon accomplish tasks reserved until recently for desktop computers and other equipment with larger processors. . . .

These advances are the latest in a series of fundamental improvements in chip design that have long driven the technology revolution. According to the tenet known as Moore's Law, named for Intel co-founder Gordon E. Moore, progress in building chips doubles the power of computer processors about every 18 months.

But this axiom is more a historical observation than a guarantee, and engineers had recently become increasingly skeptical about whether the rate of process could be maintained. Intel's announcement signaled that the pace could continue for the time being.

—Alan Sipress

Source: *The Washington Post*, January 28, 2007, p. A 10. © 2007, The Washington Post. Used with permission by PARS International Corp.

Analysis: A steady stream of inventions and innovations advances worker productivity, raising the potential for continued economic growth.

web analysis

The National Science Foundation tracks R&D spending. Visit **www. nsf.gov** and click on "Science and Engineering Statistics."

New Growth Theory. The evident contribution of "advances in knowledge" to economic growth has spawned a new perspective called "new growth theory." "Old growth theory," it is said, emphasized the importance of bricks and mortar, that is, saving and investing in new plant and equipment. By contrast, "new" growth theory emphasizes the importance of investing in ideas. Paul Romer, a Stanford economist, asserts that new ideas and the spread of knowledge are the primary engines of growth. Unfortunately, neither Romer nor anyone else is exactly sure how one spawns new ideas or best disseminates knowledge. The only evident policy lever appears to be the support of research and development, a staple of "old" growth theory.

There's an important link between R&D and capital investment. As noted earlier, part of each year's gross investment compensates for the depreciation of existing plant and equipment. However, new machines are rarely identical to the ones they replace. When you get a new computer, you're not just *replacing* an old one; you're *upgrading* your computing capabilities with more memory, faster speed, and a lot of new features. Indeed, the availability of *better* technology is often the motive for such capital investment. The same kind of motivation spurs businesses to upgrade machines and structures. Hence, advances in technology and capital investment typically go hand in hand.

POLICY TOOLS

As we've observed, economic growth is reflected in rightward shifts of the long-run aggregate supply curve (Figure 17.2). It should not surprise you, then, that growth policy makes liberal use of the tools in the supply-side toolbox (Chapter 16). The challenge for growth policy is to select those tools that will give the economy *long*-run increases in productive capacity.

Since *workers* are the ultimate source of output and productivity growth, the first place to look for growth-accelerating tools is in the area of human-capital development.

Increasing Human-Capital Investment

Governments at all levels already play a tremendous role in human-capital development by building, operating, and subsidizing schools. The quantity and quality of continuing investments in America's schools will have a major effect on future productivity. Government policy also plays an *indirect* role in schooling decisions by offering subsidized loans for college and vocational education.

Immigration policy is also a determinant of the nation's stock of human capital. At least 1 million immigrants enter the United States every year. Most of the *legal* immigrants are relatives of people already living in the United States as permanent residents (with green cards) or naturalized citizens. In addition to these *family-based* visas, the United States also grants a much smaller number of *employment-based* visas. The H-1B program offers temporary (3-year) visas to highly skilled foreigners who want to work in U.S. firms. By admitting highly skilled workers, the United States gains valuable human capital and relieves some structural unemployment. Only 65,000 H-1B visas are available each year, however—a tiny percent of the U.S. labor force. Temporary visas for agricultural (H-2A) and other less-skilled workers (H-2B) are smaller still. To accelerate our productivity and GDP growth, observers urge us to expand these programs.

Increasing Physical-Capital Investment

As in the case of human capital, the possibilities for increasing physical-capital investment are also many and diverse.

Investment Incentives. The tax code is a mechanism for stimulating investment. Faster depreciation schedules, tax credits for new investments, and lower business tax rates all encourage increased investment in physical capital. The 2002 and 2003 tax cuts were designed for this very purpose. President Obama's 2009 stimulus program also provided increased tax incentives for investment in both human and physical capital.

Savings Incentives. In principle, the government can also deepen the savings pool that finances investment. Here again, the tax code offers some policy levers. Tax preferences for Individual Retirement Accounts and other pension savings may increase the marginal propensity to save or at least redirect savings flows to longer-term investments. The Bush 2001 tax package (Chapter 11) included not only a *short-run* fiscal stimulus (e.g., tax rebates) but also enhanced incentives for *long-term* savings (retirement and college savings accounts).

Infrastructure Development. The government also directly affects the level of physical capital through its public works spending. As we observed in Chapter 16, the $2 trillion already invested in bridges, highways, airports, sewer systems, and other infrastructure is an important part of America's capital stock. In 2004, Congress passed a new Highway bill that authorized nearly $300 billion in infrastructure spending. And President Obama's 2009 stimulus program vastly increased spending on roads, bridges, power sources, and educational facilities. Investments of that sort reduce transportation costs, increase market efficiency, and expand potential output.

Fiscal Responsibility. In addition to these many supply-side interventions, the government's *macro* policies also affect the rate of investment and growth. Of particular interest in this regard is the federal government's budget balance. As we've seen, budget deficits may be a useful mechanism for attaining short-run macro stability. Those same deficits, however, may have negative long-run effects. If Uncle Sam borrows more funds from the national savings pool, other borrowers may end up with less. As we saw in Chapter 12, there's no guarantee that federal deficits will result in the **crowding out** of private investment. Let's recognize the risk of such an outcome, however. Hence, *fiscal and monetary policies must be evaluated in terms of their impact not only on (short-run) aggregate demand but also on long-run aggregate supply.*

In this regard, the transformation of federal budget deficits to budget surpluses after 1997 facilitated the **crowding in** of private investment. After 1997, more funds were available

crowding out: A reduction in private-sector borrowing (and spending) caused by increased government borrowing.

crowding in: An increase in private-sector borrowing (and spending) caused by decreased government borrowing.

to private investors and at lower interest rates. This surely contributed to the accelerated growth of capital investment in 1996–2000. Since then, budget balances have swung sharply into the red (see Figure 12.1).

Maintaining Stable Expectations

The position of the long-run AS curve also depends on a broader assessment of the economic outlook. Expectations are a critical factor in both consumption and investment behavior. People who expect to lose their job next year are unlikely to buy a new car or house this year. Likewise, if investors expect interest rates to jump next year, they may be less willing to initiate long-run capital projects.

A sense of political and economic stability is critical to any long-run current trend. Within that context, however, specific perceptions of government policy may also alter investment plans. Investors may look to the Fed for a sense of monetary stability. They may be looking for a greater commitment to long-run price stability than to short-run adjustments of aggregate demand. In the fiscal policy area the same kind of commitment to long-run fiscal discipline rather than to short-run stimulus may be sought. Such possibilities imply that macro policy must be sensitive to long-run expectations.

Institutional Context

Last, but not least, the prospects for economic growth depend on the institutional context of a nation's economy. We first encountered this proposition in Chapter 1. In the World View on page 15, nations were ranked on the basis of an Index of Freedom. Studies have shown how greater economic freedom—secure property rights, open trade, lower taxes, less regulation—typically fosters faster growth. In less regulated economies there's more scope for entrepreneurship and more opportunity to invest. Recognizing this, nations around the world, from India to China, to Russia, to Latin America, have deregulated industries, privatized state enterprises, and promoted more open trade and investment.

THE ECONOMY TOMORROW

LIMITLESS GROWTH?

Suppose we pulled all the right policy levers and were able to keep the economy on a fast-paced growth track. Could the economy keep growing forever? Wouldn't we use up all available resources and ruin the environment in the process? How much long-term growth is really possible—or even desirable?

The Malthusian Formula for Destruction. The prospect of an eventual limit to economic growth originated in the eighteenth-century warnings of the Reverend Thomas Malthus. Malthus argued that continued economic growth was impossible because food production couldn't keep pace with population growth. His dire projections earned the economics profession its characterization as the "dismal science."

When Malthus first issued his warnings, in 1798, the population of England (including Wales) was about 9 million. Annual production of barley, oats, and related grains was approximately 162 million bushels, and wheat production was around 50 million bushels, just about enough to feed the English population (a little had to be imported from other countries). Although the relationship between food and population was satisfactory in 1798, Malthus reasoned that starvation was not far off. First of all, he observed that "population, when unchecked, goes on doubling itself every 25 years, or increases in a geometrical ratio."[1] Thus, he foresaw the English population increasing to 36 million people by 1850, 144 million by 1900, and more than 1 billion by 1975, unless some social or natural restraints were imposed on population growth.

Limits to Food Production. One natural population check that Malthus foresaw was a scarcity of food. England had only a limited amount of land available for cultivation and

---

[1]Thomas Malthus, *An Essay on the Principle of Population* (1798; reprint ed., Homewood, IL: Richard D. Irwin, 1963), p. 4.

FIGURE 17.6
The Malthusian Doomsday

By projecting the growth rates of population and food output into the future, Malthus foresaw England's doomsday. At that time, the amount of available food per capita would be too small to sustain human life. Fortunately, Malthus overestimated population growth and underestimated productivity growth.

Source: Mathus's arithmetic applied to actual data for 1800 (see text).

geometric growth: An increase in quantity by a constant proportion each year.

arithmetic growth: An increase in quantity by a constant amount each year.

was already farming the most fertile tracts. Before long, all available land would be in use and only improvements in agricultural productivity (output per acre) could increase food supplies. Some productivity increases were possible, Malthus concluded, but "the means of subsistence, under circumstances the most favorable to human industry, could not possibly be made to increase faster than in an arithmetical ratio."[2]

With population increasing at a *geometric* rate and food supplies at an *arithmetic* rate, the eventual outcome is evident. Figure 17.6 illustrates how the difference between a **geometric growth** path and an **arithmetic growth** path ultimately leads to starvation. As Malthus calculated it, per capita wheat output would decline from 5.5 bushels in 1800 to only 1.7 bushels in 1900 (Figure 17.5*b*). This wasn't enough food to feed the English people. According to Malthus's projections, either England died off about 100 years ago or it has been maintained at the brink of starvation for more than a century only by recurrent plagues, wars, or the kind of "moral restraint" that's commonly associated with Victorian preachments.

Malthus's logic was impeccable. As long as population increased at a geometric rate while output increased at an arithmetic rate, England's doomsday was as certain as two plus two equals four. Malthus's error was not in his logic but in his empirical assumptions. He didn't know how fast output would increase over time, any more than we know whether people will be wearing electronic wings in the year 2203. He had to make an educated guess about future productivity trends. He based his estimates on his own experiences at the very beginning of the Industrial Revolution. As it turned out (fortunately), he had no knowledge of the innovations that would change the world, and he grossly underestimated the rate at which productivity would increase. *Output, including agricultural products, has increased at a geometric rate, not at the much slower arithmetic rate foreseen by Malthus.* As we observed earlier, U.S. output has grown at a long-term rate of roughly 3 percent a year. This *geometric* growth has doubled output every 25 years or so. That rate of economic growth is more than enough to raise living standards for a population growing by only 1 percent a year.

[2]Ibid., p. 5.

Resource Constraints. As Yale historian Paul Kennedy has suggested, maybe Malthus's doomsday predictions were just premature, not wrong. Maybe growth will come to a screeching halt when we run out of arable land, water, oil, or some other vital resource.

Malthus focused on arable land as the ultimate resource constraint. Other doomsday prophets have focused on the supply of whale oil, coal, oil, potatoes, and other "essential" resources. All such predictions ignore the role of markets in both promoting more efficient uses of scarce resources and finding substitutes for them. If, for example, the world were really running out of oil, what would happen to oil prices? Oil prices would rise substantially, prompting consumers to use oil more efficiently and prompting producers to develop alternative fuel sources.

If productivity and the availability of substitutes increase fast enough, the price of "scarce" resources might actually fall rather than rise. This possibility prompted a famous "Doomsday bet" between University of Maryland business professor Julian Simon and Stanford ecologist Paul Ehrlich. In 1980, Paul Ehrlich identified five metals that he predicted would become so scarce as to slow economic growth. Simon wagered that the price of those metals would actually *decline* over the ensuing decade as productivity and available substitutes increased. In 1990, their prices had fallen, and Ehrlich paid Simon for the bet.

Environmental Destruction. The market's ability to circumvent resource constraints would seem to augur well for our future. Doomsayers warn, though, that other limits to growth will emerge, even in a world of "unlimited" resources and unending productivity advance. The villain this time is pollution. Over 30 years ago, Paul Ehrlich warned about this second problem:

> Attempts to increase food production further will tend to accelerate the deterioration of our environment, which in turn will eventually *reduce* the capacity of the Earth to produce food. It is not clear whether environmental decay has now gone so far as to be essentially irreversible; it is possible that the capacity of the planet to support human life has been permanently impaired. Such technological "successes" as automobiles, pesticides, and inorganic nitrogen fertilizers are major contributors to environmental deterioration.[3]

The "inevitability" of environmental destruction led G. Evelyn Hutchinson to conclude in 1970 that the limits of habitable existence on Earth would be measured "in decades."[4]

It's not difficult for anyone with the basic five senses to comprehend the pollution problem. Pollution is as close these days as the air we breathe. Moreover, we can't fail to observe a distinct tendency for pollution levels to rise along with GDP and population expansion. Scientists are also alarmed by the global warming that has accompanied population and output growth. If one projects past warming and pollution trends into the future, things are bound to look pretty ugly.

Although pollution is universally acknowledged to be an important and annoying problem, we can't assume that the *rate* of pollution will continue unabated. On the contrary, the growing awareness of the pollution problem has prompted significant abatement efforts. The Environmental Protection Agency (EPA), for example, is unquestionably a force working for cleaner air and water. Indeed, active policies to curb pollution are as familiar as auto-exhaust controls, DDT bans, and tradable CO_2 and SO_2 permits. A computer programmed 10 or 20 years ago to project present pollution levels wouldn't have foreseen these abatement efforts and would thus have overestimated current pollution levels.

This isn't to say that we have in any final way "solved" the pollution problem or that we're even doing the best job we possibly can. It simply says that geometric increases in pollution aren't inevitable. There's simply no compelling reason why we have to continue polluting the environment; if we stop, another doomsday can be averted.

---

[3]Paul R. Ehrlich and Anne H. Ehrlich, *Population, Resources, Environment: Issues in Human Ecology,* 2nd ed. (San Francisco: W. H. Freeman, 1972), p. 442.
[4]Evelyn Hutchinson, "The Biosphere," *Scientific American,* September 1970, p. 53: Dennis L. Meadows et al., *The Limits to Growth* (New York: Universe Books, 1972), Chapter 4.

The Possibility of Growth. The misplaced focus on doomsday scenarios has a distinct opportunity cost. As Robert Solow summed up the issue:

> My real complaint about the Doomsday school [is that] it diverts attention from the really important things that can actually be done, step by step, to make things better. The end of the world is at hand—the earth, if you take the long view, will fall into the sun in a few billion years anyway, unless some other disaster happens first. In the meantime, I think we'd be better off passing a strong sulfur-emissions tax, or getting some Highway Trust Fund money allocated to mass transit, or building a humane and decent floor under family incomes, or overriding President Nixon's veto of a strong Water Quality Act, or reforming the tax system, or fending off starvation in Bengal—instead of worrying about the generalized "predicament of mankind."[5]

Karl Marx expressed these same thoughts nearly a century earlier. Marx chastised "the contemptible Malthus" for turning the attention of the working class away from what he regarded as the immediate problem of capitalist exploitation to some distant and ill-founded anxiety about "natural" disaster.[6]

The Desirability of Growth. Let's concede, then, that continued, perhaps even "limit-less" growth is *possible.* Can we also agree that it's *desirable?* Those of us who commute on congested highways, worry about global warming, breathe foul air, and can't find a secluded camping site may raise a loud chorus of nos. But before reaching a conclusion let's at least determine what it is people don't like about the prospect of continued growth. Is it really economic growth per se that people object to, or instead the specific ways GDP has grown in the past?

First of all, let's distinguish very clearly between economic growth and population growth. Congested neighborhoods, dining halls, and highways are the consequence of too many people, not of too many goods and services. Indeed, if we had *more* goods and services—if we had more houses and transit systems—much of the population congestion we now experience might be relieved. Maybe if we had enough resources to meet our existing demands *and* to build a solar-generated "new town" in the middle of Montana, people might move out of the crowded neighborhoods of Chicago and St. Louis. Well, probably not, but at least one thing is certain; with fewer goods and services, more people will have to share any given quantity of output.

"And so, extrapolating from the best figures available, we see that current trends, unless dramatically reversed, will inevitably lead to a situation in which the sky will fall."

Analysis: Most doomsday predictions fail to recognize the possibilities for behavioral change—or the role of market incentives in encouraging it.

[5]Robert M. Solow, "Is the End of the World at Hand?" *Challenge,* March 1973, p. 50.
[6]Cited by John Maddox in *The Doomsday Syndrome* (New York: McGraw-Hill, 1972), pp. 40 and 45.

Which brings us back to the really essential measure of growth, GDP per capita. Are there any serious grounds for desiring *less* GDP per capita, a reduced standard of living? And don't say yes just because you think we already have too many cars on our roads or calories in our bellies. That argument refers to the *mix* of output again and doesn't answer the question of whether we want *any* more goods or services per person. Increasing GDP per capita can take a million forms, including the educational services you're now consuming. The rejection of economic growth per se implies that none of those forms is desirable in the economy tomorrow.

SUMMARY

- Economic growth refers to increases in real GDP. Short-run growth may result from increases in capacity utilization (like less unemployment). In the long run, however, growth requires increases in capacity itself—rightward shifts of the long-run aggregate supply curve. LO1
- GDP per capita is a basic measure of living standards. GDP per worker is a basic measure of productivity. LO1
- The rate of economic growth is set by the growth rate of the labor force *plus* the growth rate of output per worker (productivity). Over time, increases in productivity have been the primary cause of rising living standards. LO1
- Productivity gains come from many sources, including better labor quality, increased capital investment, research and development, improved management, and supportive government policies. LO2
- Supply-side policies increase both the short- and long-run capacity to produce. Monetary and fiscal policies may also affect capital investment and thus the rate of economic growth. LO2

- Productivity growth accelerated in 1995–2008 due to fast investment growth, especially in information technology. Sustaining rapid productivity gains is the critical challenge for long-run GDP growth. LO1
- Recent U.S. investment growth has been financed with business saving and foreign investment. U.S. households save very little. LO1
- The argument that there are identifiable and imminent limits to growth—perhaps even a cataclysmic doomsday—are founded on one of two concerns: (1) the depletion of resources and (2) pollution of the ecosystem. LO3
- The flaw in doomsday arguments is that they regard existing patterns of resource use or pollution as unalterable. They consistently underestimate the possibilities for technological advance or market adaptation. LO3
- Continued economic growth is desirable as long as it brings a higher standard of living for people and an increased ability to produce and consume socially desirable goods and services. LO3

Key Terms

production possibilities	GDP per capita	net investment
economic growth	labor force	crowding out
real GDP	employment rate	crowding in
base year	productivity	geometric growth
growth rate	human capital	arithmetic growth

Questions for Discussion

1. In what specific ways (if any) does a college education increase a worker's productivity? LO1
2. Why do productivity gains slow down in recessions? (See Figure 17.5.) LO1
3. Why don't we consume all our current output instead of sacrificing some present consumption for investment? LO1
4. Should we grant immigration rights based on potential contributions to economic growth as Canada does? LO2

5. How would a growing federal budget surplus affect the prospects for long-run economic growth? Why might a growing surplus *not* be desirable? LO2
6. Should fiscal policy encourage more consumption or more saving? Does it matter? LO2
7. In 1866, Stanley Jevons predicted that economic growth would come to a halt when England ran out of coal, a doomsday that he reckoned would occur in the mid-1970s. How did we avert that projection? Will we avert an "oil crisis" in the same way? LO3

8. Fertility rates in the United States have dropped so low that we're approaching zero population growth, a condition that France has maintained for decades. How will this affect our economic growth? Our standard of living?   LO1

9. Is limitless growth really possible? What forces do you think will be most important in slowing or halting economic growth?   LO3

10 Why do some nations grow and prosper while others stagnate?   LO1

 web activities to accompany this chapter can be found on the Online Learning Center:
http://www.mhhe.com/schiller12e

LO1   1. According to the Rule of 72 (Table 17.1), how many years will it take for GDP to double if the economy is growing at:

                            (*a*) 2 percent a year? _____

                            (*b*) 3.5 percent a year? _____

LO1   2. According to the Rule of 72 (Table 17.1) and recent growth rates (World View, p. 365) how long will it be before GDP doubles in

                            (*a*) The United States? _____

                            (*b*) China? _____

                            (*c*) Ivory Coast? _____

LO1   3. If real GDP is growing at 2 percent a year, how long will it take for
(*a*) Real GDP to double? _____
(*b*) Real GDP per capita to double if the population is increasing each year by

                            (*i*) 0 percent? _____

                            (*ii*) 1 percent? _____

                            (*iii*) 2 percent? _____

LO3   4. According to Figure 17.3, in how many years since 1970 has GDP grown

                            (*a*) Faster than the population? _____

                            (*b*) Slower than the population? _____

LO1   5. If the labor force increases by 1.1 percent each year and productivity increases by 2.6 percent, how fast will output grow? _____

LO1   6. In 2008, approximately 62 percent of the adult population (230 million) was employed. If the employment rate increased to 64 percent,
(*a*) How many more people would be working? _____
(*b*) By how much would output increase if per worker GDP is $90,000? _____

LO1   7. If output per worker is now $100,000 per year, how much will the average worker produce 10 years from now if productivity improves by

                            (*a*) 1.0 percent per year? _____

                            (*b*) 2.0 percent per year? _____

LO1   8. The real (inflation-adjusted) value of U.S. manufacturing output and related manufacturing employment was

	Output	Employment
1998	$1,356 billion	17,560,000
2008	$1,685 billion	13,431,000

(*a*) How many manufacturing jobs were lost between 1998 and 2008? _____
(*b*) How much did output increase? _____
(*c*) What was average manufacturing productivity in

                            (*i*) 1998? _____

                            (*ii*) 2008? _____

LO1   9. What is the annual rate of productivity advance implied by Moore's Law (News, p. 367)? _____

LO1 10. Suppose that every additional five percentage points in the investment rate ($I \div GDP$) boost
economic growth by one percentage point. Assume also that all investment must be financed
with consumer saving. The economy is now assumed to be fully employed at

GDP	$6 trillion
Consumption	5 trillion
Saving	1 trillion
Investment	1 trillion

If the goal is to raise the growth rate by 1 percent,
(*a*) By how much must investment increase? _____
(*b*) By how much must consumption decline for this to occur? _____

LO3 11. Using data from the endcovers of this book, graph real GDP and population growth since 2000,
setting 2000 values to an index base of 100.

Lowest _____

376

PART 7 Policy Constraints

Macro theories often provide conflicting advice about whether and how the government ought to intervene. To make matters worse, the information needed to make a decision is typically incomplete. Politics muddies the waters too by changing priorities and restricting the use of policy tools. Finally, there's the inescapable reality that everything changes at once—there's no *ceteris paribus* in the real world. Chapter 18 surveys the entire panoply of real-world factors that infringe on macroeconomic policy decisions.

Theory versus Reality

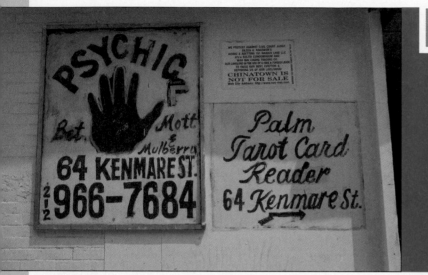

18

After reading this chapter, you should be able to:

LO1. Identify the tools of macro policy.

LO2. Explain how macro tools should work.

LO3. Discuss the constraints on policy effectiveness.

There is no one solution. It isn't just a question of the budget. It isn't just the question of inflationary labor rates. It isn't just the question of sticky prices. It isn't just the question of what the Government does to keep prices up or to make regulations that tend to be inflationary. It isn't just the weather or just the drought.

It is all these things. The interaction of these various factors is what is so terribly difficult for us to understand and, of course, what is so terribly difficult for us to deal with.

—Former Secretary of the Treasury W. Michael Blumenthal

Macroeconomic theory is supposed to explain the business cycle and show policymakers how to control it. But something is obviously wrong. Despite our relative prosperity, we haven't consistently achieved the goals of full employment, price stability, and vigorous economic growth. All too often, either unemployment or inflation surges or economic growth slows down. No matter how hard we try to eliminate it, the business cycle seems to persist, as we witnessed again in the last couple of years.

What accounts for this gap between the promises of economic theory and the reality of economic performance? Are the theories inadequate? Or is sound economic advice being ignored?

Many people blame the economists. They point to the conflicting advice of Keynesians, monetarists, and supply-siders and wonder what theory is supposed to be followed. If economists themselves can't agree, it is asked, why should anyone else listen to them?

Not surprisingly, economists see things a bit differently. First, they point out, the **business cycle** isn't as bad as it used to be.

Since World War II, the economy has had many ups and downs, but none as severe as the Great Depression or earlier catastrophes. Second, economists complain that "politics" often takes precedence over good economic advice. Politicians are reluctant, for example, to raise taxes, cut spending, or slow money growth in order to control inflation. Their concern is winning the next election, not solving the country's economic problems.

When President Jimmy Carter was in office, he anguished over another problem: the complexity of economic decision making. In the real world, neither theory nor politics can keep up with all our economic goals. As President Carter observed: "We cannot concentrate just on inflation or just on unemployment or just on deficits in the federal budget or our international payments. Nor can we act in isolation from other countries. We must deal with all of these problems simultaneously and on a worldwide basis."

No president learned this lesson faster or more forcefully than George W. Bush. Just as he was putting the final touches on a bipartisan consensus on taxes, spending, and debt reduction, terrorists destroyed the World Trade Center and damaged the Pentagon. In response to those attacks, all major economic policy decisions had to be revised. President Obama also had to revise his economic plans as soon as he took office. An acceleration of the 2008–9 downturn forced him to abandon promised tax increases and health-care reforms. Fiscal stimulus was the urgent priority.

As if the burdens of a continuously changing world weren't enough, the president must also contend with sharply differing economic theories and advice, a slow and frequently hostile Congress, a massive and often unresponsive bureaucracy, and a complete lack of knowledge about the future.

This chapter confronts these and other frustrations of the real world head on. In so doing, we provide answers to the following questions:

- **What's the ideal "package" of macro policies?**
- **How well does our macro performance live up to the promises of that package?**
- **What kinds of obstacles prevent us from doing better?**

The answers to these questions may shed some light on a broader concern that has long troubled students and policymakers alike, namely, "If economists are so smart, why is the economy always in such a mess?"

POLICY TOOLS

Table 18.1 summarizes the macroeconomic tools available to policymakers. Although this list is brief, we hardly need a reminder at this point of how powerful each instrument can be. Every one of these major policy instruments can significantly change our answers to the basic economic questions of WHAT, HOW, and FOR WHOM to produce.

The basic tools of **fiscal policy** are contained in the federal budget. Tax cuts are supposed to increase aggregate demand by putting more income in the hands of consumers and businesses. Tax increases are intended to curtail spending and reduce inflationary pressures. Table 18.2 summarizes some of the major tax changes of recent years.

The expenditure side of the federal budget is another fiscal policy tool. From a Keynesian perspective, increases in government spending raise aggregate demand and so encourage more production. A slowdown in government spending is supposed to restrain aggregate demand and lessen inflationary pressures.

Who Makes Fiscal Policy? As we first observed in Chapter 11, changes in taxes and government spending originate both in economic events and explicit policy decisions. When the economy slows, tax revenues decline, and government spending increases automatically. Conversely, when real GDP grows, tax revenues automatically rise, and government transfer payments decline. These **automatic stabilizers** are a basic countercyclical feature of the federal budget. They don't represent active fiscal policy. On the contrary, *fiscal policy refers to deliberate changes in tax or spending legislation.* These changes can be made only by the U.S. Congress. Every year the president proposes specific budget and tax changes, negotiates with Congress, then accepts or vetoes specific acts that Congress has passed. The resulting policy decisions represent "discretionary" fiscal policy. Those policy decisions expand or shrink the **structural deficit** and thus give the economy a shot of **fiscal stimulus** or **fiscal restraint.**

Type of Policy	Policy Tools
Fiscal	• Tax cuts and increases • Changes in government spending
Monetary	• Open market operations • Reserve requirements • Discount rates
Supply-side	• Tax incentives for investment and saving • Deregulation • Human-capital investment • Infrastructure development • Free trade • Immigration

business cycle: Alternating periods of economic growth and contraction.

fiscal policy: The use of government taxes and spending to alter macroeconomic outcomes.

Fiscal Policy

automatic stabilizer: Federal expenditure or revenue item that automatically responds countercyclically to changes in national income—such as unemployment benefits and income taxes.

structural deficit: Federal revenues at full employment minus expenditures at full employment under prevailing fiscal policy.

fiscal stimulus: Tax cuts or spending hikes intended to increase (shift) aggregate demand.

fiscal restraint: Tax hikes or spending cuts intended to reduce (shift) aggregate demand.

TABLE 18.1
The Policy Tools

Economic policymakers have access to a variety of policy instruments. The challenge is to choose the right tools at the right time.

TABLE 18.2
Fiscal Policy Milestones

web analysis

The Library of Congress maintains a summary of recent congressional tax legislation at **http://thomas. loc.gov.** Go to "Bills, Resolutions," then "Bill Summary, Status." Enter "taxes."

1986	Tax Reform Act	Major reduction in tax rates coupled with broadening of tax base
1990	Budget Enforcement Act	Limits set on discretionary spending; pay-as-you-go financing required
1993	Clinton "New Direction"	Tax increases and spending cuts to achieve $300 billion deficit reduction
1994	Contract with America	Republican-led Congress cuts spending, sets 7-year target for balanced budget
1997	Balanced Budget Act, Taxpayer Relief Act	Package of tax cuts and spending cuts to balance budget by 2002
2001	Economic Growth and Tax Relief Act	Eight-year, $1.35 trillion in personal tax cuts
2002	Job Creation and Worker Assistance Act	Business investment tax cuts
2003	Jobs and Growth Tax Relief Act	Cuts in dividend and capital-gains taxes
2004	Working Families Tax Relief Act	Extended 2001–3 tax cuts until 2008–10
2008	Economic Stimulus Act	$168 billion of tax rebates
2009	American Recovery and Reinvestment Act	$787 billion package of spending and tax cuts

Monetary Policy

monetary policy: The use of money and credit controls to influence macroeconomic outcomes.

natural rate of unemployment: Long-term rate of unemployment determined by structural forces in labor and product markets.

supply-side policy: The use of tax incentives, (de)regulation, and other mechanisms to increase the ability and willingness to produce goods and services.

Supply-Side Policy

The policy arsenal in Table 18.1 also contains monetary tools. Tools of **monetary policy** include open market operations, discount rate changes, and reserve requirements.

As we saw in Chapter 15, there are disagreements over how these monetary tools should be used. Keynesians believe that interest rates are the critical policy lever. In their view, the money supply should be expanded or curtailed in order to achieve whatever interest rate is needed to shift aggregate demand. Monetarists, on the other hand, contend that the money supply itself is the critical policy tool and that it should be expanded at a steady and predictable rate. This policy, they believe, will ensure price stability and a **natural rate of unemployment.**

Who Makes Monetary Policy? Actual monetary policy decisions are made by the Federal Reserve's Board of Governors. Twice a year the Fed provides Congress with a broad overview of the economic outlook and monetary objectives. The Fed's assessment of the economy is updated at meetings of the Federal Open Market Committee (FOMC). The FOMC decides which monetary policy levers to pull.

Table 18.3 depicts milestones in recent monetary policy. Of particular interest is the October 1979 decision to adopt a pure monetarist approach. This involved an exclusive focus on the money supply, without regard for interest rates. After interest rates soared and the economy appeared on the brink of a depression, the Fed abandoned the monetarist approach and again began keeping an eye on both interest rates (the Keynesian focus) and the money supply.

Monetarists contend that the Fed never fully embraced their policy. The money supply grew at a very uneven pace in 1980, they argue, not at the steady, predictable rate that they demanded. Nevertheless, the policy shifts of 1979 and 1982 were distinctive and had dramatic effects.

A quick review of Table 18.3 reveals that such monetary policy reversals have been quite frequent. There were U-turns in monetary policy between 1982 and 1983, 1989 and 1991, 1998 and 1999, 2000 and 2001, 2003 and 2004, and again between 2007 and 2008.

Supply-side theory offers the third major set of policy tools. The focus of **supply-side policy** is to provide incentives to work, invest, and produce. Of particular concern are high tax rates and regulations that reduce supply incentives. Supply-siders argue that marginal tax rates and government regulation must be reduced in order to get more output without added inflation.

In the 1980s tax rates were reduced dramatically. The maximum marginal tax rate on individuals was cut from 70 to 50 percent in 1981, and then still further, to 28 percent, in

		TABLE 18.3 **Monetary Policy Milestones**
October 1979	Fed adopts monetarist approach, focusing exclusively on money supply; interest rates soar	
July 1982	Deep into recession, Fed votes to ease monetary restraint	
October 1982	Fed abandons pure monetarist approach and expands money supply rapidly	
May 1983	Fed reverses policy and begins slowing money supply growth	
1985	Fed increases money supply with discount-rate cuts and open market purchases	
1987	Fed abandons money supply targets as policy guides; money supply growth decreases; discount rate increases	
1989	Greenspan announces goal of "zero inflation," tightens policy	
1991	Deep in recession, the Fed begins to ease monetary restraint	
1994	Fed slows M2 growth to 1 percent; raises federal funds rate by three percentage points as economy nears full employment	
1995	Greenspan trumpets "soft landing" and eases monetary restraint	
1998	Fed cuts interest rates to cushion U.S. from Asian crisis	
1999–2000	Fed raises interest rates six times	
2001–2003	Fed cuts interest rates 13 times	
2004–2006	Fed raises fed funds rate 17 times	
2007–2008	Fed cuts interest rates 10 times	
2008–2009	Treasury acquires partial ownership of failing banks; FDIC increases deposit guarantees	

1987. The 1980s also witnessed major milestones in the deregulation of airlines, trucking, telephone service, and other industries (see Table 18.4 on the next page).

Some of the momentum toward less regulation was reversed during the 1990s. New regulatory costs on business were created by the Americans with Disabilities Act, the 1990 amendments to the Clean Air Act, and the Family Leave Act of 1993. All three laws provide important benefits to workers or the environment. At the same time, however, they make supplying goods and services more expensive.

The Obama administration broadened supply-side efforts to include infrastructure development and increased investment in human capital (through education and skill training programs). These activities increase the capacity to produce and so shift the aggregate supply curve rightward. The Obama administration also toughened environmental regulation, however, and sought legislation that would require employers to provide more fringe benefits (like health insurance), initiatives that shift the aggregate supply curve leftward.

Who Makes Supply-Side Policy? Because tax rates are a basic tool of supply-side policy, fiscal and supply-side policies are often intertwined. When Congress changes the tax laws, it almost always alters marginal tax rates and thus changes production incentives. Notice, for example, that tax legislation appears in Table 18.4 as well as in Table 18.2. The Taxpayer Relief Act of 1997 not only changed total tax revenues (fiscal policy) but also restructured production and investment incentives (supply-side policy). The 2001–3 tax cuts also had both demand-side and supply-side provisions.

Supply-side and fiscal policies also interact on the outlay side of the budget. The Transportation Equity Act of 2000, for example, authorized accelerated public works spending (fiscal stimulus) on infrastructure development (increase in supply capacity). President Obama's Recovery and Reinvestment program also affected both aggregate demand and aggregate supply. ***Deciding whether to increase spending is a fiscal policy decision; deciding how to spend available funds may entail supply-side policy.***

TABLE 18.4
Supply-Side Milestones

1990	Social Security Act amendments	Increased payroll tax to 7.65 percent
1990	Americans with Disabilities Act	Required employers to provide greater access for disabled individuals
1990	Immigration Act	Increased immigration, especially for highly skilled workers
1990	Clean Air Act amendments	Increased pollution controls
1993	Rebuild America Program	Increased spending on infrastructure and human-capital investment
	Family Leave Act	Required employers to provide unpaid leaves of absence for workers
	NAFTA	Lowered North American trade barriers
1994	GATT renewed	Lowered world trade barriers
1996	Telecommunications Act	Permitted greater competition in cable and telephone industries
1996	Personal Responsibility and Work Opportunity Act	Required more welfare recipients to work
1997	Taxpayer Relief Act	Created tuition tax credits, cut capital-gains tax
1998	Workforce Investment Act	Increased funds for skills training
2000	Transportation Equity Act	Provided new funding for highways, rails
2001	Economic Growth and Tax Relief Act	Increased savings incentives; reduced marginal tax rates
2002	Job Creation and Worker Assistance Act	Provided more tax incentives for investment
2003	Jobs and Growth Tax Relief Act	Reduced taxes on capital gains and dividends
2007	Minimum wage hike	Raised from $5.15 to $7.15 in 2009
2009	American Recovery and Reinvestment Act	Calls for major infrastructure development

Regulatory policy is also fashioned by Congress. The president and executive agencies play a critical role in this supply-side area in the day-to-day decisions on how to interpret and enforce regulatory policies.

IDEALIZED USES

These fiscal, monetary, and supply-side tools are potentially powerful levers for controlling the economy. In principle, they can cure the excesses of the business cycle and promote faster economic growth. To see how, let's review their use in three distinct macroeconomic settings.

Case 1: Recession

recessionary GDP gap: The amount by which equilibrium GDP falls short of full-employment GDP.

multiplier: The multiple by which an initial change in aggregate spending will alter total expenditure after an infinite number of spending cycles; 1/(1 − MPC).

When output and employment levels fall far short of the economy's full-employment potential, the mandate for public policy is clear. Aggregate demand must be increased so that producers can sell more goods, hire more workers, and move the economy toward its productive capacity. At such times the most urgent need is to get people back to work and close the **recessionary GDP gap.**

How can the government end a recession? Keynesians emphasize the need to increase aggregate demand by cutting taxes or boosting government spending. The resulting stimulus will set off a **multiplier** reaction. If the initial stimulus and multiplier are large enough, the recessionary GDP gap can be closed, propelling the economy to full employment.

Modern Keynesians acknowledge that monetary policy might also help. Specifically, increases in the money supply may lower interest rates and thus give investment spending a further boost. To give the economy a really powerful stimulus, we might want to pull all these

The Washington Post, © 2001 The Washington Post. Used with permission by PARS International Corp.

Analysis: When the economy is flat on its back, it may need both monetary and fiscal stimulus.

policy levers at the same time. That's what the government did in early 2001—using tax cuts, lower interest rates, and increased spending to jump start the economy (see cartoon).

Monetarists would proceed differently. First, they see no point in toying with the federal budget. In the pure monetarist model, changes in taxes or government spending may alter the mix of output but not its level. So long as the **velocity of money (V)** is constant, fiscal policy doesn't matter. In this view, the appropriate policy response to a recession is patience. As sales and output slow, interest rates will decline, and new investment will be stimulated.

Supply-siders emphasize the need to improve production incentives. They urge cuts in marginal tax rates on investment and labor. They also look for ways to reduce government regulation. Finally, they urge that any increase in government spending (fiscal stimulus) focus on long-run capacity expansion such as infrastructure development.

An overheated economy provides as clear a policy mandate as does a sluggish one. In this case, the immediate goal is to restrain aggregate demand until the rate of total expenditure is compatible with the productive capacity of the economy. This entails shifting the aggregate demand curve to the left in order to close the **inflationary GDP gap.** Keynesians would do this by raising taxes and cutting government spending. Keynesians would also see the desirability of increasing interest rates to curb investment spending.

Monetarists would simply cut the money supply. In their view, the short-run aggregate supply curve is unknown and unstable. The only predictable response is reflected in the vertical, long-run aggregate supply curve. According to this view, changes in the money supply alter prices, not output. Inflation is seen simply as "too much money chasing too few goods." Monetarists would turn off the money spigot. The Fed's job in this situation isn't only to reduce money supply growth but to convince market participants that a more cautious monetary policy will be continued. This was the intent of Chairman Greenspan's 1989 public commitment to zero inflation (Table 18.3).

Supply-siders would point out that inflation implies both "too much money" *and* "not enough goods." They'd look at the supply side of the market for ways to expand productive capacity. In a highly inflationary setting, they'd propose more incentives to save. The additional savings would automatically reduce consumption while creating a larger pool of investable funds. Supply-siders would also cut taxes and regulations that raise production costs and lower import barriers that keep out cheaper foreign goods.

Although serious inflations and recessions provide clear mandates for economic policy, there's a vast gray area between these extremes. Occasionally, the economy suffers from

velocity of money (V): The number of times per year, on average, that a dollar is used to purchase final goods and services; $PQ \div M$.

Case 2: Inflation

inflationary GDP gap: The amount by which equilibrium GDP exceeds full-employment GDP.

Case 3: Stagflation

stagflation: The simultaneous occurrence of substantial unemployment and inflation.

both inflation and unemployment at the same time, a condition called **stagflation.** In 1980, for example, the unemployment rate (7.1 percent) and the inflation rate (12.5 percent) were both too high. With an upward-sloping aggregate supply curve, the easy policy options were foreclosed. If aggregate demand were stimulated to reduce unemployment, the resultant pressure on prices might fuel the existing inflation. And if fiscal and monetary restraints were used to reduce inflationary pressures, unemployment might worsen. In such a situation, there are no simple solutions.

Knowing the causes of stagflation will help achieve the desired balance. If prices are rising before full employment is reached, some degree of structural unemployment is likely. An appropriate policy response might include more vocational training in skill-shortage areas as well as a redirection of aggregate demand toward labor-surplus sectors.

High tax rates or costly regulations might also contribute to stagflation. If either constraint exists, high prices (inflation) may not be a sufficient incentive for increased output. In this case, reductions in tax rates and regulation might help reduce both unemployment and inflation, which is the basic strategy of supply-side policies.

Stagflation may also arise from a temporary contraction of aggregate supply that both reduces output and drives up prices. In this case, neither structural unemployment nor excessive demand is the culprit. Rather, an "external shock" (such as a natural disaster or a terrorist attack) or an abrupt change in world trade (such as a spike in oil prices) is likely to be the cause of the policy dilemma. Accordingly, none of our familiar policy tools is likely to provide a complete "cure." In most cases, the economy simply has to adjust to a temporary setback.

Fine-Tuning

fine-tuning: Adjustments in economic policy designed to counteract small changes in economic outcomes; continuous responses to changing economic conditions.

The apparently inexhaustible potential of public policy to alter the economy's performance has often generated optimistic expectations about the efficacy of fiscal, monetary, and supply-side tools. In the early 1960s, such optimism pervaded even the highest levels of government. Those were the days when prices were relatively stable, unemployment rates were falling, the economy was growing rapidly, and preparations were being made for the first trip into space. The potential of economic policy looked great indeed. It was also during the 1960s that a lot of people (mostly economists) spoke of the potential for **fine-tuning,** or altering economic outcomes to fit very exacting specifications. Flexible responses to changing market conditions, it was argued, could ensure fulfillment of our economic goals. The prescription was simple: When unemployment is the problem, simply give the economy a jolt of fiscal or monetary stimulus; when inflation is worrisome, simply tap on the fiscal or monetary brakes. To fulfill our goals for content and distribution, simply pick the right target for stimulus or restraint. With a little attention and experience, the right speed could be found and the economy guided successfully down the road to prosperity. As the economic expansion of the 1990s stretched into the record books, the same kind of economic mastery was claimed. More than a few prominent economists claimed the business cycle was dead.

THE ECONOMIC RECORD

The economy's track record doesn't live up to these high expectations. To be sure, the economy has continued to grow and we've attained an impressive standard of living. We can't lose sight of the fact that our per capita income greatly exceeds the realities and even the expectations in most other countries of the world. Nevertheless, we must also recognize that our economic history is punctuated by periods of recession, high unemployment, inflation, and recurring concern for the distribution of income and mix of output.

The graphs in Figure 18.1 provide a quick summary of the gap between the theory and reality of economic policy. The Employment Act of 1946 committed the federal government to macro stability. It's evident that we haven't kept that commitment. In the 1970s we rarely came close. Although we approached all three goals in the mid-1980s, our achievements were short-lived. Economic growth ground to a halt in 1989, and the economy slipped into yet another recession in 1990. Although inflation stayed low, unemployment rates jumped.

The economy performed very well again from 1992 until early 2000. After that, however, growth came to an abrupt halt again. With the economy teetering on recession, the

Analysis: There are different theories about when and how the government should "fix" the economy. Policymakers must decide which advice to follow in specific situations.

By MAL, Associated Features, Inc.

FIGURE 18.1

The Economic Record

The Full Employment and Balanced Growth Act of 1978 established specific goals for unemployment (4 percent), inflation (3 percent), and economic growth (4 percent). We've rarely attained those goals, however, as these graphs illustrate. Measurement, design, and policy implementation problems help explain these shortcomings.

Source: *Economic Report of the President, 2009 and Congressional Budget Office.*

unemployment rate started rising in mid-2000. Some of the people who had proclaimed the business cycle to be dead were out of work. Then the economy was hit by the external shock of a terrorist attack that suspended economic activity and shook investor and consumer confidence. It took 2 years to get unemployment rates back down into the "full-employment" range (4–6 percent). The cycle began to reverse at the end of 2007, leading to the recession of 2008–9.

Looking back over the entire postwar period, the record includes 10 years of outright recession (actual declines in output) and another 22 years of **growth recession** (growth of less than 3 percent). Moreover, the distribution of income in 2008 looked worse than that of 1946, and more than 35 million people were still officially counted as poor in the later year.

Despite many setbacks, recent economic performance of the United States has been better than that of other Western nations. Other economies haven't grown as fast as the U.S. nor reduced unemployment as much. But, as the World View on the next page shows, some countries did a better job of restraining prices.

When one looks at the specific policy initiatives of various administrations, the gap between theory and practice is even larger. The Fed's decision to reduce the money supply on repeated occasions during the Great Depression was colossally perverse. Only slightly less so was the Fed's decision to expand the money supply rapidly in 1978, despite evidence that inflationary pressures were already building up. During 1980–81 and again in 1989–90, the Fed slowed money supply growth much more and far longer than was justified. As a consequence, the economy suffered two consecutive recessions in the early 1980s and another one in the early 1990s. Pretty much the same sequence occurred in 1999–2001.

growth recession: A period during which real GDP grows, but at a rate below the long-term trend of 3 percent.

WORLD VIEW

Comparative Macro Performance

The performance of the U.S. economy in the 2000s was better than most developed economies. Japan had the greatest success in restraining inflation (*minus* 1.2 percent) but suffered from sluggish growth (1.7 percent per year). The United States grew faster and also experienced less unemployment than most European countries.

Performance, 2000–2007 (annual average percentage)	U.S.	Japan	Germany	United Kingdom	France	Canada
Real growth	2.7	1.7	1.1	2.6	1.7	2.7
Inflation	2.6	−1.2	1.0	2.6	2.0	2.0
Unemployment	5.0	4.8	9.3	5.2	7.9	6.3

Source: World Bank, *World Development Report, 2009* (**www.worldbank.org**) and U.S. Bureau of Labor Statistics.

Analysis: Macroeconomic performance varies a lot, both over time and across countries. In the 2000s, U.S. economic performance was above average on most measures.

On the fiscal side of the ledger, we must recall President Roosevelt's timid efforts to expand aggregate demand during the Great Depression. Also worth remembering is President Johnson's refusal to pay for the Vietnam War by either raising taxes or cutting non-military expenditures. The resulting strain on the economy's capacity kindled inflationary pressures that lasted for years. For his part, President Carter increased labor costs (higher payroll taxes and minimum wages), farm prices, and government spending at a time when inflation was a foremost policy concern. President Reagan made his share of mistakes too, including the pursuit of deep budget cuts in the early stages of a recession. President George H. Bush ignored the recession for an entire year, believing that "self-adjustment" would ensure recovery. That mistake cost him his job.

President Clinton pushed through a tax increase in 1993 that helped subdue the recovery from the 1990–91 recession. He also caused the aggregate supply curve to shift upward by forcing employers to pay higher labor costs. President George W. Bush cut taxes and regulation to shift both aggregate supply and aggregate demand in the right direction. But his insistence on cutting the growth of federal spending in the midst of the 2001 recession was ill-timed (and ultimately reversed). Later he balked at using tax increases to help pay for the Iraq war, forcing the Fed to assume the entire burden of AD restraint.

President Obama promised to make job creation his first priority. But among the first actions he took included raising mileage standards on cars, tripling the tax on cigarettes, and delaying the digital TV transition; all interventions that raised production costs or reduced employment. He also rejected supply-side tax cuts that would have stimulated job creation.

WHY THINGS DON'T ALWAYS WORK

There's plenty of blame to go around for all the blemishes on our economic record. Some people blame the Fed, others blame Congress, still others blame China or Mexico. Some forces, however, constrain economic policy even when no one is specifically to blame. In this regard, we can distinguish *four obstacles to policy success:*

- *Goal conflicts*
- *Measurement problems*
- *Design problems*
- *Implementation problems*

Goal Conflicts

The first factor to take note of is potential conflicts in policy priorities. President Clinton had to confront this problem his first day in office. He had pledged to create new jobs by increasing public infrastructure spending and offering a middle-class tax cut. He had also promised to reduce the deficit, however. This created a clear goal conflict. In the end, President Clinton had to settle for a smaller increase in infrastructure spending and a tax *increase*. President George W. Bush confronted similar problems. In the 2000 presidential campaign he had promised a big increase in federal spending on education. By the time he took office, however, the federal budget surplus was rapidly shrinking, and the goal of preserving the non–Social Security ("on budget") surplus took precedence. The conflict between spending priorities and budget balancing became much more intense when President Bush decided to attack Iraq. We noted earlier how President Obama had to set aside some campaign promises (e.g., raising taxes on capital gains, estates, and "the rich") when confronted on day 1 with the urgent need to stimulate aggregate demand.

These and other goal conflicts have their roots in the short-run trade-off between unemployment and inflation. Should we try to cure inflation, unemployment, or just a bit of both? Answers are likely to vary. Unemployed people put the highest priority on attaining full employment. Labor unions press for faster economic growth. Bankers, creditors, and people on fixed incomes demand an end to inflation.

This goal conflict is often institutionalized in the decision-making process. The Fed is traditionally viewed as the guardian of price stability. The president and Congress worry more about people's jobs and government programs, so they are less willing to raise taxes or cut spending.

Distributional goals may also conflict with macro objectives. Anti-inflationary policies may require cutbacks in programs for the poor, the elderly, or needy students. These cutbacks may be politically impossible (see News below). Likewise, tight-money policies may be viewed as too great a burden for small businesses, home builders, and auto manufacturers.

IN THE NEWS

Deficit-Cutting Wilts in Heat from Voters

Entitlements Remain Mostly Off-Limits

In April, Sen. Pete V. Domenici (R-N.M.) suggested a plan for digging out of the massive federal deficit. His idea seemed modest on its face but was revolutionary by Washington standards.

Domenici proposed capping cost-of-living increases in entitlement programs, the automatic spending engines such as Medicaid, Medicare and federal retirement that are exempt from annual congressional review. . . .

Even before his proposal took shape, more than 3,000 New Mexico constituents sent him identical postcards opposing any effort to cap entitlement programs.

The National Council of Senior Citizens dubbed the plan "the most outrageous attack on the elderly we have seen in years." The Veterans of Foreign Wars expressed "shock and outrage." Milk producers accused Domenici of trying to balance the budget "on the back of farmers."

That was enough for the Senate, which voted 69 to 28 to reject the proposal.

—Eric Pianin

Source: *The Washington Post*, August 4, 1992. © 1992 The Washington Post. Used with permission by PARS International Corp.

Analysis: Changes in economic policy inevitably alter incomes and stir political opposition. Cuts in government spending are particularly difficult to enact.

Although the policy tools in Table 18.1 are powerful, they can't grant all our wishes. Since we still live in a world of scarce resources, ***all policy decisions entail opportunity costs,*** which means that we'll always be confronted with trade-offs. The best we can hope for is a set of compromises that yields *optimal* outcomes, not ideal ones.

Measurement Problems

One reason firefighters are pretty successful in putting out fires before entire cities burn down is that fires are highly visible phenomena. But such visibility isn't characteristic of economic problems. An increase in the unemployment rate from 5 to 6 percent, for example, isn't the kind of thing you notice while crossing the street. Unless you work in the unemployment insurance office or lose your own job, the increase in unemployment isn't likely to attract your attention. The same is true of prices; small increases in product prices aren't likely to ring many alarms. Hence, both inflation and unemployment may worsen considerably before anyone takes serious notice. Were we as slow and ill-equipped to notice fires, whole neighborhoods would burn before someone rang the alarm.

Measurement problems are a very basic policy constraint. To formulate appropriate economic policy, we must first determine the nature of our problems. To do so, we must measure employment changes, output changes, price changes, and other macro outcomes. The old adage that governments are willing and able to solve only those problems they can measure is relevant here. Indeed, before the Great Depression, a fundamental constraint on public policy was the lack of statistics on what was happening in the economy. One lasting benefit of that experience is that we now try to keep informed on changing economic conditions. The information at hand, however, is always dated and incomplete. *At best, we know what was happening in the economy last month or last week.* The processes of data collection, assembly, and presentation take time, even in this age of high-speed computers. The average recession lasts about 11 months, but official data generally don't even confirm the existence of a recession until 8 months after a downturn starts! As the accompanying News reveals, the 2001 recession ended nearly 2 years before researchers confirmed its demise!

IN THE NEWS

The Recession Is Finally Declared Officially Over

The National Bureau of Economic Research said the U.S. economic recession that began in March 2001 ended eight months later, not long after the Sept. 11 terrorist attacks.

Most economists concluded more than a year ago that the recession ended in late 2001. But yesterday's declaration by the NBER—a private, nonprofit economic research group that is considered the official arbiter of recession timing—came after a lengthy internal debate over whether there can be an economic recovery if the labor market continues to contract. The bureau's answer: a decisive yes. . . .

The NBER committee is notoriously slow in making its declarations on the timing of the business cycle. Still, the 20 months it waited to declare the recession's end was slightly shorter than the 21 months it took to declare the end of the 1990–91 recession. That, too, was a so-called jobless recovery, though the job losses weren't as severe as they have been lately.

—Jon E. Hilsenrath

Source: *The Wall Street Journal*, July 18, 2003. Copyright 2003 by Dow Jones & Company, Inc. Reproduced with permission of Dow Jones & Company, Inc. in the format Textbook via Copyright Clearance Center.

Analysis: In the absence of timely information, today's policy decisions are inevitably based on yesterday's perceptions.

web analysis

For more on the NBER's recession dating procedure, go to **www. nber.org** and search "recession dating."

Forecasts. In an ideal world, policymakers wouldn't just *respond* to economic problems but would also *anticipate* their occurrence. If an inflationary GDP gap is emerging, for example, we want to take immediate action to keep aggregate spending from increasing. That is, the successful firefighter not only responds to a fire but also looks for hazards that might start one.

Unfortunately, economic policymakers are again at a disadvantage. Their knowledge of future problems is even worse than their knowledge of current problems. *In designing policy, policymakers must depend on economic forecasts,* that is, informed guesses about what the economy will look like in future periods.

Macro Models. Those guesses are often based on complex computer models of how the economy works. These models—referred to as *econometric macro models*—are mathematical summaries of the economy's performance. The models try to identify the key determinants of macro performance and then show what happens to macro outcomes when they change. The apparent precision of such computer models may disguise inherent guess work, however.

An economist "feeds" the computer two essential inputs. One is a quantitative model of how the economy allegedly works. A Keynesian model, for example, includes equations that show multiplier spending responses to tax cuts. A monetarist model shows that tax cuts raise interest rates, not total spending ("crowding out"), and a supply-side model stipulates labor-supply and production responses. The computer can't tell which theory is right; it just predicts what it's programmed to see. In other words, the computer sees the world through the eyes of its economic master.

The second essential input in a computer forecast is the assumed values for critical variables. A Keynesian model, for example, must specify how large a multiplier to expect. All the computer does is carry out the required mathematical routines, once it's told that the multiplier is relevant and what its value is. It can't discern the true multiplier any better than it can pick the right theory.

Given the dependence of computers on the theories and perceptions of their economic masters, it's not surprising that computer forecasts often differ greatly. It's also not surprising that they're often wrong. Even policymakers who are familiar with both economic theory and computer models can make some pretty bad calls. In January 1990, Fed chairman Alan Greenspan assured Congress that the risk of a recession was as low as 20 percent. Although he said he "wouldn't bet the ranch" on such a low probability, he was confident that the odds of a recession were below 50 percent. Five months after his testimony, the 1990–91 recession began. Greenspan's successor, Ben Bernanke, lost the same bet in 2008 (see News below).

IN THE NEWS

No Recession, Bernanke Says

WASHINGTON—Federal Reserve Chairman Ben Bernanke said Thursday that the USA will avoid a recession. . . .

In his first public comments since the Fed slashed interest rates in January, the chairman said a softer job market, high energy prices, stock market turmoil and declining home values likely were weighing on consumers. Their spending accounts for more than two-thirds of all U.S. economic activity.

"My baseline outlook involves a period of sluggish growth, followed by a somewhat stronger pace of growth starting later this year as the effects of (Fed) and fiscal stimulus begin to be felt," Bernanke told committee members. . . .

In judging the effects of Fed rate cuts on the economy, Bernanke said the central bank is looking for stabilization in housing, the job market and credit markets. A significant worsening in the availability and affordability of credit "would certainly be a warning bell" that more rate cuts were needed, he said. . . .

On the plus side, Bernanke said export growth and the fiscal stimulus package signed into law by President Bush on Wednesday should help. The Fed chairman said the impact of the stimulus should be felt in the July–September quarter, if not before.

—Barbara Hagenbaugh

Source: USA TODAY. February 15, 2008, B1. Reprinted with Permission.

Analysis: Policy decisions are based on forecasts of economic performance. Bad forecasts can lead to delayed or wrong policy actions.

The Council of Economic Advisers has made similar blunders. The CEA was forecasting 2–3 percent growth just as the economy was falling into the 2001 recession. In early 2008, the Bush White House was predicting a growth pickup later in the year. In fact the downturn *accelerated* in the final months of that year.

Leading Indicators. Given the complexity of macro models, many people prefer to use simpler tools for divining the future. One of the most popular is the Index of Leading Economic Indicators. As noted in Chapter 9 (see Table 9.2), the Leading Indicators are things we can observe today that are logically linked to future production (e.g., orders for new equipment). Unfortunately, the logical sequence of events doesn't always unfold as anticipated. All too often, the links in the chain of Leading Indicators are broken by changing expectations and unanticipated events.

Crystal Balls. In view of the fragile foundations and spotty record of computer and index-based forecasts, many people shun them altogether, preferring to use their own "crystal balls." The Foundation for the Study of Cycles has identified 4,000 different crystal balls that people use to gauge the health of the economy, including the ratio of used-car to new-car sales (it rises in recession); the number of divorce petitions (it rises in bad times); animal population cycles (they peak just before economic downturns); and even the optimism/pessimism content of popular music (a reflection of consumer confidence). Corporate executives claim that such crystal balls are as valuable as professional economic forecasts. In a Gallup survey of CEOs, most respondents said economists' forecasts had little or no influence on company plans or policies. The head of one large company said, "I go out of my way to ignore them." The general public apparently shares this view, giving higher marks to the forecasts of sportswriters and weather forecasters than to those of economists.

Economic forecasters defend themselves in two ways. First, they note that economic policy decisions are inevitably based on anticipated changes in the economy's performance. The decision to stimulate or restrain the economy can't be made by a flip of a coin; *someone* must try to foresee the future course of the economy. Second, forecasters claim that their quantitative approach is the only honest one. Because forecasting models require specific behavioral assumptions and estimates, they force people to spell out their versions of the future. Less rigorous ("gut feeling") approaches are too ambiguous and often inconsistent.

These are valid arguments. Still, one must be careful to distinguish the precision of computers from the inevitable uncertainties of their spoon-fed models. The basic law of the computer is GIGO: garbage in, garbage out. If the underlying models and assumptions are no good, the computer's forecasts won't be any better.

Policy and Forecasts. The task of forecasting the economic future is made still more complex by the interdependency of forecasts, policy decisions, and economic outcomes (see Figure 18.2). First, a forecast is made, based on current economic conditions, likely

FIGURE 18.2
The Mutual Dependence of Forecasts and Policy

Because tax revenues and government spending are sensitive to economic conditions, budget projections must rely on economic forecasts. The budget projections may alter policy decisions, however, and so change the basis for the initial forecasts. This interdependence among macro forecasts, budget projections, and policy decisions is virtually inevitable.

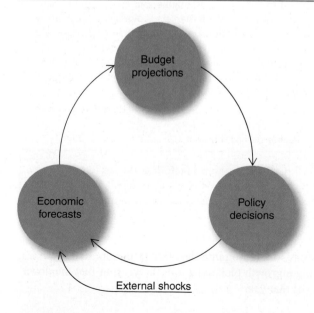

disturbances to the economy, and anticipated economic policy. These forecasts are then used to project likely budget deficits and other policy variables. Congress and the president react to these projections by revising fiscal, monetary, or supply-side policies. These changes, in turn, alter the basis for the initial forecasts.

This interdependence among forecasts, budget projections, and policy decisions was superbly illustrated in the early months of the George W. Bush presidency. At the beginning of 2001, both the White House and the Congress were forecasting enormous budget surpluses. The central policy debate focused on what to do with those surpluses. The Democrats wanted to spend the surplus; the Republicans wanted to give it back to households with larger tax cuts. As the debate dragged on, however, the weakening economy shrunk the surplus. In August 2001, the Congressional Budget Office (CBO) announced that the "on-budget" (non Social Security) surplus it had forecast just 7 months earlier had vanished. This forced both political parties to change their policy proposals. Protecting the vanishing surplus became the political priority. Spending proposals were scaled back, as were hopes of debt repayment.

President Obama used dire forecasts of the economy to build support for his stimulus proposals. He claimed that the 2008–9 recession was the worst since the Great Depression and that the economy might *never* recover unless his stimulus package was implemented. The resulting fear and uncertainty increased public support for his stimulus plan, which Congress authorized within the first month of his presidency.

External Shocks. Even accurate forecasts can be knocked astray by external shocks. The budget decisions reached in early 2001 didn't anticipate the September 11 terrorist attacks. Nor did economic forecasters in 2005 anticipate the ravages of Hurricanes Katrina and Rita. The very nature of external *shocks* is that they are *unanticipated*. Hence, even if we knew enough about the economy to forecast "shockless" outcomes perfectly, an external shock could always disrupt the economy and ruin our forecasts. In reality, forecasting methods aren't even good enough to predict the behavior of a "shockless" economy with precision.

As the accompanying News reveals, the CBO's forecasting errors in 2001 and 2005 were not an exception; they were the norm. When policymakers rely on such forecasts, they are likely to fail all too often.

IN THE NEWS

CBO's Flawed Forecasts

Every year the Congressional Budget Office (CBO) forecasts the federal budget balance for the next 5 years. Those forecasts are rarely accurate. The typical CBO forecasting error for the *current* fiscal year amounts to 0.5 percent of GDP, or about $70 billion. Moreover, the errors widen for future years: For the *fifth* year out, CBO's forecasts typically miss the actual budget balance by a startling 3 percent of GDP. This implies that CBO's January 2009 forecast of the 2014 budget balance (a $250 billion deficit) may be off the mark by $500 billion!

Since 1981, CBO has both over- and underestimated federal budget balances. There has been a slightly pessimistic bias, however, especially in the boom years of 1992–2000 and 2003–2007. Forecasts from the president's Office of Management and Budget (OMB) haven't been any better.

Source: Congressional Budget Office, *The Budget and Economic Outlook, Fiscal Years 2009–2019.* January 2009.

> **Analysis:** The economic and budget forecasts that guide policy decisions are often flawed. This reduces the chances of policy success.

web analysis

For an overview of the forecasting model the Congressional Budget Office uses, visit **www.cbo.gov.**

Design Problems

Assume for the moment that we somehow are able to get a reliable forecast of where the economy is headed. The outlook, let's suppose, is bad. Now we're in the driver's seat to steer the economy past looming dangers. We need to chart our course—to design an economic plan. What action should we take? Which theory of macro behavior should guide us? How will the marketplace respond to any specific action we take?

Suppose, for example, that we adopt a Keynesian approach to ending a recession. Specifically, we want to use fiscal policy to boost aggregate demand. Should we cut taxes or increase government spending? This was a core decision President Obama confronted as he developed his stimulus program (see News below). The choice depends in part on the efficacy of either policy tool. Will tax cuts stimulate aggregate demand? In 1998, Japanese households used their tax cut to increase *savings* rather than consumption. In 2001, U.S. households were also slow to spend their tax rebates. When consumers don't respond as anticipated, the intended fiscal stimulus doesn't materialize. Such behavioral responses frustrate even the best-intentioned policy. The successful policymaker needs a very good crystal ball, one that will also foretell how market participants are going to respond to any specific actions taken.

IN THE NEWS

Stimulus: Spend or Cut Taxes?

Most Economists Agree That Both Are Needed. The Debate Comes When They Ask How to Split It.

New York (Fortune)—As President-elect Barack Obama prepares to take office, the incoming administration and Congress continue to shape a massive stimulus package to help the struggling economy. . . .

While the final breakdown of the package remains to be seen, much of the debate centers on the effectiveness of government spending versus tax cuts as means of reviving the economy. Currently, the plan includes roughly $550 billion in spending and $275 billion in tax cuts. . . .

Most economists support the emphasis on spending, saying government expenditure does more to boost gross domestic product, a key indicator of fiscal health.

In other words, spending delivers more bang for the buck because each dollar paid to a worker building a wind turbine, for example, is then re-spent on groceries or clothing, causing a fiscal ripple-effect. Conversely, a worker might save a third of the money he is given in a tax cut, with some of the spending going toward imports, which would also reduce the stimulus to GDP.

According to a Jan. 6 study by Mark Zandi, chief economist at Moody's Economy.com, GDP grows by $1.59 for every dollar spent on infrastructure, while the increase from a corporate tax cut is only $0.30. . . .

Based on Zandi's study, some of the most efficient ways to spend government money are temporarily increasing food stamps (a $1.73 GDP increase per dollar), extending unemployment benefits ($1.63), increasing infrastructure spending ($1.59) and upping direct aid to financially strapped states ($1.38). . . .

Some research shows the positive effect of tax cuts on GDP gets short shrift. Christina Romer, who studied the subject while a professor at the University of California, Berkeley—and who Obama chose as Chairwoman of his Council of Economic Advisers—says don't underestimate them as an effective means of stimulating the economy.

—Alyssa Abkowitz and Lawrence Delevingne

Analysis: Agreement on the *need* for fiscal stimulus doesn't assure consensus on the *content* of fiscal stimulus. What mix of tax cuts, increased government spending, and income transfers should be selected?

Implementation Problems

Measurement and design problems can break the spirit of even the best policymaker (or the policymaker's economic advisers). Yet measurement and design problems are only part of the story. A good idea is of little value unless someone puts it to use. Accordingly, to understand fully why things go wrong, we must also consider the difficulties of *implementing* a well-designed policy.

Congressional Deliberations. Suppose that the president and his Council of Economic Advisers (perhaps in conjunction with the National Economic Council, the secretary of the

Treasury, and the director of the Office of Management and Budget) decide that a tax cut is necessary to stimulate demand for goods and services. Can they simply go ahead and cut tax rates? No, because only Congress can legislate tax changes. Once the president decides on the appropriate policy, he must ask Congress for authority to take the required action, which means a delay in implementing policy or possibly no policy at all.

At the very least, the president must convince Congress of the wisdom of his proposed policy. The tax proposal must work its way through separate committees of both the House of Representatives and the Senate, get on the congressional calendar, and be approved in each chamber. If there are important differences in Senate and House versions of the tax-cut legislation, they must be compromised in a joint conference. The modified proposal must then be returned to each chamber for approval.

The same kind of process applies to the outlay side of the budget. Once the president has submitted his budget proposals (in January), Congress reviews them, then sets its own spending goals. After that, the budget is broken down into 13 different categories, and a separate appropriations bill is written for each one. These bills spell out in detail how much can be spent and for what purposes. Once Congress passes them, they go to the president for acceptance or veto.

Budget legislation requires Congress to finish these deliberations by October 1 (the beginning of the federal fiscal year), but Congress rarely meets this deadline. In most years, the budget debate continues well into the fiscal year. In some years, the budget debate isn't resolved until the fiscal year is nearly over! The final budget legislation is typically more than 1,000 pages long and so complex that few people understand all its dimensions.

Time Lags. This description of congressional activity isn't an outline for a civics course; rather, it's an important explanation of why economic policy isn't fully effective. ***Even if the right policy is formulated to solve an emerging economic problem, there's no assurance that it will be implemented. And if it's implemented, there's no assurance that it will take effect at the right time.*** One of the most frightening prospects for economic policy is that a policy design intended to serve a specific problem will be implemented much later, when economic conditions have changed. This isn't a remote danger. According to Christina Romer and Paul Romer, the Fed doesn't pull the monetary-stimulus lever until a recession is under way, and Congress is even slower in responding to an economic downturn. Indeed, a U.S. Treasury Department study concluded that almost every postwar fiscal stimulus package was enacted well after the end of the recession it was intended to cure!

Figure 18.3 is a schematic view of why macro policies don't always work as intended. There are always delays between the time a problem emerges and the time it's recognized. There are additional delays between recognition and response design, between design and implementation, and finally between implementation and impact. Not only may mistakes be made at each juncture, but even correct decisions may be overcome by changing economic conditions.

Politics vs. Economics. Politics often contributes to delayed and ill-designed policy interventions. Especially noteworthy in this regard is the potential conflict of economic policy

FIGURE 18.3
Policy Response: A Series of Time Lags

Even the best-intentioned economic policy can be frustrated by time lags. It takes time for a problem to be recognized, time to formulate a policy response, and still more time to implement

that policy. By the time the policy begins to affect the economy, the underlying problem may have changed.

SHOE JEFF MacNELLY

Analysis: Budget cuts are not popular with voters—even when economic conditions warrant fiscal restraint.

with political objectives. The president and Congress are always reluctant to impose fiscal restraints (tax increases or budget cutbacks) in election years, regardless of economic circumstances. As the cartoon above emphasizes, fiscal restraint is never popular.

The tendency of Congress to hold fiscal policy hostage to electoral concerns has created a pattern of short-run stops and starts—a kind of policy-induced business cycle. Indeed, some argue that the business cycle has been replaced with the political cycle: The economy is stimulated in the year of an election and then restrained in the postelection year. The conflict between the urgent need to get reelected and the necessity to manage the economy results in a seesaw kind of instability.

Even when the need for fiscal *stimulus* seems urgent—like after the September 11 terrorist attacks—politics can slow and distort the policy response. Two months after the attacks Republican and Democrat lawmakers were still far apart on how much fiscal stimulus to provide and what form the stimulus should take. Critics feared that by the time Congress acted, the stimulus would be too late and possibly excessive.

Politics was also a major factor in designing the 2009 stimulus program (the American Recovery and Reinvestment Act, Table 18.2). President Obama had chastised the Bush "tax cuts for the rich" and characterized stimulative tax cuts as "tired old dogma." He wasn't about to include new tax cuts in his stimulus package. Besides, he wanted to use the fiscal opportunity to advance his social agenda. Republicans fought him tooth and nail, arguing that added government spending would expand Big Government, undermine market incentives, and lead to larger budget deficits down the road. Not a single Republican member of the House voted for his stimulus package; in the Senate Obama got only three Republican votes—just enough to win passage.

Political considerations affect not only the broad dimensions of a stimulus package but also all of its details. A stimulus program of tax cuts and spending is an open invitation to award special interests. Lobbyists for corporations, state and local governments, hospitals, and even universities flock to Capitol Hill to claim a piece of the stimulus pie (see News on the following page). The resulting mix of tax cuts and spending may be more responsive to political pressures than economic policies.

In theory, the political independence of the Fed's Board of Governors provides some protection from ill-advised but politically advantageous policy initiatives. In practice, however, the Fed's relative obscurity and independence may backfire. The president and the Congress know that if they don't take effective action against inflation—by raising taxes or cutting government spending—the Fed can and will take stronger action to restrain aggregate demand. This is a classic case of having one's cake and eating it too. Elected officials win votes for not raising taxes or cutting some constituent's favorite spending program. They then take credit for any reduction in the rate of inflation brought about by Federal Reserve policies. To top it off, Congress and the president can also blame the Fed for driving up interest rates or starting a recession if monetary policy becomes too restrictive!

IN THE NEWS

Lobbyists Flock As Businesses Seek Share of the Stimulus Pie

WASHINGTON—President-elect Barack Obama's stimulus plan aims to help Main Street, but it is already sparking boom times on K Street as lobbyists from a host of U.S. industries seek a share of the projected $800 billion package.

Wind farms want permanent tax credits. The steel industry wants "Buy American" protection for infrastructure projects in the bill. Home builders want a national low mortgage rate, guaranteed by Uncle Sam. Universities want money for campus repairs, as well as $700 more per student in federal grants.

The spending requests total many times the likely size of the package. Environmentalists alone put together a wish list of 80 projects that add up to $405 billion.

With a fight likely over a pie that, however large, isn't big enough for all, industries are crafting creative pitches to show that assistance to them would provide the fastest, broadest or most comprehensive stimulus. . . .

—Elizabeth Williamson and Brody Mullins

Source: *The Wall Street Journal*, January 6, 2009. Copyright 2009 by Dow Jones & Company, Inc. Reproduced with permission of Dow Jones & Company, Inc. in the format Textbook via Copyright Clearance Center.

Analysis: Fiscal stimulus implies income gains for specific businesses, governments, and nonprofit institutions. They all lobby for a slice of the stimulus pie, thereby changing its size and content.

Finally, we must recognize that policy design is obstructed by a certain attention deficit (see cartoon below). Neither people on the street nor elected public officials focus constantly on economic goals and activities. Even students enrolled in economics courses have a hard time keeping their minds on the economy and its problems. The executive and legislative branches of government, for their part, are likely to focus on economic concerns only when economic problems become serious or voters demand action. Otherwise, policymakers are apt to be complacent about economic policy as long as economic performance is within a tolerable range of desired outcomes.

AMERICA'S PROBLEM:

Analysis: Economic problems often don't arouse public or policy interest until they become severe.

HANDS ON OR HANDS OFF?

In view of the goal conflicts and the measurement, design, and implementation problems that policymakers confront, it's less surprising that things sometimes go wrong than that things so often work out right. The maze of obstacles through which theory must pass before it becomes policy explains many economic disappointments. On this basis alone, we may conclude that *consistent fine-tuning of the economy isn't compatible with either our design capabilities or our decision-making procedures.* We have exhibited a strong capability to avoid major economic disruptions in the last four decades. We haven't, however, been able to make all the minor adjustments necessary to fulfill our goals completely. As Arthur Burns, former chairman of the Fed's Board of Governors, said:

> There has been much loose talk of "fine tuning" when the state of knowledge permits us to predict only within a fairly broad level the course of economic development and the results of policy actions.[1]

Hands Off. Some critics of economic policy take this argument a few steps further. If fine-tuning isn't really possible, they say, we should abandon discretionary policies altogether and follow fixed rules for fiscal and monetary intervention.

As we saw in Chapter 15, pure monetarism would require the Fed to increase the money supply at a constant rate. Critics of fiscal policy would require the government to maintain balanced budgets, or at least to offset deficits in sluggish years with surpluses in years of high growth. Such rules would prevent policymakers from over- or understimulating the economy. Such rules would also add a dose of certainty to the economic outlook.

Milton Friedman was one of the most persistent advocates of fixed policy rules. With discretionary authority, Friedman argued:

> the wrong decision is likely to be made in a large fraction of cases because the decision-makers are examining only a limited area and not taking into account the cumulative consequences of the policy as a whole. On the other hand, if a general rule is adopted for a group of cases as a bundle, the existence of that rule has favorable effects on people's attitudes and beliefs and expectations that would not follow even from the discretionary adoption of precisely the same policy on a series of separate occasions.[2]

The case for a hands-off policy stance is based on practical, not theoretical, arguments. *Everyone agrees that flexible, discretionary policies* could *result in better economic performance. But Friedman and others argue that the practical requirements of monetary and fiscal management are too demanding and thus prone to failure.* Moreover, required policies may be compromised by political pressures.

New Classical Economics. Monetarist critiques of discretionary policy are echoed by a new perspective referred to as new classical economics (NCE). Classical economists saw no need for discretionary macro policy. In their view, the private sector is inherently stable and government intervention serves no purpose. New classical economics reaches the same conclusion. As Robert Barro, a proponent of NCE, put it: "It is best for the government to provide a stable environment, and then mainly stay out of the way."[3] Barro and other NCE economists based this laissez-faire conclusion on the intriguing notion of **rational expectations.** This notion contends that people make decisions on the basis of all available information, including the *future* effects of *current* government policy.

Suppose, for example, that the Fed decided to increase the money supply in order to boost output. If people had rational expectations, they'd anticipate that this money supply growth will fuel inflation. To protect themselves, they'd immediately demand higher prices and wages. As a result, the stimulative monetary policy would fail to boost real output.

rational expectations:
Hypothesis that people's spending decisions are based on all available information, including the anticipated effects of government intervention.

[1]*Newsweek,* August 27, 1973, p. 4.
[2]Milton Friedman, *Capitalism and Freedom* (Chicago: University of Chicago Press, 1962), p. 53.
[3]Robert Barro, "Don't Fool with Money, Cut Taxes," *The Wall Street Journal,* November 21, 1991, p. A14.

(Monetarists reach the same conclusion but for different reasons; for monetarists, the countervailing forces are technological and institutional rather than rational expectations.)

Discretionary fiscal policy could be equally ineffective. Suppose Congress accelerated government spending in an effort to boost aggregate demand. Monetarists contend that the accompanying increase in the deficit would push interest rates up and crowd out private investment and consumption. New classical economists again reach the same conclusion via a different route. They contend that people with rational expectations would anticipate that a larger deficit now will necessitate tax increases in later years. To prepare for later tax bills, consumers will reduce spending now, thereby saving more. This "rational" reduction in consumption will offset the increased government expenditure, thus rendering fiscal policy ineffective.

If the new classical economists are right, then the only policy that works is one that surprises people—one that consumers and investors don't anticipate. But a policy based on surprises isn't very practical. Accordingly, new classical economists conclude that minimal policy intervention is best. This conclusion provides yet another guideline for policy decisions. See Table 18.5 for a roster of competing theories.

Hands On. *Proponents of a hands-on policy strategy acknowledge the possibility of occasional blunders. They emphasize, however, the greater risks of doing nothing when the economy is faltering.* Some proponents of the quick fix even turn the new classical economics argument on its head. Even the wrong policy, they argue, might be better than doing nothing if enough market participants believed that *change* implied *progress*. They cite the jump in consumer confidence that followed the election of Bill Clinton, who had emphasized the need for a *change* in policy but hadn't spelled out the details of that change. The surge in confidence itself stimulated consumer purchases, even before President Clinton took office. The same kind of response occurred after the September 11, 2001, terrorist attacks. Consumers were dazed and insecure. There was a serious risk that they would curtail spending if the government didn't *do something*. Details aside, they just wanted reassurance that someone was taking charge of events. Quick responses by the Fed (increasing the money

Keynesians	Keynesians believe that the private sector is inherently unstable and prone to stagnate at low levels of output and employment. They want the government to manage aggregate demand with changes in taxes and government's spending.
Modern ("neo") Keynesians	Post–World War II followers of Keynes worry about inflation as well as recession. They urge budgetary restraint to cool an overheated economy. They also use monetary policy to change interest rates.
Monetarists	The money supply is their only heavy hitter. By changing the money supply, they can raise or lower the price level. Pure monetarists shun active policy, believing that it destabilizes the otherwise stable private sector. Output and employment gravitate to their natural levels.
Supply-siders	Incentives to work, invest, and produce are the key to their plays. Cuts in marginal tax rates and government regulation are used to expand production capacity, thereby increasing output and reducing inflationary pressures.
New classical economists	They say fine-tuning won't work because once the private sector realizes what the government is doing, it will act to offset it. They also question the credibility of quick-fix promises. They favor steady, predictable policies.
Marxists	Marxists contend that the failures of the economy are inherent in its capitalist structure. The owners of capital won't strive for full employment or a more equitable income distribution. Workers, without any capital, have little incentive to excel. This team proposes starting a new game, with entirely different rules.

TABLE 18.5
Who's on First? Labeling Economists

It's sometimes hard to tell who's on what side in economic debates. Although some economists are proud to wear the colors of monetarists, Keynesians, or other teams, many economists shun such allegiances. Indeed, economists are often accused of playing on one team one day and on another team the next, making it hard to tell which team is at bat. To simplify matters, this guide may be used for quick identification of the players. Closer observation is advised, however, before choosing up teams.

supply), the Congress (authorizing more spending), and President Bush (mobilizing security and military forces) kept consumer confidence from plunging. President Obama argued that a similar situation existed in early 2009. Claiming that the economy would slide into another Depression if Congress didn't act, he said doing *something*—even if not perfect—was better than doing *nothing*.

Just doing *something* isn't the purpose of a hands-on policy, of course. Policy activists believe that we have enough knowledge about how the economy works to pull the right policy levers most of the time. They also point to the historical record. Our economic track record may not be perfect, but the historical record of prices, employment, and growth has improved since active fiscal and monetary policies were adopted. Without flexibility in the money supply and the budget, they argue, the economy would be less stable and our economic goals would remain unfulfilled.

The historical evidence for discretionary policy is ambiguous. Victor Zarnowitz showed that the U.S. economy has been much more stable since 1946 than it was in earlier periods (1875–1918 and 1919–1945). Recessions have gotten shorter and economic expansions longer. But a variety of factors—including a shift from manufacturing to services, a larger government sector, and automatic stabilizers—has contributed to this improved macro performance. The contribution of discretionary macro policy is less clear. It's easy to observe what actually happened but almost impossible to determine what would have occurred in other circumstances.

Finally, one must contend with the difficulties inherent in adhering to any fixed rules. How is the Fed, for example, supposed to maintain a steady rate of growth in the money supply? As we observed in Chapter 13, people move their funds back and forth between different kinds of "money." Also, the demand for money is subject to unpredictable shifts. To maintain a steady rate of growth in M2 or any other measure of money would require superhuman foresight and responses. As former Fed Chairman Paul Volcker told Congress, it would be "exceedingly dangerous and in fact practically impossible to eliminate substantial elements of discretion in the conduct of Federal Reserve policy."

The same is true of fiscal policy. Government spending and taxes are directly influenced by changes in unemployment, inflation, interest rates, and growth. These automatic stabilizers make it virtually impossible to maintain any fixed rule for budget balancing. Moreover, if we eliminated the automatic stabilizers, we'd risk greater instability.

Modest Expectations. The clamor for fixed policy rules is more a rebuke of past policy than a viable policy alternative. We really have no choice but to pursue discretionary policies. Recognition of measurement, design, and implementation problems is important for an understanding of the way the economy functions. Even though it's impossible to reach all our goals, we can't abandon conscientious attempts to get as close as possible to goal fulfillment. If public policy can create a few more jobs, a better mix of output, a little more growth and price stability, or an improved distribution of income in the economy tomorrow, those initiatives are worthwhile.

SUMMARY

- The government possesses an array of macro policy tools, each of which can significantly alter economic outcomes. To end a recession, we can cut taxes, expand the money supply, or increase government spending. To curb inflation, we can reverse each of these policy tools. To overcome stagflation, we can combine fiscal and monetary levers with improved supply-side incentives.   LO1, LO2

- Although the potential of economic theory seems impressive, the economic record doesn't look as good. Persistent unemployment, recurring economic slowdowns, and nagging inflation suggest that the realities of policymaking are more difficult than theory implies.   LO3

- To some extent, the failures of economic policy are a reflection of scarce resources and competing goals. Even when consensus exists, however, serious obstacles to effective economic policy remain. These obstacles include

(*a*) Measurement problems. Our knowledge of economic performance is always dated and incomplete.

(*b*) Design problems. We don't know exactly how the economy will respond to specific policies.

(*c*) Implementation problems. It takes time for Congress and the president to agree on an appropriate plan of action. Moreover, political needs may take precedence over economic needs.

For all these reasons, discretionary policy rarely lives up to its theoretical potential. LO3

- Monetarists and new classical economists favor rules rather than discretionary macro policies. They argue that discretionary policies are unlikely to work and risk being wrong. Critics respond that discretionary policies are needed to cope with ever-changing economic circumstances. LO3

Key Terms

business cycle
fiscal policy
automatic stabilizer
structural deficit
fiscal stimulus
fiscal restraint

monetary policy
natural rate of unemployment
supply-side policy
recessionary GDP gap
multiplier
velocity of money (*V*)

inflationary GDP gap
stagflation
fine-tuning
growth recession
rational expectations

Questions for Discussion

1. What policies would Keynesians, monetarists, and supply-siders advocate for (*a*) restraining inflation and (*b*) reducing unemployment? LO1

2. Why did Fed Chairman Bernanke expect there would be no recession in 2008 (see News, p. 389)? Why was he wrong? LO3

3. If policymakers have instant data on the economy's performance, should they respond immediately? Why or why not? LO3

4. Suppose it's an election year and aggregate demand is growing so fast that it threatens to set off an inflationary movement. Why might Congress and the president hesitate to cut back on government spending or raise taxes, as economic theory suggests is appropriate? LO3

5. Should military spending be subject to macroeconomic constraints? What programs should be expanded or contracted to bring about needed changes in the budget? Is this feasible? LO2

6. Why is the multiplier higher for unemployment benefits than infrastructure spending (News, p. 392)? Which occurs faster? LO2

7. Suppose the government proposes to cut taxes while maintaining the current level of government expenditures. To finance this deficit, it may either (*a*) sell bonds to the public or (*b*) print new money (via Federal Reserve cooperation). What are the likely effects of each of these alternatives on each of the following? Would Keynesians, monetarists, and supply-siders give the same answers? LO2
   (*a*) Interest rates
   (*b*) Consumer spending
   (*c*) Business investment
   (*d*) Aggregate demand

8. Suppose the economy is slumping into recession and needs a fiscal policy boost. Voters, however, are opposed to larger federal deficits. What should policymakers do? LO2

9. What are the pros and cons of tax cuts or increased government spending as stimulative tools (News, p. 392)? LO3

10. Why are the dimensions of the consumption and investment functions so important for policy design? LO2

 web activities to accompany this chapter can be found on the Online Learning Center:
http://www.mhhe.com/schiller12e

LO3 1. If the Congressional Budget Office makes its average error this year, by how much will
it underestimate next year's budget deficit? (See News on p. 391) _____%

LO1 2. If the unemployment rate stays two percentage points above full employment for an entire year,
(a) How many jobs will be lost in a labor force of 160 million? _____
(b) If the average worker produces $100,000 of output, how much output will be lost? _____

LO1 3. According to the World View on page 386,
(a) Which country had the greatest macro misery in the 2000s? (Compute the
"misery index" from Chapter 16.) _____
(b) Who had the fastest growth? _____

LO1 4. What MPC for tax cuts is assumed in the News on page 392? _____

LO2 5. According to the News on page 392, what is the implied value of the multiplier for
(a) Increased unemployment benefits? _____
(b) Infrastructure spending? _____

LO3 6. The following table displays Congressional Budget Office forecasts of federal budget balances
for the following fiscal year. Compare these forecasts with *actual* surplus and deficits for those
same years (see Table 12.3 for data).

Year:	2000	2001	2002	2003	2004	2005	2006	2007	2008	2009
Deficit forecast (in billions of dollars)	+161	+268	+176	−315	−480	−348	−314	−285	−155	−438

(a) In how many years was CBO too optimistic (underestimating the deficit or
overestimating the surplus)? _____
(b) In how many years was CBO too pessimistic? _____

LO2 7. Complete the following chart by summarizing the policy prescriptions of various economic theories:

	Policy Prescription for	
Policy Approach	Recession	Inflation
Fiscal	_____	_____
Classical	_____	_____
Keynesian	_____	_____
Monetarist	_____	_____
Monetary	_____	_____
Keynesian	_____	_____
Monetarist	_____	_____
Supply Side	_____	_____

PART 8

International Economics

Our interactions with the rest of the world have a profound impact on the mix of output (WHAT), the methods of production (HOW), and the distribution of income (FOR WHOM). Trade and global money flows can also affect the stability of the macro economy. Chapters 19 and 20 explore the motives, the nature, and the effects of international trade and finance.

Chapter 21 examines one of the world's most urgent problems—the deprivation that afflicts nearly 3 billion people worldwide. In this last chapter, the dimensions, causes, and potential cures for global poverty are discussed.

International Trade

19

LEARNING OBJECTIVES

After reading this chapter, you should be able to:

LO1. Discuss what comparative advantage is.

LO2. Assess what the gains from trade are.

LO3. Explain how trade barriers affect prices, output, and incomes.

The **2008 World Series** between the Philadelphia Phillies and the Tampa Bay Rays was played with Japanese gloves, baseballs made in Costa Rica, and Mexican bats. Most of the players were wearing shoes made in Korea or China. And during the regular season, many of the games throughout the major leagues were played on artificial grass made in Taiwan. Baseball, it seems, has become something less than the "all-American" game.

Imported goods have made inroads into other activities as well. All DVDs, camphones, and video-game machines are imported, as are most televisions, fax machines, personal computers, and iPhones. Most of these imported goods could have been produced in the United States. Why did we purchase them from other countries? For that matter, why does the rest of the world buy computers, tractors, chemicals, airplanes, and wheat from us rather than produce such products for themselves? Wouldn't we all be better off relying on ourselves for the goods we consume (and the jobs we need) rather than buying and selling products in international markets? Or is there some advantage to be gained from international trade?

This chapter begins with a survey of international trade patterns—what goods and services we trade, and with whom. Then we address basic issues related to such trade:

- **What benefit, if any, do we get from international trade?**
- **How much harm do imports cause, and to whom?**
- **Should we protect ourselves from "unfair" trade by limiting imports?**

After examining the arguments for and against international trade, we draw some general conclusions about trade policy. As we'll see, international trade tends to increase *average* incomes, although it may diminish the job and income opportunities for specific industries and workers.

U.S. TRADE PATTERNS

The United States is by far the largest player in global product and resource markets. In 2008, we purchased 20 percent of the world's exports and sold 15 percent of the same total.

In dollar terms, our imports in 2008 exceeded $2.5 trillion. These **imports** included the consumer items mentioned earlier as well as capital equipment, raw materials, and food. Table 19.1 is a sampler of the goods and services we purchase from foreign suppliers.

Although imports represent only 18 percent of total GDP, they account for larger shares of specific product markets. Coffee is a familiar example. Since virtually all coffee is imported (except for a tiny amount produced in Hawaii), Americans would have a harder time staying awake without imports. Likewise, there'd be no aluminum if we didn't import bauxite, no chrome bumpers if we didn't import chromium, no tin cans without imported tin, and a lot fewer computers without imported components. We couldn't even play the all-American game of baseball without imports, since baseballs are no longer made in the United States.

We import *services* as well as *goods*. If you fly to Europe on Virgin Airways you're importing transportation services. If you stay in a London hotel, you're importing lodging services. When you go to Barclay's Bank to cash traveler's checks, you're importing foreign financial services. These and other services now account for one-sixth of U.S. imports.

While we're buying goods (merchandise) and services from the rest of the world, global consumers are buying our **exports.** In 2008, we exported $1.3 trillion of *goods,* including farm products (wheat, corn, soybeans), tobacco, machinery (computers), aircraft, automobiles and auto parts, raw materials (lumber, iron ore), and chemicals (see Table 19.1 for a

Imports

imports: Goods and services purchased from international sources.

[handwritten annotation: net exports = exports − net imports]

[handwritten annotation: we have a trade deficit]

Exports

exports: Goods and services sold to foreign buyers.

Country	Imports from	Exports to
Australia	Beef Alumina Autos	Airplanes Computers Auto parts
Belgium	Jewelry Cars Optical glass	Cigarettes Airplanes Diamonds
Canada	Cars Trucks Paper	Auto parts Cars Computers
China	Toys Shoes Clothes	Fertilizer Airplanes Cotton
Germany	Cars Engines Auto parts	Airplanes Computers Cars
Japan	Cars Computers Telephones	Airplanes Computers Timber
Russia	Oil Platinum Artworks	Corn Wheat Oil seeds
South Korea	Shoes Cars Computers	Airplanes Leather Iron ingots and oxides

Source: U.S. Department of Commerce.

web analysis

After long-standing trade sanctions, the U.S. has reconvened trade with Cuba in recent years. For information on trade with Cuba, see **www.cubatrade.org.**

TABLE 19.1
A U.S. Trade Sampler

The United States imports and exports a staggering array of goods and services. Shown here are the top exports and imports with various countries. Notice that we export many of the same goods we import (such as cars and computers). What's the purpose of trading goods we produce ourselves?

sample of U.S. merchandise exports). We also exported $544 billion of services (movies, software licenses, tourism, engineering, financial services, etc.).

Although the United States is the world's largest exporter of goods and services, exports represent a relatively modest fraction of our total output. As the World View below illustrates, other nations export much larger proportions of their GDP. Belgium is one of the most export-oriented countries, with tourist services and diamond exports pushing its export ratio to an incredible 89 percent. By contrast, Myanmar (Burma) is basically a closed economy, with few exports (other than opium and other drugs traded in the black market).

WORLD VIEW

Export Ratios

Very poor countries often have little to export and thus low export ratios. Saudi Arabia, by contrast, depends heavily on its oil exports. Fast-developing countries in Asia also rely on exports to enlarge their markets and raise incomes. The U.S. export ratio is low by international standards.

web analysis

Find the most recent trends in trade statistics at **http://tse.export.gov.**

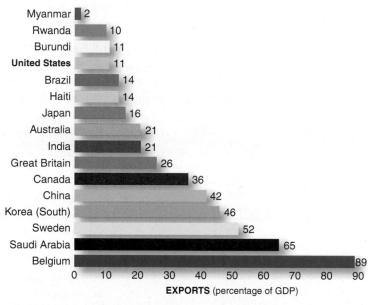

Country	Exports (% of GDP)
Myanmar	2
Rwanda	10
Burundi	11
United States	11
Brazil	14
Haiti	14
Japan	16
Australia	21
India	21
Great Britain	26
Canada	36
China	42
Korea (South)	46
Sweden	52
Saudi Arabia	65
Belgium	89

EXPORTS (percentage of GDP)

Source: World Bank, *World Development Indicators 2009*. **www.worldbank.org**.

Analysis: The relatively low U.S. export ratio reflects the vast size of our domestic market and our relative self-sufficiency in food and resources. European nations are smaller and highly interdependent.

The low U.S. export ratio (11 percent) disguises our heavy dependence on exports in specific industries. We export 25 to 50 percent of our rice, corn, and wheat production each year, and still more of our soybeans. Clearly, a decision by international consumers to stop eating U.S. agricultural products could devastate a lot of American farmers. Such companies as Boeing (planes), Caterpillar Tractor (construction and farm machinery), Weyerhaeuser (logs, lumber), Eastman Kodak (film), Dow (chemicals), and Sun Microsystems (computer workstations) sell over one-fourth of their output in foreign markets. McDonald's sells hamburgers to nearly 60 million people a day in 128 countries around the world; to do so, the company exports management and marketing services (as well as frozen food) from the United States. The Walt Disney Company produces the most popular TV shows in Russia and Germany, publishes Italy's best-selling weekly magazine, and has the most popular tourist attraction in Japan (Tokyo Disneyland). The 500,000 foreign students attending U.S. universities are purchasing $5 billion of American educational services. All these activities are part of America's service exports.

Product Category	Exports ($ billions)	Imports ($ billions)	Surplus (Deficit) ($ billions)
Merchandise	$1,291	$2,112	$(821)
Services	544	405	139
Total trade	$1,835	$2,517	$(682)

Source: U.S. Department of Commerce.

TABLE 19.2
Trade Balances

Both merchandise (goods) and services are traded between countries. The United States typically has a merchandise deficit and a services surplus. When combined, an overall trade deficit remained in 2008.

Trade Balances

Although we export a lot of products, we usually have an imbalance in our trade flows. The trade balance is the difference between the value of exports and imports; that is,

$$\text{Trade balance} = \text{exports} - \text{imports}$$

During 2008, we imported much more than we exported and so had a *negative* trade balance. A negative trade balance is called a **trade deficit.**

Although the overall trade balance includes both goods and services, these flows are usually reported separately, with the *merchandise* trade balance distinguished from the *services* trade balance. As Table 19.2 shows, the United States had a merchandise (goods) trade deficit of $821 billion in 2008 and a *services* trade *surplus* of $139 billion, leaving the overall trade balance in the red.

When the United States has a trade deficit with the rest of the world, other countries must have an offsetting **trade surplus.** On a global scale, imports must equal exports, since every good exported by one country must be imported by another. Hence, *any imbalance in America's trade must be offset by reverse imbalances elsewhere.*

Whatever the overall balance in our trade accounts, bilateral balances vary greatly. Table 19.3 shows, for example, that our 2008 aggregate trade deficit ($682 billion) incorporated huge bilateral trade deficits with Japan and China. In the same year, however, we had trade surpluses with the Netherlands, Belgium, Australia, Hong Kong, and the United Arab Emirates.

trade deficit: The amount by which the value of imports exceeds the value of exports in a given time period.

trade surplus: The amount by which the value of exports exceeds the value of imports in a given time period.

MOTIVATION TO TRADE

Many people wonder why we trade so much, particularly since (1) we import many of the things we also export (like computers, airplanes, clothes), (2) we *could* produce many of the other things we import, and (3) we worry so much about trade imbalances. Why not just import those few things that we can't produce ourselves, and export just enough to balance that trade?

Country	Exports to ($ billions)	Imports from ($ billions)	Trade Balance ($ billions)
Top Deficit Countries			
China	$71	$337	−$266
Canada	261	336	−75
Japan	67	139	−72
Mexico	152	216	−64
Germany	55	98	−43
Top Surplus Countries			
Netherlands	40	21	+19
Hong Kong	22	6	+16
United Arab Emirates	15	1	+14
Belgium	29	17	+12
Australia	22	11	+11

Source: U.S. Department of Commerce, International Trade Administration.

TABLE 19.3
Bilateral Trade Balances

The U.S. trade deficit is the net result of bilateral deficits and surpluses. We had huge trade deficits with Japan and China in 2008, for example, but small trade surpluses with the Netherlands, Belgium, Australia, and Hong Kong. International trade is *multi*national, with surpluses in some countries being offset by trade deficits elsewhere.

Specialization

Although it might seem strange to be importing goods we could produce ourselves, such trade is entirely rational. Our decision to trade with other countries arises from the same considerations that motivate individuals to specialize in production: satisfying their remaining needs in the marketplace. Why don't you become self-sufficient, growing all your own food, building your own shelter, recording your own songs? Presumably because you've found that you can enjoy a much higher standard of living (and better music) by working at just one job and then buying other goods in the marketplace. When you do so, you're no longer self-sufficient. Instead, you are *specializing* in production, relying on others to produce the array of goods and services you want. When countries trade goods and services, they are doing the same thing—*specializing* in production, and then *trading* for other desired goods. Why do they do this? Because **specialization increases total output.**

To see how nations benefit from trade, we'll examine the production possibilities of two countries. We want to demonstrate that two countries that trade can together produce more output than they could in the absence of trade. If they can, **the gain from trade is increased world output and a higher standard of living in all trading countries.** This is the essential message of the *theory of comparative advantage.*

Production and Consumption without Trade

production possibilities: The alternative combinations of final goods and services that could be produced in a given time period with all available resources and technology.

Consider the production and consumption possibilities of just two countries—say, the United States and France. For the sake of illustration, assume that both countries produce only two goods: bread and wine. Let's also set aside worries about the law of diminishing returns and the substitutability of resources, thus transforming the familiar **production possibilities** curve into a straight line, as in Figure 19.1.

The "curves" in Figure 19.1 suggest that the United States is capable of producing much more bread than France. With our greater abundance of labor, land, and other resources, we assume that the United States is capable of producing up to 100 zillion loaves of bread per year. To do so, we'd have to devote all our resources to that purpose. This capability is indicated by point A in Figure 19.1a and in row A of the accompanying production possibilities schedule. France (Figure 19.1b), on the other hand, confronts a *maximum* bread production of only 15 zillion loaves per year (point G) because it has little available land, less fuel, and fewer potential workers.

The capacities of the two countries for wine production are 50 zillion barrels for us (point F) and 60 zillion for France (point L), largely reflecting France's greater experience in tending vines. Both countries are also capable of producing alternative *combinations* of bread and wine, as evidenced by their respective production possibilities curves (points A–F for the United States and G–L for France).

closed economy: A nation that doesn't engage in international trade.

A nation that doesn't trade with other countries is called a **closed economy.** In the absence of contact with the outside world, the production possibilities curve for a closed economy also defines its **consumption possibilities.** Without imports, a country cannot consume more than it produces. Thus, the only immediate issue in a closed economy is which mix of output to choose—*what* to produce and consume—out of the domestic choices available.

consumption possibilities: The alternative combinations of goods and services that a country could consume in a given time period.

Assume that Americans choose point D on their production possibilities curve, producing and consuming 40 zillion loaves of bread and 30 zillion barrels of wine. The French, on the other hand, prefer the mix of output represented by point I on their production possibilities curve. At that point they produce and consume 9 zillion loaves of bread and 24 zillion barrels of wine.

To assess the potential gain from trade, we must focus the *combined* output of the United States and France. In this case, total world output (points D and I) comes to 49 zillion loaves of bread and 54 zillion barrels of wine. What we want to know is whether world output would increase if France and the United States abandoned their isolation and started trading. Could either country, or both, consume more output by engaging in a little trade?

Production and Consumption with Trade

Because both countries are saddled with limited production possibilities, trying to eke out a little extra wine and bread from this situation might not appear very promising. Such a conclusion is unwarranted, however. Take another look at the production possibilities

In a closed economy, production possibilities and consumption possibilities are identical.

U.S. Production Possibilities		
Bread (zillions of loaves)	**+**	**Wine** (zillions of barrels)
A	100	+	0
B	80	+	10
C	60	+	20
D	40	+	30
E	20	+	40
F	0	+	50

French Production Possibilities		
Bread (zillions of loaves)	**+**	**Wine** (zillions of barrels)
G	15	+	0
H	12	+	12
I	9	+	24
J	6	+	36
K	3	+	48
L	0	+	60

FIGURE 19.1
Consumption Possibilities without Trade

In the absence of trade, a country's consumption possibilities are identical to its production possibilities. The assumed production possibilities of the United States and France are illustrated in the graphs and the corresponding schedules. Before entering into trade, the United States chose to produce and consume at point *D*, with 40 zillion loaves of bread and 30 zillion barrels of wine. France chose point *I* on its own production possibilities curve. By trading, each country hopes to increase its consumption beyond these levels.

confronting the United States, as reproduced in Figure 19.2. Suppose the United States were to produce at point *C* rather than point *D*. At point *C* we could produce 60 zillion loaves of bread and 20 zillion barrels of wine. That combination is clearly *possible,* since it lies on the production possibilities curve. We didn't choose that point earlier because we assumed the mix of output at point *D* was preferable. The mix of output at point *C* could be produced, however.

We could also change the mix of output in France. Assume that France moved from point *I* to point *K*, producing 48 zillion barrels of wine and only 3 zillion loaves of bread.

Two observations are now called for. The first is simply that output mixes have changed in each country. The second, and more interesting, is that total world output has increased. Notice how this works. When the United States and France were at points *D* and *I*, their *combined* output consisted of

	Bread (zillions of loaves)	Wine (zillions of barrels)
United States (at point *D*)	40	30
France (at point *I*)	9	24
Total pretrade output	49	54

After they moved along their respective production possibilities curves to points *C* and *K*, the combined world output became

	Bread (zillions of loaves)	Wine (zillions of barrels)
United States (at point *C*)	60	20
France (at point *K*)	3	48
Total output with trade	63	68

Total world output has increased by 14 zillion loaves of bread and 14 zillion barrels of wine. ***Just by changing the mix of output in each country, we've increased total world output.*** This additional output creates the potential for making both countries better off than they were in the absence of trade.

The United States and France weren't producing at points *C* and *K* before because they simply didn't want to *consume* those particular output combinations. Nevertheless, our discovery that points *C* and *K* allow us to produce *more* output suggests that everybody can consume more goods and services if we change the mix of output in each country. This is our first clue as to how specialization and trade can benefit an **open economy**—a nation that engages in international trade.

open economy: A nation that engages in international trade.

Suppose we Americans are the first to discover the potential benefits from trade. Using Figure 19.2 as our guide, we suggest to the French that they move their mix of output from point I to point K. As an incentive for making such a move, we promise to give them 6 zillion loaves of bread in exchange for 20 zillion barrels of wine. This would leave them at point M, with as much bread to consume as they used to have, plus an extra 4 zillion barrels of wine. At point I they had 9 zillion loaves of bread and 24 zillion barrels of wine. At point M they can have 9 zillion loaves of bread and 28 zillion barrels of wine. Thus, by altering their mix of output (from point I to point K) and then trading (point K to point M), the French end up with more goods and services than they had in the beginning. Notice in particular that this new consumption possibility (point M) lies *outside* France's domestic production possibilities curve.

The French will be quite pleased with the extra output they get from trading. But where does this leave us? Does France's gain imply a loss for us? Or do we gain from trade as well?

As it turns out, *both* the United States and France gain by trading. The United States, too, ends up consuming a mix of output that lies outside our production possibilities curve.

Mutual Gains

Note that at point C we produce 60 zillion loaves of bread per year and 20 zillion barrels of wine. We then export 6 zillion loaves to France. This leaves us with 54 zillion loaves of bread to consume.

In return for our exported bread, the French give us 20 zillion barrels of wine. These imports, plus our domestic production, permit us to *consume* 40 zillion barrels of wine. Hence, we end up consuming at point N, enjoying 54 zillion loaves of bread and 40 zillion barrels of wine. Thus, by first changing our mix of output (from point D to point C), then trading (point C to point N), we end up with 14 zillion more loaves of bread and 10 zillion more barrels of wine than we started with. International trade has made us better off, too.

Table 19.4 recaps the gains from trade for both countries. Notice that U.S. imports match French exports and vice versa. Also notice how the trade-facilitated consumption in each country exceeds no-trade levels.

There's no sleight of hand going on here; the gains from trade are due to specialization in production. When each country goes it alone, it's a prisoner of its own production possibilities curve; it must make production decisions on the basis of its own consumption desires. When international trade is permitted, however, each country can concentrate on the exploitation of its production capabilities. ***Each country produces those goods it makes best and then trades with other countries to acquire the goods it desires to consume.***

	Production and Consumption with Trade					Production and Consumption with No Trade
	Production	+ Imports	− Exports	= Consumption		
United States at . . .	Point C				Point N	Point D
Bread	60	+ 0	− 6	=	54	40
Wine	20	+ 20	− 0	=	40	30
France at . . .	Point K				Point M	Point I
Bread	3	+ 6	− 0	=	9	9
Wine	48	+ 0	− 20	=	28	24

TABLE 19.4
Gains from Trade

When nations specialize in production, they can export one good and import another and end up with *more* total goods to consume than they had without trade. In this case, the United States special-izes in bread production. Notice how U.S. *consumption* of both goods increases (compare point D and point N totals).

The resultant specialization increases total world output. In the process, each country is able to escape the confines of its own production possibilities curve, to reach beyond it for a larger basket of consumption goods. ***When a country engages in international trade, its consumption possibilities always exceed its production possibilities.*** These enhanced consumption possibilities are emphasized by the positions of points *N* and *M* outside the production possibilities curves (Figure 19.2). If it weren't possible for countries to increase their consumption by trading, there'd be no incentive for trading, and thus no trade.

PURSUIT OF COMPARATIVE ADVANTAGE

Although international trade can make everyone better off, it's not so obvious which goods should be traded, or on what terms. In our previous illustration, the United States ended up trading bread for wine in terms that were decidedly favorable to us. Why did we export bread rather than wine, and how did we end up getting such a good deal?

Opportunity Costs

> **comparative advantage:** The ability of a country to produce a specific good at a lower opportunity cost than its trading partners.
>
> • Doing what you do best

> **opportunity cost:** The most desired goods or services that are forgone in order to obtain something else.

The decision to export bread is based on **comparative advantage,** that is, the *relative* cost of producing different goods. Recall that we can produce a maximum of 100 zillion loaves of bread per year or 50 zillion barrels of wine. Thus, the domestic **opportunity cost** of producing 100 zillion loaves of bread is the 50 zillion barrels of wine we forsake in order to devote our resources to bread production. In fact, at every point on the U.S. production possibilities curve (Figure 19.2a), the opportunity cost of a loaf of bread is ½ barrel of wine. We're effectively paying half a barrel of wine to get a loaf of bread.

Although the cost of bread production in the United States might appear outrageous, even higher opportunity costs prevail in France. According to Figure 19.2b, the opportunity cost of producing a loaf of bread in France is a staggering 4 barrels of wine. To produce a loaf of bread, the French must use factors of production that could otherwise be used to produce 4 barrels of wine.

Comparative Advantage. A comparison of the opportunity costs prevailing in each country exposes the nature of comparative advantage. The United States has a comparative advantage in bread production because less wine has to be given up to produce bread in the United States than in France. In other words, the opportunity costs of bread production are lower in the United States than in France. ***Comparative advantage refers to the relative (opportunity) costs of producing particular goods.***

A country should specialize in what it's *relatively* efficient at producing, that is, goods for which it has the lowest opportunity costs. In this case, the United States should produce bread because its opportunity cost (½ barrel of wine) is less than France's (4 barrels of wine). Were you the production manager for the whole world, you'd certainly want each country to exploit its relative abilities, thus maximizing world output. Each country can arrive at that same decision itself by comparing its own opportunity costs to those prevailing elsewhere. ***World output, and thus the potential gains from trade, will be maximized when each country pursues its comparative advantage.*** Each country does so by exporting goods that entail relatively low domestic opportunity costs and importing goods that involve relatively high domestic opportunity costs. That's the kind of situation depicted in Table 19.4.

Absolute Costs Don't Count

> **absolute advantage:** The ability of a country to produce a specific good with fewer resources (per unit of output) than other countries.

• doing something better than everyone else.

In assessing the nature of comparative advantage, notice that we needn't know anything about the actual costs involved in production. Have you seen any data suggesting how much labor, land, or capital is required to produce a loaf of bread in either France or the United States? For all you and I know, the French may be able to produce both a loaf of bread and a barrel of wine with fewer resources than we're using. Such an **absolute advantage** in production might exist because of their much longer experience in cultivating both grapes and wheat or simply because they have more talent.

We can envy such productivity, and even try to emulate it, but it shouldn't alter our production or trade decisions. All we really care about are *opportunity costs*—what *we* have to give up in order to get more of a desired good. If we can get a barrel of wine for less bread in trade than in production, we have a comparative advantage in producing bread. As long as we have a *comparative* advantage in bread production we should exploit it. It doesn't matter to us whether France could produce either good with fewer resources. For that matter, even if France had an absolute advantage in *both* goods, we'd still have a *comparative* advantage in bread production, as we've already confirmed. The absolute costs of production were omitted from the previous illustration because they were irrelevant.

To clarify the distinction between absolute advantage and comparative advantage, consider this example. When Charlie Osgood joined the Willamette Warriors football team, he was the fastest runner ever to play football in Willamette. He could also throw the ball farther than most people could see. In other words, he had an *absolute advantage* in both throwing and running. Charlie would have made the greatest quarterback or the greatest end ever to play football. *Would have.* The problem was that he could play only one position at a time. Thus, the Willamette coach had to play Charlie either as a quarterback or as an end. He reasoned that Charlie could throw only a bit farther than some of the other top quarterbacks but could far outdistance all the other ends. In other words, Charlie had a *comparative advantage* in running and was assigned to play as an end.

TERMS OF TRADE

It definitely pays to pursue one's comparative advantage by specializing in production. It may not yet be clear, however, how we got such a good deal with France. We're clever traders but, beyond that, is there any way to determine the **terms of trade,** the quantity of good A that must be given up in exchange for good B? In our previous illustration, the terms of trade were very favorable to us; we exchanged only 6 zillion loaves of bread for 20 zillion barrels of wine (Table 19.4). The terms of trade were thus 6 loaves = 20 barrels.

The terms of trade with France were determined by our offer and France's ready acceptance. But why did France accept those terms? France was willing to accept our offer because the terms of trade permitted France to increase its wine consumption without giving up any bread consumption. Our offer of 6 loaves for 20 barrels was an improvement over France's domestic opportunity costs. France's domestic possibilities required it to give up 24 barrels of wine in order to produce 6 loaves of bread (see Figure 19.2*b*). Getting bread via trade was simply cheaper for France than producing bread at home. France ended up with an extra 4 zillion barrels of wine (take another look at the last two columns in Table 19.4).

Our first clue to the terms of trade, then, lies in each country's domestic opportunity costs. ***A country won't trade unless the terms of trade are superior to domestic opportunities.*** In our example, the opportunity cost of 1 barrel of wine in the United States is 2 loaves of bread. Accordingly, we won't *export* bread unless we get at least 1 barrel of wine in exchange for every 2 loaves of bread we ship overseas.

All countries want to gain from trade. Hence, we can predict that ***the terms of trade between any two countries will lie somewhere between their respective opportunity costs in production.*** That is, a loaf of bread in international trade will be worth at least ½ barrel of wine (the U.S. opportunity cost) but no more than 4 barrels (the French opportunity cost). In our example, the terms of trade ended up at 1 loaf = 3.33 barrels (that is, at 6 loaves = 20 barrels). This represented a very large gain for the United States and a small gain for France. Figure 19.3 illustrates this outcome and several other possibilities.

Relatively little trade is subject to such direct negotiations between countries. More often than not, the decision to import or export a particular good is left up to the market decisions of individual consumers and producers.

Individual consumers and producers aren't much impressed by such abstractions as comparative advantage. Market participants tend to focus on prices, always trying to allocate their resources in order to maximize profits or personal satisfaction. Consumers tend to buy the products that deliver the most utility per dollar of expenditure, while producers try to get the most output per dollar of cost. Everybody's looking for a bargain.

So what does this have to do with international trade? Well, suppose that Henri, an enterprising Frenchman, visited the United States before the advent of international trade. He observed that bread was relatively cheap while wine was relatively expensive—the

terms of trade: The rate at which goods are exchanged; the amount of good A given up for good B in trade.

Limits to the Terms of Trade

The Role of Markets and Prices

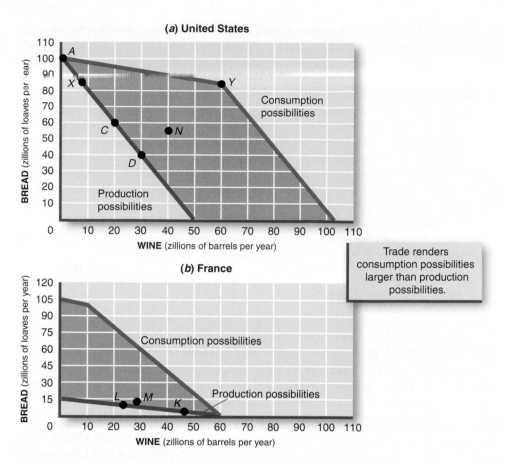

Trade renders consumption possibilities larger than production possibilities.

FIGURE 19.3

Searching for the Terms of Trade

Assume the United States can produce 100 zillion loaves of bread per year (point *A*). If we reduce output to only 85 zillion loaves, we could move to point *X*. At point *X* we have 7.5 zillion barrels of wine and 85 zillion loaves of bread.

Trade increases consumption possibilities. If we continued to produce 100 zillion loaves of bread, we could trade 15 zillion loaves to France in exchange for as much as 60 zillion barrels of wine. This would leave us *producing* at point *A* but *consuming* at point *Y*. At point *Y* we have more wine and no less bread than we had at point *X*.

A country will end up on its consumption possibilities curve only if it gets *all* the gains from trade. It will remain on its production possibilities curve only if it gets *none* of the gains from trade. The terms of trade determine how the gains from trade are distributed, and thus at what point in the shaded area each country ends up.

Note: The kink in the consumption possibilities curve at point *Y* occurs because France is unable to produce more than 60 zillion barrels of wine.

---

opposite of the price relationship prevailing in France. These price comparisons brought to his mind the opportunity for making a fast euro. All he had to do was bring over some French wine and trade it in the United States for a large quantity of bread. Then he could return to France and exchange the bread for a greater quantity of wine. *Alors!* Were he to do this a few times, he'd amass substantial profits.

Henri's entrepreneurial exploits will not only enrich him but will also move each country toward its comparative advantage. The United States ends up exporting bread to France, and France ends up exporting wine to the United States, exactly as the theory of comparative advantage suggests. The activating agent isn't the Ministry of Trade and its 620 trained economists but simply one enterprising French trader. He's aided and encouraged, of course, by consumers and producers in each country. American consumers are happy to trade their bread for his wines. They thereby end up paying less for wine (in terms of bread) than they'd otherwise have to. In other words, the terms of trade Henri offers are more attractive than the prevailing (domestic) relative prices. On the other side of the Atlantic, Henri's welcome is equally warm. French consumers are able to get a better deal by trading their wine for his imported bread than by trading with the local bakers.

Even some producers are happy. The wheat farmers and bakers in the United States are eager to deal with Henri. He's willing to buy a lot of bread and even to pay a premium price for it. Indeed, bread production has become so profitable in the United States that a lot of people who used to grow and mash grapes are now growing wheat and kneading dough. This alters the mix of U.S. output in the direction of more bread, exactly as suggested in Figure 19.2a.

In France, the opposite kind of production shift is taking place. French wheat farmers are planting more grape vines so they can take advantage of Henri's generous purchases. Thus, Henri is able to lead each country in the direction of its comparative advantage while raking in a substantial profit for himself along the way.

Where the terms of trade and the volume of exports and imports end up depends partly on how good a trader Henri is. It will also depend on the behavior of the thousands of individual consumers and producers who participate in the market exchanges. In other words, trade flows depend on both the supply and the demand for bread and wine in each country. ***The terms of trade, like the price of any good, depend on the willingness of market participants to buy or sell at various prices.*** All we know for sure is that the terms of trade will end up somewhere between the limits set by each country's opportunity costs.

PROTECTIONIST PRESSURES

Although the potential gains from world trade are impressive, not everyone will smile at the Franco-American trade celebration. On the contrary, some people will be upset about the trade routes that Henri has established. They'll not only boycott the celebration but actively seek to discourage us from continuing to trade with France.

Consider, for example, the winegrowers in western New York. Do you think they're going to be happy about Henri's entrepreneurship? Americans can now buy wine more cheaply from France than they can from New York. Before long we may hear talk about unfair foreign competition or about the greater nutritional value of American grapes (see News on the next page). The New York winegrowers may also emphasize the importance of maintaining an adequate grape supply and a strong wine industry at home, just in case of terrorist attacks.

Microeconomic Pressures

Import-Competing Industries. Joining with the growers will be the farm workers and the other producers and merchants whose livelihood depends on the New York wine industry. If they're clever enough, the growers will also get the governor of the state to join their demonstration. After all, the governor must recognize the needs of his people, and his people definitely don't include the wheat farmers in Kansas who are making a bundle from international trade. New York consumers are of course benefiting from lower wine prices, but they're unlikely to demonstrate over a few cents a bottle. On the other hand, those few extra pennies translate into millions of dollars for domestic wine producers.

The wheat farmers in France are no happier about international trade than are the winegrowers in the United States. They'd dearly love to sink all those boats bringing wheat from America, thereby protecting their own market position.

If we're to make sense of trade policies, then, we must recognize one central fact of life: Some producers have a vested interest in restricting international trade. In particular, ***workers and producers who compete with imported products—who work in import-competing industries— have an economic interest in restricting trade.*** This helps explain why GM, Ford, and Chrysler are unhappy about auto imports and why workers in Massachusetts want to end the importation of Italian shoes. It also explains why textile producers in South Carolina think China is behaving irresponsibly when it sells cotton shirts and dresses in the United States.

IN THE NEWS

California Grape Growers Protest Mixing Foreign Wine

California wine grape growers are growing increasingly frustrated and angry at each market percentage point gain of foreign wine in the U.S. wine market.

By the end of the year, burgeoning wine imports are expected to account for 30 percent of the U.S. market.

As the overall wine market in the U.S. grows at a healthy 2 percent to 5 percent annual clip, California grape growers continue to rip out vineyards. More than 100,000 acres in the Central Valley have been destroyed in the past five years. Growers are beyond weary of prices offered less than production costs. . . .

Rubbing salt into the open economic sore this season includes record bulk, inexpensive wine imports that are being blended with California wines and sold by California wineries as "American" appellation wine. . . .

"California grape growers made a significant investment in wine grape vineyards on the signals from wineries that there was a bright future in California wine." Those same growers are seeing at least some of that bright future being taken by imports.

—Harry Cline

Source: *Western Farm Press,* December 6, 2006. Reprinted with permission by Penton Media, Inc.

Analysis: Although trade increases consumption possibilities, imports typically compete with a domestic industry. The affected industries will try to restrict imports in order to preserve their own jobs and incomes.

Export Industries. Although imports typically mean fewer jobs and less income for some domestic industries, exports represent increased jobs and income for other industries. Producers and workers in export industries gain from trade. Thus, on a microeconomic level there are identifiable gainers and losers from international trade. *Trade not only alters the mix of output but also redistributes income from import-competing industries to export industries.* This potential redistribution is the source of political and economic friction.

Net Gain. We must be careful to note, however, that the microeconomic gains from trade are greater than the microeconomic losses. It's not simply a question of robbing Peter to enrich Paul. We must remind ourselves that consumers in general enjoy a higher standard of living as a result of international trade. As we saw earlier, trade increases world efficiency and total output. Accordingly, we end up slicing up a larger pie rather than just re-slicing the same old smaller pie.

The gains from trade will mean nothing to workers who end up with a smaller slice of the (larger) pie. It's important to remember, however, that the gains from trade are large enough to make everybody better off. Whether we actually choose to distribute the gains from trade in this way is a separate question, to which we shall return shortly. Note here, however, that *trade restrictions designed to protect specific microeconomic interests reduce the total gains from trade.* Trade restrictions leave us with a smaller pie to split up.

Additional Pressures

Import-competing industries are the principal obstacle to expanded international trade. Selfish micro interests aren't the only source of trade restrictions, however. Other arguments are also used to restrict trade.

National Security. The national security argument for trade restrictions is twofold. We can't depend on foreign suppliers to provide us with essential defense-related goods, it is said, because that would leave us vulnerable in time of war. The machine tool industry used this argument to protect itself from imports. In 1991, the Pentagon again sided with the toolmakers, citing the need for the United States to "gear up military production quickly in case of war," a contingency that couldn't be assured if weapons manufacturers relied on imported lathes, milling machines, and other tools. After the September 11, 2001, terrorist attacks on the World Trade Center and Pentagon, U.S. farmers convinced Congress to safeguard the nation's food supply with additional subsidies. The steel industry emphasized the importance of not depending on foreign suppliers.

Dumping. Another argument against free trade arises from the practice of **dumping.** Foreign producers "dump" their goods when they sell them in the United States at prices lower than those prevailing in their own country, perhaps even below the costs of production.

Dumping may be unfair to import-competing producers, but it isn't necessarily unwelcome to the rest of us. As long as foreign producers continue dumping, we're getting foreign products at low prices. How bad can that be? There's a legitimate worry, however. Foreign producers might hold prices down only until domestic producers are driven out of business. Then we might be compelled to pay the foreign producers higher prices for their products. In that case, dumping could consolidate market power and lead to monopoly-type pricing. The fear of dumping, then, is analogous to the fear of predatory pricing.

The potential costs of dumping are serious. It's not always easy to determine when dumping occurs, however. Those who compete with imports have an uncanny ability to associate any and all low prices with predatory dumping. The United States has used dumping *charges* to restrict imports of Chinese shrimp, furniture, lingerie, and other products in which China has an evident comparative advantage. The Chinese have retaliated with dozens of their own dumping investigations, including the fiber-optic cable case. As the accompanying World View explains, such actions slow imports and protect domestic producers.

Infant Industries. Actual dumping threatens to damage already established domestic industries. Even normal import prices, however, may make it difficult or impossible for a new domestic industry to develop. Infant industries are often burdened with abnormally high

> **dumping:** The sale of goods in export markets at prices below domestic prices.

WORLD VIEW

China Accuses Corning of "Dumping"

Corning Inc., the big U.S. fiber-optic and glass maker, said the Chinese government has charged it with selling optical-fiber products in China at an unfairly low price that damaged Chinese producers, a practice known as dumping.

Corning denied the charge, which followed a nearly yearlong investigation by China's Ministry of Commerce after two Chinese companies alleged that optical-fiber imports were priced below what market conditions justified. . . .

Since it joined the WTO, China has brought about 25 dumping cases against foreign companies, according to a King & Spalding estimate. In that same period, U.S. companies have brought 24 dumping cases against China, according to the International Trade Commission. . . .

Recent U.S. trade actions against China, most notably an antidumping case launched in October against $1 billion worth of Chinese wood and bedroom furniture imports, have likely played a role, too, according to trade experts.

The high-profile U.S. furniture case against China and China's charge against fiber makers such as Corning also exemplify the chief economic concerns in each economy: The U.S. is preoccupied with protecting workers in its hard-hit manufacturing sector, while China is interested in nurturing its technology industry. . . .

With the filing of the Chinese charges, Corning customers in China will have to pay a 16% deposit on the purchase price of the company's products, starting immediately. That money will be held in an escrow account until the matter is resolved.

Source: *The Wall Street Journal,* June 17, 2004. Copyright 2004 by Dow Jones & Company, Inc. Reproduced with permission of Dow Jones & Company, Inc. in the format Textbook via Copyright Clearance Center.

Analysis: *Dumping* means that a foreign producer is selling exports at prices below cost or below prices in the home market, putting import-competing industries at a competitive disadvantage. *Accusations* of dumping are an effective trade barrier.

start-up costs. These high costs may arise from the need to train a whole workforce and the expenses of establishing new marketing channels. With time to grow, however, an infant industry might experience substantial cost reductions and establish a comparative advantage. When this is the case, trade restrictions might help nurture an industry in its infancy. Trade restrictions are justified, however, only if there's tangible evidence that the industry can develop a comparative advantage reasonably quickly.

Improving the Terms of Trade. A final argument for restricting trade rests on how the gains from trade are distributed. As we observed, the distribution of the gains from trade depends on the terms of trade. If we were to buy fewer imports, foreign producers might lower their prices. If that happened, the terms of trade would move in our favor, and we'd end up with a larger share of the gains from trade.

One way to bring about this sequence of events is to put restrictions on imports, making it more difficult or expensive for Americans to buy foreign products. Such restrictions will reduce the volume of imports, thereby inducing foreign producers to lower their prices. Unfortunately, this strategy can easily backfire: Retaliatory restrictions on imports, each designed to improve the terms of trade, will ultimately eliminate all trade and therewith all the gains people were competing for in the first place.

BARRIERS TO TRADE

The microeconomic losses associated with imports give rise to a constant clamor for trade restrictions. People whose jobs and incomes are threatened by international trade tend to organize quickly and air their grievances. The World View below depicts the efforts of farmers in the Czech Republic to limit imports of Austrian pork in 2007. They hope to convince their government to impose restrictions on imports. More often than not, governments grant the wishes of these well-organized and well-financed special interests.

WORLD VIEW

Meat Imports "Threaten" Farmers

Around 200 Czech farmers held a protest action March 26 on the Czech-Austrian border crossing in Dolní Dvořiště, South Bohemia, against meat imports. The protest was to draw attention to the situation of Czech pig breeders who claim they are threatened by growing pork imports to Czech retail chains and low purchasing prices.

Representatives of the Agricultural Chamber (AK) said it was a token protest, but didn't rule out further actions.

"We will . . . send an appeal to the Ministry of Agriculture, the Chamber of Deputies and the Senate, asking them for public support of Czech farmers and Czech food," said Jan Veleba, president of the AK. . . .

Minister of Agriculture Petr Gandalovič said blockades won't resolve the situation and would probably only worsen relations between the Czech Republic and Austria.

Source: *Czech Business Weekly*, April 2, 2007. Used with permission.

Analysis: Import-competing industries cite lots of reasons for restricting trade. Their primary concern, however, is to protect their own jobs and profits.

Embargoes

embargo: A prohibition on exports or imports.

The surefire way to restrict trade is simply to eliminate it. To do so, a country need only impose an embargo on exports or imports, or both. An **embargo** is nothing more than a prohibition against trading particular goods.

In 1951, Senator Joseph McCarthy convinced the U.S. Senate to impose an embargo on Soviet mink, fox, and five other furs. He argued that such imports helped finance world communism. Senator McCarthy also represented the state of Wisconsin, where most U.S. minks are raised. The Reagan administration tried to end the fur embargo in 1987 but met with stiff congressional opposition. By then, U.S. mink ranchers had developed a $120 million per year industry.

The United States has also maintained an embargo on Cuban goods since 1959, when Fidel Castro took power there. This embargo severely damaged Cuba's sugar industry and deprived American smokers of the famed Havana cigars. It also fostered the development of U.S. sugar beet and tobacco farmers, who now have a vested interest in maintaining the embargo.

A more frequent trade restriction is a **tariff,** a special tax imposed on imported goods. Tariffs, also called *customs duties,* were once the principal source of revenue for governments. In the eighteenth century, tariffs on tea, glass, wine, lead, and paper were imposed on the American colonies to provide extra revenue for the British government. The tariff on tea led to the Boston Tea Party in 1773 and gave added momentum to the American independence movement. In modern times, tariffs have been used primarily as a means to protect specific industries from import competition. The current U.S. tariff code specifies tariffs on over 9,000 different products—nearly 50 percent of all U.S. imports. Although the average tariff is less than 5 percent, individual tariffs vary widely. The tariff on cars, for example, is only 2.5 percent, while cotton sweaters confront a 17.8 percent tariff.

The attraction of tariffs to import-competing industries should be obvious. *A tariff on imported goods makes them more expensive to domestic consumers and thus less competitive with domestically produced goods.* Among familiar tariffs in effect in 2009 were 50 cents per gallon on Scotch whiskey and 76 cents per gallon on imported champagne. These tariffs made American-produced spirits look relatively cheap and thus contributed to higher sales and profits for domestic distillers and grape growers. In the same manner, imported baby food is taxed at 34.6 percent, maple sugar at 9.4 percent, golf shoes at 8.5 percent, and imported sailboats at 1.5 percent. In each case, domestic producers in import-competing industries gain. The losers are domestic consumers, who end up paying higher prices. The tariff on orange juice, for example, raises the price of drinking orange juice by $525 million a year. Tariffs also hurt foreign producers, who lose business, and world efficiency, as trade is reduced.

"Beggar Thy Neighbor." Microeconomic interests aren't the only source of pressure for tariff protection. Imports represent leakage from the domestic circular flow and a potential loss of jobs at home. From this perspective, the curtailment of imports looks like an easy solution to the problem of domestic unemployment. Just get people to "buy American" instead of buying imported products, so the argument goes, and domestic output and employment will surely expand. President Obama used this argument to include "buy American" rules in his 2009 stimulus package.

Congressman Willis Hawley used this same argument in 1930. He assured his colleagues that higher tariffs would "bring about the growth and development in this country that has followed every other tariff bill, bringing as it does a new prosperity in which all people, in all sections, will increase their comforts, their enjoyment, and their happiness."[1] Congress responded by passing the Smoot-Hawley Tariff Act of 1930, which raised tariffs to an average of nearly 60 percent, effectively cutting off most imports.

Tariffs designed to expand domestic employment are more likely to fail than to succeed. If a tariff wall does stem the flow of imports, it effectively transfers the unemployment problem to other countries, a phenomenon often referred to as "beggar thy neighbor." The resultant loss of business in other countries leaves them less able to purchase our exports. The imported unemployment also creates intense political pressures for retaliatory action. That's exactly what happened in the 1930s. Other countries erected trade barriers to compensate for the effects of the Smoot-Hawley tariff. World trade subsequently fell from $60 billion in 1928 to a mere $25 billion in 1938. This trade contraction increased the severity of the Great Depression (see World View on next page).

Tariffs

> **tariff:** A tax (duty) imposed on imported goods.

---

[1] *The New York Times,* June 15, 1930, p. 25.

WORLD VIEW

"Beggar-Thy-Neighbor" Policies in the 1930s

President Herbert Hoover, ignoring the pleas of 1,028 economists to veto it, signed the Smoot-Hawley Tariff Act on June 17, 1930. It was a hollow celebration. The day before, anticipating the signing, the stock market suffered its worst collapse since November 1929, and the law quickly helped push the Great Depression deeper.

The new tariffs, which by 1932 rose to an all-time high of 59 percent of the average value of imports (today it's 5 percent), were designed to save American jobs by restricting foreign competition. Economists warned that angry nations would retaliate, and they did.

- Spain passed the Wais tariff in July in reaction to U.S. tariffs on grapes, oranges, cork, and onions.
- Switzerland, objecting to new U.S. tariffs on watches, embroideries, and shoes, boycotted American exports.
- Italy retaliated against tariffs on hats and olive oil with high tariffs on U.S. and French automobiles in June 1930.
- Canada reacted to high duties on many food products, logs, and timber by raising tariffs threefold in August 1932.
- Australia, Cuba, France, Mexico, and New Zealand also joined in the tariff wars.

From 1930 to 1931 U.S. imports dropped 29 percent, but U.S. exports fell even more, 33 percent, and continued their collapse to a modern-day low of $2.4 billion in 1933. World trade contracted by similar proportions, spreading unemployment around the globe.

In 1934 the U.S. Congress passed the Reciprocal Trade Agreements Act to empower the president to reduce tariffs by half the 1930 rates in return for like cuts in foreign duties on U.S. goods. The "beggar-thy-neighbor" policy was dead. Since then, the nations of the world have been reducing tariffs and other trade barriers.

Source: World Bank, *World Development Report 1987.* **www.worldbank.org;** and *The Wall Street Journal,* April 28, 1989. Copyright 1989 by Dow Jones & Company, Inc. Reproduced with permission of Dow Jones & Company, Inc. in the format Textbook via Copyright Clearance Center.

Analysis: Tariffs inflict harm on foreign producers. If foreign countries retaliate with tariffs of their own, world trade will shrink and unemployment will increase in all countries.

web analysis

The tariff schedule for imported products is available online from the U.S. International Trade Commission. Go to **www.usitc.gov** and click on "Publications" and then "Official Harmonized Tariff Schedule."

The same kind of macroeconomic threat surfaced in 2009. The "buy American" provisions introduced by the Obama administration angered foreign nations that would lose export sales. When they threatened to retaliate with trade barriers of their own, President Obama had to offer reassurances about America's commitment to "free trade." In the interim, of course, President Obama gained crucial political support for his stimulus proposals from important domestic unions, industries, and regions.

Quotas

quota: A limit on the quantity of a good that may be imported in a given time period.

Tariffs reduce the flow of imports by raising import prices. The same outcome can be attained more directly by imposing import **quotas,** numerical restrictions on the quantity of a particular good that may be imported. The United States limits the quantity of ice cream imported from Jamaica to 950 gallons a year. Only 1.4 million kilograms of Australian cheddar cheese and no more than 7,730 tons of Haitian sugar can be imported. Textile quotas are imposed on every country that wants to ship textiles to the U.S. market. According to the U.S. Department of State, approximately 12 percent of our imports are subject to import quotas.

Comparative Effects

Quotas, like all barriers to trade, reduce world efficiency and invite retaliatory action. Moreover, their impact can be even more damaging than tariffs. To see this, we may compare market outcomes in four different contexts: no trade, free trade, tariff-restricted trade, and quota-restricted trade.

No-Trade Equilibrium. Figure 19.4*a* depicts the supply-and-demand relationships that would prevail in an economy that imposed a trade *embargo* on foreign textiles. In this situation,

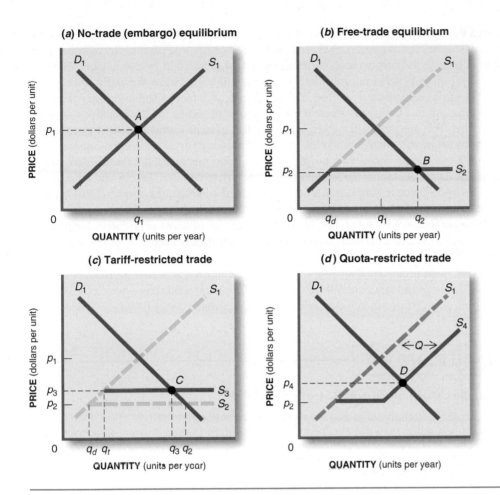

(a) No-trade (embargo) equilibrium

(b) Free-trade equilibrium

(c) Tariff-restricted trade

(d) Quota-restricted trade

FIGURE 19.4

The Impact of Trade Restrictions

In the *absence of trade,* the domestic price and sales of a good will be determined by domestic supply and demand curves (point *A* in part *a*). Once trade is permitted, the market supply curve will be altered by the availability of imports. With *free trade* and unlimited availability of imports at price p_2, a new market equilibrium will be established at world prices (point *B*).

Tariffs raise domestic prices and reduce the quantity sold (point *C*). *Quotas* put an absolute limit on imported sales and thus give domestic producers a great opportunity to raise the market price (point *D*).

---

equilibrium price: The price at which the quantity of a good demanded in a given time period equals the quantity supplied.

the **equilibrium price** of textiles is completely determined by domestic demand and supply curves. The no-trade equilibrium price is p_1, and the quantity of textiles consumed is q_1.

Free-Trade Equilibrium. Suppose now that the embargo is lifted. The immediate effect of this decision will be a rightward shift of the market supply curve, as foreign supplies are added to domestic supplies (Figure 19.4*b*). If an unlimited quantity of textiles can be bought in world markets at a price of p_2, the new supply curve will look like S_2 (infinitely elastic at p_2). The new supply curve (S_2) intersects the old demand curve (D_1) at a new equilibrium price of p_2 and an expanded consumption of q_2. At this new equilibrium, domestic producers are supplying the quantity q_d while foreign producers are supplying the rest ($q_2 - q_d$). Comparing the new equilibrium to the old one, we see that ***free trade results in reduced prices and increased consumption.***

Domestic textile producers are unhappy, of course, with their foreign competition. In the absence of trade, the domestic producers would sell more output (q_1) and get higher prices (p_1). Once trade is opened up, the willingness of foreign producers to sell unlimited quantities of textiles at the price p_2 puts a lid on domestic prices. Domestic producers hate this.

Tariff-Restricted Trade. Figure 19.4*c* illustrates what would happen to prices and sales if the United Textile Producers were successful in persuading the government to impose a tariff. Assume that the tariff raises imported textile prices from p_2 to p_3, making it more difficult for foreign producers to undersell domestic producers. Domestic production expands from q_d to q_1, imports are reduced from $q_2 - q_d$ to $q_3 - q_t$, and the market price of textiles rises. Domestic textile producers are clearly better off. So is the U.S. Treasury, which will collect increased tariff revenues. Unfortunately, domestic consumers are worse off (higher prices), as are foreign producers (reduced sales).

"TELL ME AGAIN HOW THE QUOTAS ON JAPANESE CARS HAVE PROTECTED US"

Analysis: Trade restrictions that protect import-competing industries also raise consumer prices.

Quota-Restricted Trade. Now consider the impact of a textile *quota*. Suppose we eliminate tariffs but decree that imports can't exceed the quantity Q. Because the quantity of imports can never exceed Q, the supply curve is effectively shifted to the right by that amount. The new curve S_4 (Figure 19.4*d*) indicates that no imports will occur below the world price p_2 and above that price the quantity Q will be imported. Thus, the *domestic* demand curve determines subsequent prices. Foreign producers are precluded from selling greater quantities as prices rise further. This outcome is in marked contrast to that of tariff-restricted trade (Figure 19.4*c*), which at least permits foreign producers to respond to rising prices. Accordingly, *quotas are a greater threat to competition than tariffs, because quotas preclude additional imports at any price.* The actual quotas on textile imports raise the prices of shirts, towels, and other textile products by 58 percent. As a result, a $10 shirt ends up costing consumers $15.80. All told, U.S. consumers end up paying an extra $25 billion a year for textile products.

The sugar industry is one of the greatest beneficiaries of quota restrictions. By limiting imports to 15 percent of domestic consumption, sugar quotas keep U.S. prices artificially high (see News below). This costs consumers nearly $2 billion a year in higher prices. Candy and soda producers lose sales and profits. Foreign sugar producers (mainly in poor nations) lose sales and income. Who gains? Domestic sugar producers—who, coincidently, are highly concentrated in key electoral states like Florida.

IN THE NEWS

Some See Bush Sheltering Sugar for Votes

The Bush administration is shielding the sugar industry from competition in a new trade pact with Australia, rather than damage the president's re-election hopes in swing states such as Florida and Michigan, industry groups say. . . .

"It all boils down to electoral politics. It's very raw," says Sarah Thorn, a lobbyist at the Grocery Manufacturers of America. . . .

President Bush edged Al Gore four years ago after the Supreme Court ruled on the vote in Florida, the biggest sugar-producing state. Michigan and Minnesota, home to thousands of sugar beet growers, are considered up for grabs this fall.

The industry is among the largest contributors to both parties. Growers and processors, along with makers of corn-based sweetener, made $25.5 million in political action committee contributions and soft money gifts between 1997 and June 2003, Common Cause says.

The sugar industry is protected by quotas that restrict imports to about 15% of the U.S. market. The government also has a price-support program and offers loans to sugar processors, who can repay in sugar rather than cash if prices fall. . . .

Critics of the program say U.S. growers and processors aren't globally competitive. They say the program hurts sugar users such as candymakers and forces consumers to pay inflated prices. U.S. sugar prices last year were 21.4 cents a pound, nearly three times the world price of 7.5 cents a pound.

—James Cox

Source: USA TODAY. February 11, 2004, 3B. Reprinted with Permission.

Analysis: Import quotas preclude increased foreign competition when domestic prices rise. Protected domestic producers enjoy higher prices and profits while consumers pay higher prices.

Voluntary Restraint Agreements

voluntary restraint agreement (VRA): An agreement to reduce the volume of trade in a specific good; a voluntary quota.

A slight variant of quotas has been used in recent years. Rather than impose quotas on imports, the U.S. government asks foreign producers to "voluntarily" limit their exports. These so-called **voluntary restraint agreements** have been negotiated with producers in Japan, South Korea, Taiwan, China, the European Union, and other countries. Korea, for example, agreed to reduce its annual shoe exports to the United States from 44 million pairs to 33 million pairs. Taiwan reduced its shoe exports from 156 million pairs to 122 million pairs per year. In 2005, China agreed to slow its exports of clothing, limiting its sales growth to 8–17 percent a year. For their part, the Japanese agreed to reduce sales of color TV sets in the United States from 2.8 million to 1.75 million per year. In 2006, Mexico agreed to limit its cement exports to the U.S. to 3 million tons a year.

All these voluntary export restraints, as they're often called, represent an informal type of quota. The only difference is that they're negotiated rather than imposed. But these differences are lost on consumers, who end up paying higher prices for these goods. The voluntary limit on Japanese auto exports to the United States alone cost consumers $15.7 billion in only 4 years.

Tariffs and quotas are the most visible barriers to trade, but they're only the tip of the iceberg. Indeed, the variety of protectionist measures that have been devised is testimony to the ingenuity of the human mind. At the turn of the century, the Germans were committed to a most-favored-nation policy, a policy of extending equal treatment to all trading partners. The Germans, however, wanted to lower the tariff on cattle imports from Denmark without extending the same break to Switzerland. Such a preferential tariff would have violated the most-favored-nation policy. Accordingly, the Germans created a new and higher tariff on "brown and dappled cows reared at a level of at least 300 meters above sea level and passing at least one month in every summer at an altitude of at least 800 meters." The new tariff was, of course, applied equally to all countries. But Danish cows never climb that high, so they weren't burdened with the new tariff.

With the decline in tariffs over the last 20 years, nontariff barriers have increased. The United States uses product standards, licensing restrictions, restrictive procurement practices, and other nontariff barriers to restrict roughly 15 percent of imports. In 1999–2000, the European Union banned imports of U.S. beef, arguing that the use of hormones on U.S. ranches created a health hazard for European consumers. Although both the U.S. government and the World Trade Organization disputed that claim, the ban was a highly effective nontariff trade barrier. The United States responded by slapping 100 percent tariffs on dozens of European products.

Mexican Trucks. One of the more flagrant examples of nontariff barriers is the use of safety regulations to block Mexican trucking companies from using U.S. roads to deliver goods. The resulting trade barrier forces Mexican trucks to unload their cargoes at the U.S. border, and then reload them into U.S. (Teamster-driven) trucks for shipment to U.S. destinations. The U.S. agreed to lift that restriction in 1995, but didn't. In 2009, President Obama actually solidified the Mexican roadblock, despite the fact that Mexican trucks passed all 22 safety (nontariff) regulations the U.S. Department of Transportation had imposed. In so doing, President Obama secured more jobs for Teamster-union drivers, but raised costs for U.S. shippers and consumers and drove down sales and employment for Mexican trucking companies. Fed up with U.S. protectionism, Mexico retaliated by slapping tariffs on 90 U.S. export products (see World View below).

WORLD VIEW

Mexico Retaliates for Loss of Truck Program

Mexico announced Monday it will increase tariffs on 90 U.S. industrial and agricultural goods in reprisal for the United States canceling a test program that gave Mexican trucks access to U.S. highways. Mexican Economy Minister Gerardo Ruiz said around $2.4 billion worth of U.S. exports would be affected and that the government would soon publish a list. U.S. labor, highway safety and consumer groups have opposed the truck access permitted under the North American Free Trade Agreement.

Source: USA TODAY. March 17, 2009, B1. Reprinted with Permission.

Analysis: Nontariff barriers like extraordinary safety requirements on Mexican trucks limit import competition and invite retaliation.

Nontariff Barriers

AN INCREASINGLY GLOBAL MARKET

Proponents of free trade and representatives of special interests that profit from trade protection are in constant conflict. But most of the time the trade-policy deck seems stacked in favor of the special interests. Because the interests of import-competing firms and workers are highly concentrated, they're quick to mobilize politically. By contrast, the benefits of freer trade are less direct and spread over millions of consumers. As a consequence, the beneficiaries of freer trade are less likely to monitor trade policy—much less lobby actively to change it. Hence, the political odds favor the spread of trade barriers.

Multilateral Trade Pacts. Despite these odds, the long-term trend is toward *lowering* trade barriers, thereby increasing global competition. Two forces encourage this trend. ***The principal barrier to protectionist policies is worldwide recognition of the gains from freer trade.*** Since world nations now understand that trade barriers are ultimately self-defeating, they're more willing to rise above the din of protectionist cries and dismantle trade barriers. They diffuse political opposition by creating across-the-board trade pacts that seem to spread the pain (and gain) from freer trade across a broad swath of industries. Such pacts also incorporate multiyear timetables that give affected industries time to adjust.

Trade liberalization has also been encouraged by firms that *export* products or use imported inputs in their own production. Tariffs on imported steel raise product costs for U.S.-based auto producers and construction companies. In 2007 the European Union eliminated a tariff on frozen Chinese strawberries, largely due to complaints from EU yogurt and jam producers.

Global Pacts: GATT and WTO. The granddaddy of the multilateral, multiyear free-trade pacts was the 1947 *General Agreement on Tariffs and Trade (GATT)*. Twenty-three nations pledged to reduce trade barriers and give all GATT nations equal access to their domestic markets.

Since the first GATT pact, seven more "rounds" of negotiations have expanded the scope of GATT: 117 nations signed the 1994 pact. As a result of these GATT pacts, average tariff rates in developed countries have fallen from 40 percent in 1948 to less than 4 percent today.

WTO. The 1994 GATT pact also created the *World Trade Organization (WTO)* to enforce free-trade rules. If a nation feels its exports are being unfairly excluded from another country's market, it can file a complaint with the WTO. This is exactly what the United States did when the EU banned U.S. beef imports. The WTO ruled in favor of the United States. When the EU failed to lift its import ban, the WTO authorized the United States to impose retaliatory tariffs on European exports.

The EU turned the tables on the United States in 2003. It complained to the WTO that U.S. tariffs on steel violated trade rules. The WTO agreed and gave the EU permission to impose retaliatory tariffs on $2.2 billion of U.S. exports. That prompted the Bush administration to scale back the tariffs in December 2003.

In effect, the WTO is now the world's trade police force. It is empowered to cite nations that violate trade agreements and even to impose remedial action when violations persist. Why do sovereign nations give the WTO such power? Because they are all convinced that free trade is the surest route to GDP growth.

WTO Protests. Although freer trade clearly boosts economic growth, some people say that it does more harm than good. Environmentalists question the very desirability of continued economic growth. They worry about the depletion of resources, congestion and pollution, and the social friction that growth often promotes. Labor organizations worry that global competition will depress wages and working conditions. And many Third World nations are concerned about playing by trade rules that always seem to benefit rich nations (e.g., copyright protection, import protection, farm subsidies).

Despite some tumultuous street protests (e.g., Seattle in 1999, Hong Kong in 2005), WTO members continue the difficult process of dismantling trade barriers. The latest round of negotiations began in Doha, Qatar, in 2001. The key issue in the "Doha Round" was farm subsidies in rich nations. Poor nations protest that farm subsidies in the United States and Europe not only limit their exports but also lower global farm prices (hurting farmers in developing nations). After 8 *years* of negotiations, the industrial nations had still not agreed to reduce those farm subsidies significantly.

Regional Pacts. Because worldwide trade pacts are so complex, many nations have also pursued *regional* free-trade agreements.

NAFTA. In December 1992, the United States, Canada, and Mexico signed the *North American Free Trade Agreement (NAFTA),* a 1,000-page document covering more than 9,000 products. The ultimate goal of NAFTA is to eliminate all trade barriers between these three countries. At the time of signing, intraregional tariffs averaged 11 percent in Mexico, 5 percent in Canada, and 4 percent in the United States. NAFTA requires that all tariffs among the three countries be eliminated. The pact also requires the elimination of specific nontariff barriers.

The NAFTA-initiated reduction in trade barriers substantially increased trade flows between Mexico, Canada, and the United States. It also prompted a wave of foreign investment in Mexico, where both cheap labor and NAFTA access were available. Overall, NAFTA accelerated economic growth and reduced inflationary pressures in all three nations. Some industries (like construction and apparel) suffered from the freer trade, but others (like trucking, farming, and finance) reaped huge gains (see News below).

IN THE NEWS

NAFTA Reallocates Labor: Comparative Advantage at Work

More Jobs in These Industries		but . . .	Few Jobs in These Industries	
Agriculture	+10,600		Construction	−12,800
Metal products	+6,100		Medicine	−6,000
Electrical appliances	+5,200		Apparel	−5,900
Business services	+5,000		Lumber	−1,200
Motor vehicles	+5,000		Furniture	−400

Source: Congressional Budget Office.

The lowering of trade barriers between Mexico and the United States is changing the mix of output in both countries. New export opportunities create jobs in some industries while increased imports eliminate jobs in other industries. (Estimated gains and losses are during the first five years of NAFTA.)

Analysis: The specialization encouraged by free trade creates new jobs in export but reduces employment in import-competing industries. In the process, total world output increases.

CAFTA. The success of NAFTA prompted a similar 2005 agreement between the United States and Central American nations. The Central American Free Trade Agreement (CAFTA) aims to standardize trade and investment policies in CAFTA nations, while eliminating tariffs on thousands of products.

European Union. The *European Union* is another regional pact, but one that virtually eliminates national boundaries among 27 countries. The EU not only eliminates trade barriers but also enhances full intercountry mobility of workers and capital. In effect, Europe has become one large, unified market.

As trade barriers continue to fall around the world, the global marketplace is likely to become more like an open bazaar as well. The resulting increase in competition should spur efficiency and growth in the economy tomorrow.

SUMMARY

- International trade permits each country to specialize in areas of relative efficiency, increasing world output. For each country, the gains from trade are reflected in consumption possibilities that exceed production possibilities. LO2

- One way to determine where comparative advantage lies is to compare the quantity of good A that must be given up in order to get a given quantity of good B from domestic production. If the same quantity of B can be obtained for less A by engaging in world trade, we have a comparative advantage in the production of good A. Comparative advantage rests on a comparison of relative opportunity costs. LO1

- The terms of trade—the rate at which goods are exchanged—are subject to the forces of international supply and demand. The terms of trade will lie somewhere between the opportunity costs of the trading partners. The terms of trade determine how the gains from trade are shared. LO2

- Resistance to trade emanates from workers and firms that must compete with imports. Even though the country as a whole stands to benefit from trade, these individuals and companies may lose jobs and incomes in the process. LO3

- Trade barriers take many forms. Embargoes are outright prohibitions against import or export of particular goods. Quotas limit the quantity of a good imported or exported. Tariffs discourage imports by making them more expensive. Other nontariff barriers make trade too costly or time-consuming. LO3

- The World Trade Organization (WTO) seeks to reduce worldwide trade barriers and enforce trade rules. Regional accords such as the European Union (EU), the North American Free Trade Agreement (NAFTA), and the Central American Free Trade Agreement (CAFTA) pursue similar objectives among fewer countries. LO3

Key Terms

imports	consumption possibilities	dumping
exports	open economy	embargo
trade deficit	comparative advantage	tariff
trade surplus	opportunity cost	quota
production possibilities	absolute advantage	equilibrium price
closed economy	terms of trade	voluntary restraint agreement (VRA)

Questions for Discussion

1. Suppose a lawyer can type faster than any secretary. Should the lawyer do her own typing? Can you demonstrate the validity of your answer? LO1

2. What would be the effects of a law requiring bilateral trade balances? LO2

3. If a nation exported much of its output but imported little, would it be better or worse off? How about the reverse, that is, exporting little but importing a lot? LO2

4. How does international trade restrain the price behavior of domestic firms? LO3

5. Suppose we refused to sell goods to any country that reduced or halted its exports to us. Who would benefit and who would lose from such retaliation? Can you suggest alternative ways to ensure import supplies? LO2

6. Domestic producers often base their claim for import protection on the fact that workers in country X are paid substandard wages. Is this a valid argument for protection? LO1

7. On the basis of News on page 423, how do U.S. furniture manufacturers feel about NAFTA? How about farmers? LO3

8. Why did President Obama pursue "Buy American" rules if they actually hurt the economy? LO3

9. Who gains and who loses from nontariff barriers to Mexican trucks (World View, p. 421)? LO3

10. Which consumers benefited from the dumping cases mentioned in the World View on page 415? LO3

web activities to accompany this chapter can be found on the Online Learning Center:
http://www.mhhe.com/schiller12e

connect
|ECONOMICS

LO2   1. Which countries are the two largest export markets for the United States? (See Table 19.3.)   _____
    _____

LO1   2. Suppose a country can produce a maximum of 10,000 jumbo airliners or 2,000 aircraft carriers.
    (*a*) What is the opportunity cost of an aircraft carrier?   _____
    (*b*) If another country offers to trade six planes for one aircraft carrier, should the offer be
    accepted?   _____
    (*c*) What is the implied price of the carrier in trade?   _____

LO1   3. If it takes 48 farm workers to harvest 1 ton of strawberries and 8 farm workers to harvest
    1 ton of wheat, what is the opportunity cost of 5 tons of strawberries?   _____

LO1   4. Alpha and Beta, two tiny islands off the east coast of Tricoli, produce pearls and pineapples. The
LO2   following production possibilities schedules describe their potential output in tons per year.

Alpha		Beta	
Pearls	Pineapples	Pearls	Pineapples
0	30	0	20
2	25	10	16
4	20	20	12
6	15	30	8
8	10	40	4
10	5	45	2
12	0	50	0

    (*a*) Graph the production possibilities confronting each island.
    (*b*) What is the opportunity cost of pineapples on each island (before trade)?   Alpha: _____
    Beta: _____

    (*c*) Which island has a comparative advantage in pearl production?   _____
    (*d*) Graph the consumption possibilities of each island with free trade.
    (*e*) If Beta produced only pearls,
       (*i*) How many could it produce?   _____
       (*ii*) How many pearls would it have to export to get 20 pineapples in return?   _____
       (*iii*) What is the net gain to Beta in this case?   _____

LO3   5. (*a*) How much more are U.S. consumers paying for the 20 billion pounds of sugar they consume
       each year as a result of the quotas on sugar imports? (See News, p. 720.)   _____
    (*b*) How much sales revenue are foreign sugar producers losing as a result of those same quotas?   _____

LO2 6. Suppose the two islands in Problem 4 agree that the terms of trade will be one for one and
exchange 10 pearls for 10 pineapples.

    (*a*) If Alpha produced 6 pearls and 15 pineapples while Beta produced 30 pearls and
        8 pineapple's before they decided to trade, how many pearls would each be producing
        after trade? Assume that the two countries specialize according to their comparative
        advantage.

        Alpha: _____
        Beta: _____

    (*b*) How much would the combined production of pineapples increase for the two islands
        due to specialization? _____

    (*c*) How much would the combined production of pearls increase? _____

LO2
LO3
 7. Suppose the following table reflects the domestic supply and demand for compact disks (CDs):

Price($)	18	16	14	12	10	8	6	4
Quantity supplied	8	7	6	5	4	3	2	1
Quantity demanded	2	4	6	8	10	12	14	16

    (*a*) Graph these market conditions and identify
        (*i*) The equilibrium price. _____
        (*ii*) The equilibrium quantity. _____

    (*b*) Now suppose that foreigners enter the market, offering to sell an unlimited supply of CDs for
        $6 apiece. Illustrate and identify
        (*i*) The new market price. _____
        (*ii*) Domestic consumption. _____
        (*iii*) Domestic production. _____

    (*c*) If a tariff of $2 per CD is imposed, what will happen to
        (*i*) The market price? _____
        (*ii*) Domestic consumption? _____
        (*iii*) Domestic production? _____

Graph your answers.

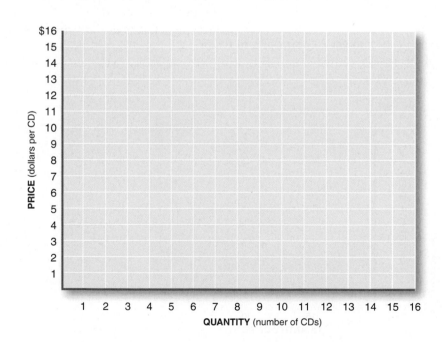

20 International Finance

LEARNING OBJECTIVES

After reading this chapter, you should be able to:

LO1. Identify the sources of foreign-exchange demand and supply.

LO2. Explain how exchange rates are established.

LO3. Summarize how changes in exchange rates affect prices, output, and trade flows.

U.S. textile, furniture, and shrimp producers want China to increase the value of the yuan. They say China's undervalued currency makes Chinese exports too cheap, undercutting American firms. On the other hand, Wal-Mart thinks a cheap yuan is a good thing, as it keeps prices low for the $16 *billion* of toys, tools, linens, and other goods it buys from China each year. Those low import prices help Wal-Mart keep its prices low and sales volume high.

This chapter examines how currency values affect trade patterns and ultimately the core questions of WHAT, HOW, and FOR WHOM to produce. We focus on the following questions:

- **What determines the value of one country's money as compared to the value of another's?**
- **What causes the international value of currencies to change?**
- **Should governments intervene to limit currency fluctuations?**

EXCHANGE RATES: THE GLOBAL LINK

As we saw in Chapter 19, the United States exports and imports a staggering volume of goods and services. Although we trade with nearly 200 nations around the world, we seldom give much thought to where imports come from and much less to how we acquire them. Most of the time, all we want to know is which products are available and at what price.

Suppose you want to buy a Magnavox DVD player. You don't have to know that Magnavox players are produced by the Dutch company Philips Electronics. And you certainly don't have to fly to the Netherlands to pick it up. All you have to do is drive to the nearest electronics store; or you can just "click and buy" at the Internet's virtual mall.

But you may wonder how the purchase of an imported product was so simple. Dutch companies sell their products in euros, the currency of Europe. But you purchase the DVD player in dollars. How is this possible?

There's a chain of distribution between your dollar purchase in the United States and the euro-denominated sale in the Netherlands. Somewhere along that chain someone has to convert your dollars into euros. The critical question for everybody concerned is how many euros we can get for our dollars—that is, what the **exchange rate** is. If we can get two euros for every dollar, the exchange rate is 2 euros = 1 dollar. Alternatively, we could note that the price of a euro is 50 U.S. cents when the exchange rate is 2 to 1. Thus, *an exchange rate is the price of one currency in terms of another.*

> **exchange rate:** The price of one country's currency expressed in terms of another's; the domestic price of a foreign currency.

FOREIGN-EXCHANGE MARKETS

Most exchange rates are determined in foreign-exchange markets. Stop thinking of money as some sort of magical substance, and instead view it as a useful commodity that facilitates market exchanges. From that perspective, an exchange rate—the price of money—is subject to the same influences that determine all market prices: demand and supply.

The Demand for Dollars

Euros depreciated causes price to go up on their products

When the Japanese Toshiba Corporation bought Westinghouse Electric Co. in 2006, it paid $5.4 billion. When Belgian beer maker InBev bought Anheuser-Busch (Budweiser, etc.) in 2008, it also needed dollars—over 50 billion of them! In both cases, the objective of the foreign investor was to acquire an American business. To attain their objectives, however, the buyers first had to buy *dollars.* The Japanese and Belgian buyers had to exchange their own currency for American dollars.

Canadian tourists also need American dollars. Few American restaurants or hotels accept Canadian currency as payment for goods and services; they want to be paid in U.S. dollars. Accordingly, Canadian tourists must buy American dollars if they want to see the United States.

Europeans love iPods. The Apple Corporation, however, wants to be paid in U.S. dollars. Hence, European consumers must exchange their euros for U.S. dollars if they want an iPod. Individual consumers can spend euros at their local electronics store. When they do so, however, they're initiating a series of market transactions that will end when Apple Corporation gets paid in U.S. dollars. In this case, some intermediary exchanges the European currency for American dollars.

Some foreign investors also buy U.S. dollars for speculative purposes. When the ruble collapsed, Russians feared that the value of the ruble would drop further and preferred to hold U.S. dollars. Barclay's Bank also speculates in dollars on occasions when it fears that the value of the British pound will drop.

All these motivations give rise to a demand for U.S. dollars. Specifically, *the market demand for U.S. dollars originates in*

- *Foreign demand for American exports* (including tourism).
- *Foreign demand for American investments.*
- *Speculation.*

Governments may also create a demand for dollars through currency *swaps* and other activities.

The *supply* of dollars arises from similar sources. On the supply side, however, it's Americans who initiate most of the exchanges. Suppose you take a trip to Mexico. You'll need to buy Mexican pesos at some point. When you do, you'll be offering to *buy* pesos by offering to *sell* dollars. In other words, **the demand *for foreign currency represents a* supply *of U.S. dollars.***

When Americans buy BMW cars, they also supply U.S. dollars. American consumers pay for their BMWs in dollars. Somewhere down the road, however, those dollars will be exchanged for European euros. At that exchange, dollars are being *supplied* and euros *demanded.*

American corporations demand foreign exchange too. General Motors builds cars in Germany, Coca-Cola produces Coke in China, Exxon produces and refines oil all over the world. In nearly every such case, the U.S. firm must first build or buy some plant and equipment, using another country's factors of production. This activity requires foreign currency and thus becomes another component of our demand for foreign currency.

We may summarize these market activities by noting that **the supply of dollars originates in**

- **American demand for imports** (including tourism).
- **American investments in foreign countries.**
- **Speculation.**

As on the demand side, government intervention can also contribute to the supply of dollars.

Whether American consumers will choose to buy an imported BMW depends partly on what the car costs. The price tag isn't always apparent in international transactions. Remember that the German BMW producer and workers want to be paid in their own currency. Hence, the *dollar* price of an imported BMW depends on two factors: (1) the German price of a BMW and (2) the *exchange rate* between U.S. dollars and euros. Specifically, the U.S. price of a BMW is

$$\frac{\text{Dollar price}}{\text{of BMW}} = \frac{\text{euro price}}{\text{of BMW}} \times \frac{\text{dollar price}}{\text{of euro}}$$

Suppose the BMW company is prepared to sell a German-built BMW for 100,000 euros and that the current exchange rate is 2 euros = $1. At these rates, a BMW will cost you

$$\frac{\text{Dollar price}}{\text{of BMW}} = 100,000 \text{ euros} \times \frac{\$1}{2 \text{ euros}}$$

$$= \$50,000$$

If you're willing to pay this much for a shiny new German-built BMW, you may do so at current exchange rates.

Now suppose the exchange rate changes from 2 euros = $1 to 1 euro = $1. Now you're getting only 1 euro for your dollar rather than 2 euros. In other words, euros have become more expensive. *A higher dollar price for euros will raise the dollar costs of European goods.* In this case, the dollar price of a euro increases from $0.50 to $1. At this new exchange rate, the BMW plant in Germany is still willing to sell BMWs at 100,000 euros apiece. And German consumers continue to buy BMWs at that price. But this constant euro price now translates into a higher *dollar* price. Thus that same BMW that you previously could buy for $50,000 now costs you $100,000.

As the dollar price of a BMW rises, the number of BMWs sold in the United States will decline. As BMW sales decline, the quantity of euros demanded may decline as well. Thus, the quantity of foreign currency demanded declines when the exchange rate rises because foreign goods become more expensive and imports decline.[1] When the dollar price of European currencies actually increased in 1992, BMW decided to start producing cars in South Carolina. A year later Mercedes-Benz decided to produce cars in the United States as well.

---

[1]The extent to which imports decline as the cost of foreign currency rises depends on the *price elasticity of demand.*

The Foreign-Exchange Market

The foreign-exchange market operates like other markets. In this case, the "good" bought and sold is dollars (foreign exchange). The price and quantity of dollars actually exchanged are determined by the intersection of market supply and demand.

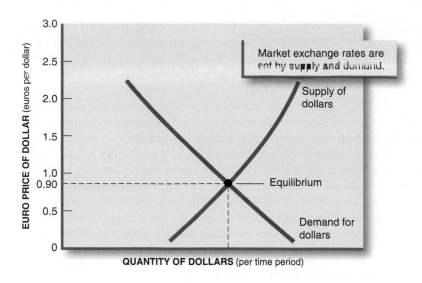

Market exchange rates are set by supply and demand.

Sales of American-made BMWs and Mercedes no longer depend on the exchange rate of the U.S. dollars.

The Supply Curve. These market responses suggest that the supply of dollars is upward-sloping. If the value of the dollar rises, Americans will be able to buy more euros. As a result, the dollar price of imported BMWs will decline. American consumers will respond by demanding more imports, thereby supplying a larger quantity of dollars. The supply curve in Figure 20.1 shows how the quantity of dollars supplied rises as the value of the dollar increases.

The Demand Curve. The demand for dollars can be explained in similar terms. Remember that the demand for dollars arises from the foreign demand for U.S. exports and investments. If the exchange rate moves from 2 euros = $1 to 1 euro = $1, the euro price of dollars falls. As dollars become cheaper for Germans, all American exports effectively fall in price. Germans will buy more American products (including trips to Disney World) and therefore demand a greater quantity of dollars. In addition, foreign investors will perceive in a cheaper dollar the opportunity to buy U.S. stocks, businesses, and property at fire-sale prices. Accordingly, they join foreign consumers in demanding more dollars. Not all these behavioral responses will occur overnight, but they're reasonably predictable over a brief period of time.

Equilibrium

equilibrium price: The price at which the quantity of a good demanded in a given time period equals the quantity supplied.

Given market demand and supply curves, we can predict the **equilibrium price** of any commodity, that is, the price at which the quantity demanded will equal the quantity supplied. This occurs in Figure 20.1 where the two curves cross. At that equilibrium, the value of the dollar (the exchange rate) is established. In this case, the euro price of the dollar turns out to be 0.90.

The value of the dollar can also be expressed in terms of other currencies. The following World View displays a sampling of dollar exchange rates in March 2009. (Notice how many Indonesian rupiah you could buy for $1.) The *average* value of the dollar is a weighted mean of the exchange rates between the U.S. dollar and all these currencies. The value of the dollar is "high" when its foreign-exchange price is above recent levels, "low" when it is below recent averages.

The Balance of Payments

The equilibrium depicted in Figure 20.1 determines not only the *price* of the dollar but also a specific *quantity* of international transactions. Those transactions include the exports, imports, international investments, and other sources of dollar supply and demand. A

WORLD VIEW

Foreign-Exchange Rates

The foreign-exchange mid-range rates below show (a) how many U.S. dollars are needed to buy one unit of foreign currency and (b) how many units of foreign currency are needed to buy one U.S. dollar.

Country	(a) U.S. Dollar per Unit (dollar price of foreign currency)	(b) Currency per U.S. Dollar (foreign price of U.S. dollar)
Brazil (real)	0.4433	2.2560
Britain (pound)	1.4600	0.6849
Canada (dollar)	0.8130	1.2300
China (yuan)	0.1464	6.8309
Indonesia (rupiah)	0.0001	11675.0000
Japan (yen)	0.0102	97.9991
Mexico (peso)	0.0696	14.3700
Russia (ruble)	0.0297	33.6527
Euroland (euro)	1.3494	0.7411

Source: March 25, 2009, data from Federal Reserve Board of Governors.

web analysis

What's a euro? Read more about the European currency at **www.ecb.int**.

Analysis: The exchange rates between currencies are determined by supply and demand in foreign-exchange markets. The rates reported here represent the equilibrium exchange rates on a particular day.

summary of all those international money flows is contained in the **balance of payments**—an accounting statement of all international money flows in a given period of time.

balance of payments: A summary record of a country's international economic transactions in a given period of time.

Trade Balance. Table 20.1 depicts the U.S. balance of payments for 2008. Notice first how the millions of separate transactions are classified into a few summary measures. The trade balance is the difference between exports and imports of goods (merchandise) and services. In 2008, the United States imported over $2.5 trillion of goods and services but

web analysis

The latest statistics on the balance of payments are available from the Bureau of Economic Analysis at **www.bea.gov**.

Item	Amount ($ billions)
1. Merchandise exports	$1,291
2. Merchandise imports	(2,112)
3. Service exports	544
4. Service imports	(405)
Trade balance (items 1–4)	−682
5. Income from U.S. overseas investments	755
6. Income outflow for foreign-owned U.S. investments	(628)
7. Net U.S. government grants	(42)
8. Net private transfers and pensions	(77)
Current-account balance (items 1–8)	−674
9. U.S. capital inflow – *money put in by foreign*	178
10. U.S. capital outflow – *money spent outside US*	(47)
11. Increase in U.S. official reserves	(5)
12. Increase in foreign official assets in U.S.	421
Capital-account balance (items 9–12)	547
13. Statistical discrepancy – *where is the $ put*	127
Net balance (items 1–13)	0

Source: U.S. Department of Commerce (2008 data).

TABLE 20.1
The U.S. Balance of Payments

The balance of payments is a summary statement of a country's international transactions. The major components of that activity are the trade balance (merchandise exports minus merchandise imports), the current-account balance (trade, services, and transfers), and the capital-account balance. The net total of these balances must equal zero, since the quantity of dollars paid must equal the quantity received.

trade deficit: The amount by which the value of imports exceeds the value of exports in a given time period.

exported only $1.8 trillion. This created a **trade deficit** of $682 billion. That trade deficit represents a net outflow of dollars to the rest of the world.

$$\text{Trade balance} = \text{exports} - \text{imports}$$

The excess supply of dollars created by the trade gap widened further by other net outflows. U.S. government grants to foreign nations (line 7 in Table 20.1) contributed $42 billion to the net *supply* of dollars.

Current-Account Balance. The current-account balance is a subtotal in Table 20.1. It includes the merchandise, services, and investment balances as well as government grants and private transfers such as wages sent home by foreign citizens working in the United States.

$$\frac{\text{Current-account}}{\text{balance}} = \frac{\text{trade}}{\text{balance}} + \frac{\text{unilateral}}{\text{transfers}}$$

The current-account balance is the most comprehensive summary of our trade relations. As indicated in Table 20.1, the United States had a current-account deficit of $674 billion in 2008.

Capital-Account Balance. The current-account deficit is offset by the capital-account surplus. The capital-account balance takes into consideration assets bought and sold across international borders; that is,

$$\frac{\text{Capital-account}}{\text{balance}} = \frac{\text{foreign purchases}}{\text{of U.S. assets}} - \frac{\text{U.S. purchases}}{\text{of foreign assets}}$$

As Table 20.1 shows, foreign consumers demanded $178 billion in 2008 to buy farms and factories as well as U.S. bonds, stocks, and other investments (item 9). This exceeded the flow of U.S. dollars going overseas to purchase foreign assets (item 10). In addition, the United States and foreign governments bought and sold dollars, creating an additional inflow of dollars (items 11 and 12).

The net capital inflows were essential in financing the U.S. trade deficit (negative trade balance). As in any market, the number of dollars demanded must equal the number of dollars supplied. Thus, ***the capital-account surplus must equal the current-account deficit.*** In other words, there can't be any dollars left lying around unaccounted for. Item 13 in Table 20.1 reminds us that our accounting system isn't perfect—that we can't identify every transaction. Nevertheless, all the accounts must eventually "balance out":

$$\frac{\text{Net balance}}{\text{of payments}} = \frac{\text{current-account}}{\text{balance}} + \frac{\text{capital-account}}{\text{balance}} = 0$$

That's the character of a market *equilibrium:* The quantity of dollars demanded equals the quantity of dollars supplied.

MARKET DYNAMICS

The interesting thing about markets isn't their character in equilibrium but the fact that prices and quantities are always changing in response to shifts in demand and supply. The U.S. demand for BMWs shifted overnight when Japan introduced a new line of sleek, competitively priced cars (e.g., Lexus). The reduced demand for BMWs shifted the supply of dollars leftward. That supply shift raised the value of the dollar vis-à-vis the euro, as illustrated in Figure 20.2. (It also increased the demand for Japanese yen, causing the yen value of the dollar to *fall.*)

depreciation (currency): A fall in the price of one currency relative to another.

Depreciation and Appreciation

Exchange-rate changes have their own terminology. **Depreciation** of a currency occurs when one currency becomes cheaper in terms of another currency. In our earlier discussion of exchange rates, for example, we assumed that the exchange rate between euros and dollars

(a) Dollar-euro market

(b) Dollar-yen market

FIGURE 20.2

Shifts in Foreign-Exchange Markets

When the Japanese introduced luxury autos into the United States, the American demand for German cars fell. As a consequence, the supply of dollars in the dollar-euro market (part *a*) shifted to the left and the euro value of the dollar rose. At the same time, the increased American demand for Japanese cars shifted the dollar supply curve in the yen market (part *b*) to the right, reducing the yen price of the dollar.

---

changed from 2 euros — $1 to 1 euro = $1, making the euro price of a dollar cheaper. In this case, the dollar *depreciated* with respect to the euro.

The other side of depreciation is **appreciation,** an increase in value of one currency as expressed in another country's currency. ***Whenever one currency depreciates, another currency must appreciate.*** When the exchange rate changed from 2 euros = $1 to 1 euro = $1, not only did the euro price of a dollar fall, but also the dollar price of a euro rose. Hence, the euro appreciated as the dollar depreciated.

Figure 20.3 illustrates actual changes in the exchange rate of the U.S. dollar since 1980. The trade-adjusted value of the U.S. dollar is the (weighted) average of all exchange rates for the dollar. Between 1980 and 1985, the U.S. dollar appreciated over 80 percent. This appreciation greatly reduced the price of imports and thus increased their quantity. At the same time, the dollar appreciation raised the foreign price of U.S. exports and so reduced their volume. U.S. farmers, aircraft manufacturers, and tourist services suffered huge sales losses. The trade deficit ballooned.

The value of the dollar reversed course after 1985. This brief dollar depreciation set in motion forces that reduced the trade deficit in the late 1980s. Then the dollar started appreciating again, slowing export growth and increasing imports throughout the 1990s. After a long steep appreciation, the dollar started losing value in 2003. This was good for U.S. exporters, but bad for U.S. tourists and foreign producers (see World View on the next page).

Exchange rates change for the same reasons that any market price changes: The underlying supply or demand (or both) has shifted. Among the more important sources of such shifts are

- ***Relative income changes.*** If incomes are increasing faster in country A than in country B, consumers in A will tend to spend more, thus increasing the demand for B's exports and currency. B's currency will appreciate.
- ***Relative price changes.*** If domestic prices are rising rapidly in country A, consumers will seek out lower-priced imports. The demand for B's exports and currency will increase. B's currency will appreciate.

appreciation: A rise in the price of one currency relative to another.

Market Forces

FIGURE 20.3

Changing Values of U.S. Dollar

Since 1973, exchange rates have been flexible. As a result, the value of the U.S. dollar has fluctuated with international differences in inflation, interest rates, and economic growth. U.S. economic stability has given the U.S. dollar increasing value over time.

Source: Federal Reserve Board of Governers.

web analysis

How much are 100 Japanese yen worth in U.S. dollars? Find out at the currency converter at **www.xe.com/ucc.**

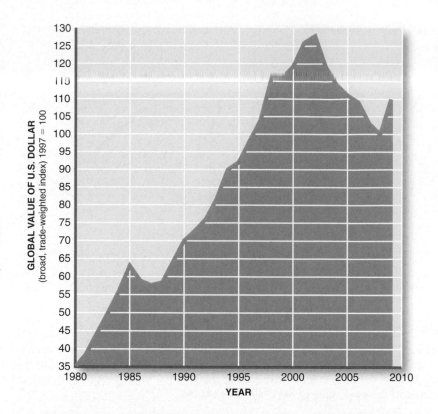

WORLD VIEW

Weak Dollar Helps U.S. Firms

The dollar's precipitous decline against European currencies has brought overseas customers to Al Lubrano's small Rhode Island manufacturing firm that he hasn't heard from in five years.

Gerry Letendre's manufacturing plant in New Hampshire just hired five employees to keep up with growing European demand, two and a half years after Letendre laid off a quarter of his work force.

The dollar's slide has made U.S. goods far cheaper for European consumers, and European exports considerably more expensive here. Letendre's Diamond Casting and Machine Co. in Hollis, N.H., has already boosted shipments of its circuit board printing equipment and industrial valves to Europe by 30 percent. Lubrano, president of Technical Materials Inc., in Lincoln, R.I., said his export business should jump as much as 25 percent this year.

"On balance, the weak dollar has been tremendous for us," Lubrano said.

—Jonathan Weisman

Source: *The Washington Post,* January 26, 2004. © 2004 The Washington Post. Used with permission by PARS International Corp.

Dollar's Fall Puts Big Crimp in European Tourism

ROME—As the euro continues to strengthen against the battered U.S. dollar, tourists, businesses and Americans living abroad complain that Europe is pricing itself out of the market.

"It has become so expensive it almost makes me ill," says Nancy Oliveira, 55, an American living in Rome on what she says was once a "comfortable fixed income.". . .

The Italian National Tourist office reports a 15% decline in the number of Americans visiting from 2000 to 2002. . . .

Companies that rely on tourists and visitors estimate business is down 20% to 30%. . . .

Sales at Florence Moon, a leather store in Rome that caters primarily to Americans, are down 50%, says Farshad Shahabadi, whose family owns the store. "If it's bad for us, then it must be bad for everyone else, too," Shahabadi says.

—Ellen Hale

Source: USA TODAY. February 20, 2004, 3B. Reprinted with Permission.

Analysis: Depreciation of a nation's currency is good for that nation's exporters but bad for that nation's importers (including its tourists).

- *Changes in product availability.* If country A experiences a disastrous wheat crop failure, it will have to increase its food imports. B's currency will appreciate.
- *Relative interest rate changes.* If interest rates rise in country A, people in country B will want to move their deposits to A. Demand for A's currency will rise and it will appreciate.
- *Speculation.* If speculators anticipate an increase in the price of A's currency, for the preceding reasons or any other, they'll begin buying it, thus pushing its price up. A's currency will appreciate.

All these various changes are taking place every minute of every day, thus keeping **foreign-exchange markets** active. On an average day, over *$1 trillion* of foreign exchange is bought and sold in the market. Significant changes occur in currency values, however, only when several of these forces move in the same direction at the same time. This is what caused the Asian crisis of 1997–98.

foreign-exchange markets: Places where foreign currencies are bought and sold.

The Asian Crisis of 1997-98

In July 1997, the Thai government decided the baht was overvalued and let market forces find a new equilibrium. Within days, the dollar prices of the baht plunged 25 percent. This sharp decline in the value of the Thai baht simultaneously increased the Thai price of the U.S. dollar. As a consequence, Thais could no longer afford to buy as many American products.

The devaluation of the baht had a domino effect on other Asian currencies. The plunge in the baht shook confidence in the Malaysian ringget, the Indonesian rupiah, and even the Korean won. People wanted to hold "hard" currencies like the U.S. dollar. As people rushed to buy U.S. dollars with their local currencies, the value of those currencies plunged. At one point the Indonesian rupiah had lost 80 percent of its dollar value, making U.S. exports five times more expensive for Indonesians. As a result, Indonesians could no longer afford to buy imported rice, machinery, cars, or pork. Indonesian students attending U.S. colleges could no longer afford to pay tuition. The sudden surge in prices and scarcity of goods led to street demonstrations and a change in government. Similar problems erupted throughout Southeast Asia.

The "Asian contagion" unfortunately wasn't confined to that area of the world. Hog farmers in the United States saw foreign demand for their pork evaporate. Koreans stopped taking vacations in Hawaii. Thai Airways canceled orders for Boeing jets. And Japanese consumers bought fewer Washington state apples and California oranges. This loss of export markets slowed economic growth in the United States, Europe, Japan, and other nations.

RESISTANCE TO EXCHANGE-RATE CHANGES

Given the scope and depth of the Asian crisis of 1997–98, it's easy to understand why people crave *stable* exchange rates. The resistance to exchange-rate fluctuations originates in various micro and macroeconomic interests.

Micro Interests

The microeconomic resistance to changes in the value of the dollar arises from two concerns. First, people who trade or invest in world markets want a solid basis for forecasting future costs, prices, and profits. Forecasts are always uncertain, but they're even less dependable when the value of money is subject to change. An American firm that invests $2 million in a ski factory in Sweden expects not only to make a profit on the production there but also to return that profit to the United States. If the Swedish krona depreciates sharply in the interim, however, the profits amassed in Sweden may dwindle to a mere trickle, or even a loss, when the kronor are exchanged back into dollars. Even the Nobel Prize loses a bit of its luster when the krona depreciates (see World View on the next page). From this view, the uncertainty associated with fluctuating exchange rates is an unwanted burden.

Even when the direction of an exchange rate move is certain, those who stand to lose from the change are prone to resist. *A change in the price of a country's money automatically alters the price of all its exports and imports.* When the Russian ruble and Japanese yen depreciated in 2000–2001, for example, the dollar price of Russian and Japanese

WORLD VIEW

Nobel Prize Was Nobler in October

STOCKHOLM—Winners of the four Nobel science awards said yesterday that the honor is more important than the money, so it does not matter much that each award has lost $242,000 in value since October.

"If we had been more intelligent, we would have done some hedging," said Gary S. Becker, 61, a University of Chicago professor and a Nobel economics laureate. Sweden's decision last month to let the krona float caused the prizes' value to drop from $1.2 million each when announced in October to $958,000 when King Carl XVI Gustaf presents them Thursday.

The recipients are Becker; American Rudolph A. Marcus, the chemistry laureate; Frenchman Georges Charpak, the physics laureate; and medicine prize winners Edmond Fischer and Edwin Krebs of the University of Washington in Seattle.

—Associated Press

Source: *Boston Globe*, December 8, 1992. Used with permission by The Associated Press. All rights reserved.

Analysis: Currency depreciation reduces the external value of domestic income and assets. The dollar value of the Nobel Prize fell when the Swedish krona depreciated.

web analysis

For a history of the dollar to krona exchange rate, visit **http://finance.yahoo.com** and search "USD/SEK."

steel declined as well. This prompted U.S. steelmakers to accuse Russia and Japan of "dumping" steel. Steel companies and unions appealed to Washington to protect their sales and jobs.

Even in the country whose currency becomes cheaper, there'll be opposition to exchange-rate movements. When the U.S. dollar appreciates, Americans buy more foreign products. This increased U.S. demand for imports may drive up prices in other countries. In addition, foreign firms may take advantage of the reduced American competition by raising their prices. In either case, some inflation will result. The consumer's insistence that the government "do something" about rising prices may turn into a political force for "correcting" foreign-exchange rates.

Macro Interests

Any microeconomic problem that becomes widespread enough can turn into a macroeconomic problem. The huge U.S. trade deficits of the 1980s effectively exported jobs to foreign nations. Although the U.S. economy expanded rapidly in 1983–85, the unemployment rate stayed high, partly because American consumers were spending more of their income on imports. Yet fear of renewed inflation precluded more stimulative fiscal and monetary policies.

The U.S. trade deficits of the 1980s were offset by huge capital-account surpluses. Foreign investors sought to participate in the U.S. economic expansion by buying land, plant, and equipment and by lending money in U.S. financial markets. These capital inflows complicated monetary policy, however, and greatly increased U.S. foreign debt and interest costs.

U.S. a Net Debtor

The inflow of foreign investment also raised anxieties about "selling off" America. As Japanese and other foreign investors increased their purchases of farmland, factories, and real estate (e.g., Rockefeller Center), many Americans worried that foreign investors were taking control of the U.S. economy.

Fueling these fears was the dramatic change in America's international financial position. From 1914 to 1984, the United States had been a net creditor in the world economy. We owned more assets abroad than foreign investors owned in the United States. Our financial position changed in 1985. Continuing trade deficits and offsetting capital inflows transformed the United States into a net debtor in that year. Since then, foreigners have owned more U.S. assets than Americans own of foreign assets.

America's new debtor status can complicate domestic policy. A sudden flight from U.S. assets could severely weaken the dollar and disrupt the domestic economy. To prevent that from occurring, policymakers must consider the impact of their decisions on foreign investors. This may necessitate difficult policy choices.

There's a silver lining to this cloud, however. The inflow of foreign investment is a reflection of confidence in the U.S. economy. Foreign investors want to share in our growth and profitability. In the process, their investments (like BMW's auto plant) expand America's production possibilities and stimulate still more economic growth.

Foreign investors actually assume substantial risk when they invest in the United States. If the dollar falls, the foreign value of *their* U.S. investments will decline. Hence, foreigners who've already invested in the United States have no incentive to start a flight from the dollar. On the contrary, a strong dollar protects the value of their U.S. holdings.

EXCHANGE-RATE INTERVENTION

Given the potential opposition to exchange-rate movements, governments often feel compelled to intervene in foreign-exchange markets. The intervention is usually intended to achieve greater exchange-rate stability. But such stability may itself give rise to undesirable micro- and macroeconomic effects.

One way to eliminate fluctuations in exchange rates is to fix the rate's value. To fix exchange rates, each country may simply proclaim that its currency is worth so much in relation to that of other countries. The easiest way to do this is for each country to define the worth of its currency in terms of some common standard. Under a **gold standard,** each country determines that its currency is worth so much gold. In so doing, it implicitly defines the worth of its currency in terms of all other currencies, which also have a fixed gold value. In 1944, the major trading nations met at Bretton Woods, New Hampshire, and agreed that each currency was worth so much gold. The value of the U.S. dollar was defined as being equal to 0.0294 ounce of gold, while the British pound was defined as being worth 0.0823 ounce of gold. Thus, the exchange rate between British pounds and U.S. dollars was effectively fixed at $1 = 0.357$ pound, or 1 pound $= \$2.80$ (or $\$2.80/0.0823 = \$1/0.0294$).

Fixed Exchange Rates

> **gold standard:** An agreement by countries to fix the price of their currencies in terms of gold; a mechanism for fixing exchange rates.

Balance-of-Payments Problems. It's one thing to proclaim the worth of a country's currency; it's quite another to *maintain* the fixed rate of exchange. As we've observed, foreign-exchange rates are subject to continual and often unpredictable changes in supply and demand. Hence, two countries that seek to stabilize their exchange rate at some fixed value are going to find it necessary to compensate for such foreign-exchange market pressures.

Suppose the exchange rate officially established by the United States and Great Britain is equal to e_1, as illustrated in Figure 20.4. As is apparent, that particular exchange rate is consistent with the then-prevailing demand and supply conditions in the foreign-exchange market (as indicated by curves D_1 and S_1).

QUANTITY OF POUNDS (per year)

FIGURE 20.4
Fixed Rates and Market Imbalance

If exchange rates are fixed, they can't adjust to changes in market supply and demand. Suppose the exchange rate is initially fixed at e_1. When the demand for British pounds increases (shifts to the right), an excess demand for pounds emerges. More pounds are demanded (q_D) at the rate e_1 than are supplied (q_S). This causes a balance-of-payments deficit for the United States.

Now suppose that Americans suddenly acquire a greater taste for British cars and start spending more income on Jaguars and Mini Coopers. As U.S. purchases of British goods increase, the demand for British currency will *shift* from D_1 to D_2 in Figure 20.4. Were exchange rates allowed to respond to market influences, the dollar price of a British pound would rise, in this case to the rate e_2. But we've assumed that government intervention has fixed the exchange rate at e_1. Unfortunately, at e_1, American consumers want to buy more pounds (q_D) than the British are willing to supply (q_S). The difference between the quantity demanded and the quantity supplied in the market at the rate e_1 represents a **market shortage** of British pounds.

The excess demand for pounds implies a **balance-of-payments deficit** for the United States: More dollars are flowing out of the country than into it. The same disequilibrium represents a **balance-of-payments surplus** for Britain, because its outward flow of pounds is less than its incoming flow.

Basically, there are only two solutions to balance-of-payments problems brought about by the attempt to fix exchange rates:

- Allow exchange rates to rise to e_2 (Figure 20.4), thereby eliminating the excess demand for pounds.
- Alter market supply or demand so that they intersect at the fixed rate e_1.

Since fixed exchange rates were the initial objective of policy, only the second alternative is of immediate interest.

The Need for Reserves. One way to alter market conditions would be for someone simply to supply British pounds to American consumers. The U.S. Treasury could have accumulated a reserve of foreign exchange in earlier periods. By selling some of those **foreign-exchange reserves** now, the Treasury could help to stabilize market conditions at the officially established exchange rate. The rightward shift of the pound supply curve in Figure 20.5 illustrates the sale of accumulated British pounds—and related purchase of U.S. dollars—by the U.S. Treasury. (In 2008, the U.S. Treasury reduced foreign-exchange reserves by $5 billion; see item 11 in Table 20.1.)

Although foreign-exchange reserves can be used to fix exchange rates, such reserves may not be adequate. Indeed, Figure 20.6 should be testimony enough to the fact that today's deficit isn't always offset by tomorrow's surplus. A principal reason that fixed exchange rates didn't live up to their expectations is that the United States had balance-of-payments deficits for 22 consecutive years. This long-term deficit overwhelmed our stock of foreign-exchange reserves.

The Role of Gold. Gold reserves are a potential substitute for foreign-exchange reserves. As long as each country's money has a value defined in terms of gold, we can use gold to buy

---

market shortage: The amount by which the quantity demanded exceeds the quantity supplied at a given price; excess demand.

balance-of-payments deficit: An excess demand for foreign currency at current exchange rates.

balance-of-payments surplus: An excess demand for domestic currency at current exchange rates.

foreign-exchange reserves: Holdings of foreign exchange by official government agencies, usually the central bank or treasury.

FIGURE 20.5

The Impact of Monetary Intervention

If the U.S. Treasury holds reserves of British pounds, it can use them to buy U.S. dollars in foreign-exchange markets. As it does so, the supply of pounds will shift to the right, to S_2, thereby maintaining the desired exchange rate, e_1. The Bank of England could bring about the same result by offering to buy U.S. dollars with pounds.

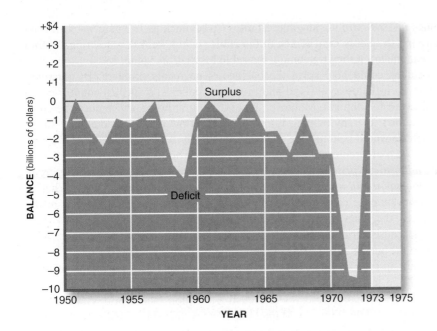

FIGURE 20.6
The U.S. Balance of Payments, 1950–1973

The United States had a balance-of-payments deficit for 22 consecutive years. During this period, the foreign-exchange reserves of the U.S. Treasury were sharply reduced. Fixed exchange rates were maintained by the willingness of foreign countries to accumulate large reserves of U.S. dollars. However, neither the Treasury's reserves nor the willingness of foreigners to accumulate dollars was unlimited. In 1973, fixed exchange rates were abandoned.

British pounds, thereby restocking our foreign-exchange reserves. Or we can simply use the gold to purchase U.S. dollars in foreign-exchange markets. In either case, the exchange value of the dollar will tend to rise. However, we must have **gold reserves** available for this purpose. Unfortunately, the continuing U.S. balance-of-payments deficits recorded in Figure 20.6 exceeded even the hoards of gold buried under Fort Knox. As a consequence, our gold reserves lost their credibility as a potential guarantee of fixed exchange rates.

gold reserves: Stocks of gold held by a government to purchase foreign exchange.

Domestic Adjustments. The supply and demand for foreign exchange can also be shifted by changes in basic fiscal, monetary, or trade policies. With respect to trade policy, *trade protection can be used to prop up fixed exchange rates.* We could eliminate the excess demand for pounds (Figure 20.4), for example, by imposing quotas and tariffs on British goods. Such trade restrictions would reduce British imports to the United States and thus the demand for British pounds. In August 1971, President Nixon imposed an emergency 10 percent surcharge on all imported goods to help reduce the payments deficit that fixed exchange rates had spawned. Such restrictions on international trade, however, violate the principle of comparative advantage and thus reduce total world output. Trade protection also invites retaliatory trade restrictions (see World View on Mexico's 2009 retaliation against U.S. trade barriers, p. 421).

Fiscal policy is another way out of the imbalance. An increase in U.S. income tax rates will reduce disposable income and have a negative effect on the demand for all goods, including imports. A reduction in government spending will have similar effects. In general, *deflationary (or restrictive) policies help correct a balance-of-payments deficit by lowering domestic incomes and thus the demand for imports.*

Monetary policies in a deficit country could follow the same restrictive course. A reduction in the money supply raises interest rates. The balance of payments will benefit in two ways. The resultant slowdown in spending will reduce import demand. In addition, higher interest rates may induce international investors to move more of their funds into the deficit country. Such moves will provide immediate relief to the payments imbalance.[2] Russia

[2]Before 1930, not only were foreign-exchange rates fixed, but domestic monetary supplies were tied to gold stocks as well. Countries experiencing a balance-of-payments deficit were thus forced to contract their money supply, and countries experiencing a payments surplus were forced to expand their money supply by a set amount. Monetary authorities were powerless to control domestic money supplies except by erecting barriers to trade. The system was abandoned when the world economy collapsed into the Great Depression.

tried this strategy in 1998, tripling key interest rates (to as much as 150 percent). But even that wasn't enough to restore confidence in the ruble, which kept depreciating. Within 3 months of the monetary policy tightening, the ruble lost half its value.

A surplus country could help solve the balance-of-payments problem by pursuing expansionary—even inflationary—fiscal and monetary policies, a surplus country could stimulate the demand for imports. Moreover, any inflation at home will reduce the competitiveness of exports, thereby helping to restrain the inflow of foreign demand. Taken together, such efforts would help reverse an international payments imbalance.

Even under the best of circumstances, domestic economic adjustments entail significant costs. In effect, ***domestic adjustments to payments imbalances require a deficit country to forsake full employment and a surplus country to forsake price stability***. China has had to grapple with these domestic consequences of fixing the value of its currency. The artificially low value of the yuan promoted Chinese exports and accelerated China's GDP growth. It has also caused prices in China to rise faster than the government desires, however. To maintain the yuan's fixed exchange rate, the Chinese government had to adopt restrictive monetary and fiscal policies to keep inflation in check. The Chinese government also had to be willing to accumulate the inflow of U.S. dollars and other currencies. By 2009, China's foreign-exchange reserves exceeded $1 trillion (see World View below). There's no easy way out of this impasse. Market imbalances caused by fixed exchange rates can be corrected only with abundant supplies of foreign-exchange reserves or deliberate changes in fiscal, monetary, or trade policies. At some point, it may become easier to let a currency adjust to market equilibrium.

The Euro Fix. The original 12 nations of the European Monetary Union (EMU) fixed their exchange rates in 1999. They went far beyond the kind of exchange-rate fix we're discussing here. Members of the EMU *eliminated* their national currencies, making the euro the

WORLD VIEW

Foreign Currency Piles Up in China

SHANGHAI, Jan. 16—China's state media on Monday reported that the country's foreign currency reserves swelled by more than one-third last year to a record $819 billion as its factories churned out goods for markets around the world, heightening the likelihood of fresh trade tensions with the United States.

Coupled with news only days earlier that China's world trade surplus tripled last year, to $102 billion, the country's burgeoning foreign exchange reserves seemed certain to intensify demands that China increase the value of its currency, the yuan, the worth of which is linked to the dollar. U.S. manufacturing groups argue that China's currency is priced too low, making its goods unfairly cheap on world markets. . . .

China is loath to increase the yuan enough to dampen growth in its coastal factories. Exports are a key source of jobs in a country that must find tens of millions of them for poor farmers and workers laid off by bankrupt state factories in the continued transition from communism to capitalism. . . .

Still, some economists said China's reserves were now growing so huge as to compel the central bank to deliver a significant revaluation. Otherwise, China risks that its reserves will leak into the banking system and be lent out for speculative investments that will only worsen a feared glut of real estate and factory capacity.

"The renminbi [yuan] is fundamentally undervalued," said Ha Jiming, chief economist at China International Capital Corp., a giant state-owned investment bank. "As foreign exchange continues to grow, it will force a revaluation."

—Peter S. Goodman

Source: *The Washington Post*, January 17, 2006, p. D1. © 2006 The Washington Post. Used with permission by PARS International Corp.

Analysis: When a currency is deliberately undervalued, strong export demand may kindle inflation. The trade surplus that results also increases foreign-exchange reserves.

common currency of Euroland. They don't have to worry about reserve balances or domestic adjustments. However, they do have to reconcile their varied national interests to a single monetary authority, which may prove to be difficult politically in times of economic stress.

Flexible Exchange Rates

flexible exchange rates: A system in which exchange rates are permitted to vary with market supply-and-demand conditions; floating exchange rates.

Balance-of-payments problems wouldn't arise in the first place if exchange rates were allowed to respond to market forces. Under a system of **flexible exchange rates** (often called floating exchange rates), the exchange rate moves up or down to choke off any excess supply of or demand for foreign exchange. Notice again in Figure 20.4 that the exchange-rate move from e_1 to e_2 prevents any excess demand from emerging. *With flexible exchange rates, the quantity of foreign exchange demanded always equals the quantity supplied,* and there's no imbalance. For the same reason, there's no need for foreign-exchange reserves.

Although flexible exchange rates eliminate balance-of-payments and foreign-exchange reserves problems, they don't solve all of a country's international trade problems. *Exchange-rate movements associated with flexible rates alter relative prices and may disrupt import and export flows.* As noted before, depreciation of the dollar raises the price of all imported goods. The price increases may contribute to domestic cost-push inflation. Also, domestic businesses that sell imported goods or use them as production inputs may suffer sales losses. On the other hand, appreciation of the dollar raises the foreign price of U.S. goods and reduces the sales of American exporters. Hence, *someone is always hurt, and others are helped, by exchange-rate movements.* The resistance to flexible exchange rates originates in these potential losses. Such resistance creates pressure for official intervention in foreign-exchange markets or increased trade barriers.

The United States and its major trading partners abandoned fixed exchange rates in 1973. Although exchange rates are now able to fluctuate freely, it shouldn't be assumed that they necessarily undergo wild gyrations. On the contrary, experience with flexible rates since 1973 suggests that some semblance of stability is possible even when exchange rates are free to change in response to market forces.

Speculation. One force that often helps maintain stability in a flexible exchange-rate system is speculation. Speculators often counteract short-term changes in foreign-exchange supply and demand. If an exchange rate temporarily rises above its long-term equilibrium, speculators will move in to sell foreign exchange. By selling at high prices and later buying at lower prices, speculators hope to make a profit. In the process, they also help stabilize foreign-exchange rates.

"Damn it! How can I relax, knowing that out there, somewhere, somehow, someone's attacking the dollar?"

Analysis: A "weak" dollar reduces the buying power of American tourists.

Speculation isn't always stabilizing, however. Speculators may not correctly gauge the long-term equilibrium. Instead, they may move "with the market" and help push exchange rates far out of kilter. This kind of destabilizing speculation sharply lowered the international value of the U.S. dollar in 1987, forcing the Reagan administration to intervene in foreign-exchange markets, borrowing foreign currencies to buy U.S. dollars. In 1997, the Clinton administration intervened for the opposite purpose: stemming the rise in the U.S. dollar. The Bush administration was more willing to stay on the sidelines, letting global markets set the exchange rates for the U.S. dollar.

Managed Exchange Rates. Governments can intervene in foreign-exchange markets without completely fixing exchange rates. That is, they may buy and sell foreign exchange for the purpose of *narrowing* rather than *eliminating* exchange-rate movements. Such limited intervention in foreign-exchange markets is often referred to as **managed exchange rates,** or, popularly, "dirty floats."

> **managed exchange rates:** A system in which governments intervene in foreign-exchange markets to limit but not eliminate exchange-rate fluctuations; "dirty floats."

The basic objective of exchange-rate management is to provide a stabilizing force. The U.S. Treasury, for example, may use its foreign-exchange reserves to buy dollars when they're depreciating too much. Or it may buy foreign exchange if the dollar is rising too fast. From this perspective, exchange-rate management appears as a fail-safe system for the private market. Unfortunately, the motivation for official intervention is sometimes suspect. Private speculators buy and sell foreign exchange for the sole purpose of making a profit. But government sales and purchases may be motivated by other considerations. A falling exchange rate increases the competitive advantage of a country's exports. A rising exchange rate makes international investment less expensive. Hence, a country's efforts to manage exchange-rate movements may arouse suspicion and outright hostility in its trading partners.

Although managed exchange rates would seem to be an ideal compromise between fixed rates and flexible rates, they can work only when some acceptable "rules of the game" and mutual trust have been established. As Sherman Maisel, a former governor of the Federal Reserve Board, put it, "Monetary systems are based on credit and faith: If these are lacking, a . . . crisis occurs."[3]

THE ECONOMY TOMORROW

CURRENCY BAILOUTS

The world has witnessed a string of currency crises, including the one in Asia during 1997–98, the Brazilian crisis of 1999, the Argentine crisis of 2001–2, recurrent ruble crises in Russia, and periodic panics in Mexico and South America. In every instance, the country in trouble pleads for external help. In most cases, a currency "bailout" is arranged, whereby global monetary authorities lend the troubled nation enough reserves (such as U.S. dollars) to defend its currency. Typically, the International Monetary Fund (IMF) heads the rescue party, joined by the central banks of the strongest economies.

The Case for Bailouts. The argument for currency bailouts typically rests on the domino theory. Weakness in one currency can undermine another. This seemed to be the case during the 1997–98 Asian crisis. After the **devaluation** of the Thai baht, global investors began worrying about currency values in other Asian nations. Choosing to be safe rather than sorry, they moved funds out of Korea, Malaysia, and the Philippines and invested in U.S. and European markets (notice in Figure 20.3 the 1997–98 appreciation of the U.S. dollar).

> **devaluation:** An abrupt depreciation of a currency whose value was fixed or managed by the government.

The initial baht devaluation also weakened the competitive trade position of these same economies. Thai exports became cheaper, diverting export demand from other Asian nations. To prevent loss of export markets, Thailand's neighbors felt they had to devalue as well. Speculators who foresaw these effects accelerated the domino effect by selling the region's currencies.

---

[3]Sherman Maisel, *Managing the Dollar* (New York: W. W. Norton, 1973), p. 196.

When Brazil devalued its currency (the *real*) in January 1999, global investors worried that a "samba effect" might sweep across Latin America. The domino effect could reach across the ocean and damage U.S. and European exports as well. Hence, the industrial countries often offer a currency bailout as a form of self-defense.

The Case against Bailouts. Critics of bailouts argue that such interventions are ultimately self-defeating. They say that once a country knows for sure that currency bailouts are in the wings, it doesn't have to pursue the domestic policy adjustments that might stabilize its currency. A nation can avoid politically unpopular options such as high interest rates, tax hikes, or cutbacks in government spending. It can also turn a blind eye to trade barriers, monopoly power, lax lending policies, and other constraints on productive growth. Hence, the expectation of readily available bailouts may foster the very conditions that cause currency crises.

Future Bailouts? The decision to bail out a depreciating currency isn't as simple as it appears. To minimize the ill effects of bailouts, the IMF and other institutions typically require the crisis nation to pledge more prudent monetary, fiscal, and trade policies. Usually there's a lot of debate about what kinds of adjustments will be made—and how soon. As long as the crisis nation is confident of an eventual bailout, however, it has a lot of bargaining power to resist policy changes. Only after the IMF finally said no to further bailouts in 2001 did Argentina devalue its currency and pursue more domestic reforms.

SUMMARY

- Money serves the same purposes in international trade as it does in the domestic economy, namely, to facilitate productive specialization and market exchanges. The basic challenge of international finance is to create acceptable standards of value from the various currencies maintained by separate countries. LO1
- Exchange rates are the mechanism for translating the value of one national currency into the equivalent value of another. An exchange rate of $1 = 2 euros means that one dollar is worth two euros in foreign-exchange markets. LO2
- Foreign currencies have value because they can be used to acquire goods and resources from other countries. Accordingly, the supply of and demand for foreign currency reflect the demands for imports and exports, for international investment, and for overseas activities of governments. LO1
- The balance of payments summarizes a country's international transactions. Its components are the trade balance, the current-account balance, and the capital-account balance. The current and capital accounts must offset each other. LO1
- The equilibrium exchange rate is subject to any and all shifts of supply and demand for foreign exchange. If relative incomes, prices, or interest rates change, the demand for foreign exchange will be affected. A depreciation is a

- change in market exchange rates that makes one country's currency cheaper in terms of another currency. An appreciation is the opposite kind of change. LO2
- Changes in exchange rates are often resisted. Producers of export goods don't want their currencies to rise in value (appreciate); importers and tourists dislike it when their currencies fall in value (depreciate). LO3
- Under a system of fixed exchange rates, changes in the supply and demand for foreign exchange can't be expressed in exchange-rate movements. Instead, such shifts will be reflected in excess demand for or excess supply of foreign exchange. Such market imbalances are referred to as balance-of-payments deficits or surpluses. LO2
- To maintain fixed exchange rates, monetary authorities must enter the market to buy and sell foreign exchange. In order to do so, deficit countries must have foreign-exchange reserves. In the absence of sufficient reserves, a country can maintain fixed exchange rates only if it's willing to alter basic fiscal, monetary, or trade policies. LO3
- Flexible exchange rates eliminate balance-of-payments problems and the crises that accompany them. But complete flexibility can lead to excessive changes. To avoid this contingency, many countries prefer to adopt managed exchange rates, that is, rates determined by the market but subject to government intervention. LO3

Key Terms

exchange rate
equilibrium price
balance of payments
trade deficit
depreciation (currency)
appreciation

foreign-exchange markets
gold standard
market shortage
balance-of-payments deficit
balance-of-payments surplus

foreign-exchange reserves
gold reserves
flexible exchange rates
managed exchange rates
devaluation

Questions for Discussion

1. Why would a decline in the value of the dollar prompt foreign manufacturers such as BMW to build production plants in the United States? LO3

2. How do changes in the foreign value of the U.S. dollar affect foreign enrollments at U.S. colleges? LO3

3. How would rapid inflation in Canada alter our demand for travel to Canada and for Canadian imports? Does it make any difference whether the exchange rate between Canadian and U.S. dollars is fixed or flexible? LO2

4. Under what conditions would a country welcome a balance-of-payments deficit? When would it *not* want a deficit? LO3

5. In what sense do fixed exchange rates permit a country to "export its inflation"? LO1

6. In the World View on page 434, who is Farshad Shahabadi referring to as "everyone else"? LO1

7. If a nation's currency depreciates, are the reduced export prices that result "unfair"? LO3

8. How would each of these events affect the supply or demand for Japanese yen? LO1
    (*a*) Stronger U.S. economic growth.
    (*b*) A decline in Japanese interest rates.
    (*c*) Higher inflation in the USA.

9. Is a stronger dollar good or bad for America? Explain. LO3

10. What can China do with its U.S. dollar reserves? What impact will that have? LO3

! web activities to accompany this chapter can be found on the Online Learning Center:
http://www.mhhe.com/schiller12e

PROBLEMS FOR CHAPTER 20

Name: _____

connect |ECONOMICS

LO2 1. According to the World View on page 431, which nation had
    (*a*) The cheapest currency? _____
    (*b*) The most expensive currency? _____

LO2 2. If a euro is worth $1.20, what is the euro price of a dollar? _____

LO3 3. If a pound of U.S. pork cost 50 rupiah in Indonesia before the Asian crisis, how much did it cost when the dollar value of the rupiah fell by 80 percent? _____

LO2 4. If a PlayStation 3 costs 30,000 yen in Japan, how much will it cost in U.S. dollars if the exchange rate is
LO3
    (*a*) 120 yen = $1? _____
    (*b*) 1 yen = $0.00833? _____
    (*c*) 100 yen = $1? _____

LO2 5. Between 1980 and 1985, by how much did the dollar appreciate (Figure 20.3)? _____%

LO1 6. If inflation raises U.S. prices by 3 percent and the U.S. dollar appreciates by 4 percent, by how
LO3 much does the foreign price of U.S. exports change? _____%

LO2 7. According to the World View on page 431, what was the peso price of a euro in March 2009? _____

LO1 8. For each of the following possible events, indicate whether the global value of the U.S. dollar
LO2 will A: rise or B: fall.
LO3
    (*a*) American cars become suddenly more popular abroad. _____

    (*b*) Inflation rates in the United States accelerate. _____

    (*c*) The United States falls into a depression. _____

    (*d*) Interest rates in the United States drop. _____

    (*e*) The United States suddenly experiences rapid increases in productivity. _____

    (*f*) Anticipating a return to the gold standard, Americans suddenly rush to buy gold from the two big producers, South Africa and the Soviet Union. _____

    (*g*) War is declared in the Middle East. _____

    (*h*) The stock markets in the United States suddenly collapse. _____

LO1
LO2
LO3

9. The following schedules summarize the supply and demand for trifflings, the national currency of Tricoli:

Triffling price (U.S. dollars per triffling)	0	$4	$8	$12	$16	$20	$24
Quantity demanded (per year)	40	38	36	34	32	30	28
Quantity supplied (per year)	1	11	21	31	41	51	61

Use the above schedules for the following:
(*a*) Graph the supply and demand curves.
(*b*) Determine the equilibrium exchange rate.   _____
(*c*) Determine the size of the excess supply or excess demand that would exist if the Tricolian government fixed the exchange rate at $22 = 1 triffling.   _____
(*d*) Which of the following events would help reduce the payments imbalance? Which would not? (A = helps; B = doesn't help)
   (*i*) Domestic inflation.   _____
   (*ii*) Foreign inflation.   _____
   (*iii*) Slower domestic growth.   _____
   (*iv*) Faster domestic growth.   _____

21

Global Poverty

After reading this chapter, you should be able to:

LO1. Explain how U.S. and global poverty are defined.

LO2. Classify how many people in the world are poor.

LO3. Discuss how global poverty can be reduced.

Bono, the lead singer for the rock group U2, has performed concerts around the world to raise awareness of global poverty. He doesn't have a specific agenda for eradicating poverty. He does believe, though, that greater awareness of global poverty will raise assistance levels and spawn more ideas for combating global hunger, disease, and isolation.

The dimensions of global poverty are staggering. According to the World Bank, roughly a third of the world's population lacks even the barest of life's necessities. *Billions* of people are persistently malnourished, poorly sheltered, minimally clothed, and at constant risk of debilitating diseases. Life expectancies among the globally poor population still hover in the range of 40–50 years, far below the norm (70 80 years) of the rich, developed nations.

In this chapter we follow Bono's suggestion and take a closer look at global poverty. We address the following issues:

- **What income thresholds define "poverty"?**
- **How many people are poor?**
- **What actions can be taken to reduce global poverty?**

In the process of answering these questions, we get another opportunity to examine what makes economies "tick"—particularly what forces foster faster economic growth for some nations and slower economic growth for others.

AMERICAN POVERTY

Poverty, like beauty, is often in the eye of the beholder. Many Americans feel "poor" if they can't buy a new car, live in a fancy home, or take an exotic vacation. Indeed, the average American asserts that a family needs at least $35,000 a year "just to get by." With that much income, however, few people would go hungry or be forced to live in the streets.

Official Poverty Thresholds

To develop a more objective standard of poverty, the U.S. government assessed how much money a U.S. family needs to purchase a "minimally adequate" diet. Back in 1963, they concluded that $1,000 per year was needed for that purpose alone. Then they asked how much income was needed to purchase other basic necessities like housing, clothes, transportation, etc. They figured all those *non*food necessities would cost twice as much as the food staples. So they concluded that a budget of $3,000 per year would fund a "minimally adequate" living standard for a U.S. family of four. That standard became the official **U.S. poverty threshold** in 1963.

> **poverty threshold (U.S.):** Annual income of less than $22,000 for a family of four (2009, inflation adjusted).

Inflation Adjustments. Since 1963, prices have risen every year. As a result, the price of the poverty "basket" has risen as well. In 2009, it cost roughly $22,000 to purchase those same basic necessities for a family of four that cost only $3,000 in 1963.

Twenty-two thousand dollars might sound like a lot of money, especially if you're not paying your own rent or feeding a family. If you break the budget down, however, it doesn't look so generous. Only a third of the budget goes for food. And that portion has to feed four people. So the official U.S. poverty standard provides only $5 per day for an individual's food. That just about covers a single Big Mac combo at McDonald's. There's no money in the poverty budget for dining out. And the implied rent money is only $700 a month (for the whole family). So the official U.S. poverty standard isn't that generous—certainly not by *American* standards (where the *average* family has an income of nearly $80,000 per year and eats outside their $240,000 home three times a week).

U.S. Poverty Count

The Census Bureau counted over 38 million Americans as "poor" in 2008 according to the official U.S. thresholds (as adjusted for family size). This was one out of eight U.S. households, for a **poverty rate** of roughly 12.5 percent. According to the Census Bureau, the official U.S. poverty rate has been in a narrow range of 11–15 percent for the last 40 years.

> **poverty rate:** Percentage of the population counted as poor.

How Poor Is U.S. "Poor"?

Many observers criticize these official U.S. poverty statistics. They say that far fewer Americans meet the government standard of poverty and even fewer are really destitute.

In-Kind Income. A major flaw in the official tally is that the government counts only *cash* income in defining poverty. Since the 1960s, however, the U.S. has developed an extensive system of **in-kind transfers** that augment cash incomes. Food stamps, for example, can be used just as easily as cash to purchase groceries. Medicaid and Medicare pay doctor and hospital bills, reducing the need for cash income. Government rent subsidies and public housing allow poor families to have more housing than their cash incomes would permit. These in-kind transfers allow "poor" families to enjoy a higher living standard than their cash incomes imply. Adding those transfers to cash incomes would bring the U.S. poverty count down into the 9–11 percent range.

> **in-kind transfers:** Direct transfers of goods and services rather than cash, e.g., food stamps, Medicaid benefits, and housing subsidies.

Material Possessions. Even those families who remain "poor" after counting in-kind transfers aren't necessarily destitute. Over 40 percent of America's "poor" families own their own home, 70 percent own a car or truck, and 30 percent own at least *two* vehicles. Telephones, color TVs, dishwashers, clothes dryers, air conditioners, and microwave ovens are commonplace in America's poor households.

America's poor families themselves report few acute problems in everyday living. Fewer than 14 percent report missing a rent or mortgage payment, and fewer than 8 percent report a food deficiency. So American poverty isn't synonymous with homelessness, malnutrition, chronic illness, or even social isolation. These problems exist among America's poverty population, but don't define American poverty.

GLOBAL POVERTY

Poverty in the rest of the world is much different from poverty in America. *American poverty is more about* relative *deprivation than* absolute *deprivation. In the rest of the world, poverty is all about* absolute *deprivation.*

As a starting point for assessing global poverty consider how *average* incomes in the rest of the world stack up against U.S. levels. By global standards, the U.S. is unquestionably a very rich nation. As we observed in Chapter 2 (World View, p. 29), U.S. GDP per capita is five times larger than the world average. Over three-fourths of the world's population lives in what the World Bank calls "low-income" or "lower-middle-income" nations. In those nations the *average* income is under $4,000 a year, less than *one-tenth* of America's per capita GDP. Average incomes are lower yet in Haiti, Nigeria, Ethiopia, and other desperately poor nations. By American standards, virtually all the people in these nations would be poor. By *their* standards, no American would be poor.

Because national poverty lines are so diverse and culture-bound, the World Bank decided to establish a uniform standard for assessing global poverty. And it set the bar amazingly low. In fact, the World Bank regularly uses two thresholds, namely $1 per day for **"extreme" poverty** and a higher $2 per day standard for less "severe" poverty.

The World Bank thresholds are incomprehensively low by American standards. How much could you buy for $1 a day? A little rice, maybe, and perhaps some milk? Certainly not a Big Mac. And part of that dollar would have to go for rent. Clearly, this isn't going to work. Doubling the World Bank standard to $2 per day **(severe poverty)** doesn't reach a whole lot further.

The World Bank, of course, wasn't defining "poverty" in the context of American affluence. They were instead trying to define a rock-bottom threshold of absolute poverty—a threshold of physical deprivation that people everywhere would acknowledge as the barest "minimum"— a condition of "unacceptable deprivation."

Inflation Adjustments. The World Bank lines were established in the context of 1985 prices and translated into local currencies (based on purchasing power equivalents, not official currency exchange rates). Like official U.S. poverty lines, the World Bank's global poverty lines are adjusted each year for inflation. They are also recalculated on occasion (e.g., 1993) to reflect changing consumption patterns. In today's dollars, the "$1" standard of 1985 is actually about $1.50 per day in U.S. currency. That works out to $2,190 per year for a family of four—a *tenth* of the official U.S. poverty threshold. Despite continuing inflation adjustments, the World Bank standard is still referred to as the "dollar-a-day" index of extreme poverty.

extreme poverty (world): World Bank income standard of less than $1 per day per person (inflation adjusted).

severe poverty (world): World Bank income standard of $2 per day per person (inflation adjusted).

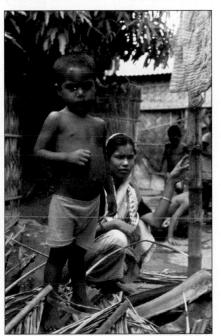

Analysis: Global poverty is defined in terms of absolute deprivation.

FIGURE 21.1

Geography of Extreme Poverty

Over a billion people around the world are in "extreme" poverty. In smaller, poor nations, deprivation is commonplace.

Source: World Bank, *World Development Report 2009.* **www.worldbank.org**

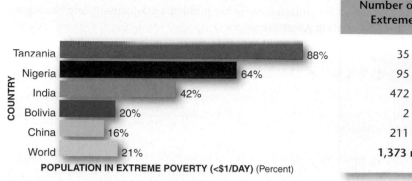

Country	POPULATION IN EXTREME POVERTY (<$1/DAY) (Percent)	Number of People in Extreme Poverty
Tanzania	88%	35 million
Nigeria	64%	95 million
India	42%	472 million
Bolivia	20%	2 million
China	16%	211 million
World	21%	**1,373 million**

Global Poverty Counts

On the basis of household surveys in over 100 nations, *the World Bank classifies over a billion people as being in "extreme" poverty (<$1/day) and nearly 3 billion people as being in "severe" poverty (<$2/day).*

Figure 21.1 shows where concentrations of extreme poverty are the greatest. Concentrations of extreme poverty are alarmingly high in dozens of smaller, less developed nations like Mali, Haiti, and Zambia, where average incomes are also shockingly low. However, the greatest *number* of extremely poor people reside in the world's largest countries. China and India alone contain a third of the world's population and half of the world's extreme poverty.

Table 21.1 reveals that the distribution of severe poverty (<$2/day) is similar. The incidence of this higher poverty threshold is, of course, much greater. Severe poverty afflicts over 80 percent of the population in dozens of nations and even reaches over 90 percent of the population in some (e.g., Tanzania). By contrast, less than 13 percent of the U.S. population falls below the official *American* poverty threshold and *virtually no American household has an income below the* global *poverty threshold.*

Social Indicators

The levels of poverty depicted in Figure 21.1 and Table 21.1 imply levels of physical and social deprivation few Americans can comprehend. Living on less than a dollar or two a day means always being hungry, malnourished, ill-clothed, dirty, and unhealthy. The problems associated with such deprivation begin even before birth. Pregnant women often fail to get enough nutrition or medical attention. In low-income countries only a third of all births are attended by a skilled health practitioner. If something goes awry, both the mother and the baby are at fatal risk. Nearly all of the children in global poverty are in a state of chronic malnutrition. At least 1 out of 10 children in low-income nations will actually die before reaching age five. In the

TABLE 21.1

Population in Severe Poverty (<$2/day)

Nearly half the world's population has income of less than $2 per person per day. Such poverty is pervasive in low-income nations.

Country	Percent	Number
Tanzania	97%	39 million
Rwanda	90	9
Nigeria	84	124
Bangladesh	81	129
Ethiopia	78	62
India	76	855
China	36	474
World	**39%**	**2,560**

Source: World Bank, *World Development Report 2009.* **www.worldbank.org**

poorest sectors of the population infant and child mortality rates are often two to three times higher than that. Children often remain unimmunized to preventable diseases. And AIDS is rampant among both children and adults in the poorest nations. All of these factors contribute to a frighteningly short life expectancy—less than half that in the developed nations.

Fewer than one out of two children from extremely poor households is likely to stay in school past the eighth grade. Women and minority ethnic and religious groups are often wholly excluded from educational opportunities. As a consequence, great stocks of human capital remain undeveloped: In low-income nations only one out of two women is literate and only two out of three men.

Global poverty is not only more desperate than American poverty, but also more permanent. In India, a rigid caste system still defines differential opportunities for millions of rich and poor villagers. Studies in Brazil, South Africa, Peru, and Ecuador document barriers that block access to health care, education, and jobs for children of poor families. Hence, inequalities in poor nations are not only more severe than in developed nations but also tend to be more permanent.

Persistent Poverty

Economic stagnation also keeps a lid on upward mobility. President John F. Kennedy observed that "a rising tide lifts all boats," referring to the power of a growing economy to raise everyone's income. In a growing economy, one person's income *gain* is not another person's *loss*. By contrast, a stagnant economy intensifies class warfare, with everyone jealously protecting whatever gains they have made. The *haves* strive to keep the *have-nots* at bay. Unfortunately, this is the reality in many low-income nations. As we observed in Chapter 2 (Table 2.1), in some of the poorest nations in the world output grows more slowly than the population, intensifying the competition for resources.

GOALS AND STRATEGIES

Global poverty is so extensive that no policy approach offers a quick solution. Even the World Bank doesn't see an end to global poverty. The United Nations set a much more modest goal back in 2000. The U.N. established a **Millennium Poverty Goal** of cutting the incidence of extreme global poverty in half by 2015 (from 30 percent in 1990 to 15 percent in 2015). Even that seemingly modest goal wouldn't greatly decrease the *number* of people in poverty. The world's population keeps growing at upward of 80–100 million people a year. By the year 2015, there will be close to 7.2 billion people on this planet. Fifteen percent of that population would still leave over a *billion* people in extreme global poverty.

The U.N. Millennium Goal

Millennium Poverty Goal: United Nations goal of reducing global rate of extreme poverty to 15 percent by 2015.

Why should we care? After all, America has its own poverty problems and a slew of other domestic concerns. So why should an American—or, for that matter, an affluent Canadian, French, or German citizen—embrace the U.N.'s Millennium Poverty Goal? For starters, one might embrace the notion that a poor child in sub-Saharan Africa or Borneo is no less worthy than a poor child elsewhere. And a child's death in Bangladesh is just as tragic as a child's death in Buffalo, New York. In other words, humanitarianism is a starting point for *global* concern for poor people. Then there are pragmatic concerns. Poverty and inequality sow the seeds of social tension both within and across national borders. Poverty in other nations also limits potential markets for international trade. Last but not least, undeveloped human capital anywhere limits human creativity. For all these reasons, the U.N. feels the Millennium Poverty Goal should be universally embraced.

To reach even this modest goal will be difficult, however. In principle, ***there are only two general approaches to global poverty reduction, namely,***

Policy Strategies

- *Redistribution* of incomes within and across nations.
- *Economic growth* that raises average incomes.

The following sections explore the potential of these strategies for eliminating global poverty.

INCOME REDISTRIBUTION

Many people suggest that the quickest route to eliminating global poverty is simply to *redistribute* incomes and assets, both within and across countries. The potential for redistribution is often exaggerated, however, and its risks underestimated.

Within-Nation Redistribution

Take another look at those nations with the highest concentrations of extreme poverty. Tanzania tops the list in Figure 21.1, with an incredible 88 percent of its population in extreme poverty and 97 percent in severe poverty. Yet the other 3 percent of the population lives fairly well, taking in 20 percent of that nation's income. So what would happen if we somehow forced Tanzania's richest households to share that wealth? Sure, Tanzania's poorest households would be better off. But the gains wouldn't be spectacular: the *average* income in Tanzania is less than $1,200 a year. Nigeria, Haiti, Zambia, and Madagascar also have such low *average* incomes that outright redistribution doesn't hold great hope for income gains by the poor.

WORLD VIEW

Glaring Inequalities

Inequality tends to diminish as a country develops. In poor nations, the richest tenth of the population typically gets 40 to 50 percent of all income—sometimes, even more. In developed countries, the richest tenth gets 20 to 30 percent of total income.

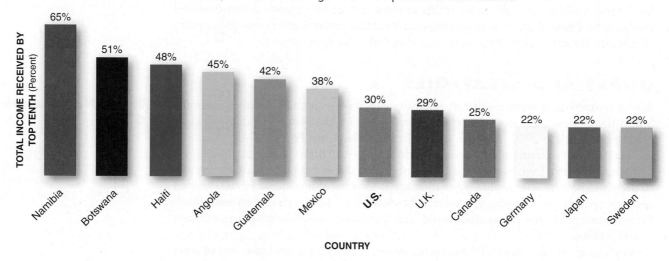

Source: World Bank, *World Development Indicators, 2009*. **www.worldbank.org**.

Analysis: The FOR WHOM question is reflected in the distribution of income. Although the U.S. income distribution is very unequal, inequalities loom even larger in most poor countries.

Economic Risks. Then there's the downside to direct redistribution. How is the income pie going to be resliced? Will the incomes or assets of the rich be confiscated? How will underlying jobs, stocks, land, and businesses be distributed to the poor? How will *total* output (and income) be affected by the redistribution? If savings are confiscated, people will no longer want to save and invest. If large, efficient farms are divided up into small parcels, who will manage them? After Zimbabwe confiscated and fragmented that nation's farms in 2000, its agricultural productivity plummeted. If the government expropriates factories, mills, farms, or businesses, who will run them? If the *rewards* to saving, investment, entrepreneurship, and management are expropriated, who will undertake these economic activities?

This is not to suggest that *no* redistribution of income or assets is appropriate. More progressive taxes and land reforms can reduce inequalities and poverty. But the potential of direct within-nation redistribution is often exaggerated. Historically, nations have often been forced to reverse land, tax, and property reforms that have slowed economic growth and reduced average incomes.

Expenditure Reallocation. In addition to directly redistributing private income and wealth, governments can also reduce poverty by reallocating direct government expenditures. As we observed in Chapter 1 (Figure 1.3), some poor nations devote a large share of output to the military. If more of those resources were channeled into schools, health services, and infrastructure, the poor would surely benefit. Governments in poor nations also tend to give priority to urban development (where the government and middle class reside), to the neglect of rural development (where the poor reside). Redirecting more resources to rural development and core infrastructure (roads, electricity, and water) would accelerate poverty reduction.

Redistribution *across* national borders could make even bigger dents in global poverty. After all, the United States and other industrialized nations are so rich that they could transfer a lot of income to the globally poor if they chose to.

Across-Nation Redistribution

Foreign Aid. Currently, developed nations give poorer nations $80–$100 billion a year in "official development assistance." That's a lot of money. But even if it were distributed exclusively to globally poor households, it would amount to less than $35 per year per person.

Developed nations have set a goal of delivering more aid. The United Nations' **Millennium Aid Goal** is to raise foreign aid levels to 0.7 percent of donor-country GDP. That may not sound too ambitious, but it's a much larger flow than at present. As Table 21.2 reveals, few "rich" nations now come close to this goal. Although the United States is by far the world's largest aid donor, its aid equals only 0.16 percent of U.S. total output. For all developed nations, the aid ratio averages around 0.28 percent—just over a third of the U.N. goal.

Given the history of foreign aid, the U.N. goal is unlikely to be met anytime soon. But what if it were? What if foreign aid *tripled*? Would that cure global poverty? No. Tripling foreign aid would generate only $100 a year for each of the nearly 3 billion people now in global poverty. Even that figure is optimistic, as it assumes all aid is distributed to the poor in a form (e.g., food, clothes, and medicine) that directly addresses their basic needs.

> **Millennium Aid Goal:** United Nations goal of raising foreign aid levels to 0.7 percent of donor-country GDP.

Nongovernmental Aid. Official development assistance is augmented by private charities and other nongovernmental organizations (NGOs). The Gates Foundation, for example, spends upward of $1 billion a year on health care for the globally poor, focusing on treatable diseases like malaria, tuberculosis, and HIV infection (see World View on the next page). Religious organizations operate schools and health clinics in areas of extreme poverty. The International Red Cross brings medical care, shelter, and food in emergencies.

Country	Total Aid ($ billions)	Percent of Donor Total Income
Australia	$ 2	0.32%
Canada	4	0.29
Denmark	2	0.81
France	10	0.38
Japan	14	0.17
Italy	4	0.19
Norway	3	0.95
United Kingdom	10	0.36
United States	22	0.16
22-Nation Total	**$108**	**0.28%**

Source: World Bank, *World Development Indicators 2009* (2007 data). **www.worldbank.org.**

TABLE 21.2
Foreign Aid

Rich nations give roughly $100–120 billion to poor nations every year. This is a tiny fraction of donor GDP, however.

WORLD VIEW

The Way We Give

Philanthropy Can Step In Where Market Forces Don't

One day my wife Melinda and I were reading about millions of children dying from diseases in poor countries that were eliminated in this country . . .

Malaria has been known for a long time. In 1902, in 1907, Nobel Prizes were given for advances in understanding the malaria parasite and how it was transmitted. But here we are a hundred years later and malaria is setting new records, infecting over 400 million people every year, and killing over a million people every year. That's a number that's increasing every year, and every day it's over 2,000 African children . . .

And this would extend to tuberculosis, yellow fever, AIDS vaccine, acute diarrheal illnesses, respiratory illnesses; you know, millions of children die from these things every year, and yet the advances we have in biology have not been applied because rich countries don't have these diseases. The private sector really isn't involved in developing vaccines and medicines for these diseases because the developing countries can't buy them . . .

And so if left to themselves, these market forces create a world, which is the situation today, where over 90 percent of the money spent on health research is spent on those who are the healthiest. An example of that is the billion a year spent on combating baldness. That's great for some people, but perhaps it should get behind malaria in terms of its priority ranking . . .

So philanthropy can step in where market forces are not there . . . It can get the people who have the expertise and draw them in. It can use awards, it can use novel arrangements with private companies, it can partner with the universities . . . And every year the platform of science that we have to do this on gets better.

—Bill Gates

Analysis: When markets fail to provide for basic human needs, additional institutions and incentives may be needed.

web analysis

Go to **www.nptrust.org** and visit the "Philanthropy Statistics" link under "About Philanthropy" for data on giving in the United States.

As with official development assistance, the content of NGO aid can be as important as its level. Relatively low-cost immunizations, for example, can improve health conditions more than an expensive, high-tech health clinic can. Teaching basic literacy to a community of young children can be more effective than equipping a single high school with Internet capabilities. Distributing drought-resistant seeds to farmers can be more effective than donating advanced farm equipment (which may become useless when it needs to be repaired).

ECONOMIC GROWTH

No matter how well designed foreign aid and philanthropy might be, across-nation transfers alone cannot eliminate global poverty. As Bill Gates observed, the entire endowment of the Gates Foundation would meet the health needs of the globally poor for only 1 year. The World Bank concurs: "Developing nations hold the keys to their prosperity; global action cannot substitute for equitable and efficient domestic policies and institutions."[1] So as important as international assistance is, it will never fully suffice.

Increasing Total Income

The "key" to ending global poverty is, of course, **economic growth.** As we've observed, *redistributing existing incomes doesn't do the job;* total *income has to increase.* This is what economic growth is all about.

economic growth: An increase in output (real GDP); an expansion of production possibilities.

Unique Needs. The generic prescription for economic growth is simple: more resources and better technology. But this growth formula takes on a new meaning in the poorest nations. Rich nations can focus on research, technology, and the spread of "brain power." Poor nations need the basics—the "bricks and mortar" elements of an economy such as water

---

[1]World Bank, *World Development Report, 2006* (Washington, DC: World Bank, 2006), p. 206.

systems, roads, schools, and legal systems. Bill Gates learned this firsthand in his early philanthropic efforts. In 1996 Microsoft donated a computer for a community center in Soweto, one of the poorest areas in South Africa. When he visited the center in 1997 he discovered the center had no electricity. He quickly realized that growth-policy priorities for poor nations are different from those for rich nations.

Growth Potential

The potential of economic growth to reduce poverty in poor nations is impressive. The 61 nations classified as "low-income" by the World Bank have a combined output of nearly $1.5 trillion. "Lower-middle-income" nations like China, Brazil, Egypt, and Sri Lanka produce another $4 trillion or so of annual output. Hence, every one percentage point of economic growth increases total income in these combined nations by roughly $55 billion. According to the World Bank, if these nations could grow their economies by just 3.8 percent a year (an extra $200 billion of output in the first year and increasing thereafter), global poverty *could* be cut in half by 2015.

China has demonstrated just how effective economic growth can be in reducing poverty. Since 1990, China has been the world's fastest-growing economy, with annual GDP growth rates routinely in the 8–10 percent range. This sensational growth has not only raised *average* incomes but has also dramatically reduced the incidence of poverty. In fact, *the observed success in reducing global poverty from 30 percent in 1990 to 21 percent in 2008 is almost entirely due to the decline in Chinese poverty.* By contrast, slow economic growth in Africa, Latin America, and South Asia has *increased* their respective poverty populations.

Reducing Population Growth

China not only has enjoyed exceptionally fast GDP growth but also has benefited from relatively slow population growth (now around 0.9 percent a year). This has allowed *aggregate* GDP growth to lift *average* incomes more quickly. In other poor nations, population growth is much faster, making poverty reduction more difficult. As Table 21.3 shows, population growth is in the range of 2–3 percent in some of the poorest nations (e.g., Ethiopia, Nigeria, Angola, Mali, Niger, and Somalia). *Reducing population growth rates in the poorest nations is one of the critical keys to reducing global poverty.*

Birth control in some form may have to be part of any antipoverty strategy. In the poorest population groups in the poorest nations, contraceptives are virtually nonexistent. Yet,

	Average Annual Growth Rate (2000–2007) of		
	GDP	Population	Per Capita GDP
High-income countries			
United States	2.7	0.9	1.8
Canada	2.7	1.0	1.7
Japan	1.7	0.1	1.6
France	1.7	0.7	1.0
Low-income countries			
China	10.2	0.6	9.6
India	7.8	1.4	6.4
Nigeria	6.7	2.4	4.3
Ethiopia	7.5	2.6	4.9
Venezuela	4.7	1.7	3.0
Madagascar	3.3	2.8	0.5
Burundi	2.7	3.5	−0.8
Haiti	0.2	1.6	−1.4
West Bank/Gaza	0.4	3.8	−3.4
Zimbabwe	−4.4	0.8	−5.2

Source: World Bank, *World Development Report, 2009.* **www.worldbank.org.**

TABLE 21.3
Growth Rates in Selected Countries, 2000–2007

The relationship between GDP growth and population growth is very different in rich and poor countries. The populations of rich countries are growing very slowly, and gains in per capita GDP are easily achieved. In the poorest countries, population is still increasing rapidly, making it difficult to raise living standards. Notice how per capita incomes are declining in many poor countries (such as Zimbabwe and Haiti).

within those same nations, contraceptive use is much more common in the richest segments of the population. This suggests that limited access, not cultural norms or religious values, constrains the use of contraceptives. To encourage more birth control, China also used tax incentives and penalties to limit families to one child.

Human Capital Development

human capital: The knowledge and skills possessed by the workforce.

Reducing population growth makes poverty reduction easier, but not certain. The next key is to make the existing population more productive, that is, to increase **human capital.**

Education. In poor nations, the need for human capital development is evident. Only 71 percent of the population in low-income nations complete even elementary school. Even fewer people are *literate*, that is, able to read and write a short, simple statement about everyday life (e.g., "We ate rice for breakfast"). Educational deficiencies are greatest for females, who are often prevented from attending school by cultural, social, or economic concerns (see World View below). In Chad and Liberia, fewer than one out of six girls completes primary school. Primary-school completion rates for girls are in the 25–35 percent range in most of the poor nations of sub-Saharan Africa.

WORLD VIEW

The Female "Inequality Trap"

In many poor nations, women are viewed as such a financial liability that female fetuses are aborted, female infants are killed, and female children are so neglected that they have significantly higher mortality rates. The "burden" females pose results from social norms that restrict the ability of women to earn income, accumulate wealth, or even decide their own marital status. In many of the poorest nations, women

- have restricted property rights,
- can't inherit wealth,
- are prohibited or discouraged from working outside the home,
- are prohibited or discouraged from going to school,
- are prevented from voting,
- are denied the right to divorce,
- are paid less than men if they do work outside the home,
- are often expected to bring a financial dowry to the marriage,
- may be beaten if they fail to obey their husbands.

These social practices create an "inequality trap" that keeps returns on female human capital investment low. Without adequate education or training, they can't get productive jobs. Without access to good jobs, they have no incentive to get an education or training. This kind of vicious cycle creates an inequality trap that keeps women and their communities poor.

Source: World Bank, *World Development Report 2006*, pp. 51–54. **www.worldbank.org.**

inequality trap: Institutional barriers that impede human and physical capital investment, particularly by the poorest segments of society.

In Niger and Mali, only one out of five *teenage* girls is literate. This lack of literacy creates an **inequality trap** that restricts the employment opportunities for young women to simple, routine, manual jobs (e.g., carpet weaving and sewing). With so few skills and little education, they are destined to remain poor.

The already low levels of *average* education are compounded by unequal access to schools. Families in extreme poverty typically live in rural areas, with primitive transportation and communication facilities. *Physical* access to schools itself is problematic. On top of that, the poorest families often need their children to work, either within the family or in paid employment. As Figure 21.2 shows, these forces often foreclose school attendance for the poorest children.

Health. In poor nations, basic health care is also a critical dimension of human capital development. Immunizations against measles, diphtheria, and tetanus are more the exception

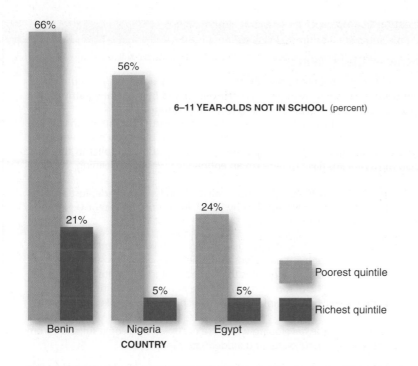

6–11 YEAR-OLDS NOT IN SCHOOL (percent)

66%
56%
24%
21%
5%
5%

Poorest quintile

Richest quintile

Benin   Nigeria   Egypt
COUNTRY

FIGURE 21.2
School Attendance

In developing countries the poorest children often don't attend school at all. Illiteracy is common in these extremely poor families.

Source: World Bank, *World Development Indicators 2009*. **www.worldbank.org.**

than the rule in Somalia, Nigeria, Afghanistan, Congo, the Central African Republic, and many other poor nations. For all low-income nations taken together, the child immunization rate is only 67 percent (versus 96 percent in the United States). Access and education—not money—are the principal barriers to greater immunizations.

Water and sanitation facilities are also in short supply. The World Bank defines "adequate water access" as a protected water source of at least 20 liters per person a day within 1 kilometer of the home dwelling. We're not limited to indoor plumbing with this definition: A public water pipe a half a mile from one's home is considered adequate. Yet, only three out of four households in low-income nations even meet this minimum threshold of water adequacy (see World View on next page). In Afghanistan, Ethiopia, and Somalia only one out of four households has even that much water access. Access to sanitation facilities (ranging from pit latrines to flush toilets) is less common still (on average one out of three low-income-nation households). In Ethiopia, only 6 percent of the population is so privileged.

When illness strikes, professional health care is hard to find. In the United States, there is one doctor for every 180 people. In Sierra Leone, there is one doctor for every 10,000 people! For low-income nations as a group, there are 2,500 people for every available doctor.

These glaring inadequacies in health conditions breed high rates of illness and death. In the United States, only 8 out of every 1,000 children die before age five. In Angola, 260 of every 1,000 children die that young. For all low-income nations, the under-five mortality rate is 13.5 percent (nearly one out of seven). Those children who live are commonly so malnourished (either severely underweight and/or short) that they can't develop fully (another inequality trap).

AIDS takes a huge toll as well. Only 0.6 percent of the U.S. adult population has HIV. In Botswana, Lesotho, Swaziland, and Zimbabwe, over 25 percent of the adult population is HIV-infected. As a result of these problems, life expectancies are inordinately low. In Zambia, only 16 percent of the population live to age 65. In Botswana, life expectancy at birth is 35 years (versus 78 years in the United States). For low-income nations as a group, life expectancy is a mere 57 years.

Associated Press

Analysis: Unsafe water is a common problem for the globally poor.

WORLD VIEW

Dying for a Drink of Clean Water

In the United States and Europe, people take it for granted that when they turn on their taps, clean water will flow out. But for those living in U.S. cities devastated by Hurricane Katrina, as in large parts of the world, obtaining safe water requires a constant struggle.

Water is essential to all aspects of life, yet 99 percent of water on Earth is unsafe or unavailable to drink. About 1.2 billion people lack safe water to consume and 2.6 billion do not have access to adequate sanitation. There are also stark comparisons: Just one flush of a toilet in the West uses more water than most Africans have to perform an entire day's washing, cleaning, cooking, and drinking.

Unsafe water and sanitation is now the single largest cause of illness worldwide, just as it has been a major threat to the health of people affected by Hurricane Katrina. A recent U.N. report estimated that:

- At least 2 million people, most of them children, die annually from water-borne diseases such as diarrhea, cholera, dysentery, typhoid, guinea worm and hepatitis as well as such illnesses as malaria and West Nile virus carried by mosquitoes that breed in stagnant water.
- Many of the 10 million child deaths that occurred last year were linked to unsafe water and lack of sanitation. Children can't fight off infections if their bodies are weakened by water-borne diseases.
- Over half of the hospital beds in the developing world are occupied by people suffering from preventable diseases caused by unsafe water and inadequate sanitation.

When poor people are asked what would most improve their lives, water and sanitation is repeatedly one of the highest priorities. We should heed their call.

—Jan Eliasson and Susan Blumenthal

Source: *The Washington Post,* September 20, 2005, p. A23. From *The Washington Post,* September 20, 2005. Reprinted with permission by Jan Eliasson through Monica Lundkrist.

Analysis: Access to safe water and sanitation is one of the most basic foundations for economic growth. The U.N.'s millennium water goal is to reduce by 2015 half the percentage of people without safe water.

web analysis

To assess water sanitation in your area, visit **www.scorecard.org** and link to "Clean Water Act."

Rostow's 5 Stages of Development

In view of these glaring human-capital deficiencies, one might wonder how poor nations could possibly grow enough to reduce their extreme poverty. After surveying diverse growth experiences, Walt Rostow, an M.I.T. economist, discerned five distinct stages in the development process, as summarized in Table 21.4. Many of the poorest nations are still stuck in stage 1, the "traditional society," with minimal core infrastructure, especially in the rural areas where the poorest households reside. To get beyond that stage, poor nations have to

TABLE 21.4
Five Stages of Economic Development

Walt Rostow distinguished these five sequential stages of economic development:

- Stage 1: *Traditional society.* Rigid institutions, low productivity, little infrastructure, dependence on subsistence agriculture.
- Stage 2: *Preconditions for takeoff.* Improved institutional structure, increased agricultural productivity, emergence of an entrepreneurial class.
- Stage 3: *Takeoff into sustained growth.* Increased saving and investment, rapid industrialization, growth-enhancing policies.
- Stage 4: *Drive to maturity.* Spread of growth process to lagging industrial sectors.
- Stage 5: *High mass consumption.* High per capita GDP attained and accessible to most of population.

Source: World Bank, *World Development Indicators 2005,* Table 2.11a. **www.worldbank.org.**

create the "preconditions for takeoff"—to channel more resources into basic education and health services, while dismantling critical inequality traps.

Meeting Basic Needs. *To get beyond Rostow's stage 1, poor nations must substantially improve the health and education of the mass of poor people.* Cuba was highly successful in following this approach. Although Cuba was a very poor country when Fidel Castro took power in 1959, his government placed high priority on delivering basic educational and health services to the entire population. Within a decade, health and educational standards approached that of industrialized nations.

Implied Costs. The amount of money needed to meet the basic needs of poor nations is surprisingly modest. Malaria vaccinations cost less than 20 cents a shot. Bringing safe water to the poor would cost around $4 billion per year. Bringing both safe water and sanitation would cost about $23 billion annually. Providing universal primary education would cost about $8 billion a year. These costs aren't prohibitive. After all, U.S. consumers spend $20 billion a year on pet food and $100 billion on alcohol. The challenge for poor nations is to get the necessary resources applied to their basic needs.

Capital Investment

To reach stages 2 and 3 in Rostow's scenario, poor nations also need sharply increased capital investment, in both the public and private sectors. Transportation and communications systems must be expanded and upgraded so that markets can function. Capital equipment and upgraded technology must flow into both agricultural and industrial enterprises.

Internal Financing. Acquiring the capital resources needed to boost productivity and accelerate economic growth is not an easy task. Domestically, freeing up scarce resources for capital investment requires cutbacks in domestic consumption. In the 1920s, Stalin used near-totalitarian powers to cut domestic consumption in Russia (by limiting output of consumer goods) and raise Russia's **investment rate** to as much as 30 percent of output. This elevated rate of investment pushed Russia into stage 3, but at a high cost in terms of consumer deprivation.

> **investment rate:** The percentage of total output (GDP) allocated to the production of new plant, equipment, and structures

Other nations haven't had the power or the desire to make such a sacrifice. China spent two decades trying to raise consumption standards before it gave higher priority to investment. Once it did so, however, economic growth accelerated sharply. Table 21.5 documents the low investment rates that continue to plague other poor nations.

Pervasive poverty in poor nations sharply limits the potential for increased savings. Nevertheless, governments can encourage more saving with improved banking facilities, transparent capital markets, and education and saving incentives. And there is mounting evidence that even small dabs of financing can make a big difference. Extending a small loan that enables a poor farmer to buy improved seeds or a plow can have substantial effects on productivity. Financing small equipment or inventory for an entrepreneur can get a new business rolling. Such **"microfinance"** can be a critical key to escaping poverty (see World View on the next page).

> **microfinance:** The granting of small ("micro"), unsecured loans to small businesses and entrepreneurs.

Some nations have also used inflation as a tool for shifting resources from consumption to investment. By financing public works projects and private investment with an increased money supply, governments can increase the inflation rate. As prices rise faster than

Angola	14%
Central African Republic	9
Congo	18
EL Salvador	16
Zimbabwe	17
Bolivia	13
China	44
India	38

Source: World Bank, *World Development Report 2009* (2007 data). **www.worldbank.org.**

TABLE 21.5
Low Investment Rates

Low investment rates limit economic growth. China has attained gross investment rates as high as 44 percent—and exceptionally fast economic growth.

WORLD VIEW

Muhammad Yunus: Microloans

Teach a man to fish, and he'll eat for a lifetime. But only if he can afford the fishing rod. More than 30 years ago in Bangladesh, economics Professor Muhammad Yunus recognized that millions of his countrymen were trapped in poverty because they were unable to scrape together the tiny sums they needed to buy productive essentials such as a loom, a plow, an ox, or a rod. So he gave small loans to his poor neighbors, secured by nothing more than their promise to repay.

Microcredit, as it's now known, became a macro success in 2006, reaching two huge milestones. The number of the world's poorest people with outstanding microloans—mostly in amounts of $15 to $150—was projected to reach 100 million. And Yunus, 66, shared the Nobel Peace Prize with the Grameen Bank he founded. The Nobel Committee honored his grassroots strategy as "development from below."

You know an idea's time has come when people start yanking it in directions its originator never imagined. Some, like Citigroup, are making for-profit loans, contrary to Yunus' break-even vision. Others, like Bangladesh's BRAC, are nonprofit but have a more holistic vision than Grameen, offering health care and social services in addition to loans.

Source: Reprinted from December 18, 2006, issue of *BusinessWeek* by special permission. Copyright © 2006 by The McGraw-Hill Companies, Inc.

Analysis: "Microloans" focus on tiny loans to small businesses and farmers that enable them to increase output and productivity.

web analysis

Go to **www.grameenfoundation. org** for more information on microcredit.

consumer incomes, households are forced to curtail their purchases. This "inflation tax" ultimately backfires, however, when both domestic and foreign market participants lose confidence in the nation's currency. Periodic currency collapses have destabilized many South and Central American economies and governments. Inflation financing also fails to distinguish good investment ideas from bad ones.

External Financing. Given the constraints on internal financing, poor nations have to seek external funding to lift their investment rate. In fact, Columbia University economist Jeffrey Sachs has argued that external financing is not only necessary but, if generous enough, also sufficient for *eliminating* global poverty (see World View below). As we've observed, however, actual foreign aid flows are far below the "Big Money" threshold that

WORLD VIEW

Jeffrey Sachs: Big Money, Big Plans

Columbia University economics professor Jeffrey Sachs has seen the ravages of poverty around the world. As director of the UN Millennium Project, he is committed to attaining the UN's goal of reducing global poverty rates by half by 2015. In fact, Professor Sachs thinks we can do even better: the complete *elimination* of extreme poverty by 2025.

How will the world do this? First, rich nations must double their foreign aid flows now, and then double them again in ten years. Second, poor nations must develop full-scale, comprehensive plans for poverty reduction. This "shock therapy" approach must address all dimensions of the poverty problem simultaneously and quickly, sweeping all inequality traps out of the way.

Critics have called Sachs's vision utopian. They point to the spotty history of foreign aid projects and the failure of many top-down, Big Plan development initiatives. But they still applaud Sachs for mobilizing public opinion and economic resources to fight global poverty.

Source: Jeffrey Sachs, *The End of Poverty*, Penguin, 2006.

Analysis: World poverty can't be eliminated without committing far more resources. Jeff Sachs favors an externally financed, comprehensive Big Plan approach.

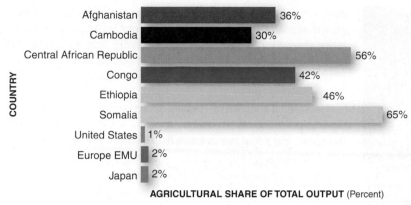

AGRICULTURAL SHARE OF TOTAL OUTPUT (Percent)

FIGURE 21.3
Agricultural Share of Output

In poor nations, agriculture accounts for a very large share of total output.

Source: World Bank (*World Development Report 2009*). www.worldbank.org.

Sachs envisions. Skeptics also question whether more foreign aid would really solve the problem, given the mixed results of previous foreign aid flows. They suggest that more emphasis should be placed on increasing *private* investment flows. Private investment typically entails *direct foreign investment* in new plants, equipment, and technology, or the purchase of ownership stakes in existing enterprises.

When we think about capital investment, we tend to picture new factories, gleaming office buildings, and computerized machinery. In discussing global poverty, however, we have to remind ourselves of how dependent poor nations are on agriculture. As Figure 21.3 illustrates, 65 percent of Somalia's income originates in agriculture. Agricultural shares in the range of 35–55 percent are common in the poorest nations. By contrast, only 1 percent of America's output now comes from farms.

Agricultural Development

Low Farm Productivity. What keeps poor nations so dependent on agriculture is their incredibly low **productivity.** Subsistence farmers are often forced to plow their own fields by hand, with wooden plows. Irrigation systems are primitive and farm machinery is scarce or nonexistent. While high-tech U.S. farms produce nearly $42,000 of output per worker, Ethiopian farms produce a shockingly low $158 of output per worker (see Figure 21.4). Farmers in Zimbabwe produce only 676 kilograms of cereal per hectare, compared with 6,444 kilos per hectare in the United States.

> **productivity:** Output per unit of input, e.g., output per labor-hour.

To grow their economies—to rise out of stage 1—poor nations have to invest in agricultural development. Farm productivity has to rise beyond subsistence levels so that workers can migrate to other industries and expand production possibilities. One of the catapults to China's growth was an exponential increase in farm productivity that freed up labor for industrial production. (China now produces nearly 5,000 kilos of cereal per hectare.) To achieve greater farm productivity, poor nations need capital investment, technological know-how, and improved infrastructure.

The five stages of economic growth envisioned by Rostow imply significant discontinuities in the development process. Nations need some critical mass—some spark—to jump from one stage to the next. That's where the kind of "shock therapy" envisioned by Jeff Sachs

Institutional Reform

VALUE OF FARM OUTPUT PER WORKER (U.S. dollars)

FIGURE 21.4
Low Agricultural Productivity

Farmers in poor nations suffer from low productivity. They are handicapped by low education, inferior technology, primitive infrastructure, and a lack of machinery.

Source: World Bank (*World Development Report 2009*). www.worldbank.org.

Punchstock/DAL

Analysis: Lack of capital, technology, and markets keeps farm productivity low.

comes in. But not everyone embraces this view. Surely, economic growth won't occur automatically, as centuries of global poverty make clear. But growth doesn't necessarily have to follow the sequence of Rostow's five stages either. Moreover, even a series of capital infusions (rather than one massive shock) might promote development.

The critical thing is to get enough resources and use them in the best possible way. To do that, **a *nation needs an institutional structure that promotes economic growth.***

Property Rights. Land, property, and contract rights have to be established before farmers will voluntarily improve their land or invest in agricultural technology. China saw how agricultural productivity jumped when it transformed government-run communal farms into local enterprises and privately managed farms, beginning in 1978. China is using the lessons of that experience to now extend ownership rights to farmers.

Entrepreneurial Incentives. Unleashing the "animal spirits" of the marketplace is also critical. People *do* respond to incentives. If farmers see the potential for profit—and the opportunity to keep that profit—they will pursue productivity gains with more vigor. To encourage that response, governments need to assure the legitimacy of profits and their fair tax treatment. In 1992 the Chinese government acknowledged the role of profits and entrepreneurship in fostering economic advancement. Before then, successful entrepreneurs ran the risk of offending the government with conspicuous consumption that highlighted growing inequalities. The government even punished some entrepreneurs and confiscated their wealth. Once "profits" were legitimized, however, entrepreneurship and foreign investment accelerated, pushing China well into Rostow's stage 3.

Cuba stopped short of legitimizing private property and profits. Although Fidel Castro periodically permitted some private enterprises (e.g., family restaurants), he always withdrew that permission when entrepreneurial ventures succeeded. As a consequence, Cuba didn't advance from stage 2 to stage 3. Venezuela has recently moved further in that direction, expropriating and nationalizing private enterprises (see World View below), thereby discouraging private investment and entrepreneurship.

Equity. What disturbed both Castro and Venezuelan President Chávez was the way capitalism intensified income inequalities. Entrepreneurs got rich while the mass of people remained

WORLD VIEW

Chávez Sets Plans for Nationalization

BOGOTA, Colombia, Jan. 8—Venezuelan President Hugo Chávez on Monday announced plans to nationalize the country's electrical and telecommunications companies, take control of the once-independent Central Bank and seek special constitutional powers permitting him to pass economic laws by decree.

"We're heading toward socialism, and nothing and no one can prevent it," Chávez, who won a third term in a landslide election in December, said in a speech in Caracas, in the Venezuelan capital.

Chávez also said Monday that the government would soon exert more control over the Central Bank, one of the few Venezuelan institutions that has shown itself to be independent of the Chávez administration. Two of the seven directors of the bank's board, including Domingo Maza Zavala, who often criticized government economic policy, are on their way out.

"The Central Bank must not be autonomous," Chávez said. "That is a neoliberal idea."

—Juan Forero

Source: *The Washington Post,* January 9, 2007, p. A10. © 2007 The Washington Post. Used with permission by PARS International Corp.

Analysis: By restricting private ownership, governments curb the entrepreneurship and investment that may be essential for economic development.

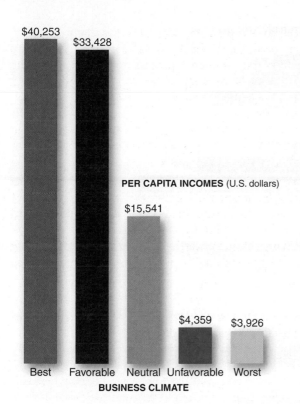

FIGURE 21.5
Business Climates Affect Growth

Nations that offer more secure property rights, less regulation, and lower taxes grow faster and enjoy higher per capita incomes.

Source: Adapted from Heritage Foundation, *2009 Index of Economic Freedom*, p. 7. Washington, DC. Used with permission.

Note: Business climate in 183 nations gauged by 50 measures of government tax, regulatory, and legal policy.

poor. For Castro, the goal of equity was more important than the goal of efficiency. A nation where everyone was equally poor was preferred to a nation of haves and have-nots. Chávez thought he could pursue both equity and efficiency with government-managed enterprises.

In many of today's poorest nations policy interests are not so noble. A small elite often holds extraordinary political power and uses that power to protect its privileges. Greed restricts the flow of resources to the poorest segments of the population, leaving them to fend for themselves. These inequalities in power, wealth, and opportunity create inequality traps that restrain human capital development, capital investment, entrepreneurship, and, ultimately, economic growth.

Business Climate. To encourage capital investment and entrepreneurship, governments have to assure a secure and supportive business climate. Investors and business start-ups want to know what the rules of the game are and how they will be enforced. They also want assurances that contracts will be enforced and that debts can be collected. They want their property protected from crime and government corruption. They want minimal interference from government regulation and taxes.

As the annual surveys by the Heritage Foundation document, nations that offer a more receptive business climate grow at a faster pace. Figure 21.5 illustrates this connection. Notice that nations with the most pro-business climate (e.g., Hong Kong, Singapore, Iceland, USA, and Denmark) enjoy living standards far superior to those in nations with hostile business climates (e.g., North Korea, Congo, Sudan, Zimbabwe, and Myanmar). This is no accident; *pro-business climates encourage the capital investment, the entrepreneurship, and the human capital investment that drive economic growth.*

Unfortunately, some of the poorest nations still fail to provide a pro-business environment. Figure 21.6 illustrates how specific dimensions of the business climate differ across fast-growing nations (China) and perpetually poor ones (Cambodia and Kenya). A biannual survey of 26,000 international firms elicits their views of how different government policies restrain their investment decisions. Notice how China offers a more certain policy environment, less corruption, more secure property rights, and less crime. Given these business conditions, where would you invest?

The good news about the business climate is that it doesn't require huge investments to fix. It does require, however, a lot of political capital.

FIGURE 21.6
Investment Climate

International investors gravitate toward nations with business-friendly policies. Shown here are the percentages of international firms citing specific elements of the business climate that deter their investment in the named countries.

Source: World Bank, *World Development Indicators 2006*. **www.worldbank.org.**

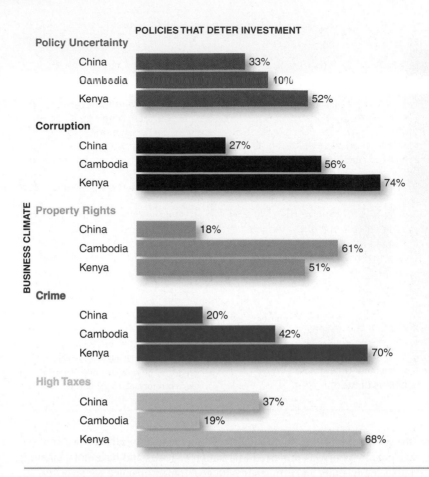

POLICIES THAT DETER INVESTMENT

World Trade

comparative advantage: The ability of a country to produce a specific good at a lower opportunity cost than its trading partners.

import quota: A limit on the quantity of a good that may be imported in a given time period.

When it comes to political capital, poor nations have a complaint of their own. They say that rich nations lock them out of their most important markets—particularly agricultural export markets. Poor nations typically have a **comparative advantage** in the production of agricultural products. Their farm productivity may be low (see Figure 21.4), but their low labor costs keep their farm output competitive. They can't fully exploit that advantage in export markets, however. The United States, the European Union, and Japan heavily subsidize their own farmers. This keeps farm prices low in the rich nations, eliminating the cost advantage of farmers in poor nations. To further protect their own farmers from global competition, rich nations erect trade barriers to stem the inflow of Third World products. The United States, for example, enforces an **import quota** on foreign sugar. This trade barrier has fostered a high-cost, domestic beet-sugar industry (see World View, p. 465), while denying poor nations the opportunity to sell more sugar and grow their economies faster.

Poor nations need export markets. Export sales generate the hard currency (dollars, euros, and yen) that is needed to purchase capital equipment in global markets. Export sales also allow farmers in poor nations to expand production, exploit economies of scale, and invest in improved technology. Ironically, *trade barriers in rich nations impede poor nations from pursuing the agricultural development that is a* **prerequisite** *for growth.* The latest round of multilateral trade negotiations (the "Doha" round; see p. 422) dragged on forever because of the resistance of rich nations to open their agricultural markets. Poor nations plead that "trade, not aid" is their surest path to economic growth.

A 2004 study estimated that 440 million people would be lifted out of severe poverty if all trade barriers were dismantled.[2] China has demonstrated how a vibrant export sector can propel economic growth; South Korea, Taiwan, Malaysia, India, and Costa Rica have also successfully used exports to advance into the higher stages of economic growth.

[2]William Cline, *Trade Policy and Global Poverty* (Washington, DC: Institute for International Economics, 2004).

WORLD VIEW

African Sugar Production Ramps Up

EU Plan to Cut Tariffs Shows How Developing Nations Can Benefit

BRUSSELS—The developing world has been adamant that rich nations abandon farm subsidies in order to get a global trade deal both sides say they want. A flood of investment pouring into Southern Africa's sugar industry demonstrates why the poor countries won't back down on this demand.

The hundreds of millions of dollars being spent to ramp up African sugar production is a direct response to European Union plans to slash import duties and subsidies that for years have locked out farmers in developing countries. . . .

The expansion shows how the EU's gradual opening of its farm sector can boost production in some developing countries. . . .

The impact of the planned opening of the EU's sugar market suggests those changes could trigger significant investment in some of the world's poorest rural economies.

Sugar concern Tongaat-Hulett Group Ltd. of South Africa says it will spend $180 million over the next two years to plant roughly an additional 21,250 acres of sugar cane, install modern technology in existing mills and hire 8,800 more workers. . . .

"It's not easy to find reasons to invest in countries like Mozambique," said Tongaat-Hulett Chief Executive Peter Staude in an interview. "The civil war just ended, and there are land mines and machine guns all over." One of the company's executives was shot at recently when his plane landed near the sugar mill in Xinavane.

Two things made the investment possible, he said. One is that Mozambique has two functional harbors connected to rail lines, infrastructure that doesn't exist in many other poor African countries, Mr. Staude said. The other was the planned changes to EU sugar tariffs and subsidies. "Above all, we want a platform to sell into the EU," he said.

—John W. Miller

Source: *The Wall Street Journal,* February 12, 2007, p. A4. Copyright 2007 by Dow Jones & Company, Inc. Reproduced with permission of Dow Jones & Company, Inc. in the format Textbook via Copyright Clearance Center.

Analysis: Poor nations need access to markets in rich nations in order to encourage investment in domestic production. They demand "trade, not aid."

Mozambique is demonstrating how even a small window of export opportunity can make a real difference in investment and productivity rates (see World View above). Other poor nations want the same opportunity.

THE ECONOMY TOMORROW

UNLEASHING ENTREPRENEURSHIP

The traditional approach to economic development emphasizes the potential for government policy to reallocate resources and increase capital investment. External financing of capital investment was always at or near the top of the policy agenda (see World View, bottom of p. 460). This approach has been criticized for neglecting the power of people and markets.

One of the most influential critics is the Peruvian economist Hernando de Soto. When he returned to his native Peru after years of commercial success in Europe, he was struck by the dichotomy in his country. The "official" economy was mired in bureaucratic red tape and stagnant. Most of the vitality of the Peruvian economy was contained in the unofficial "underground" economy. The underground economy included trade in drugs but was overwhelmingly oriented to meeting the everyday demands of Peruvian consumers and households. The

© David Zurich/DAL

Analysis: Markets exist but struggle in poor nations.

underground economy wasn't hidden from view; it flourished on the streets, in outdoor markets, and in transport services. The only thing that forced this thriving economy underground was the failure of the government to recognize it and give it legitimate status. Government restrictions on prices, business activities, finance, and trade—a slew of inequality traps—forced entrepreneurs to operate "underground."

De Soto concluded that countries like Peru could grow more quickly if governments encouraged rather than suppressed these entrepreneurial resources. In his best-selling book, *The Other Path,* he urged poor countries to refocus their development policies. This "other path" entails improving the business climate by

- Reducing bureaucratic barriers to free enterprise.
- Spreading private ownership.
- Developing and enforcing legal safeguards for property, income, and wealth.
- Developing infrastructure that facilitates business activity.

Yunus's "microloans" (World View, p. 460) would also fit comfortably on this other path.

De Soto's book has been translated into several languages and has encouraged market-oriented reforms in Peru, Argentina, Mexico, Russia, Vietnam, and elsewhere. In India the government is drastically reducing both regulation and taxes in order to pursue De Soto's other path. The basic message of his other path is that poor nations should exploit the one resource that is abundant in even the poorest countries—entrepreneurship.

SUMMARY

- Definitions of "poverty" are culturally based. Poverty in the United States is defined largely in *relative* terms, whereas global poverty is tied more to *absolute* levels of subsistence. LO1
- About 12 percent of the U.S. population (nearly 38 million people) are officially counted as poor. Poor people in America suffer from *relative* deprivation, not *absolute* deprivation, as in global poverty. LO1
- Global poverty thresholds are about one-tenth of U.S. standards. "Extreme" poverty is defined as less than $1 per day per person; "severe" poverty is less than $2 per day (inflation adjusted). LO1
- One billion people around the world are in extreme poverty; close to 3 billion are in severe poverty. In low-income nations global poverty rates are as high as 70–90 percent. LO2
- The United Nations' Millennium Poverty Goal is to cut the global poverty rate in half, to 15 percent by 2015. LO3

- Redistribution of incomes *within* poor nations doesn't have much potential for reducing poverty, given their low *average* incomes. *Across*-nation redistributions (e.g., foreign aid) can make a small dent, however. LO3
- Economic growth is the key to global poverty reduction. Many poor nations are stuck in stage 1 of development, with undeveloped human capital, primitive infrastructure, and subsistence agriculture. To grow more quickly, they need to meet basic human needs (health and education), increase agricultural productivity, and encourage investment. LO3
- To move into sustained economic growth, poor nations need capital investment and institutional reforms that promote both equity and entrepreneurship. LO3
- Poor nations also need "trade, not aid," that is, access to rich-nation markets, particularly in farm products. LO3

Key Terms

poverty threshold (U.S.)	Millennium Poverty Goal	investment rate
poverty rate	Millennium Aid Goal	microfinance
in-kind transfers	economic growth	productivity
extreme poverty (world)	human capital	comparative advantage
severe poverty (world)	inequality trap	import quota

Questions for Discussion

1. Why should Americans care about extreme poverty in Haiti, Ethiopia, or Bangladesh?   LO2
2. If you had only $14 to spend per day (the U.S. poverty threshold), how would you spend it? What if you had only $2 a day (the World Bank "severe poverty" threshold)?   LO1
3. If a poor nation must choose between building an airport, some schools, or a steel plant, which one should it choose? Why?   LO3
4. Why are incomes so much more unequal in poor nations than in developed ones? (See World View, p. 452.)   LO1
5. How do more children per family either restrain or expand income-earning potential?   LO3
6. Are property rights a perquisite for economic growth? Explain.   LO3
7. How do unequal rights for women affect economic growth?   LO3
8. Identify "inequality traps" that might inhibit economic growth.   LO3
9. Could a nation reorder Rostow's five stages of development and still grow? Explain.   LO3
10. How does microfinance alter prospects for economic growth? The distribution of political power?   LO3
11. Can poor nations develop without substantial increases in agricultural productivity? (See Figure 21.3.) How?   LO3
12. Would you invest in Cambodia or Kenya on the basis of the information in Figure 21.6?   LO3
13. How might Bolivia match China's investment rate? (See Table 21.4.)   LO2
14. Why do economists put so much emphasis on entrepreneurship? How can poor nations encourage it?   LO3
15. How do nations expect nationalization of basic industries to foster economic growth?   LO3
16. If economic growth reduced poverty but widened inequalities, would it still be desirable?   LO3
17. What market failure does Bill Gates (World View, p. 454) cite as the motivation for global philanthropy?   LO3

---

 web activities to accompany this chapter can be found on the Online Learning Center:
http://www.mhhe.com/schiller12e

LO1 1. Adjusted for inflation, the World Bank's threshold for "extreme" poverty is now close to $1.50 per person per day.
   (a) How much *annual* income does this imply? $_____
   (b) What portion of the official U.S. poverty threshold (roughly $22,000 for a family of four) is met by the Bank's measure?   _____%

LO2 2. Close to half the world's population of 6 billion people is in "severe" poverty with less than $3 of income per day (with inflation adjustments).
   (a) What is the maximum *combined* income of this "severely" poor population? $_____
   (b) What percentage of the world's *total* income (roughly $70 trillion) does this represent?   _____%

LO2 3. In Namibia,
   (a) What percent of total output is received by the richest 10 percent of households? (See World View, p. 452.)   _____%
   (b) How much output did this share amount to in 2007, when Namibia's GDP was $11 billion? $_____
   (c) With a total population of 2 million, what was the implied per capita income of
     (i) The richest 10 percent of the population? $_____
     (ii) The remaining 90 percent? $_____

LO3 4. (a) How much foreign aid does the U.S. now provide? (See Table 21.2.) $_____
   (b) How much more is required to satisfy the U.N.'s Millennium Aid Goal if U.S. GDP = $15 trillion? $_____

LO3 5. If the industrialized nations were to satisfy the U.N.'s Millennium Aid Goal, how much *more* foreign aid would they give annually? (See Table 21.2.) $_____

LO3 6. According to Table 21.3, now many years will it take for per capita GDP to double in
   (a) China?   _____
   (b) Madagascar?   _____
   (c) Zimbabwe?   _____

LO3 7. (a) Which low-income nation in Table 21.3 has GDP growth equal to the United States?   _____
   (b) How much faster is that nation's population growth?   _____%
   (c) How much lower is its per capita GDP growth?   _____%

LO3 8. According to the World View on page 454,
   (a) How much money is spent annually to combat baldness? $_____
   (b) How much medical care would that money buy for each child who dies from malaria each year? $_____

PHOTO CREDITS

Note: Numbers in parentheses indicate the chapters in which the definitions appear.

absolute advantage: The ability of a country to produce a specific good with fewer resources (per unit of output) than other countries. (19)

AD excess: The amount by which aggregate demand must be reduced to achieve full-employment equilibrium after allowing for price-level changes. (11)

AD shortfall: The amount of additional aggregate demand needed to achieve full employment after allowing for price-level changes. (11)

adjustable-rate mortgage (ARM): A mortgage (home loan) that adjusts the nominal interest rate to changing rates of inflation. (7)

aggregate demand (AD): The total quantity of output (real GDP) demanded at alternative price levels in a given time period, *ceteris paribus.* (8, 9, 10, 11, 13, 15)

aggregate supply (AS): The total quantity of output (real GDP) producers are willing and able to supply at alternative price levels in a given time period, *ceteris paribus.* (8, 9, 11, 16)

antitrust: Government intervention to alter market structure or prevent abuse of market power. (4)

appreciation: A rise in the price of one currency relative to another. (20)

arithmetic growth: An increase in quantity by a constant amount each year. (17)

asset: Anything having exchange value in the marketplace; wealth. (12)

automatic stabilizer: Federal expenditure or revenue item that automatically responds countercyclically to changes in national income, like unemployment benefits, income taxes. (12, 18)

average propensity to consume (APC): Total consumption in a given period divided by total disposable income. (9)

balance of payments: A summary record of a country's international economic transactions in a given period of time. (20)

balance-of-payments deficit: An excess demand for foreign currency at current exchange rates. (20)

balance-of-payments surplus: An excess demand for domestic currency at current exchange rates. (20)

bank reserves: Assets held by a bank to fulfill its deposit obligations. (13)

barter: The direct exchange of one good for another, without the use of money. (13)

base year: The time period used for comparative analysis; the basis for indexing, e.g., of price changes. (5, 7, 17)

bond: A certificate acknowledging a debt and the amount of interest to be paid each year until repayment; an IOU. (14)

bracket creep: The movement of taxpayers into higher tax brackets (rates) as nominal incomes grow. (7)

budget deficit: Amount by which government spending exceeds government revenue in a given time period. (12)

budget surplus: An excess of government revenues over government expenditures in a given time period. (12)

business cycle: Alternating periods of economic growth and contraction. (8, 9, 18)

capital: Final goods produced for use in the production of other goods, e.g., equipment, structures. (1)

capital-intensive: Production processes that use a high ratio of capital to labor inputs. (2)

ceteris paribus: The assumption of nothing else changing. (1, 3)

closed economy: A nation that doesn't engage in international trade. (19)

comparative advantage: The ability of a country to produce a specific good at a lower opportunity cost than its trading partners. (19, 21)

complementary goods: Goods frequently consumed in combination; when the price of good *x* rises, the demand for good *y* falls, *ceteris paribus.* (3)

Consumer Price Index (CPI): A measure (index) of changes in the average price of consumer goods and services. (7)

consumption: Expenditure by consumers on final goods and services. (9)

consumption function: A mathematical relationship indicating the rate of desired consumer spending at various income levels. (9)

consumption possibilities: The alternative combinations of goods and services that a country could consume in a given time period. (20)

core inflation rate: Changes in CPI, excluding food and energy prices. (7)

cost-of-living adjustment (COLA): Automatic adjustments of nominal income to the rate of inflation. (7)

crowding in: An increase in private-sector borrowing (and spending) caused by decreased government borrowing. (12, 17)

crowding out: A reduction in private-sector borrowing (and spending) caused by increased government borrowing. (11, 12, 15, 17)

cyclical deficit: That portion of the budget deficit attributable to unemployment or inflation. (12)

cyclical unemployment: Unemployment attributable to a lack of job vacancies, that is, to inadequate aggregate demand. (6, 9, 10)

debt ceiling: An explicit, legislated limit on the amount of outstanding national debt. (12)

debt service: The interest required to be paid each year on outstanding debt. (12)

deficit ceiling: An explicit, legislated limitation on the size of the budget deficit. (12)

deficit spending: The use of borrowed funds to finance government expenditures that exceed tax revenues. (12)

deflation: A decrease in the average level of prices of goods and services. (7)

demand: The willingness and ability to buy specific quantities of a good at alternative prices in a given time period, *ceteris paribus.* (3)

demand curve: A curve describing the quantities of a good a consumer is willing and able to buy at alternative prices in a given time period, *ceteris paribus.* (3)

demand for money: The quantities of money people are willing and able to hold at alternative interest rates, *ceteris paribus.* (15)

demand-pull inflation: An increase in the price level initiated by excessive aggregate demand. (9, 10)

demand schedule: A table showing the quantities of a good a consumer is willing and able to buy at alternative prices in a given time period, *ceteris paribus.* (3)

deposit creation: The creation of transactions deposits by bank lending. (13)

depreciation: The consumption of capital in the production process; the wearing out of plant and equipment. (5)

depreciation (currency): A fall in the price of one currency relative to another. (20)

devaluation: An abrupt depreciation of a currency whose value was fixed or managed by the government. (20)

discount rate: The rate of interest the Federal Reserve charges for lending reserves to private banks. (14)

discounting: Federal Reserve lending of reserves to private banks. (14)

discouraged worker: An individual who isn't actively seeking employment but would look for or accept a job if one were available. (6)

discretionary fiscal spending: Those elements of the federal budget not determined by past legislative or executive commitments. (12)

disposable income (DI): After-tax income of households; personal income less personal taxes. (5, 9, 10, 11)

dissaving: Consumption expenditure in excess of disposable income; a negative saving flow. (9)

dumping: The sale of goods in export markets at prices below domestic prices. (19)

economic growth: An increase in output (real GDP); an expansion of production possibilities. (1, 2, 17, 21)

economics: The study of how best to allocate scarce resources among competing uses. (1)

efficiency: Maximum output of a good from the resources used in production. (1)

embargo: A prohibition on exports or imports. (19)

employment rate: The percentage of the adult population that is employed. (17)

entrepreneurship: The assembling of resources to produce new or improved products and technologies. (1)

equation of exchange: Money supply (M) times velocity of circulation (V) equals level of aggregate spending ($P \times Q$). (15)

equilibrium (macro): The combination of price level and real output that is compatible with both aggregate demand and aggregate supply. (8, 9, 11)

equilibrium GDP: The value of total output (real GDP) produced at macro equilibrium (AS–AD). (9, 10)

equilibrium price: The price at which the quantity of a good demanded in a given time period equals the quantity supplied. (3, 19, 20)

equilibrium rate of interest: The interest rate at which the quantity of money demanded in a given time period equals the quantity of money supplied. (15)

excess reserves: Bank reserves in excess of required reserves. (13, 14)

exchange rate: The price of one country's currency expressed in terms of another's; the domestic price of a foreign currency. (20)

expenditure equilibrium: The rate of output at which desired spending equals the value of output. (9)

exports: Goods and services sold to foreign buyers. (5, 19)

external debt: U.S. government debt (Treasury bonds) held by foreign households and institutions. (12)

externalities: Costs (or benefits) of a market activity borne by a third party; the difference between the social and private costs (benefits) of a market activity. (2, 4)

extreme poverty (world): World Bank income standard of less than $1 per day per person (inflation adjusted). (21)

factor market: Any place where factors of production (e.g., land, labor, capital) are bought and sold. (3)

factors of production: Resource inputs used to produce goods and services, e.g., land, labor, capital, entrepreneurship. (1, 2)

federal funds rate: The interest rate for interbank reserve loans. (14, 15)

fine-tuning: Adjustments in economic policy designed to counteract small changes in economic outcomes; continuous responses to changing economic conditions. (18)

fiscal policy: The use of government taxes and spending to alter macroeconomic outcomes. (8, 11, 12, 18)

fiscal restraint: Tax hikes or spending cuts intended to reduce (shift) aggregate demand. (11, 12, 18)

fiscal stimulus: Tax cuts or spending hikes intended to increase (shift) aggregate demand. (11, 12, 18)

fiscal year (FY): The 12-month period used for accounting purposes; begins October 1 for the federal government. (12)

flexible exchange rates: A system in which exchange rates are permitted to vary with market supply-and-demand conditions; floating exchange rates. (20)

foreign-exchange markets: Places where foreign currencies are bought and sold. (20)

foreign-exchange reserves: Holdings of foreign exchange by official government agencies, usually the central bank or treasury. (20)

free rider: An individual who reaps direct benefits from someone else's purchase (consumption) of a public good. (4)

frictional unemployment: Brief periods of unemployment experienced by people moving between jobs or into the labor market. (6)

full employment: The lowest rate of unemployment compatible with price stability; variously estimated at between 4 and 6 percent unemployment. (6, 10)

full-employment GDP: The value of total market output (real GDP) produced at full employment. (8, 9, 10)

GDP deflator: A price index that refers to all goods and services included in GDP. (7)

GDP gap (real): The difference between full-employment GDP and equilibrium GDP. (11, 18)

GDP per capita: Total GDP divided by total population; average GDP. (5, 17)

geometric growth: An increase in quantity by a constant proportion each year. (17)

gold reserves: Stocks of gold held by a government to purchase foreign exchange. (20)

gold standard: An agreement by countries to fix the price of their currencies in terms of gold; a mechanism for fixing exchange rates. (20)

government failure: Government intervention that fails to improve economic outcomes. (1, 4)

gross business saving: Depreciation allowances and retained earnings. (10)

gross domestic product (GDP): The total market value of all final goods and services produced within a nation's borders in a given time period. (2, 5)

gross investment: Total investment expenditure in a given time period. (5)

growth rate: Percentage change in real output from one period to another. (17)

growth recession: A period during which real GDP grows but at a rate below the long-term trend of 3 percent. (8, 18)

human capital: The knowledge and skills possessed by the workforce. (2, 16, 17, 21)

hyperinflation: Inflation rate in excess of 200 percent, lasting at least one year. (7)

imports: Goods and services purchased from international sources. (5, 19)

import quota: A limit on the quantity of a good that may be imported in a given time period. (22)

income quintile: One-fifth of the population, rank-ordered by income (e.g., top fifth). (2)

income transfers: Payments to individuals for which no current goods or services are exchanged, e.g., Social Security, welfare, unemployment benefits. (11, 12)

income velocity of money (V): The number of times per year, on average, a dollar is used to purchase final goods and services; $PQ \div M$. (15)

inequality trap: Institutional barriers that impede human and physical capital investment, particularly by the poorest segments of society. (21)

inflation: An increase in the average level of prices of goods and services. (4, 5, 7, 8)

inflation rate: The annual percentage rate of increase in the average price level. (7)

inflation targeting: The use of an inflation ceiling ("target") to signal the need for monetary policy adjustments. (15)

inflationary flashpoint: The rate of output at which inflationary pressures intensify; point of inflection on the AS curve. (16)

inflationary GDP gap: The amount by which equilibrium GDP exceeds full-employment GDP. (9, 10, 11, 18)

in-kind transfers: Direct transfers of goods and services rather than cash; e.g., food stamps, Medicaid benefits, and housing subsidies. (21)

infrastructure: The transportation, communications, education, judicial, and other institutional systems that facilitate market exchanges. (16)

injection: An addition of spending to the circular flow of income. (10)

interest rate: The price paid for the use of money. (15)

intermediate goods: Goods or services purchased for use as input in the production of final goods or in services. (5)

internal debt: U.S. government debt (Treasury bonds) held by U.S. households and institutions. (12)

investment: Expenditures on (production of) new plant, equipment, and structures (capital) in a given time period, plus changes in business inventories. (5, 9, 16)

investment rate: The percentage of total output (GDP) allocated to the production of new plant, equipment, and structures. (21)

item weight: The percentage of total expenditure spent on a specific product; used to compute inflation indexes. (7)

labor force: All persons over age 16 who are either working for pay or actively seeking paid employment. (6, 17)

labor-force participation rate: The percentage of the working-age population working or seeking employment. (6)

labor productivity: Amount of output produced by a worker in a given period of time; output per hour (or day, etc.). (16)

laissez faire: The doctrine of "leave it alone," of nonintervention by government in the market mechanism. (l, 8)

law of demand: The quantity of a good demanded in a given time period increases as its price falls, *ceteris paribus*. (3, 8)

law of supply: The quantity of a good supplied in a given time period increases as its price increases, *ceteris paribus*. (3)

leakage: Income not spent directly on domestic output but instead diverted from the circular flow, e.g., saving, imports, taxes. (10)

liability: An obligation to make future payment; debt. (12)

liquidity trap: The portion of the money demand curve that is horizontal; people are willing to hold unlimited amounts of money at some (low) interest rate. (15)

macroeconomics: The study of aggregate economic behavior, of the economy as a whole. (1, 8)

managed exchange rates: A system in which governments intervene in foreign-exchange markets to limit but not eliminate exchange-rate fluctuations; "dirty floats." (20)

marginal propensity to consume (MPC): The fraction of each additional (marginal) dollar of disposable income spent on consumption; the change in consumption divided by the change in disposable income. (9, 10, 11)

marginal propensity to save (MPS): The fraction of each additional (marginal) dollar of disposable income not spent on consumption; 1 – MPC. (9)

marginal tax rate: The tax rate imposed on the last (marginal) dollar of income. (16)

market demand: The total quantities of a good or service people are willing and able to buy at alternative prices in a given time period; the sum of individual demands. (3)

market failure: An imperfection in the market mechanism that prevents optimal outcomes. (1, 4)

market mechanism: The use of market prices and sales to signal desired outputs (or resource allocations). (1, 3, 4)

market power: The ability to alter the market price of a good or service. (4)

market shortage: The amount by which the quantity demanded exceeds the quantity supplied at a given price; excess demand. (3, 20)

market supply: The total quantities of a good that sellers are willing and able to sell at alternative prices in a given time period, *ceteris paribus*. (3)

merit good: A good or service society deems everyone is entitled to some minimal quantity of. (4)

microeconomics: The study of individual behavior in the economy, of the components of the larger economy. (1)

microfinance: The granting of small ("micro"), unsecured loans to small businesses and entrepreneurs. (21)

Millennium Aid Goal: United Nations goal of raising foreign aid levels to 0.7 percent of donor-country GDP. (21)

Millennium Poverty Goal: United Nations goal of reducing global rate of extreme poverty to 15 percent by 2015. (21)

mixed economy: An economy that uses both market signals and government directives to allocate goods and resources. (1)

monetary policy: The use of money and credit controls to influence macroeconomic outcomes. (8, 14, 15, 18)

money: Anything generally accepted as a medium of exchange. (13)

money illusion: The use of nominal dollars rather than real dollars to gauge changes in one's income or wealth. (7)

money multiplier: The number of deposit (loan) dollars that the banking system can create from $1 of excess reserves; equal to 1 ÷ required reserve ratio. (13, 14)

money supply (M1): Currency held by the public, plus balances in transactions accounts. (13, 14, 15)

money supply (M2): M1 plus balances in most savings accounts and money market funds. (13, 14, 15)

monopoly: A firm that produces the entire market supply of a particular good or service. (2, 4)

multiplier: The multiple by which an initial change in aggregate spending will alter total expenditure after an infinite number of spending cycles; 1/(1 – MPC). (10, 11, 18)

national debt: Accumulated debt of the federal government. (12)

national income (NI): Total income earned by current factors of production: GDP less depreciation and indirect business taxes, plus net foreign factor income. (5)

national-income accounting: The measurement of aggregate economic activity, particularly national income and its components. (5)

natural monopoly: An industry in which one firm can achieve economies of scale over the entire range of market supply. (4)

natural rate of unemployment: Long-term rate of unemployment determined by structural forces in labor and product markets. (6, 15, 18)

net domestic product (NDP): GDP less depreciation. (5)

net exports: The value of exports minus the value of imports: $(X - M)$. (5)

net investment: Gross investment less depreciation. (5, 17)

nominal GDP: The value of final output produced in a given period, measured in the prices of that period (current prices). (5, 7)

nominal income: The amount of money income received in a given time period, measured in current dollars. (7)

Okun's Law: One percent more unemployment is estimated to equal 2 percent less output. (6)

open economy: A nation that engages in international trade. (19)

open market operations: Federal Reserve purchases and sales of government bonds for the purpose of altering bank reserves. (14)

opportunity cost: The most desired goods or services that are forgone in order to obtain something else. (1, 3, 4, 12, 19)

optimal mix of output: The most desirable combination of output attainable with existing resources, technology, and social values. (4, 12)

outsourcing: The relocation of production to foreign countries. (6)

per capita GDP: The dollar value of GDP divided by total population; average GDP. (2)

personal income (PI): Income received by households before payment of personal taxes. (5)

Phillips curve: An historical (inverse) relationship between the rate of unemployment and the rate of inflation; commonly expresses a trade-off between the two. (16)

portfolio decision: The choice of how (where) to hold idle funds. (14, 15)

poverty rate: Percentage of the population counted as poor. (21)

poverty threshold (U.S.): Annual income of less than $22,000 for family of four (2009, inflation adjusted). (21)

precautionary demand for money: Money held for unexpected market transactions or for emergencies. (15)

price ceiling: Upper limit imposed on the price of a good. (3)

price floor: Lower limit set for the price of a good. (3)

price stability: The absence of significant changes in the average price level; officially defined as a rate of inflation of less than 3 percent. (7)

private good: A good or service whose consumption by one person excludes consumption by others. (4)

product market: Any place where finished goods and services (products) are bought and sold. (3)

production possibilities: The alternative combinations of final goods and services that could be produced in a given time period with all available resources and technology (1, 5, 6, 17, 19)

productivity: Output per unit of input, e.g., output per labor-hour. (2, 17, 21)

progressive tax: A tax system in which tax rates rise as incomes rise. (4)

proportional tax: A tax that levies the same rate on every dollar of income. (4)

public choice: Theory of public-sector behavior emphasizing rational self-interest of decision makers and voters. (4)

public good: A good or service whose consumption by one person does not exclude consumption by others. (4)

quota: A limit on the quantity of a good that may be imported in a given time period. (19)

rational expectations: Hypothesis that people's spending decisions are based on all available information, including the anticipated effects of government intervention. (18)

real GDP: The value of final output produced in a given period, adjusted for changing prices. (5, 7, 8, 17)

real income: Income in constant dollars; nominal income adjusted for inflation. (7)

real interest rate: The nominal interest rate minus the anticipated inflation rate. (7, 15)

recession: A decline in total output (real GDP) for two or more consecutive quarters. (8)

recessionary GDP gap: The amount by which equilibrium GDP falls short of full-employment GDP. (9, 10, 11, 18)

refinancing: The issuance of new debt in payment of debt issued earlier. (12)

regressive tax: A tax system in which tax rates fall as incomes rise. (4)

relative price: The price of one good in comparison with the price of other goods. (7)

required reserves: The minimum amount of reserves a bank is required to hold; equal to required reserve ratio times transactions deposits. (13, 14)

reserve ratio: The ratio of a bank's reserves to its total transactions deposits. (13)

saving: That part of disposable income not spent on current consumption; disposable income less consumption. (5, 9, 16)

Say's Law: Supply creates its own demand. (8)

scarcity: Lack of enough resources to satisfy all desired uses of those resources. (1)

seasonal unemployment: Unemployment due to seasonal changes in employment or labor supply. (6)

severe poverty (world): World Bank income standard of $2 per day per person (inflation adjusted). (21)

shift in demand: A change in the quantity demanded at any (every) given price. (3)

speculative demand for money: Money held for speculative purposes, for later financial opportunities. (15)

stagflation: The simultaneous occurrence of substantial unemployment and inflation. (16, 18)

structural deficit: Federal revenues at full employment minus expenditures at full employment under prevailing fiscal policy. (12, 18)

structural unemployment: Unemployment caused by a mismatch between the skills (or location) of job seekers and the requirements (or location) of available jobs. (6, 16)

substitute goods: Goods that substitute for each other; when the price of good x rises, the demand for good y increases, *ceteris paribus*. (3)

supply: The ability and willingness to sell (produce) specific quantities of a good at alternative prices in a given time period, *ceteris paribus*. (3)

supply-side policy: The use of tax incentives, (de)regulation, and other mechanisms to increase the ability and willingness to produce goods and services. (8, 18)

tariff: A tax (duty) imposed on imported goods. (19)

tax elasticity of supply: The percentage change in quantity supplied divided by the percentage change in tax rates. (16)

tax rebate: A lump-sum refund of taxes paid. (16)

terms of trade: The rate at which goods are exchanged; the amount of good A given up for good B in trade. (19)

trade deficit: The amount by which the value of imports exceeds the value of exports in a given time period (negative net exports). (19, 20)

trade surplus: The amount by which the value of exports exceeds the value of imports in a given time period (positive net exports). (19)

transactions account: A bank account that permits direct payment to a third party, for example, with a check. (13)

transactions demand for money: Money held for the purpose of making everyday market purchases. (15)

transfer payments: Payments to individuals for which no current goods or services are exchanged, like Social Security, welfare, unemployment benefits. (4, 16)

Treasury bonds: Promissory notes (IOUs) issued by the U.S. Treasury. (12)

underemployment: People seeking full-time paid employment who work only part-time or are employed at jobs below their capability. (6)

unemployment: The inability of labor-force participants to find jobs. (4, 6)

unemployment rate: The proportion of the labor force that is unemployed. (6)

value added: The increase in the market value of a product that takes place at each stage of the production process. (5)

velocity of money (V): The number of times per year, on average, that a dollar is used to purchase final goods and services; $PQ \div M$. (18)

voluntary restraint agreement (VRA): An agreement to reduce the volume of trade in a specific good; a "voluntary" quota. (19)

wealth effect: A change in consumer spending caused by a change in the value of owned assets. (9)

yield: The rate of return on a bond; the annual interest payment divided by the bond's price. (14)

INDEX

Note: **Bold** page numbers indicate definitions; page numbers followed by *n* indicate material in notes.

REAL GROSS DOMESTIC PRODUCT IN CHAIN-WEIGHTED DOLLARS, 1929–2008 (2000 = 100)

Year	GDP	Personal Consumption Expenditures Total	Gross Private Domestic Investment Total	Net Exports — Net	Net Exports — Exports	Net Exports — Imports	Government Purchases — Total	Federal — Total	Federal — National Defense	Federal — Non-Defense	State and Local	Percent Change from Prior Year GDP
1929	865	661	91	—	35	44	121	25	—	—	104	—
1930	791	626	61	−10	29	39	133	28	—	—	111	−8.9
1931	740	607	38	−10	24	34	139	28	—	—	115	−7.7
1932	644	553	12	−9	19	28	134	27	—	—	108	−13.3
1933	636	541	17	−10	19	29	129	35	—	—	101	−2.1
1934	704	579	31	−9	21	30	146	45	—	—	94	7.7
1935	767	615	57	−17	22	39	156	46	—	—	113	7.7
1936	867	677	73	−15	23	38	175	72	—	—	109	14.2
1937	911	702	91	−14	29	43	167	67	—	—	112	4.3
1938	880	670	60	−15	29	34	180	71	—	—	114	−4.0
1939	951	729	77	−4	31	35	196	97	17	56	124	7.9
1940	1,034	767	108	−1	35	36	202	87	45	54	119	7.8
1941	1,211	822	132	−9	36	45	335	215	169	40	114	18.2
1942	1,435	803	70	−16	24	40	789	564	484	28	107	20.0
1943	1,671	826	41	−31	20	51	1,173	895	781	17	99	19.9
1944	1,807	850	51	−32	21	53	1,321	1,014	882	21	96	8.4
1945	1,786	903	67	−27	30	57	1,153	852	748	12	99	−4.0
1946	1,589	1,013	172	18	65	47	397	201	166	29	109	−20.8
1947	1,575	1,032	165	29	74	45	337	127	97	33	124	−1.5
1948	1,643	1,054	211	6	58	52	362	144	94	50	131	3.8
1949	1,635	1,083	161	8	58	50	405	160	105	54	147	.4
1950	1,777	1,153	228	−9	50	59	405	167	125	41	159	8.7
1951	1,915	1,171	228	0	62	62	554	294	257	36	161	8.8
1952	1,988	1,208	267	−8	59	67	666	372	326	45	164	4.3
1953	2,080	1,266	216	−18	55	73	714	389	329	60	172	3.7
1954	2,065	1,291	206	−12	58	70	665	335	288	47	174	−.7
1955	2,213	1,386	257	−14	64	78	641	307	267	40	198	5.6
1956	2,256	1,425	253	−11	74	85	641	303	266	37	205	2.0
1957	2,301	1,461	242	−7	81	88	670	316	279	37	217	1.8
1958	2,279	1,472	222	−12	70	92	691	312	265	46	234	−.5
1959	2,441	1,554	266	34	77	101	714	395	325	65	260	7.1
1960	2,501	1,597	266	−21	90	103	715	380	322	58	275	2.5
1961	2,560	1,630	264	−19	91	102	751	395	332	63	298	2.3
1962	2,715	1,711	298	−26	95	114	797	423	345	78	306	6.1
1963	2,834	1,781	318	−22	102	117	818	425	338	82	322	4.4
1964	2,998	1,888	344	15	114	120	836	410	320	95	344	5.0
1965	3,191	2,007	393	−26	117	136	861	424	321	98	367	6.4
1966	3,399	2,121	427	−40	126	157	937	466	362	99	391	6.5
1967	3,484	2,185	408	−49	128	168	1,008	504	404	100	418	2.5
1968	3,652	2,310	431	−78	139	193	1,040	514	415	95	442	4.8
1969	3,765	2,396	457	−70	145	204	1,038	493	391	98	459	3.1
1970	3,771	2,451	427	−64	161	213	1,012	456	354	98	471	.2
1971	3,898	2,545	475	−75	164	224	990	426	324	102	484	3.4
1972	4,105	2,701	532	−88	176	250	983	423	315	108	487	5.3
1973	4,341	2,833	594	−62	209	261	980	402	294	104	506	5.8
1974	4,319	2,812	550	−36	226	255	1,004	396	284	109	528	−.5
1975	4,311	2,876	453	−7	224	227	1,027	397	279	115	545	−.2
1976	4,540	3,035	544	−41	234	271	1,031	393	277	115	548	5.3
1977	4,750	3,164	627	−66	240	301	1,043	404	280	122	548	4.6
1978	5,015	3,303	702	−67	265	327	1,074	412	285	127	568	5.6
1979	5,173	3,383	725	−45	292	333	1,094	420	291	129	579	3.2
1980	5,161	3,374	645	+10	323	310	1,115	439	303	134	581	−.2
1981	5,291	3,422	704	+5	327	319	1,125	459	322	137	570	2.5
1982	5,189	3,470	606	−15	302	315	1,145	477	349	128	567	−1.9
1983	5,423	3,668	662	−64	294	354	1,187	506	371	135	575	4.5
1984	5,813	3,863	857	−129	318	441	1,227	525	395	129	593	7.2
1985	6,053	4,064	849	−149	328	469	1,312	560	423	137	629	4.1
1986	6,263	4,228	843	−165	353	510	1,392	586	445	141	669	3.5
1987	6,475	4,369	870	−156	391	540	1,426	597	450	146	695	3.4
1988	6,742	4,546	890	−112	454	561	1,445	586	446	138	721	4.1
1989	6,981	4,675	926	−79	506	586	1,482	594	443	150	749	3.5
1990	7,112	4,770	895	−54	552	607	1,530	659	479	178	868	1.9
1991	7,100	4,778	822	−14	589	603	1,547	658	474	182	886	−.2
1992	7,336	4,934	889	−15	629	645	1,555	646	450	195	906	3.3
1993	7,532	5,099	968	−52	650	702	1,541	619	425	194	919	2.7
1994	7,835	5,290	1,099	−79	706	785	1,541	596	404	191	943	4.0
1995	8,031	5,433	1,134	−71	778	849	1,549	580	389	191	968	2.5
1996	8,328	5,619	1,234	−79	843	923	1,564	573	383	189	990	3.7
1997	8,703	5,831	1,387	−104	943	1,048	1,594	567	373	194	1,025	4.5
1998	9,066	6,125	1,524	−203	966	1,170	1,624	561	365	195	1,063	4.2
1999	9,470	6,438	1,642	−296	1,008	1,304	1,686	573	372	201	1,113	4.5
2000	9,817	6,739	1,735	−379	1,096	1,475	1,721	578	370	208	1,142	3.7
2001	9,890	6,910	1,598	−399	1,036	1,435	1,780	601	384	216	1,179	.8
2002	10,048	7,099	1,557	−471	1,013	1,484	1,858	643	413	230	1,215	1.6
2003	10,301	7,295	1,613	−518	1,026	1,545	1,904	687	449	238	1,217	2.5
2004	10,676	7,561	1,770	−594	1,126	1,720	1,932	716	475	241	1,216	3.6
2005	10,990	7,792	1,874	−617	1,205	1,822	1,939	725	482	242	1,214	2.9
2006	11,295	8,029	1,913	−616	1,315	1,931	1,971	741	490	251	1,230	2.8
2007	11,524	8,253	1,810	−547	1,426	1,972	2,012	753	502	250	1,259	2.0
2008	11,652	8,272	1,689	−390	1,514	1,904	2,070	798	538	260	1,273	1.1

Source: U.S. Department of Commerce.

Note: Subtotals within Government Purchases based on 1992 prices for years 1929–1989.

CONSUMER PRICE INDEX, 1925–2008 (1982–84=100)

Year	Index (all items)	Percent Change
1925	17.5	0.8
1926	17.7	−1.1
1927	17.4	−2.3
1928	17.1	−1.2
1929	17.1	0.6
1930	16.7	−6.4
1931	15.2	−9.3
1932	13.7	−10.3
1933	13.0	0.8
1934	13.4	1.5
1935	13.7	3.0
1936	13.9	1.4
1937	14.4	2.9
1938	14.1	−2.8
1939	13.9	0.0
1940	14.0	0.7
1941	14.7	9.9
1942	16.3	9.0
1943	17.3	3.0
1944	17.6	2.3
1945	18.0	2.2
1946	19.5	18.1
1947	22.3	8.8
1948	24.1	3.0
1949	23.8	−2.1
1950	24.1	5.9
1951	26.0	6.0
1952	26.5	0.8
1953	26.7	0.7
1954	26.9	−0.7
1955	26.8	0.4
1956	27.2	3.0
1957	28.1	2.9
1958	28.9	1.8
1959	29.1	1.7
1960	29.6	1.4
1961	29.9	0.7
1962	30.2	1.3
1963	30.6	1.6
1964	31.0	1.0
1965	31.5	1.9
1966	32.4	3.5
1967	33.4	3.0
1968	34.8	4.7
1969	36.7	6.2
1970	38.8	5.6
1971	40.5	3.3
1972	41.8	3.4
1973	44.4	8.7
1974	49.3	12.3
1975	53.8	6.9
1976	56.9	4.9
1977	60.6	6.7
1978	65.2	9.0
1979	72.6	13.3
1980	82.4	12.5
1981	90.9	8.9
1982	96.5	3.8
1983	99.6	3.8
1984	103.9	3.9
1985	107.6	3.8
1986	109.6	1.1
1987	113.6	4.4
1988	118.3	4.6
1989	124.0	4.6
1990	130.7	6.1
1991	136.2	3.1
1992	140.3	2.9
1993	144.5	2.7
1994	148.2	2.7
1995	152.4	2.5

Note: Data beginning 1978 are for all urban consumers: earlier data are for urban wage earners and clerical workers.

Source: U.S. Department of Labor. Bureau of Statistics.

CONSUMER PRICE INDEX, 1925–2008 (continued)

Year	Index (all items)	Percent Change
1996	156.9	2.9
1997	160.5	1.7
1998	163.0	1.6
1999	166.6	2.7
2000	172.2	3.4
2001	177.1	2.8
2002	179.7	1.6
2003	184.0	2.6
2004	188.9	2.7
2005	195.3	3.4
2006	201.6	3.2
2007	207.3	2.8
2008	215.3	3.8

CHAIN-WEIGHTED PRICE DEFLATORS FOR GROSS DOMESTIC PRODUCT, 1959–2008 (2000=100)

Year	Index (all items)	Percent Change
1959	20.7	1.2
1960	21.0	1.4
1961	21.2	1.1
1962	21.5	1.4
1963	21.8	1.1
1964	22.1	1.5
1965	22.5	1.8
1966	23.1	2.8
1967	23.8	3.1
1968	24.9	4.3
1969	26.1	5.0
1970	27.5	5.3
1971	28.9	5.0
1972	30.1	4.3
1973	31.8	5.6
1974	34.7	9.0
1975	38.0	9.5
1976	40.2	5.8
1977	42.7	6.4
1978	45.7	7.0
1979	49.5	8.3
1980	54.0	9.1
1981	59.1	9.4
1982	62.7	6.1
1983	65.2	3.9
1984	67.6	3.8
1985	69.7	3.0
1986	71.2	2.2
1987	73.2	2.7
1988	75.7	3.4
1989	78.5	3.8
1990	81.6	3.9
1991	84.4	3.5
1992	86.4	2.3
1993	88.3	2.3
1994	90.2	2.1
1995	92.1	2.0
1996	93.8	1.9
1997	95.4	1.7
1998	96.4	1.1
1999	97.8	1.4
2000	100.0	2.2
2001	102.3	2.4
2002	104.1	1.7
2003	106.0	1.8
2004	109.5	2.8
2005	113.0	3.0
2006	116.7	2.9
2007	119.8	2.7
2008	122.5	2.3

Source: U.S. Department of Commerce, Bureau of Economic Analysis.

INTEREST RATES, 1929–2008 (percent per annum)

Year	Prime Rate Charged by Banks	Discount Rate, Federal Reserve Bank of New York
1929	5.50–6.00	5.16
1933	1.50–4.00	2.56
1939	1.50	1.00
1940	1.50	1.00
1941	1.50	1.00
1942	1.50	1.00
1943	1.50	1.00
1944	1.50	1.00
1945	1.50	1.00
1946	1.50	1.00
1947	1.50–1.75	1.00
1948	1.75–2.00	1.34
1949	2.00	1.50
1950	2.07	1.59
1951	2.56	1.75
1952	3.00	1.75
1953	3.17	1.99
1954	3.05	1.60
1955	3.16	1.89
1956	3.77	2.77
1957	4.20	3.12
1958	3.83	2.15
1959	4.48	3.36
1960	4.82	3.53
1961	4.50	3.00
1962	4.50	3.00
1963	4.50	3.23
1964	4.50	3.55
1965	4.54	4.04
1966	5.63	4.50
1967	5.61	4.19
1968	6.30	5.16
1969	7.96	5.87
1970	7.91	5.95
1971	5.72	4.88
1972	5.25	4.50
1973	8.03	6.44
1974	10.81	7.83
1975	7.86	6.25
1976	6.84	5.50
1977	6.83	5.46
1978	9.06	7.46
1979	12.67	10.28
1980	15.27	11.77
1981	18.87	13.42
1982	14.86	11.02
1983	10.79	8.50
1984	12.04	8.80
1985	9.93	7.69
1986	8.83	6.33
1987	8.21	5.66
1988	9.32	6.20
1989	10.87	6.93
1990	10.01	6.98
1991	8.46	5.45
1992	6.25	3.25
1993	6.00	3.00
1994	7.15	3.60
1995	8.83	5.21
1996	8.27	5.02
1997	8.44	5.00
1998	8.35	4.92
1999	8.00	4.62
2000	9.23	5.73
2001	6.91	3.40
2002	4.67	1.17
2003	4.12	1.15
2004	4.34	2.34
2005	6.19	4.19
2006	7.96	5.96
2007	8.05	5.86
2008	5.09	2.39

Source: Board of Governors of the Federal Reserve System.